TOWARD NUCLEAR ABOLITION

A History of the World Nuclear Disarmament Movement, 1971 to the Present

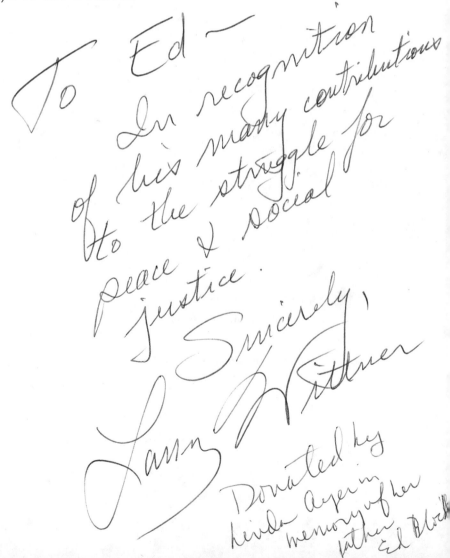

To Ed —

In recognition of his many contributions to the struggle for peace & social justice.

Sincerely,

Larry Wittner

Donated by Linda Ayer in memory of her father, Ed Block

VOLUME THREE

THE STRUGGLE AGAINST THE BOMB

TOWARD NUCLEAR ABOLITION

A History of the World Nuclear Disarmament Movement, 1971 to the Present

LAWRENCE S. WITTNER

Stanford University Press, Stanford, California, 2003

Stanford University Press
Stanford, California
© 2003 by the Board of Trustees of the
Leland Stanford Junior University
Printed in the United States of America

Library of Congress Cataloging-in-Publication Data

Wittner, Lawrence S.
    The struggle against the bomb / Lawrence S. Wittner.
      p. cm. — (Stanford nuclear age series)
    Includes bibliographical references and index.
    Contents: v. 3. Toward nuclear abolition: A history of the world nuclear
disarmament movement, 1971 to the present
    ISBN 0-8047-4861-6 (cloth : alk. paper) —
    ISBN 0-8047-4862-4 (pbk. : alk. paper)
    1. Nuclear disarmament—History. 2. Antinuclear movement—History.
I. Title. II. Series.

JX.1974.7W575   1993
327'.1'74'09—dc20   92-28026

This book is printed on acid-free, archival-quality paper.

Original printing 2003

Last figure below indicates year of this printing:
12   11   10   09   08   07   06   05   04   03

Typeset in 10/12.5 Times

To Benjamin and Elizabeth

The Stanford
Nuclear Age Series

Conceived by scientists, delivered by the military, and adopted by policy-makers, nuclear weapons emerged from the ashes of Hiroshima and Nagasaki to dominate our time. The politics, diplomacy, economy, and culture of the Cold War nurtured the nuclear arms race and, in turn, have been altered by it. "We have had the bomb on our minds since 1945," E. L. Doctorow observes. "It was first our weaponry and then our diplomacy, and now it's our economy. How can we suppose that something so monstrously powerful would not, after forty years, compose our identity? The great golem we have made against our enemies is our culture, our bomb culture—its logic, its faith, its vision."

The pervasive, transformative potential of nuclear weapons was foreseen by their creators. When Secretary of War Henry L. Stimson assembled a committee in May 1945 to discuss postwar atomic energy planning, he spoke of the atomic bomb as a "revolutionary change in the relations of man to the universe." Believing that it could mean "the doom of civilization," he warned President Truman that this weapon "has placed a certain moral responsibility upon us which we cannot shirk without very serious responsibility for any disaster to civilization."

In the decades since World War II that responsibility has weighed heavily on American civilization. Whether or not we have met it is a matter of heated debate. But that we must meet it, and, moreover, that we must also prepare the next generation of leaders to meet it as well, is beyond question.

Today, over half a century into the nuclear age the pervasive impact of the nuclear arms race has stimulated a fundamental reevaluation of the role of nuclear armaments and strategic polices. But mainstream scholarly work in strategic studies has tended to focus on questions related to the development, the deployment, and the diplomacy of nuclear arsenals. Such an exclusively managerial focus cannot probe the universal revolutionary changes about which Stimson spoke, and the need to address these changes is urgent. If the academic community is to contribute imaginatively and helpfully to the increasingly complex problems of the nuclear age, then the base of scholarship and pedagogy in the national security–arms control field must be broadened. It is this goal that the Stanford Nuclear Age Series is intended to support, with paperback reissues of important out-of-print works and original publication of new scholarship in the humanities and social sciences.

Martin J. Sherwin
General Editor

Preface

> In all modesty, but with all the determination of our spirit as well, let us here and now pledge to conceive and assemble an ark of memory capable of withstanding the atomic deluge.
>
> Gabriel Garcia Marquez, 1987

For more than half a century, the world has teetered on the brink of collective suicide. With the development of nuclear weapons, that terrible fate has loomed consistently before us—not as a preferred choice, but as the logical outcome of the ancient practice of waging war.

How we have avoided that disaster provides the focus of this book. In a number of ways, it is a heartening story, filled with examples of how concerned citizens around the world—through intelligence, courage, and determination—have altered the course of history. But it is also a cautionary tale for, although their achievement has been substantial, their success has been limited. Nuclear weapons still exist in the tens of thousands, ready to be employed in yet another of humanity's many murderous conflicts. Thus, even as we celebrate human achievement, we would do well to reflect upon our own responsibility to complete the important task that others have begun.

I am well aware of the traditional explanation for nuclear restraint. Indeed, how could one avoid it? Again and again, government officials have told us how fortunate we have been to have benefited from their wise leadership, a leadership devoted to fostering national security through the amassing of overwhelming military power. Paradoxically, they argue, it has been their willingness to develop, deploy, and use nuclear weapons that has limited the nuclear arms race and averted nuclear war. In one of their favorite phrases, they have secured "peace through strength."

Leaving aside the issue of peace—dubious enough in an era of constant wars that have consumed the lives of tens of millions of people—a careful examination of nuclear weapons policy shows that nuclear restraint was not their choice, at least for their own nations. Instead, as this study indicates, they usually championed a nuclear buildup and an increased willingness to wage nuclear war. This is not because they were particularly evil people, but because they were locked into a traditional system of national defense in a world of competing nation-states. It took an especially far-sighted statesman—for example, Mikhail Gorbachev—to recognize how dangerous this traditional system was and to move beyond it. And even Gorbachev, as we shall see, drew much of his "new thinking" from the citizens' campaign for nuclear disarmament.

As the alert reader already may have surmised, this is an unusual book. Along with the two volumes that have preceded it in this trilogy—*One World or None* and *Resisting the Bomb*—it examines a phenomenon not usually considered an appropriate part of the history of diplomacy or of national security policy. As academic fields of study are now defined, popular resistance to nuclear weapons doesn't quite "fit." But, as we shall see, it is impossible to explain the course of nuclear arms control and disarmament policy without it. As I suggested in *Resisting the Bomb*, recounting the history of nuclear arms control and disarmament without referring to the antinuclear movement is like telling the story of civil rights legislation without referring to the civil rights movement.

This book is unusual in other respects, too. Although it draws upon a "Realist" analysis of the international system, it rejects the pessimistic assumption of many "Realist" scholars that the system cannot be altered. Instead, this book, like its predecessors, implicitly argues that the international system—often in the face of furious resistance by national security managers—has been changed in some important ways. Furthermore, although historians are supposed to describe and analyze the past, they do not usually wrestle with the future. But, while giving talks in a number of venues on the history of nuclear disarmament efforts, I have been struck by the fact that my listeners also have wanted some advice. After all, they seemed to be saying, you have studied the nuclear arms race for years. Don't you have *anything* to suggest that we can do about it? And, to be honest, I do have some suggestions. Accordingly, I have sketched them briefly in this book's "Conclusion." Readers who cannot bear these departures from standard scholarly practice are urged to skip the offending passages or to forgo reading this book, to which the guardians of propriety surely will assign a "U" (i.e. Unorthodox) rating, if they deign to notice it at all.

Doing research for this book was challenging. In part, this reflected the difficulties inherent in writing a global history. Specifically, there are too many nations, actors, and languages for any individual to do complete justice to such a project. Furthermore, national security officials have built a wall between their decision-making process and the public that they do not want the researcher—or anyone—to breach. Thus, although there are plenty of government records dealing with nuclear issues, the vast bulk of them generated during the past three decades remain officially closed. Even so, thanks to the collapse of some governments and to loopholes in the classification policies of others, I have obtained access to a surprising array of government documents, many of which I never expected to see. These range from records of the central committee of the Communist Party of the Soviet Union, to surveillance reports of the Stasi (the East German secret police), to summaries of White House telephone conversations of Ronald Reagan. I have supplemented them with well over a hundred interviews with former government officials and nuclear disarmament movement leaders, with the papers of numerous individuals and organizations, with government and organizational publications, with memoirs, and with scholarly works. But there remains considerable room for additional research, especially in government records. When most of the latter finally are declassified—if they ever are—they seem likely to reveal greater government responsiveness to antinuclear campaigns than government officials have admitted in their memoirs or in after-the-fact interviews.

Securing adequate funding for this study also posed some difficulties. To judge from their cool response, a good number of foundations and institutions would have preferred a more conventional project. Ultimately, however, it attracted a grant from the Nonprofit Sector Research Fund of the Aspen Institute that facilitated the research and a senior fellowship from the U.S. Institute of Peace and a grant from the John D. and Catherine T. MacArthur Foundation that facilitated the writing. I am very grateful for this support, and I hope this book will justify it.

Other kinds of support were vital, as well. Dana Frye, Heather Sheeley, and Carol Taylor served as my research assistants, and did an excellent job of it. Many individuals provided me with useful research suggestions or materials, including Graham Barker-Benfield, Donald Birn, Helen Caldicott, David Cortright, John Crist, Sanford Gottlieb, Walter Hooke, Glenn Inghram, Bruce Kent, Anne Kjelling, Robert Musil, Christopher Paine, David Patterson, Rob Prince, Natalia Romashkina, Mark Selden, Dhirendra Sharma, Martin Sherwin, Mark Solomon, Ralph Summy, Frank von Hippel, and Peter Zheutlin. Michael Bess, Randall Forsberg, Sheila Jones, Daryl Kimball, and Günter Wernicke were particularly helpful in this regard. For assistance in translating materials from Dutch, German, Russian, Spanish, and Uighur, I am grateful to George Berger, Dana Frye, Linda McNell, Natalia Romashkina, Corinna Ruth Unger, Kate Vanovitch, Andrea Walter, and Michael Weinberg. So many librarians aided me that it is impossible to list them all here, but Wendy

Chmielewski and the staff of the Swarthmore College Peace Collection deserve special praise. Martin Sherwin, the editor of Stanford's Nuclear Age series, played a key role in this project from its inception. Muriel Bell and Carmen Borbón-Wu of Stanford University Press did much to carry it through to completion. I am also thankful for the computer wizardry of my colleague, Gerry Zahavi, and for the untiring assistance of two staff members of my department, Debra Neuls and Harriet Temps. Colin Archer, Graham Barker-Benfield, John W. Chambers, Bruce Kent, Daryl Kimball, Robert Musil, David Patterson, and Ralph Summy read portions of the book manuscript and made many useful suggestions for revision. Deb Cavanaugh prepared the index. In addition, there is a broad network of peace researchers who, through their example, have contributed to this book. Gathered in such organizations as the Peace History Society and the International Peace Research Association, they have assisted and sustained me throughout the research and writing process.

My deepest thanks go to my wife, Dorothy Tristman, who has not only encouraged the writing of this book, but the building of the kind of world that it envisions.

L.S.W.

Contents

10 pages of photographs follow page 288

Dr. Rieux resolved to compile this chronicle . . . to state quite simply what we learn in a time of pestilence. . . . He knew that the tale he had to tell could not be one of a final victory. It could be only the record of what had had to be done . . . by all who . . . strive their utmost to be healers.

Albert Camus, 1947

Largely Forgotten

The Arms Race and the Movement, 1971-76

> The nuclear arms race . . . continues unhampered.
> Competition for ever more destructive technologies is
> steadily accelerating. A frightening new momentum is
> spreading nuclear weapons capabilities to more and
> more countries.
>
> Alva Myrdal, 1976

During the early 1970s, nuclear weapons went largely unnoticed and, there-fore, unresisted. In contrast to earlier upsurges of public concern and anti-nuclear activism—first, in the late 1940s and, subsequently, in the late 1950s and early 1960s[1]—there was relatively little popular protest against nuclear weapons in the early 1970s. This public complacency about nuclear dangers is particularly striking when set against the fact that, at the time, nuclear powers were expanding their nuclear arsenals while would-be nuclear pow-ers were working to acquire them—all of them with the intention of better preparing themselves for nuclear war. Perceptions, though, do not always correspond to realities. And the contemporary perception—bolstered by So-viet-American détente and well-publicized arms control negotiations—was that the world was gradually taming the nuclear menace. In this context, the general public gave government officials a fairly easy time of it, at least when it came to integrating nuclear weapons into their ongoing interna-tional rivalries. Even most peace and disarmament groups, dwindling in size and obsessed with the Vietnam War, put up only a feeble resistance to the Bomb. Only in the South Pacific did they wage a lively antinuclear cam-paign. In hindsight, the result was predictable enough: a gradually escalat-ing nuclear arms race.

The Fizzling of the Disarmament Decade, 1971-76

Ever since the nuclear arms control breakthroughs of the 1960s—most notably the Limited Test Ban Treaty of 1963 and the Nuclear Nonproliferation
Treaty of 1968—there had been a widespread popular assumption that the
nations of the world were acting to remove nuclear dangers. Based on this
assumption, as well as on the promise made by the Soviet and U.S. governments in the nonproliferation treaty to take concrete action toward eliminating nuclear weapons, the United Nations had proclaimed the 1970s the
"Disarmament Decade." Against this backdrop, during the early 1970s the
two great powers held numerous rounds of nuclear arms control negotiations. These negotiations resulted in the 1972 Strategic Arms Limitation
Treaty—or SALT I, as it became known—which limited the deployment of
intercontinental and sea-launched ballistic missiles and, also, the deployment of anti-ballistic missile (ABM) systems. "With this step," declared
U.S. President Richard Nixon, "we have begun to check the wasteful and
dangerous spiral of nuclear arms which has dominated relations between our
two countries." According to Henry Kissinger, his national security advisor,
the SALT I agreements represented "a major contribution to strategic stability," as well as an important step toward further nuclear arms limitations.
In fact, SALT II proved harder to negotiate, but an interim measure—the
Vladivostok Accord, signed in November 1974—did set additional nuclear
limits.[2]

Furthermore, the two governments successfully negotiated agreements
that called for averting the use of nuclear weapons. Meeting in May 1972 in
Moscow, Nixon and Soviet party secretary Leonid Brezhnev signed an
agreement, "Basic Principles of Relations," in which the U.S. and Soviet
governments pledged to do "their utmost to avoid military confrontation and
to prevent the outbreak of nuclear war." In this accord, they proclaimed "the
recognition of the security interests" of both nations "based on the principle
of equality and the renunciation of the use or threat of force." A little more
than a year later, the two governments signed the Prevention of Nuclear
War agreement, which bound them to "act in such a manner as to . . . exclude the outbreak of nuclear war between them and between either of the
Parties and other countries." Kissinger acclaimed this as "a significant step
toward the prevention of nuclear war" and a potentially "significant landmark" in the relations between the United States and the Soviet Union and
in their relationships with "all other countries in the world."[3]

Whatever the other virtues of these agreements, they did not foster nuclear disarmament. Indeed, the worldwide nuclear arms race proceeded

without serious interruption. SALT I did not control the replacement of old weapons by new ones and, also, placed no restrictions on the Multiple Independently Targetable Re-Entry Vehicle (MIRV), which enabled a missile to carry numerous nuclear warheads. In fact, on the very day the SALT I treaty was signed, U.S. Secretary of Defense Melvin Laird announced a major new plan for "modernization and improvement" of U.S. strategic forces, including the acceleration of the Trident nuclear submarine program. Moreover, the Vladivostok Accord set very high ceilings on missiles and placed no ceilings at all on nuclear warheads. As a result, between 1972 and 1977 the U.S. government increased the number of its strategic nuclear warheads and bombs from about 4,500 to about 9,000, while the Soviet Union increased its strategic arsenal from some 2,500 to 3,650. Meanwhile, the United States began developing a new class of strategic weapons—cruise missiles—and the Soviet Union commenced deploying more than three new models of intercontinental ballistic missiles (ICBMs) and assorted versions of a new submarine ballistic missile system. In addition, both Cold War camps possessed even larger numbers of tactical nuclear weapons. By the mid-1970s, the United States alone was estimated to have some 22,000 of these, dispersed for action around the globe.[4]

Nor was the nuclear arms race limited to the two superpowers. The British, French, and Chinese governments had made the breakthrough to nuclear weapons status years before, and during the early 1970s devoted themselves to testing, upgrading, and increasing their nuclear arsenals. Having developed the Bomb in the late 1960s, the Israeli government, though careful to maintain ambiguity about its nuclear status, also cultivated its weaponry. In 1974, the Indian government conducted what it called a "peaceful nuclear explosion," but few were fooled by the rhetorical sugar-coating. Denouncing this "fateful development," Pakistan's prime minister, Zulfikar Ali Bhutto, spurred on his own country's program to develop nuclear weapons. Indeed, an estimated ten nations stood in line for entry into the once-exclusive nuclear club. Despite their professed desire for nuclear disarmament, these lesser and would-be nuclear powers showed no more interest than the United States and the Soviet Union in taking this route or, indeed, accepting anything that would significantly limit their nuclear options. France rejected the partial test ban treaty and—along with China, Israel, India, and South Africa—refused to sign the Nuclear Nonproliferation Treaty. China would not even take part in nuclear arms control or disarmament negotiations.[5]

Although the buildup of nuclear arsenals did not necessarily reflect an eagerness to use them, there was little doubt that the nuclear powers remained ready and willing to wage nuclear war. NATO policy was to reply to a Warsaw Pact conventional attack upon Western Europe with the initiation of nuclear war against the Soviet Union and its allies. The Soviet government sometimes professed greater reluctance to initiate a nuclear war, but stated repeatedly that it stood ready to respond to Western "aggression" by fighting and winning a nuclear conflict.[6] The Kremlin apparently considered the signing of the Prevention of Nuclear War agreement an important event, but U.S. officials did not take it seriously. Kissinger referred to it contemptuously in his memoirs as "a bland set of principles that had been systematically stripped of all implications harmful to our interests." In both nations, insiders prepared themselves for a nuclear holocaust. A White House official recalled that "personal activities were designed according to the time it would take a nuclear missile to fly from Russia to the United States. The rule was: The President should never be more than two minutes from a telephone. Even the White House press corps designed its daily life around the possibility that the President might push the nuclear button at any moment."[7]

Sometimes, in fact, that moment seemed perilously close. In April 1972, Nixon suggested to Kissinger that the time might have arrived in the Vietnam War to "use the nuclear bomb." When Kissinger responded coolly to the idea, Nixon remarked: "I just want you to think big."[8] The use of nuclear weapons came up again in late October 1973. In the midst of a war between Israel and Egypt that appeared to be spiraling out of control, the Soviet government sent a tough message to Washington suggesting joint— or, if necessary, Soviet—military action to end the conflict. With Nixon reeling from the Watergate scandal and drunk in the White House, his top national security advisors (Kissinger and Defense Secretary James Schlesinger) responded by ordering a worldwide alert of U.S. military forces, including U.S. nuclear forces. Aghast at this sudden escalation of the dispute to the nuclear level by their American counterparts, Soviet Politburo members asked: "Are they crazy?" Fortunately, the Russians refused to rise to this military challenge, and the crisis was resolved without a nuclear war. Nevertheless, it was the most dangerous nuclear confrontation between the great powers since the Cuban missile crisis. Furthermore, this time it occurred during a period of Soviet-American détente.[9]

This preparation for nuclear war reflected the centuries-old conflict among nations and their traditional solution to the resulting national security dilemma: military power. In retrospect, former Soviet officials conceded that their nuclear buildup of the time was foolish and provocative, but insisted that it was undertaken as a defensive measure. According to Anatoly Chernyaev, then an official in the International Department of the Central Committee of the Communist Party, the Soviet Union was not "planning to organize or begin a nuclear war. Among our elders, there was not a single person . . . seriously preparing for a nuclear war with the United States." And yet, their brains were infused with a "military-psychology setup," derived from World War II. Nikolai Detinov, an arms control expert in the Soviet Ministry of Defense, agreed that World War II provided the crucial ingredient in official thinking. Kremlin leaders "witnessed the defeat of the Soviet army because we didn't have enough arms, they saw the cities and towns burning, they saw our divisions marching toward the east in retreat. And so they sought . . . the promise of security" through military strength. Georgi Arbatov, a member of the Central Committee of the Communist Party, recalled: "In the light of the bitter experience of the Soviet people, the preservation of peace was in no way a propagandistic slogan . . . but a serious political motive. . . . More often than not the top people sincerely believed" that "the generous financing of military programs" served "the cause of peace."[10]

This attachment to nuclear weapons was reinforced by the background and attitudes of Soviet party leader Leonid Brezhnev. Poorly educated and intellectually limited, Brezhnev was marked, according to Arbatov, by "his conservatism, his traditionalism, and his downright allergy to anything new." These traits were tempered by "an absence of any inclination toward extremist or adventurous decisions," which, in terms of foreign policy, meant "sincere support for the relaxing of international tensions" and cautious moves toward nuclear arms control. Furthermore, according to Anatoly Dobrynin, the longtime Soviet ambassador to the United States, Brezhnev believed that "a nuclear war was utterly unacceptable." In 1971, addressing the twenty-fourth Soviet Party Congress, Brezhnev unveiled a peace program, featuring his first use of the word "détente." Even so, as Arbatov noted, "I often heard Brezhnev repeat the line 'Defense is sacrosanct,' explaining his generosity toward the military." As a result, the Soviet government was "not yet ready to discuss the issue of arms limitation in a businesslike manner, if only because no one had ever demanded that the Ministry of Defense or the defense industry care about disarmament. They were concerned with catching up with the Americans in arms, not with arms control." Indeed, "the military-industrial complex was a state within a state," with Brezhnev "accustomed to granting the generals and the military industrialists what they wanted. And the thing that they wanted most was no agreements tying their hands."[11]

Furthermore, even with the best intentions on the part of Soviet arms negotiators, arms control issues were tricky and difficult to resolve. Soviet leaders believed that their country was entitled to nuclear parity with the United States. But, in the quest for parity, how did one assess the significance of different types of weapons and their destructiveness? U.S. nuclear weapons were more accurate and more sophisticated. To offset this "performance edge," Soviet leaders built bigger missiles and warheads with a higher destructive yield. Furthermore, how did one evaluate differences in nuclear deployment? During the SALT negotiations, Soviet leaders were acutely conscious of the dangers their nation faced from U.S. "forward-based systems": nuclear bombers close to Soviet borders, aircraft carrier-based planes that could hit Soviet territory, bases in Scotland and Spain where submarines were armed with nuclear missiles, and increasing numbers of British and French strategic nuclear weapons. Thus, to compensate for the U.S. superiority in nuclear forces stationed on the periphery of the Soviet Union, Soviet leaders thought they were entitled to an advantage in the number of land-based ballistic missiles. This was a reasonable approach, they felt, and they could not quite understand why the U.S. government proved so unyielding on the point of Soviet vulnerability to forward-based systems. Indeed, as two Soviet arms control negotiators recalled, although Soviet leaders had "a general conviction that the arms race had to be curbed," they feared that the U.S. government sought to gain a military advantage through arms treaties. "Behind the Soviet leadership's rather conservative steps towards arms limitation," they noted, "lay a worst-case scenario."[12]

The U.S. government, too, was trapped by its fear and suspicion of other nations, particularly the Soviet Union. To be sure, Nixon, his national security advisor (and, later, secretary of state) Henry Kissinger, and his successor as President, Gerald Ford, while not enthusiastic about reducing nuclear stockpiles, did publicly champion détente and nuclear arms controls.[13] In practice, however, both Nixon and Kissinger shared a hardboiled, "Realist" approach to foreign policy that made them deeply suspicious of other nations and practitioners of power politics. Although they lacked the ideologically inflamed anti-Communism that characterized so much of the Republican Party, they held the traditional view that, ultimately, securing U.S. interests depended upon military strength and the determination to use it. Indeed, Kissinger began his meteoric rise in national security circles through books that advocated a greater U.S. willingness to employ nuclear weapons in world affairs.[14] Thus, although Nixon, Ford, and Kissinger talked much of détente, especially from 1972 to 1975, and reluctantly accepted Soviet nuclear parity, they practiced a tough-minded policy of competition with and containment of the Soviet Union. Furthermore, these American leaders had only a minimal interest in controlling nuclear weapons. From their standpoint, arms control treaties were valuable primarily for garnering domestic political support and for dampening Soviet challenges to the role of the United States in world affairs.[15]

Not surprisingly, then, nuclear arms control treaties between the great powers remained within the comfort zone. During negotiations for SALT I, when the United States possessed MIRV technology and the Russians did not, Nixon and Kissinger successfully insisted upon leaving MIRVs out of the agreement. In turn, this concession to Washington effectively undermined the chances for securing a concession from Moscow that the U.S. government would have welcomed: reducing the Soviet arsenal of ICBMs. In this fashion, both nations ended up holding onto their security blankets; the Americans multiplied the nuclear warheads on their missiles and the Russians retained their land-based, heavy missile force. For the most part, Soviet-American treaties limited items that were not useful. Only when the U.S. Senate refused to fund a nationwide ABM deployment did Nixon and Kissinger agree to ban it through the ABM treaty. Similarly, Nixon accepted a bilateral Threshold Test Ban Treaty in 1974 principally because its 150-kiloton limit on underground testing accommodated the nuclear testing requirements of the United States. The low priority accorded by the administration to curbing the nuclear arms race was further exemplified when Nixon—shortly after his 1972 re-election—began a sweeping purge of the top ranks of his SALT delegation and of the Arms Control and Disarmament Agency.[16]

Thereafter, in fact, nuclear arms controls and détente began to lose their appeal. During the mid-1970s, the SALT II negotiations became bogged down over conflicting American and Soviet demands. Furthermore, in 1976, pressed by a hawkish challenge within the Republican Party to Ford's renomination—led by California Governor Ronald Reagan—the President shelved the SALT negotiations. Taking up his opponent's rhetoric, Ford now began to champion a policy of "peace through strength."[17] Although, in principle, he supported the goal of a comprehensive nuclear test ban treaty, he did not conduct negotiations for it but, instead, sponsored a considerably more modest measure to limit nuclear testing: a Peaceful Nuclear Explosions Treaty, which he and Brezhnev signed in 1976. The latter was designed to supplement the Threshold Test Ban Treaty by eliminating the possibility that "peaceful" explosions might be substituted for weapons tests exceeding the 150-kiloton limit. Both, however, became dead letters when, with the approach of the Republican convention, Ford decided not to submit them to the Senate for ratification. By the time of the 1976 election campaign, the President had even dropped the word "détente" from his speeches.[18]

A Movement in the Doldrums, 1971-74

Another key reason for the nuclear buildup of the early 1970s lay in the enfeebled state of the nuclear disarmament movement. During the late 1950s and early 1960s, the antinuclear movement and the public opinion it had mobilized in nations around the world had provided the motor force behind curbing the nuclear arms race and averting nuclear war. But, in the late 1960s, the movement went into serious decline thanks to a combination of over-optimistic expectations about changes in government policies, exhaustion of activists after years of intense struggle, and the peace constituency's preoccupation with the Vietnam War.[19] The movement's condition further deteriorated in the years thereafter, as halting the murderous Vietnam conflict became an obsession, leaving little time or energy for anything else. In this context, nuclear disarmament organizations died, dwindled, or changed their focus, and their mass base melted away. Although the movement did not disappear entirely in the years from 1971 to 1974, it was certainly in the doldrums.

Britain's once-powerful Campaign for Nuclear Disarmament (CND) survived during these years, but just barely. Once Britain's largest and most dynamic mass movement, with yearly Aldermaston marches that, at their zenith, drew over 100,000 people, CND, in the early 1970s, had a relatively quiescent membership that barely topped two thousand. Despite a major publicity and organizational effort behind the 1974 Aldermaston march (including 65,000 leaflets, 7,000 posters, and 12,000 stickers), only about 200 people began the march and some 2,000 attended the culminating rally. According to CND's own assessment, the organization was "'overtaken' by other campaigns—most notably the one to end the Vietnam war and . . . the student and youth movement."[20] Nevertheless, CND continued to protest nuclear testing, organized Hiroshima Day events, and held small meetings of the antinuclear faithful around the country.[21] Scotland provided one of Britain's most supportive regions, and a Scottish CND demonstration in June 1974, led by Glasgow city officials, drew an assemblage of 1,200. It included a small march to the Holy Loch Polaris nuclear submarine base, where CND presented a "notice to quit" to the military guardians. Nevertheless, in the words of Zoë Fairbairns, a CND staffer, this was a "lean time for CND." When telling strangers whom she worked for, she would add: "Yes, it is still going."[22]

In France, the situation was no better. The Socialist and Communist parties agreed in 1972 on a Common Program that, among other things, repudiated nuclear weapons. But, thereafter, given the expectation that a Left government would abolish France's nuclear arms, the *force de frappe*, a sense of complacency demobilized antinuclear activists. To be sure, in 1973 small groups of protesters, including several Catholic priests and a French general, did sail into the South Pacific in an attempt to disrupt French nuclear testing. Moreover, in 1974, French pacifists—hoping to link nonviolent action to antimilitarism and social justice—formed the Movement for a Nonviolent Alternative (Mouvement pour une Alternative non-violente). But these were very small ventures, and failed to jolt the French public out of its overall complacency about French nuclear testing and nuclear weapons.[23]

Elsewhere in Western Europe, the movement also persisted, but without much energy or a mass base. In the Netherlands, an Interchurch Peace Council (Interkerkelijk Vredesberaad, IKV), formed in 1966 by the powerful Protestant and Catholic churches, had considerable potential. But, as late as 1974, its activities were quite restrained, involving little more than organizing an annual Peace Week.[24] In neighboring Belgium, peace activists divided between the French-speaking (Walloon) and the Dutch-speaking (Flemish) communities. During the early 1970s, a National Action Committee for Peace and Development (Comité National d'Action pour la Paix et le Développement, CNAPD) did emerge as a coordinating body for French-speaking youth organizations, peace groups, and Third World campaigns, but no comparable body developed among Dutch-speaking groups. Furthermore, the priorities of groups on both sides of the linguistic divide remained diverse, without an emphasis upon nuclear weapons.[25] In Scandinavia, too, the once-powerful antinuclear movement had dissipated. The venerable Swedish Peace and Arbitration Society (Svenska Freds- och Skiljedoms Föreningen) continued its operations but, by 1974, its membership was down to about 4,000 and nuclear weapons did not rank among its major concerns. In Norway, a leading antinuclear campaigner recalled, "the movement fell asleep."[26]

In the United States, where the peace and disarmament community focused on the Vietnam War, nuclear issues were marginalized. Pacifist groups like the American Friends Service Committee (AFSC), the Fellowship of Reconciliation (FOR), the War Resisters League (WRL), and the Women's International League for Peace and Freedom (WILPF) threw themselves into the antiwar struggle. According to Ron Young, the director of the Peace Education Division of the AFSC, "Vietnam sort of took over." In 1974, a poll at the biennial WILPF meeting indicated 30 items on which members wanted to work, but none of them dealt with nuclear weapons or disarmament.[27] Even among the larger, non-pacifist groups that had led the mass movement against nuclear weapons during the late 1950s and early 1960s, such as the National Committee for a Sane Nuclear Policy (SANE) and Women Strike for Peace (WSP), the Vietnam War had a profound impact. According to Sandy Gottlieb, SANE's executive director, his organization was "consumed" by the war. Ethel Taylor of WSP recalled: "We were sidetracked by the war in Vietnam. Even though we knew that . . . the nuclear arms race would continue, we had to make a choice on what issue we would deal with immediately. There was no question" that it would be the war, "because this was so urgent." Ironically, however, despite their adaptation to the demands of the era, the era was not kind to them. Membership and participation plummeted. "About '73 or '74," recalled David Cortright, a leading antiwar activist among American soldiers, "you could hardly find the peace movement."[28]

Nevertheless, despite the distraction of the war and their weakness, U.S. peace and disarmament groups did, on occasion, assail aspects of the arms race. The WRL attacked nuclear testing, SANE criticized the "overkill capacity" of the great powers, and WSP launched an International Demand Disarmament Day.[29] In late 1973, the AFSC—anxious to challenge the military-industrial complex—hired a young antiwar activist, Terry Provance, to head up a program to stop the B-1 bomber, a proposed $50 billion Pentagon weapons system with both nuclear and conventional capabilities. Working closely with the non-pacifist Clergy and Laity Concerned, which agreed to co-sponsor the project, Provance developed a nationwide Stop the B-1 Bomber campaign during the following year, with 75 local groups.[30] Another peace movement project with antinuclear implications began at Rocky Flats, Colorado, sixteen miles northwest of Denver. Here local peace and environmental activists started to investigate plutonium contamination in the vicinity of the U.S. nuclear weapons plant. In 1974, taking up the issue, AFSC staff members Pam Solo and Judy Danielson organized the Rocky Flats Action Group, a coalition of local peace, environmental, religious, and community organizations that demanded the plant's closure.[31]

Nor were these the only signs of life in the movement. Long the mainstay of scientific opposition to the nuclear arms race, the Federation of American Scientists was down to about a thousand members and an annual budget of $7,000 by 1969, when it decided to hire Jeremy Stone as its di-

rector. Beginning work in mid-1970 as the organization's first full-time staffer in 22 years, Stone set about rejuvenating it. By 1974, the FAS had significantly raised its profile, established permanent headquarters in Washington, recruited a substantial crop of Nobel Prize winners, and increased its
membership by 450 percent. Meanwhile, the FAS went to work attacking
the arms race, especially the ABM system and the first use of nuclear weapons. It also began a campaign to defend Andrei Sakharov, the Soviet Union's best-known advocate of nuclear disarmament, from government harassment.[32] Another sign that the movement had not died was the growth of
the Union of Concerned Scientists (UCS), a group initiated by students and
faculty at MIT in 1969. At first, UCS focused on opposing ABM and MIRV,
but in the early 1970s it began a devastating critique of nuclear reactor
safety.[33]

Probably the most unusual of the new peace groups was the Center for
Defense Information (CDI), founded in 1972 by Admiral Gene LaRocque.
Working as a U.S. government nuclear war planner since 1957, LaRocque
ultimately concluded that "planning, training, arming, and practicing for
nuclear war . . . bordered on insanity." Consequently, upon his retirement
from active duty in March 1972, he established the CDI as a means of providing the information crucial to fostering nuclear arms controls and,
thereby, averting nuclear war. Staffed largely by former U.S. military officers and drawing upon a prestigious board of directors that disarmament-
oriented businessman Harold Willens brought in from a group that he had
organized previously—Business Executives Move for a Vietnam Peace—
the CDI constituted an unusually credible peace organization. Even so, like
its U.S. counterparts, it did not have a mass base.[34]

The nuclear disarmament movement also lacked a powerful presence in
Asia. India had never mustered a substantial antinuclear movement and,
consequently, it was hardly surprising that the government's "peaceful nuclear explosion" of May 1974 failed to provoke widespread resistance. Indeed, initially it seemed to provide a significant political boost for Indian
Prime Minister Indira Gandhi. Overcome by nationalist fervor, even the opposition sang her praises and most of the Indian press greeted the event ec-
statically. "Indian Genius Triumphs," read one headline. Another proclaimed: "Thrilled Nation Lauds Feat." As things turned out, her triumph
was short-lived. That fall, the misery of the Indian lower classes, combined
with growing economic difficulties, sank her standing in the polls to an all-
time low. This discontent, however, was not accompanied by a significant
nuclear disarmament campaign.[35]

Even in Japan, where a far larger and better-organized antinuclear movement existed, it remained at low tide. Ever since the mid-1960s, it had been divided into two feuding groups with quite different approaches: the Japan Congress Against A- and H-Bombs (Gensuikin, controlled by the Socialist Party and its close trade union ally, Sohyo) and the Japan Council Against A- and H-Bombs (Gensuikyo, controlled by the Communist Party). Gensuikin opposed all nuclear weapons, as well as all nuclear power. Gensuikyo, on the other hand, as befit its leadership, drew a distinction between the nuclear weapons and nuclear power plants in Communist and non-Communist nations. This organizational rivalry not only kept the Japanese antinuclear movement divided, but dissuaded many ordinary, non-political people from becoming involved in what they considered a sectarian campaign. Determined to avoid recreating this situation, peace activists organized a new organization, Beheiren, to oppose the Vietnam War. Thus, although both groups sustained an array of activities in the early 1970s—including resistance to the war, demonstrations against the entry of nuclear-armed U.S. warships, and rival world conferences for activists—the Japanese antinuclear movement lacked strength and influence.[36]

The world's liveliest antinuclear protest occurred in the South Pacific, largely thanks to persistent French atmospheric nuclear testing. Spurning the partial test ban treaty of 1963, the French government, between 1966 and 1974, conducted 41 nuclear tests in the atmosphere over Moruroa Atoll in French Polynesia. From this site, radioactive clouds drifted across small Pacific island nations to New Zealand and Australia, depositing their deadly nuclear fallout. During 1972, New Zealand activists, as part of a Peace Media project, defied the French government by sailing small vessels into the test danger zone. With New Zealand's conservative government waffling on the French testing issue, the opposition Labour Party took a more principled stand, which contributed to its election victory that November. By 1973, New Zealand's movement was flourishing. Growing crowds of supporters dispatched protest ships with songs and cheers, while the New Zealand Federation of Labour pledged a strict ban on French goods.[37] In Australia, thousands of people, outraged by plans for a new round of French tests in 1972, joined marches held in Adelaide, Melbourne, Brisbane, and Sydney; scientists wrote editorials and issued statements demanding an end to the tests; readers filled whole pages of newspapers with angry letters; and consumers boycotted French products. Australian unions played a leading role, with their members refusing to load French ships, service French planes, or carry French mail. Polls found that up to 90 percent of the Australian public opposed French nuclear testing.[38]

Coupled with opposition to other regional ventures by the nuclear powers, French nuclear testing also spurred resistance in the small island nations of the Pacific. In May 1970, after some 600 people in Suva, Fiji turned out for a public meeting on nuclear tests, an Against Testing on Moruroa (ATOM) organization was established. Drawing together representatives from the Fiji Council of Churches, the YWCA, and the University of the South Pacific Students Association, ATOM focused on publicizing the growing resistance within French Polynesia to nuclear testing, building an antinuclear alliance among churches, unions, and the government, and linking up with antinuclear groups elsewhere in the Pacific. It also sought to influence the South Pacific Forum, a regional body bringing together representatives of governments.[39] Meanwhile, other antinuclear efforts developed elsewhere in the Pacific. On Tinian, an island in Micronesia where the U.S. government sought to eject the entire native population to make way for an expanded U.S. Air Force base housing nuclear weapons, vigorous opposition emerged, including public meetings, anti-military demonstrations, and official protests to the United Nations. On Tahiti, an island in Polynesia, a 1973 antinuclear rally of over 5,000 people issued an appeal to all French men and women "to join with us in doing everything they can to stop this crazy nuclear testing." Aware of the rising tide of protest and determined to halt the "Pacific colonialism" of the nuclear powers, ATOM began planning in 1974 for a Nuclear-Free Pacific movement, to be launched by an international conference of activists the following year. By November, the conference had secured the sponsorship not only of a broad range of groups in Fiji, but of the Pacific Conference of Churches, the University of the South Pacific Students Association, and antinuclear groups in Australia, France, Japan, New Zealand, and the United States.[40]

For the most part, however, the movement was far more subdued in the early 1970s. In Canada, the Voice of Women (VOW), which had been founded in 1960 to protest against the nuclear arms race, almost totally dropped the subject from its agenda, focusing instead on a variety of international issues, especially ending the Vietnam War.[41] In the Soviet Union, antimilitary ideas and themes appeared here and there among elements of the artistic and scientific intelligentsia. Numerous Soviet scientists shared Sakharov's antinuclear views, and many others kept up with arms control and disarmament issues through America's *Bulletin of the Atomic Scientists* and through the international Pugwash conferences. An antimilitary movement of Soviet "hippies" also commenced, especially in big cities. On June 1, 1971, nearly 150 of these countercultural demonstrators gathered in Moscow under the banner "Make Love Not War." But these activities did not get very far. In Moscow, the planned protest march was broken up by waiting militiamen, who seized the demonstrators. Furthermore, with Soviet party conservatives waging a fierce counterattack against the libertarian and antimilitary trends unleashed in the late 1950s and early 1960s, Sakharov and other reformers found themselves preoccupied with defending human rights.[42]

Thanks to decades of pacifist and antinuclear agitation in many nations, by the early 1970s there also existed a number of international organizations that addressed nuclear issues. Among pacifist groups these included the International Fellowship of Reconciliation (IFOR), which brought together religious pacifists; the War Resisters' International (WRI), which appealed to secular pacifists; and the Women's International League for Peace and Freedom (WILPF), which, for the most part, mobilized female pacifists. However, although they maintained sections in dozens of nations, they did not have a mass base. Furthermore, their critique of nuclear weapons was diluted by their multiplicity of concerns. To focus on the arms race, many pacifists joined other antinuclear groups, like Britain's CND and America's SANE, which also drew upon peace-oriented non-pacifists. These more diverse groups, plus some of the pacifist organizations, often were affiliated with the International Confederation for Disarmament and Peace (ICDP), founded in 1963, when the antinuclear campaign was in full bloom. By the early 1970s, however, the ICDP was in dire straits—undermined by the disintegration of the antinuclear movement and desperately short of money and staff. Moreover, like most of its constituent groups, it was obsessed with the struggle against the Vietnam War and, therefore, unable to do very much for the cause of nuclear disarmament.[43] Other peace-oriented internationals existed for specific religions (e.g. Pax Christi, for Catholics) and for interfaith groups (e.g. the World Conference on Religion and Peace), but none was flourishing.[44] Even the Pugwash movement, which had mobilized scientists in East and West against the arms race since its founding in 1957, was languishing; furthermore, during these years it branched out to other issues, such as economic development and the Vietnam War.[45]

Perhaps because of this scant attention to the nuclear danger, a new antinuclear international began to arise at the grassroots level. In 1971, Jim Bohlen and Irving Stowe, two antiwar Americans who had moved with their families to Vancouver, Canada, to ensure that their sons would not be drafted for the Vietnam War, were promoting local opposition to U.S. government plans to explode nuclear weapons on Amchitka Island, off Alaska. After a few frustrating meetings on the issue, Bohlen's wife, Marie, suggested that "somebody sail a boat up there and park right next to the bomb." The idea caught on, and in September, six antinuclear activists, three journalists, and a cameraman—whose presence was viewed as a possible deterrent to the sinking of the vessel by the U.S. Navy—set off on a rusting fishing trawler, the *Phyllis Cormack*, for Alaska. During the journey, one of the journalists read a collection of the legends of North American Indians. They included a Cree grandmother's 200-year-old prophecy that, because of white people's greed, there would come a time when the birds would fall from the skies, the fish would die in their streams, and the seas would be destroyed. Ultimately, however, all the races of the world would unite as Rainbow Warriors, going forth to end the destruction of the earth. The crew discussed this legend and, given its commitment to the preservation of life, found it deeply moving. Indeed, across the vessel, it had already hoisted a sail, adorned with peace and ecology symbols, and proclaiming: "Greenpeace."[46]

Within a short time, this small effort touched off an international movement. Although the U.S. coast guard arrested the crew of the *Phyllis Cormack* as it approached the nuclear test site, thousands of supporters cheered the crew members upon their return to Vancouver. Furthermore, Bohlen and Stowe found another ship to continue the voyage, and when they asked for volunteers for the crew, 400 people signed up. This second Greenpeace vessel failed to reach Amchitka before the U.S. government exploded its nuclear bomb—240 times as powerful as the one it had used to destroy Hiroshima. But the movement against nuclear tests was spreading. In New Zealand, a former Canadian businessman, David McTaggart, convinced Canada's Greenpeace group that he should sail his yacht, *Vega*, across several thousand miles of the Pacific Ocean into the France's unilaterally proclaimed 100,000 square mile nuclear testing zone around Moruroa. Accompanied by two crew members, from Britain and Australia, McTaggart arrived there in June 1972, dropping anchor in international waters. At the orders of the French government, a French minesweeper rammed and crippled the *Vega* that July, but this did not stop McTaggart. A year later, he returned to the test site in his repaired ship, with a new crew.[47] These antinuclear efforts were reinforced by the establishment of Greenpeace groups in Australia and New Zealand. In 1973 and 1974, they campaigned against French nuclear testing and dispatched yet another yacht, the *Fri*, into the test zone and on a "Peace Odyssey" throughout the Pacific.[48]

These freewheeling attitudes and activities—based on a disdain for all nuclear weapons—contrasted with the assumptions and operations of another kind of international peace movement, the World Peace Council (WPC). Launched in 1950, the WPC brought together more than a hundred national peace organizations that were controlled by local Communist parties. Like most of the world Communist movement, the WPC was dominated by the Soviet Communist Party, which, operating through its agent, the Soviet Peace Committee, paid nearly all of the very substantial costs of the WPC's worldwide operations. Through subsidies to other Communist parties, the Soviet party also covered the costs of most WPC affiliates. The only rival force in the organization, the Chinese Communist Party, contemptuously abandoned the WPC in the mid-1960s, as the Chinese and Soviet governments increasingly clashed over foreign policy issues. Although some non-Communists were active in WPC affiliates, Communists dominated the movement. In East Germany, for example, the president of the German Peace Council, Professor Günther Drefahl, was not a Communist. But, before a German Peace Council meeting began, the Communist leaders met and made decisions on the important matters. Then they would invite Drefahl in and commence the official meeting.[49]

Communist control did not mean that every stand taken by the WPC and its affiliates was a hard-line, dogmatic one. On a variety of occasions, these groups proved willing, even eager, to make vague statements about supporting peace and opposing the arms race. After all, mouthing appealing platitudes risked nothing and furthered the chances of attracting non-Communists to their ranks.[50] But Communist control did mean that, when it came to the specifics of world affairs, the WPC ritually took the side of the Soviet Union. According to Rob Prince, a former member of the WPC secretariat, the organization had a "nakedly pro-Soviet approach." Nor was this surprising, for its Communist leaders were convinced that the Soviet Union provided the world's greatest force for peace and human progress. Consequently, as Mark Solomon, a former member of the WPC's presidential committee, recalled, "the WPC . . . was never going to take a position in direct confrontation with Soviet policy." WPC affiliates adopted much the same stance. A characteristic statement, issued by the East German Peace Council in August 1974, lauded "the policy of peace pursued by the Soviet Union and the community of socialist states," while assailing "militarist NATO quarters." The Peace Council concluded that "we consider the strengthening of socialism to be our paramount mission."[51]

Despite its very substantial resources, the WPC provided little support for the nuclear disarmament campaign. One reason was that, ever since the mid-1950s, the WPC's Soviet partisanship had been narrowing its appeal, especially in Europe and North America.[52] But, in the early 1970s, at least as important a factor was that the WPC was thoroughly dedicated to what its Bulgarian affiliate called the "victory of the heroic Vietnamese people over the American aggressors." This enthusiasm for burying "the US imperialists" in the jungles of Vietnam reflected not only the usual Cold War bias of the WPC, but the growing recognition of Communist leaders that the war—in which the U.S. government mobilized massive military power to destroy a poor, Asian peasant nation—provided a body blow to American influence (and, it was assumed, a boost to Soviet influence) in Third World nations. In line with this assessment, in 1966 the Kremlin tapped Romesh Chandra, an Indian Communist, to become the WPC's secretary-general—the first to come from the Third World. Although inept at building the WPC in industrial nations, Chandra proved skillful at exploiting Third World anger at the United States. Together with U.S. napalming of villages in Vietnam, this WPC emphasis upon Third World sufferings and national liberation struggles encouraged a substantial flow of Asian, African, and Latin American recruits to the WPC, which in the early 1960s had seemed close to extinction. But it had the drawback of dissipating pressure for Soviet-American arms accords and for détente.[53]

Not surprisingly, relations between this Soviet-aligned peace movement and its nonaligned counterpart were often quite strained. Usually, nonaligned disarmament groups spurned the annual world peace congresses organized by the WPC, considering them little more than pro-Soviet propaganda extravaganzas. In 1973, however, Chandra called for an end to the "cold war" among peace groups and the WPC made extraordinary efforts to lure independent disarmament activists to its "World Congress of Peace Forces," in Moscow. As a result, despite lingering suspicions, small delegations of independent activists made plans to attend the gathering. Some were never admitted to it. In the aftermath of a SANE letter of protest to the Soviet embassy about Soviet human rights violations, the Soviet government denied visas to the SANE delegation. The vice-chair of the Moscow Congress, Michael Zimyanin, explained that "fascists, racists, and openly aggressive organizations," as well as "enemies of peace, democracy, and national independence have no place in this Congress."[54] Others, who attended, were appalled by the intimidating atmosphere of the Moscow meeting, where plain-clothes vigilantes ripped suspiciously independent badges off delegates and party faithful destroyed independent literature. When a defense of Soviet dissidents, signed by a galaxy of American peace movement leaders (including Daniel Berrigan, David McReynolds, Grace Paley, David Dellinger, and Noam Chomsky), was read to the convention's Commission on Social Problems and Human Rights by the Rev. Paul Mayer, he was quickly gaveled out of order, told that there were no political prisoners in the Soviet Union, and censured by the U.S. delegation, most of whom were WPC stalwarts. By contrast, Leonid Brezhnev's dreary two-

and-a-half-hour justification of Soviet foreign and military policy was greeted with what the convention minutes called "stormy, prolonged applause." Naturally, the Moscow Congress did little to alter the chilly relations between nonaligned and pro-Soviet peace activists.[55]

Government Response, 1971-76

Given their commitment to a nuclear buildup, the nuclear powers reacted with considerable hostility to the activities of antinuclear groups. Thoroughly contemptuous of what he derided as "peacenik views," especially in the midst of the Vietnam War, Nixon stepped up FBI and CIA spying upon peace organizations and the disruption of their activities. By the early 1970s, the CIA's Operation Chaos, conducted in violation of that agency's charter, had targeted over a thousand U.S. organizations and 200,000 individuals. The President also initiated the legal prosecution of numerous activists. Not surprisingly, the White House placed both SANE and its executive director, Sandy Gottlieb, upon the President's "Enemies List."[56] Irked by the opposition of scientists to nuclear tests on Amchitka and to other administration programs, Nixon secured his revenge by abolishing the President's Science Advisory Committee. He also vetoed the nomination of Franklin Long, a leading chemist who had criticized the government's ABM program, as director of the National Science Foundation.[57]

Antinuclear activists also faced grave difficulties in the Soviet Union. To be sure, government officials continued their strong support for the Communist party's official peace operation. Dispatching a message to the Soviet ambassadors in 58 nations in June 1976, the central committee of the Soviet party told them to transmit to Communist parties its appreciation of the WPC's "mass worldwide campaign for cessation of the arms race and for disarmament." The WPC's recent appeal to ban atomic weapons had "unanimous approval" in the Soviet Union, where "special placards," "special films," and the mass media would ensure its success, and it was the duty of Communists elsewhere to promote the campaign in their own nations.[58] Furthermore, the Kremlim granted unusual latitude to those Soviet scientists it allowed to attend the Pugwash conferences. Indeed, Kremlin officials respected these Soviet scientists sufficiently to accept their critique of missile defense—based, in turn, on the analysis provided by Western antinuclear scientists—and, consequently, sign the ABM treaty.[59] But this was the limit of Soviet tolerance. Fearful of the plans of independent activists to support the rights of Soviet dissenters, Moscow denied a visa in 1973 not only to SANE's Gottlieb, but to the War Resisters' International's Michael

Randle. When other Western peace activists, who did reach Moscow, went to the GUM department store and distributed leaflets demanding the right of free expression, they were arrested. Similarly, Soviet police regularly dispersed gatherings of Soviet pacifists or arrested their participants. When Sakharov was awarded the Nobel Peace Prize in 1975, Kremlin officials barred his travel to Oslo and denounced him as "a judas," a "laboratory rat of the West."[60]

The French government, particularly, seemed determined to silence its critics. When David McTaggart of Greenpeace, having survived the ramming of his yacht, returned with the *Vega* to France's nuclear testing zone in the South Pacific in August 1973, the French authorities were waiting for him. A French military ship heaved to and dispatched sailors, who stormed aboard the *Vega*. Although McTaggart pointed out that his ship was moored in international waters and, of course, was private property, the French sailors attacked him and the other male crew member, beating them savagely with truncheons. The sailors also threw cameras and other equipment overboard. But a female crew member, spared the initial assault, managed to take pictures of the attack and, then, to elude pursuing sailors long enough to hide her camera. As a result, although the French government later claimed that McTaggart had "fallen and injured himself" and, then, requested medical help from France, her pictures revealed what had really happened. Two of the pictures were picked up by the wire services and published in at least twenty countries, thereby adding to the furor over France's policy of atmospheric nuclear testing.[61]

Indeed, as international pressure grew, French policy could no longer be sustained. In late 1972, the new Labour Prime Minister of New Zealand, Norman Kirk, dispatched a stiff letter of protest to the French government about nuclear testing, contending that the deep-seated opposition of New Zealanders simply had to be heeded by a democratic government. Not taking this lightly, the French government responded by threatening to undermine New Zealand's economy. In early 1973, New Zealand and Australia, which now also had elected a Labour government, sought an injunction from the International Court of Justice to halt French nuclear testing. Although the court issued a preliminary ruling in June calling upon that nation to avoid nuclear tests in the atmosphere until the case was decided, France refused to accept the court's jurisdiction. Following the trail blazed by antinuclear activists, New Zealand's government now dispatched two protest frigates to the French nuclear testing zone, one with a cabinet minister on board. To Kirk, his government's campaign had become a moral crusade, "shaking alive the conscience of the world as to the danger of expanding the stockpile and manufacture of deadly nuclear weapons." Although neither the interim injunction of the International Court nor the fleet of protest vessels stopped France's nuclear tests that year or—despite New Zealand's further action before the International Court—during the first part of 1974, the French government grew increasingly rattled. Near the end of that year, it proclaimed that it had finally abandoned atmospheric nuclear testing.[62]

For a time, in fact, it seemed that the antinuclear tide in the South Pacific would sweep further; but this did not prove to be the case. In July 1975, the South Pacific Forum had agreed to press for the creation of a nuclear-free zone in the region. Accordingly, that October, New Zealand's government brought the nuclear-free zone proposal to the United Nations, where it secured the co-sponsorship of Fiji and Papua New Guinea. And, in December, the United Nations endorsed a South Pacific Nuclear Weapon Free Zone. However, countervailing pressure from the U.S. government and political shifts in two key countries quickly undermined the plan. In November, elections in New Zealand brought to power the more hawkish National Party, which two days later disavowed the nuclear-free zone proposal. In Australia, as well, elections in late 1975 produced a conservative government firmly committed to maintaining the West's nuclear options in the region. Consequently, despite its promising beginning, the South Pacific nuclear-free zone plan collapsed. Indeed, the new administration in New Zealand went still further and reversed the Labour government's ban on the admission of nuclear-armed warships to its ports. Furthermore, French nuclear testing continued underground.[63]

Nevertheless, the popular mobilization in the Pacific and, ultimately, the success in ending France's atmospheric nuclear testing, like the more impressive arms control advances of the 1960s, suggest that, when stirred to action, antinuclear campaigners could be effective. Even the hostile Nixon administration, acting for what a U.S. government spokesperson called "political and other reasons," responded to the Greenpeace campaign by canceling the remaining U.S. nuclear tests on Amchitka and, eventually, turning the island into a bird sanctuary.[64] For the most part, however, the early 1970s was a time of relatively little movement activity and, consequently, few victories.

The Movement Begins
to Revive, 1975-78

> The primary task before us is disarmament.
> David McReynolds, 1977

Between 1975 and 1978, the world antinuclear movement began to awaken from its torpor. In part, its revival reflected the end of the Vietnam War in April 1975. This event released many peace groups and activists from their preoccupation with that conflict, thereby enabling them to confront the nuclear menace. But the stirrings in the movement also resulted from a number of factors that heightened awareness of the ongoing nuclear arms race. With public concern growing about the dangers of nuclear power plants—including releases of radioactivity, disposal of nuclear waste, and production of fissionable material for nuclear weapons—people were reminded of the fact that the Bomb also existed and, in fact, posed an even greater threat to human survival. Indeed, many activists already perceived a perilously close relationship between the two kinds of "nukes." Furthermore, the U.S. government's plan, revealed in 1977, to produce and deploy an enhanced radiation warhead—better known as the neutron bomb—seemed to millions of people a particularly disgusting escalation of the nuclear arms race. Finally, in 1978 the United Nations held a Special Session on Disarmament in New York City. This high-level conclave not only helped to focus the energies of peace groups on the nuclear question, but gave them the opportunity to gather with one another for meetings, strategy sessions, and demonstrations. It also raised the salience of the nuclear issue among the general public. Together with developments unique to specific nations, these factors gave a new impetus to nuclear disarmament activism.

Western Europe

Probably the most significant outbreak of antinuclear agitation during these years occurred in the Netherlands. By late 1976, the Interchurch Peace Council (IKV) had concluded that the nuclear powers were not moving toward the elimination of nuclear weapons but, rather, were continuing the nuclear arms race. Consequently, in September 1977 it embarked on a disarmament campaign epitomized by its new slogan: "Help rid the world of nuclear weapons; let it begin in the Netherlands." The assumption was that the denuclearization of the Netherlands would not upset the overall strategic balance, but would provide a dramatic first step toward worldwide nuclear disarmament.[1] By mid-1978, IKV had organized over 200 local groups around its campaign. Although the Dutch political parties remained wary of this venture, a poll that October showed that it had the support of 58 percent of the population.[2] IKV played a less prominent role in yet another antinuclear campaign launched in late 1977, the "Halt the Neutron Bomb" movement. With popular outrage widespread at the U.S. plan for building and deploying the new weapon, the Netherlands was swept by fierce anti-neutron bomb activity, including a protest demonstration with 50,000 participants in March 1978 and a petition to the Dutch parliament, signed by 1.2 million people.[3]

The movement also showed a new liveliness in Britain. CND protested against Chinese nuclear testing, called attention to the dangers of nuclear proliferation,[4] and acquired an attractive new leader in 1977, when Monsignor Bruce Kent—a Catholic prelate with strong social convictions—became chair of the organization. Furthermore, it also screened *The War Game*—a chilling docudrama on nuclear war—before university and other public audiences around the country. Students proved especially interested in the film, which the BBC had banned from television since 1965.[5] Many Britons in these years also were caught up in the campaign against nuclear power plants. Friends of the Earth, an environmentalist group, played a leading role, especially during the Windscale power plant inquiry of 1977. Although, initially, this crusade stayed clear of the nuclear weapons question, the connections between the two nuclear issues, highlighted by CND's participation, enhanced environmentalist and public concern about the Bomb.[6] Even more important, CND launched a spirited campaign against the neutron bomb, turning it into a major issue. Attacking plans for the new weapon, CND produced thousands of leaflets and posters, held meetings and demonstrations, and circulated a petition that drew 161,000 signatures. In May 1978, polls found that, of Britons who had heard of the neutron bomb, 72 percent opposed its deployment in their country.[7] When added to interest stirred up by the U.N. Special Session on Disarmament,[8] these factors produced the first significant growth in CND for years. By 1978, though CND still had only 3,220 members and 3½ paid staff, it claimed 102 local groups, 293 affiliated organizations, and a new dynamism.[9]

Although the nuclear disarmament movement in West Germany was far less unified and visible, it, too, started to revive. During the 1970s, veterans of the Federal Republic's youthful, leftwing extra-parliamentary opposition began to gravitate into local citizens' initiatives (*Bürgerinitiativen*), where they continued their anti-Establishment activities on a grassroots level. Many of these citizens' initiatives related to environmental protection, and none proved more dramatic than the struggle against nuclear power. In 1975, storming the nuclear reactor site at Wyhl, some 20,000 activists tore down the surrounding fence and proceeded to occupy it for the next month—organizing study groups, running a "people's school," and hosting students and other activists from all over Western Europe. In the West German campaign against nuclear power, as elsewhere, the nuclear weapons issue kept peeping through. A popular photo book showed a mushroom cloud rising out of a power plant cooling tower. A key slogan of the activists was: "Better Active Today than Radioactive Tomorrow!"[10] Within church circles, as well, there was a growing concern about nuclear weapons, fostered in part by the neutron bomb issue and by the activities of IKV in the Netherlands. As a result, two peace groups, Action Reconciliation/Peace Service (Aktion Sühnezeichen/Friedensdienste) among Protestants and Pax Christi among Catholics, decided to address disarmament issues. In 1978, a group of Protestant pacifists—responding to a 1975 critique of the arms race by the World Council of Churches—organized a new peace group, Live Without Armaments (Ohne Rüstung Leben), whose members signed a statement proclaiming that, henceforth, they would "support the political development of the idea of peace without weapons in our country." Like the protesters against nuclear power, they found themselves drawn into a growing nuclear disarmament campaign.[11]

Disarmament activism also began to flourish in the Nordic countries. Plans for the neutron bomb touched off a wave of concern in Denmark and, especially, in Norway, where a Campaign Against the Neutron Bomb was formally launched in January 1978. Drawing the support of 20 Norwegian organizations—including nearly all the major political youth groups and a number of peace organizations—the Norwegian campaign protested the development of the bomb and urged the Norwegian government to oppose the weapon's production and deployment in Europe.[12] The U.N. Special Session on Disarmament also had a significant impact on peace groups and public opinion throughout the region. In Sweden, it led to the convening of a "people's parliament" to prepare for the gathering, with participation by the WILPF section and other peace organizations. In the wake of the U.N. conclave, Swedish activists, together with their Danish and Norwegian counterparts, convened a follow-up meeting in Göteborg.[13] After the end of the Vietnam War, Sweden also experienced a substantial upsurge of activism against nuclear power plants—a campaign that formed the basis for later mobilizations against nuclear weapons. Meanwhile, in Finland, the defunct Committee of 100—a veteran of the nuclear disarmament crusade of the early 1960s—was revived in late 1976 and 1977. It became the key component of the Finnish Peace Union, which in 1978 began playing a more active role by serving as an umbrella organization for Finland's small, independent peace organizations.[14]

Elsewhere in Western Europe, the movement was also stirring. Reviving in 1975 after the fall of the Greek military dictatorship, the Greek Committee for Nuclear Disarmament and Peace issued a call, signed by prominent personalities, to make the Mediterranean a "sea of peace," free of nuclear weapons. In Italy, the small Radical Party organized a series of anti-militarist marches.[15] In Belgium, peace groups mobilized public opinion against the neutron bomb and, led by CNAPD and inspired by the U.N. Special Session, turned out 10,000 demonstrators in Brussels during May 1978 around the slogan "Disarm to Survive."[16] The most surprising upsurge occurred in Turkey, where a broad-based peace organization had never existed. In April 1977, during a time of substantial democratization in Turkish life, the Istanbul Bar Association helped launch the Turkish Peace Association (TPA). Within a short time, the TPA's governing body consisted of representatives from almost 50 groups, including professional bodies and Turkey's largest labor, women's, and youth organizations. In its first year, the TPA held more than 40 public meetings in the country's major cities, published a monthly journal, and participated in conferences at home and overseas. Campaigning for nuclear disarmament, the TPA sharply criticized the proposal to site the neutron bomb in Turkey's U.S. and NATO military bases.[17]

Throughout Western Europe, the only country in which the movement suffered a serious setback was France. For a time, developments there seemed promising enough, with a rising opposition to nuclear power cresting in 1976 and 1977. Assailing the French government's enthusiasm for nuclear-based energy, some 50,000 protesters turned out in late July 1977 to demonstrate against the French breeder reactor at Malville.[18] In other ways, however, the tide was turning against critics of the Bomb. Starting in 1977,

Socialist and Communist delegates stopped attending meetings of the action committee against French nuclear testing in Polynesia—a body that also drew representatives of several small peace groups—because both parties had decided to abandon their opposition to nuclear weapons. Their political reversal was based, in part, upon the existence of the *force de frappe*; in part, on a desire for the foreign policy independence that it provided for France. It also reflected political opportunism, for it would free these proponents of a government of the Left of the charge that they would surrender France to the Soviet Union and would lessen the possibility that the French military, fond of its new weapons, would stage a *coup* to prevent their taking office. Although leaders of both parties had difficulties selling the new, pro-nuclear position to their rank and file, ultimately it prevailed.[19]

North America

In the United States, the antinuclear movement was growing. With the Vietnam war at an end, opposition to nuclear weapons became a top issue among pacifists. WILPF renewed its emphasis on disarmament with a number of disarmament seminars in May 1975 and, thereafter, sought to build support for the U.N. disarmament conference.[20] In 1976, the War Resisters League took the lead in organizing a Continental Walk for Disarmament and Social Justice, in which "the case for disarmament" was "taken to the people, town by town." During the following summer, its national committee voted to make "Disarmament and Peace Conversion" its highest priority for the next year. In September 1978, War Resisters League members staged simultaneous demonstrations in Red Square and on the White House lawn, where they unfurled banners calling upon the two Cold War antagonists to disarm.[21] Similarly, in early 1978 the FOR national council—after a discussion of nuclear disarmament, the U.N. special session, and activities at Rocky Flats—voted to "reaffirm disarmament as our major priority." The group's magazine, *Fellowship*, explained: "Our membership and leadership are agreed that, in view of the accelerating arms race between the US and the USSR and their client states, other programmatic concerns must, for the moment, take second place."[22]

As the AFSC's resources and staff dwarfed those of other pacifist groups, its change of priorities was particularly important. Ron Young, then the AFSC peace education secretary, recalled that, with the end of the Vietnam War in 1975, AFSC leaders asked themselves: "OK, now what do we do?" For older staffers, who had cut their teeth in the antinuclear campaigns of the 1950s and early 1960s, the answer was easy: agitate for nuclear disarmament. But younger staffers, whose experience was limited to the intense struggle against the Vietnam War, were somewhat reluctant to return to a disarmament agenda, which they initially viewed as somewhat old-fashioned and nebulous. Ultimately, however, they accepted it as one of the AFSC's top priorities. Young recalled that, in their eyes, nuclear war was "what happened to the Vietnamese writ large. If you look at images of Hiroshima, Asian people, and also burned people, buildings down, and whole villages destroyed, there was a carryover. If we created a holocaust for Vietnam, nuclear war was a holocaust for everybody." Consequently, the AFSC stepped up its support for the nationwide campaign against the B-1 bomber and expanded its local organizing efforts against nuclear weapons facilities—efforts that were beginning to take hold.[23] In 1975, the Rocky Flats Action Group held its first demonstration, with 25 people. Three years later, it turned out some 6,000.[24]

America's non-pacifist groups were also gravitating toward a nuclear disarmament agenda. Women Strike for Peace urged the Chinese to stop nuclear testing, demanded a test ban treaty, assailed the neutron bomb, and distributed a brochure entitled "Human Beings are an Endangered Species." It also petitioned President Carter—who, at the outset of his administration, it rather liked—to enter into negotiations to end the arms race.[25] Clergy and Laity Concerned, faced with developing a new focus after the Vietnam War, plunged not only into the campaign against the B-1 bomber, but into opposition to nuclear facilities and nuclear weapons.[26] Similarly, the American branch of Pax Christi, founded in 1973 and reorganized in 1975, produced newsletters and other publications that dealt principally with nuclear issues.[27] Meanwhile, the Center for Defense Information played an active role in opposing the B-1 bomber, criticizing the neutron bomb, and promoting a nuclear test ban.[28] New Directions, a peace organization designed to serve as a Common Cause for foreign policy, focused heavily on mobilizing support for nuclear arms controls.[29]

As for SANE, in the aftermath of the Vietnam War it denounced the Ford administration's nuclear policies, publicly protested China's atmospheric nuclear tests, and, in testimony before the platform committee at the 1976 Democratic national convention, assailed "strategic arms competition and nuclear proliferation." Quoting the party's presidential candidate, Jimmy Carter, it demanded "control, then reduction, and ultimately, elimination of nuclear arsenals."[30] Like WSP, SANE found Carter an appealing candidate, and nearly endorsed him; instead, as things turned out, SANE's executive director, Sandy Gottlieb, took a leave from his job and went to work in Carter's campaign. Of course, at the time, SANE had little weight in U.S. politics. When David Cortright became executive director the following year, the disarmament group was at a low point organizationally, with only about 4,000 members. But it gradually began to revive, assisted by the public furor over the neutron bomb, the growing concern about nuclear power, and a closer relationship with organized labor. Thanks largely to the election of the peace-oriented William Winpisinger as president of the International Association of Machinists, this emerging labor-peace alliance pushed SANE into the forefront of economic conversion efforts—an attack upon America's military-industrial complex with antinuclear implications.[31]

Antinuclear activities were also heating up within the American scientific community. The Federation of American Scientists continued its efforts to defend Andrei Sakharov. Arranging for a meeting with the dissident Soviet physicist—in whom Jeremy Stone "saw the mirror image of the movement that had created FAS"—the FAS pressed the Soviet government for Sakharov's inclusion in Pugwash meetings and, pending his better treatment, organized a boycott by individual scientists of Soviet scientific events. In addition, the FAS issued a vigorous challenge to the American government's "linkage" of a SALT II agreement to Soviet behavior in other areas.[32] Although the rapidly-growing Union of Concerned Scientists continued to emphasize the issue of nuclear reactor safety, in 1978 it issued a "Declaration on the Nuclear Arms Race" that called for U.S. initiatives to halt the production of nuclear weapons. Signed by thousands of scientists, engineers, and other professionals, the Declaration was followed up by another UCS petition calling for ratification of the SALT II treaty.[33] Meanwhile, pointing to the "rough strategic nuclear parity" between the United States and the Soviet Union, the *Bulletin of the Atomic Scientists* suggested that the U.S. government simply *"stop* the race in accumulation of new weapons and weapon delivery systems," on a temporary basis, to see if the Soviet Union would follow its example.[34]

Many of these groups, plus others, worked together amicably in the Coalition for a New Foreign and Military Policy, the successor to the Vietnam-era Coalition to Stop Funding the War. For the most part, the new Coalition served as the congressional lobbying arm of the American peace movement. During these years, it focused especially on the congressional passage of "transfer amendments" that would shift billions of dollars in federal funding from military to social programs. In this way, it was hoped, organizations devoted to expanding the nation's health, housing, education, mass transit, and welfare facilities would join with critics of the arms race to limit the Pentagon's expensive weapons programs. Although Congress repeatedly rejected these "transfer amendments," they did draw substantial support from liberal legislators.[35] In addition, in 1976, peace organizations formed an Ad Hoc Working Group for Disarmament that, in early 1977, became the Coalition's Disarmament Working Group. By mid-1978, this Washington-based Disarmament Working Group consisted of more than forty national religious, labor, peace, research, and social action organizations.[36]

For the time being, the biggest joint disarmament project taken on by U.S. peace groups was the campaign against the B-1 bomber. By the end of 1975, Terry Provance had organized Stop the B-1 Bomber groups in 180 American cities. Meanwhile, in Washington, the AFSC had drawn together a broad coalition of groups to lobby against the weapons program, ranging from peace groups like WSP, the FAS, and the Council for a Livable World, to Environmental Action and Common Cause. Although Gerald Ford, faced with primary challenges from the hawkish Ronald Reagan, put himself clearly on record as favoring the B-1, Carter seemed more open to influence. Consequently, peace activists bird-dogged him at every campaign stop, pressing him to scrap plans for the nuclear bomber. Meanwhile, thanks to movement lobbying, many Democrats in Congress came out against the weapon. As a result, during the Democratic primaries Carter committed himself to opposing the B-1—a position that, despite later equivocation on his part, activists did not let him forget. Shortly after Carter's election victory, they held a vigil outside his home in Plains, Georgia. And two days after Carter's inauguration as President, activists staged anti–B-1 demonstrations in 145 cities, including Washington, D.C. "If Carter builds the B-1, it will be a breach of faith," a WILPF activist declared. With 33 national organizations working against the B-1 during early 1977, the White House was flooded with telephone calls, letters, and appeals, including an anti–B-1 petition signed by 29 mayors.[37]

American peace groups also worked together on the 1978 U.N. Special Session on Disarmament. Recognizing its potential for mobilizing public opinion and changing public policy, U.S. and overseas disarmament groups promoted public awareness of the event, met together frequently, issued disarmament proposals, lobbied government officials, and even hosted seminars on disarmament for the official U.N. delegations from small nations. On May 27, they staged a march through Manhattan and rally for nuclear disarmament outside the United Nations buildings that drew an estimated 15,000 to 20,000 people—probably the largest disarmament demonstration up to that point in American history.[38] Although the U.N. Special Session did not lead to a breakthrough in the realm of public policy, it secured an agreement by the U.N. delegates that the arms race jeopardized the security of all nations, enhanced the role of disarmament NGOs in U.N. affairs, focused the energies of disparate groups, and raised public consciousness. Furthermore, from the standpoint of peace groups, the U.N. Special Session produced an excellent Final Document—the result, in part, of their lobbying—which they championed thereafter.[39]

This new concern with disarmament intersected with rising U.S. activism against nuclear power. Organized by the Clamshell Alliance, thousands of antinuclear demonstrators staged a nonviolent occupation of the Seabrook, New Hampshire, nuclear reactor site in April of 1977, leading to 1,400 arrests. Most of the arrested refused bail, and had to be held in jail for days or weeks. This dramatic incident led to the appearance of similar antinuclear power groups in other regions, including the Catfish Alliance in Alabama, the Oystershell Alliance in New Orleans, the Cactus Alliance in Utah and Arizona, the Red Clover Alliance in Vermont, the Palmetto Alliance in South Carolina, the Abalone Alliance in California, and the Crabshell Alliance in Seattle. The struggle at Seabrook was now reenacted nationwide. Although, superficially, this was an environmental movement, the underlying reality was that many of the activists viewed nuclear reactors as extensions of nuclear weapons. Bumper stickers, books, and buttons depicted nuclear power as the "silent bomb," while activists referred to both nuclear reactors and nuclear weapons simply as "nukes." The graphics used in the campaign also emphasized the nuclear connection: mushroom clouds rising from reactor cooling towers, or a reactor shaped like an egg cracking open and giving birth to the Bomb.[40]

The underlying revulsion against nuclear weapons can also be seen in the backgrounds of individual activists. Randy Kehler, one of those arrested at Seabrook, recalled that nuclear war "was the shadow that hung over my life" since the early 1960s. Helen Caldicott, an Australian pediatrician who moved to the United States in the late 1970s and produced a cutting critique of nuclear power (*Nuclear Madness*), recalled that she had "grown up with the fear of imminent annihilation by nuclear holocaust"; consequently, she had become a leader in the campaigns against French nuclear testing and Australian uranium mining.[41] Chuck Johnson, who participated in two occupations of the Trojan nuclear power plant site outside of Portland, recalled that, "ever since I was a kid, I worried about" nuclear weapons, "thought about them, and wanted to do something about them." Peter Bergel, another leader of the Portland campaign, had opposed nuclear weapons testing as a college student in the 1960s and, during the 1970s, had wanted to sail a ship into the French nuclear testing zone. Frank von Hippel, a physicist who produced devastating studies of nuclear reactor safety, was the grandson of James Franck, one of the earliest critics of the Bomb. He recalled: "I guess I was always focused on nuclear weapons issues," but "didn't become active until I . . . became involved . . . in the nuclear energy issue." A key reason for assailing nuclear reactors at this time was that, by contrast to the weapons, banning them seemed feasible. As one critic of nuclear power observed: "I can't do anything about bombs, but I can do something about reactors." Taking on nuclear weapons, recalled Johnson, felt like "too much." Bergel regarded stopping nuclear power as "a winnable issue, which was one of the things I liked about it."[42]

The kinship of the two campaigns was recognized by a new organization that united them in a nationwide movement: Mobilization for Survival. Organized at an April 1977 gathering in Philadelphia by representatives of 49 organizations, mostly peace and anti-nuclear power groups, Mobilization for Survival was officially launched in mid-year around four goals: "Zero Nuclear Weapons"; "Ban Nuclear Power"; "Stop the Arms Race"; and "Fund Human Needs." As might be expected, the first two proved the most important foci of its subsequent activities. That August, in commemoration of the Hiroshima and Nagasaki bombings, the Mobilization sponsored more than a hundred public gatherings. In the fall, it organized over 200 teach-ins across the country; though some drew as few as thirty people, many attracted hundreds, and at least two (in Boston and San Francisco) drew more than a thousand participants. By the time of its first nationwide conference in December, the Mobilization claimed 330 affiliates, many of them small but militant groups formed to campaign against nuclear power plants. Assailing the idea of peaceful nuclear power, Caldicott warned the gathering: "Every country that builds a nuclear reactor can build a bomb." In May 1978, the Mobilization played the central role in organizing the demonstration at the U.N. Special Session on Disarmament.[43]

Although the impact of these developments upon the broader society was modest, they did contribute to a fairly dovish mood. Between March 1975 and March 1978, polls found that the percentage of Americans favoring increased military spending never topped 29 percent. In 1977 and 1978, some three-quarters of the population approved of a nuclear test ban treaty. In July 1978, a Harris poll found that 71 percent of respondents favored a SALT II treaty. By 52 to 30 percent, Americans believed that it was "morally wrong" for a nation "to use nuclear weapons in war if it has to." Only on the issue of deploying the neutron bomb was there an even split in popular sentiment.[44] In Congress, a substantial bloc of liberal Democrats challenged Pentagon priorities. Some of them, like U.S. Senator George McGovern, of South Dakota, had warm relations with peace groups.[45] In 1976, when President Ford requested funding to start production of the B-1 bomber, these congressional Democrats passed a measure drawn up by the Stop the B-1 Bomber Campaign and its close congressional allies to block action. Though not killing the project, it delayed a decision on production until the following year, when many hoped that a Democratic President would slay the B-1 dragon.[46]

This seemed quite possible. During his 1976 campaign, the Democratic presidential candidate, Jimmy Carter, not only proclaimed his opposition to the B-1, but called for curbs on nuclear power and proliferation, a comprehensive nuclear test ban, and movement toward the elimination of all nuclear weapons. In part, these positions reflected Carter's humane, religious convictions, which led him to believe that mass killing was immoral. In addition, his experience as a nuclear engineer gave him a sophisticated understanding of nuclear dangers.[47] But Carter's dovish stands on nuclear issues also reflected his interaction with Democratic Party and peace activists that year. During the primaries, he recalled, small groups of people met with him, and "I listened to . . . their suggestions about . . . defense matters, what they were concerned about in SALT and non-proliferation. So I began to expand my mind a little bit further." For example, Carter became a good friend that year of Harold Willens, the California businessman who had long been a vigorous opponent of nuclear weapons and a staunch supporter of peace groups. Willens recalled that Carter "was very anxious to have me become a spokesman for him because he was not well-known among northern progressives." In private, they discussed the dangers of the nuclear arms race at length, and, according to Willens, Carter "was really a soul-mate." Shortly after Carter's election, the President-elect invited Willens and his dovish associate, the actor Paul Newman, to meet with him in Washington. Here, over dinner, Willens noted, "we talked a lot about what . . . Carter could do as President" to deal with the nuclear menace. "And he . . . made certain commitments."[48]

The nuclear disarmament campaign also began to gather momentum in Canada. With the Vietnam War at an end, the Voice of Women (VOW), like so many other peace groups, joined the struggle against nuclear power, which in the Canadian case meant opposing the manufacture, promotion, and sale of Canadian reactors abroad. However, as the U.N. Special Session approached, it focused more directly on the nuclear arms race. VOW sent a substantial delegation to New York City for the event, at which it lobbied, discussed disarmament strategy with its overseas counterparts, and demonstrated.[49] The U.N. Special Session also helped set the priorities of a new Canadian peace organization, Project Ploughshares. During 1976, religious pacifists and experts on Third World economic development began discussions on the relationship between disarmament and development. On January 1, 1977, they launched Project Ploughshares, a study and action group whose name was taken from the biblical verse that spoke of beating swords into plowshares and spears into pruning hooks. The Canadian Council of Churches found the venture attractive and, in the middle of that year, adopted Project Ploughshares, whose sponsorship and funding henceforth came from twelve church and civic groups. Although Project Ploughshares initially critiqued aspects of the Canadian military budget, the advent of the U.N. Special Session redirected its energies toward highlighting the Soviet-American arms race.[50] In August 1978, asked how they would vote on nuclear weapons if a worldwide referendum were held, Canadians—by a ratio of three to one—responded that they would vote in favor of complete nuclear disarmament.[51]

Asia and the Pacific

Although the Australian nuclear disarmament movement had less public presence than the North American during these years, it, too, was reviving. In part, this revival, like the flurries of activity in Western Europe and North America, emerged obliquely, thanks to the growth of widespread public opposition to uranium mining. Indeed, the campaign against uranium mining was the Australian counterpart to the campaign against nuclear power in Western Europe and United States. In this uranium-rich country, critics of uranium mining pointed out that it caused radioactive contamination of the environment, encouraged the growth of dangerous nuclear reactors, and provided the raw material for the building of nuclear weapons. Launched in 1975 by environmentalists, peace activists, and assorted radicals, the crusade against uranium mining was soon loosely coordinated by a National Uranium Moratorium Campaign. By 1977, the campaign had become a mass movement, with frequent demonstrations held by a far-flung network of local groups. It also won the backing of the Australian Labor Party and of many unions, whose members recognized all too well what uranium mining did to workers. As Helen Caldicott quipped: "They were more concerned about their testicles than their jobs."[52] In addition, in 1978 more direct disarmament activity emerged in connection with the U.N. Special Session. That April, peace groups convened "Australian People's Disarmament" conferences in Melbourne and Sydney. Meanwhile, the Australian Peace Liaison Committee circulated a "Australian Disarmament Declaration" setting out "seven concrete ways in which Australia could contribute to halting the arms race." These methods included fostering a treaty to ban the use of nuclear weapons and halting the mining and export of uranium.[53]

In New Zealand, public protest developed over the visits of U.S. nuclear-armed and nuclear-powered warships. From 1973 to 1975, New Zealand's Labour government had banned such visits. But pressure from the U.S. government to resume them led, in mid-1975, to the idea of Peace Squadrons, small flotillas of private boats that would block the entry of nuclear warships into New Zealand's harbors. Their originator was the Rev. George Armstrong, a peace activist and theologian who launched the venture in Auckland that October. It would be "a creative, affirmative, non-violent action," he said—"a symbolic gesture of resistance to the destruction of humanity" and something that "could make New Zealand an island of sanity in an ocean of peace." Their commitment was soon tested, for, the following month, Labour was defeated at the polls by the conservative National Party, which reinstituted visits by the nuclear warships. Anticipating difficulties in Auckland, the government arranged for the first U.S. nuclear warship, the *Truxton*, to arrive at Wellington. It was met there by a small Wellington Peace Squadron, as well as by a union ban on the waterfront, which prevented it from berthing. In October 1976, when the U.S. nuclear cruiser *Long Beach* arrived at Auckland, a more substantial Peace Squadron of some 150 small yachts, dinghies, canoes, and kayaks obstructed its passage, as did individual surfboarders, flying the nuclear disarmament symbol.[54]

Attracting very substantial publicity in New Zealand and overseas, Peace Squadron activism continued thereafter, increasingly setting the terms for public debate. In early 1978, a fleet of 100 protest vessels met the U.S. nuclear submarine *Pintado*. Although navy and police vessels and helicopters managed to disrupt the peace flotilla, capsizing several protest boats, the event produced dramatic confrontations. The commander of the *Pintado*, disturbed by the sight of a mother holding a baby in her arms in a small protest craft before the ship's bow, told the press: "She was holding that baby to her, and I'll never forget the way she looked at me. . . . We were like that for 30 seconds—30 years—who knows? It seemed a long time." With the announcement by the government of another nuclear submarine visit, Friends of the Earth, Greenpeace, CND, the New Zealand Foundation for Peace Studies, and the Auckland branch of the United Nations Association joined the Peace Squadrons in seeking a supreme court injunction to block it. The leader of the Labour opposition, Bill Rowling, charged that the National Party was making New Zealand "a doormat for the larger powers. . . . New Zealand should not be sucked into their war games." Committing the Labour Party to the struggle for a nuclear-free Pacific, he declared that the region provided "the last remaining opportunity to take a stand against the escalation of the arms race."[55]

These events added momentum to the emerging nuclear-free movement throughout the Pacific. In early April 1975, thanks primarily to the efforts of Fiji's ATOM and antinuclear organizations in New Zealand, Tahiti, Australia, and France, 88 delegates representing 85 organizations in twenty Pacific and two European countries met in Suva, Fiji, for a week-long Conference for a Nuclear Free Pacific. Discussing the French government's use of Moruroa for nuclear testing, the U.S. government's use of Micronesia for nuclear testing and nuclear weapons bases, and other great power uses of the region for their military purposes, the conferees agreed "that racism, colonialism, and imperialism lie at the core of . . . the activities of the nuclear powers in the Pacific. The Pacific peoples and their environment continue to be exploited because Pacific Islanders are considered insignificant in numbers and inferior as people." This emphasis barely papered over a division in the movement between those emphasizing nuclear issues (usually from predominantly white nations) and those emphasizing independence issues (usually from predominantly non-white colonies or recent colonies). Even so, the conference did launch the Nuclear Free Pacific Movement, with a People's Charter that called for prohibiting: the tests of nuclear weapons and delivery systems; the presence of such weapons, support systems, or bases, nuclear reactors and waste storage; and uranium mining. In 1978, the movement held another international conference at Ponape, in the Caroline Islands. Although this gathering, like the one in 1975, was plagued by the difficulty of reconciling antinuclear and independence emphases, the delegates did endorse a new People's Treaty for a Nuclear-Free Pacific. The latter charged that "our environment continues to be despoiled by foreign powers developing nuclear weapons for a strategy of warfare that has no winners, no liberators, and imperils the survival of all humankind."[56]

In Japan, too, the movement was on the upswing. The Soka Gakkai, a peace-oriented Buddhist group, held antinuclear exhibitions in Japan's cities and gathered 10 million signatures on petitions calling for the abolition of nuclear weapons. Increasing numbers of Japanese people visited the Hiroshima and Nagasaki peace memorials which, by the end of 1978, had attracted more than 38 million visitors.[57] Furthermore, the growing use of nuclear reactors in Japan stirred widespread resistance.[58] The most important factor behind the antinuclear revival, however, was the shift toward greater unity in the divided nuclear disarmament movement, spurred on by the entreaties of non-political citizens' antinuclear groups and by the approach of the U.N. Special Session. In May 1977, Gensuikyo and Gensuikin agreed to hold a united world conference against atomic and hydrogen bombs, to establish a united delegation for the U.N. conclave, and to work toward organizational unity. Although tensions persisted between the two antinuclear organizations, Japanese activists considered the U.N. Special Session a great success. Japan's 500-member peace delegation provided the largest overseas contingent. Moreover, it presented a nuclear abolition petition to the U.N. with nearly 19 million signatures, and it came away delighted by the official U.N. declaration. When Gensuikyo and Gensuikin held another united world conference in Hiroshima on August 6, 1978, the gathering attracted the participation of numerous citizen action groups that had abandoned these kinds of meetings fifteen years before.[59]

Elsewhere

In substantial portions of the world, however, the nuclear disarmament movement remained far weaker. Latin America—located on the outer fringes of the Soviet-American nuclear arms race and plagued by repressive governments—experienced very little antinuclear activity during these years, although a small group in Brazil did seek to combat its government's moves toward developing nuclear weapons.[60] In the Middle East and Africa, where conditions were similar, the movement remained somnolent.

Communist nations also had dictatorial governments that circumscribed the opportunities for citizen activism, but they were considerably closer to the front lines of the nuclear confrontation. Thus, given the looming possibility of nuclear war and a respect for Western activists, small-scale antinuclear activity did emerge there. In a message dispatched to the Fall 1975 Pugwash symposium on "New Designs for Complete Nuclear Disarmament," Andrei Sakharov pointed out that he shared the views of participants that "the problems of disarmament have an evident priority over other problems confronting mankind now." Indeed, he favored "the total prohibition of nuclear weaponry" through step-by-step measures. At the same time, however, he warned that disarmament could not be achieved "without strengthening international confidence, without overcoming the closed attitude of the socialist countries, and in isolation from other aspects of détente." Like most other Soviet dissidents, Sakharov strongly opposed a return to Cold War confrontation, arguing—in a 1977 interview—that "only détente created the possibility of exerting even minimal influence on both the domestic and foreign policies" of Communist countries.[61] Within the Communist party, as well, reformers defended détente and disarmament against what they called "Stalinist conservatism." In articles published in

1978, Georgi Arbatov argued that there would be no winners in a nuclear war and that "no one will return" from one—statements that rankled in official circles.[62]

Dissent from the official peace through strength position also began to appear in Communist East Germany. In June 1978, an announcement by Education Minister Margot Honecker of a government plan to introduce compulsory military education into the ninth- and tenth-grade curriculum touched off major protests by parents, youth groups, and members of the clergy. The Evangelical Church sent a letter to its parishioners stating its strong opposition to the measure and, in addition, set up Peace Education initiatives at parish and regional levels. These stirrings of dissent were encouraged by the rise of the West European nuclear disarmament movement. Watching reports on the Western antinuclear demonstrations on West German television broadcasts, which could be viewed equally well in East Germany, many citizens of the German Democratic Republic, and especially the young, were favorably impressed. Furthermore, since 1977, the Evangelical Church had been widening its contacts with the antinuclear Dutch Interchurch Peace Council.[63]

The Peace Movement Internationals: Nonaligned and Aligned

During these years, the nonaligned peace internationals, reflecting the ferment in their own national sections, began to place more emphasis on nuclear issues. At the April 1977 council meeting of the War Resisters' International (WRI), David McReynolds of America's War Resisters League, pointing to the growing demonstrations and the forthcoming U.N. Special Session, persuaded the organization to give a high priority to disarmament, with nuclear disarmament as the first step. The following year, at its July meeting, the WRI council added opposition to nuclear energy to the organization's agenda, citing "the inevitable link between the production of nuclear power and nuclear weapons."[64] The faith-based internationals, ranging from the World Conference on Religion and Peace to the International FOR, confronted the nuclear issue as well. In a statement issued on August 6, 1977, the 32nd anniversary of the Hiroshima bombing, Pax Christi International called on "all governments of the world to immediately disarm all existing nuclear weapons and to discontinue the development of even more terrible weapons of destruction."[65] That same month, as scientists and scholars from around the world gathered for the 27th meeting of the Pugwash Conferences on Science and World Affairs, the organization's governing council warned of new weapons of mass destruction, nuclear proliferation, and the impasse in nuclear arms control. It called on the leaders of concerned governments, particularly those of the United States and the USSR, "to halt new weapons deployment and reverse the arms race" and "on men and women everywhere to redouble their efforts to make their governments understand and act in the face of our common peril."[66]

For the time being, however, these international peace organizations had little power to implement their recommendations. Not only were they divided by constituency, but their resources remained quite minimal. In mid-1977, the WRI had only two full-time staff members. Indeed, the WRI and the International FOR were so weak that, in the mid-1970s, pacifist leaders suggested a merger of the two groups as a means of keeping them afloat.[67] After the end of the Vietnam War, the International Confederation for Disarmament and Peace, with its roots in the antinuclear campaign of the early 1960s and its broad mix of constituencies, had greater potential for drawing these scattered groups together into a global disarmament movement. And it did show a renewed interest in nuclear disarmament, particularly with the approach of the U.N. Special Session.[68] But, perhaps because of its debilitated condition, antinuclear campaigners chose to make a new start.

On August 6, 1977, leading activists announced the establishment of an International Mobilization for Survival at press conferences held simultaneously in Stockholm, Washington, San Francisco, and Hiroshima. In a joint statement, the top leaders of the ICDP, the IFOR, WILPF, the WRI, Pax Christi, the World Council of Churches, and other groups called upon "the people of every nation to mobilize for survival," to "require their governments to move beyond the rhetoric of disarmament toward concrete action." They concluded: "Let the year ahead be a time of determined actions toward the abolition of all nuclear weapons and the end of the arms race. Let the year ahead affirm our common humanity and our ability to solve our differences peacefully." Nevertheless, although the new international maintained reasonably good momentum through the meeting of the U.N. Special Session, during which it hosted strategy sessions and the mass public rally in New York City, it remained a short-term, consultative venture rather than a long-term, structured organization. After the U.N. events, it disintegrated, leaving its American namesake as the sole survivor of the 1977–78 upsurge.[69]

Unlike its independent rivals, the Communist-led World Peace Council seemed quite able to provide international coordination for its sector of the world peace movement. In June 1975, with the Vietnam War at an end, the WPC launched a mass petition campaign called the New Stockholm Appeal, which demanded an end to the arms race. Eventually, the WPC claimed to have obtained 450 million signatures on this statement.[70] The WPC also threw itself into the anti-neutron bomb campaign—one that, with its emphasis upon the fiendishness of an exclusively American weapon, possessed particular appeal for these pro-Soviet activists. "The mobilization of the public of the world against the neutron bomb is the central question of the fight for peace," observed WPC vice president Albert Norden. Beating the drum for global protest, the WPC called upon the people of the world to unite and "say 'No'" to the U.S. government's "horror-bomb."[71] In addition, the WPC championed the U.N. Special Session, declaring that the WPC "and the national organisations in it from more than 130 countries of the world will do their best to mobilize public opinion" to "ensure that the Special Session achieves its full potentialities."[72]

In fact, however, the WPC was a much less effective organization than it appeared. Its strongest and most powerful affiliates existed in Soviet bloc nations, where they were bolstered by the enormous power of party and state. Certainly, this accounted for the vast number of signatures on the New Stockholm Appeal. In tiny Hungary alone, the Hungarian Peace Council claimed to have obtained 7.5 million signatures.[73] But, outside of these friendly environs, the WPC could rarely field a significant peace group; indeed, many WPC affiliates existed only on paper. The world peace conferences of the WPC drew massive attendance because they provided free airline tickets, room, and board to people around the world who—often lacking any organizational base in their homelands—availed themselves of the opportunity for an all-expenses-paid junket to Soviet bloc nations. Even some WPC officials recognized that this procedure encouraged people to avoid doing any serious organizing in their own countries.[74] Furthermore, the Vietnam War, which had provided the most popular boost to the WPC in its history, came to an end, thus leading to a considerable loss of momentum in the organization.[75] Also, when it came to mobilizing for disarmament in non-Communist nations, the WPC was no match for the new, nonaligned organizations.

In addition, despite the overlapping concern with disarmament issues, Communist peace activists could not count on nonaligned activists for support. For one thing, there remained the continuing scandal of WPC partisanship. In 1975, when the WPC presented a special Peace Medal to Leonid Brezhnev, WPC president Romesh Chandra called the award, as two Polish enthusiasts recalled, an "expression of the highest esteem for a man who had devoted all his life and all his political activity to the cause of preserving peace" and "a token of the high evaluation placed . . . upon the consistent foreign policy of the CPSU in the service of peace."[76] By contrast, nonaligned peace groups not only freely criticized the militarism of both Cold War blocs and their leaders, but—unlike the WPC, which viewed human rights in Communist nations as cynically as did Kremlin officials[77]—persistently criticized human rights violations.[78] As a result of these and other incompatibilities, even in those few places where Communist Party activists had secured a foothold in nonaligned groups, they soon lost it. In Britain, CND's dwindling membership during the early 1970s had magnified the influence of the Communists (and the Quakers) in the organization. A few British Communists—albeit those willing to criticize Soviet policy, then called Eurocommunists—even emerged as CND leaders. But, in 1977, with the organization undergoing a growth spurt, non-Communists began to shoulder them aside. Thereafter, as CND turned into a mass movement, the small Communist element became ever more marginal.[79]

Nor, for that matter, was the WPC especially fond of nonaligned peace activists. After all, the WPC would not have existed if Communist officials had viewed independent peace groups as politically reliable. Sometimes, in fact, it sharply attacked independent groups as imperialist agents. Charging that Mobilization for Survival was no more than a CIA front, Chandra waged a fierce public campaign against it.[80] Most of the time, however, the WPC approach was more subtle. Where independent peace groups existed, it usually either tried to lure them into WPC operations (for example, through invitations to attend its world conferences)[81] or encouraged the development of alternative organizations with a pro-Soviet perspective. Thus, in the United States, where the WPC viewed groups like SANE as politically retrograde, efforts to create a U.S. affiliate of the WPC commenced among WPC loyalists in 1976. Rob Prince, a district organizer for the Communist Party USA and a member of its national council for fifteen years, recalled that he was "part of a nucleus of Communist Party activists" that formed a new Communist-led group, the U.S. Peace Council. Although the founding conference did not occur until 1979, the organization was in operation by 1978, pulling together U.S. Communists and others willing to work with them organizationally. Members of the U.S. Peace Council were eager to link up their efforts with the WPC, which in turn finally had what it considered a politically acceptable branch in the United States.[82]

Conclusion

Thus, between 1975 and 1978, a nuclear disarmament campaign once more took shape across substantial portions of the globe. However, despite the clear signs of its progress, the campaign remained weak and, even in 1978, few could predict that it had much of a future. After all, in many nations, the antinuclear movement barely existed or did not exist at all. And even where it was beginning to develop a substantial presence, it dissipated its slender resources and energies among scattered causes. Furthermore, international coordination of the movement was almost entirely lacking—except, of course, from the World Peace Council, which most of the new, non-Communist activists considered hopelessly one-sided and corrupt. In this context, what is surprising is that, in a world that seemed to be suffering from nuclear amnesia, a relatively small group of people accomplished as much as they did. The growing success of their mobilization effort attested both to their determination and to the profound danger that had inspired it: the ongoing nuclear peril.

Signs of Progress

Public Policy Shifts, 1977-78

> We will move this year a step toward our ultimate
> goal—the elimination of all nuclear weapons from this
> earth. We urge all other people to join us, for success
> can mean life instead of death.
>
> > Jimmy Carter, 1977

With this upsurge of nuclear disarmament activism, governments began to grapple more seriously with the nuclear arms race—a process that led to canceling some weapons systems, seriously negotiating limits on others, taking measures to halt nuclear proliferation, and restraining the first use of nuclear weapons. Part of this antinuclear tilt in public policy can be attributed to the advent of a more antinuclear leadership at the governmental level in a number of key countries, most notably the United States. Even so, these new officials, like their more traditional counterparts, were sensitive to popular agitation against nuclear weapons, and this public pressure contributed to their emphasis upon nuclear arms controls and disarmament. The result was a higher level of governmental commitment to nuclear restraint.

The New Leaders and the Old

From the standpoint of curbing the nuclear arms race, the beginning of Jimmy Carter's presidency, in January 1977, represented the most significant shift in national authority. To be sure, not all of Carter's national security policies were quite as dovish as his later reputation as a man of peace would imply. For example, within four months of taking office, he badgered NATO governments into agreeing to at least a 3 percent annual increase in their military budgets.[1] Nevertheless, when it came to nuclear weapons, few other government leaders could match Carter's antinuclear zeal. During the

1976 election campaign, he had proclaimed a goal of abolishing nuclear weapons, albeit one step at a time, and as early as January 26, 1977, he informed Brezhnev that "my solid objective is to liquidate nuclear weapons completely." This commitment was deeply rooted in Carter's moral and religious values, as well as in his recognition of the murderous potential of nuclear arms. "The unbelievable destruction they represented," he wrote in his memoirs, "was constantly on my mind."[2]

Although most officials in the Carter administration did not share the new President's stark antinuclear determination, they did not directly challenge it either. Perhaps the most hawkish of them was Carter's National Security Advisor, Zbigniew Brzezinski. Deeply suspicious of the Soviet Union and anxious to strengthen U.S. military power, Brzezinski did not oppose arms control and disarmament measures, but argued that they should be contingent upon peaceful Soviet conduct in world affairs.[3] By contrast, the new Secretary of State, Cyrus Vance, and the new director of the Arms Control and Disarmament Agency, Paul Warnke, rejected linkage and thought nuclear arms control and disarmament were crucial in their own right.[4] Carter's Secretary of Defense, Harold Brown, formerly director of the Livermore weapons lab and Secretary of the Air Force, fell somewhere in between, agreeable to some measure of arms control and disarmament but wary of any plan to carry this forward to the point of nuclear abolition. All were loyal to the new President, and his priorities were clearly to reduce nuclear weapons, nuclear proliferation, and the danger of nuclear war.[5]

In most other NATO nations, the governments of the time also leaned toward nuclear disarmament, largely because they were led by relatively antinuclear Center-Left parties. In Scandinavia, where the Social Democrats had seen to it that their nations would neither manufacture nor deploy nuclear weapons, government officials regularly assailed the nuclear arms race. In April 1978, Danish Prime Minister Anker Jorgensen condemned nuclear weapons as "the devil's work," and demanded that their production be halted.[6] That same year, in a dramatic speech to the U.N. Special Session, Canadian Prime Minister Pierre Elliot Trudeau, a Liberal, reported that his country was divesting itself of nuclear weapons and, furthermore, outlined a "Strategy of Suffocation" for the nuclear arms race.[7] To be sure, two leading Social Democrats—Prime Minister James Callaghan of Britain and Chancellor Helmut Schmidt of West Germany—fearful of Soviet military power, quietly accepted the maintenance of nuclear weapons in their countries. But with substantial portions of their parties favoring antinuclear action, they were careful to advocate arms control and disarmament, as well. Michael Foot, a champion of CND within the British Labour Party, recalled that, although Callaghan had "never been interested" in nuclear disarmament, in 1978 he dispatched to the U.N. conference an official delegation that proposed an impressive plan for the eventual abolition of nuclear weapons.[8]

The prospects for antinuclear action also improved in the Third World. In India, the international backlash against the "peaceful nuclear explosion" of 1974 and the failure of the nuclear program to enhance Prime Minister Indira Gandhi's popularity led her to reassess the situation and to oppose additional Indian nuclear tests. Furthermore, in March 1977, her Congress Party was trounced by the opposition in parliamentary elections. And the new prime minister, Morarji Desai, a Gandhian with a long history of opposition to nuclear weapons, promptly declared that his government opposed them and would not manufacture them. At the 1978 U.N. Special Session, Desai reiterated this pledge, adding that India abjured even peaceful nuclear explosions. This position meshed nicely with Third World support for what was called the New International Economic Order. According to its proponents, Third World economic development was being undermined by the squandering of great power resources on the nuclear arms race. Although the depth of Third World antinuclearism remained in question, linking disarmament to development did enhance its appeal to the nations of Asia, Africa, and Latin America. Indeed, the U.N. Special Session resulted from an August 1976 initiative by the Non-Aligned Movement, a leading forum for Third World countries.[9]

Although Communist nations continued to talk of détente and disarmament, their leaders were mired in more traditional ways of thinking. Committed to the blend of ideological, military, and, especially, national interests that had driven their foreign and defense policies throughout the years, they showed little genuine interest in creating a world without the Bomb. During 1977–78, Chinese Communist leaders, driven by fierce hostility toward the Soviet Union, consistently applauded the Carter administration's plan to build neutron bombs. In April 1978, when Carter announced that he was scuttling the project, the New China News Agency responded tartly that his decision would never "satisfy Moscow's appetite"; rather, it would lead the Kremlin to "exert greater pressure" for further U.S. "concessions." Soviet-American treaties on nuclear weapons provoked similar Chinese scorn. In meetings with U.S. government leaders during 1977, Chinese officials professed to desire the abolition of nuclear weapons, but warned against concluding arms control agreements with the Soviet government, which they claimed was thoroughly untrustworthy.[10]

Actually, Soviet officials were less treacherous than the Chinese maintained, but seemed incapable of changing course and confronting the problems that plagued their country and the world. "Through its blind adherence to old dogmas and obsolete ideas," recalled Mikhail Gorbachev, "the leadership overlooked the far-reaching changes that were taking place." Meanwhile, "the arms race continued, gaining momentum even after achieving military and strategic parity with the United States."[11] Although Soviet officials proclaimed their commitment to banning the Bomb, the reality was that they were relatively comfortable with it. Concerned primarily with maintaining a rough nuclear balance between the United States and the Soviet Union—the strategic stability that they believed would safeguard their society from external attack—they favored arms control rather than disarmament.[12] And even this modest goal seemed beyond their limited capabilities. Advancing age and illness took their toll on the party leadership, with party secretary Leonid Brezhnev increasingly enfeebled. Looking back on these years, Anatoly Chernyaev recalled the Brezhnev era as "a stagnation period," a time of "the gradual dying of our society." Leaving meetings of the party secretariat, "we were depressed by the helpless nature of the decisions we made and the helpless nature of the individuals who made these decisions."[13]

Government Response to Nuclear Disarmament Agitation

In general, governments reacted to the revival of nuclear disarmament agitation in direct proportion to their commitment to nuclear disarmament. Developing nations, recognizing that antinuclear groups shared their position on the arms race, pressed to have their leaders address meetings at the U.N. Special Session and drew eagerly upon their expertise. The Social Democratic Nordic countries were also fairly open to exchanges with disarmament NGOs, as was the Social Democratic government of Turkey. Upon its advent in 1978, Turkey's new administration began sending observers and representatives to many of the seminars and international symposia organized by the Turkish Peace Association.[14] By contrast, the conservative-led government of the Netherlands was less forthcoming, with the Dutch foreign minister telling Brzezinski in the spring of 1978 that he was "worried about the emergence of new 'ban the bomb' movements." Although Britain's Prime Minister Callaghan had a negative view of CND, the strength of antinuclear sentiment within his Labour Party led him to avoid direct clashes with it over nuclear weapons.[15]

The Soviet Union, of course, faced a somewhat more complex situation, given its own extensive operations in the area of peace and disarmament agitation. Greeting delegates to the WPC's January 1977 world conference with his wishes for "fresh, big successes in your lofty activity," Brezhnev thanked them "from the bottom of my heart." Meanwhile, the Soviet Communist Party appropriated substantial additional funds for WPC activities and, if the CIA is to be believed, spent more than $100 million campaigning against the neutron bomb.[16] As before, Soviet authorities took a considerably less charitable view of independent peace activism. Indeed, solely on the basis of Soviet objections, the United Nations denied NGO status to the nonaligned International Confederation for Disarmament and Peace. The Soviet government also worked to keep independent peace groups out of the 1978 U.N. Special Session on Disarmament—the only government to do so. Although Soviet authorities continued to allow select groups of Soviet scientists to attend the Pugwash conferences, they did not appoint them to the USSR's official disarmament delegations.[17]

In the United States, peace groups enjoyed unusual access to power after the advent of the Carter administration. Officials at the Arms Control and Disarmament Agency, the State Department, and the White House met with leaders of the disarmament movement, providing them with briefings on key issues, and, on occasion, soliciting their opinions.[18] Administration officials not only considered them an important Democratic constituency, but— on occasion—a useful force for promoting the Carter administration's disarmament agenda. "I thought they were a plus," recalled Paul Warnke; "certainly Cy Vance did, too." When it came to mobilizing support for the SALT II treaty, "we were counting very heavily on them."[19] Particularly during 1977, U.S. peace groups spent more time commending the Carter administration than criticizing it. They were particularly heartened by his talk of abolishing nuclear weapons.[20] In turn, the President warmly thanked WSP for its disarmament efforts, issued a public testimonial for SANE, and appointed peace group leaders as members of the official U.S. delegation to the U.N. Special Session. In March 1978, both the State Department and the Arms Control and Disarmament Agency held regular meetings with the leaders of more than 100 NGOs and solicited their proposals for the U.N. Special Session.[21]

Curiously, though, Carter kept aloof from most antinuclear campaigners. Although WSP leaders tried repeatedly to meet with the new President, they were rebuffed every time. Eventually, they concluded that the administration lacked a sincere interest in nuclear disarmament and was only trying to "coopt" them.[22] Other peace groups also found that, although they had some measure of entrée to a variety of government officials, they had no access to the President. Even Harold Willens, who had been very close to Carter during his 1976 presidential campaign, found the White House door "locked" to him by the President's top aides. He recalled: "You could only walk through it holding the hand—metaphorically speaking—of Jody Powell or Hamilton Jordan. And they blocked everything that I wanted to get done and that Jimmy Carter himself had indicated that he wanted to get done." A case in point, Willens contended, was Carter's personal absence from the U.N. Special Session. Horrified, Willens and Paul Newman met with Vice President Walter Mondale about this. "Deeply impressed about our frustration," the Vice President "promised to do anything that he could to change Jimmy Carter's mind, but he failed." As a result, Carter never spoke on "what was really an historic occasion"—a "source of great disappointment and frustration" to Willens and other peace group leaders.[23]

Carter's failure to play a direct role in cultivating people who were his natural allies on arms control and disarmament issues is puzzling. Part of the explanation probably lies in the fact that a number of top administration officials, such as Brzezinski and Brown, had mixed feelings about disarmament activism. "On some issues," Brzezinski recalled, disarmament groups "were helpful. On some issues, they were a pain in the ass."[24] Administration displeasure was particularly keen when intense opposition emerged to its plan to deploy the neutron bomb. In early 1978, to counter such opposition in Western Europe, the administration worked through the CIA to initiate a covert program of financial and other incentives to encourage the West European press corps to provide favorable coverage of the weapon.[25] Furthermore, some degree of political calculation seems likely to have contributed to Carter's coy behavior. Beginning in the fall of 1977, reports from Brzezinski and from the President's pollster, Patrick Caddell, emphasized growing public dismay at America's "weakness" in the face of Soviet military power. According to Brzezinski, U.S. foreign policy was "seen as 'soft.'"[26] In these circumstances, White House political operatives had a strong incentive to discourage presidential meetings with leaders of peace groups.

The Impact on Nuclear Weapons Policy: NATO

Even so, during the first years of his Presidency, Carter proved remarkably responsive to the positions taken by antinuclear activists. As a follow-up to his 1976 campaign pledge to scrap the B-1 bomber, Carter met twice in the White House with Terry Provance of the Stop the B-1 Bomber Campaign. Provance also received frequent correspondence on this subject from the President, the Secretary of State, and White House officials. In addition,

Carter met with leaders of the anti-B-1 liberal bloc in Congress, who pointed to polls showing majority opposition to the weapon. Moreover, some of the President's top advisors believed that, in an age of missile technology, nuclear-capable aircraft were superfluous. Nevertheless, after years of lobbying for the B-1, the Rockwell corporation and the Air Force had built up a powerful army of supporters in Congress and in the many parts of the country eager to secure defense contracts. And numerous Pentagon weapons projects of dubious value had been approved in the past.[27] Consequently, Carter acted cautiously, ordering a Pentagon study of the B-1. Ultimately, the Joint Chiefs of Staff (JCS) argued for building it, as did Defense Secretary Brown, who contended that the project should be developed on a very limited basis. Carter fretted that, if he opposed the weapons system, Congress would not sustain his position. The expectation grew that the B-1 would go forward, though perhaps in a reduced form. Then, on June 30, 1977, as Pentagon generals reportedly were ordering champagne to celebrate their victory, Carter startled political observers by canceling the project. The President had concluded that the weapons system was expensive and unnecessary, and that building it would violate his campaign pledge. Senator McGovern called it Carter's "finest hour."[28]

Antinuclear pressures were even more decisive when it came to the neutron bomb. On June 6, 1977, an article in the *Washington Post* revealed administration procurement plans for an enhanced radiation warhead for the U.S. Army's short-range Lance missile, stationed in Western Europe. This misnamed "neutron bomb" was a carryover from the Ford administration, and was designed to offset the Warsaw Pact's three-to-one advantage in tank forces. But the *Post* article, which emphasized this weapon as the first with the explicit purpose of killing people through radiation, touched off what Brzezinski called "a political explosion that reverberated throughout the United States and Europe." Most of the administration's top national security officials had never heard of the neutron bomb. But when the storm of protest broke, they rallied behind its development, claiming that it did not significantly alter the strategic situation. Furthermore, they said, by reducing the heat and blast produced by the explosion of tactical nuclear weapons, it would reduce civilian casualties in a war. The furor grew, however, and quickly spread to Congress, where liberals sought to block funding for the weapon. Although, that July, the administration won the battle over congressional funding, the neutron bomb issue remained unsettled for Carter, who—noting that it had "generated a great deal of controversy"—was reluctant to give the order for production.[29]

From mid-July through mid-November 1977, the issue seemed even more problematic in Western Europe. News of the neutron bomb had "set off an explosive political and public reaction," Vance recalled, led by "antinuclear groups." In this context, West European government leaders shied away from requesting deployment. On July 22, Brzezinski complained to the President that, although NATO officials wanted the new weapon, "they are terrified by the political consequences of seeming to approve nuclear warfare on their territory and of endorsing a weapon which . . . seems to have acquired a particularly odious image." Responding to Carter's request for additional information on European attitudes, State Department reports from West Germany and the Netherlands stressed uneasiness about the neutron bomb, forecasting a "strong emotional, negative response" in these nations to any attempt to deploy the weapon there.[30] With West European leaders refusing to share responsibility for the neutron bomb, Carter found himself in a very uncomfortable position. At an August 17 meeting with Vance, Brown, and Brzezinski, the latter noted in his diary, Carter told them "he did not wish the world to think of him as an ogre, and we agreed that we will press the Europeans to show greater interest in having the bomb and therefore willingness to absorb some of the political flak or we will use European disinterest as a basis for a negative decision." That September, Carter himself warned West German Chancellor Helmut Schmidt: "It would be difficult for me to make a decision to deploy this weapon in Europe without strong European desire for such deployment."[31]

With neither Carter nor West European leaders willing to accept primary responsibility for the unpopular neutron bomb, Brzezinski orchestrated what he considered a compromise strategy. As he recalled: "It was clear to me that the European governments needed some help in making the issue more palatable politically." At the center of Brzezinski's "help" lay the political situation in West Germany, where the ruling Social Democratic Party (SPD) demanded that conditions should be created to make the deployment of the neutron bomb unnecessary. The political palliative, it seemed, was to link the decision for armament with an option for disarmament. Thus, the new U.S. position, hammered out between November 1977 and January 1978, included a U.S. government decision to produce the neutron bomb, a willingness to forgo deployment if—during the following two years—the Soviet Union would agree to forgo deployment of its SS-20 intermediate range ballistic missile, and a public NATO statement of agreement with this plan.[32] This would minimize the political burden for the U.S. government of deploying the neutron bomb by spreading responsibility to NATO allies and, if the arms control talks failed, to the Soviet Union. But would the West European governments go along with it?

Although U.S. officials reported some progress, developments in early 1978 led Carter, in his words, "to question the advisability of our proceeding with the highly unpopular and very expensive project." In February, Brzezinski told him that the British "turned out to have a lot of trouble with publicly supporting a decision to produce and deploy. . . . The Labour Party was split" and the Cabinet ministers "would prefer to avoid a decision." On February 22, the Danish prime minister informed Carter that he would not support deployment. The following day, the West German government announced that "the forthcoming decision on the production of neutron weapons falls into the exclusive responsibility of the United States." On March 4, in the midst of parliamentary deliberations on the neutron bomb, the Dutch defense minister, R. J. H. Kruisinga, a Christian Democrat, resigned in protest, saying that he could not support production or deployment. Four days later, the Dutch parliament passed a resolution declaring that production of the neutron bomb was undesirable, and the prime minister reported to Washington that, in these circumstances, he could not agree to deployment. Although U.S. officials continued to argue that they could secure a public commitment to deployment by West European governments, by March 18 Carter was ready to abandon the venture. His willingness to cancel production of the weapon was reinforced on March 23, when British Prime Minister Callaghan told him that it would be "the greatest relief in the world" if Carter scrapped it, as otherwise it would provide "a very difficult political issue" for him. Consequently, on April 7, 1978, Carter announced that he was deferring production of the neutron bomb—a position that meant, in effect, canceling plans for its production.[33]

Thus, although it seems likely that, as some of Carter's aides have emphasized, the President felt morally uncomfortable with the idea of the neutron bomb,[34] his decision to scrap the project was based primarily on the strong political pressures against it in Western Europe—what the State Department, in its secret explanation for the decision, termed "the political problem that ERW has created in most allied countries." On numerous occasions, Carter indicated that he was willing to order production of the neutron bomb if other government leaders would bear some share of the responsibility for this unpopular decision. However, facing substantial popular resistance, often within their own parties, other government leaders were not willing to meet this condition. And this abdication of responsibility left Carter in a politically awkward position. According to Vance, the President "felt that the burden and political liability for this weapon . . . was being placed on his shoulders." Or, as Carter himself fumed: "Why should I go forward and take all the onus for having produced this infamous weapon, if they're not prepared to take their fair share of the opprobrium?" The result was a clear-cut victory for the nuclear disarmament movement.[35]

Other curbs on the nuclear arms race evoked greater enthusiasm within the Carter administration, although they, too, were shaped in part by public pressure. Both Carter and Vance were deeply concerned about the proliferation of nuclear weapons, particularly through sales of allegedly peaceful nuclear technology to would-be nuclear nations. Accordingly, Carter pressed forward with a new, more restrictive policy, despite the fact that it placed the U.S. government at odds with a number of its allies, including West Germany and Japan. Congress, though, was already stirred up on the proliferation issue, and seemed likely to adopt *more* restrictive policies than the administration desired. Brzezinski recalled that, by 1977, there were several draft bills on Capitol Hill "that we felt were excessively tough. To head them off and to prevent further legislative initiatives, we introduced our own bill, the Nuclear Nonproliferation Act." Passed in March 1978 by overwhelming majorities in both houses, the legislation set criteria for licensing export of nuclear material and prohibited U.S. nuclear exports to any country not accepting international safeguards on its nuclear plants. Later in the year, U.S. nonproliferation policy was strengthened by an amendment to the Foreign Assistance Act which provided that U.S. economic aid would be halted to any nation not accepting safeguards on dangerous nuclear technology.[36]

Another area in which public opinion had some impact on the Carter administration's nuclear policy lay in the use of nuclear weapons. Although Carter did not want to undermine the credibility of a U.S. nuclear response to a conventional Soviet attack upon Western Europe, he did favor some softening in the U.S. policy of first use of nuclear weapons. On July 22, 1977, in response to a query from Carter, Brzezinski proposed that the President issue "a statement to the effect that we would not be the first to use nuclear weapons, except as a response to the invasion of territory of the U.S. or of U.S. Allies." This "would highlight the notion that nuclear weapons are designed only for defensive purposes and it would throw the burden of nuclear responsibility on the party initiating military hostilities." Remarking that "this is a good public position to take," Carter asked Brzezinski, Vance, and Mondale to work out the details. That September, he ran the idea past Schmidt, noting that, "in anticipation" of the convening in Belgrade of the Conference on Security and Cooperation in Europe and of the U.N. General Assembly, he had "given some thought as to how we might take the initiative on such matters as . . . non-use of nuclear weapons." Such a statement would "be regarded as a further sign of our serious interest in reducing the dangers of nuclear war" and would "also deprive the Soviet Union of its propaganda monopoly over this issue."[37] Finally, in June 1978—after strong pressure for a U.S. disarmament initiative from the U.S. delegation to the U.N. Special Session on Disarmament and from ACDA—the administration used the U.N. conference to unveil its modification of first use doctrine.[38]

Public pressure also played a role in government efforts to end nuclear testing. At the inception of his presidency, Carter told journalists of his plan "to proceed quickly and aggressively with a comprehensive test ban treaty" (CTBT). In the fall of 1977, U.S.-British-Soviet negotiations began, with the hope that the signing of a tri-partite agreement would impel France and China to join it.[39] Behind the U.S. initiative in this area lay not only the goal of inhibiting nuclear advances by the existing nuclear powers, but of limiting nuclear proliferation to additional nations. Indeed, the Nuclear Nonproliferation Treaty made restraint by non-nuclear nations contingent upon moves toward nuclear disarmament by nuclear nations. As the Soviet government proved unusually open to compromise, the negotiations made substantial progress. However, there was a sharp division on this issue within the Carter administration, with the Joint Chiefs of Staff, the directors of the weapons laboratories, and the energy secretary (James Schlesinger) vigorously opposed to a CTBT. They waged a fierce battle within the bureaucracy to eviscerate or block a treaty, and mobilized hawkish members of Congress along similar lines.[40] Vance, though, countered that "there is substantial support in the country" for a CTBT. On another occasion, he and Warnke told Carter that, if the CTBT negotiations were abandoned, the Russians "will saddle us with the blame" and "the non-aligned countries, probably led by India, will complain that they have been misled." Moreover, "domestically, there is both a congressional and private constituency that puts a comprehensive test ban high on its priority list. These constituencies will be disappointed and vocal."[41]

In these circumstances, Carter made a number of compromises. To placate the critics of the CTBT, he accepted revision of the U.S. proposal to a treaty of three years, after which its signers would re-evaluate it, and, furthermore, one that permitted small nuclear experiments.[42] Furthermore, he agreed to delay the signing of the CTBT and the battle for its Senate ratification until the completion of the same process for the SALT II treaty. Carter's White House aides pressed this strategy of delay very forcefully upon him, arguing that SALT enjoyed substantially more support within the administration than did the CTBT. Thus, leading off with the CTBT would jeopardize the chances for both, while beginning with SALT would pave the way for passage of the CTBT. Hamilton Jordan went a step further, arguing that, "if we ratify a SALT II agreement in 1979, and the economy is in reasonably good shape, I believe that it will insure your re-election in 1980." As a result, Carter agreed to give a higher priority to the SALT II treaty. Although these administration compromises resulted in formulating a less than comprehensive CTBT and in putting it on a slow track, they did keep the treaty process alive.[43]

As the internal debate over the CTBT implied, securing a SALT II agreement was a top objective—perhaps *the* top objective—of the Carter administration. Carter called it his "most difficult and important task." In his opinion, it was imperative to deal with the threat to human survival posed by the thousands of Soviet and American ICBMs. During a meeting with the Joint Chiefs of Staff prior to his inauguration, Carter startled them by asking about the possibility of reducing Soviet and American nuclear arsenals to 200 ICBMs each.[44] The President also believed, however, that championing nuclear arms controls as an alternative to cynical, balance-of-power style diplomacy was good politics. This assumption helped set the tone of his 1976 campaign and, as Jordan's remarks about the importance of a SALT treaty to Carter's re-election indicated, continued to pervade the thinking of his closest advisors. Furthermore, Carter thought that, given the strength of antinuclear sentiment in many nations, embracing nuclear arms controls provided the United States with a useful position in world affairs. As he wrote in his memoirs:

It was important not to appear as a warmonger, interested only in potential military solutions to the intractable problems we faced. Such a posture would drive away some of our European allies, alienate the nonaligned countries of the world, and tend to isolate the United States within the community of nations. The Soviet Union had already reaped a great propaganda harvest by claiming falsely that it was the only world power that truly wanted peace and was eager to control the buildup of nuclear arsenals. . . . Our unequivocal commitment to nuclear arms control . . . would signal that America was a peaceful and reliable country.

Vance, too, recalled that "a SALT agreement would . . . be important in maintaining the confidence of our Western European allies." Thus, Carter decided to press for "deep cuts" in strategic arsenals through the SALT II negotiations and, then, push on to a minimum deterrent of several hundred missiles through SALT III—points he made in a White House meeting with Soviet Ambassador Anatoly Dobrynin on February 1, 1977.[45]

Within a month, the Carter administration was ready to reopen the stalled talks on SALT II, and in March 1977 dispatched Vance to Moscow with two alternative proposals. One would have modified the Kissinger-

Brezhnev understandings at Vladivostok, and the other—preferred by the administration—would have slashed very substantially the number of strategic missiles, imposed stringent limits on their improvement, and prohibited the deployment of new ones. These proposals appealed to differing currents of opinion in the United States. Disarmers liked the proposal for deep cuts, which would move the arms control process well beyond the modest limitations of the Nixon-Ford-Kissinger years to actual disarmament. Hawks liked them both, for the former scrapped the concessions on the Soviet Backfire bomber and U.S. cruise missiles that the Russians claimed they had secured at Vladivostok, while the latter called for most of the weapons cuts to come from the Soviet Union's heavy, land-based ICBMs.[46] Apparently as a means of rallying popular support for the deep cuts proposal, at home and abroad, Carter went public with elements of it, even before Soviet officials had been briefed. Angered by the proposals and by the process, the Kremlin rudely rejected them.[47] In retrospect, White House officials thought that the administration had been "too ambitious" and that Vance's March 1977 mission had been "a mistake."[48]

The collapse of the administration's early SALT proposals shattered the alliance between hawks and doves on strategic arms control policy, exposing their differences. During the late spring and early summer of 1977, Callaghan and Schmidt pressed Carter for a more conciliatory approach to Brezhnev on nuclear issues, arguing that it was vital to get the SALT talks back on track. Within the Carter administration, Vance and Warnke lobbied for a similar position.[49] Their key opponent was Brzezinski, who argued that it was impossible to separate the SALT negotiations from other aspects of the U.S.-Soviet relationship. Without good behavior by the Soviet Union, he insisted, the U.S. government should take a hard line on the SALT II treaty.[50] In a report to Carter on April 7, 1978, Brzezinski argued that the latest Vance mission to Moscow should "not be merely a negotiating session devoted to the specifics of SALT," but should "address other issues in the US/Soviet relationship." Sometimes, in fact, he played upon the possibility that the SALT treaty would not be ratified to press Carter for a more anti-Soviet position. On April 14, 1978, he told Carter that, "to help SALT, you will have to take some decision in the near future that conveys clearly your toughness in dealing with the Russians." Within the White House, Hamilton Jordan promoted this line of thought. According to Vance, although Carter "resisted . . . linking the SALT negotiations to overall U.S.-Soviet relations," the "political pressures on him to be harder on the Soviets were intense."[51]

This hawkish pressure was counter-balanced by the strength of antinuclear sentiment. To be sure, Carter's White House aides warned him that he "should not underestimate the difficulty we will have getting a SALT II Treaty ratified by two-thirds of the United States Senate." A test case was provided by the confirmation vote on the dovish Warnke as SALT negotiator, for it fell nine votes short of the total needed for SALT II ratification.[52] Moreover, in the winter of 1977–78, Republican leaders—including Ford, Kissinger, and GOP Senate leader Howard Baker—told the President, as he recalled, that "they would never support SALT II, no matter what was in it." Even so, as he noted, "my hope, and . . . my expectation then, was that I could so thoroughly convince the public about the advisability of the SALT II treaty that the Republicans would change their minds and support SALT II in their own best political interest."[53] This did not seem at all far-fetched for, as one White House aide reported happily in April 1978, "there is broad public support for arms control," and "public support for SALT can be quickly organized to take effective political action." The following month, the President's aides took note of a Harris poll showing 75 to 12 percent backing for a SALT arms control agreement, up 9 percent over the preceding fourteen months.[54] Beginning with the existing base of disarmament groups, the administration expanded SALT's support network very substantially, using Americans for SALT as the umbrella organization. As a result, until well into 1979, the administration expected to prevail in any Senate battle over SALT ratification.[55]

Bolstered by the popularity of arms control and disarmament, the administration moved forward with the SALT negotiations. In May 1977, it brought new, less ambitious proposals to the bargaining table, and the Soviet government found them considerably more palatable than those of two months before. Although the SALT I treaty was scheduled to expire in October, U.S. and Soviet leaders agreed to honor its terms until SALT II was implemented.[56] Even as the negotiations made slow progress, Brzezinski continued to press for linkage of the treaty to Soviet good behavior. In addition, he and Brown teamed up to stiffen the U.S. negotiating position on a number of issues. The Russian negotiators also proved remarkably difficult. Nevertheless, over time, both sides narrowed their differences—accepting limits on the number of missile launchers (which would result in a reduction of 10 percent by the Soviet Union), trading acceptance of the Soviet Union's land-based ICBMs for limits on MIRVing them, and working out solutions to the thorny issue of air-launched cruise missiles.[57] By September 1978, Carter considered the SALT II negotiations "about over," and planning began for a Carter-Brezhnev summit meeting to sign the treaty and promote it. In fact, lingering disagreements dragged the negotiations on into 1979. But by late 1978 Carter and his associates were well on their way to realizing the administration's top priority.[58]

Progress in limiting intermediate-range nuclear forces (INF) was considerably more problematic. As some Western nuclear programs were curbed—the B-1 bomber, the neutron bomb, and strategic nuclear weapons—the remaining nuclear options assumed added importance.[59] Furthermore, ever since the mid-1970s, NATO military planners had been gravitating toward the deployment in Western Europe of cruise missiles—slow but highly accurate rockets that could fly at low altitudes and, thereby, evade radar and air defenses. Cruise missiles seemed particularly useful for implementing the latest version of NATO's "flexible response" strategy. Drawn up by U.S. Defense Secretary James Schlesinger in late 1973 and approved by Nixon in early 1974, it expanded U.S. possibilities for waging limited nuclear war.[60] Pressures to upgrade NATO's theater nuclear forces grew dramatically after 1976, when the Soviet Union began to replace its increasingly obsolete SS-4 and SS-5 missiles with a considerably upgraded model, the SS-20, which was mobile, much more accurate, and possessed three MIRVed warheads. Worried by what he considered a tilt in the "Eurostrategic" balance that would open the way for Soviet political blackmail of Western Europe, Schmidt raised the SS-20 issue with Carter and his aides, but without much effect. In October 1977, he went public with this concern in a speech to the International Institute for Strategic Studies, in London.[61]

Although Schmidt's well-publicized speech heightened the pressure for NATO's deployment of a new generation of nuclear missiles, other factors constrained this policy. Schmidt, for example, did not favor such deployment. As he later explained, he "did not pursue the goal of responding to Soviet preliminary arming with Western rearming; rather, I demanded that . . . Eurostrategic nuclear weapons . . . be included in the arms limitation the two superpowers were striving to achieve in SALT II." Indeed, Schmidt followed up with concrete proposals for such an arms control agreement.[62] As late as October 1978, in a meeting with Brzezinski, he continued to complain that, although the United States and the Soviet Union were limiting strategic nuclear weapons through SALT, there existed "no limitation on medium-range missiles." Although, at this time, he expressed a willingness to accept cruise missile deployment in West Germany, he qualified this by adding: "If no other country would take them . . . this would be very difficult." Even Brzezinski showed little enthusiasm for deploying the cruise missile. "There clearly would be considerable political fallout in reaction to such a weapon," he told the German chancellor. Furthermore, "how would deployment relate to arms control? . . . Should we go into arms talks first and hold up deployment, or should there be a combination of hardware deployment and arms talks?" A few days later, in a meeting with the Belgian foreign minister, Brzezinski expressed similar concerns. What would be the "political consequences" of deployment, he asked. And "what should be the timing of an arms control proposal in relation to weapons decision? . . . This is not just a military issue; it is a highly sensitive political issue."[63] Thus, at the end of 1978, the resolution of the INF question remained unclear.

The Impact on Nuclear Weapons Policy:
Warsaw Pact

For the time being, Soviet nuclear weapons policy remained more contradictory. Underneath Soviet propaganda calls for banning the Bomb, there did lurk a genuine, if more modest, Kremlin interest in détente and nuclear arms control. This attempt to set limits to the nuclear arms race and reduce the danger of nuclear war was reflected in the intense negotiations with the U.S. government over the SALT II treaty. The Soviet government was also quite serious about a CTBT, apparently based on its fear of nuclear proliferation and its desire to curb nuclear advances by China. The United States and the Soviet Union should "work more vigorously in the direction of reliable prevention of nuclear weapons proliferation," Gromyko told Carter in September 1977; "we are ready for it." This was further illustrated when it announced a moratorium on "peaceful nuclear explosions," accepted the U.S. proposal for a CTBT of indefinite duration, and accepted provisions for verification through national seismic stations and even through some types of on-site inspection.[64] In addition, in January 1977, speaking at Tula, Brezhnev broke new ground for a Soviet leader by declaring the impossibility of victory in a nuclear war. According to Dobrynin, this speech "was made as a signal of goodwill from Moscow to the new President," with the hope that it would breathe new life into détente and the SALT process. Moreover, the "Tula line"—an implicit concession that nuclear war would be an unmitigated disaster—became official policy, and was reiterated by Brezhnev at the 26th Soviet Party Congress of February 1981.[65]

At the same time, however, in areas not covered by arms control treaties or Kremlin promises, the Soviet Union continued its steady military build-up. Although Soviet defense spending in the late 1970s increased at a lower level than CIA and other U.S. officials estimated at the time, it nonetheless continued to rise after 1976. During these years, the Soviet government also deployed a new generation of ICBMs with improved accuracy and MIRVed warheads, as well as improved longer-range, sea-launched ballistic missiles.

In addition, it moved forward with the deployment of its intermediate range SS-20 missiles. At the suggestion of Soviet Defense Minister Dmitri Ustinov, the Kremlin adopted the SS-20 program for what it claimed was the modernization of similar missiles in the Soviet Union. But, as Gorbachev later wrote, the SS-20s were "far superior to their predecessors in terms of range, precision, guidance and all other properties." Moreover, "the Soviet leadership failed to take into account the probable reaction of the Western countries," despite the appeals against deployment by the West German political leadership. In retrospect, Gorbachev considered the deployment of the SS-20 missiles "an unforgivable adventure, embarked on . . . under pressure from the military-industrial complex."[66]

Nor did other Soviet policies indicate a dramatic departure from the priorities of the past. Although, during these years, the Kremlin was on relatively good behavior vis-à-vis Western Europe and Japan, it engaged in a variety of military activities in the Third World. Channeling arms and other aid to "national liberation" movements and friendly governments in underdeveloped nations, especially in Africa, it contributed thereby to an atmosphere of international insecurity. Dobrynin recalled that he tried to explain to Soviet officials "how our Third World adventures undermined our relations with Washington," but they invariably responded: "Why does the United States raise such complaints about us when they are themselves so active around the globe?" Therefore, at Politburo meetings dealing with Angola, Somalia, and Ethiopia, "American complaints were not even seriously considered."[67] Even when wooed by relatively dovish officials within the Carter administration, the Kremlin could not shake off its adversarial approach to the United States or, for that matter, develop a cordial relationship with Carter. Despite repeated efforts by Carter to improve U.S.-Soviet relations through summit meetings with Brezhnev, the Kremlin stubbornly insisted upon making such conclaves contingent upon the successful conclusion of a SALT II agreement.[68]

The contradictions in Soviet policy were exemplified by the aging, increasingly decrepit Brezhnev, caught in a bind between his revulsion at nuclear war and his fear of U.S. aggression. According to Dobrynin, the Soviet party secretary "remained firmly convinced of the necessity of improving our relations with Washington." Moreover, "he completely excluded any possibility of a war with the United States, for this would amount to 'the end of the world.'" Nevertheless, although "détente in Soviet-American relations was Brezhnev's true objective . . . he failed to comprehend fully what it entailed. His credo was based on the traditional Marxist-Leninist 'class approach' to foreign policy, which cast even peaceful relations into a mould of confrontation, although not necessarily on the battlefield." The United States "remained for Brezhnev the principal opponent which strove to undermine the socialist order inside the Soviet Union and the socialist camp as a whole. Détente, therefore, had to have its limits." He "saw no need of any major corrections" in Soviet policy, despite the fact that "reality demanded changes." Such "stagnation of thought, ideological inertia, and lack of flexibility could not but lead to . . . an ultimate deadlock in Soviet policy."[69]

In this context, the initial Soviet response to the Carter administration was quite hostile. Given the Kremlin's innate conservatism, during the 1976 presidential campaign it had preferred a known U.S. government official like Ford to an unpredictable outsider like Carter. And the new President's early actions rapidly heightened its anxieties. His criticism of human rights abuses in the Soviet Union, typified by his 1977 exchange of letters on the subject with Andrei Sakharov, outraged Soviet officials, who not only re-garded it as meddling in their country's internal affairs but also as an indi-cation of the U.S. government's return to a policy of Cold War confronta-tion. Soviet Foreign Minister Andrei Gromyko irritably told Carter that September: "When you or other American politicians begin to talk about 'human rights,' we . . . in the Soviet leadership have a kind of automatic . . . reflex: we expect that some shots will be made towards the Soviet Union. . . . Why is it being done?"[70] In retrospect, officials from both East and West concluded that Carter's human rights emphasis dramatically raised the level of Soviet mistrust and, therefore, undermined Soviet willingness to negoti-ate seriously over nuclear arms controls with the new administration.[71]

Carter's March 1977 SALT proposals proved even more divisive. In the eyes of Soviet leaders, these proposals were outrageous, for they scrapped the understandings they had reached with Kissinger at Vladivostok in 1974. Meeting in late March 1977 with Vance, Gromyko demanded to know if "the next government of the USA" would "just as easily throw everything that we are able to agree upon now into the trash?"[72] In addition, as Do-brynin told Brzezinski that June, Soviet leaders believed that "the United States is deliberately attempting to significantly affect the central compo-nent of the Soviet nuclear force, namely, ground-based missiles." Unlike the United States, the Soviet Union did not have its strategic weapons in a bal-anced land-sea-air triad. Instead, the Soviet Union's land-based missiles constituted about two thirds of its total nuclear weapons force. Finally, as old hands at antinuclear propaganda, Kremlin officials suspected that Carter was simply trying to turn antinuclear opinion against the Soviet Union. Do-brynin recalled: "The very fact of publicizing the basic content of American proposals before Vance presented them to the Soviet leadership was taken in Moscow as an indication that Carter's intentions were not serious, and that he was merely trying to achieve a propaganda victory."[73]

Ironically, then, as Brzezinski recalled, despite the new President's sincere desire to reduce the dangers of the Soviet-American nuclear confrontation, the Russians "were very suspicious of Carter's motives." They seemed to think that the initial U.S. SALT proposals "were designed less for humanistic reasons and more for strategic reasons. They did not, I think, fully understand the depth of his commitment to arms control." Indeed, in his June 1977 meeting with Brzezinski, Dobrynin emphasized that "Soviet leaders are very perplexed about what it is that the Carter administration is trying to do."[74] In August, when Senator McGovern conferred with Soviet officials, they complained bitterly to him about new U.S. weapons systems and about the administration's rejection of the Vladivostok understandings. That September, Gromyko insisted plaintively to Carter that "the entire Soviet leadership . . . and all our people sincerely aspire to maintain good, friendly relations with the USA." But, although Carter, in some of his speeches, had "emphasized the importance of mutual understanding and cooperation with the Soviet Union," in others "you criticized the Soviet Union . . . I repeat, criticized it." Consequently, "we ponder which of these statements reflect your true policy."[75]

Subsequently, Soviet leaders, recognizing that they had judged the new administration somewhat hastily, settled down to working with it satisfactorily on some issues. Indeed, the Russians perked up considerably after new SALT proposals were made by the U.S. government later in the spring of 1977, for these indicated greater flexibility than they had assumed in the U.S. position on strategic nuclear weapons. As the talks recommenced, the Soviet side accepted compromises on the MIRVing of missiles, the Backfire bomber, and other sensitive issues. Soviet leaders also recognized that they shared a common interest with the U.S. government when it came to the CTBT and issues of non-proliferation. In 1977, when the Soviet government warned Washington that the South African government was about to test a nuclear weapon, the U.S. government applied enough pressure on the Pretoria regime to get it to cancel the test. Another common interest, they hoped, lay in dealing with China. Soviet relations with the Chinese were "tense," Gromyko admitted to Carter, and he warned the American President to "be on guard so that they do not pull you into games dirty and dangerous for both our countries."[76]

The working relationship that Soviet officials developed with the Carter administration, especially on arms control issues, reflected, overwhelmingly, their pursuit of what they considered their national security interests, with relatively little attention paid to the nuclear disarmament campaign. After all, the Kremlin set the agenda for the World Peace Council, rather than vice versa, and the independent antinuclear efforts of the time were small-scale and confined almost entirely to the West. Even so, the Soviet government had made a substantial investment of its resources in WPC propaganda portraying the Soviet Union as the paragon of peace and arms control. Furthermore, the pesky independent nuclear disarmament movement was beginning to nip uncomfortably at its heels, reminding people that the Warsaw Pact, too, maintained dangerous nuclear weapons. Therefore, like the U.S. government, the Soviet government was loath to tarnish what it considered its good name by displaying a belligerent face to the world. Instead, it took every opportunity to portray itself as the champion of peaceful coexistence. Characteristically, Brezhnev proclaimed: "We counter the 'doctrine' of war hysteria and frantic arms race with the doctrine of a steady drive for peace and security on earth."[77]

Nevertheless, despite the development of a working relationship with the Carter administration, Soviet leaders remained deeply suspicious of it. In the spring of 1978, they blamed Washington repeatedly for undermining U.S.-Soviet relations.[78] These gloomy assessments reached a zenith on June 8, the day after a tough speech by Carter, in an address that Brezhnev delivered to the Central Committee of the Soviet Communist Party. "We are experiencing a very complicated period in the development of international relations," he declared. "A serious deterioration and exacerbation of the situation has occurred. And the primary source of this deterioration is the growing aggression of the foreign policy of the Carter government, the continually more sharply anti-Soviet character of the statements of the President himself and of his closest colleagues," primarily "those of Brzezinski." Carter was "not simply falling under the usual influence of the most shameless anti-Soviet types and ringleaders of the military-industrial complex of the USA, but is intent upon struggling for his election to a new term as President . . . under the banner of anti-Soviet policy and a return to the 'cold war.'" According to Brezhnev, "under the curtain of lies and slander on the USSR and other socialist countries, concrete matters are being . . . directed against peace and détente." For example, "the course of negotiations with the Soviet Union on the limitations of strategic arms is intentionally being retarded. Attempts at clumsy interference in our internal affairs are being perpetrated. . . . New extensive plans for the arms race are being made, and for decades in advance, at the very time when the peoples hoped for disarmament."[79]

Even so, Brezhnev did not use this harsh assessment to argue for a Soviet military buildup, but, rather, to advocate a peace policy, with substantial attention to public opinion. "We must fight actively and persistently for peace and détente," he told the party leaders at the same gathering. Although "there is an attempt to impose on us a continually broader competition in arms," the Soviet government must "decisively come forward for keeping in check the arms race, for concrete agreements on these questions in all forums." The Soviet Union would do everything possible "for the successful completion of negotiations with the USA concerning SALT." As part of this peace policy, the Soviet government would produce informational materials that would put Western hawks on the defensive, for "it is necessary to show both to other countries and to communities in the USA itself, just how dangerous a game Carter, Brzezinski, and their likes are starting." In line with this propaganda campaign, the Soviet government would "develop work through other channels as well—along the lines of connections with fraternal parties" and with "international social organizations." The U.N. Special Session was also important in this light, and the Soviet government "should likewise support all that is healthy and constructive" in its operations and "should expose the maneuvers of the opponents to disarmament."[80]

A similar policy, based on a more sophisticated analysis, was advanced a month later by the Soviet embassy in Washington. Reviewing U.S.-Soviet relations in a message to Moscow of July 11, 1978, Ambassador Dobrynin criticized the Carter administration for "a selective, half-hearted conception of détente." The Carter administration, he charged, had "imposed a definite barrier to the possible improvement in our relations," which included "strengthening NATO, the arms game," and "the game with China." Even so, he noted, "it would not be in our interests to pass by specific positive aspects of Carter's approach to relations with the Soviet Union—in the first place his great personal interest in a meeting with L.I. Brezhnev" and "his support in principle for a treaty on SALT. . . . Appropriate positive reactions from our side . . . would strengthen the positions of those individuals and circles which are trying to influence the President from the perspective of the need for the development of Soviet-American relations over the long term." Therefore, Dobrynin concluded, it was important "to continue to energetically pursue the working out of agreements on SALT and a total ban on nuclear tests." These steps would provide "the political perquisites for a Soviet-American summit meeting which could have decisive significance for normalization and then for improvement of our relations."[81]

In short, during 1977–78, the Soviet government, like the U.S. government, genuinely desired to strengthen Soviet-American détente and to foster nuclear arms controls. The problem was that, dominated by tradition-bound, authoritarian, and sickly leaders and shielded, to a great degree, from popular pressures, it was incapable of changing course and taking the necessary action. Unable to depart substantially from its adversarial approach to foreign and military policy, it failed to grasp fully the unusual opportunities along these lines presented by the dovish orientation of key figures in the Carter administration and, behind them, the force of antinuclear public opinion. Arbatov recalled, in retrospect: "We didn't need to build all those missiles or deploy the SS-20s in Europe. . . . There was no need to ship so many arms to the Third World." When "Vance came to Moscow with a set of arms control proposals quite different from what had been agreed on," the Soviet government "shouldn't have rejected them out of hand." Pondering the "mistakes" of both nations, he concluded that "Jimmy Carter's presidency was a period of lost opportunities."[82]

A Time of Modest Progress

Nevertheless, despite obstacles erected by the Soviet government and by hawkish forces in the United States, 1977–78 was a time of modest progress in bringing the nuclear arms race under control. Some nuclear weapons systems were scrapped unilaterally. Others—notably strategic nuclear weapons—provided the subject of good faith arms control negotiations, with treaties well on their way. Governmental efforts were also made to restrain nuclear proliferation and to raise the threshold for the use of nuclear weapons. Although these nuclear arms control and disarmament policies were certainly linked to national security concerns, at key junctures they were also affected by the pressure of antinuclear public opinion and by its organizational expression, the antinuclear movement. Indeed, at this potential turning point in the arms race, substantially more might have been accomplished toward taming the nuclear menace had the movement been stronger and public officials wiser.

Escalating Activism, 1979-80

We must learn to be loyal, not to "East" or "West," but
to each other.

Appeal for European Nuclear Disarmament, 1980

During 1979–80, escalating great power suspicion and rivalry led to the deterioration of the U.S.-Soviet relationship and to the reversal of the modest
progress against the nuclear arms race made in preceding years. The Soviet
Union's continued buildup of dangerous SS-20 missiles in Eastern Europe
was matched by a NATO decision to install threatening intermediate range
nuclear missiles in Britain, West Germany, the Netherlands, Belgium, and
Italy. In addition, the U.S. government pressed forward with the development of a new strategic weapons system, the MX missile. Although the
SALT II treaty was finally signed, efforts to secure its ratification were
abandoned—along with efforts to negotiate an already debilitated CTBT—
after the beginning of Soviet military intervention in Afghanistan. Furthermore, as détente crumbled, the Carter administration unveiled a plan for
fighting a prolonged, escalating nuclear war. In 1980, world military expenditures reached the unprecedented figure of $500 billion a year, and there
existed over 60,000 nuclear warheads with the overall destructive power of
1.3 million Hiroshima-style bombs. At the end of that fateful year, the editors of the *Bulletin of the Atomic Scientists* decided to move the hands of
their famous "doomsday clock" three minutes closer to midnight.[1]

These ominous developments provided a spur to further growth and development of the nuclear disarmament movement. Some of the gathering
antinuclear campaigners were veterans of past efforts who had dropped
away years before. Others were new recruits. Meanwhile, the scattered antinuclear activism that had emerged previously began to coalesce into coordinated ventures. In Western Europe, this took the form of rallying behind a
European Nuclear Disarmament campaign to block the deployment of Soviet and NATO Euromissiles. In the United States, peace organizations

gravitated toward a Nuclear Freeze campaign—an attempt to halt further testing, production, and deployment of nuclear weapons. Although this expanding antinuclear movement was not strong enough to halt the surging nuclear arms race, in a number of countries it began to take on mass dimensions, influencing important constituencies and mainstream organizations.

Western Europe

The movement's revival was nowhere more evident than in Western Europe, where, in 1979–80, it made substantial strides toward renewing the mass participation it had enjoyed during the early 1960s.

In Britain, the Campaign for Nuclear Disarmament was once again growing rapidly. By late 1980, membership stood at some 9,000—double that of 1979 and nearly triple the membership of 1978. Bruce Kent, who had taken leave of his pastoral duties with the Roman Catholic Church to become CND general secretary, reported in late 1980 that "hundreds of new groups have formed" on the local level, "and many other organizations have affiliated." These statistics, however, do not provide a full picture of CND's revival. Week by week, Kent recalled, there "arrived more letters, more membership applications, more callers, more journalists, more requests for speakers, more orders for badges and leaflets." CND's showings of *The War Game* played before packed audiences every night. Its two tiny office rooms became jammed with volunteers, while lines formed outside its door. Early in 1980, CND had rejected an offer of new office space on the grounds that it was too large. Then it changed its mind and moved to the new office, only to find, by the end of the year, that this space, too, was becoming too small.[2]

Having, with some difficulty, filled a 600-seat hall for a mass meeting in 1979, CND's leaders initially were wary of proceeding with a proposed fall 1980 disarmament march. Organized in honor of U.N. Disarmament Week and scheduled to run from Hyde Park to Trafalgar Square, it might produce only a few hundred demonstrators, thus humiliating CND before the press and the public. But, sensing that a turning point had arrived, CND's leaders plunged ahead. On the morning of October 26, the day of the demonstration, Kent recalled, "we already knew that we were on to a winner. Coaches were coming from all over the country, trains had been booked, and there was an astonishing feeling of expectation." Suddenly, "Labour MPs of all sorts were popping up, anxious to be photographed in front of the march." Trafalgar Square "was full and kept on filling. As many as 80,000 people turned out that day. Great banners kept on flowing down from Piccadilly like the sails of ships. By half past four it was already getting near dusk, and still they came." Addressing the rally, the historian E. P. Thompson sent a surge of energy through the antinuclear throng, the largest since CND's marches of the early 1960s, as he cried out: "Feel your strength!"[3]

Most historians and movement leaders are agreed on the major factors behind what the London *Times* called "the second coming of CND." The most important was probably NATO's December 1979 decision to install cruise and Pershing II missiles in Western Europe. As a substantial number of the cruise missiles were slated for deployment in Britain, this brought the new round in the nuclear arms race home to Britons very directly. In addition, however, the Soviet invasion of Afghanistan, the British government's decision to upgrade its "independent" nuclear force by replacing its aging Polaris nuclear submarines with the Trident variety, the shift in U.S. nuclear doctrine from deterrence to war-fighting, and the overall collapse of détente helped convince many members of the public that the nuclear arms race was getting out of hand.[4] This belief was reinforced when the British government published *Protect and Survive*, a little manual on how to survive a future nuclear war. When Professor Michael Howard, defending the pamphlet, argued that the public should be prepared for nuclear war's "disagreeable consequences," Thompson, who had withdrawn from CND activities some years before, returned to the fray with a scathing, highly publicized riposte, *Protest and Survive*, that appeared in April 1980. It quickly became a CND best seller that, along with his fiery speeches, helped mobilize the new army of resistance.[5]

CND's activities mirrored these concerns. To call attention to Britain's own nuclear weapons program, in the spring of 1979 it staged a march from the atomic weapons research site at Aldermaston, in southern England, to the Polaris base in Faslane, Scotland. The seven-week march, organized around the theme of "scrap Polaris," drew about 5,000 participants along the way, and culminated in a protest demonstration of some 1,000 people. As CND was not enthusiastic about the SALT II agreement, which it considered sadly insufficient and likely to spread false optimism about progress toward disarmament, the organization did little to promote it. CND was far more active in campaigning against what it called "the civil defense sham," distributing Thompson's pamphlet and another prepared by a CND stalwart, *Civil Defense—the Cruelist Confidence Trick*.[6] As a participant in the National Peace Council, the umbrella organization for Britain's peace organizations, CND joined in condemning the Soviet war in Afghanistan. Fearing a Soviet invasion of Poland, it even prepared a draft resolution assailing that hypothetical event. By 1980, however, CND was focusing increasingly on the Euromissile issue, which, together with the Thatcher government's decision to acquire Trident nuclear submarines, provided the centerpiece for the massive London protest rally that October.[7]

Although CND stood in the forefront of Britain's reviving nuclear disarmament movement, other groups were also becoming involved. Originally opposed only to nuclear power, Britain's Anti Nuclear Campaign resolved, in 1980, to broaden its aims to include opposition to nuclear weapons. Toward this end, it decided to oppose the siting of cruise missiles in Britain, to reject the planned purchase of Trident missiles, "to emphasize . . . the link between nuclear weapons and nuclear power," and to rally around "a broad-based campaign for unilateral disarmament."[8] Church bodies were also gravitating in an antinuclear direction. At its November 1979 Assembly, the British Council of Churches voted overwhelmingly to oppose replacing Britain's Polaris submarine fleet with an upgraded version—a position echoed by the National Pastoral Congress of the Roman Catholic Church in early 1980.[9] Moreover, in June 1980, the Labour Party, deeply disturbed by the deployment of INF missiles in Europe, organized an "Against Nuclear Weapons" rally and march in downtown London. Despite rainy weather, the event drew some 20,000 participants. CND's influence in the Labour Party had been dwindling since the early 1960s, but the revival of public concern about nuclear weapons helped restore the relationship. In the fall of 1980, the Labour Party's national convention passed a range of strong antinuclear resolutions, including statements opposing Polaris, Trident, and cruise missiles.[10]

Sometimes, the condemnation of nuclear weapons was to be expected, as when Lords Fenner Brockway and Philip Noel-Baker, two venerable peace activists, held the founding meeting of their World Disarmament Campaign—an event that drew some 2,600 people to Central Hall, Westminster, in April 1980. Although emphasizing multilateral nuclear disarmament, the new organization enjoyed reasonably good relations with the unilateralist CND, and helped focus popular attention upon the dangers of nuclear weapons.[11] Sometimes, however, the new surge of protest came from more unusual sources. On November 15, 1980, the prestigious British medical journal, *The Lancet*, ran a lead article entitled "The Threat of Nuclear War." That year, a group of health care workers launched the British Medical Campaign Against Nuclear Weapons. Even the mass media, long indifferent or unfriendly to antinuclear activism, began to churn out interviews with CND leaders and to put them on radio and television programs.[12] Polls found substantial support among Britons for new limits on nuclear weapons and a speed-up of strategic arms talks.[13] By the end of 1980, the nuclear disarmament movement was becoming a force once again in British life.

The movement was already a force in the Netherlands. Throughout 1979, the principal disarmament group, the Interchurch Peace Council (IKV), continued its meteoric growth. Polls showed overwhelming support for its proposal to remove all nuclear weapons from Dutch territory as a first step in worldwide nuclear disarmament. That April, the powerful Social Democratic Party officially adopted the IKV proposal as party policy. By January 1980, IKV had more than 350 local branches in operation. But its long-term campaign was overtaken in 1979 by the NATO plan to deploy cruise and Pershing II missiles in Western Europe, and this caused a redirection of its efforts and those of its allies in Pax Christi and the Stop the Neutron Bomb organization. IKV sparked countless parish meetings, marches, vigils, and picket lines against the missile deployment. The National Council of Churches raised its voice against the missile plan, as did the synods of the two largest Protestant churches and the Catholic bishops. On November 24, 1979, some 25,000 people turned out for an anti-missile demonstration organized by IKV, the Stop the Neutron Bomb group, the Social Democrats, and other opposition parties. With even the ruling Christian Democrats split on missile deployment, there was a clear parliamentary majority against the NATO deployment decision.[14]

Moreover, on the broader—and more radical—issue of withdrawing nuclear weapons from the Netherlands, Dutch public opinion was overwhelmingly antinuclear. In 1979, polls found that only 26 percent of respondents wanted the Dutch armed forces equipped with nuclear weapons, and that 56 percent did not. An October 1980 opinion survey found that 65 percent of the public desired the removal of nuclear weapons from the Netherlands, while only 28 percent favored their continued presence.[15]

Although, for a time, INF missile deployment seemed less controversial in Belgium, this situation changed dramatically in the fall of 1979. CNAPD began to mobilize peace movement resistance in the French-speaking regions of the country, while a new coalition, the Flemish Action Committee Against Nuclear Weapons (Vlaams Aktiekomitee tegen Atoomwapens, VAKA) arose to agitate in the Flemish regions. Pax Christi was particularly influential in the latter. News conferences, torchlight demonstrations, debates, hunger strikes, and petitions demanding removal of the SS-20s and non-deployment of the cruise and Pershing IIs highlighted the growing opposition. Both the Flemish and the French Socialist parties came out against the missiles. On December 6, the Belgian bishops issued a statement calling for an end to the arms race. Three days later, an anti-missile demonstration organized by CNAPD, VAKA, and their allies brought approximately 50,000 people to downtown Brussels in the driving rain. Drawn from

throughout Belgium and from neighboring countries, they demanded sus-
pension of the NATO missile deployment decision, as well as negotiations
for removal of the Soviet SS-20 missiles and all other nuclear weapons in
Eastern and Western Europe. Opinion polls reported that 64 percent of the
population opposed installation of the new missiles in Belgium.[16]

The new movement also showed substantial strength in Scandinavia.
During late 1979, a massive campaign emerged spontaneously in Norway
against NATO plans for missile deployment. Publicly launched by veteran
peace activists on October 20, the campaign published appeals against intermediate range missiles—both American and Soviet—in newspapers, issued a petition signed by prominent personalities, held public meetings,
and, by November, had organized fifteen to twenty local groups in Norway's major cities and towns. Within a short time, union federations, most
branches of the ruling Labour Party, and other small parties of the Center-
Left endorsed the campaign. In addition, some 70,000 Norwegians signed
campaign petitions against the missiles. Polls found that a substantial plurality of the population (44 percent) opposed the NATO missile decision,
and that 80 percent opposed deployment of the missiles in Norway. In the
aftermath of the NATO decision, campaign activists met in January 1980
and reorganized their venture as a broader, non-hierarchical disarmament
movement, No to Nuclear Weapons (Nei til Atomvåpen). Later that year,
the new group committed itself to working for a ban on nuclear weapons in
Norway in peace or war, a nuclear-free zone in the Nordic countries, and
the gradual dismantling of nuclear weapons in East and West. With polls in
late 1980 showing that only about 10 percent of the population thought it
would be advantageous for Norway to rely upon nuclear weapons for its defense, No to Nuclear Weapons grew rapidly.[17]

Much the same thing happened in Denmark. In the fall of 1979, as the
Danish parliament debated the issue of NATO missile deployment, a small
group of peace activists, including veterans of the earlier anti-Vietnam War
and antinuclear movements, began a campaign against nuclear armaments.
They circulated a petition, calling upon the Danish parliament "to repudiate
the nuclear arms build-up in both the Warsaw Pact and NATO" and to postpone the NATO deployment decision, thus providing the opportunity for a
negotiated settlement of the gathering Euromissile crisis. When 5,000 people signed their petition and contributed funds to publish it, they took out
full-page advertisements in two daily newspapers that November. The
popular response was "overwhelming," they recalled, and the campaign
surged forward. Protest marches were held in several cities on the weekend
before the NATO decision, including a torchlight parade in Copenhagen

that drew over 10,000 people. Polls showed a plurality (43 percent) of Danes opposed to missile deployment and 63 percent opposed to deployment in Denmark. The popularity of the anti-missile campaign, together with NATO's decision to deploy, led stalwarts to hold a meeting in mid-January 1980 to found a new grassroots organization, No to Nuclear Weapons (Nej til Atomvåben). The choice of name probably reflected the influence of the Norwegian movement, with which many of the initiators had had contact. Its grassroots, non-hierarchical structure, lacking formal membership, probably also owed something to the Norwegian movement, as well as to the experience of many youthful activists with protests against nuclear power plants.[18]

In both Norway and Denmark, a new women's peace group also played a key role in the developing antinuclear campaign. In the aftermath of the NATO missile decision and the Soviet invasion of Afghanistan, and with a U.N. women's conference scheduled to open in Copenhagen in the summer of 1980, Danish women launched Women for Peace (Kvinder for Fred) on February 15, 1980. Without formal leadership or membership, Women for Peace quickly spread to Norway and other neighboring countries. The first project of the new movement was a petition, declaring that "women of the Nordic countries have had it. Enough is enough!" They would "no longer tacitly accept the power struggle between the superpowers. All acts of aggression must be stopped immediately and the disarmament negotiations must be resumed at once, resulting in action." That July, when the U.N. conference convened, Women for Peace presented it with 500,000 signatures on this petition, including 200,000 from Denmark and 70,000 from Norway. Although Women for Peace had a more emotive, less analytical style than No to Nuclear Weapons, the two movements worked together against the nuclear arms race in both countries. However, Women for Peace never became a powerful movement in Norway, largely because No to Nuclear Weapons in that country constantly sought to bring women's disarmament activism under its auspices.[19]

Although weaker in West Germany, the nuclear disarmament movement there gathered strength throughout 1979–80. Initially, opposition to NATO missile plans had little visibility in the Federal Republic. Protest among Social Democrats was muted because, after Chancellor Schmidt had made concessions to his party's doves, he had secured a grudging party acceptance of the NATO decision. Even so, in November 1979, a group called Christians for Disarmament called upon West Germany's churches to lead a struggle for disarmament and upon NATO governments to break through the vicious circle of the arms race by refusing to go along with missile buildup plans. Furthermore, throughout 1980, peace and anti-missile demonstrations began to erupt in West Germany's cities and towns, some drawing as many as 15,000 participants. Both Pax Christi and Action Reconciliation began major disarmament programs.[20] Building upon this growing resistance, antinuclear leaders launched the Krefeld Appeal—a critique of the NATO missile deployment—that November. Moreover, young activists organized a new political party, the Greens (Die Grünen), in 1979. Committed to ecological balance, feminism, and peace, the Greens—led by the dynamic Petra Kelly—began to emerge as a leading force for nuclear disarmament in electoral politics and in the streets. Although polls in November 1979 showed a slight plurality of West Germans (38 percent) in favor of NATO missile deployment, these new developments made it increasingly controversial.[21]

The movement was weaker yet in NATO countries along the Mediterranean. In Italy, the Catholic Church hierarchy tacitly accepted cruise missile deployment, which was strongly supported by the ruling Christian Democrats. Even so, in October 1979, eight religious groups published an open letter on the arms race; though avoiding any explicit mention of the NATO missiles, it denounced "the new threat imposed by the political policy of the 'balance of terror.'" The tiny Radical Party engaged in more straightforward opposition to the missiles, including marches and demonstrations, as it did to all military ventures. Also moving into action, the much larger Communist Party called upon the Soviet Union to halt construction of its SS-20 missiles and upon NATO to delay its missile decision by six months.[22] In France, the decision of the Socialist and Communist parties to support the French *force de frappe* severely undermined the influence of antinuclear campaigners, and the independent peace movement barely survived. Nevertheless, the small Movement for Disarmament, Peace and Liberty (Mouvement pour le Désarmement, la Paix et la Liberté) continued small-scale antinuclear activities, including opposing French nuclear testing in Polynesia and calling for a Europe free of nuclear weapons.[23] Meanwhile, at the eastern end of the Mediterranean, the Turkish Peace Association campaigned against the idea of deploying NATO missiles in its country.[24]

In West European countries outside of NATO, the movement fared somewhat better. Irish CND had dwindled away in the 1960s, but it was revived in October 1979. Thereafter, focusing on the dangers of the nuclear arms race and the need for disarmament, it grew rapidly in membership and influence.[25] In Finland, peace organizations used U.N. Disarmament Week in 1980 to stage demonstrations in various parts of the country, drawing some 15,000 participants. Under the slogan "Act Before the Weapons Act," more than 6,000 people staged an antinuclear march through the center of Helsinki. Although Women for Peace made its debut in Finland during early 1980, for the most part this upsurge of activism was not launched by new organizations, but, instead, by the nation's oldest peace movement, the Peace Union of Finland.[26] Sweden, too, experienced an upsurge of protest against nuclear weapons, particularly after NATO's missile deployment decision of 1979. Much of it became channeled into a campaign for a Nordic nuclear-free zone. The upsurge included the founding of a Women for Peace group that, like its counterparts in the other Nordic countries, widely circulated the women's petition assailing the nuclear arms race. As in Finland, the primary peace movement beneficiary of Sweden's new wave of protest turned out to be the senior organization, the Swedish Peace and Arbitration Society. But the rising campaign did sweep in a new, and much younger, leadership.[27]

North America

As Canada was not a site for deployment of the new NATO missiles, the Canadian disarmament movement had less focus, but nonetheless underwent substantial growth. During 1979, the United Church took a leading role in criticizing the NATO decision, warning that it would have "a seriously destabilizing effect upon an already precarious world." Taking a dim view of the nuclear power industry, the Voice of Women mounted protests against the development of nuclear power plants in Canada, while a Canadian-based committee, No Candu for Argentina, protested the sale of Canada's Candu nuclear reactors and the shipment of nuclear materials to that country. By the fall of 1980, the Canadian movement was beginning to show some strength. Coordinated by Project Ploughshares, its 1980 Disarmament Week involved more than 10,000 Canadians in 160 events held in all ten provinces. Churches and religious organizations emphasized disarmament education. Disarmament events took place on the campuses of 22 Canadian universities. In Vancouver, the mayor of that city, citing the final document of the 1978 U.N. Special Session, issued a disarmament proclamation. Similar proclamations were made by mayors or city councils in other cities and towns. In Winnipeg, medical doctors published a half-page advertisement on the medical implications of nuclear war. Films like *War Without Winners*, *Dr. Strangelove*, and *Who's in Charge Here?* were widely shown. Although the national communications media gave these events virtually no coverage, they did receive media attention at the local and regional levels.[28]

Protest against the nuclear arms race grew apace in the United States, with religious groups increasingly vocal. The AFSC took a strong stand against NATO missile deployment, observing that, just as past campaigns had defeated "civil defense shelters, the ABM, atmospheric testing of nuclear weapons, the B-1 bomber and the neutron bomb, now, together with European peace forces, there is a very good possibility of defeating the deployment of Eurostrategic weapons." More surprisingly, in testimony before the Senate Foreign Relations Committee in September 1979, the U.S. Catholic Conference, the organization representing 350 bishops, condemned threats to use nuclear weapons and demanded the complete phasing out of nuclear deterrence. Writing in the FOR's magazine in early 1980, Homer Jack, the secretary general of the World Conference on Religion and Peace and a former SANE leader, urged religious groups to "take the lead in launching a worldwide moral and religious crusade . . . to say 'no' to nuclear war and 'no' to the nuclear arms race."[29]

Although there was little sign of mainstream religious leadership along these lines in the following months, small groups of religious pacifists did begin to take nonviolent direct action against nuclear weapons. The best known of the incidents occurred in September 1980, near Philadelphia. Entering the General Electric plant in the town of King of Prussia, eight Catholic pacifists—including the priest Daniel Berrigan and his brother Philip—followed the Biblical injunction to beat swords into plowshares by hammering nuclear missile cones out of shape and, then, pouring blood upon missile blueprints, work orders, and equipment. Their work finished, they knelt, joined hands, and sang hymns. Eventually, the "Plowshares Eight" were tried and convicted, receiving three- to ten-year prison terms. But they were not repentant. "Who expects politicians, generals, and bomb makers to disarm?" asked Philip Berrigan. "People must disarm the bombs."[30]

American women were also becoming increasingly focused on disarmament. Determined to create a nuclear-free world, the U.S. branch of WILPF made ratification of the SALT II treaty a major organizational priority and worked to defeat plans for funding and deployment of the MX missile.[31] The nation's largest feminist organization, the National Organization for Women, participated alongside peace and social justice groups in the May 17, 1980 March for Jobs, Peace, and Justice in Washington, D.C. On June 1, 1980, Women Strike for Peace took out a full-page antinuclear advertisement in the *New York Times*. The many signers declared that "we are angered by the continuing build-up of arsenals which threaten the world with nuclear extinction by plan or accident" and "at the spectacle of men who claim they are for peace while they build for war." These women's groups and many others backed the Women's Pentagon Action, a day of protest and resistance held in mid-November. "We want an end to the arms race," their official statement declared. "No more bombs. No more amazing inventions of death." Marching behind huge, eerie puppets, about 1,900 women slowly circled the Pentagon, drums beating, women raging and moaning. Eventually, they blocked three of the five entrances to the building. Police arrested 150 women and drove them off to federal prison—"wired up," as their guards phrased it, in handcuffs and leg irons, and chained together at the waist.[32]

Although, previously, physicians had involved themselves in U.S. anti-nuclear efforts to a limited degree,[33] in the late 1970s they emerged as a key element. In the summer of 1978, the Australian pediatrician Helen Caldicott was working at Harvard Medical School, doing research on the health effects of radiation from nuclear power plants. When a young doctor stopped by to consult her on the issue, she responded: "This is a medical problem. Let's start a medical group!" At a meeting for this purpose about a week later, one of the physicians present recalled that a now-defunct organization, Physicians for Social Responsibility (PSR), which had worked to stop nuclear testing in the early 1960s, was still incorporated in Massachusetts. Consequently, they adopted this name and invited leaders of the former organization to join their venture. During 1979, PSR gathered momentum, helped along by the fortuitous appearance of a full-page ad it placed in the *New England Journal of Medicine* about nuclear dangers. Appearing on the day after the Three Mile Island nuclear reactor experienced a near-meltdown, the ad inspired a flood of letters and PSR quickly became a national organization.[34] With the deterioration of Soviet-American relations, PSR shifted its focus from nuclear power to nuclear war, and that, too, proved a prescient move. In February 1980, PSR held a symposium at Harvard Medical School on the medical consequences of nuclear war. The organizers expected minimal attendance, but, to their surprise, an overflow crowd of more than a thousand people showed up and the national media covered the event. After two days of discussing horrifying scenarios, sixty physicians sent a telegram to Carter and Brezhnev, warning them that "recovery from nuclear war would be impossible." Subsequently, PSR sent a delegation of prominent figures to hold a press conference in Washington and to meet with White House and Soviet embassy officials. The only way to deal with a nuclear war, they argued, was to prevent it.[35]

PSR's rapid mobilization of American physicians owed a great deal not only to timing, but to the enormous energy and persuasiveness of Caldicott. Articulate, strong-willed, and emotional, she did more than anyone else to establish PSR as a powerful, nationwide organization. Resigning her position at Harvard, she barnstormed across the country, addressing groups of doctors and the general public and leaving vigorous PSR chapters in her wake. By late 1980, PSR had 10,000 members. Judy Lipton, at the time a young psychiatrist, recalled that she was part of the tiny, ineffectual PSR group in Seattle when, in 1980, Caldicott phoned her and said: "Set me up to do some grand rounds." New to her practice, Lipton replied that she had no idea how to arrange that. Caldicott responded: "Just do it!" Impressed by Caldicott's determination, Lipton arranged these meetings with doctors at area hospitals that September, along with a host of Caldicott media interviews and speeches. Lipton chauffeured her everywhere for five days and, as she recalled, "by the end of the time, I was a hysterical, raving, totally decompensated lunatic, because I had heard her describe the effects of nuclear war . . . about twelve times. . . . I couldn't look at a window without seeing firestorms. I just lost it. I really lost it. And I had kind of a conversion experience." Although she had just had a baby, was in the process of moving, and was beginning her career, "I couldn't think of anything but nuclear war." As a result, she quit her teaching position, halted her research, and began to organize the city of Seattle against the nuclear arms race.[36]

The major weapons issue for U.S. peace groups was the building and deployment of the MX missile. The Euromissile decision was too Europe-focused to become a top priority, while the SALT II treaty was too limited to inspire much affection.[37] By contrast, the MX missile had a direct impact upon American life, and defeating it seemed feasible. Considering the MX a dangerous, first-strike weapon, SANE organized a powerful resistance coalition, the National Campaign to Stop the MX. It brought together not only peace groups like the AFSC and Clergy and Laity Concerned, but local ranchers, Native Americans, environmental organizations, and unions. As peace activists publicized the fact that, under the MX basing plan, nuclear missile sites would cover a substantial portion of Utah and Nevada, the normally super-patriotic residents of these states grew increasingly uncomfortable with the project. The military was "talking about the land mode, the sea mode, and the air mode for basing the MX," declared a local cowboy and popular orator. "I'd like to suggest another solution—let's put it in the commode!" Local organizers placed MX referenda on the ballot in eight rural counties in Nevada and, in the 1980 elections, voters rejected the MX by two-to-one. Meeting with Mormon Church leaders, perhaps the most influential group in Utah politics, Admiral LaRocque and Harold Willens of the Center for Defense Information convinced them of the dangers of the MX and of the immorality of the nuclear arms race.[38]

As in previous years, the nuclear disarmament movement received a boost from the growing concern about the hazards of nuclear power. In the dazed aftermath of the Three Mile Island disaster, as the nation reassessed its love affair with the "peaceful atom," Mobilization for Survival brought an estimated 100,000 protesters to Washington for the largest demonstration against nuclear power in American history. In 1980, activists in Oregon placed a measure on the ballot to halt all future nuclear power plant construction in the state, and it passed—one of three state referenda pushed through to victory that year by antinuclear forces. Other states passed laws that barred new reactors until the creation of a means to dispose of nuclear wastes permanently.[39] The widespread public fear of nuclear reactors fed into popular dismay with the nuclear arms race, for many people saw the connections. In April 1979, the month after the near meltdown at Three Mile Island, 15,000 demonstrators appeared at the Rocky Flats nuclear weapons facility to demand its conversion to peaceful production. Their theme was "Local hazards, global threats." In July, the mayor of Harrisburg, Pennsylvania—the city nearest the devastated Three Mile Island plant—proposed a sister city affiliation with Hiroshima. Through its constant agitation, Mobilization for Survival continued to meld the causes of banning nuclear power and banning nuclear weapons.[40] Other groups went over entirely to the struggle against the Bomb. In Oregon, the activists behind the successful ballot initiative against nuclear power met in late 1980 and formed Citizens Action for Lasting Security, which became the Oregon branch of the Nuclear Weapons Freeze Campaign.[41]

The Freeze campaign was the brainchild of Randall Forsberg, a young defense and disarmament researcher. Committed to nuclear arms control and disarmament, Forsberg had been giving talks to peace groups since 1975. Along the way, she discovered that these groups "were extremely splintered and diverse in terms of their kinds of goals and demands." Concluding that they needed greater unity and an attainable goal, she began suggesting action along these lines, but with little success. Finally, in mid-1979, she took matters into her own hands and commenced proposing a Nuclear Freeze and a non-intervention policy—two positions that, though not requiring precipitous U.S. disarmament, would "fundamentally change the nature of government policies." That December, when addressing the annual meeting of Mobilization for Survival, she decided to drop the non-intervention idea and focus upon the Nuclear Freeze, "for it was going to be hard enough to unify the peace movement around one goal, let alone two." In fact, Mobilization for Survival—and the major groups behind it (the AFSC, Clergy and Laity Concerned, and the FOR)—had begun earlier that year to champion a "moratorium" on nuclear weapons production and deployment. Therefore, as Forsberg recalled, what she did at the conference was to say: "All you need to do is take this unilateral moratorium and make it bilateral. The great majority of the American people would completely agree with you. And you could change the world!"[42]

Thereafter, the Nuclear Freeze idea caught fire. Extremely enthusiastic, leaders of these groups implored her to draw up a proposal "so we can give it to people and think about running with it." In late December 1979, Forsberg began drafting a "Call to Halt the Nuclear Arms Race," which was widely circulated among leading peace activists. Proposing a U.S.-Soviet agreement to stop the testing, production, and deployment of nuclear weapons, the "Call" emphasized that the Freeze would retain "the existing nuclear parity between the United States and the Soviet Union" and open the way for the drastic reduction or elimination of nuclear weapons in the future. In April 1980, having obtained considerable feedback and individual endorsements, the AFSC, CALC, the FOR, and Forsberg's own Institute for Defense and Disarmament Studies published the "Call" and began lining up endorsements from peace groups.[43] A newly organized Nuclear Freeze Steering Committee took steps to implement a strategic plan for the period from 1980 to 1984, drawn up by Forsberg and peace activist George Sommaripa. Starting with obtaining the support of peace organizations, it called for moving on to secure the backing of major interest groups, to mount a widespread public education campaign for converting "middle America," and, finally, to inject the issue into mainstream politics.[44] The potential of the campaign was shown in western Massachusetts, where, prematurely, a Freeze referendum was placed on the November 1980 election ballot. Thanks to the efforts of Randy Kehler, Frances Crowe, and other local peace activists, the Freeze emerged victorious in 59 of the 62 towns that voted on it.[45]

Thus, at the end of the decade, the U.S. disarmament movement again emerged as a significant force, albeit one that remained proportionately smaller and less influential than its counterparts in Western Europe. New organizations like PSR grew by leaps and bounds, while several older ones, like SANE, underwent revivals in membership and energy. In 1980, eight leading organizations joined to coordinate their Washington lobbying efforts for disarmament in what became known as the Monday Lobby Group.[46] Furthermore, careful planning for a coalition venture, the Nuclear Weapons Freeze Campaign, laid the groundwork for what became the greatest outburst of disarmament activism in American history.

Undergirding this organizational network lay a solid base of public support for nuclear arms control and disarmament. Although the deterioration of Soviet-American relations, plus relentless Republican attacks, undermined popular backing for the SALT II treaty, polls found that, as late as March 1980—after the administration had abandoned it—a plurality of Americans who knew of the treaty still favored its ratification. Asked, more abstractly, if they favored "a new agreement between the United States and Russia which would limit nuclear weapons," Americans responded in the affirmative by ratios that varied from nearly six to one in January 1979 to more than two to one in September 1979, when the polling on this question stopped. Nor did public opinion support the use of nuclear weapons, even when such use was U.S. government policy. Asked in April 1979 if they favored employing nuclear weapons against the Soviet Union "if Western Europe were threatened with a Russian take-over," a majority of Americans responded negatively.[47] Despite the inflamed state of public opinion on questions like the safety of U.S. hostages in Iran, when it came to nuclear issues, Americans were quite dovish.

Asia, the Pacific, Latin America, Africa, and the Middle East

In Japan, the antinuclear campaign also continued its revival. Thanks to the growing cooperation between the nation's two leading disarmament groups, Gensuikyo and Gensuikin, the 1979 and 1980 World Conferences Against Atomic and Hydrogen Bombs proved the most united yet held. They took up such issues as an international treaty to prohibit nuclear weapons and ban their use, the enforcement of Japan's three non-nuclear principles, the establishment of nuclear-free zones, peace education, and measures for relief of the Japanese *hibakusha*. Nevertheless, organizational unity between the rival groups remained elusive, for wide differences remained between them on specific issues. The question of nuclear power was particularly divisive, for the Socialist-oriented Gensuikin was determined to oppose it, unlike the Communist-dominated Gensuikyo. Consequently, the two groups remained organizationally distinct and sponsored separate events.[48] Even so, the movement was lively and visible. It sponsored widespread demonstrations against participation by the Japanese armed forces in RIMPAC (Rim of the Pacific) military exercises, which it claimed would pull Japan into a nuclear war. Furthermore, in October 1980, it mobilized some 10,000 people for rallies and demonstrations against nuclear power plants and against nuclear waste dumping in the Pacific.[49]

Elsewhere in the Pacific, a variety of nuclear hazards contributed to the growth of disarmament activism. In the Philippines, a lively, popular antinuclear campaign was organized in the late 1970s, to protest the construc-

tion of a giant Westinghouse nuclear power plant on the slope of a live vol-
cano in Morong, Bataan. Although constrained by the martial law imposed
by the Marcos dictatorship, the movement mobilized thousands of local
Filipinos against the project and, gradually, began taking on nuclear weapons issues, as well.[50] In Australia, the National Uranium Moratorium Campaign in 1979 became the Movement Against Uranium Mining (MAUM),
which drew substantial backing from the Australian labor movement, including the Australian Congress of Trade Unions. MAUM did not just campaign against the mining of uranium but came around to championing nuclear disarmament. Indeed, it joined Australia's disarmament groups in
protesting French nuclear testing, calling for a nuclear-free Pacific, and
sponsoring Hiroshima Day activities. In turn, disarmament groups endorsed
MAUM's anti-uranium campaign. The two themes for the 1980 Hiroshima
Day march and rally in Sydney were: "Keep uranium in the ground" and
"No to nuclear war." These ideas had considerable popularity. Later that
year, the Sydney city council officially proclaimed Sydney nuclear-free, an
action similar to that taken by numerous other municipal councils throughout Australia.[51]

In New Zealand, the antinuclear efforts already underway grew more
widespread. In January 1979, when a U.S. nuclear submarine, the *Haddo*, arrived at Auckland harbor, a large protest fleet, organized by the Peace
Squadron, sought to block its entry. The *Haddo*, although slowing down,
pressed forward, sinking a number of the kayaks and other small protest
craft. Nevertheless, to the delight of the protesters and many other New
Zealanders, one activist managed to board the nuclear submarine. According to a news account: "Like Zorba the Greek he began a dance, half of defiance, half of joy on the very nose of the incoming sub. . . . The image was
a powerful one—the lone figure in his life jacket, arms raised in anger on
the back of this strange sea creature." For the next four-and-a-half years, the
U.S. government did not send another nuclear ship to Auckland. Stimulated
by the antinuclear activities of the Peace Squadron, the Campaign for Nuclear Disarmament, and Greenpeace, as well as by the revival of the movement in Europe and North America, large numbers of nuclear disarmament
groups emerged around the country. By 1980, the necessity for some sort of
overall coordination became clear, and meetings began for the purpose of
organizing a nationwide antinuclear movement.[52]

The antinuclear campaign was also taking off in the small island nations
of the Pacific. During 1979, in the Marshall Islands—governed by the
United States as a "trust territory"—some 500 people staged a non-violent
occupation of eight islands from which they had been forcibly removed

years before by the U.S. military to accommodate tests of U.S. nuclear missiles. That same year, in Palau—another small island "trust territory," located in the Caroline Islands—92 percent of the voters in a U.N. referendum gave their support to a constitution, drafted in preparation for independence, that would make the island nuclear-free. As U.S. officials were planning to use the island as a repair station for Trident nuclear submarines, they were greatly disturbed by the nuclear-free constitution, the first in world history. Consequently, they declared the U.N. referendum unofficial and sponsored a second vote that year on a constitution, this time without the antinuclear provision. Despite a massive U.S. public relations campaign, Palau's voters rejected this U.S.-imposed constitution and, then, proceeded to adopt yet another nuclear-free charter for the island.[53]

Building on these and other antinuclear efforts, the Nuclear Free Pacific Movement held its third conference in May 1980, in Honolulu. Sponsored by over 50 organizations from 20 Pacific and Pacific rim nations, the conference voted to establish a Pacific Concerns Resource Center in Hawaii; to enlist the aid of doctors to examine the people of the Marshall Islands and French Polynesia for radiation-caused illness; to mobilize international support for Palau; to back the independence of the Pacific's indigenous peoples; to oppose the presence of Trident nuclear submarines, RIMPAC military exercises, and French nuclear tests in the Pacific; and to work for a nuclear-free Pacific treaty. Activists were particularly outraged at the dumping of nuclear waste in the Pacific by the great powers, which they perceived as yet another aspect of the colonialist exploitation of native peoples. A popular Nuclear Free Pacific poster read: "If it's so safe, Dump it in Tokyo, Test it in Paris, Store it in Washington."[54]

As before, the nations of Latin America, Africa, and the Middle East underwent relatively little antinuclear agitation. In Brazil, to be sure, the combination of its massive import of nuclear technology, the beginning of its missile program, government talk of conducting a "peaceful" nuclear explosion, and its refusal to sign the nuclear nonproliferation treaty did begin to stir fears among the citizens of that nation. Founded years before to take on social problems, the group Ecological Resistance (Resistência Ecologica) became active in publicizing the ominous possibilities of this new situation. Another group campaigning against Brazil's development of a nuclear weapons capacity, the Anti-Nuclear Movement, expanded to over 400 members.[55] For the most part, however, the nations of these regions remained untouched by the antinuclear revival.

Eastern Europe

Against considerable odds, disarmament activism continued to make headway in Eastern Europe. In the Soviet Union, the Afghan war, though not directly affecting attitudes toward nuclear weapons, gave a strong impetus to a broader current of anti-militarism. Although most people did not dare to speak out against the Soviet invasion, the nation's most famous nuclear critic, Andrei Sakharov, issued a public condemnation. Determined to silence the dissident physicist, the regime exiled him to Gorky, where he and his wife endured life under virtual house arrest. Other disarmament proponents criticized the crackdown upon Sakharov, including the prominent Soviet physicist, Peter Kapitza. Despite his incarceration, Sakharov continued to champion antinuclear measures, and emphasized "the similarity of my position on questions of disarmament" with that of the Federation of American Scientists.[56] In 1980, when Western activists issued a call for the removal of all nuclear weapons—Soviet and American—from Europe, the dissident Soviet historian Roy Medvedev responded publicly that he believed that "the peoples of the USSR and Eastern Europe are also, in their hearts, enthusiastic for this campaign." But "our voice is not heard as yours is, because here there remain in force many restrictions on freedom of organization, meetings and expression. . . . I hope the movement will make its influence felt here as well."[57]

Other Soviet intellectuals resisted the arms race in more cautious, less confrontational ways. Bernard Lown, a prominent American cardiologist who had founded the original PSR and had returned to it upon its revival, was eager to mobilize Soviet physicians in the antinuclear cause. In early 1979, he sent a highly emotional letter urging joint action against the arms race to a distinguished Soviet cardiologist, Evgenii Chazov, with whom he had become acquainted professionally over the years. Lown chose Chazov because of his influence as the personal physician to the Kremlin's top leaders, including Brezhnev, for he felt that "unless you're very high in the pecking order, there's nothing you can do and there's nothing you dare do." Chazov did not respond, so Lown tried again five months later, this time proposing to a young Soviet physician working in Boston that she carry his letter back to Chazov in Moscow. When it became clear that she was frightened at the prospect of serving as a courier, he had her open the message and read it. Poring over the letter and its meaning, she began to cry and promised to deliver it. In October 1979, Chazov responded positively, and Lown traveled to Moscow to meet with him.[58]

The physicians' project now moved forward, though not without some major difficulties. When Lown arrived in Moscow in April 1980, it became clear that Chazov had grown reluctant to proceed. The Soviet cardiologist said that Lown's plan would destroy his career and sacrifice the modern hospital he was building—all for a clearly quixotic venture. Infuriated, Lown called him an opportunist and stormed out of the room. But the next day, Chazov phoned and suggested that they talk some more about it. What had happened was that he had returned home after the confrontation with Lown and related it to his daughter, also a physician. She thought about it for some time, and then said that he should take on the project—"not because of me, not because of you, but because of your six month old grandson. You owe it to him." Lown remembered that Chazov told him that "he spent the whole night . . . thinking of his career, his life's work, what medicine is all about, what it meant to him. And he decided, what the hell, he's going to go with me into this misadventure." Accordingly, in December 1980, three American physicians and three of their Soviet counterparts met in Geneva and worked out plans for a new disarmament organization: International Physicians for the Prevention of Nuclear War. Although even this meeting was stormy, given a backlog of Cold War suspicions, the new movement was launched, providing the basis for substantial participation by Soviet doctors.[59]

Elsewhere in Eastern Europe, antinuclear activism had more of a dissident quality. In Hungary, following the teachings of György Bulanyi, a Catholic priest, Catholic "base communities" developed rapidly in the late 1970s, preaching not only a new way of life, but resistance to militarism. Although the Catholic Church hierarchy condemned these ventures, many young priests and Catholic laypersons became involved in them. Furthermore, prominent independent voices risked imprisonment by lending their support to the European nuclear disarmament campaign.[60] In East Germany, the Protestant Evangelical Church widened its peace activities. Together with the Evangelical Church in West Germany, it issued a "Statement on Peace" in September 1979 that called for peace education in the schools. In November 1980, it organized a "Peace Week" under the slogan "Make Peace Without Weapons." As part of this "Peace Week," the Church produced a sew-on badge with this slogan, together with the words "Swords into Plowshares" and an accompanying emblem. Particularly among young people, there developed an informal "Swords into Plowshares" movement, in which supporters identified themselves by wearing the symbol. Although the "Swords into Plowshares" symbol merely replicated the statue donated to the United Nations by the Soviet Union, wearing it came to be regarded by the young as a subversive activity.[61]

International Organization: Nonaligned

As nuclear disarmament campaigns sprang up in numerous countries, they built connections across national boundaries. The leaders of the major organizations corresponded with one another, arranging for exchanges of speakers and nuclear information.[62] Launched in Britain in 1980, the World Disarmament Campaign worked to develop other national initiatives for implementation of recommendations made by the 1978 U.N. Special Session, although without much success. In early 1980, a more modest project of communication among the new nuclear disarmament groups was undertaken by the group Nonviolent Alternatives, located in Antwerp, with the publication of an international newsletter, *Disarmament Campaigns*. Reporting on nuclear disarmament activism around the world, the newsletter ultimately became a project of the International Peace Communication and Coordination Center, a networking group in The Hague.[63] Of course, important disarmament work across national lines continued to be provided by the WRI, WILPF, and the International FOR, but these internationals remained relatively small, confined to pacifists, and involved with multiple issues.[64]

As the development of IPPNW indicated, the movement's efforts at international coordination fared somewhat better on the constituency level. The Pugwash movement focused increasingly on current issues in the nuclear arms race. Meeting in August 1980 at the 30th Pugwash Conference on Science and World Affairs, scientists from around the world issued a statement warning: "Never before has mankind been in such grave peril. A major nuclear war would mean the end of civilization and could lead to the extinction of the human race. And yet, throughout the world, militarily powerful nations with obscenely large stockpiles of nuclear weapons seem unable to compose their differences by accommodation and negotiation."[65] Meanwhile, Pax Christi, the international Catholic peace movement, played an important role in stirring concern among its co-religionists about the nuclear arms race. In late 1979, it issued a powerful statement condemning both the NATO missile deployment decision and the Soviet SS-20 deployment. "The whole present system of deterrence-equilibrium, and its inevitable arms race," declared the organization, "can only lead ultimately to a total collapse of this system and to the destruction of the world community." In 1980, Pax Christi International laid plans for making 1981–82 "a year for an international disarmament campaign," and called upon all its national sections to give the campaign top priority. Many, in fact, were already in the thick of the rising struggle against nuclear weapons.[66]

Women, too, were emerging as an increasingly self-conscious disarmament constituency. During the spring of 1980, Women for Peace groups sprang up not only in the Nordic countries, but in West Germany, the Netherlands, and Switzerland. Among these groups and among the many women flocking to the mixed gender antinuclear campaign, the belief was widespread that it was quite natural for women to be in the vanguard of the new resistance movement. "Women all over the world are rising up, and infusing the anti-nuclear and peace movements . . . with a vitality and creativity never before seen," declared Petra Kelly. "Woman must lead the efforts . . . for peace awareness, because only she . . . can go back to her womb, her institution, her roots, her natural rhythms, her inner search for harmony and peace, while men, most of them anyway, are continually bound to their power struggle, to the exploitation of nature and to ego trips toward military power and so-called security."[67]

Social Democratic parties also strengthened their efforts for disarmament on the international level. In 1976, Willy Brandt of West Germany was elected the president of the Socialist International (SI), the world body of Social Democratic parties, and in his inaugural address he listed "an offensive for a secure peace" as the first of three challenges then confronting the organization. Two years later, the SI established a study group on disarmament led by Kalevi Sorsa, chair of the Finnish Social Democrats. Sorsa's study group, plus the revival of the nuclear arms race, made disarmament one of the principal topics of discussion within the SI and its national affiliates. Taking up the disarmament issue at its November 1980 congress in Madrid, the SI called for efforts to strengthen nuclear non-proliferation and set forth an "ultimate goal" of "the total elimination of all nuclear weapons." In the meantime, it declared, the development of new weapons should be limited by agreement, and, during arms control negotiations, "all parties should refrain from developing and testing new arms and delivery systems."[68]

The best known of the new international movements was the European Nuclear Disarmament (END) campaign. In early 1980, a group of veteran British antinuclear activists, convinced that the time had come for mass mobilization against the arms race, began to work on an Appeal for European Nuclear Disarmament. The immediate backdrop was the NATO missile decision, which, together with the Soviet SS-20 deployment, they believed, called for a Europe-wide response. Drafted by E. P. Thompson, the document was subsequently edited or revised by Ken Coates (director of the Bertrand Russell Peace Foundation), Mary Kaldor (a young armament and disarmament researcher), and other movement stalwarts, some from the continent. Released at a press conference in the House of Commons in late

April 1980, the Appeal provided a devastating critique of great power irresponsibility. "We are entering the most dangerous decade in human history," capped by "a demented arms race," it noted. "In Europe, the main geographical stage for the East-West confrontation, new generations of ever more deadly weapons are appearing." Appraising this situation, "we do not wish to apportion guilt between the political and military leaders of East and West. Guilt lies squarely upon both parties. Both parties have adopted menacing postures and committed aggressive actions in different parts of the world."[69]

The genuinely novel part of the END Appeal was its dramatic call for a people's movement to reverse the deadly momentum of the arms race—what, some months earlier, Thompson had denounced as "exterminism." As little could be expected of missile-wielding governments, "the remedy lies in our own hands. We must act together to free the entire territory of Europe, from Poland to Portugal, from nuclear weapons." Indeed, "we must commence to act as if a united, neutral and pacific Europe already exists. We must learn to be loyal, not to 'East' or 'West,' but to each other, and we must disregard the prohibitions and limitations imposed by any national state." Along the way, "we must defend and extend the right of all citizens, East or West, to take part in this common movement and to engage in every kind of exchange." Furthermore, "we must resist any attempt by the statesmen of East and West to manipulate this movement to their own advantage. . . . Our objectives must be to free Europe from confrontation, to enforce détente between the United States and the Soviet Union and, ultimately, to dissolve both great power alliances."[70]

If the Appeal for European Nuclear Disarmament seemed rather sweeping and utopian, that was because it genuinely reflected the deep-seated anti-militarist, democratic, and internationalist ideals of its drafters. Thompson and Coates, Kaldor later remarked, believed in the creation of "a peaceful, united, democratic socialist Europe" and "therefore, the link between democracy, disarmament, human rights, and peace, the notion of a transcontinental movement of citizens—those were all crucial elements." Kaldor recalled that "we wanted to be much more internationalist" than other peace movements. Moreover, "we wanted to make clear our commitment to democracy and human rights." In certain ways, she noted, END "followed the women's movement" by assuming that "we were going to win not by getting our people in power but . . . when our ideas won. It was about changing the relationship between state and society." In a discussion of END published the following year, Thompson himself emphasized the transcendent nature of the new movement. "The militarization of the continent can only be resisted by a commitment among citizens as profound as that of the Resistance in World War II," he declared. END proposed "nothing less than the creation of a spirit of popular anti-militarist internationalism."[71]

Perhaps because of its daring proposal, the END Appeal generated substantial enthusiasm. At its launching, it was endorsed by 68 British MPs and by nearly 200 other major public figures. Thereafter, the Appeal, circulated by the Bertrand Russell Peace Foundation, garnered the signatures of thousands of prominent individuals in the West and of a small, courageous group of people in the East. Even more important, the new antinuclear organizations in Europe, as well as some of the old, now rallied to the new campaign. Delegates from CND, branches of Pax Christi, No to Nuclear Weapons (Norway), No to Nuclear Weapons (Denmark), Irish CND, and other nuclear disarmament organizations began to meet together under END's auspices. END chapters sprang up throughout Britain, though, eventually, END left British activism to CND and focused, instead, on coordinating the burgeoning antinuclear campaign across Europe. Enormous demands began to be made on END's very slender resources and rather inchoate organizational structure. But, whatever the difficulties, END's first months of operations, Thompson reported, were "successful beyond our expectations," and the END Appeal "became a charter of the nonaligned Western peace movements." Throughout Europe, new energy surged through the nuclear disarmament campaign, with signs springing up to proclaim END's popular slogan: "No Cruise, No SS-20s!"[72]

International Organization: Aligned

The Communist-led World Peace Council, by contrast, continued its partisan approach to the international crisis. Without ever uttering a word of protest against Soviet military policy, it leveled a ceaseless attack upon the actions of the United States, NATO, Japan, and China. In February 1979, denouncing "imperialist circles . . . who try to curb détente under the pretext of 'Soviet military threat,'" a special session of the WPC urged people to "demand" that "NATO countries . . . renounce . . . their decision to further increase their military potential . . . which provokes new acceleration in the arms race." That December, another special session of the WPC assailed NATO's Euromissile decision as "a most serious threat to peace, détente, and the future of the world." Romesh Chandra, the WPC president, made a fervent appeal for mass action to prevent the implementation of NATO's decision—a decision that the WPC journal, *Peace Courier*, claimed "casts the shadow of nuclear holocaust over Europe." *Peace Courier*—like the WPC—did not criticize or even mention the deployment of Soviet SS-20 missiles; instead, it praised what it called the Soviet "peace initiative" in the controversy. Within WPC ranks, the faith in unblemished Soviet virtue remained unshakeable. In 1980, as Soviet troops poured into Afghanistan, Chandra blithely told a WPC gathering: "We all know that the Soviet Union has been and is the best friend of all the countries of the third world."[73]

Indeed, the WPC's reaction to Soviet intervention in Afghanistan was so partisan that it might well have been scripted by Kremlin officials. In August 1979, not long after the Communist coup in that country, the WPC held an International Conference of Solidarity with the People of Afghanistan in Kabul, which unanimously passed a lengthy, adoring resolution concluding that "the world's peace forces stand solidly with Afghanistan— today and tomorrow and for all time. . . . GLORY TO THE SAUR REVOLUTION!"[74] As things turned out, however, the people of Afghanistan proved less enthusiastic about the new Communist rulers, leading to internal upheaval and, that December, to Soviet military intervention. In response, the WPC portrayed the Soviet invasion as an act of solidarity in the face of external aggression. According to Chandra: "The problem of Afghanistan is that of an armed intervention by the United States, backed by China and reactionary forces inside Pakistan. It is an intervention by outside forces against . . . all that the Afghanistan revolution has achieved." After all, Leonid Brezhnev had said "that the Soviet forces went there for the purpose of fighting this armed intervention and that they would withdraw the moment this armed intervention is halted. This statement has been welcomed widely in all parts of the world by . . . all those who stand for peace." At the WPC's March 1980 International Conference for Peace and Security in Asia, the delegates unanimously supported a resolution condemning American and Chinese intervention in Afghanistan and praising "the proposals made by the government of Afghanistan and the Soviet Union" in facilitating what was termed "a political solution."[75]

The attitudes were virtually the same in the WPC's affiliates. Yuri Zhukov, chair of the Soviet Peace Committee (SPC), was thoroughly orthodox in his thinking, viewing the arms race as entirely the fault of the United States. In an article published in 1980, Nikolai Blokhin, another member of the SPC, had nothing to say in praise of Western officials, but claimed that "the consistent and vigorous efforts of the Communist Party of the Soviet Union for peace, détente, and disarmament . . . have blazed the trail to détente in international relations and comprehensive and fruitful cooperation among peoples." Yet another SPC member, Nikolai Inozemtsev, maintained that same year that the "threat to peace . . . lies . . . in the actions of imperialist forces, the United States above all." By contrast, "the Soviet Union . . . is filled with determination to continue its peace policy."[76] In East Germany, the Peace Council sponsored massive mobilizations in support of Soviet foreign policy. During the autumn of 1979, practically every adult in the country signed a Peace Council petition backing Soviet disarmament proposals. Condemning the new NATO missiles, Günther Drefahl, the Peace Council president, displayed quite a different attitude toward Soviet military measures. "As long as the imperialist threat continues to exist," he argued, Communist countries "have no other alternative but to protect their achievements."[77]

Although the WPC's affiliates in Western countries were substantially weaker, their political orientation was much the same. At most WPC conventions, there was no dissent by Western delegates, and the resolutions passed unanimously. In Australia, the Australian Peace Committee loyally supported Soviet intervention in Afghanistan. To be sure, in the United States, the U.S. Peace Council, officially launched in November 1979, championed numerous ventures in line with the program of mainstream disarmament groups: negotiating a SALT treaty, blocking the MX missile, and opposing cruise and Pershing II missile deployment. Nevertheless, unlike other U.S. peace groups, the U.S. Peace Council worked closely with the WPC and with its driving force, the Soviet Peace Committee. Moreover, it directed its fire exclusively at the U.S. government and its Western allies.[78] The U.S. Peace Council's official response to the Soviet war in Afghanistan, issued at the end of January 1980, had nothing critical to say of Soviet policy. Instead, it charged that "the frenzied cry over a 'Russian expansionist threat to our vital interests' is a disguised (and gravely dangerous) effort to conceal shameless US interventionism in behalf of the oil monopolies." The same Americans "who brought us the Cold War, the Korean War, the Vietnam war, and soaring military budgets and assorted 'Soviet threats' are now creating a new crisis." In the midst of the most devastating military assault upon Third World people ever conducted by the Soviet Union, the U.S. Peace Council statement concluded: "NO TO THE USE OF U.S. MILITARY FORCES AGAINST THE OPPRESSED PEOPLES OF THE WORLD."[79]

Given this orientation, the WPC, its affiliates, and their Communist backers remained deeply ambivalent about the rise of the nonaligned disarmament movement. Calling attention to the "broad social movements and organizations" that were "tackling peace-related problems," a Soviet Peace Committee leader concluded that "the world public has become a real force in the . . . struggle against the arms race." On the other hand, the willingness of independent peace activists to take Communist nations to task exasperated the party faithful. In the United States, the U.S. Peace Council published an ad assailing Joan Baez and other pacifists for criticizing Vietnam's abuses of human rights. "We are appalled at your recent attack on Vietnam and embarrassed by the ignorance it displays," declared the Peace Council. In Britain, the Communist Party endorsed the END Appeal, but with strong objections to its critique of the Soviet government, which it insisted behaved on a higher plane of morality than its U.S. counterpart. E. P. Thompson complained of the attack upon END from both Communist Party and Trotskyist groups who "criticize END for proposing 'symmetry' between the two super-powers. They counter-propose that Soviet weaponry is 'primarily defensive,' and that the thrust towards war comes only from 'Western imperialism.'" Although Eurocommunists might occasionally criticize "the 'mistakes' of Soviet policies, in effect the only peace campaigning that is required is against NATO weaponry."[80]

Not surprisingly, the attitudes of nonaligned groups to their WPC counterparts also remained chilly. In Denmark, anti-missile activists—alienated by the pro-Soviet orientation of the Communist-led Cooperation Committee for Peace and Security—spurned working through it. Consequently, they founded a new group, No to Nuclear Weapons.[81] In the United States, the Coalition for a New Foreign and Military Policy rejected the U.S. Peace Council's application for membership in 1980. Eight peace organizations voted in favor of its admission to this peace movement coordinating body, but eighteen others voted against it and four abstained. Even among the supporters of admission, the motive was primarily libertarian rather than agreement with the group's orientation. David McReynolds of the War Resisters League, one of the keenest backers of admission, believed that the Peace Council was "effectively dominated by the American Communist Party" and "substantially aligned with the Soviet Bloc," but thought nonaligned groups should "fight it out internally with those in this country who support the Soviet position." In August 1980, outlining the next steps for END, Thompson insisted that "the thrust against both NATO and Warsaw Pact positions be steadily maintained." And that meant that "we must keep our nose clean of any association with official Soviet-sponsored 'peace' organizations."[82]

By the late 1970s, the WPC was clearly on the wane. Although supporters billed it as a powerful organization—"the largest non-governmental peace organization in the world, encompassing 125 national peace movements with their tens of millions of members"—its popular appeal was limited and dwindling. Soviet military intervention in Afghanistan, like Soviet deployment of the SS-20s, chilled public confidence in the Communist-led peace movement's central message: the Kremlin's peaceful intentions. Furthermore, the WPC's fervent support of Soviet intervention badly damaged its own credibility. Nor did the rise of popular protest against the Bomb benefit the WPC. Indeed, the vibrancy and mass mobilization of its nonaligned competitor merely exposed WPC weakness and marginality. Even some of its affiliates, like the powerful East German Peace Council, began to lose faith—not in the WPC's perspective, which they continued to share, but in its effectiveness. Thus, the Communist-led peace campaign, infused with a triumphal spirit at the start of the 1970s, concluded the decade with a recognition that, as one of its leaders recalled, it "was on the sidelines."[83]

Conclusion

By late 1980, the nuclear disarmament movement was once again well underway. Although the Communist-led campaign fared poorly in the final years of the decade, the nonaligned movement experienced an organizational revival, mobilized important constituencies and political parties, and stirred up public opinion against nuclear weapons in numerous countries. Admittedly, the antinuclear movement had not, as yet, developed significant organizations in many nations, built up a mass membership in nations where such organizations already existed, or put together a coordinated international campaign. But, at the end of the decade, spurred on by the sharp deterioration of the international situation, it had moved from obscurity to increasing visibility.

Big Defeats, Small Victories, 1979-80

> Two nations and their leaders, each of which seemed in
> early 1977 to desire . . . a reduction of the nuclear dan-
> ger, had by early 1980 arrived at a situation in which . . .
> détente had collapsed, a nuclear arms reduction treaty
> lay unratified . . . and the groundwork was laid for a
> revival of intense Cold War rhetoric and confrontation.
>
> Anatoly Dobrynin, 1995

The simultaneous growth of the nuclear disarmament movement and of the nuclear arms race in the final years of the decade presents an apparent paradox. But, actually, this synchronism is less puzzling than it seems. The explanation is that the movement's growth, which occurred in direct response to the heightening nuclear danger, was not yet sufficient to halt the unraveling of détente and the acceleration of the nuclear arms race. Even so, the movement had grown strong enough to provide governments with an appreciation of its potential. And, in the West at least, this enhanced appreciation led to some public policy concessions from uneasy government officials. Thus, although the movement's defeats were resounding and substantially outnumbered its victories in these years, it did have some impact upon public policy—an impact that persisted in the form of treaties and other public commitments by government leaders. Consequently, the government concessions of 1979–80 to antinuclear activism, largely overlooked at this time of deteriorating international relations, lay the foundation for nuclear arms control and disarmament policies in the future.

Ambivalence Toward the Movement

As NATO officials returned to Cold War concerns, they found the rising tide of antinuclear activism increasingly irritating. To be sure, the Carter administration viewed disarmament groups as vital to its ratification campaign for the SALT II treaty. The list of eighteen U.S. organizations favorable to SALT, developed for the campaign, included the Coalition for a New Foreign and Military Policy, the Center for Defense Information, the Council for a Livable World, the FAS, SANE, WILPF, WSP, the Union of Concerned Scientists, and New Directions. Furthermore, the administration placed the AFSC, Clergy and Laity Concerned, and the Friends Committee on National legislation within the Religious Committee on SALT. Clearly, the influence of these groups could not be ignored. In October 1979, Carter sent a note of appreciation to WSP for its petition against the nuclear arms race, accompanied by the admonition that "all of us must work together to ensure the ratification of SALT II."[1] Nevertheless, the response was cool when a delegation of U.S. peace group leaders—including Helen Caldicott and William Sloane Coffin, Jr.—expressed their concerns about the nuclear weapons spiral to U.S. embassy staffers in Moscow. It was even chillier when a delegation from WILPF met with NATO officials in December 1979 to oppose the Western alliance's deployment of cruise and Pershing II missiles.[2]

Where new, conservative forces came to power in NATO nations, governments regarded opposition to nuclear programs in a particularly unkindly light. In Turkey, a 1980 military takeover of the government led to the dissolution of the Turkish Peace Association, the seizure of its files, and to a government investigation of its leaders. In Britain, the May 1979 election victory of the Conservatives also opened the door for government surveillance of antinuclear activists. In 1977, Britain's foreign secretary had abolished the Information Research Department, the Foreign Office's secret propaganda arm that had worked closely with Britain's intelligence agencies in spying upon and discrediting opponents of the Cold War. Such activities might have come to a halt entirely had not diehard Cold Warriors from IRD and allied intelligence bureaus reacted by establishing "The 61," a secret, private sector intelligence agency that continued its operations. According to Brian Crozier, a leader in these efforts, The 61 was "beholden to no government, but at the disposal of allied or friendly governments for certain tasks which . . . they were no longer able to tackle." Funding for the group came from "big companies," from "a few . . . corporations," and from "some very rich men." After the Tory victory, Crozier and other leaders of The 61 had many meetings with the new prime minister, Margaret Thatcher, providing her with reports on the activities of allegedly dangerous dissident groups, including CND, in which The 61 placed a "mole."[3]

Soviet officials also had mixed feelings about the nuclear disarmament

campaign. Western antinuclear activism drew the respectful attention of Soviet diplomats like Aleksandr Yakovlev, whose suspiciously independent
ideas had led the Kremlin to farm him out to Canada as ambassador. Impressed by PSR's September 1980 conference, Medical Consequences of
Nuclear Weapons and Nuclear War, the counselor at the Soviet mission to
the United Nations emphasized that it drew a large crowd, distinguished
speakers, and good coverage by the mass media. He also observed that PSR
was growing into a strong organization, with branches in 37 states and influence upon the American Medical Association. On the other hand, Soviet officials continued to regard the Western movement as having serious defi-
ciencies. Some conference statements "showed a misunderstanding and lack
of information of some speakers on our position on the question of ceasing
the nuclear arms race," the counselor noted. Moreover, Soviet officials believed that the Western movement was simply too weak to accomplish very
much. In 1979, after a positive appraisal of the attitudes of "bourgeois-
liberal activists . . . in numerous public pacifist, religious, and disarmament
organizations," a Soviet embassy dispatch from Washington concluded that
"they do not have enough influence on the Senate and among the public at
large to discontinue or to brake a little the powerful campaign to prepare the
American public for a new twist to the arms race."[4]

Consequently, in 1980, when the Kremlin geared up to fight an all-out
battle against NATO missile deployment, it did not base its campaign upon
the nonaligned movement. Admittedly, public statements by Soviet officials
did praise both WPC and nonaligned ventures. "World public opinion has
shown itself in recent years to be an increasingly active force in the struggle
for the constructive solution of international issues, including . . . disarmament," wrote the deputy head of the International Department of the Central
Committee of the Soviet Communist Party. "The contemporary movement
of the peace-loving public" was "capable not only of showing the danger
and senselessness of continuing the arms race in the nuclear age but also of
actively promoting the isolation of those who foment it." Even so, in its secret meetings, the party leadership decided to lean heavily upon its tried and
true Communist propaganda apparatus. In April 1980, to mount a massive
"public effort" against NATO missile deployment, the Central Committee
ordered a major propaganda offensive against the NATO plan based upon
the efforts of Soviet public organizations, the Soviet mass media, and "fraternal parties."[5]

Furthermore, Communist governments continued to regard disarmament
activism as far more acceptable in the West than in the East. To be sure, the
authorities tolerated the early meetings of Chazov and his medical col-

leagues with Lown and others from PSR. But Chazov was careful to keep Soviet officials abreast of the discussions and to clear plans with the party's Central Committee. The Soviet physician was "tightrope walking," Lown recalled, "and he was a consummate artist at that."[6] By contrast, Sakharov was far less careful and, after his public condemnation of the Soviet invasion of Afghanistan, Soviet security police seized him in January 1980. Thereafter, the authorities stripped him of his rights, awards, and privileges and flew him to Gorky. Here, in a city ruled off-limits to foreigners, he was confined to an isolated apartment, often without a telephone, and kept under constant police surveillance, harassment, and threats for the next seven years. When Jeremy Stone of the FAS sought to travel to Moscow to express the disarmament organization's concern over Sakharov's house arrest, the Soviet embassy refused to grant him a visa.[7]

Communist Policy

Not surprisingly, then, the policies of Communist nations remained relatively unaffected by the upsurge of nonaligned nuclear disarmament activism. Although Chinese policy toward the West softened, particularly with the normalization of relations between Washington and Beijing, the Chinese government continued to deprecate nuclear arms control and disarmament negotiations. Like France, China did not participate in the CTBT discussions, and made it clear that, if invited, it would not participate. In early 1979, amid talks in Washington with top U.S. policymakers, Chinese Vice-Premier Deng Xiaoping issued public statements assailing the Soviet Union and, along the way, questioning the value of a SALT treaty and threatening Vietnam, its Communist neighbor. That February, in fact, China shocked believers in its peaceful intentions by beginning a military invasion of Vietnam. According to Deng, this show of force would teach that Soviet-aligned country a "lesson." The invasion might also have been designed to upset Soviet-American plans for an early summit conference and SALT agreement. When Britain's CND dispatched a letter to the Chinese embassy in London, protesting the Chinese invasion, the embassy simply refused to accept it.[8]

Meanwhile, Soviet government fears of the West continued to grow. A nation like Norway, which had never deployed nuclear arms and was an unlikely aggressor, came under Kremlin suspicion as a staging area for a U.S. invasion of the Soviet Union.[9] Even the signing of the SALT II treaty left Soviet officials wary of the future. From Washington, the Soviet embassy reported that Senate hearings on the treaty showed the need for "serious vigilance." In its opinion, most of "the US ruling elite in the Senate, mass media, and in the military departments of the US administration was dissatisfied by the loss of US military superiority," and feared "that SALT II ratification will encourage a mood of détente among the American public and will prevent a new twist to the arms race . . . planned by the US military complex. These ruling élites are ready to support the treaty," but only "after the passage of all strategic and conventional military programs which aren't banned by the SALT II treaty." Speaking with East German Communist Party leader Erich Honecker in July 1979, Brezhnev complained that the SALT negotiations had been "very difficult" and that he had been unable to make any progress with the Carter administration on the rejection of the first use of nuclear weapons. "There are quite a few dark moments in our relationships with the USA," he concluded glumly.[10]

Soviet fear of the West grew dramatically after the December 1979 NATO decision to install intermediate range nuclear missiles—cruise and Pershing II—in Western Europe. Plans for the Pershing II missiles, especially, created great anxiety. Soviet leaders believed that these missiles, scheduled for deployment in West Germany, would enable the United States to deliver an extremely rapid, decapitating nuclear strike upon Moscow. ICBMs flying from the United States would take 25 to 35 minutes to reach their targets, but the Pershings, they concluded, could destroy the Soviet Union's command and control facilities, plus the Soviet leadership, within six minutes of their launching. By contrast, the Soviet SS-20 missiles—the official justification for Western missile deployment—could not reach the United States. Moreover, it was feared that a Pershing missile attack would prepare the way for a devastating assault upon the Soviet Union by the thousands of U.S. strategic nuclear warheads launched from U.S. submarines, ICBMs, and bombers. KGB chief Yuri Andropov warned his colleagues on the Communist party's central committee that, by installing the Pershing missiles, NATO was readying itself for a nuclear surprise attack upon the Soviet Union. According to Oleg Gordievsky, a high ranking KGB official who defected to the West in 1985: "In the face of Pershing . . . the Kremlin panicked." He had "frequently heard people ask in recent years: 'Is it possible that anyone in Moscow seriously believed that the West would commit aggression and launch a nuclear war?' The answer is, unfortunately, yes, there were such people and . . . from 1980 to 1985, they were in the majority in the political and military leadership of the U.S.S.R."[11]

Yet, despite rising Soviet fears, the leadership did not abandon the nuclear arms control process. By May 1979, an agreement on the SALT II treaty had at last been reached, establishing restrictions on the numbers of strategic nuclear weapons, their replacement, and modification. It even provided for small reductions. With the treaty in hand, Carter and Brezhnev finally held their summit meeting in June 1979, in Vienna, where they exchanged kisses at its signing. Brezhnev remarked to his associates that Carter was "quite a nice guy after all." The treaty was acceptable to the Kremlin despite the fact that, at U.S. insistence, it did not incorporate a number of key Soviet positions. These included the principle of "Equal Security," which called for a balance between the United States and the Soviet Union in weapons capable of reaching the territory of the other. The following month, in his meeting with Honecker, Brezhnev was not very enthusiastic about the SALT II treaty, commenting complacently that, even if it failed to be ratified by the U.S. Senate, "we will probably not lose politically, because then the entire world will recognize who is consistently seeking disarmament and who is working in the opposite direction." Even so, he concluded, "we all should try . . . to make sure this important matter will have a different end," for "the prospect of the failure of the treaty is not desirable."[12]

Similarly, the Soviet government moved, albeit reluctantly, toward making the question of Euromissile deployment a matter of arms control negotiations. Initially, at least, the Kremlin did not consider its deployment of SS-20 missiles an extraordinary measure, but as one providing it with a nuclear balance in Europe. As two Soviet arms control officials have written: "The leadership viewed the deployment . . . as their right, while it probably failed to comprehend the full implications." Nevertheless, growing Western complaints, and particularly the increasing likelihood of NATO counteraction, led to a change in the Soviet position. In a speech Brezhnev delivered on October 6, 1979, he spoke out against the prospect of Western missile deployments but, at the same time, announced that 20,000 Soviet troops and 1,000 tanks would be withdrawn from East Germany. Furthermore, he promised to decrease the number of Soviet intermediate range missiles in the western part of the Soviet Union, provided that NATO did not install additional intermediate range missiles in Western Europe, and implied that, within the framework of SALT III, the Soviet Union was willing to discuss overall INF limitations. To be sure, on December 14, after the NATO deployment decision, the Soviet government announced that the NATO action had destroyed the basis for INF negotiations. But, on July 1, 1980, after further criticism of SS-20 deployment by Schmidt, Brezhnev recanted and agreed to negotiate with the United States on limiting INF missiles. Negotiations began that October.[13]

And yet, Soviet participation in arms control negotiations with the United States did not hide the fact that its leadership, while anxious to maintain détente, had little interest in pushing ahead toward substantial dis-armament. At the June 1979 summit, Carter presented Brezhnev with pro-posals for major strategic arms cuts in the future. But, as Dobrynin recalled, "the Soviet leadership under Brezhnev was not prepared for such a broad approach." Defense Minister Ustinov "was dead against the proposals as too far-reaching." Politburo member Konstantin Chernenko "seconded him at once." Gromyko, somewhat more cautious, "said such questions should not be decided overnight." Reluctant to tackle new issues at the conference, Brezhnev sided with Gromyko, and Carter's proposals "were mothballed." Meanwhile, despite the opening of INF negotiations, the buildup of Soviet SS-20 missiles continued, apparently at a faster rate than before. As Do-brynin later conceded, although the Soviet Union did improve its relations with West European nations through its acceptance of West German *Ost-politik*, "we were also feverishly building up our nuclear and conventional arms in Europe beyond any reasonable measure."[14] Furthermore, in the final days of 1979, the Soviet government poured its armed forces into Afghani-stan, where they battled Afghan rebels in an attempt to prop up the Com-munist government of that nation. Although Soviet officials viewed this military intervention as a quick fix to stabilize the political situation in a friendly country on their border, Western nations—and particularly the United States—regarded it as a flagrant act of military aggression.[15]

The inability of the Soviet government to recognize that its own actions were contributing to the unraveling of the détente that it desired, was based, in part, on the poor quality of its top leadership. Brezhnev's health contin-ued to deteriorate—a fact that, together with the heavy medications he took to deal with it, rendered him sluggish, depressed, and increasingly incom-petent. At the June 1979 summit meeting, Dobrynin was struck by the con-trast between Carter's capability and Brezhnev's physical and mental de-crepitude—a situation that he blamed in large part for the failure of personal diplomacy between the two world leaders. Gorbachev, too, was disturbed by the fact that Brezhnev seemed "more dead than alive." After a Politburo meeting at which the party secretary forgot the subject of the discussion, Gorbachev spoke earnestly to Andropov about the possibility of encourag-ing Brezhnev to retire. But he found that his mentor and Politburo colleague viewed Brezhnev as irreplaceable, "even in his present state." In fact, this was the view of most Politburo members, who seemed quite content with the present arrangements, which enabled them to continue ruling their fief-doms without interference. The result, then, was a government leadership that went through the motions, but that was incapable of fully comprehend-ing the serious issues that confronted it.[16]

Western Policy

Western nuclear policy was also becoming muddled. Within the Carter administration, the growing perception of Soviet misbehavior did not totally rout the doves, but it did undermine their influence. The State Department continued to champion nuclear arms control and disarmament—first under Vance and, after he resigned in May 1980, under his successor, Edmund Muskie. On occasion, they were joined by Mondale, who claimed that Brzezinski's tough, anti-Soviet stance was endangering the SALT treaty. Increasingly, however, Brown allied himself with Brzezinski, arguing forcefully for a greater U.S. military effort. At key junctures, Carter followed their advice. Genuinely disturbed by the intransigence of Soviet officials, the President was shocked by Soviet military intervention in Afghanistan, which he condemned, emotionally, as "the greatest threat to peace since World War II." Political necessity reinforced Carter's shift toward promilitary positions, for the path to his 1980 re-election was increasingly strewn with hawkish, GOP charges that he failed to "stand up" to the Russians. At the same time, however, Carter refused to give up on the possibilities of progress toward nuclear disarmament, a position that he realized *also* had popular appeal.[17] The result was that the administration's policy grew more inconsistent, though clearly tilting in a more hawkish direction.

An even more decisive tilt in this direction occurred in Britain. In May 1979, thanks to a Conservative Party election victory, the hawkish Margaret Thatcher became prime minister. Her belief at that time, Thatcher recalled, was that "to resist the Soviet Union effectively, it would be necessary to restore our [NATO's] . . . military strength." In her view, "a nuclear weapon-free world . . . was neither attainable nor even desirable." Instead, she favored a Western nuclear buildup, including the deployment of cruise and Pershing missiles. "These weapons," she believed, "made up for Western Europe's unpreparedness to face a sudden, massive attack by the Warsaw Pact." Thus, unlike some of her arms control and disarmament-oriented NATO colleagues, Thatcher was eager for Western missile deployment, with or without the danger of Soviet SS-20 missiles. Although she professed to like Carter personally, she had little respect for him as a world leader. "In foreign affairs," she recalled, "he was over-influenced" by the idea "that the threat from communism had been exaggerated." Moreover, he had "no large vision of America's future."[18]

Given this dwindling desire for disarmament within and the deteriorating international situation without, efforts to secure a comprehensive nuclear test ban came to nought. In Washington, the Joint Chiefs of Staff and high level officials in the Department of Energy remained thoroughly opposed to a CTBT. Committed to maintaining and upgrading nuclear weapons as the cornerstone of U.S. national security, they did everything possible to sabotage progress toward a cutoff in nuclear testing. In Britain, the ministry of defense took a similar position, and, after Thatcher's election, so did the prime minister. Although the Russians continued to display genuine interest in a CTBT, their invasion of Afghanistan strengthened the hand of treaty opponents and—along with the Carter administration's preoccupation with the hostage crisis in Iran—chilled White House interest in the negotiations. Herbert York, the physicist who served as chief U.S. negotiator at the talks, recalled that "after the Soviet seizure of Kabul, it was obvious that all was lost." At the beginning of 1981, the treaty talks were adjourned, with no date set for resumption. Looking back on the CTBT negotiations of 1979–81, York concluded that they were frustrating, but that "working things out in the Washington bureaucracy was much more frustrating than dealing with the Russians."[19]

Other signs of slippage in the Western commitment to curb the nuclear arms race were numerous. Existing nuclear weapons systems were upgraded, while the U.S. government (like its Soviet counterpart) engaged in a strategic nuclear weapons buildup. By January 1981, when Carter left office, the United States and the Soviet Union possessed unprecedented numbers of strategic nuclear missiles.[20] Dramatic plans were unveiled for the future, including U.S. development of the MX missile, a new, highly accurate ICBM. Approved by Carter in June 1979, at a meeting of top administration officials just before the Vienna summit, the MX project was a massive one. It entailed building and deploying 200 MX missiles, each carrying ten nuclear warheads, in a mobile, race-track form, with thousands of missile silos dug in the desert region of the Southwest to house them on their constant travels. The largest construction project in human history, dwarfing the building of the Egyptian pyramids, it carried an estimated price-tag of up to $60 billion. Members of the Carter administration rallied behind this scheme—dubbed by critics "the shell game"—because of their belief that, having canceled the B-1 bomber, the administration had to champion an alternative nuclear weapons system. Moreover, they saw it as improving the chances for Senate ratification of the SALT II treaty. Even Vance supported the MX, explaining: "I had long felt, since the 1977 cancellation of the B-1 bomber, that ratification . . . would be unlikely without a firm commitment to the MX program."[21]

Another sign of the hawkish drift was Carter's issuance of Presidential Directive 59. Put together by Brown and Brzezinski and signed by the Presi-

dent on July 25, 1980, it outlined a new strategy for U.S. nuclear war-
fighting. Under PD-59, if deterrence failed to block Soviet aggression, U.S.
military forces would wage a slow-motion, escalating nuclear war upon Soviet targets, with sufficient destructiveness to defeat the Soviet government
at every stage. Brown contended that this approach would limit nuclear war
to the lowest-possible level of damage and, also, "convince Soviet leaders
that they cannot secure victory." Critics, on the other hand, maintained that
this limited nuclear war scenario lowered the nuclear threshold and, thus,
made nuclear war more likely. Although Brown claimed, with some justification, that this strategy represented merely an upgrading of the Schlesinger
doctrine, the fact that the administration deliberately leaked PD-59 to the
press made it seem like one further, provocative blow to Soviet-American
relations. Moreover, both hawks and doves considered its leakage an indication that, in the midst of an election campaign, the Carter administration
was cynically firming up its anti-Soviet credentials.[22]

If, however, the Carter administration made efforts to appease American
hawks, it also shaped its policies in the hope of conciliating dovish forces.
On December 12, 1979, NATO adopted what became known as its "two-
track" policy for intermediate range nuclear missiles. Track one provided
that, in the fall of 1983, the U.S. government would begin installing 464
cruise missiles and 108 Pershing II missiles in five West European nations.
But track two provided that NATO would begin negotiations with the Soviet Union for the reduction or elimination of all nuclear missiles in Europe.
Although track one reflected NATO officials' growing anxiety about what
Soviet installation of SS-20 missiles might do to "decouple" the United
States from Western Europe, track two represented a significant concession
to antinuclear sentiment. As a U.S. House of Representatives study of the
issue concluded: "The general aversion to nuclear weapons that existed
among important sections of public opinion in several European countries
was . . . an important factor in the evolution of an arms control approach.
The arms control element was considered essential in order to gain parliamentary and public support for the NATO proposal in several countries,
particularly those where the system would be based. A clear indication of
the likely public reaction to the introduction of the new missiles had already
been given by the widespread opposition to the proposed introduction of the
enhanced radiation warhead." Although cruise and Pershing missile deployment "was of a different nature than that of the 'neutron bomb,' substantial opposition could be anticipated in the leftwing of the SPD, on a
widespread basis in the Netherlands and to a lesser but unpredictable extent
in Belgium. Moreover, it could be expected that the traditional 'no nuclear'

policies of Norway and Denmark would complicate their endorsement of the proposal."[23]

Events leading up to the "two-track" decision confirm this assessment. In January 1979, when Carter met at Gaudeloupe with French President Valéry Giscard d'Estaing, Schmidt, and Callaghan—outlining a U.S. plan for deployment of the Western missiles—he complained, as he recalled, that "no European leader had been willing to accept on their soil our neutron weapons, ground-launched cruise missiles, or the Pershing 2 medium-range missiles." In response, his NATO partners, although reluctantly accepting deployment, stressed the necessity of negotiations. According to Schmidt, Callaghan said that, ultimately, missile deployment "would probably be necessary, but that it should be taken only if Soviet-American arms limitation negotiations . . . were to lead to a negative outcome. Callaghan urged that such negotiations be undertaken soon." Giscard d'Estaing agreed with Callaghan on the need for INF negotiations, although he wanted to set a time limit to them. Schmidt stressed that deployment "would not meet with undivided approval in Europe and in my own party" and, therefore, he would not only have to insist upon deployment in other nations, but upon arms control negotiations. According to Schmidt, this discussion provided "the genesis" of the December 1979 two-track decision.[24]

Thereafter, in fact, the arms control track became inseparable from the deployment decision. In May 1979, in a memo to Carter on the INF issue, Vance and Brown emphasized that "obtaining a [NATO] consensus will not be easy. . . . Each ally confronts major political problems. . . . Nuclear issues provoke strong reactions among European publics." Germany remained particularly problematic. "Schmidt's domestic situation encourages procrastination and equivocation on his part," they noted. "The left wing of his own party—the main source of his problem—wants to avoid deployments." Therefore, "Schmidt's strategy for managing this situation" included the condition that "a deployment decision must be accompanied by sincere arms control attempts." As one West German expert on the two-track decision concluded: "It was clear to all concerned that the party would not have tolerated the NATO resolution without a serious arms control offer. Just how serious Helmut Schmidt himself judged the situation to be is evident in the fact that he threatened . . . his resignation on the eve of the party congress in December 1979." The Dutch government, too—facing massive public opposition to the missiles, an internal division over deployment, and the fierce resistance of the opposition Social Democrats—insisted upon the second track.[25]

The antinuclear origins of the second track are also confirmed by the recollections of Carter administration officials. According to Vance, "the arms control aspect of this so-called two-track approach was politically essential to contain expected internal opposition to the proposed deployments within most of the member countries." Asked if the arms control track reflected an attempt to head off West European opposition to missile deployment, Brzezinski replied: "That's correct. That's correct." Brown recalled that, with "European public opinion" uneasy about the missile deployment, the Germans and the Dutch "insisted on the second track." Paul Warnke, who had left the Carter administration in late 1978 but remained well informed about its internal decision-making, recalled that there was "no question about" the decisive importance of antinuclear pressures for development of the second track. There "were always, of course, problems with Germany" and, in Britain, Labour Party opposition provided an important incentive for it. McGeorge Bundy, an administration advisor, concurred: "In order to be responsive to important antinuclear opinion in Western Europe, NATO adopted a double track." The second track "was necessary for domestic political reasons."[26]

Nor was it clear that, even with this concession to antinuclear sentiment, all NATO nations would support the two-track package. Although Thatcher, who replaced Callaghan that spring, was thoroughly committed to it, her subsequent talks with West European leaders left her appalled at their equivocation. Schmidt remained "very concerned at the effect on German public opinion of stationing more nuclear missiles on German soil," while "the Belgians were looking over their shoulder at the Dutch." In her talks with the Dutch prime minister, she recalled, he "explained to me in some detail the difficulties he was facing. Apparently, half the sermons in Dutch churches were now dealing with nuclear disarmament and the issue of deployment was endangering his government's survival." In a non-binding vote on December 6, the Dutch parliament rejected the proposed NATO decision. The Belgian government called for a postponement of the NATO decision for six months. Although Norway and Denmark were not part of the deployment plan—as they had refused ever since the late 1950s to install nuclear weapons on their soil in peacetime—even their support for action by other NATO nations seemed problematic. Indeed, the Social Democratic government of Denmark concluded that it would propose a six-month delay in the NATO deployment decision.[27]

Ultimately, given the fear of Soviet SS-20 missiles and loyalty to NATO, the two-track decision of December 1979 was unanimous, but, as Carter noted, antinuclear pressures made it very difficult to implement. Both the Dutch and Belgian governments had entered their formal reservations to the decision, and—in line with them—placed conditions upon their participation. The Dutch government postponed a decision on accepting its share of the missiles until the end of 1981. The Belgian government also began postponing a final decision on missile installation, making it dependent upon the state of Soviet-American negotiations.[28] Meanwhile, in early 1980, Schmidt began calling for a joint public declaration by Moscow and Washington to simply halt Euromissile deployment until the end of 1983. Schmidt's antimissile speeches led to a fierce altercation between the West German chancellor and Carter, who believed that Schmidt was pandering to antinuclear sentiment and undermining allied support for deployment.[29]

Furthermore, West European antinuclear pressures became so intense that they began to turn the arms control track into the most radical, farthest-reaching of its possibilities: what became known, during the Reagan presidency, as the "zero option." Most NATO officials wanted some deployment of new missiles in Western Europe, regardless of what the Russians did about the SS-20s. But the zero option—the removal of all intermediate range nuclear missiles from Europe—began to make headway, particularly after it was proposed by the West German and Dutch Social Democratic parties in the summer of 1979. Naturally, it took on an increasing political significance as protest against the missiles grew. Given the SPD's enthusiasm for the zero option, Schmidt became one of its earliest proponents among top NATO officials. "The zero solution," he recalled, was "first thought up in Bonn; I had first proposed it publicly in December 1979 and repeated it several times." With his own Labor Party badly split by the two-track decision, the Norwegian foreign minister adopted a similar approach. He, too, expressed his hope that Soviet-American negotiations would result in the zero option, for that would make it unnecessary to deploy the new Euromissiles.[30]

For a time, dovish sentiment also had a favorable impact upon attempts to reduce the number of strategic nuclear weapons. When it came to SALT, Carter would brook no compromise. "I will never have a chance so momentous to contribute to world peace as to negotiate and to see ratified this SALT treaty," he told a group of Democratic congressional legislators in May 1979. Carter's willingness to draw the line on this issue reflected not only his deep personal commitment to controlling these deadliest of nuclear weapons, but his recognition that curbing the nuclear arms race enjoyed strong public support. That same month, the President's pollster, Patrick Caddell, sent him a report on public attitudes toward the issue that observed: "One fact stands out in the recent survey on SALT—the American people stand firmly behind the idea of arms limitation and . . . behind the

SALT treaty." Among those who had heard of the treaty, it drew more than two-to-one backing, and there was "overwhelming support for the idea of limiting nuclear arms among the whole population." Indeed, "support for SALT is both broader and deeper than we would have imagined," and "the public concern over possible nuclear confrontation is much deeper than many would predict." Impressed by the report, portions of which he underlined and commented upon, Carter ordered that it be made the basis for all his speeches and those of his Cabinet.[31]

Consequently, when Carter met with Brezhnev that June for their summit meeting in Vienna, he was not only eager to sign the SALT II treaty, but ready to move beyond it to a dramatic reversal of the strategic nuclear arms race. At the meeting, he produced the lengthy list of proposals for SALT III that shocked Soviet officials, including "deep cuts in weapons," a halt to production of "nuclear warheads and launchers," and a CTBT. Moreover, he suggested an interim plan, advanced since November 1978 by Jeremy Stone of the Federation of American Scientists, who had been criticizing the SALT II limits as too high. This interim plan provided for lowering SALT II limits on strategic nuclear weapons annually by a fixed percentage.[32]

The problem for Carter was that the treaty's popularity did not necessarily translate into the two-thirds vote in the U.S. Senate required for its ratification. Although some dovish Senators indicated that they might not vote for the SALT II treaty because of its failure to foster significant nuclear arms reductions, the real danger to its ratification emerged among Senators with more hawkish views. Republican Senators, particularly, were abandoning the treaty as it became an issue in the emerging 1980 presidential campaign. Thus, the Carter administration began to follow the Brzezinski line, which maintained that a more assertive military policy would enable it to secure the necessary support for SALT II.[33] Robert Beckel, a White House congressional liaison officer, recalled that, although NATO had agreed on a 3 percent annual increase in military spending, "Carter decided to go up two more percentage points" because Brown and White House operative Lloyd Cutler "argued persuasively that it was essential to get SALT ratified." The military budget increase "would never have been five percent had it not been because of SALT." Ultimately, "Brzezinski and company used SALT as an excuse to get Carter on a hardline position on a lot of . . . things."[34]

But if the administration considered concessions to the hawks necessary to secure a two-thirds Senate vote for SALT II, it also recognized that the bottom line for the treaty remained its solid backing by an antinuclear public. "On the positive side" of the ratification struggle, Vance recalled,

"SALT enjoyed a powerful base of popular support which could be mobilized." Although some administration officials worried that mainstream community leaders might be "turned off by the Women's [sic] Strike for Peace types," they drew them both into the treaty campaign. Well before the final initialing of the agreement, the administration-organized Americans for SALT had pulled them together and was laying the groundwork for ratification with considerable effectiveness.[35] In mid-1979, Vance recalled, "the polls continued to show heavy public support for SALT," and he believed that, when the Senate vote occurred, "we could get the required 67 votes." Brown, too, thought that, by mid-summer of 1979, the Senate battle had been won. Overseas demands for arms control and disarmament also influenced administration and Senate thinking. In his diary, Carter recounted a meeting with wavering Senators at which he helped turn them around by pointing to the "terrible consequences" of the Senate's rejection of the treaty, among them the fact that "our Western allies and the rest of the world would look on us as warmongers."[36]

Ultimately, it was not the unpopularity of nuclear arms controls but, rather, the behavior of hawks in Washington and Moscow that torpedoed the prospects for SALT II treaty ratification. In early September 1979, the "discovery" of a Soviet brigade in Cuba was seized upon by opponents of arms control to argue the case for an onslaught of Moscow-backed aggression, despite the fact that the Soviet Union had maintained the brigade in Cuba, at the Cuban government's request, for nearly two decades. Although the furor over this issue gradually receded, it did delay action on SALT II for several months—enough time for top officials in the Kremlin to embark upon a genuinely aggressive act: the invasion of Afghanistan. As Carter recalled, the beginning of Soviet warfare in Afghanistan "wiped out any chance for a two-thirds vote of approval." Accordingly, in early January 1980, he had Senate supporters of the treaty defer consideration of it.[37] For all intents and purposes, the treaty ratification fight had come to an end. Carter recalled: "Our failure to ratify the SALT II treaty and to secure even more far-reaching agreements on nuclear arms control was the most profound disappointment of my Presidency." He added: "We could only hope that an aroused public—in the United States and other countries—could convince the leaders of both superpowers that they must work to remove this nuclear shadow from over the earth."[38]

All, however, was not lost. Had Carter been re-elected President in 1980, he would have renewed the treaty ratification fight and moved on to more sweeping attempts to curb the arms race and avert nuclear war.[39] And even his election defeat that year, by a far more hawkish opponent, did not bring an end to the nuclear arms limitations agreed upon in the SALT II treaty. Quite the contrary. Like the arms control track of the two-track decision, it provided an important precedent for the future. Indeed, though unratified, SALT II continued to be observed by the U.S. and Soviet governments well into the following decade. Thus, these concessions to the force of antinuclear sentiment, largely unappreciated or unnoticed at the time, would prove to be like the seed in the snow—ready to germinate in later years, when more favorable developments warmed the earth with new hope.

The Rise of the Hawks, 1976-83

> We recall the Roman maxim—if you want peace, prepare for war.
>
> Eugene V. Rostow, 1977

Failing to realize that the deterioration of U.S.-Soviet relations and the accompanying arms race resulted primarily from fear, misunderstanding, and incompetence, powerful forces on both sides of the Cold War divide assumed that they flowed from calculated aggression on the part of the rival bloc. In their view, "the other side," encouraged by their "weakness," had gone on the march, and could be stopped only by a display of military "strength." Thus, they believed that the remedy was to get tough—to scrap plans for nuclear arms control and disarmament and, instead, to launch major new weapons programs. These hawkish forces were particularly successful in the United States, where they helped to steer the Carter administration toward a more confrontational foreign and military policy and to shatter the possibilities for ratification of the SALT II treaty. In 1980, they secured their greatest victory with the successful conquest of power by Ronald Reagan and other champions of a nuclear buildup. But they also emerged in other parts of the world, particularly in Western Europe and the Soviet Union, where unrepentant hawks did their best to undermine Soviet-American détente and to spur on the efforts of their respective nations in the nuclear arms race.

Anxious Cold Warriors, 1976-80

During the 1970s, an alarm grew among hawkish elements in the United States that—thanks to a decline in U.S. military power relative to that of Communist nations—the Soviet Union stood on the verge of dominating the world. Frightened of the Soviet Union, many Americans had never accepted the idea of Soviet-American détente or of limits upon their nation's weapons program. This group included not only many conservative Republicans, but a smaller group of vigorously anti-Soviet Democrats, many of them active in the hawkish Coalition for a Democratic Majority. The best-known of the Democratic hawks was U.S. Senator Henry Jackson of Washington, whose Cold War zeal meshed nicely with the fat defense contracts he brought back to his state, leading to his description as "the Senator from Boeing." Together with his hard-line aide, Richard Perle, Jackson conscientiously opposed the efforts of Presidents Nixon, Ford, and Carter to reach agreements with the Soviet Union. In 1972, when the Senate debated ratification of the SALT I treaty, they secured passage of an amendment criticizing the administration for its acceptance of the treaty's missile limits. In 1974, when the Soviet Union sought "most favored nation" trading status with the United States, they pushed through an amendment to the Trade Act of 1974, thereby effectively torpedoing that possibility. Other hawks made their criticism of arms controls known through a report drafted in late 1976 by the CIA's "Team B" panel. Appointed by CIA director George Bush that June, the panel had been instructed to check whether earlier intelligence estimates about Soviet strategic capabilities and intentions had been overoptimistic. Chaired by the hawkish Richard Pipes of Harvard and well-stocked with hard-liners, the panel, not surprisingly, concluded that earlier estimates had been overly sanguine and that Soviet military strength presented a grave menace to America's future.[1]

These forces coalesced in late 1976 with the formation of the Committee on the Present Danger. A key figure in its development was Paul Nitze, a former deputy secretary of defense and, more recently, a member of the CIA's Team B. That year, he met with Eugene Rostow (a former under secretary of state and a Coalition for a Democratic Majority leader) and other veterans of the nation's policymaking élite who, as Nitze recalled, "shared my view that the United States was entering a dangerous period of strategic disadvantage vis-à-vis the Soviet Union, and that the American public was either unaware of or too complacent about this trend." On November 11, 1976, they launched the Committee on the Present Danger (CPD) with a statement declaring that "the principal threat to our nation, to world peace, and to the cause of human freedom is the Soviet drive for dominance based upon an unparalleled military buildup." The CPD called for increased spending for U.S. "land, sea, and air forces" and for "our strategic deterrent. . . . If we continue to drift," it declared, "we shall become second best to the Soviet Union in overall military strength. . . . Then we could find ourselves isolated in a hostile world, facing the unremitting pressures of Soviet policy backed by an overwhelming preponderance of power. Our national survival would be in peril."[2]

The CPD, chaired by Rostow, never had more than about 180 members, all of whom served on its board of directors, but—as most of them were former participants in the nation's policymaking élite and had substantial financial resources at their command—they had very considerable influence. Although, initially, press stories depicted them as "cold warriors" and "hawkish," media coverage quickly became more flattering, with the CPD henceforth described as "a public interest group" and "an organization comprised of many leading Americans from all segments of the political spectrum." Nitze recalled that, after the CPD issued a new policy statement ("What Is the Soviet Union Up To?") in the spring of 1977, "AP and UPI placed excellent and substantial stories, which were widely reprinted. Along with these basic news reports, many of the major newspapers published favorable companion editorials. Additionally, we were gaining coverage on national television. ABC-TV and CBS-TV carried special interviews with Gene Rostow and me."[3] Recognizing the power of the new group, even some of the targets of the CPD's ire tried to curry favor with its leaders. Kissinger sought out Nitze at a Time-Life-Fortune reception in Washington, D.C., and assured him: "Paul, I want you to know that I thoroughly approve and agree with what you have been doing. . . . I quite agree that we need to have a true war-fighting capability." When Nitze seemed unimpressed, Kissinger returned to him later in the evening and remarked: "Paul, you must believe that what I have said is true. Now that I am out of office, I have nothing to gain by not telling you the truth."[4]

The substantial influence of CPD and its allies became evident in the heated campaign to block the nomination of Paul Warnke as head of ACDA and of the SALT II negotiating team. The Coalition for a Democratic Majority weighed in by circulating an anonymous denunciation of Warnke, accusing him of having been "the principal advisor to George McGovern on national security issues during the 1972 presidential campaign" and with advocating unilateral disarmament. Rightwing groups also did their part, with the Committee for the Survival of a Free Congress reportedly mailing out 600,000 anti-Warnke letters. For Nitze, as he recalled, it was "a serious debate not only on the nomination of Paul Warnke but on our posture toward the Soviet Union and the entire question of arms control." Accordingly, Nitze joined the fray in appearances before the Senate Foreign Relations Committee and the Senate Armed Services Committee, calling Warnke's views on defense issues "screwball" and "absolutely asinine." When one Senator, disturbed by the harshness of Nitze's testimony, asked him if he thought he was a better American than Warnke, Nitze responded: "I really do." Rostow thanked Nitze for his "heroic labors on the Warnke front," for "you have contributed to the education of the Senate and public opinion on the grim implications of the problem, and convinced the Senate . . . that Warnke is a hypocrite and the President an opportunist." On March 9, however, the Senate confirmed Warnke for the ACDA post by a vote of 70 to 29 and for the SALT position by 58 to 40. Even so, the hawks had mustered a large number of votes—enough to defeat a SALT treaty negotiated by Warnke. Nitze recalled that this fact "should have been a warning to the Carter administration to adopt a more realistic view of the Soviet Union and of our defense needs."[5]

Well aware of the CPD's influence and stung by its attack upon the administration's SALT proposals, Carter arranged a meeting with its leaders on August 4, 1977, in the Cabinet room of the White House. As the President, Brown, and Brzezinski listened, Rostow emphasized "the Soviet menace to our security," while Nitze cast doubts on the value for the United States of *any* possible SALT treaty. "In our view," Nitze said, "the terms of the best SALT agreement now negotiable could well rule out the possibility of going ahead with a U.S. weapons program adequate to maintain rough parity and crisis stability." According to an account in the *Washington Post*, the meeting grew heated when Carter responded that public sentiment in the United States would not support a major increase in military spending. "No, no, no," Nitze murmured, whereupon the President snapped: "Paul, would you please let me finish." To share ideas and narrow their differences, Carter urged the CPD leaders to meet regularly with Brown, Brzezinski, Vance, and with him to discuss policy issues, particularly the SALT treaty.[6] In another apparent effort to mollify the CPD, Brzezinski informed Rostow in October that Presidential Directive 18 provided the framework "for our longterm competition with the Soviets and sets forth programs and policies which I think you and your associates should find congenial. We do not intend to be caught with our guard down and we will not permit erosion in the current military balance. The President's commitment to 3% annual increases in real spending for defense underlines this commitment."[7]

But the CPD remained unimpressed. Carter's foreign and defense policy team horrified CPD leaders, with Nitze complaining that "every softliner I can think of is now part of the executive branch." According to Rostow, his views on Carter's appointees were "unprintable." At least as serious, in the opinion of the CPD, was the administration's failure to follow the hawkish policy that the group championed. In November 1977, only a few months after the CPD visit with the President, Rostow complained to Averell Harriman that "so far we have had little or no visible influence. . . . I am worried about the orientation of the Carter administration, very." Shortly thereafter, he warned the CPD board of directors that the nation's situation was becoming "steadily worse," and "we must rally very, very soon, or it will indeed be too late."[8]

Subsequent developments led the CPD to adopt an ever more antagonistic stance toward the Carter administration. In a tart letter of advice to Vance in June 1978, Rostow warned him: "I cannot imagine our getting anywhere, on Africa or any other subject, without reversing the B-1, MX and neutron bomb decisions, and obtaining a supplemental appropriation for more ships, research, ready forces, tanks, and strategic weapons." In 1979, Rostow told Senator Jackson that if Carter was serious about defending the United States, "he should get rid of Vance, Brown, Brzezinski, and the 250 Tony Lakes who hold the commanding heights of the bureaucracy." Throwing down the gauntlet in January 1980, the CPD executive committee condemned the Carter administration's foreign and defense policies as "wrong," and insisted that they "must be changed unequivocally and at once." That November, reviewing the situation, Rostow seemed to border on hysteria. "A ruthless reexamination of our foreign-cum-defense policy has been our highest priority for years," he wrote, but "it has been avoided like the plague by people terrorized or traumatized by the word 'Vietnam.'" Thus, "we must undertake the task now, on a crash basis, or (quite literally) die."[9]

In fact, the CPD's talk of U.S. military weakness and its dire predictions of Soviet conquest, while sincere, proved considerably exaggerated. Although the CPD warned repeatedly of a military "spending gap" between the United States and the Soviet Union, with Soviet expenditures increasing relentlessly at 4 to 5 percent annually, CIA and NATO studies later found that, for the period after 1976, Soviet increases were only about 2 percent a year. Indeed, according to the CIA, "the Soviets did not field weapons as rapidly after 1976 as before." Although Soviet conventional forces remained larger than the American, the United States never lost its advantage in weapons technology. Furthermore, the situation with respect to nuclear weapons did not shift in favor of the Soviet Union. Between 1970 and 1980, the number of nuclear warheads in U.S. strategic forces increased from about 4,000 to some 10,000, while those of the Soviet Union increased from about 1,800 to 6,000. Looking back on the fierce outcry of the CPD years later, Stewart Udall, a former member of Congress and Secretary of the Interior, remarked: "Deluded by their anti-Communist demonology and their misreadings of postwar history, Paul Nitze and his coterie of nuclear theologians made a series of spectacular misjudgments. . . . They were dead wrong about the imminent missile gap. . . . They were wrong in their judgments about Soviet power and Soviet intentions."[10]

Nonetheless, in the late 1970s, the CPD had enough influence to seriously damage the SALT II treaty. In July 1977, the CPD's first formal critique of the SALT process ("Where We Stand on SALT") argued that, "in the short run, it is unlikely that a comprehensive and safe SALT agreement can be negotiated." In "the longer run," it maintained, a SALT agreement "might" be acceptable, but only if it was far more favorable to U.S. security interests and if it was accompanied by new U.S. nuclear weapons programs. As the treaty process moved forward, the CPD kept up a running attack upon it. In October 1978, months before the end of treaty negotiations, Rostow told Kissinger that "we remain of the view that only the crushing defeat of Warnke's agreement can clear away the illusions to which the wishful thinkers cling about the nature of our security problem." During Senate hearings on the treaty in the fall of 1979, CPD executive committee and board members testified, by invitation, on seventeen different occasions before the Senate Foreign Relations and Armed Services Committees, and with considerable effect.[11] Leveling a withering attack upon SALT II, they argued that it would reduce the United States to a position of military inferiority, leaving it ripe for conquest by the Soviet Union. Thus, although Soviet intervention in Afghanistan dealt the final blow to the treaty, the CPD, in Vance's words, "had a great deal to do with undermining SALT." Richard Allen, a CPD executive committee member, claimed even greater efficacy: "The Committee on the Present Danger . . . managed to destroy SALT II, which was our objective."[12]

In the wake of the SALT II fiasco, the CPD had few regrets about the collapse of the nuclear arms control process. Committed to a U.S. nuclear buildup and to confronting Soviet military power, the CPD and its leaders had little sympathy for arms control or disarmament. Rostow wrote in November 1980: "The nuclear weapons issue has probably gotten beyond the possibility of control through arms limitations agreements like SALT. So? What arms limitation agreements have ever done much good? The SALT I agreements have not worked at all, from any point of view—political, military, or any other. Now that the Soviets have at least caught up with us, SALT II has even less promise." The CPD had more important concerns. The following month, in a memo to another CPD member, William Casey, who headed up the Reagan White House transition team, Rostow wrote: "One question now haunts the world: Who is going to win the war we still call Cold?"[13]

Opportunity Knocks: The Election of 1980

With the rise of Ronald Reagan and the Republican Right, the hawks had an excellent opportunity to sweep arms control and détente from the board. A fervent anti-Communist and proponent of a U.S. military buildup, Reagan became a member of the CPD in 1976. He "was very skeptical about the effectiveness of arms control treaties," recalled Martin Anderson, one of his longtime campaign aides, and leaned heavily upon *The Treaty Trap*, an anti-arms control tract written by an old friend of his, Lawrence Beilenson.[14] Lauding this book and other critiques of arms controls, Reagan used his weekly radio program in 1975 to tell listeners that "we'd rather prevent a war by being well armed than by surrendering." As for détente, he remarked: "Isn't that what a farmer has with his turkey—until Thanksgiving day?" In September 1979, he asked his radio audience: "Do arms limitation agreements—even good ones—really bring or preserve peace?" He replied: "History would seem to say 'no.'" Repeatedly denouncing SALT II negotiations, Reagan called instead for "strategic superiority." He explained: "If the object of the Salt [*sic*] II talks is to reduce the possibility of war, what better way is there than to stay so far ahead in weaponry that Russia's imperialistic desires will be inhibited?" The treaty being negotiated, he argued, was "an act of appeasement."[15] Indeed, by the time of his 1980 election, Reagan had opposed *every* nuclear arms control agreement negotiated by Democratic and Republican administrations.[16]

During the late 1970s, Reagan also used his radio addresses to publicly discuss pro-nuclear and antinuclear campaigns. Lauding the CPD—these "well known men & women of both parties"—for their patriotism, Reagan expressed his full agreement with their call for military "superiority" to "stop the thunder of [Soviet] hobnailed boots on their march to world empire." By contrast, he maintained, "the ghosts from the riotous, hate-filled '60s are stalking the land. . . . Today their goal is support of the Salt [*sic*] II treaties & unilateral disarmament by the U.S." In 1978, he charged, an agent of the Soviet-dominated World Peace Council had "set up a new combine of anti-nuclear power plant people & advocates of disarmament" in the United States, Mobilization for Survival. When this group held a conference at Yale University, "the ghosts appeared—in the flesh; Dr. Spock, environmentalist Barry Commoner," and other alleged subversives. Supporting this conference, he charged, were groups like the American Friends Service Committee, the War Resisters League, and Women Strike for Peace—all part of what he claimed was a Communist-directed campaign. Having remarked that "most people" in public life were "afraid" to expose "a communist conspiracy," Reagan added, sarcastically: "You could call these Americans a suicide lobby—but for heaven's sake dont [*sic*] say conspiracy."[17]

Convinced that Communism was not a rival political or economic system, but "a form of insanity," Reagan rarely saw a military weapon that he did not want to press into service in America's Cold War crusade. Enthusiastic about the neutron bomb, Reagan called it "the dreamed of death ray weapon of science fiction" and "a moral improvement" over other means of modern war—perhaps even "the ideal deterrent weapon."[18] Even so, perhaps because he remembered an era before the advent of total war, Reagan never felt entirely comfortable with nuclear weapons. His speech to the 1976 GOP national convention warned that "we live in a world in which the great powers have poised and aimed at each other horrible missiles of destruction, that can, in a matter of minutes, arrive in each other's country and destroy virtually the civilized world we live in." But, for the time being, his anti-Soviet zeal kept his qualms at bay, and his emphasis clearly remained upon a buildup of military "strength." Consequently, the 1980 Republican Party platform unabashedly called for the development of military superiority over the Soviet Union.[19]

And certainly that was Reagan's emphasis during the 1980 presidential election campaign. On the campaign trail, he championed building the B-1 bomber, the neutron bomb, the Trident submarine, and the MX missile, as well as additional navy warships and air force planes. Refusing to put a dollar figure upon what would evidently be a vast increase in military spending, Reagan declared: "In national defense you have to spend whatever is necessary." The Russians, he explained, were "monsters," who had kept the Cold War alive by their relentless drive to spread "Godless communism." Indeed, he declared, "the Soviet Union underlies all the unrest that is going on. If they weren't engaged in this game of dominoes, there wouldn't be any hot spots in the world."[20] In these circumstances, Reagan could see little reason for nuclear constraints. Asked, in January, if the United States should oppose the development of nuclear weapons by other nations, he responded: "I just don't think it's any of our business." The SALT II treaty, he declared, was "fatally flawed," and he would not submit it for Senate ratification. Questioned about the prospect of his using nuclear weapons, Reagan declared that he would never reveal what the United States "won't do." His running mate, George Bush, insisted to an interviewer that a nuclear war was winnable.[21] Richard Allen, Reagan's chief foreign and military policy advisor, recalled that the Republican statements that year were not just campaign rhetoric, but "really promises meant to be fulfilled." They were designed to "serve as a guide to action on Day One" of the Reagan administration.[22]

Although the CPD was ostensibly nonpartisan, many of its members threw themselves into the Reagan campaign. After all, Reagan was not only a CPD member but, most important, shared their views on foreign and military policy. During previous years, Reagan had not only sprinkled his radio commentaries with laudatory references to the CPD, but had even labeled a series of broadcasts Rostow I through Rostow VI. Predictably, not only Allen, but CPD members like Jeane Kirkpatrick, Richard Pipes, and Lt. General Edward Rowny became key foreign policy advisors during the campaign. Shortly after the GOP convention, the CPD held a day-long briefing for Reagan at its headquarters. Nitze met twice and at length with Reagan on weapons issues. Indeed, during the campaign and the subsequent transition process, 46 CPD members served on the Reagan advisory task force.[23] Only a week before the election, Rostow—at this point head of a group called Democrats for Reagan—told a press conference that "no one can deny" that Carter "is an isolationist" and "an illusionist about the Soviet Union." The President, he said, was "tempting the aggressor." Joining Rostow at the press conference, Nitze denounced Carter for "crude" attempts to stress SALT II's advantages and underplay its disadvantages. For Nitze, his 1980 association with Reagan proved an exhilarating experience. "Having wandered in an arms control wilderness for so many years," he recalled, "I saw reason to hope that we stood on the threshold of a new era."[24]

Democratic strategists, on the other hand, thought that Reagan's hawkishness might provide them with an advantage in the campaign. At the time of the GOP national convention, Carter recalled, his political team believed that Reagan was "the weakest candidate the Republicans could have chosen," for his positions on issues seemed extreme. Among them were "an unprecedented increase in defense spending, a rejection of SALT," and "indifference to the proliferation of nuclear weapons." These were the kinds of things "that we thought would make him quite vulnerable." Thus, "we tried to emphasize the radical nature of his departure from the policies of my administration and from those of my predecessors in the White House." Gerald Rafshoon, a top Carter campaign official, recalled the heavy emphasis he gave to the theme that "Reagan is a mad bomber." This included a TV ad in which Carter spoke earnestly about the dangers of nuclear war and a fifteen-minute radio talk in which he charged that Reagan was bringing the United States closer to a "nuclear precipice." At times, this strategy backfired. During the October 27 TV debate, when Carter talked of his twelve-year-old daughter Amy's concern about nuclear war, he was ridiculed for it by Reagan and by reporters. Nevertheless, Rafshoon recalled, "our polls showed that even after the debate . . . we were pulling back up again. Reagan kept being knocked down because people still were worried about the risk there."[25]

In fact, Republican strategists also believed that Reagan's hawkishness could prove his undoing. As early as August 1979, one of his top campaign aides, Martin Anderson, sent Reagan a lengthy memo emphasizing the need for "avoiding an overly aggressive stance that would be counterproductive." There needed "to be a switch from the false perception that Reagan sees complex foreign policy issues in black and white" and that he favors "stockpiling nuclear weapons to blast the Soviet Union." Reagan, he argued, should stress "the fostering of world peace" and "effective arms control" as part of what "should become known in the press as 'Reagan's Peace Plan.'" After all, "relying on large increases in our strategic nuclear forces to retaliate massively in the event of Soviet attack has some serious problems. A lengthy public debate on the virtues of quantum leaps in the levels of assured nuclear destruction is apt to frighten as many people as it consoles." Indeed, "substantial increases in the attack missile capability of the United States would be a powerful, emotional issue to deal with politically—especially by Reagan." Thus, "it is important that Reagan stress his commitment to the idea of a good arms control agreement before spelling out the problems and difficulties with SALT II that make it unacceptable."[26]

During the 1980 campaign, Republican operatives realized that it had become especially important to blunt the perception of Reagan's hawkishness. The nuclear weapons issue "was clearly one of the things that we had to watch with some care," recalled Richard Wirthlin, the director of planning and strategy for the Reagan campaign. Given the public "concern about nuclear war and peace," Republican strategists had "to avoid anything that would heighten the already fairly strong perception that Reagan was not only more aggressive in foreign affairs and the development of strong defense, but also would be more likely than Carter to get us into war." In an attempt to offset this perception, GOP strategists focused the campaign on the economy. But they also moderated Reagan's approach to arms control issues. "To soften his hawkish image," the *Wall Street Journal* reported that June, Reagan told his audiences "that he would also be ready to negotiate an arms limitation treaty with the Russians—but only if they agree to real cuts in nuclear arms." By October, even this legerdemain did not work very well. According to an October 20 *New York Times* dispatch: "For the last few weeks, as national polls showed the presidential race growing tighter, Mr. Reagan, who would rather have been concentrating on what he sees as the failures of Mr. Carter's economic policies, found himself compelled to devote time in nearly every campaign appearance to deny that he had a bellicose nature." In a lengthy television speech he delivered that evening to deal with what one Reagan advisor called the "war issue," which he said had been plaguing the campaign of late, the Republican candidate complained that his views had "been distorted in what I can only conclude is an effort to scare people."[27]

Given Reagan's potential vulnerability in this area, he came off fairly well. "What was underestimated," recalled Harold Brown, was "how his hawkish . . . positions have been, in the eyes of the American public, completely redeemed by his personal attractiveness and apparent straightforwardness. . . . The style is what came across, and the style was folksy and open and friendly, even if the substance might have been unthought-out and irresponsible and dangerous." Carter, too, complained: "I did not realize then that the press and public would not believe that Reagan actually meant what he was saying." Wirthlin agreed that, despite Reagan's stand on the issues, "the persona of the man was such that he didn't really scare people down to their boots." Of course, some of what would later be called Reagan's "Teflon" aspect—the fact that nothing seemed to stick to him— reflected the unwillingness of the mass media to scrutinize his contentions. Rafshoon recalled bitterly that, in the aftermath of the October 27 presidential debate, the press ignored "the fact that Reagan lied" when "he said 'I never made the statement that nuclear proliferation is none of our business.'" Overall, the press gave Reagan "a free ride."[28] These factors limited popular anxiety about Reagan's hawkishness and contributed to his decisive victory at the polls that November. The Republican Party also captured control of the U.S. Senate.

The New Administration: Views

With the advent of the Reagan administration, the hawks took command of the U.S. executive branch. Appointed Secretary of Defense, Caspar Weinberger told his first news conference that "a strong confident America . . . is willing to fight for its freedom as the best hope for peace." Outlining his plans for a military buildup, he added: "I look forward with great enthusiasm and eagerness as we begin to rearm America." His top priority, he later stated, was "the regaining of our nuclear deterrent capability." Thus, as one administration official recalled, when it came to nuclear arms controls, "Weinberger was disinclined to negotiate on anything." The Soviet intention "is world domination," Weinberger explained; "it's just that simple."[29]

As Weinberger had no foreign or military policy experience, he leaned heavily for advice and expertise upon the new Assistant Secretary of Defense, Richard Perle. Smart, relentless, and skilled at working the government bureaucracy, Perle was a very effective advocate for hawkish policies. Like Weinberger, he consistently promoted a U.S. military buildup. Dubbed "the Prince of Darkness" by the U.S. press corps, he insisted that the Soviet Union is "a place where everyone lies all the time." Perle remarked: "The sense that we and the Russians could compose our differences, reduce them to treaty constraints . . . and then rely on compliance to produce a safer world—I don't agree with any of that." Even Reagan felt somewhat chilled by what he observed in his own Defense Department. "There were some people in the Pentagon," he recalled grimly, "who thought in terms of fighting and *winning* a nuclear war."[30]

Although, traditionally, U.S. Secretaries of State often resisted the military orientation of Secretaries of Defense, the appointment of General Alexander Haig to head up the State Department precluded this possibility. Haig was a strong proponent of military power, which, in his memoirs, he termed "the basis of foreign policy for all the nations of earth." Nuclear weapons, he insisted, did not exist "in a world of their own," but were "an expression of strength of the nation possessing them." In 1979, Haig condemned NATO's Euromissile decision not because it heightened the arms race, but because he believed it was thoroughly inadequate, representing "only political expediency and tokenism."[31] During his Senate confirmation hearings, he claimed that the Soviet military buildup had led to "perhaps the most complete reversal of global power relationship ever seen in a period of relative peace." He also opined that "there are more important things than peace . . . things we Americans should be willing to fight for." Nancy Reagan recalled that "Haig alarmed Ronnie and his top advisers with his belligerent rhetoric. Once, talking about Cuba in a meeting of the National Security Council, he turned to Ronnie and said, 'You just give me the word and I'll turn that f—— island into a parking lot.'" She concluded: "If Ronnie had given him the green light, Haig would have bombed everybody and everything."[32]

Reagan also went through a rapid succession of hawkish National Security Advisors. The first of them, Richard Allen, used his first public statement to warn against the "advocacy of arms control negotiations as a substitute for military strength." Referring to Soviet deployment of SS-20 missiles, he argued that the idea that "we can bargain the reduction of a deployed Soviet weapons system for a promise not to deploy our own" was "illusory." Although Allen was ousted from his post in 1981 for shady financial dealings,[33] his successor, William Clark, continued the emphasis upon military strength, based on what White House aide Michael Deaver called an "obsession" with the Soviet Union. Clark "saw no hope in any policy that relied on trusting the Russians, argued against any attempt to improve that relationship, and did what he could to slow it down," Deaver recalled. George Shultz, who succeeded Haig as Secretary of State, wrote that Clark "categorically opposed U.S.-Soviet contacts." Clark's assistant, Robert Mc-Farlane, who became National Security Advisor after Clark resigned in protest against what he considered insufficient militancy in Reagan's "Evil Empire" speech, was less phobic about the Soviet Union. Nevertheless, he entered the administration "passionately committed" to nuclear "modernization," as he later remarked. "Militarily, we had to modernize our force," and Reagan's commitment to military competition with the Russians was "romantically appealing."[34]

Leading hawks even took command of the Arms Control and Disarmament Agency (ACDA). Eugene Rostow, named its director, insisted that "arms control thinking drives out sound thinking." Characterizing the nation's decade of experience with SALT I and SALT II as "painful and unsatisfactory," he could see little virtue in any previous arms control treaty save for the Rush-Bagot Agreement of 1817. His "first task" as ACDA director, he promised, would be to "reassess the role of arms limitation agreements in our foreign and defense policy." This mordant view of arms control reflected Rostow's keen commitment to a massive U.S. nuclear buildup, expressed most recently during his stint as a member of the Reagan administration's transition team. He told the Senate that the United States "should persevere in our armaments program whether the news from the negotiating table is favorable or unfavorable." Even the prospect of nuclear war did not seem to dampen his enthusiasm for nuclear weapons. Asked, during the hearings, if the United States or the Soviet Union could survive a full-scale nuclear exchange, he responded: "Japan . . . not only survived but flourished after the nuclear attack." Pressed to comment on the results of a *full* nuclear exchange, he stated: "The human race is very resilient."[35] Rostow's successor as ACDA director, Kenneth Adelman, did not differ with him in any substantial respect, and defined himself as "a card-carrying skeptic on arms control." Nuclear weapons, Adelman believed, were "the final guarantor of our national security."[36]

Most other Reagan appointees shared this belief. Appointed the administration's chief arms control negotiator, Lt. General Edward Rowny had resigned from the SALT II talks because of his opposition to the emerging treaty. In 1980, he told a National Defense University conference: "We have put too much emphasis on the *control* of arms and too little on the *provision* of arms." During Senate confirmation hearings, he remarked that he saw "nothing sacrosanct about the ABM Treaty."[37] Paul Nitze, appointed chief negotiator for theater nuclear forces in Europe, was an inveterate foe of nuclear arms control treaties and a keen supporter of a nuclear buildup. Richard Pipes, appointed to direct Soviet affairs for the National Security Council, argued that in a Soviet-American nuclear war, the "country better prepared could win and emerge a viable society." Colin Gray, another defense advisor for the administration, argued that, in a full-scale nuclear war with the Soviet Union, the United States could keep its casualties down "to approximately 20 million" and, thus, emerge the "victor." Others, like William Casey (appointed director of the CIA) and Jeane Kirkpatrick (appointed U.S. ambassador to the United Nations), were full-blown Cold War ideologues.[38]

Thus, Reagan's 1980 victory placed leading hawks in command of U.S. foreign and military policy. Admittedly, not all Reagan appointees fit this characterization. On the White House staff, less ideological, more pragmatic types like Deaver and James Baker teamed up to oppose hard-liners like Clark and White House Counsel Edwin Meese. Nancy Reagan frequently took the side of the moderates. When some of the President's staff "wanted him to get tough with the Soviets," recalled Deaver, "she argued that he should soften his language," for "he had been painted as strident and unyielding to the point of being a warmonger."[39] For the most part, however, the hawks held sway. By November 1981, 32 of the 182 members of the CPD occupied key posts in the Reagan administration. According to a *New York Times* report, they had achieved "a virtual takeover of the nation's national security apparatus." By 1984, the number of CPD members that had served in the Reagan administration reached 60. They included Adelman, Allen, Anderson, Casey, Max Kampelman, Kirkpatrick, Nitze, Perle, Pipes, Rostow, Donald Rumsfeld, Shultz, and Edward Teller. Moreover, another CPD member, Ronald Reagan, was now President of the United States.[40]

Although, in his memoirs, Reagan claimed that, upon entering the White House, he was deeply uneasy about the nuclear arms race and even began to dream of "a world free of nuclear weapons,"[41] there is no evidence to sustain this contention. Addressing the Corps of Cadets at West Point in May 1981, Reagan contended that any argument in his administration over U.S. national security policy "will be over which weapons, not whether we should forsake weaponry for treaties and agreements." At early Cabinet meetings, when the majority expressed dismay at the massive military buildup called for by Weinberger and supported by Haig and Casey, Reagan came out forcefully in favor of it, declaring: "Look, I am the President of the United States, the Commander-in-Chief. . . . We're going to go ahead with these programs." In line with his promises, arms control treaties were accorded a very low priority. He later explained: "I wanted peace through strength, not peace through a piece of paper." Thus, when it came to the Russians, "we were going to spend whatever it took to stay ahead of them in the arms race."[42]

Behind Reagan's commitment to winning the arms race lay his continued belief that the United States faced a satanic enemy. Only nine days after taking office, he declared in his first press conference that the Russians reserved the right "to commit any crime, to lie, to cheat" in a relentless campaign to promote "world revolution and a one-world socialist or communist state." The *Los Angeles Times* called it "the harshest Cold War attack to come from the White House in two decades." His strident pronouncements culminated in a public address on March 8, 1983, in which he denounced the Soviet Union as "the focus of evil in the modern world," an "evil empire." Conflict between the United States and the Soviet Union, he said, was nothing less than an apocalyptic "struggle between right and wrong and good and evil."[43]

This Manichean view of the world meshed well with the evangelical Protestantism, often laced with visions of global annihilation, that infused elements of the new administration. Asked in 1982 about his belief in Biblical prophecy, Weinberger replied: "I have read the Book of Revelation and yes, I believe the world is going to end—by an act of God, I hope," and "every day I think that time is running out." Questioned during his confirmation hearings about preserving the environment, Interior Secretary-designate James Watt responded: "I do not know how many future generations we can count on before the Lord returns." The President himself had developed a belief in Biblical prophecy during his youth, and it deepened in the 1960s and 1970s thanks to his contacts with Billy Graham and others who shared this faith. At a 1971 political dinner shortly after a coup in Libya, Reagan declared: "That's a sign that the day of Armageddon isn't far off. . . . Everything is falling into place. It can't be long now. Ezekial says that fire and brimstone will be rained down upon the enemies of God's people. That must mean that they'll be destroyed by nuclear weapons." Reagan continued to express these views during his White House years. In 1983, he told a lobbyist: "I turn back to . . . the signs foretelling Armageddon, and I find myself wondering if we're the generation that's going to see that come about. . . . These prophecies . . . certainly describe the times we're going through."[44]

The New Administration: Early Policies

Not surprisingly, the Reagan administration moved to implement its hawk-ish beliefs with a vast nuclear weapons buildup. Warning of what they called a "window of vulnerability"—a period of Soviet advantage in strate-gic nuclear forces—Weinberger and other officials championed a program designed to provide the U.S. government with clear nuclear superiority over its Soviet rival. Announced in October 1981, the Pentagon's program called for simultaneous across-the-board modernization of all U.S. strategic forces, including cruise missiles, the MX missile, and the Trident submarine. Fur-thermore, the administration laid out plans to produce the once-canceled B-1 bomber. Weinberger added that "we have also placed high priority on up-grading our stockpiles of nuclear artillery, short-range missiles, bombs, and sea-based weapons." Even the once-discredited neutron bomb was resur-rected. Responding to criticism of its manufacture, he declared that there was "no reason to consult anyone" about it. James Wade, the assistant sec-retary of defense, promised that "over the next 5 years there will be an in-crease in the total number of nuclear warheads deployed, both strategic and tactical, on the order of several thousand." And, in fact, during its first year in office, the administration did secure a 25 percent real increase in the Pentagon's budget to fund these and other military programs.[45]

These programs for a nuclear weapons buildup were accompanied by statements and plans that displayed a rather relaxed attitude toward the waging of nuclear war. In October 1981, drawn into a discussion of the fea-sibility of "limited" nuclear war, Reagan told a group of newspaper editors that he thought a future nuclear war might be confined to Europe. Sensitive to the wave of European criticism that followed, the White House followed up with a "clarification" that the United States would not "consider fighting a nuclear war at Europe's expense." But, only a few days later, Weinberger declared that "it is possible that with nuclear weapons there can be some use of them—in a connection with what is up to that time a war solely within a European theater." In November, Haig declared that NATO contingency planning for a conventional war in Europe called for the explosion of a nu-clear weapon for "demonstrative purposes." Weinberger denied this, and the President said he did not know.[46] The following May, when the administra-tion's first Defense Guidance was leaked to the press, it revealed that the administration was readying itself for a "protracted" nuclear war with the Soviet Union, in which American nuclear forces "must prevail and be able to force the Soviet Union to seek earliest termination of hostilities on terms favorable to the United States." U.S. military forces must be able to "render ineffective the total Soviet (and Soviet-allied) military and political power structure" and be capable "of supporting controlled nuclear counterattacks over a protracted period while maintaining a reserve of nuclear forces sufficient for trans- and post-attack protection and coercion."[47]

In these circumstances, nuclear arms control and disarmament agreements received a very low priority. As Gerard Smith, President Nixon's director of ACDA, observed: "From the beginning of the Reagan regime, a bias against arms control was basic to its strategic thinking." In 1982, the administration decided to end U.S. participation in the negotiations for a comprehensive test ban treaty, which dated back to the 1950s. A CTBT, Reagan decided, was not in the national interest. Thereafter, the Reagan administration increased the frequency of U.S. nuclear testing and initiated a policy of not announcing some of its tests. The administration also abandoned the Threshold Test Ban Treaty, announcing that the verification procedures agreed to by his Republican predecessors were inadequate. SALT II, of course, remained unmentionable, and the administration never submitted the treaty to the U.S. Senate for ratification.[48] In June 1981, Rostow declared that he did not think the Reagan administration would be able to begin formal negotiations with the Soviet Union to limit strategic nuclear weapons until March 1982, adding: "I don't know anyone who knows what it is yet that we want to negotiate about." Paul Nitze told an interviewer in May 1981 that "there could be serious arms control negotiations, but only after we have built up our forces," a process that he predicted would take ten years. Within the National Security Council, McFarlane recalled, Perle and Weinberger teamed up to paralyze progress on arms controls, "stopping any movement before it got started."[49]

Many of these early attitudes and programs fed into National Security Decision Directive 75 (NSDD 75), drawn up by an NSC team during 1982 and signed by Reagan in January 1983. According to McFarlane, who directed the preparation of NSDD 75, it signaled a "clean break with the Soviet policy of the past," for it "repudiated the policy of détente." The document declared that the U.S. task was "competing effectively on a sustained basis with the Soviet Union in all international arenas—particularly in the overall military balance." The United States "must modernize its military forces—both nuclear and conventional," and must sustain "steady, long-term growth in U.S. defense spending and capabilities. . . . This is the most important way of conveying to the Soviets U.S. resolve." Arms control agreements were "not an end in themselves," but should "serve U.S. national security objectives." Thus, "U.S. arms control proposals will be consistent with necessary force modernization plans." In Soviet-American relations, "the U.S. should insist that Moscow address the full range of U.S. concerns . . . and should continue to resist Soviet efforts to return to a U.S.-Soviet agenda focused primarily on arms control."[50] Although NSDD 75 provided a more measured approach to U.S. foreign and military policy than did the administration's glib, off-the-cuff remarks about nuclear war, the priorities were clear enough.

On the March in Other Nations

Although, during these years, the hawks made their greatest political advances in the United States, they were also on the march elsewhere and, particularly, within NATO nations. NATO's military command had disliked the alliance's two-track decision, for the disarmament track left an opportunity open for canceling the deployment of U.S. intermediate range nuclear missiles in Western Europe. Denis Healey, the British Labour government's defense secretary until mid-1979, recalled that "the NATO strategic mafia . . . had recommended the deployment of cruise and Pershing as a necessary step on the ladder of nuclear deterrence . . . and wanted to keep these intermediate range missiles in Europe, even if Russia dismantled the SS-20 missiles to which they were supposed to be a response." Thus, "they opposed the disarmament part of the Dual Track decision; indeed General [Bernard] Rogers at SACEUR said it gave him gas pains."[51] Furthermore, as in the United States, their pressure for a nuclear buildup was given powerful support by conservative parties and governments.

Nowhere was this more evident than in Britain, where the victory of Margaret Thatcher's Conservatives in the spring of 1979 caused a defense policy turnabout as dramatic as the one in the United States. By the beginning of the new decade, the British government had come out against the CTBT, warned about the Russian proposals for compromises on the Euromissiles, expressed skepticism about the value of an early summit meeting, and laid plans for a nuclear buildup, including the deployment of Trident submarines and cruise missiles. Addressing the 1982 U.N. Special Session on Disarmament, Thatcher lashed out at the idea that nuclear weapons endangered the world. She was "convinced," as she recalled, "that much cant was spoken about the arms race, as if by slowing down the process of improving our defenses we would make peace more certain. History had repeatedly demonstrated quite the opposite." Naturally, as McFarlane noted, she and Reagan "were ideological soulmates and had a strong relationship." When she first met Reagan, Thatcher recalled, "I knew that I was talking to someone who instinctively felt and thought as I did." And, with his election,

"I regarded it as my duty to do everything I could to reinforce and further President Reagan's bold strategy to win the Cold War." Indeed, "I was perhaps his principal cheerleader in NATO."[52]

Opponents of arms control were also on the move in West Germany. During the SALT II debate in the United States, German hardliners sought to kill the treaty by leaking information that the German military was opposed to it. Furthermore, the conservative Christian Democrats, out of power at the time of NATO's two-track decision, championed deployment of Western nuclear missiles, regardless of what the Russians might do about the SS-20s. Until the fall of 1981, Christian Democratic leaders scorned the idea of a "zero option" as nonsense, claiming that it merely distracted attention from the necessity of missile deployment. Manfred Wörner, the party's defense spokesperson, assailed the "total illusion of a so-called zero option." During the 1980 election campaign, the Christian Democrats charged that the Social Democratic government's security policies were "halfhearted and insufficient," and that Chancellor Schmidt was "a security risk" to the Atlantic Alliance. Although defeated at the polls, they felt a new surge of hope with Reagan's election. Organizing a pro-Reagan rally in June 1982, they castigated antinuclear demonstrators. A party spokesperson maintained that "a lot" of nuclear disarmament activists were in the pay of the East German regime, and even the "honest people" were "being misled and betrayed." Finally, in October, a change in political alliance by the small Free Democratic Party toppled the Social Democratic–led government and enabled the Christian Democrats to take power.[53]

In other nations, too, military-oriented forces were on the ascendant. In Japan, the hawkish (and misleadingly named) Liberal Democratic Party underwent a revival in the late 1970s, routing its antinuclear rivals on the local level and, in 1980, winning an overwhelming victory in parliamentary elections. Continuing a program begun in 1974, South Africa's apartheid government pressed forward with the development of nuclear weapons.[54] In France, even the Left parties adopted a more hawkish stance. Until 1981, the French Socialist Party had continued to proclaim its opposition to the nuclear arms race, the installation of new missile systems, and the dangers of the bloc system. But the party's victory at the polls that year largely brought an end to this approach. Thereafter, French President François Mitterrand declared his support for installation of Western Euromissiles and NATO rearmament and castigated tendencies toward what he called "neutralism" in Western Europe. The two French Socialist signers of the END Appeal were persuaded by party leaders to withdraw their signatures. Sharing power in the French government, the Communist Party did its best to avoid the nuclear issue or to obscure its views on the subject. Meanwhile, France's non-Communist press assailed disarmament initiatives as pro-Soviet, neutralist, or naive.[55]

Within the Soviet Union, the government leadership did not change substantially, but hawkish tendencies grew. Arbatov recalled that, in the late 1970s, "our military policy and arms industry completely escaped political control. The leadership made the decisions, but the military and the military-industrial agencies prompted those decisions and even managed to 'preprogram' the political leadership." The "military-industrial complex" increased its "strength and influence and . . . skillfully put Brezhnev's patronage and weaknesses to its own good use." Brezhnev viewed the military "as a very important power base" and, also, had a "sentimental" attachment to it, "which grew in proportion to his age and illness." Indeed, the Soviet party secretary "had a passion for military ranks and awards, especially military decorations, something that made him the subject of ridicule." In addition, "Dmitri Ustinov, particularly after he became minister of defense, matched Brezhnev in his sycophancy toward the military. It seemed as if he were trying to prove that a civilian minister could get even more for the military than a professional officer could." This did not translate into reckless military aggression but, rather, into a weapons buildup and a foreign policy lacking in sensitivity to the fears of other nations. Reflecting upon a meeting with Soviet officials in July 1980, Schmidt observed: "Calling them militarists would be an oversimplification. They were merely callous in pursuing Soviet security interests and seemed genuinely surprised that the world reacted by speaking of a Soviet expansionist drive."[56]

With the advent of the Reagan administration, these hawkish tendencies escalated dramatically. In May 1981, amidst the new President's anti-Soviet tirades, Brezhnev delivered a secret address to a major KGB conclave in Moscow, denouncing Reagan's policies and warning that the Soviet Union and the United States stood on the brink of nuclear war. The Soviet premier was followed by Andropov, the KGB director, who told the gathering that the new U.S. administration was actively preparing for nuclear war, including the possible launching of a nuclear first strike. Accordingly, the Politburo had decided that the top priority of Soviet foreign intelligence operations must be the collection of military-strategic data on the looming threat of a U.S. nuclear attack. The Kremlin thus began Operation RYAN—whose Soviet acronym meant Surprise Nuclear Missile Attack—the largest peacetime military intelligence operation in Soviet history. For years thereafter, KGB stations around the world diligently explored every sign that might reveal the imminence of a Western nuclear attack, including increased purchases of blood and rises in the price paid for it. In London, the KGB was ordered to conduct a regular census of lighted windows at all government buildings and military installations involved in preparing for nuclear war, and to report immediately any deviations from the norm. Meanwhile, the Kremlin's ICBMs stood ready, every day, to respond to Western preparations by launching a devastating missile strike.[57]

This KGB alert was paralleled by a rapid buildup and mobilization of Soviet military might. Arbatov recalled: "The strengthening and consolidation of the conservative forces in the United States exercised an influence on the political situation in the Soviet Union. This forced us to spend more on defense and to pay even greater heed to the opinions of the military." To counter deployment of Pershing II missiles, Soviet officials decided to preserve the ABM system around Moscow (which had been allowed under the ABM treaty, but which they were planning to dismantle), to build a new, ground-launched, high-speed missile (Skorost) to attack them, and to place SS-20 missiles in a position where they could devastate the northwestern United States. According to Vladimir Slipchenko, who served on the Soviet General Staff, Reagan's "evil empire" speech was widely noticed in the Soviet Union. "The military, the armed forces . . . really used this declaration," he recalled, "as a reason to begin a very intense preparation inside the military for a state of war. . . . A very intense inspection plan was started to be sure that our arms were ready for action." In addition, "we started to run huge strategic exercises. . . . These were the first military exercises in which we really tested our mobilization. We didn't just exercise the ground forces but also the strategic arms." Thus, "for the military, the period when we were called the evil empire was actually very good and useful, because we achieved a very high military readiness. . . . We also rehearsed the situation when a non-nuclear war might turn into a nuclear war."[58]

Not surprisingly, then, in the early 1980s U.S.-Soviet diplomatic relations went into a deep freeze. By mid-1982, recalled Secretary of State Shultz, "relations between the two superpowers were not simply bad; they were virtually nonexistent." Under different circumstances, Soviet policy might have softened somewhat thereafter, for Brezhnev died that November and was succeeded as party secretary by Andropov. Although a committed Communist, Andropov was an intelligent, sophisticated political figure who had kept his lines out to party reformers, shielding them on occasion from conservative attack. Furthermore, unlike Brezhnev, he was not especially close to the military. Nevertheless, like his predecessors, he deeply distrusted the West, which he believed threatened the Soviet Union with war. Moreover, as indicated by the KGB's unprecedented campaign to locate signs of a NATO surprise nuclear attack, the advent of the Reagan administration raised his level of paranoia substantially. Speaking with his young protégé, Gorbachev, Andropov remarked bitterly: "With this administration we cannot do anything."[59]

The Meaning of Victory

Consequently, thanks to the rise of the hawks, the world moved ever closer to the brink of catastrophe. By late 1983, progress on nuclear arms controls had ground to a halt. Indeed, that fall, nuclear arms control negotiations were abandoned entirely. Although the world's stockpile of nuclear weapons, 97 percent of them possessed by the United States and the Soviet Union, had a destructiveness equivalent to 2,700 times the explosive energy released in all the battles of World War II,[60] both countries, viewing these as inadequate to meet their needs, pressed forward with plans for the development of new nuclear weapons—faster, deadlier, and more accurate than ever before. Moreover, in the midst of glib official talk of nuclear war and increasing planning for it, such a war seemed ever more likely. Even the Reagan administration, while pursuing its nuclear buildup, recognized the seriousness of the situation. In March 1983, the President proposed a Strategic Defense Initiative—soon dubbed "Star Wars"—to defend the United States from a nuclear attack. Implicit in this program was the assumption that nuclear deterrence no longer worked and, therefore, that the nation must prepare itself for nuclear war.[61]

These nuclear policies, however, did not rest upon a strong base of popular support, for the rise of the hawks was unrelated to their stand on nuclear weapons. In the United States, as Wirthlin noted, the 1980 campaign was "fought primarily on the grounds of economic issues," specifically "the fact that the Carter administration failed so miserably in terms of unemployment and inflation." Furthermore, although it is true that, between 1977 and 1980, the percentage of Americans believing that too little was spent on defense rose from 24 to 56 percent, this appears to have reflected the growing sense of frustration Americans felt in dealing with a world beyond their control. The Iranian hostage crisis, more than any other foreign policy issue, contributed to this turnabout and to Carter's political demise. But the crisis in Iran had nothing to do with nuclear weapons. Moreover, its devastating effect on Carter's political fortunes did not override the public's deep-seated fear of Reagan's hawkishness. Thus, although polls showed that the public favored Reagan over Carter as the candidate who would preserve America's military strength, the public also believed—by a margin of 28 points—that

Reagan was "most likely to get the United States into another war." Consequently, when the two candidates were compared on foreign policy, polls showed Carter with a small advantage. As one public opinion analyst has concluded: "Ronald Reagan won the 1980 presidential election despite widespread public reservations about his foreign policy."[62]

The hawkish rise elsewhere also had no connection with nuclear weapons. In Britain, as opinion polls indicated, during Margaret Thatcher's first years in office, she was a very unpopular prime minister. However, in the aftermath of the Falklands War—which, in the spring of 1982, led to a decisive British military victory over Argentina—her standing in the polls doubled. In her memoirs, even Thatcher gave Britain's victory credit for her substantially improved political standing. "The outcome of the Falklands War transformed the British political scene," she wrote. "I could feel the impact of the victory wherever I went." Her political fortunes were also enhanced very considerably when a breakaway group from the opposition Labour Party organized a third party that siphoned off large numbers of Labour votes.[63] Similarly, in West Germany, Franz Josef Straus—whose hawkish views led to his image as an extremist—was resoundingly defeated by the more moderate Schmidt in the 1980 election for chancellor. In Japan, the ruling conservatives carefully avoided challenging the antinuclear consensus in the country, including the government's proclaimed "three non-nuclear principles," by insisting, apparently falsely, that U.S. warships did not bring nuclear weapons into Japanese ports.[64]

Even in NATO nations, the public much preferred arms controls to a nuclear buildup. In March 1981, a U.S. government-sponsored poll asked respondents in six West European countries about the best way for their country to improve its security: "by pushing harder for arms control negotiations to try to reduce military forces on both sides" or "by strengthening its military forces to help NATO maintain a balance of military power with the East." The results were not encouraging for supporters of strengthening the West's nuclear weapons capabilities. The arms controllers outnumbered the weapons proponents by 40 to 31 percent in Britain, 50 to 18 percent in France, 60 to 22 percent in Italy, 44 to 21 percent in the Netherlands, and 35 to 21 percent in West Germany. Only in Norway—where there was an even split—did the arms controllers fail to predominate.[65]

Thus, by the early 1980s, although hawkish forces held office in a number of powerful countries, their ability to fully implement their program for a nuclear buildup and, if necessary, nuclear war, remained problematic. Much of the public—and certainly the nuclear disarmament movement, which was beginning to gain popular attention and sympathy—preferred

nuclear arms controls. And many viewed such a buildup as a dangerous escalation of the nuclear arms race. Therefore, the potential existed for very
substantial conflict between hawkish governments on the hand and an antinuclear public on the other. After all, it was one thing to provide for the
common defense and quite another to make serious plans for the waging of
nuclear war. Much of the public knew the difference, even if many of the
hawks did not.

Revolt of the Doves

The Movement in Northern Europe, 1981-85

> We are becoming good democrats, rising up non-
> violently against the arms race in East and West. . . .
> No Euroshima!
>
> Petra Kelly, 1982

During the early 1980s, the reaction to the rise of the hawks was widespread and stormy, especially in Northern Europe. Here, despite the commitment of most governments to NATO's nuclear buildup, peace and disarmament groups burgeoned into mass movements of unprecedented size and intensity. Major cities were swept by vast nuclear disarmament marches and rallies—in many cases, the largest political demonstrations in their history.[1] Furthermore, powerful social institutions—including labor federations, religious bodies, and Social Democratic parties—threw their weight behind the antinuclear campaigns. The strength of these campaigns and the willingness of mainstream social institutions to support them both reflected and encouraged the development of antinuclear opinion. Repeated surveys of Britain, the Netherlands, Norway, and West Germany found substantial portions of their populations listing nuclear weapons as among their "greatest concerns."[2] Majorities or pluralities of Northern Europeans also opposed the deployment of cruise, Pershing II, and SS-20 missiles and preferred negotiating arms controls to maintaining a military balance with the Soviet Union.[3] Although the Euromissiles provided a focal point of protest up to November 1983, when the NATO deployment began, even thereafter they stirred large numbers of people to resistance.

Behind this protest campaign lay not only widespread opposition to the nuclear buildup, but a belief that, with nuclear weapons enthusiasts controlling major governments, a nuclear conflagration was becoming more likely.

Surveys of Northern European opinion found a dramatic rise in fears of war and, particularly, of nuclear war. Between 1977 and 1980, the percentage of people expecting a nuclear war within the next decade rose from 13 to 39 percent in Britain, and from 14 to 34 percent throughout the European Economic Community. Thereafter, with the advent of the Reagan administration, which large numbers of Northern Europeans viewed as dangerous and irresponsible, the fear of nuclear war escalated. There had "been decisions about new weapons systems before, and people didn't get so upset," recalled END's Mary Kaldor. But "now an American administration was really talking about fighting . . . a nuclear war in Europe. That brought it home very vividly."[4] Confronted with what they felt was an imminent nuclear catastrophe, millions of irate Europeans mobilized to roll back the nuclear menace.

Britain

In Britain, the general public, appalled by the militarist rhetoric and policies of the early 1980s, flooded into the Campaign for Nuclear Disarmament. CND's national membership soared from 9,000 in 1980 to over 100,000 by early 1985, and local membership, dispersed in more than a thousand local groups, was reported to number in the hundreds of thousands.[5] In October 1981, CND turned out an unprecedented 250,000 antinuclear demonstrators for a rally in Hyde Park. In June 1982, to protest the visit of President Reagan, it repeated the feat—a remarkable show of strength at the height of the popular Falklands War.[6] Other demonstrations, while smaller, were nonetheless dramatic. In April 1983, CND mobilized 70,000 Britons—ranging from well-dressed grandmothers to babies in strollers—to form a 14-mile human chain that linked three government nuclear weapons centers.[7] As membership climbed, CND developed specialist sections that sponsored their own activities and did outreach work to specific constituencies; they included Labour CND, Green CND, Liberal CND, Trade Union CND, and Christian CND.[8] CND leaflets drew on testimonials from prominent figures in the nation's cultural life, such as actress Susannah York and writer Salman Rushdie. Under the dynamic leadership of Joan Ruddock (chair) and Bruce Kent (secretary), CND became the largest, most active, single issue organization in Britain.[9]

Although CND's membership in the early 1980s was much larger than during its upsurge in the late 1950s and early 1960s, its constituency remained much the same. Surveys found that CND members came overwhelmingly from the middle class, particularly the well-educated middle class, with occupations heavily concentrated in the education, human welfare, and creative sectors. Indeed, a survey in 1982 found that half of CND members could be categorized as "professionals," and that another 20 percent were students. Only about 5 percent were blue collar workers. In politics, CND members usually could be found clustered on the left side of the spectrum; 67 percent voted for the Labour Party, another 15 percent voted for the more moderate Social Democratic and Liberal Party Alliance, and 10 percent for the Greens, with the balance scattered among the smaller parties. Exactly half of CND members were women, and nearly half fell into the 25- to 40-year-old age group. When asked why they joined CND, many members cited moral revulsion at weapons of mass destruction; others just responded "Thatcher" or "Reagan." Survey after survey found that the people most likely to join CND were youthful, socially concerned members of the university-educated middle class.[10]

When it came to program, CND often downplayed unilateralism in favor of more modest demands. Its literature pointed out that it favored *both* unilateral and multilateral nuclear disarmament as steps toward the creation of a nuclear-free world. In 1985, there was an effort to amend the CND constitution by replacing the call for Britain's unilateral nuclear disarmament with a call for "independent" British action, but purists insisted upon retaining the reference to unilateralism.[11] Furthermore, during these years, CND devoted most of its energy to opposing the latest round in the nuclear arms race—the deployment of cruise, Pershing II, and SS-20 nuclear missiles in Europe and Britain's purchase of Trident nuclear submarines.[12] It also threw itself into opposing civil defense exercises. Work on the latter was facilitated by sympathetic local city councils, which, starting with Manchester's council in November 1980, began to declare their cities nuclear-free zones. In 1982, CND and the nuclear-free zone movement—which had grown to more than 120 local jurisdictions, including all of Wales—joined forces to block government plans for a nationwide civil defense drill.[13]

For the most part, CND's leaders worked, successfully, to avoid extraneous issues, however worthy, and to keep the organization focused on the necessity for nuclear disarmament. Although CND did criticize the British war in the Falklands, U.S. policy toward Nicaragua, and martial law in Poland, it did so in the context of associated nuclear dangers.[14] As condemning government abuses of human rights also raised the specter of distracting CND from its central concern, it generally kept clear of such issues. But it did consider the defense of "peace rights" appropriate, and consequently protested repeatedly against government persecution of independent disarmament activists in Eastern Europe (e.g. in the Soviet Union and East Germany) and Western Europe (e.g. in Turkey).[15] Some tangential projects never got off the ground. In light of the fact that NATO was a nuclear-armed alliance, delegates at CND national conferences approved British withdrawal from NATO by a very narrow margin. But the measure lacked support from most CND leaders and members and, consequently, never became a serious organizational priority.[16] Ultimately, as most activists recognized, what CND did best was to arouse the nation to the dangers of the nuclear arms race. Through a blizzard of meetings, demonstrations, leaflets, public statements, and other forms of popular agitation, it helped create a widespread debate within Britain on nuclear weapons and nuclear war.[17]

Although CND was by far the largest and most powerful of Britain's nuclear disarmament organizations, others also flourished in the early 1980s, particularly within the professions. Among them were Teachers for Peace, Journalists Against Nuclear Extermination, Lawyers for Nuclear Disarmament, the Medical Campaign Against Nuclear Weapons, Scientists Against Nuclear Arms, Clergy Against Nuclear Arms, Pax Christi, and Women for Peace.[18] Scientists Against Nuclear Arms played an important role in opposing civil defense exercises, while groups of antinuclear teachers—often supported by students and parents—created peace education programs in the schools. To popularize the cause of nuclear disarmament, sympathetic musicians organized No Nukes Music, which by mid-1981 had 18 affiliated groups.[19] Meanwhile, antinuclear defense intellectuals—some of them veteran peace activists—participated in an Alternative Defense Commission which, in 1983, published a massive study, *Defense Without the Bomb*.[20] Although the World Disarmament Campaign remained in the shadow of the far more dynamic CND, it did gather 2.25 million British signatures on a petition calling for multilateral nuclear disarmament; moreover, a variety of peace groups continued to use its literature.[21] Similarly, a Nuclear Freeze campaign, modeled on the American, emerged in Britain in 1983 and 1984. Although it failed to produce much activism, it did appeal briefly to some of the more "moderate" peace groups.[22]

The best-known disarmament venture that developed independently of CND was the women's peace camp at Greenham Common. In August 1981, a group of 36 women, calling themselves Women for Life on Earth, set out on a 120-mile walk from Cardiff, Wales, to the proposed cruise missile deployment site: the U.S. air force base at Greenham Common, England. Upon their arrival, they demanded a debate with the British government on nuclear weapons. When the government ignored them, the women established a peace camp outside the base. In 1982, amid rising feminist agitation against the missiles, the Greenham Common peace camp became a women-only site, with activists declaring that it was time to "take the toys away from the boys." Protests and demonstrations multiplied, leading to a growing number of arrests. On December 12, 1982, in response to a call for action, 30,000 women from across the nation appeared at the nine-mile military fence surrounding the base, adorning it with children's pictures and other decorations—symbols of the life the nuclear missiles would destroy. Later that day, they linked arms to "embrace the base," and that night television news carried aerial shots of the miles of women holding glowing candles and encircling it. In the ensuing months and years, thousands of women activists settled in at Greenham Common to continue resistance efforts—blocking the gates with their bodies, cutting or pulling down the perimeter fence (including four miles of it on October 29, 1983), painting peace symbols on U.S. planes, and even dancing and singing defiantly atop the cruise missile silos. Buffeted by icy storms in winter, evicted from their tent colonies repeatedly (and sometimes brutally), assailed as bizarre and disreputable by the mass media, the women of Greenham Common hung on tenaciously.[23]

By refusing to disperse and let the government get on with its nuclear war preparations, the Greenham women also posed a challenge to Britain's nuclear disarmament movement. Was a "women's peace movement"—one that excluded men—really a good idea? After all, plenty of men were antinuclear activists. Furthermore, women comprised half of the CND leadership and played a very important role in its operations. The dilemma posed by events at Greenham seemed to be symbolized by the scene on December 12, 1982, in which male peace movement activists looked on, uselessly, from the surrounding woods, as their wives, daughters, lovers, and friends confronted the police. Furthermore, activism at Greenham raised the issue of civil disobedience, which had created a serious rift within CND during the early 1960s. Ultimately, though, both issues were resolved satisfactorily. Whatever their qualms about gender segregation within the movement, CND leaders sympathized with the Greenham women's sprightly resistance to the nuclear arms race. Also, they were impressed by the enormous energy it unleashed among women—not only at Greenham Common, but at Molesworth and throughout the rest of Britain, where similar peace camps emerged. Moreover, although most CND members preferred educational to illegal activities, CND did vote to support "well-considered" non-violent resistance. As a result, male CND activists adapted to the women's peace camps—ferrying in supplies, making tea for the women, and taking on childcare responsibilities at home—while CND leaders joined in civil disobedience actions.[24]

As the nuclear disarmament movement swept forward, it won major victories among British unions and political parties. At the 1981 annual conference of the Trades Union Congress, delegates adopted a resolution calling for Britain's unilateral nuclear disarmament, and followed that up in 1982 and 1983 with resolutions demanding the removal of all nuclear bases from Britain. Although the rank and file did not always share this antinuclear fervor, it was certainly dominant among union activists and leaders. By 1985, some 28 national unions, representing a majority of British union members, had formally affiliated with CND. In turn, CND's strength within the unions had a substantial impact on the Labour Party, which passed antinuclear resolutions at its 1981 annual conference and, in 1982, adopted a unilateralist resolution by a two-thirds majority. This overwhelming support by the delegates for the creation of a non-nuclear Britain, combined with the election of Michael Foot, a longtime CND activist, as party leader, made it certain that unilateralism would provide a key component of the Labour Party platform in the forthcoming election. Foot and deputy party leader Denis Healey also proposed multilateralist measures, including, in 1981, a "zero option" for the Euromissiles. However, that fall, when they suggested it to Brezhnev, his response was negative and the Conservative press denounced it.[25] In addition, the smaller parties of the Center developed their own nuclear critique. The Liberal Party, though rejecting unilateralism, committed itself to abandoning the independent British nuclear deterrent and split on cruise missile deployment. The Social Democratic Party, formed in 1981 by bolters from the Labour Party, opposed the Trident program. Both parties, which joined together for election purposes as the Alliance, condemned the Thatcher government for escalating the nuclear arms race and called for multilateral nuclear disarmament.[26]

Criticism of nuclear weapons also made headway among religious groups. Polls found that church members comprised 23 percent of CND's constituency, and Christian CND played a very active role in mobilizing them—holding antinuclear religious services and publishing its own magazine. Furthermore, a number of the smaller Protestant denominations took unilateralist stands, including the Society of Friends, the Church of Scotland, the United Reform Church, and the Baptist Church. The Methodist Church opposed the deployment of cruise missiles, the acquisition of Trident, and the use (though not the possession) of nuclear weapons in any circumstances.[27] But the far larger and more powerful Church of England—sometimes described as the Tory party at prayer—was considerably less critical of official nuclear policy. Although, in 1982, a church working party published a report, *The Church and the Bomb*, that called for Britain's unilateral renunciation of nuclear weapons, a meeting of the General Synod in

February 1983 rejected it by a vote of more than three to one. On the other hand, while endorsing nuclear deterrence, the Church of England proclaimed that "there is a moral obligation on all countries publicly to forswear the first use of nuclear weapons."[28] Although Roman Catholics—like other members of Britain's minority churches—were disproportionately numerous among CND's church members, the official church position on nuclear weapons combined expressions of dismay at the arms race with an endorsement of deterrence as a temporary measure. The church hierarchy viewed Monsignor Bruce Kent's prominent role in CND with some embarrassment, though it did defend him against the papal nuncio's charge that he and other people who supported unilateral nuclear disarmament were "useful idiots" of the Kremlin. Overall, the center of gravity among Britain's religious bodies fell somewhere between CND's position and that of the government.[29]

By contrast, the ruling Conservative Party took a staunchly pro-nuclear position, and denounced CND at every opportunity. Its chair, John Selwyn Gummer, played a key role in lobbying the Church of England on behalf of government policy. Often, it functioned through a network of "New Right" organizations directed by Conservative MPs and operatives. Producing masses of literature and frequent public statements, these groups charged that Britain's disarmament campaign was "manipulated by pro-Soviet apologists in one of the most brilliantly orchestrated propaganda offensives." The "well-dressed CND activist," they claimed, wore a "KGB hat" and carried an appeasement umbrella that was "standard issue" from the "Bulgarian secret service." Overprinting the peace sign with the hammer and sickle, they termed it "the symbol of Communists, Neutralists, Defeatists." One of the key groups, the Coalition for Peace through Security, used loudspeakers to disrupt CND events, denounced Bruce Kent as a supporter of IRA terrorism, and flew a plane over CND's April 1983 demonstration trailing a banner that proclaimed: "CND—Kremlin's April Fools." It also placed a spy—a flying saucer enthusiast who claimed to have been a youth affairs advisor to President Nixon—in CND's office.[30] Winston Churchill, grandson of the wartime prime minister and a Conservative Party spokesman on arms issues, helped coordinate the activities of these New Right groups, charging that CND was "stuffed full of Communists, Marxists, and International Socialists." Although these Conservative front groups often refused to reveal their sources of funding, some, at least, obtained it from conservative organizations in the United States, with which they worked closely, and, directly or indirectly, from the British and American governments.[31]

Britain's communications media also worked at undermining the antinuclear campaign. Although CND received respectful attention in the *Guardian*, probably the nation's best newspaper, almost all the rest of the press either failed to cover its activities or trivialized it by ignoring its arguments and emphasizing bizarre behavior. As one CND press officer complained, what most of the press wanted and produced was "Blondes Boobs Bollocks." Occasionally, the press defamed CND through scurrilous attacks. In late 1983, the *Evening Standard* produced the banner headline: "CND Holds Hands with the IRA." Although the newspaper subsequently apologized, it later published an article claiming that Kent, among other disarmament activists, saw only one paradise left in Eastern Europe: Albania. "Having never maintained that there were any paradises in Eastern Europe, let alone Albania," recalled Kent, "I felt somewhat miffed." In the conservative press, the Greenham Common women were described as radicals, lesbians, communists, traitors, deserters of their families, and "cut-priced Delilahs."[32] Radio and television were fairer, but not much. In 1981, the BBC withdrew its invitation to E. P. Thompson to deliver the prestigious Dimbleby Lecture, and kept him off the air thereafter. Although the massive CND and Greenham Common demonstrations of 1982 and 1983 did draw television news coverage, it tended to concentrate on *what* happened rather than *why* it happened. Rarely were TV viewers allowed to hear what the speakers at CND rallies actually said.[33]

Although CND was frequently depicted by Conservatives—and sometimes by the mass media—as funded by the Kremlin and dominated by Communists, the reality was quite different. CND's income—never very great—came in small amounts from its members and from its sale of literature. To dispel Conservative charges of Moscow funding, Bruce Kent even offered a prize of 100 pounds to anyone who could produce evidence of it. The prize was never claimed. Of course, as a citizens' organization, CND was open to people of all political persuasions. And some Communists did join it, though not very many. A 1985 survey of CND members found that only 0.3 percent were Communist Party members and that only 1 percent favored Communist candidates in elections. Nor did Communists succeed in capturing the top CND leadership posts. Joan Ruddock, a Labour Party supporter, soundly defeated a Communist candidate for the post of CND chair in 1981. In 1985, when Ruddock left this position to seek election to Parliament, another Communist ran for the post of CND chair, only to place a distant last in a field of five candidates.[34] Although Trotskyites occasionally created internal difficulties for CND, particularly within its youth division, CND's leaders worked to limit their influence. Scoffing at those who assumed that "Moscow organized us all," Kent observed: "It's dim, really."[35]

Given CND's rapid growth and increasing clout, Britain's June 1983 parliamentary election results came as a blow to antinuclear activists.[36] Led by Michael Foot, the Labour Party stood by its commitment to unilateralism, although it emphasized canceling Trident, cruise missile deployment, and the development of all new nuclear weapons as the first steps in building a non-nuclear Britain. The Conservatives and most of the press pilloried Labour mercilessly for what they claimed were one-sided disarmament, the abandonment of the nation's defense, and playing Moscow's game. "The only alternative to nuclear deterrence," argued Thatcher, "is surrender or capitulation." The Tories and the press also hammered away at divisions within the Labour Party, particularly after former Labour Prime Minister James Callaghan issued a statement dissociating himself from Labour's defense policy.[37] These factors, together with an inept campaign by Labour, the popularity of the Falklands war, and a swing by voters to the new Liberal-Social Democratic Alliance, led to a stunning defeat for the Labour Party, whose share of the vote dropped from 36.9 percent in 1979 to 28.3 percent in 1983. And yet, although the Conservatives secured an overwhelming majority in parliament, the election was not an endorsement of the government's nuclear policy, either. Polls found that unemployment outranked nuclear disarmament by far as the most important issue for voters. Furthermore, the Conservative share of the vote *also* declined, from 47 to 44 percent. Indeed, the new Alliance Party had done almost as well as the Labour Party, and together these two antinuclear groups had substantially outpolled the Conservatives.[38]

In the immediate aftermath of the election, Defense Minister Michael Heseltine proclaimed happily that CND was dead and buried. But, in fact, the antinuclear movement continued to grow and to inspire support. Between 1983 and 1985, CND's national membership expanded from 75,000 to over 100,000. With the exception of the Conservative Party, CND had attained the largest membership of any political organization in Britain. Furthermore, during these years its annual income rose from 461,000 pounds to 782,000 pounds and the number of its paid staff to a record forty.[39] In October 1983, when CND held an antinuclear rally in Hyde Park, an estimated 400,000 people participated in what may have been the largest demonstration in British history.[40] Nor, despite the depressing election outcome, did the Labour Party jettison its support for Britain's unilateral nuclear disarmament. Neil Kinnock, chosen to succeed Foot as party leader, spoke at CND's October 1983 rally and, the following year, guided the Labour Party toward a clarification of its stand in favor of a non-nuclear Britain, a position convention delegates endorsed by a four-to-one margin.[41] Meanwhile, the number of localities declaring themselves nuclear-free zones continued to grow, reaching 155 by October 1983, and they continued their close liaison with CND. Eventually, the national government found itself so embattled with some of these elected authorities on civil defense and related issues that it began to abolish them.[42]

Public sentiment, as well, frequently conflicted with national government policy. To be sure, opinion polls in the early 1980s consistently found that substantial majorities opposed Britain's unilateral nuclear disarmament and, moreover, favored maintaining the nuclear weapons already located in Britain.[43] Furthermore, probably as a result of the media attacks, public sympathy for antinuclear demonstrators—which polls reported at 52 percent in November 1981 and 54 percent in February 1983—declined somewhat thereafter, particularly with respect to the women at Greenham Common.[44] Even so, in nearly every instance polls found pluralities or majorities of the public—ranging from 48 to 61 percent—opposed to the deployment of cruise missiles in Britain. A large majority of Britons also opposed the purchase of Trident nuclear submarines. On both issues, women proved more antinuclear than men.[45] In addition, although NATO policy was to employ nuclear weapons to respond to a conventional attack upon Western Europe, a May 1984 poll found that 24 percent of the public would not use them under any circumstances, 51 percent would use them only if the Soviets used them first, and only 18 percent would use them "against an overwhelming conventional attack." Large number of Britons believed that a nuclear war was likely—reaching a peak of 49 percent in February 1983—and many blamed this on the policies of the Reagan administration.[46] That December, 70 percent said that U.S. policies increased the risks of war. In October 1983, a *Guardian* poll reported that 65 percent of Britons thought the United States and the Soviet Union were equally to blame for the arms race, while a *Times* poll found that only 16 percent trusted the Americans and 5 percent the Russians. Furthermore, during the early 1980s, British opinion gradually shifted from a belief that the U.S. government was making a genuine effort to reach an arms control agreement to a belief that it was not.[47]

The Netherlands

In the Netherlands, the antinuclear movement was even stronger. The Interchurch Peace Council (IKV), headed by a young mathematician, Mient Jan Faber, expanded to some 400 groups functioning on a local or parish level. Championing a step-by-step approach "away from the dynamics of the nuclear arms race and from the brink of nuclear disaster," IKV played the dominant role in the massive Dutch antinuclear effort. But other major peace organizations in the campaign included the still-powerful Stop the Neutron Bomb movement, the 28,000 member Pax Christi, and Women for Peace, the Dutch branch of the emerging women's peace movement. Working together, some nine peace groups, seven political parties, and the nation's trade union federation formed the No Cruise Missiles Committee (Komitee Kruisraketten Nee, KKN). It staged anti-missile rallies of 400,000 people in Amsterdam in November 1981 and 550,000 people in The Hague in October 1983—the largest demonstrations ever held in the Netherlands. (Demonstrations with an equivalent portion of the U.S. population would number 6.2 million and 8.5 million people.) In 1985, 3.75 million people signed an anti-missile petition presented to the prime minister—an all-time record for a Dutch petition. Attending an IKV meeting in Haarlem, a *Wall Street Journal* reporter found himself surrounded by earnest, typical Dutch citizens who had no use whatsoever for the new U.S. and Soviet nuclear missiles. "Why on earth are they making these weapons?" a fruit seller remarked. "They'd be better off making something else."[48]

The Dutch movement's primary effort went into pressuring the nation's parliament to reject NATO's plan for deployment of cruise missiles in the country—an effort that continued throughout the early 1980s, as the parliament stalled rather than give the go-ahead.[49] But the campaign also had wider dimensions. In early May 1984, KKN organized a nationwide action week to illustrate the broad popular resistance to Euromissile deployment. Reportedly, about 560 local groups put together 2,000 antinuclear ventures in cities and villages throughout the country, including special church services and vigils, a strike staged by union members and joined by students, and demonstrations at military bases and in provincial capitals. This local focus to much of the campaign resulted in a significant impact on the grassroots level, and some 200 Dutch townships declared themselves nuclear-free zones. They included Woensdrecht, the proposed site for cruise missile deployment.[50] IKV also fostered an international program—protesting government repression of peace groups in Eastern Europe and Turkey[51] and, in addition, defending the rights of dissident movements like Solidarity in Poland and Charter 77 in Czechoslovakia.[52] Indeed, IKV became the leading force within the world peace movement for bypassing national governments and generating "détente from below."[53] In addition, small nonviolent direct action groups employed civil disobedience on a few occasions—for example, in June 1984, when some 8,000 protesters blockaded the entrances to the military base at Woensdrecht. But IKV, Pax Christi, and most other groups in KKN opposed direct action, fearing that it would upset the coalition, antagonize potential supporters, and fail to have much political impact; as a result, civil disobedience did not become a major element in the Dutch campaign.[54]

That campaign made extraordinary progress within major social institutions. After 1981, the Federation of Netherlands Labor Unions became an active participant in the KKN, backing national anti-missile demonstrations and local peace initiatives. Women's organizations, including those with a traditional orientation, also emerged as an important component of the antinuclear struggle.[55] The greatest source of the movement's strength, however, lay in the support it mobilized within the Dutch churches. Prodded by IKV, which had been created by the churches and which continued to enjoy their support, the synods of the two main Protestant bodies continued their antinuclear stand in the early 1980s, coming out with public proclamations opposing cruise missile deployment. Meanwhile, Pax Christi pressed the Roman Catholic Church to end its "tolerance" of nuclear weapons. In response, the Roman Catholic bishops issued a pastoral letter in June 1983 that opposed the deployment of new missiles, said that the use of nuclear weapons was impermissible, and approved unilateral steps as one means to halt the arms race. These strong antinuclear positions, together with that of the National Council of Churches, created substantial internal polarization, causing the Dutch churches, by 1985, to be less vocal in expressing their nuclear critique. Even so, in a nation with a substantial majority of churchgoers, the support of all the major churches gave the movement, and certainly IKV, enormous legitimacy.[56]

Despite the movement's strength within the Christian churches, it had far less impact upon the Christian Democrats—the churches' electoral arm—than on the secular parties to their left. Thanks to proportional representation, the Netherlands had a multitude of political parties, but three blocs, led by the three largest parties, maneuvered for power. Occupying the political Center, the Christian Democrats usually played the key role in forming a coalition government with the major party to their left (the Social Democrats) or to their right (the Liberals). As things turned out, the antinuclear movement made its greatest headway within the parties of the Left—most significantly, the Social Democratic party, which staunchly opposed the deployment of cruise missiles. By contrast, the Christian Democratic Party was split, with a clear majority favoring deployment and a minority opposing it. According to a poll taken at the October 1983 antinuclear rally, 91.8 percent of the demonstrators backed the Social Democrats and the smaller leftwing parties, while only 1.3 percent supported the Christian Democrats. The Liberals enthusiastically endorsed missile deployment. In

the elections of 1982—in which views on Euromissiles did not seem to affect voting behavior—the Social Democrats emerged as the largest party,
but their rivals had more than enough seats to form a Center-Right coalition
government. Even so, because a small bloc of Christian Democratic deputies threatened to vote with the Social Democrats against missile deployment, the governing coalition of Christian Democrats and Liberals lacked
the votes necessary to push the measure through parliament.[57]

Behind the deadlock in parliament lay the antinuclear state of public
opinion. Between 1981 and 1985, polls found that the public opposed cruise
missile deployment by about two-to-one, with opposition fluctuating from
slightly over 50 percent to about 70 percent of the population. Polls on the
neutron bomb showed opposition ranging between three-to-one and six-to-
one.[58] Nor did the population favor the NATO policy of responding to an
overwhelming Soviet conventional attack with nuclear weapons. Surveys
found that only 11 to 19 percent of the population supported this position,
while pluralities ranging from 36 to 50 percent said that nuclear weapons
should not be used under any circumstances.[59] Naturally, these attitudes
translated into unfavorable views of the U.S. nuclear buildup. Asked in
April 1981 whether they thought "the foreign policy direction taken by the
United States under President Reagan is more likely to improve or more
likely to harm East-West relations," 14 percent chose the former and 48 percent the latter. That December, asked how much confidence they had "in
the ability of the United States to deal responsibly with world problems," 56
percent responded "not very much" or "none at all." In a 1983 survey, 49
percent said that the United States presented just as great a threat to world
peace as did the Soviet Union. A May 1984 survey reported that the Dutch
public, by 44 to 14 percent, believed that U.S. policies during the past year
had done more to increase the risk of war than to promote peace.[60]

As poll after poll indicated, nuclear arms control and disarmament had
very substantial backing in the Netherlands. Asked in March 1981 if they favored "pushing harder for arms control negotiations to try to reduce military
forces on both sides" or strengthening "military forces to help NATO
maintain a balance of power with the East," the Dutch chose the former by
44 to 21 percent. Similarly, that July, 56 percent said the West should begin
arms control talks as soon as possible, while only 10 percent favored
strengthening its nuclear forces first. Polls found that up to 85 percent of the
Dutch population favored the removal of all nuclear weapons from the
Netherlands through multilateral action, and that as much as 56 percent
backed it through unilateral action.[61] Such sentiments fed into very favorable appraisals of the nuclear disarmament movement. In late 1981, after the

first of the massive anti-missile demonstrations, polls reported that 79 percent of Dutch respondents were sympathetic to the demonstrators. Shortly before the October 1983 rally, another survey found 62 percent in sympathy with them.[62] Yet, although action for nuclear disarmament enjoyed broad popular support, polls found antinuclear sentiments strongest among the best educated, women, young people, humanists, people without a religion, and those with a leftwing orientation. Opinion analysts discovered that the percentage of the population with antinuclear views did not increase during this period; instead, it remained rather stable. But, thanks to the nuclear disarmament campaign, antinuclear sentiment did become more salient.[63]

Belgium

In neighboring Belgium, the movement was nearly as strong. The Flemish north was more pacifist in orientation than the Walloon south and, perhaps for this reason, the Flemish VAKA tended to favor unilateral steps while the Francophone CNAPD emphasized bilateral moves toward nuclear disarmament. Nevertheless, VAKA and CNAPD—both coalitions of peace groups, unions, churches, and political organizations—worked closely together to oppose the deployment of nuclear missiles in Western Europe, to support the dismantling of SS-20 missiles in Eastern Europe, to call for the creation of a European denuclearized zone, and to demand an independent peace policy by their country. In October 1981, they mobilized 200,000 people for an antinuclear protest in Brussels, the largest demonstration in Belgium's history. Two years later, once again in Brussels, they doubled that turnout.[64] In April 1984, VAKA and CNAPD drew some 20,000 people to the proposed cruise missile site at Florennes, where they formed a human chain around its ten-mile perimeter. As in the Netherlands, local committees did much of the antinuclear work—organizing meetings, promoting peace education, and distributing circulars, posters, and petitions. By the fall of 1982, more than 150 Belgian townships had declared themselves nuclear-free zones.[65]

The antinuclear campaign also made substantial progress within Belgium's mainstream institutions. Labor unions placed their influence behind it and, in July 1983, the Catholic bishops weighed in with an official statement, "Disarmament for Peace," that buttressed the campaign's legitimacy. Although the bishops did not completely reject nuclear deterrence, they sanctioned it only as a temporary stage on the road to nuclear disarmament, which they said could be achieved by unilateral and multilateral steps.[66] Belgium's political parties took positions on nuclear issues roughly along the lines of their counterparts in the Netherlands, with the exception that, as a reflection of the split of the parties along Flemish and Walloon lines, there were two of each kind. Thus, the nation's two Socialist parties (leaders of the Left), took an anti-missile stand, and its two Liberal parties (leaders of the Right) fully backed missile deployment. Belgium's two Christian Democratic parties (the major Center parties) were divided on the missile issue, with the leadership supporting deployment and the labor and youth wings opposing it. Although, after 1981, Belgium was governed by a Center-Right coalition, the declining political fortunes of the Christian Democrats, combined with their internal divisions, led the government to adopt a policy of ambiguity and delay on the issue of cruise missile deployment.[67]

Avoiding a pro-nuclear commitment made good sense from the stand-point of Belgian opinion. In October 1981, a poll found that 84 percent of the population opposed cruise missile deployment in Belgium, while only 14 percent supported it. In general, surveys during the early 1980s reported that opposition to such deployment ranged between 60 and 78 percent. Further-more, this was just the tip of the antinuclear iceberg. Polls found that a ma-jority of Belgians opposed any nuclear armament for their country. Indeed, when asked why they opposed deployment of the additional missiles, 82 percent responded that "all nuclear weapons should be abolished." Between 1981 and 1984, support for NATO's policy of using nuclear weapons to repel a Soviet conventional attack never topped 16 percent; by contrast, from 35 to 51 percent of Belgians told pollsters that NATO should not use nuclear weapons under any circumstances. Not surprisingly, then, most Belgians had a favorable view of nuclear disarmament activism. Polled in 1983, 63 percent said that the new movements made "a positive contribution to peace."[68]

West Germany

In West Germany, an unusually diverse, decentralized, and powerful move-ment shook yet another NATO nation slated for missile deployment. Al-though no single organization predominated, political parties, religious groups, unions, women's groups, pacifists, youth groups, and the citizens' environmental initiative movement worked together to produce unprece-dented outpourings of antinuclear sentiment. In October 1981, 300,000 peo-ple protested in Bonn against the Euromissiles—the largest political demon-stration in West Germany's history.[69] Thousands of small, activist groups began operations on the local level. In 1983, when a loose Coordinating Committee brought together thirty of the major organizations, it was able to produce a national week of action against missile deployment that drew an estimated three million participants nationwide. It culminated on October 23 in rallies staged in four cities and attracting over a million people. Addressing an assemblage of 500,000 at Bonn, former Chancellor Willy Brandt charged that nuclear disarmament had been blocked because NATO officials had decided that it was more important to station missiles in Western Europe than to get rid of Soviet SS-20s. Meanwhile, the antinuclear Krefeld Appeal attracted broad public support and, ultimately, was signed by five million West Germans. By late 1983, the antinuclear campaign had become the largest extraparliamentary movement in the history of the Federal Republic.[70]

Although this startling upsurge of protest focused on Euromissile deployment, the roots of antinuclear activism went much deeper. The escalating nuclear arms race and the breakdown of Soviet-American détente fostered widespread public dismay. Furthermore, the advent of the Reagan administration—with its demand for nuclear superiority, its rejection of arms controls, and its loose talk of fighting and winning a nuclear war—deeply disturbed many Germans. Finally, Germany had a front line status in a future nuclear war, with thousands of nuclear weapons already stationed on its territory. When the magazine *Der Stern* published a map showing the Federal Republic's many nuclear sites—which, in a future war, would also be nuclear targets—it underscored for many readers the fact that Germans lived on the edge of the nuclear abyss. "We . . . have little time left to stop the nuclear madness," declared Petra Kelly, chair of the Green Party, for "we are a country which can only be defended in the atomic age at the price of its total destruction." Antinuclear activism "does not mean negative protest," she insisted. "It is necessarily pro-environment, pro-woods and fields, pro-rivers and oceans, pro-plants and animals . . . and above all, *pro-people.* . . . We are the dreamers of brotherhood and sisterhood; of beauty; of nonviolence; of survival. We must act together. Now. Before it is too late."[71]

The movement's constituency in West Germany was rather typical. As was the case elsewhere in Western Europe, it attracted a disproportionate number of the nation's best educated people. Polled in the fall of 1983 about activity in the West German antinuclear movement, 10 percent of respondents with a higher education reported that they were already active, as compared to 4 percent with an intermediate education and 1 percent with a primary education. Furthermore, another 21 percent of those with a higher education said they intended to be active, as compared to lower percentages among the more poorly educated. Polls also found disproportionate activism and support for the movement among the young. A 1982 survey of youth reported that 11 percent regarded themselves as part of the peace movement, another 64 percent agreed with its aims, and that virtually no one disapproved of it. Politically, movement participants were usually on the Left. Looking at the percentage of peace movement activists within political parties, a November 1981 survey concluded that activists comprised 70 percent of the Greens, 10 percent of the Social Democrats, 9 percent of the Free Democrats, and 4 percent of the Christian Democrats.[72]

Religious organizations played a central role in the Federal Republic's antinuclear campaign. In response to the strong current of disarmament concern that swept through West Germany's Catholic churches, the Catholic Church Assembly of September 1982 met under the slogan, "Turn Around—Disarm Yourself." At the gathering, three church-linked groups— Pax Christi, Christians Against Nuclear Armaments, and the Church Initiative from Below—urged Catholics to join forces with Protestants in crusading against the Euromissiles. Furthermore, the 650,000 member Catholic Youth Organization adopted "Peace and Justice" as its key theme for three years. Against this backdrop, the April 1983 response of the Catholic Bishops, a pastoral letter entitled "Out of Justice, Peace," was rather tepid. Although criticizing the arms race, it did not discuss current weapons policies, such as cruise and Pershing missile deployment. Nor did it repudiate first use of nuclear weapons or nuclear deterrence. Nonetheless, during these years, German Catholicism—which previously had taken a very orthodox stand on foreign and military policy issues—moved closer to the position of the antinuclear movement, and many young Catholics participated in antinuclear demonstrations.[73]

Considerably greater support for the antinuclear campaign came from the Protestant (Evangelical) Church. Two Protestant peace groups, Action Reconciliation and Action Committee, played the leading roles in organizing the massive October 1981 anti-missile demonstration and, thereafter, served on the antinuclear Coordinating Committee. Furthermore, the Peace Week that they had organized in 1980 became an annual event, held every November with ever-greater participation. In 1982, over 5,000 Protestant parishes (more than 50 percent of the total), plus hundreds of villages and cities, hosted Peace Weeks, which emphasized the dangers of missile deployment and the need for nuclear-free zones.[74] In turn, this antinuclear ferment, particularly among the young, led to the transformation of the Kirchentags, the nation's biannual Protestant lay conferences. Previously sedentary gatherings of church elders, they were transformed in the early 1980s, as tens of thousands of youthful activists flooded in, turning them into vast antinuclear festivals. In September 1983, on the eve of NATO missile deployment, the national council of the Evangelical church issued a statement condemning nuclear deterrence and first use of nuclear weapons, championing a halt to the development, testing, production, and deployment of nuclear weapons, and calling for a "drastic reduction in Eurostrategic nuclear weapons." "For the Christian conscience," it declared, "the use of mass destruction weapons is unbearable."[75]

Other major social groups also contributed substantially to the growth of the West German campaign. Drawing upon a feminist peace philosophy, the women's movement, including Women for Peace and Women in the Army—We Say No!, served as an important component. Petra Kelly argued that "the nuclear arms race is in large part underwritten by masculine behavior" and, thus, "humanity's long term future depends on a radical re-evaluation of masculine institutions and ideologies." Thousands of women activists formed "peace chains" linking the Soviet and American consulates in West Berlin and, also, established peace camps near cruise missile sites.[76] Furthermore, as large numbers of professionals turned against the nuclear arms race, they organized new disarmament groups of their own, including Doctors Against Nuclear Arms, Artists for Peace, Teachers Against Arms Insanity, and Scientists for Peace.[77] Initially, the labor movement kept its distance from the antinuclear campaign, but when the Social Democrats moved into opposition to Euromissile deployment, the eight-million-member German trade union federation, the DGB, followed their lead. In October 1983, warning of the missile danger, the DGB staged a five-minute strike (symbolizing "five minutes to midnight") in factories around the country. Union leaders and members became actively involved in the antinuclear movement.[78]

The movement also made dramatic gains within West Germany's political party system. Thoroughly identifying themselves with the antinuclear movement, the Greens campaigned for unilateral rejection of Euromissile deployment and for the withdrawal of all nuclear weapons from the territory of the Federal Republic. Like END, the Greens championed the dismantling of NATO and of the Warsaw Pact, thus producing a Europe freed from superpower militarism and domination. Unlike other West German parties, they played a key role in West Germany's antimissile demonstrations and, also, publicly demonstrated in East Berlin and in Moscow against Soviet SS-20 missiles and government repression of independent peace activists. In the 1983 elections, the Green vote rose above the 5 percent hurdle, producing the new party's first parliamentary delegation, a group of 27 antinuclear activists.[79] Although the Greens sniped at their much larger rivals on the Left, the Social Democrats, for compromises with NATO militarism,[80] the latter, in fact, were running to catch up with the antinuclear movement. After the fall of 1982, when the Social Democrats were forced out of office thanks to abandonment by their centrist coalition partner, the long-suppressed opposition within their ranks to the NATO missile decision came surging to the fore. During the summer and fall of 1983, Social Democratic regional assemblies came out overwhelmingly against missile deployment. That November, at a nationwide party congress in Cologne, the Social Democrats voted to reject the stationing of the U.S. missiles on the territory of the Federal Republic and to call upon the Soviet Union to begin the reduction of its SS-20 missiles.[81]

The movement had considerably less impact on West Germany's other parties. Within the small, centrist Free Democratic Party—whose 1982 defection to the Christian Democrats had toppled the Social Democratic-led government—its early commitment to missile deployment inspired heated debate. But, after a threat by party leader (and West German Foreign Minister) Hans-Dietrich Genscher to resign if missile deployment were not reaffirmed, pro-nuclear forces carried the vote at party conferences by a two-to-one margin. The Free Democrats' coalition partners after late 1982, the conservative Christian Democrats, headed by the new Chancellor, Helmut Kohl, were considerably more enthusiastic about missile deployment. They staged pro-missile rallies (which drew far fewer participants than antinuclear rallies) and denounced antinuclear demonstrators. "Everyone who joins the ranks of the Easter marchers," declared party secretary Heiner Geissler, "becomes, whether he wants to or not, the tool of Soviet foreign policy."[82] As in so many other countries, the eagerness of the political parties for Euromissile deployment was directly proportional to how far to the Right they were on the political spectrum.

Although the Christian Democrats and the Free Democrats emerged victorious in the March 1983 elections, securing a parliamentary majority, this did not reflect a popular endorsement of their stand on nuclear weapons. Opinion polls in early 1983 indicated majority West German opposition to Euromissile deployment.[83] Furthermore, although the Social Democrats' percentage of the vote fell off in 1983, most of the defectors went to the more sharply antinuclear Greens, who secured the largest vote yet in their brief history. Indeed, *all* of West Germany's traditional political parties entered the elections committed to missile deployment. Finally, in early 1983, other issues were of greater concern to voters. Indeed, during the early 1980s, surveys indicated that foreign and defense policy issues were rated by West Germans as of far less importance than domestic issues, among them the economic situation. Thus, it seems likely that the Christian Democrats and the Free Democrats won their 1983 victory in spite of their pro-nuclear stand, rather than because of it.[84] Nonetheless, it did enable them to continue their coalition government and, later that year, to deploy the missiles.

Such policies were in sharp conflict with public opinion. Although polls usually showed a majority of West German respondents favoring NATO's two-track missile deployment decision if the question emphasized the negotiations track, when West Germans were asked simply whether they approved of the deployment of cruise and Pershing missiles in their country, they consistently responded in the negative, sometimes by a ratio of more than four to one. Indeed, according to a Harris poll, public acceptance of the Euromissiles dropped to a mere 15 percent by late 1983. Asked about the Reagan administration's proposal to produce the neutron bomb, 69 percent of West Germans said they opposed deploying it in their country. According to these polls, the most antinuclear groups were almost invariably women, the well-educated, and (ironically, given the movement's strength in the churches) those who seldom or never attended church.[85] Furthermore, between July 1981 and May 1984, the percentage of West Germans opposed to NATO's use of nuclear weapons "under any circumstances" rose from 29 to 44 percent, while the percentage willing to employ them to defend against an overwhelming conventional attack (i.e. the NATO position) declined from 17 to 11 percent.[86]

Other opinion surveys, too, could hardly bring much cheer to Germany's conservative rulers. West Germans gave U.S. defense policy a remarkably negative assessment, with 43 percent of respondents in a February 1982 poll stating that they thought the Reagan administration's policy toward the East was too hard-line and another 39 percent agreeing partially with this view. Asked in December 1983 if they had confidence in the ability of the United States to deal responsibly with world problems, 34 percent said "Yes" and 53 percent "No." Between July 1982 and December 1983, four separate USIA polls found pluralities of West Germans stating that U.S. policies did more to increase the risk of war than to promote peace.[87] By contrast, the antinuclear movement received rather favorable ratings. Polled in November 1981 about the antinuclear demonstrations sweeping through Western Europe, 59 percent of West German respondents reported themselves sympathetic; 65 percent approved of the demonstration in Bonn. A May 1983 poll found that 47 percent of respondents viewed the peace movement as "necessary," 24 percent "superfluous," and only 7 percent "detrimental." In the fall of 1983, yet another poll found that, when queried about the peace movement's demands, 14 percent of the population fully supported them and another 50 percent were generally sympathetic.[88]

This kind of popular support meant that West Germany's antinuclear campaign continued even after cruise and Pershing II missiles were deployed in late 1983. To be sure, the arrival of the missiles had a dispiriting effect upon the movement, and the mammoth protests gave way to smaller demonstrations. Within the Greens, conflicts erupted between the party's "realist," "fundamentalist," and Marxist factions. Moreover, differences emerged within the movement over future strategy, with some groups (such as the Greens) promoting nonviolent resistance and others (such as Action Reconciliation and Action Committee) more traditional tactics. As a result, the movement produced a "shopping list" of national activities in the fall of 1984, without the mass impact of the preceding years. Even so, it remained organizationally strong and active, especially at the grassroots level.[89] Furthermore, the Social Democrats kept to their new, antinuclear course, raising hopes for the advent of a Social Democratic–Green government that would implement many of the peace movement's demands. Perhaps most important, as Jo Leinen, chair of the citizens' initiatives movement remarked, the antinuclear campaign had succeeded in "removing the taboo" from public debate about nuclear policy and in "building up . . . a mass movement that sits deep in the population."[90]

The Nordic Countries

In the small Nordic countries, the new movement attracted a larger following than had any previous antinuclear campaign. Appealing disproportionately to the educated middle class, and particularly to that portion of it with avant garde political, social, and cultural views, the new movement developed affiliates among teachers, journalists, doctors, engineers, psychologists, architects, artists, and lawyers. In addition, powerful Social Democratic parties, labor federations, and women's organizations backed the antinuclear campaign, as did many religious bodies. Women for Peace groups sprang up all over Scandinavia in support of an antinuclear Copenhagen to Paris march in 1981, which was followed the next year by a women's march from Sweden to Minsk. Although none of these countries was slated for missile deployment, the antinuclear campaign made such deployment a key issue. Furthermore, a Nordic nuclear weapons–free zone had enormous appeal, and, by June 1982, petitions calling for its creation had been signed by 2.75 million people throughout the region. In October 1981, simultaneous demonstrations in 54 Finnish cities and towns demanding a Nordic nuclear-free zone, as well as a nuclear-free Europe, drew 130,000 participants.[91]

The movement made tremendous strides in Norway. In this country of only four million people, No to Nuclear Weapons mushroomed into an organization with a membership that topped 100,000, operating in about 300 local groups. With branches situated in almost every Norwegian community, No to Nuclear Weapons was able to forge direct links with the bulk of the population by placing its newspaper in 80 to 90 percent of the mailboxes. Conducting one of the largest petition campaigns ever seen in Norway, No to Nuclear Weapons gathered 540,000 signatures on its call for a Nordic nuclear-free zone. In October 1983, together with other peace groups, it turned out 20,000 people for a torchlight antinuclear march in Oslo, the largest demonstration in that country's history.[92] Powerful social institutions were swept up in the antinuclear tide. In May 1981, No to Nuclear Weapons was officially endorsed by the Norwegian Trade Union Congress, which subsequently played an important role in the antinuclear campaign. Although the Norwegian Labor Party—unlike the small parties to its left—had supported the NATO two-track decision in December 1979, substantial internal turmoil followed over the issue. In the fall of 1982, the Labor Party—now out of power—began leading the fight in parliament against funding for missile deployment and, in 1983, for blocking deployment while INF negotiations continued. Even though each of these efforts failed by one vote, antinuclear activists were heartened by the Labor Party's turnabout on this issue, by its backing for a Nordic nuclear-free zone (first proclaimed in 1981), and by the prospect of its return to office. By late 1983, they could also point to 11 Norwegian counties (out of 19) and 93 municipalities (out of 440) that had adopted nuclear-free zone resolutions.[93]

Events unfolded in a similar fashion in Denmark. Growing into a powerful organization, No to Nuclear Weapons soon had some 45 local branches scattered about the country. Together with Women for Peace and pacifist groups, it encouraged the development of disarmament groups within the professions, dispatched speakers to schools and other institutions, and fostered widespread opposition to the arms race. As antinuclear fervor swept through the nation, antimissile demonstrations of about 100,000 people erupted in Copenhagen in 1981 and 1983, antinuclear Easter marches drew escalating numbers of participants (estimated at 60,000 to 100,000 in 1984), and the Danish petition for a nuclear-free zone garnered 260,000 signatures.[94] Largely thanks to the decentralized structure of the Danish churches, religious groups had little visibility in the antinuclear campaign. But union participation was more significant, and in November 1983 the Trade Union Council organized a five-minute work stoppage as a demonstration for peace and against the deployment of the Euromissiles.[95] Although the Danish Social Democrats had supported the NATO two-track decision, with the growth of the antinuclear campaign and the example of other Social Democratic parties, they began to revise their position. Out of office after September 1982, they joined two small socialist parties and one small centrist party in forming a majority in parliament that demanded a postponement of NATO missile deployment. "We dread how this lunatic rearmament will end," explained the Social Democratic chair, and even if the Russians were not as sympathetic to disarmament as they claimed, "we must be ready to go ahead of them."[96]

If the nuclear disarmament movement was somewhat smaller in Sweden, that was only because its major ideas already reigned supreme in that nation. By 1984, Sweden had more than thirty peace groups with a combined membership of about 25,000. They included Women for Peace (with 3,000 members), as well as nineteen antinuclear organizations formed among professionals, such as Physicians Against Nuclear Weapons, which enrolled more than half the nation's medical doctors. By far the largest was the Swedish Peace and Arbitration Society (SPAS), which between 1980 and 1984 grew from 6,000 to more than 15,000 members, organized in 115 local groups.[97] Championing a Nordic nuclear weapons–free zone, an idea that had originated in Sweden decades before, the antinuclear campaign gathered 750,000 Swedish signatures on its petitions. The larger demonstrations against the Euromissiles and for nuclear-free zones drew crowds that ranged from 50,000 to 100,000 people.[98] Here, as throughout the region, churches and unions took an antinuclear stand. In a petition campaign for peace and disarmament, conducted by the churches and concluding at Easter 1983, more than a million Swedes signed a statement calling for a halt to testing, development, production, and deployment of nuclear weapons, a Nordic nuclear-free zone, and support for peace work, peace research, and peace education.[99] Although all the political parties (except the Conservatives) backed at least part of the antinuclear movement's program, the sweeping election victory of the Social Democrats in September 1983 was particularly heartening to peace activists. The new prime minister, Olof Palme, had very close relations with Western Europe's antinuclear campaign. In his inaugural address, he announced his government's commitment to a Nordic nuclear-free zone within the first 60 seconds.[100]

In Finland, too, the movement's ideas permeated the society. The Peace Union and the Committee of 100 served as the major nonaligned groups, with the former attracting an older, more moderate, sedate constituency and the latter a more youthful, pacifist, and leftwing one. Both took up the issues of missile deployment and a Nordic nuclear weapon–free zone. Pacifist groups, new peace associations among professionals, and Women for Peace rounded out the roster of peace movement organizations, all of which joined the antinuclear campaign.[101] "We don't want to be the last generation in Europe," proclaimed Women for Peace; "we do not want to be exterminated because of the madness of the great powers."[102] Nevertheless, the Finnish peace movement, more broadly construed, was—as Illka Taipale, a prominent activist, termed it—"a movement of consciousness," channeled through many different organizations, including the unions, the churches, and the major political parties. Thus, the level of antinuclear mobilization was quite extraordinary. In this thinly populated nation, some 1.2 million Finns signed petitions calling for a Nordic nuclear-free zone. In November 1983, an estimated 215,000 people (about 5 percent of the population) turned out across Finland to demonstrate simultaneously against nuclear weapons—the largest demonstration in the Nordic countries since the Second World War.[103]

Throughout the Nordic region, public opinion was strikingly antinuclear. According to opinion polls, between September 1982 and October 1983 the percentage of Norwegians listing nuclear weapons as among their "greatest concerns" ranged from 38 to 42 percent. Asked in 1985 about factors threatening the future of humanity, 79 percent of Finns listed war, armaments, and nuclear weapons.[104] In Denmark, opinion surveys in 1983 reported opposition to NATO missile deployment ranging from 51 to 58 percent, with support at only about half those levels. In Norway, polls in the early 1980s found pluralities or majorities opposed to missile deployment, with very large majorities when the question did not emphasize negotiations. In August 1981, Norwegians opposed deployment by 71 to 21 percent; in November 1982, by 69 to 27 percent.[105] The idea of a Nordic nuclear-free zone enjoyed great popularity, and a survey in 1981 found Norwegians favoring it by 69 to 14 percent.[106] Given NATO's position on the use of nuclear weapons, the attitudes in the Nordic region's two NATO nations were startling. In Denmark, according to a May 1984 poll, 43 percent opposed their employment under any circumstances, while only 7 percent favored their use against a conventional attack. In Norway, an October 1983 survey reported a similar result: 48 percent opposing their employment under any circumstances and only 4 percent favoring their use to repel a conventional attack.[107]

Given this revulsion to nuclear weapons and nuclear war, Nordic attitudes toward nuclear arms control and disarmament, as well as toward the nuclear disarmament movement, were quite favorable. Asked, in 1981, if they wanted their country to do more toward arms control, Norwegians replied affirmatively by a ratio of two-to-one. In 1985, 78 percent of Finns favored general and complete disarmament as soon as possible, and only 6 percent did not.[108] That same year, 82 percent of Finns told pollsters that the peace movement decreased the possibility of war. Indeed, 52 percent said that people all over the world should participate in demonstrations against the arms race, and 45 percent said that they either had participated or would be ready to participate in them. A 1982 poll found that 60 percent of Norwegians approved of the antinuclear demonstrations, and another in 1983 reported that, by a ratio of two-to-one, Danes rejected the notion that the movement was "onesidedly favoring the Soviet Union."[109] Repeatedly, the polls found that the most antinuclear responses and the most positive assessments of the antinuclear movement came from the young, the well-educated, women, and from the Left.[110]

Revolt of the Doves

The Movement Elsewhere in Non-Communist Europe, 1981-85

> We launch an appeal . . . for a vast movement against
> war and nuclear armament, which takes its place in the
> European current and, with it, vigorously contests the
> proliferation of nuclear arms equally in the West and in
> the East.
>
> The Larzac Appeal, 1981

Elsewhere in non-Communist Europe, antinuclear activism also swelled into a mass movement of unprecedented dimensions. Triggered by the heightened great power confrontation of the late 1970s and early 1980s, it became a dynamic political force that could not be ignored. Although the movement's progress was restrained in some countries by the relatively conservative position of the Catholic Church hierarchy, by the pro-nuclear positions of some Socialist and Communist parties, and by unique national situations, it nevertheless could mobilize very substantial popular opposition to nuclear weapons. Whether in NATO or neutral countries, there was widespread public dismay at the deployment of Euromissiles, at other nuclear weapons programs, and at the prospect of nuclear war. Thus, although the antinuclear movement here often lagged behind its counterpart in Northern Europe, it could draw upon deep-seated public resistance to the nuclear arms race, particularly among the highly educated, the young, women, and those with avant garde social and political views. Furthermore, it was large enough and militant enough to send powerful tremors through the social and political fabric of most nations.

France

The French movement began the 1980s in a very discouraging context. France's four major parties all championed the nation's independent nuclear deterrent, while the nation's press ridiculed those who dared to challenge the alleged "national consensus" on the *force de frappe*. Thus, as E. P. Thompson complained, although the quest for national independence in the face of the deadly Soviet-American military confrontation encouraged the antinuclear movement in Northern Europe, it undermined the movement in France. Furthermore, the NATO double-track decision, which had done so much to spark protest elsewhere, had less relevance in France, which had withdrawn from the NATO military command years before. France had not been a party to that decision, and none of the missiles would be deployed on French soil. Moreover, in a country where citizen activism was often the work of political parties, the support for the missile deployment by all major parties except the Communists left the movement with relatively little "political space" in which to operate.[1]

One of the most significant problems faced by the French movement was that the powerful Communist Party had a near monopoly on mass peace activism. This meant not only that non-Communists shunned such activism, but that, when it occurred, it was limited to a critique of NATO policy, such as cruise and Pershing II missile deployment. In 1981, when the Communist government in Poland cracked down on the Solidarity movement by imposing martial law, the French Communists' longtime peace operation, the Movement for Peace (Mouvement de la Paix), refused to condemn the action, thereby tarnishing its reputation still further. Recognizing the isolation of the Movement for Peace, the Communist Party helped organize the Appeal of the 100 (Appel des Cent), a peace group drawing upon many of the nation's cultural and professional luminaries—including some non-Communists—in May 1982. Amid the turmoil the nuclear arms race inspired during the early 1980s, the Appeal did mobilize unprecedented numbers of antinuclear demonstrators—some 200,000 in June 1982 and 300,000 in June 1983. But these demonstrations continued the vague rhetoric on nuclear arms favored by the Communists (e.g. "I love peace"), and did not mention French nuclear weapons at all.[2]

By late 1981, inspired by the example of nonaligned nuclear disarmament movements elsewhere, France's independent activists were ready to create an alternative. A key precipitating factor was an August 1981 festival on the Larzac plateau, in southern France, where anti-militarists—ranging from pacifists, to environmentalists, to local peasants—gathered to celebrate the victory of their ten-year, grassroots campaign to block the French army from expanding a military base. Issuing the "Larzac Appeal," they called for the creation in France of a broad-based coalition of groups that would battle for European nuclear disarmament. By November of that year, some 25 groups had heeded the call, forming the Committee for Nuclear Disarmament in Europe (Comité pour le Désarmement nucléaire en Europe, CODENE). Small and diverse, they included peace and nonviolence groups (the Movement for Disarmament, Peace, and Liberty, the FOR, and the Movement for a Nonviolent Alternative), women's groups (Women for Peace), independent Left groups (the Unified Socialist Party and Trotskyite factions), religious organizations (Rural Movement of Christian Youth), most ecological organizations, and the peasants of Larzac. Officially launched in February 1982, CODENE saw itself as the French counterpart of nonaligned nuclear disarmament groups in other European nations. It opposed nuclear missiles in East and West, and called upon the French government to both halt its nuclear modernization program and work toward the dismantling of the French nuclear arsenal "within the framework of a denuclearized and non-aligned Europe."[3]

In the following years, CODENE plunged into an array of antinuclear activities. It sponsored conferences, campaigned to have cities and towns declare themselves nuclear-free, and organized its own demonstrations, including one in June 1982 that turned out 30,000 people in Paris to protest the visit of Ronald Reagan.[4] In addition, like its nonaligned counterparts in the rest of Western Europe, it established close contacts with independent peace activists in Eastern Europe. Developing warm relations with Poland's embattled Solidarity movement and with Czechoslovakia's hard-pressed Charter 77, CODENE issued a joint communiqué with Charter 77 in June 1983—probably the first public statement signed by a Western peace movement and an East bloc human rights organization.[5] That August, once again at Larzac, CODENE brought together 15,000 French activists, along with representatives from sister organizations in East and West, to hammer out plans for a nuclear-free and democratic continent. The first step, the conferees agreed, was to freeze French nuclear testing and weapons systems.[6] Although these activities enhanced the image of the nuclear disarmament campaign within France, CODENE remained relatively weak and fragmented, at least compared to movements elsewhere. Its October 1983 demonstration against the Euromissiles, while spirited, drew only about 15,000 participants. Nevertheless, CODENE's credibility and membership continued to grow, and by 1985 it claimed 78 local groups.[7]

In France, as elsewhere, important social institutions strengthened the antinuclear campaign. Although the Communist-led General Confederation of Labor remained thoroughly in line with the approach of the Communist peace movement, the French Democratic Federation of Labor (CFDT)— with its leanings toward democratic socialism, workers' control, and decentralism—gravitated toward CODENE. In September 1983, the CFDT and CODENE issued a joint declaration condemning both Cold War blocs for the arms race and calling for the destruction of Soviet SS-20s and the nondeployment of U.S. Pershing II and cruise missiles. The CFDT also joined CODENE in sponsoring the October 1983 demonstration against the Euromissiles.[8] Within religious circles, the hierarchies of the large Catholic and much smaller Protestant churches adopted sharply divergent positions. In November 1983, the French Catholic bishops issued a pastoral letter, "Winning the Peace," that endorsed nuclear deterrence and argued that French nuclear weapons protected "the weak from the strong." A number of small Catholic groups expressed their dismay at this position, as did an official Protestant assembly, which responded with its own declaration, "The Struggle for Peace." Declaring that the real issue is "life or death for the people of this planet," the Protestants asked people to refuse "to submit to the bipolarization of the world" and to support a French "nuclear freeze as the first step to a de-escalation of the arms build-up."[9]

The movement had less impact upon the political parties. After a landslide victory in the June 1981 parliamentary elections, the Socialists formed a coalition government with the Communists. François Mitterrand, France's new Socialist president, took a strong stand in favor of the *force de frappe* and the deployment of NATO missiles, and this remained the party position. The Communist Party favored French nuclear weapons and, though it was critical of NATO missile deployment, its desire to remain within the government made it wary of challenging the Socialists on this issue. As for the two conservative parties, they were both happy enough to remain within the official "consensus" on nuclear weapons. Only two small, marginal parties—the Unified Socialist Party (a longtime gadfly on the Left) and the Greens (who began party work in 1982)—were thoroughly committed to French and European nuclear disarmament. In fact, antinuclear attitudes within the Socialist Party, the activities of CODENE, and the stands taken by European Social Democratic parties did have some impact upon Socialist officials, and many were dissatisfied with the government's position on nuclear issues. Nevertheless, in the name of party unity, they usually refrained from antinuclear statements and activities.[10]

Despite the difficulties the movement faced in France, its positions enjoyed considerable popular support. Opinion surveys usually found backing for Euromissile deployment running at no more than 35 percent. Questioned in May 1983 as to whether the United States should renounce Pershing missile deployment even if the Soviet Union maintained its SS-20s, 44 percent of French respondents supported the idea, while only 34 percent opposed it.[11] Although polls revealed much stronger popular support for French nuclear weapons, ranging between 66 and 72 percent, modernization of these weapons had considerably less backing, ranging between 20 and 52 percent. Furthermore, there was considerable skepticism about their value. In 1982, 37 percent of those questioned said French nuclear weapons "protect France from war," but 44 percent remarked that "they serve no purpose because if they were used against a great power, France would . . . be wiped off the map."[12] Use of nuclear weapons inspired little enthusiasm. Between 1981 and 1983, polls showed that only 8 to 17 percent would employ them to repel a conventional military attack, while 27 to 44 percent would not use them under any circumstances. The French preferred arms controls and, between 1982 and 1984, consistently favored them by a two-to-one ratio or more over maintaining a military balance with the Soviet Union.[13] Questioned in November 1981 about the recent antinuclear demonstrations in Western Europe, 50 percent of French respondents reported themselves sympathetic. Numerous polls found that women, the young, environmentalists, and supporters of the Left parties were disproportionately antinuclear.[14]

Italy

The Italian nuclear disarmament campaign, though lacking formal leadership and direction, also burgeoned into a mass movement. In response to the Christian Democratic–led government's August 1981 announcement of definite plans to deploy cruise missiles, a loose coalition of leftwing political parties, religious groups, unions, ecologists, feminists, pacifist groups, and youth organizations turned out some 500,000 people for a protest demonstration in Rome that October. They demanded the rejection of the cruise missiles and the dismantling of the SS-20s as the first steps toward the demilitarization of Europe. Despite this promising beginning, as well as nationwide assemblies of the Italian peace movement in 1983 and 1984 that sought to develop some overall structure, activists found it difficult to agree upon a unified policymaking body for the campaign or to develop a movement independent of political parties. A key problem was that the powerful Italian Communist Party—perhaps the most independent in Europe and regularly drawing about 30 percent of the nation's vote—was vital to the movement's mass mobilization. Yet many activists feared that, given the party's attempts to enter the government through a "historic compromise" with the Christian Democrats, it would end up compromising on the Euromissiles as well. The result was that the movement, while claiming 500 local peace committees by early 1984, remained fragmented and disputatious.[15]

Nevertheless, it generated mass participation. In October 1983, a crowd estimated at from 500,000 to a million people participated in an antimissile demonstration in Rome. According to an account in the *Guardian*: "Beaming Franciscans flanked by Augustinians and nuns called for peace and goodness on earth. . . . A placard showed St. Francis of Assisi preaching to a wild beast—the contemporary wolf of nuclear weaponry. Young anarchists ignored traffic lights." They were joined by pensioners, women's and environmental groups, leftists, and youth activists. A female figure of Europe in mourning was surrounded by American and Soviet missiles. Demonstrators smeared red paint on the pavement near the Soviet embassy and left a poster denouncing Soviet intervention in Afghanistan and Poland.[16] In Sicily alone, 1.2 million people (a fourth of the population) signed a petition rejecting missile deployment.[17] When parliament ignored a movement petition calling for a nationwide popular referendum on cruise missiles, the movement organized one itself. Held in 1983–84, it drew five million votes, 80 percent of them against deployment. Furthermore, thanks to the political clout of leftwing parties in many localities, numerous cities and towns proclaimed themselves nuclear-free zones.[18]

The most intense battle of the antinuclear campaign was waged at the proposed cruise missile site, in Comiso, Sicily. Although located far from the movement's strongholds in the north, this rural region produced a remarkable resistance movement. After the government's August 1981 announcement, residents of Comiso and neighboring towns formed a local Coordinating Committee for Disarmament and Peace (CUDIP), which pulled together leftwing political parties, unions, cultural associations, church organizations, and pacifist groups into a powerful force. That October, CUDIP staged an anti-missile demonstration of 30,000 people at Comiso and, the following April, produced an international demonstration there of 60,000 or more protesters. In Comiso, itself, two-thirds of the residents signed the petition calling for cancellation of the missile base.[19] They were joined by antinuclear activists from West European nations and the United States, who, beginning in the summer of 1982, organized peace camps outside the missile base and engaged in numerous demonstrations, hunger strikes, and nonviolent blockades. In response, the mafia—which stood to benefit substantially from missile base construction contracts, as

well as subsequent prostitution and drug dealing—murdered a leading antinuclear campaigner, Pio La Torre, in April 1982. Women's groups, from Italy and from abroad, organized their own peace camps and demonstrations,
and—despite the nonviolent nature of their protests—police attacked them
brutally and razed their tent sites. Mafia and police assaults were intimidating, but, nonetheless, antinuclear demonstrators filled the public squares of
Sicily in November 1983, as Italy's parliament again debated missile deployment.[20]

The Italian antinuclear campaign drew upon constituencies similar to
those in other West European nations. Initially, the Italian labor movement,
politically divided, was rather vague about its position on the arms race.
But, by early 1983, a far more specific and pro-movement stance had been
formulated. Joining an antinuclear march called by the Italian Christian
Workers Associations that May, the labor confederation called for the extension of U.S.-Soviet negotiations, the destruction of "adequate numbers"
of Soviet 20 missiles, and the non-deployment of NATO missiles. Feminist
groups, student groups, and peace groups among scientists and physicians
also joined the campaign, although participation by intellectuals remained
rather light.[21] Given the conservative, anti-Communist views of the Italian
Catholic Church hierarchy and of the Vatican, these groups sought to discourage participation in antinuclear activities. Even so, a small number of
Catholic Church prelates supported the antinuclear campaign, as did Catholic organizations like the 500,000-member Italian Christian Workers Associations and Pax Christi. Furthermore, the small Protestant denominations
took a strong, uncompromising stand in opposition to the cruise missiles,
arguing that people still had "the possibility to choose between a race toward self-destruction and a more human development of society."[22]

Politically, the movement faced a difficult situation. All five parties in
the governing coalition favored missile deployment. They included not only
the nation's largest party, the conservative Christian Democrats, but the
only force on the Left in the cabinet, the small Socialist Party. To be sure, a
portion of the Socialist Party was critical of deployment.[23] Furthermore, in a
number of ways the large Communist Party took on the political role in Italy that Social Democratic parties played in other West European nations.
Even so, in the early 1980s, Italian Communist leaders felt ambivalent about
antinuclear activism. If they snubbed it, they might lose support to the small
parties on their Left. But, if they appeared pro-Soviet, they might lose support to the parties on their Right and, also, undermine their chances to enter
the government. In these circumstances, the Communist Party adopted a
fairly cautious approach—backing the antinuclear movement, but doing it

in a muted fashion and emphasizing the importance of maintaining an East-West "balance" of nuclear forces. Consequently, many antinuclear activists considered the Communists opportunists, and preferred the more straightforward stand of the smaller parties on the Left. Indeed, the staunchly anti-militarist Radical Party refused to work in any disarmament coalition including the Communists.[24] During the elections of June 1983, the governing parties deliberately kept the missile issue in the background. Moreover, the election results failed to change the situation. Although the Christian Democrats lost ground, the governing coalition held on to power and, soon thereafter, pressed forward with missile deployment.[25]

The government's evasion of the missile issue made good political sense. During the early 1980s, pluralities or majorities of Italians told pollsters that they unconditionally opposed cruise missile deployment in their country, with opposition peaking at two-thirds of respondents in the spring of 1984. In addition, a 1982 survey found that 78 percent of Italians opposed deployment of the neutron bomb in their country.[26] According to polls from 1981 to 1983, only 5 to 12 percent of Italians favored use of nuclear weapons to repel a Soviet conventional attack upon Western Europe, while from 38 to 55 percent opposed their use under any circumstances.[27] By a substantial majority, respondents favored strengthening Italy's security through arms controls rather than through a NATO nuclear buildup. Indeed, in 1981, as many Italians favored their nation's unilateral nuclear disarmament as opposed it.[28] Although Italy was a NATO nation—with even the Communist Party supporting membership in the U.S.-led alliance—Italians were uneasy about the priorities of the Reagan administration, and in April 1982 a poll found that a plurality of Italian respondents (44 percent) thought that U.S. policies and actions during the past year had increased the risk of war. Polls reported antinuclear sentiment at its highest among the young, the university educated, and supporters of parties on the Left.[29]

Greece

In another NATO nation, Greece, the movement also became entangled in national politics, but in a more promising context. Founded in 1955, The Greek Committee for International Détente and Peace (EEDYE), the WPC affiliate, was closely associated with Greece's traditional Communists. In 1981, dissenters within that organization broke away and formed the Non-Aligned Peace Movement (AKE). Although, unlike EEDYE, AKE organized events critical of the Soviet Union, it was not politically independent, for it was dominated by Greece's Eurocommunists. The most successful rival to the EEDYE was the Movement for National Independence, International Peace and Disarmament (KEADEA), also formed in 1981. Though not a mass movement, KEADEA was comprised of a group of prominent personalities from PASOK, the Greek Socialist Party.[30] Led by the charismatic Andreas Papandreou, the Socialists won a smashing victory at the polls in 1981 and, thereafter, KEADEA's star rose rapidly. KEADEA opposed Euromissile deployment, agitated for the closure of U.S. military bases in Greece, and championed the creation of a nuclear weapons–free zone in the Balkans—measures strongly backed by the Papandreou government—and became the leading force in the Greek antinuclear movement. In the spring of 1983, it brought together the three rival groups for a joint demonstration against U.S. military bases. The following February, it hosted an international conference in Athens on the denuclearization of Europe.[31]

Antinuclear attitudes were widespread in Greece, from the grassroots to the highest levels of power. In October 1983, 77 percent of Greeks polled said that, even if the Soviet Union failed to withdraw its SS-20s, cruise and Pershing II missiles should not be deployed. In April 1984, when Greeks were asked about Western nuclear policy, a plurality (38 percent) favored unilateral nuclear disarmament, another 17 percent were unconditionally opposed to deploying additional NATO nuclear weapons, and only 5 percent favored an attempt to attain nuclear superiority. That same month, 51 percent of Greeks polled stated that the use of nuclear weapons was not acceptable under any circumstances, and only 5 percent supported their use to repel a non-nuclear attack.[32] Given this kind of popular support, Greece's peace groups drew mass participation at antinuclear demonstrations, including one in Athens in December 1981, supporting the government's policy of opposition to nuclear weapons in the Balkans. Antinuclear attitudes also prevailed at the governmental level. Papandreou had been one of the earliest signers of the END Appeal and, once in power, he moved quickly to call for an end to the nuclear arms race and to propose an array of antinuclear measures. "Nuclear weapons," he told END's Mary Kaldor, "contribute exactly zero to our national defense. Exactly zero."[33]

Spain

Relative to other West European nations, Spain was a newcomer to antinuclear activism. After the Franco dictatorship had come to an end in 1975, Spain was ruled by a Center-Right government that, in May 1982, brought the nation into NATO's political structure. Nevertheless, in the midst of the reviving Cold War and the growing arms race, this move—which seemed but a prelude to integrating Spain into NATO's military structure—proved highly unpopular. During 1981, hundreds of thousands of Spaniards demonstrated against NATO membership, including at least 300,000 who participated in a rally for disarmament, peace, and liberty that November, in Madrid. The rising Socialist Workers Party played a leading role in the anti-NATO agitation and, during the 1982 elections, promised to freeze Spain's integration into NATO and hold a popular referendum on the subject. This position contributed to a sweeping Socialist election victory, returning the party to office for the first time since the 1930s. Once in power, however, the Socialist leader, Felipe Gonzalez, equivocated, apparently because he desired to appease the Spanish military and, thereby, prevent a coup and the restoration of military dictatorship. But the movement was not so easily contained. Although lacking in central leadership and divided by politics, it coalesced during July 1983, when representatives of 51 groups met and formed a loose umbrella organization, the National Coordinator of Peace Organizations (Coordinadora estatal de organizaciones pacifistas, CEOP). In the following years, the CEOP pulled together 400 peace groups that continued the nationwide antimilitary campaign and, especially, sought to ensure that the Socialist government held the promised referendum on NATO.[34]

Despite the fragmented nature of the Spanish movement, it had substantial strength. In October 1983, massive numbers of people—including 150,000 in Madrid—participated in peace demonstrations around the country that focused on nuclear disarmament, withdrawal from NATO, and other peace issues. In May 1984, 100,000 people in Barcelona took part in a human chain that linked the NATO consulates and Warsaw Street (symbolizing the Soviet bloc)—an event organized by numerous peace collectives, the Socialist Party, the Eurocommunists, ecologists, Pax Christi, and other groups. That June, two weeks of antimilitary agitation were capped by a rally of half a million people in Madrid. By the mid-1980s, more than 350 Spanish villages, towns, and cities had proclaimed themselves nuclear-free zones.[35] Polls indicated not only overwhelming Spanish opposition to NATO membership,[36] but a strong distaste for nuclear weapons. From 1982 to 1984, Spaniards preferred arms control measures over a military balance with the Soviet Union by ratios ranging from three-to-one to six-to-one. Indeed, an October 1983 survey found that 55 percent of Spaniards favored unilateral nuclear disarmament by the West. Questioned by pollsters that same month, only 2 percent of Spaniards supported use of nuclear weapons to repel a non-nuclear attack, while 61 percent said that they opposed use of nuclear weapons under any circumstances.[37]

Switzerland

Protest against nuclear weapons also erupted in Switzerland—a neutral country, but one whose government routinely expressed its approval of NATO policies. In previous years, there had been growing antimilitary agitation, and this fed into a major upsurge of Swiss antinuclear activism in 1981, at least partially in response to the rising antinuclear campaign elsewhere in Europe. That year, a Committee for Peace and Disarmament (Komitee für Frieden und Abrüstung) sprang up in Berne, the nation's capital, proposing to hold a national antinuclear demonstration. Ultimately, some 42 peace movement and other sympathetic organizations joined together to sponsor the event. Occurring that December, it attracted 30,000 to 40,000 participants—the largest demonstration ever held in that city. Other large marches and demonstrations quickly followed, including one in Geneva, in January 1982 (with 20,000 participants), and another through Basel, Baden, and Alsace (with 20,000–30,000 participants), in April 1982. What was referred to as the "new" peace movement crested in November 1983, when 40,000 to 50,000 peace demonstrators formed two human chains surrounding the federal building, the seat of government and parliament, as well as the embassies of the United States and the Soviet Union.[38]

Switzerland's "new" peace movement drew upon a variety of constituencies. Some, in fact, were not new at all, such as the traditional pacifist and other peace groups that worked together in the Swiss Peace Council (Schweizer Friedensrat, SFR), which had been founded in 1946. Keenly opposed to nuclear weapons, the SFR formed support committees for the demonstrators at Greenham Common and Comiso, sponsored the Basel-Baden-Alsace march, and, in November 1982, on the occasion of a meeting of the Socialist International, sought to promote a dialogue between the European peace movement and Social Democratic leaders. Much of the "new" peace movement, however, was more fragmented and decentralized. It included groups like Women for Peace which, in solidarity with the peace camps in Britain and Sicily, established a women's peace camp in the spring of 1982 at Frauenfeld. Although the official church bodies did not take a stand in support of the antinuclear movement, activists raised nuclear issues within the churches at the grassroots level. In Berne, an Ecumenical Peace Network emerged in 1983 thanks to the initiative of the Protestant Reformed Church. Among the political parties, the Social Democratic Party was the one most receptive to disarmament issues, and called for a popular referendum on defense spending decisions. Many Swiss Social Democrats were active participants in the nation's peace and disarmament movement.[39]

Austria

In neighboring Austria, another neutral country, the movement was stronger, perhaps because of the nation's location on the border between East and West. Although Austria's peace movement flared up in 1980 over plans to sell tanks to the Chilean dictatorship, it took the Euromissile issue to generate a massive surge of protest. In June 1981, the first march of the "new" peace movement, organized by independent peace and anti-nuclear power groups in Vienna, drew some 7,000 participants. They demanded a range of antimilitary measures, including a nuclear-free Europe. By May 1982, the movement had taken off, with 70,000 protesters drawn to a mass demonstration in Vienna. Organized primarily by youth and student organizations, the event was supported by several hundred groups. Its main demand was: "Prevent nuclear war—disarm!" The governing party (the Socialists) and the youth group of the conservative opposition Austrian People's Party both backed the swelling antinuclear campaign, as did numerous minor parties, notably the Greens. By October 1983, when Austrians joined citizens of other nations across Western Europe in protesting the deployment of Euromissiles, the movement seemed irresistible. According to the *New York Times*, "some 100,000 demonstrators brought Vienna to a standstill."[40]

In fact, Austria's antinuclear movement, while widespread, remained more divided than it seemed. Although a Coordinating Committee pulled together most of the activist groups, underlying tensions remained. With the major political parties playing a central role in the campaign, independent activist groups often felt marginalized and, at the least, suspicious of their motives. Many preferred participating in the activities of the Working Group of Independent Peace Initiatives (Arbeitsgemeinschaft Unabhängiger Friedens Initiativen, ARGE U.F.I.), founded in April 1982. ARGE U.F.I. brought together independent peace groups and individuals, such as anti-nuclear power activists, pacifists, non-dogmatic socialists, women, and partisans of the alternative movement. Very much in the END mold, it worked with nonaligned antimilitary and human rights organizations in the East and West. Independent groups also felt uneasy about the Linz Appeal, a petition that called upon the Austrian government to speak out against the deployment of cruise and Pershing II missiles. Issued in December 1982 and ultimately signed by some 120,000 Austrians, the petition did not mention Soviet missiles or condemn the rival military blocs. As a result, a number of independent groups, including ARGE U.F.I., refused to support it.[41]

Despite these tensions, however, Austrian activists built a powerful

movement. It not only appealed strongly to intellectuals, youth, environmentalists, and unionists, but to Catholic Church groups, such the Catholic
Youth Organization and the Catholic bishops. Indeed, in April 1983, the
Austrian Bishops' conference issued a very strong statement, declaring that
all governments and all people "must understand, once and for all, that the
violent way in which conflicts are dealt with is inhuman." Therefore, "war
can no longer be valid as a means of attaining political goals" and "means
of mass destruction . . . should be rejected." This Bishops' Appeal was immediately taken up by independent peace groups and used as a petition; circulated as an alternative to the Linz Appeal, it eventually garnered 140,000
signatures.[42] Even in the aftermath of the first Euromissile deployment that
fall, the Austrian movement remained a vigorous force. Starting in February
1984, peace activists in Villach began working on a proposal for a nuclear-
free belt around Austria, the aim of which was to remove short-range nuclear missiles from northeast Italy and western Hungary. Taking up the
"Villach proposal," many peace groups and individuals promoted it as a
means of creating a link between existing plans for nuclear-free zones in
Scandinavia and the Balkans.[43]

Ireland

Considerably farther from the front lines of the Cold War, antinuclear activism in Ireland never reached these massive dimensions; but, even so, it
became a prominent feature in the nation's political life. Revived in 1979,
Irish CND grew rapidly. By the beginning of 1983, it had over 5,000 members and 40 local branches, plus tens of thousands of other activists in affiliated groups. Irish CND commemorated the Hiroshima and Nagasaki bombings, protested against the Reagan administration's decision to deploy the
neutron bomb, and condemned Euromissile deployment and the increasing
dangers of nuclear war. In October 1983, the month of anti-missile protests
throughout Western Europe, it organized a demonstration of 4,000 people in
Dublin. In mid-1984, together with other peace groups, Irish CND created
the Irish Campaign against Reagan's Foreign Policies. This coalition organized a 10,000-person "Ring Around Reagan" as he participated in a lavish state banquet at Dublin Castle and a 5,000-person protest at the parliament, which the U.S. President addressed the following day.[44]

   As agitation against nuclear weapons spread across Ireland, powerful
forces joined the antinuclear campaign. Politicians of all political parties
joined Irish CND, as did unionists and church activists. Just before Reagan
began his speech to the nation's parliament, three members of that legisla-

tive body walked out in protest, announcing their opposition to his defense policies. In the summer of 1983, the Irish Catholic bishops issued a joint statement on nuclear war, "The Storm That Threatens," a sharp critique of the arms race and nuclear deterrence. Cities and towns rushed to declare themselves nuclear-free zones and, by the beginning of 1983, more than half the Irish population was living in such areas.[45]

Conclusion

Thus, by early 1985, West European nations had been swept up in a massive surge of antinuclear activism. In the autumn of 1983 alone, an estimated five million people in Western Europe took to the streets to demonstrate against the Euromissiles—the largest outpouring of popular protest in that region's history.[46] Furthermore, powerful religious bodies, unions, and political parties joined the antinuclear crusade. This was not an anti-American campaign, but one directed against the nuclear policies of both superpowers. Nevertheless, the level of dissent from the Reagan administration's military policy was remarkable, particularly given the fact that so much of it came from within the ranks of the Western military alliance. A May–June 1984 survey of seven West European NATO nations, conducted by the U.S. Information Agency, found that in only two of them (Britain and Italy) did a majority of the public "have at least a fair amount of confidence in the ability of the U.S. to act responsibly in world affairs." Furthermore, in six of these nations the prevailing view was that "U.S. policies have increased the risk of war."[47] Far from strengthening the Western defense alliance, the Reagan administration's nuclear policies were creating the greatest crisis in its history.

Revolt of the Doves

The Movement in the United States and Canada, 1981-85

> The hope for peace and disarmament has been stirred in
> people—and governments may yet learn that they are
> unable to kill the dream.
>
> Pam Solo, 1983

In North America, the nuclear arms race swept to the forefront of public
concerns. Amid the escalating nuclear confrontation of the early 1980s, unprecedented numbers of American and Canadian disarmament activists assailed Euromissile deployment, the development of new weapons programs
(e.g. the MX missile), the Reagan administration's Strategic Defense Initiative (SDI, better known as Star Wars), and the readiness of the great powers
to wage nuclear war. Americans rallied to an apparently more moderate en-
deavor than organized by their counterparts in Western Europe: the Nuclear
Weapons Freeze Campaign. While END supporters in Western Europe
sought to rid the continent entirely of nuclear weapons, Americans worked
to halt nuclear testing, production, and deployment as "a first step" toward
nuclear disarmament. In addition, while many END affiliates demanded
unilateral action, the Freeze championed a Soviet-American bilateral agreement. In other respects, however, American activists promoted a more
sweeping approach than did their European allies. They addressed the issue
of nuclear disarmament around the world, rather than solely in Europe.
Furthermore, while West Europeans focused upon blocking the deployment
of one particular weapons system—intermediate range nuclear missiles—
America's Freeze proponents worked at halting the entire nuclear arms race.

In the United States and Canada, as elsewhere, the surge in antinuclear
activism resulted primarily from a belief that the world was careening toward disaster. At the beginning of 1981, the editors of *Bulletin of the Atomic*

Scientists moved forward the hands of their famous "doomsday clock" to three minutes to midnight. Polls in 1981 found that 47 percent of Americans thought that it was fairly or very likely that the United States would soon be in a nuclear war; in 1982, the percentage rose to 48 percent. Between September 1982 and October 1983, the percentage of the population saying that the threat of war and fear of nuclear weapons were among their greatest concerns rose from 23 to 45 percent. Even Admiral Hyman Rickover, creator of America's nuclear navy, remarked grimly: "I think we will probably destroy ourselves."[1] Much of the apocalyptic mood was fostered by the comments and priorities of the Reagan administration. For millions of Americans, as William Sloane Coffin, Jr., recalled, the "bellicose rhetoric of Ronald Reagan" rang like an alarm bell, setting a vast antinuclear campaign in motion. Looking back upon events, John Isaacs of the Council for a Livable World concluded that the Reaganites provided "a dream team" for the movement.[2]

The United States

Some of the new concern led to intense informational activity. The Center for Defense Information held two well-publicized conferences on nuclear war—one in the Netherlands and the other in the United States—in which military and other experts testified about its terrible consequences. CDI luminaries, including Admirals Gene LaRocque and Eugene Carroll, traveled about, addressing a broad variety of peace movement and public gatherings. In these and other fora, they provided devastating critiques of the INF missiles, the neutron bomb, the MX missile, and SDI.[3] Colonel Robert Bowman, a former director of advanced space programs for the U.S. Air Force Space Command, added to the growing furor over Star Wars, portraying it as "military lunacy."[4] Meanwhile, at the Natural Resources Defense Council, which had previously dealt with nuclear environmental and proliferation dangers, Tom Cochran compiled a reference guidebook on U.S. nuclear weapons that, like CDI studies, was put to effective use by activist groups.[5] Determined to heighten popular understanding of nuclear dangers, Roger Molander, a National Security Council staffer during the Ford and Carter administrations, put together Ground Zero Week in April 1982. In some 650 cities and towns, it drew more than a million Americans to "nuclear war awareness and education" events, ranging from street theater to lectures, from town meetings to tours of the area of devastation that would result from a nuclear attack.[6]

Thanks to the work of local activists, some communities underwent a thorough immersion in nuclear issues. Inspired by the community-based work of IKV in the Netherlands, Seattle's PSR president, Judy Lipton, came up with the idea of bringing her entire metropolitan community of 1.2 million people into a concentrated nuclear colloquy. In 1982, she and other activists set out to make sure that, for a week that fall, all the city's major institutions discussed nuclear war. "No matter where people went for that week—from their local pastor to their schools to theaters or to union halls—we were going to rub their faces in it. . . . We'd leave them no choice but to think about nuclear war as a real thing" and, thus, "penetrate their denial." Meeting with business, church, and veterans' group leaders, she stated: "You don't have to agree with me; let's just have public discussion about the issue. Let's bring it out and let people make up their own minds." As a result, 67 community organizations, including the YMCA, the Municipal League, and the City Club, endorsed and participated in "Target Seattle." Programs were held in virtually every public school and in 200 churches. For the culminating event, some 25,000 people filled a downtown football stadium, where they heard speeches by Helen Caldicott and other movement luminaries. Successful beyond the organizers' hopes, Target Seattle was repeated in 1983 and 1984.[7]

Other activists adopted a more confrontational approach. A New Abolitionist Covenant, drawn up in 1981 by members of religious pacifist groups, argued that the wholesale destruction threatened by nuclear weapons "make their possession and planned use morally indefensible and an offense against God and humanity." Following the model of the Plowshares activists of 1980, religious pacifists conducted an additional seventeen nonviolent civil disobedience actions by 1985. Despite sentences that ranged up to eighteen years in prison, priests, nuns, teachers, students, anti-poverty workers, and lawyers entered nuclear weapons facilities, hammered and poured blood on MX missiles, Trident submarines, B-52 bombers, and other components of the U.S. nuclear weapons system, and often left behind "indictments" that charged the U.S. government and corporations with crimes against international law and God.[8] Other pacifist groups adopted somewhat different tactics. Reviving war tax resistance, the War Resisters League also sparked sit-ins at the diplomatic missions of the five nuclear powers and helped foster the turnout at mass antinuclear rallies.[9] The AFSC and the FOR lobbied against nuclear missiles and worked with broader coalitions to shut down nuclear weapons facilities.[10]

Like the pacifists, Mobilization for Survival was located on the "radical" end of the antinuclear spectrum. In the early 1980s, as the AFSC, the FOR, CALC, and WILPF lost interest in the Mobilization—largely because of their involvement in the Freeze campaign—it shifted from a cooperative venture of national peace organizations to a coalition comprised primarily of local antinuclear groups. Furthermore, given the nation's growing preoccupation with the nuclear arms race, "the Mobe" began to accord the struggle against nuclear war a higher priority than resistance to nuclear power.[11] In 1982, it initiated the coalition that led to a massive antinuclear rally in New York City. The following year, it organized nationwide local protests against cruise and Pershing II missile deployment. Starting in 1983, it also championed the development of nuclear-free zones and spurred the development of "Deadly Connections" conferences, which linked great power interventionism to the threat of nuclear war. Fostering such projects was difficult, for the departure of national peace groups from the Mobe left it short of financial resources. Furthermore, it was plagued by personal and strategic bickering. Nevertheless, Mobilization for Survival remained a lively, dynamic organization, with 160 affiliates. Some of them, like the Livermore Action Group, conducted major campaigns on the local level.[12]

Women's peace groups played a particularly important role in resisting the nuclear arms race. Declaring that "there is no political difference which would justify the destruction of the world," Women Strike for Peace demanded that the U.S. government call an emergency session of the heads of nuclear nations to halt the nuclear arms race and lay plans for "the dismantling of *all* nuclear weapons by *all* nuclear nations." It also produced and distributed 200,000 copies of a booklet, *A Basic Primer on 'Star Wars' for the Legitimately Confused*, and followed this up with a slide show on the same subject. WILPF, too, waged a spirited antinuclear campaign, and found its membership soaring.[13] A larger number of recently mobilized women, however, joined Women's Action for Nuclear Disarmament (WAND). Founded by Caldicott in 1980, when—during her speaking tours—she was struck by women's passionate rejection of nuclear war, WAND sought, in the words of its leaders, "to halt and reverse the nuclear arms race." It vigorously opposed Euromissile deployment and the MX missile program, and backed the Nuclear Freeze campaign. Phone calls flooded into its offices, especially after Caldicott's major speeches, and by mid-1984 it had affiliated groups in 30 states.[14]

Long dormant, SANE grew into a very significant political entity—larger and more powerful than ever before in its history. It denounced the Reagan administration's military budget increases, condemned Euromissile deployment, and backed the Freeze campaign. Its most important venture, however, remained the struggle against the MX missile, in which it continued to play a leading role. In the early 1980s, the anti-MX coalition burgeoned into a formidable force, bringing together not only disarmament groups, but Common Cause, major labor unions, and environmental, religious, black, and Hispanic organizations. SANE's executive director, David Cortright, recalled that "the letters we would send to the Hill sometimes had as many as a hundred organizations signed on." During "monumental struggles in Congress in '83 and '84," he remarked, "we would have the entire organization on emergency footing, calling everybody in the country, lobbyists battling members up on the Hill, producing the ads, doing everything we could." Leaders of the House of Representatives worked closely with the coalition, and on a number of occasions SANE dragged individual legislators from their sickbeds for key votes.[15] These and other activities contributed to SANE's meteoric revival. Between 1981 and 1984, its membership grew by 800 percent.[16]

Disarmament-oriented scientists' organizations also issued sharp critiques of the nuclear arms race. Although the Federation of American Scientists played a relatively modest role in the Euromissile crisis, it became far more deeply involved in the controversy over SDI. After the President announced the new program, the mass media mobbed Jeremy Stone of the FAS in their quest for a scientific appraisal. Criticizing SDI then and on numerous occasions thereafter, Stone and FAS specialists contended that it would accelerate the arms race, undermine the ABM treaty, and provide an unreliable defense for the United States. When the FAS was approached by Soviet scientists, also concerned about the dim future of the ABM treaty and nuclear arms control, the two groups began meeting to see what could be done to head off an arms race in space.[17] The independent *Bulletin of the Atomic Scientists*, edited by the physicist Bernard Feld, followed much the same course. Warning of a runaway nuclear arms race and nuclear war, Feld and other scientists repeatedly utilized the *Bulletin* to champion nuclear arms control and disarmament. Meanwhile, the *Bulletin* nearly doubled its number of subscribers.[18]

The largest of the scientists' disarmament groups, the Union of Concerned Scientists, played a particularly prominent role in the antinuclear campaign. In November 1981, it attracted thousands of concerned students and faculty members to nuclear weapons–focused teach-ins and convocations it organized on 151 college campuses. During 1982, the UCS expanded the convocations to more than 500 events around the theme of "Solutions to End the Arms Race." That year, it also released a report entitled "Framework for a New National Security Policy." Signed by 46 Nobel Laureates in science and medicine and more than 500 members of the National Academy of Sciences, the report called for a pledge by the United States and its allies not to be the first to use nuclear weapons, a bilateral freeze on strategic weapons and delivery systems, a comprehensive test ban treaty, deep cuts in nuclear arsenals, and a program to curtail nuclear proliferation. In November 1983, the UCS expanded its convocation program—this time designated "The New Arms Race or New Ways of Thinking?"—to a full week of events, held in a thousand locations around the United States. Like the FAS, the UCS sharply attacked SDI. Issuing an "Appeal by American Scientists to Ban Space Weapons," the UCS argued that "the development of antisatellite weapons and space-based missile defenses would increase the risk of nuclear war and stimulate a dangerous competition in offensive nuclear arms." According to Henry Kendall, the best-known UCS spokesperson, "the nuclear arms race is the most outstanding folly on which mankind has so far embarked."[19]

Like UCS, Physicians for Social Responsibility served as a key player in the burgeoning nuclear resistance. PSR held symposia on "The Medical Consequences of Nuclear Weapons and Nuclear War" in virtually every major city in the United States, often drawing crowds in the thousands. Termed by PSR insiders "the bombing run," a symposium described in chilling detail what would happen to the host city in the event of a nuclear attack. In addition, PSR widely distributed a videotape, *The Last Epidemic*, outlining the effects of nuclear war in San Francisco, and another videotape, *The Final Epidemic*, a collection of speeches given during PSR symposia. In October 1982, moving beyond this informational work, the PSR board of directors agreed to oppose those national policies that presupposed that nuclear war could be won or survived. Henceforth, PSR formally opposed civil defense planning, supported a Nuclear Freeze, advocated a comprehensive nuclear test ban, and rejected U.S. and Soviet development of a new generation of first-strike nuclear weapons. It also expanded the kinds of events it hosted to include speaker tours, antinuclear displays at medical society meetings, and community programs in coalition with other groups. As physicians had considerable prestige in American life, PSR enjoyed unusually good access to community leaders, to the mass media, and to members of Congress.[20]

During the early 1980s, PSR grew dramatically, despite a nasty internal conflict. Although Caldicott was the organization's best-known, most popular leader, at least among its rank and file, she was viewed less favorably by some senior figures in the PSR hierarchy. Uneasy with her strong personality, evangelical style, and handling of factual information, they began an attack upon her leadership and, in September 1983, succeeded in maneuvering her out of the organization's presidency. Caldicott felt terribly hurt by this treatment. Staff members and some board members, who recognized her central role in reviving PSR, were disturbed as well. Nevertheless, Caldicott retained a formal affiliation with the organization as president emeritus, and both she and her critics downplayed the conflict for some years.[21] Meanwhile, PSR continued to flourish. In the aftermath of "the bombing run" in Seattle, the local PSR chapter soared from about a hundred members to well over a thousand; it promptly opened an office, installed a telephone, and hired a staff. By 1985, the national PSR had ten times its membership of 1981. It could also point to 150 active chapters, located in every major metropolitan area of the country, as well as in many smaller cities and towns.[22]

Although PSR had a particularly high profile during these years, it was only one among dozens of disarmament groups that sprang up among professionals. In addition to the FAS, the UCS, and PSR, they included the Lawyers Alliance for Nuclear Arms Control, Educators for Social Responsibility, High Technology Professionals for Peace, Architects for Social Responsibility, Social Workers for Peace and Nuclear Disarmament, and Computer Professionals for Social Responsibility. Combining enthusiasm, influence, and expertise, they brought substantial portions of their constituencies into the antinuclear campaign. Sometimes, as in the case of the Social Workers, they were established as a component part of their professional association. Usually, however, they developed independently and, then, injected the nuclear issue into the ranks of their professions. In this role, they often could bring great prestige to bear. The outreach committee of the Lawyers Alliance contained four former presidents of the American Bar Association and a former U.N. ambassador. In addition, recognizing their considerable influence in American life, most of them campaigned publicly for nuclear arms control and disarmament measures. Three of the leading organizations—PSR, the UCS, and the Lawyers Alliance—drew together in 1983 to form the Professionals Coalition for Nuclear Arms Control, which henceforth mobilized their members for united action in congressional battles against the Reagan administration's nuclear priorities.[23]

None of these organizations, however, compared in size, popular mobilization, and impact to the Nuclear Weapons Freeze Campaign. In March 1981, Freeze organizers held their first national conference at the Center for Peace Studies at Georgetown University, in Washington, D.C. Forsberg was determined to push the gathering beyond an assemblage of marginal peace activists, for she wanted the new movement "very middle class"—working "within the system rather than alienating it from the system." Thus, despite the leading role played in the conference by pacifists and other longtime critics of military priorities, it produced a strategy and movement geared toward the political mainstream. Rejecting offers by East Coast–based peace organizations to house the Freeze, organizers decided to set up their own, independent headquarters in St. Louis, deep in the heartland of the nation. To be sure, the first Freeze coordinator, Randy Kehler—a longtime peace activist, imprisoned as a conscientious objector during the Vietnam War— was somewhat less mainstream than the desired image. Nonetheless, Kehler was a clean-cut, articulate individual, skilled as a consensus builder and determined to keep the new venture on course. By the end of 1981, the Freeze campaign, though largely unnoticed by the mass media, drew upon tens of thousands of activists in 43 states.[24]

Early Freeze campaign efforts focused, for the most part, on popularizing the Freeze idea and on influencing people at the local level. Activists distributed vast quantities of Freeze literature, initially emphasizing the magnitude and dangers of the nuclear arms race but, eventually, taking up other issues as well, such as the economic benefits of a nuclear weapons Freeze.[25] In addition, they brought Freeze resolutions before organizations with which they were personally affiliated, including religious bodies, professional associations, and unions, and also placed them before town meetings, city councils, and state legislatures. Through local petition drives, they gathered signatures in a nationwide campaign and, in addition, placed Freeze referenda on the ballot in cities, counties, and states throughout the country. Efforts to win passage of these referenda proved time-consuming, but they gave activists a local issue around which to organize. The local meetings sponsored by the UCS and PSR on campuses and in communities wove nicely into the pattern of Freeze organizing, for the Freeze campaign provided the many thousands of attendees with what appeared to be a reasonable channel for their heightened concern. Although Freeze activism was more prevalent in Northern and Western states than in the conservative South, by June 1982 it had taken root in 75 percent of the nation's congressional districts.[26]

Within a short time, these efforts produced an unprecedented outpouring of American support for an end to the nuclear arms race. On March 2, 1982, 159 out of 180 Vermont town meetings voted to back a U.S.-U.S.S.R nuclear weapons Freeze. When a broad coalition of peace groups sponsored an antinuclear demonstration in New York City on June 12, 1982, around the theme "Freeze the Arms Race—Fund Human Needs," it turned into the largest political rally in American history, with nearly a million participants. The Freeze campaign's petitions, delivered to the U.S. and Soviet missions to the United Nations, were signed by more than 2.3 million Americans. The most stunning display of antinuclear sentiment occurred that fall, when Freeze referenda appeared on the ballot in ten states, the District of Columbia, and 37 cities and counties around the nation. Despite the intense opposition of the Reagan administration, which campaigned hard to defeat these referenda, the Freeze emerged victorious in nine out of ten states (including the President's home state of California) and in all but three localities. In this largest referendum on a single issue in American history, covering about a third of the U.S. electorate, over 60 percent of the voters supported the Freeze.[27] Opinion surveys revealed that the Freeze had the backing of large majorities of Americans. Five polls taken during 1983 found an average of 72 percent support and 20 percent opposition—results virtually unchanged from six polls in 1982.[28]

Endorsements of the Freeze reflected this widespread popularity. Within a short time, hundreds of national organizations—many never before involved with national defense issues—gave it their stamp of approval. In addition to church bodies and labor unions, they included the American Association of School Administrators, the American Association of University Women, the American Public Health Association, the American Nurses Association, the American Pediatric Society, Friends of the Earth, the National Council of La Raza, the National Education Association, the U.S. Conference of Mayors, and the Young Women's Christian Association. Furthermore, by November 1983, the Freeze had been endorsed by more than 370 city councils (including those of New York, Chicago, Atlanta, Tucson, Philadelphia, Detroit, New Orleans, Baltimore, Pittsburgh, Terre Haute, and St. Petersburg), 71 county councils, and by one or both houses of 23 state legislatures.[29] Although Mobilization for Survival and the War Resisters League sniped at what they considered the shallowness of the Freeze campaign, virtually all American peace and disarmament organizations ultimately gave it their backing and, in most cases, focused their efforts upon it.[30] Explaining the widespread support for the Nuclear Freeze, Forsberg told the press: "People have decided enough is enough."[31]

Most American peace groups also worked together in opposition to the Euromissiles. From the start, they perceived the danger of cruise, Pershing II, and SS-20 deployment, but also recognized that it was an issue with less resonance among the American people than the MX missile (slated to be deployed on U.S. territory) or the Freeze. Consequently, in May 1981, when SANE held a small anti-missile demonstration in Washington, D.C., only two other national peace organizations participated: WSP and WILPF. That winter, although other peace groups—including the AFSC, the Coalition for a New Foreign and Military Policy, the FOR, Mobilization for Survival, and the War Resisters League—joined them in a critique of the Reagan administration's Euromissile negotiating proposal, the campaign remained limited.[32] By early 1983, however, amid massive anti-missile demonstrations in Western Europe and the imminent U.S. deployment of the cruise and Pershing II missiles, the situation had changed. Mary Kaldor of END received a standing ovation at the February 1983 Freeze convention when she asked for American support in that "year of decision." Proclaiming that cruise and Pershing II missiles introduced a "new, qualitatively different, and greater danger of nuclear war," the delegates voted to oppose their deployment, to call upon the Soviet Union to reduce its deployment of SS-20 missiles, and to follow the recommendation of an FOR-AFSC task force to join anti-missile demonstrations that October.[33]

Despite the growth of anti-missile activism, it never reached the massive dimensions of the Freeze campaign. A key problem was that, unlike the Freeze, it seemed to lead down a unilateral path, such as cutting off U.S. congressional funding for cruise and Pershing II missile deployment. Freeze leaders found themselves wrestling uneasily with this issue, which they feared would jeopardize their mainstream support. On the other hand, U.S. missile deployment would deliver a serious blow to their hopes for halting the arms race and, furthermore, tamely accepting it would undermine the morale of their activist base.[34] Ultimately, the Freeze campaign rallied behind congressional legislation, also supported by other peace groups, to urge the President to delay missile deployment for a year while arms negotiators worked out an agreement to substantially reduce Soviet SS-20s and, thereby, render new missiles unnecessary. Although defeated in Congress, this proposal did secure 101 votes in the House of Representatives.[35] It also provided the core of Freeze appeals to Reagan and Andropov that September. In October, a broad range of peace groups, including the Freeze, sponsored the planned demonstrations. Calling for "an immediate halt to all efforts to deploy cruise and Pershing II missiles" and support of European peace movement efforts "to create a nuclear-free Europe, East and West," some 200 of these anti-missile rallies occurred in communities around the nation, with total participation estimated at over 110,000 people.[36]

Like their counterparts in Western Europe, American antinuclear groups also worked to oppose the repression of nonaligned peace activists by Communist governments. During the summer of 1982, sixteen U.S. peace groups publicly condemned the Soviet regime's harassment of the independent Moscow Trust Group. In September, twenty prominent U.S. antinuclear leaders—among them Henry Kendall (UCS), Randall Forsberg (Freeze), Helen Caldicott (PSR), Jerome Grossman (Council for a Livable World), and Frank von Hippel (Federation of American Scientists)—issued a letter of protest against Soviet mistreatment of the struggling organization. Expressing their dismay that "the Soviet government has chosen to harass and persecute this tiny group," they called for the release of its chair, Sergei Batovrin, from a psychiatric hospital, where Soviet authorities had incarcerated him.[37] In June 1983, many of these leaders—plus others from Mobilization for Survival, Clergy and Laity Concerned, and END—hosted a public reception for Batovrin in New York City after his expulsion from the Soviet Union. Meanwhile, as Andrei Sakharov conducted hunger strikes to challenge Soviet mistreatment of his family, the FAS protested repeatedly to Soviet authorities, sparked stories in the press about his situation, and helped generate an international support campaign.[38]

The vast majority of American antinuclear leaders considered backing for human rights thoroughly consonant with their goals. Having returned from a spring 1984 visit to the Soviet Union, where she met with a Trust Group activist on the verge of a three year sentence to a labor camp, Pam Solo, a leader of the AFSC's disarmament program, had no hesitation about championing a defense of nonaligned Soviet and East German peace groups. "These groups are . . . extremely important for the internal dynamics of their societies and for the international peace movement as a whole," she told AFSC leaders. "We have an obligation and important political reasons to relate to them and support them. . . . I cannot imagine that the peace and disarmament we seek can be isolated from the human struggle for dignity and self determination in the East." Indeed, in 1982, another U.S. peace activist, Joanne Landy, organized a new group, the Campaign for Peace and Democracy/East and West, to blend peace and human rights issues. In April 1983, the Campaign placed an ad in the *New York Times* attacking the Polish government's plans to put Solidarity movement leaders on trial. Signed by an array of U.S. social activists, including numerous disarmament movement luminaries, the ad declared that "it is our profound conviction that . . . the freedom to organize democratic movements without official interference, and to communicate openly, are essential if humanity is ever to progress to a just and peaceful world."[39]

As the antinuclear campaign gathered steam in the early 1980s, mainstream religious bodies threw their weight behind it. The National Council of Churches endorsed the Nuclear Freeze and, in the spring of 1983, sponsored a nationwide "Peace with Justice" week that focused on the negative implications of the Reagan administration's military policy. Bishop James Armstrong, the National Council president, declared that "Jesus Christ stands in direct opposition to everything nuclear weapons represent." The more liberal Protestant denominations—including the United Presbyterian Church, the United Methodist Church, the United Church of Christ, the Episcopalians, and the Lutherans—also endorsed the Freeze and condemned nuclear war, with the Presbyterians exhorting the United States to "never again be the first nation to use nuclear weaponry." Although fundamentalist denominations generally stayed clear of the antinuclear movement, even the Southern Baptists gravitated toward a critique of the arms race and, after some hesitation, endorsed nuclear disarmament.[40] Among Jewish groups, the Conservative Rabbinical Assembly of America endorsed the Freeze, as did its Reform counterpart, the Union of American Hebrew Congregations (UAHC), which also demanded a 50 percent cut in nuclear stockpiles. In February 1983, the Synagogue Council of America, a loose umbrella group for all branches of Judaism, called upon Reagan and Andropov "to implement a bilateral mutual cessation of the production and deployment of nuclear weapons." Rabbi Alexander Schindler, president of the UAHC, declared that the nuclear arms race was the "central moral issue of our day."[41]

The most dramatic breakthrough among religious groups, however, involved American Catholics. With 51 million adherents, Roman Catholicism not only constituted the largest religious denomination in the United States, but one that, during most of the twentieth century, had been quite hawkish. Nevertheless, the Catholic Church's position began to shift during the Vietnam War and, by 1982, 57 Catholic bishops belonged to Pax Christi. Appalled by nuclear war, Archbishop Raymond Hunthausen of Seattle urged parishioners to withhold part of their income taxes, while Bishop Leroy Matthiesen of Amarillo, Texas, urged workers at the nearby Pantex nuclear weapons assembly plant to quit their jobs.[42] In November 1981, the National Conference of Catholic Bishops appointed a five-member commission to define American Catholic responsibilities in light of the Reagan administration's massive arms buildup and talk of winnable nuclear war. On May 3, 1983, in a clear-cut victory for antinuclear advocates, the Catholic bishops adopted the resulting pastoral letter, *The Challenge of Peace*, by a vote of 238 to 9. "We feel that our world and nation are headed in the wrong direction," it declared. Although not rejecting the temporary possession of nuclear weapons, the pastoral letter insisted that ultimately they must be eliminated and that "the first imperative is to prevent any use of nuclear weapons." Indeed, "our 'No' to nuclear war must . . . be definitive and decisive." Furthermore, the bishops' letter deplored the arms race and recommended support for a Nuclear Freeze, "deep cuts in the arsenals of both superpowers," and a comprehensive nuclear test ban treaty.[43]

Naturally, the stands taken by mainstream religious organizations proved of considerable value to the nuclear disarmament movement. Reinforcing the credibility of the antinuclear campaign, they helped shield it from rightwing charges that it was a marginal, Soviet-sponsored element in American life. Moreover, numerous religious bodies engaged in follow-up activities among their parishioners, often through the creation of peace commissions, thus spreading the campaign's message among their adherents.[44] Actually, many religious believers were *already* uneasy about the nuclear arms race. In May 1983, when the Catholic bishops adopted their pastoral letter, polls reported that 82 percent of Jews, 78 percent of Catholics, and 57 percent of Protestants supported a Nuclear Freeze. Nevertheless, the additional institutional backing certainly helped widen support among parishioners, just as it helped facilitate the movement's progress among politicians. Recalling his efforts in Congress to block the Reagan administration's nuclear weapons programs, David Cohen, head of the Professionals Coalition, emphasized how useful the backing of the nation's religious leadership was in bolstering his agenda, even when the churches did not formally lobby for it.[45]

Another breakthrough for the antinuclear campaign came when, unexpectedly, many of the nation's major unions joined it. Although most of the top leaders of the AFL-CIO—including its president, Lane Kirkland—had been rather hawkish, the situation within organized labor underwent significant changes in the early 1980s. Recognizing the harmful effects of military spending upon workers and battered by the conservative, anti-union policies of the Reagan administration, leaders of the more liberal unions joined the Machinists' president William Winpisinger (then co-chair of SANE) in challenging Pentagon budget increases. Although Kirkland sought to block endorsements of the Freeze campaign, by the fall of 1982 key AFL-CIO unions had begun to line up behind it. They included the Amalgamated Clothing and Textile Workers, the American Federation of State, County, and Municipal Employees, the Communications Workers of America, the Service Employees International Union, the United Farm Workers, and the United Food and Commercial Workers. The United Auto Workers (which soon came on board) used the July 1982 issue of its magazine, *Solidarity*, for a cover story on the threat of nuclear war, adorned by a picture of a worker wearing a button proclaiming: "Jobs not Bombs." In California, 77 local unions threw their support behind the Freeze referendum. The flood of union endorsements for the Freeze became so great that, in October 1983, the AFL-CIO executive council voted unanimously to add its own and to call for "radical reductions" in nuclear arsenals. Ultimately, 25 national unions joined the Freeze campaign, and six major national unions came out against the MX missile program.[46]

The nuclear disarmament movement was even stronger among professionals. Leading professional bodies—ranging from the American Historical Association, to the American Psychiatric Association, to the Association of American Geographers—endorsed the Freeze campaign, and many participated actively in the overall movement. Prodded by PSR, the American Medical Association called upon its state and local affiliates to educate physicians and the public about the medical consequences of nuclear weapons and nuclear war. Law school deans lobbied Congress on behalf of the Nuclear Freeze resolution. The staid *Journal of the American Medical Association* printed dozens of articles emphasizing post-irradiation leukemia, nuclear reactor accidents, and the prevention of nuclear war. In August 1983, the *Journal's* editors produced a special issue devoted to the Hiroshima bombing, including statements by leading antinuclear campaigners.[47] Meanwhile, America's top scientists leveled devastating criticism at Reagan administration plans for SDI, and a study by the American Physical Society cast doubt on the possibility of achieving the most modest objectives of this program. Scientists, led by the astronomer Carl Sagan, also publicized a new danger that might result from nuclear war: a "nuclear winter" that would complete the destruction of life on earth.[48] This antinuclear stance among professionals may well have reflected their advanced education. Polls found that the higher the level of education, the greater the belief that the United States already had enough nuclear weapons and the greater the support for the Freeze.[49]

The struggle against nuclear weapons had particular appeal among women. Following the example of activists at Greenham Common, American women established antinuclear "peace camps." The best-known of these emerged at Seneca Falls, New York, a town that, in 1848, had hosted the nation's first women's rights conference but, in the early 1980s, served as the site for the Seneca Army Depot, which handled transshipment of Pershing II nuclear missiles to West Germany. In July 1983, vowing to "create a women's community of resistance," thousands of activists, including some from abroad, set up a Women's Encampment for a Future of Peace and Justice about a mile-and-a-half from the depot. Thereafter, defying arrests, they organized numerous anti-missile rallies and waves of nonviolent civil disobedience at its gates. By mid-1984, feminist antinuclear activists had dug in for a determined struggle at Seneca Falls, as well as at five other peace camps in the country.[50] Other women organized special women's meetings on nuclear war, such as the "Jane Addams Conference on Security in the Nuclear Age," which drew nearly a thousand people to a Chicago gathering, addressed by women speakers, in March 1984. In general, opinion surveys found women more antinuclear than men.[51] Eleanor Smeal, the past president of the National Organization for Women, declared that, "when it comes to the military and questions of nuclear disarmament, the gender gap becomes the gender gulf."[52]

Although students provided a sympathetic audience for the antinuclear campaign, they did not play a very significant role in it. The overall movement was community based and disproportionately composed of a somewhat older generation—people between 25 and 40 years of age. Often well educated and launched on their careers, these activists possessed political views and expertise that had been honed by participation in the civil rights, anti-Vietnam War, women's, and environmental movements. To be sure, hundreds of college and university campuses provided the sites for the fall "convocations" sponsored by the UCS and other antinuclear groups, drawing audiences of 100,000 in 1981 and 150,000 in 1982.[53] United Campuses to Prevent Nuclear War (UCAM) grew out of the fall 1981 convocation and, thereafter, promoted the Freeze, opposed the MX missile, and condemned SDI. Furthermore, students at the Berkeley campus of the University of California organized spirited sit-ins at the Lawrence Livermore Laboratory, which designed the U.S. government's nuclear weapons. Nevertheless, UCAM was a relatively modest operation, which never managed to develop more than about 50 chapters. Swallowed up in a considerably larger movement, student activism was not especially noticeable.[54]

Within a short time, the momentum of the antinuclear campaign attracted congressional attention. In February 1982, as Freeze supporters gathered for a convention in Denver, U.S. Congressman Edward Markey (D-Mass.), in a message of support, informed them that, together with 35 of his colleagues, he had introduced a Freeze resolution into the House of Representatives. U.S. Senator Edward Kennedy (D-Mass.) also found the Freeze campaign appealing and, during the convention, had Jeremy Stone of the FAS fly to Washington to brief him on how he should relate to it.[55] Deciding that the time had come for "catching up with the country," Kennedy joined with Senator Mark Hatfield (R-Ore.) to develop a Freeze resolution for the Senate. Introduced on March 10, this resolution had the backing of seventeen Senators and 122 Representatives. A month later, Kennedy and Hatfield came out with a popularly written book, dedicated to the Nuclear Freeze movement, to promote the Freeze idea. Although Freeze campaign leaders had planned a much lengthier grassroots campaign before embarking upon congressional efforts, these actions forced their hand; consequently, they worked closely with their newfound congressional allies.[56]

Throughout 1982, the Freeze steadily gained political support, especially among Democrats. Addressing the House in late March 1982, Democratic majority leader Thomas (Tip) O'Neill declared that the Freeze "would provide the vehicle to stop the arms race and that, by adopting it, we will be choosing the path of life, not the path of catastrophe and destruction." By contrast, Republican minority leader Robert Michel, echoing the Reagan administration, stated that "any freeze that denies us the right to build the B-1 bomber, the MX missile or the Trident submarine is not acceptable. . . . America's possession of nuclear weapons is the only thing that has stood between us and those bent on world domination." Nevertheless, although the June 1982 midterm Democratic convention passed a carefully crafted endorsement of the Freeze idea, it was vaguely worded.[57] Moreover, many of the leading Democratic presidential hopefuls—including Walter Mondale, Gary Hart, and Alan Cranston—still either promoted their own arms control measures or refused to commit themselves specifically to this one. Even so, the movement's rapid growth had some effect. That June, nearly half the Republicans on the House Foreign Affairs Committee rejected the pleas of the administration and joined most Democrats in voting for the Freeze. Their uneasiness with administration policy was reinforced by the November 1982 elections, when Freeze referenda swept to a resounding victory, antinuclear groups played a significant role in some congressional races, and the Democrats gained 26 seats in the House. Although the Republicans held on to their 54- to 46-seat edge in the Senate, the arms control coalition in the House substantially enhanced its position.[58]

Within a short time, the rising strength of the antinuclear campaign began to produce political results. On May 4, 1983, after numerous administration-led efforts to weaken or demolish the Freeze resolution through amendments, it sailed through the House of Representatives by a vote of 278 to 149. Joining the overwhelming majority of Democrats in voting for the measure were 60 House Republicans. As expected, the administration prevailed in the Republican-controlled Senate, where the Freeze resolution was defeated that October. But even here the measure garnered 40 votes, and Senator Kennedy planned to introduce it again. In addition, the MX missile program, while surviving a House vote only three weeks after the Freeze resolution victory, was in deep trouble in Congress.[59] Moreover, with the approach of the presidential election, the leading Democratic contenders gravitated ever closer to the antinuclear movement. Campaigning for the Democratic nomination, Cranston made the Freeze the centerpiece of his race. Immediately after Cranston defeated Mondale in a straw poll at the June 1983 Wisconsin Democratic convention, the former Vice President, who previously had said little about the Freeze, announced that, if elected, it would be his top priority. Interviewed in January 1984 by the leaders of the nation's major antinuclear groups, Mondale was exceptionally forthcoming, promising to back both unilateral and bilateral measures for nuclear disarmament. That May, when Hart met with an array of antinuclear leaders, he pledged his total commitment to ending the nuclear arms race.[60]

The movement faced far greater difficulties in its dealings with the communications media. To break through the overall media blackout on its activities and issues, antinuclear groups managed to develop a number of media ventures of their own in the 1970s, including SANE's radio program, Consider the Alternatives, which by early 1981 was broadcast weekly on some 500 stations and reached millions of Americans.[61] With the March 1982 appearance of the Kennedy-Hatfield resolution, however, the mass media, as Kehler noted, "discovered" the movement and accorded it considerable attention. Even so, most of the media dropped the movement again in the spring of 1983, after House passage of the Freeze resolution. Moreover, much of the coverage given the Freeze campaign depicted it as a simple, folksy citizens' phenomenon—an emphasis that tended to trivialize it. When the *New York Times Magazine* got around to covering the Freeze in the summer of 1982, Forsberg learned that the peg for the story would be the fact that the campaign had been founded by a schoolteacher. Although she remonstrated that she had taught school for only two years, but had worked as an arms control expert for the past eleven, the story went forward with the more charming—but misleading—emphasis. Caldicott, too, found that, when she met for a discussion of nuclear issues with the *Washington Post* staff, they put her in the Style section: "How old I was, how many children I had, nice string of pearls. They would never do that to Henry Kissinger. They put *him* on the *front* page of the *Post*."[62]

The Freeze, of course, *was* a grassroots, popular phenomenon, but it was *also* a carefully crafted proposal and piece of arms control legislation, and it was this second item that the media chose to ignore or disparage. A week after the introduction of the Kennedy-Hatfield resolution, the *New York Times* editorialized that "the Freeze movement members are not lobbying for a specific piece of legislation." Instead, "they are . . . ordinary citizens, pressing for something less intricate." They wanted "to give . . . peace a chance." Although the news media defined the passage of the statewide ballot propositions as a test of the Freeze movement's power, on November 3, 1982, when the movement won these referenda overwhelmingly, CBS

Evening News—the nation's highest-rated TV newscast—devoted only 20 seconds, in the middle of its broadcast, to this extraordinary victory. A few days later, a reporter on CBS Evening News denigrated the referenda still further, referring to them as "beauty contests." In March 1983, on the eve of the movement's remarkable success in pushing the Freeze resolution through the House, CBS Evening News reported: "This is really just a game. The Freeze is a symbol. The genuine issue will come in votes on individual weapons. And the opposition there is not a rally."[63]

When it came to the content of the Freeze proposal, the mass media usually attacked it. In May 1982, the *New York Times* pontificated: "Few knowledgeable Americans actually favor a freeze or think it can work." That fall, the newspaper referred to the Freeze referenda as a "simplistic sloganeering response to a complex issue." In September 1982, noting that three-quarters of the voters in Wisconsin's primary had just endorsed the Freeze, the *Chicago Tribune* editorialized: "The freeze is a powerful political idea, but it is also a bad one." Meanwhile, on May 20, 1982, CBS carried a news analysis of the Reagan administration's case against the Freeze by pairing news anchor Dan Rather with Herman Kahn, a supposedly disinterested expert but, in fact, a figure who for decades had worked to prepare Americans for nuclear war. After showing an animated version of Soviet nuclear missiles crashing into the United States, the two men agreed that a massive U.S. nuclear buildup was absolutely essential. Rather insisted: "If we freeze now, there is no way to catch up, no way to ease the nightmare of a Russian first strike."[64]

Occasionally, the mass media could be quite unscrupulous. Shortly before the June 1982 rally in New York City, the *Wall Street Journal* published a lengthy article on peace and antinuclear groups that depicted them as pro-Soviet. Furthermore, the *Journal* so frequently misrepresented the Freeze as a "unilateral" measure that the Freeze campaign leadership ultimately appealed for relief to the journalism profession's ethics commission. Although an investigation by the commission sustained the complaint of the antinuclear organization, the communications media then neglected to report this fact.[65] Probably the most vicious story on the antinuclear movement appeared in *Reader's Digest*, a magazine with a circulation of 31 million. In a lengthy article entitled "The KGB's Magical War for 'Peace,'" published in October 1982, one of magazine's senior editors, John Barron, charged that the Freeze and its West European counterparts were all part of a Soviet government plot. According to the author, there had never been "any outcry against the relentless Soviet buildup of offensive nuclear weapons." The article was adorned with a picture of a giant Russian hand, manipulating the strings attached to grim puppets bearing signs saying "No Nukes," "Peace," and "Nuclear Freeze." Outraged at this pastiche of innuendoes, misrepresentations, and falsehoods, individuals and organizations defamed in the article complained bitterly about it, but to no effect.[66]

Given its strength in intellectual and artistic circles, the movement fared better on the cultural front. A broad array of excellent articles and books appeared on nuclear issues, with the best known of them probably Jonathan Schell's powerful meditation on nuclear war, *The Fate of the Earth*. First published in three February 1982 issues of *The New Yorker*, the book became a bestseller and sparked widespread public discussion.[67] That same year, in preparation for the massive antinuclear demonstration in New York City, James Taylor pulled together some of the nation's top singers and musicians for the event, which sparked the formation of Performers and Artists for Nuclear Disarmament. Actors and actresses worked closely with the antinuclear campaign. Colleen Dewhurst performed an original one-act play on nuclear issues, Ed Asner did a series for SANE on Star Wars, and Meryl Streep recorded spots in support of the Freeze. Hollywood for SANE, which had flourished in the late 1950s and early 1960s, was revived by an ad placed in *Variety* in December 1983, signed by more than 250 actors, producers, writers, and directors. They included Anne Bancroft, Mel Brooks, James Earl Jones, Jack Lemmon, Dana Andrews, Ralph Bellamy, Burt Lancaster, Shirley MacLaine, and Jean Stapleton. Its most successful project was the production of *Handy Dandy*, a play with an ironic commentary on the nuclear crisis that was performed simultaneously by leading Hollywood actors in fourteen theaters throughout Los Angeles in October 1984. Designed as a fundraiser for the Freeze movement, it also generated a great deal of favorable publicity.[68]

The antinuclear movement's new opportunities to reach a mass audience, as well as the remaining barriers in this direction, were revealed in the controversy over the screening of *The Day After*. Although, traditionally, television networks had avoided realistic portrayals of nuclear war, ABC broke through this barrier on November 22, 1983, with a showing of this dramatic version of what would happen to Lawrence, Kansas, should a nuclear war erupt. In the weeks preceding the event, antinuclear groups did their best to spur a large viewing audience, while enraged American hawks demonstrated outside ABC affiliates. "WHY IS ABC DOING YURI ANDROPOV'S JOB?" screamed a *New York Post* editorial. Corporate sponsors dropped away. Confronted with this backlash, as well as with strong pressures by the Reagan administration, ABC executives retreated. The movie was censored and, as its director, Nicholas Meyer observed, "barely made it on the air." Immediately after the film showing to an audience of more than 100 million Americans, Secretary of State Shultz appeared on the program and assured viewers that their government was working to avert nuclear war. Following Shultz's reassurance came a panel discussion by six alleged experts—three of whom were former U.S. national security officials (including the ubiquitous Kissinger, who dismissed the film as "simpleminded") and only one of whom supported the Freeze. The Freeze proposal came up only after 45 minutes into the program, when a questioner raised it from the floor.[69] In these circumstances, it was hardly surprising that this one television program did not change viewers' opinions dramatically. But polls did find that the publicity surrounding the film deepened public concern about nuclear war. Public support for the Freeze rose from 83 to 85 percent.[70]

In contrast to the strong backing the antinuclear campaign generated elsewhere on the political spectrum, it stirred up furious resistance on the Right. Denouncing "the freezeniks," Phyllis Schlafly contended that "moaning and groaning about the horrors of nuclear weapons . . . is evidence of juvenile immaturity." The Bomb, she believed, was "a marvelous gift that was given to our country by a wise God." Condemning the Freeze campaign, Edward Teller proclaimed that "we should pray that revolutionary students, politicians and archbishops do not make common cause in supporting an oversimplified solution which will lead to disaster."[71] The neoconservative *Commentary* published an article by Vladimir Bukovsky, a Soviet defector, who stated that "there is . . . not the slightest doubt that this motley crowd is manipulated by a handful of scoundrels instructed directly from Moscow." In another *Commentary* piece, Edward Luttwak, one of the new crop of conservative defense intellectuals, scolded the Reagan administration for "appeasing the protesters" and being unwilling to face the "reality" that nuclear war could take place with "surprisingly few dead on all sides." Writing in the *National Review*, New Right commentator Joseph Sobran despaired that, at the June 1982 rally in New York City, "so many people should gather under totalitarian auspices." *Human Events*, which billed itself as "the national conservative weekly," directed numerous blasts at activists, such as: "How Far Left Is Manipulating U.S. Nuclear 'Freeze' Movement."[72]

Mainstream conservative organizations joined the attack. In May 1982, the Heritage Foundation distributed a "Backgrounder" on "Moscow and the Peace Offensive," calling for a massive campaign to block the growth of the antinuclear movement in the United States and in Europe. Many millions of dollars, it insisted, should be spent in anti-Freeze efforts. Early in October,

Senator Jeremiah Denton (R-Ala.) charged on the Senate floor that a move to proclaim October 10 as National Peace Day, supported by 35 Senators, would "give aid and comfort to the enemies of this country." Behind it, he explained, lurked a women's group, Peace Links, headed by Betty Bumpers, the wife of Senator Dale Bumpers (D-Ark.), and that group—planning a demonstration against nuclear war—was connected to other groups that were "either Soviet controlled or openly sympathetic with . . . Communist foreign policy objectives." Although numerous angry Democratic Senators took to the floor to rebuke Denton—two of them pointing out that their wives were confederates of Ms. Bumpers—a number of rightwing Republicans sprang to his defense. Indeed, during the early 1980s, most Republican Party activists sharply assailed the Freeze campaign. The College Republicans produced posters that, across a picture of Soviet troops in Red Square, had a headline proclaiming: "The Soviet Union Needs You! Support a U.S. 'Nuclear Freeze.' "[73]

Much of the task of opposing the Freeze was shouldered by the Coalition for Peace Through Strength and the American Security Council (ASC)—two organizations that were virtually indistinguishable and shared facilities, staff, projects, and membership. By 1983, the Coalition—led by retired military officers and consisting of about 160 conservative, military, and other hawkish groups, among them the 2-million-member Veterans of Foreign Wars—had efforts underway in fifty cities to defeat local Freeze resolutions and substitute "Peace Through Strength" resolutions. The lavishly funded ASC, boasting some 230,000 members (including 290 members of Congress), stated in its June 1982 *Washington Report* that the Freeze effort—directed "by a small contingent of radical leftists and Marxist leaning 60's leftovers"—was "clearly an integral part of the massive campaign to disarm the West which the Soviets have conducted over the past five years." In an October 1982 fundraising letter, the ASC's president, John Fisher, a former FBI agent, insisted that "KGB leaders tell the Kremlin that their orchestration of the nuclear freeze movement . . . is their greatest disinformation success" and that he had heard that the KGB was spending $300 million a year on such activities in the United States. During the fall 1982 Freeze referenda battles and thereafter, a Coalition movie, *Countdown for America* (which repeated these false charges and drew upon a cameo appearance by Defense Secretary Weinberger), was widely presented on TV by the ASC and the Coalition, as were anti-Freeze ads featuring Charlton Heston.[74]

The Christian Right also threw itself into the pro-nuclear campaign. Having long associated nuclear war with the Last Judgment, Biblical prophecy enthusiasts saw no reason to interfere with the divine will. Cruise mis-

siles had arrived, wrote an eager believer, "just in time for the TRIBULA-
TION!" The Rev. Jerry Falwell, the nation's most popular evangelical
preacher and a confidant of the President, described the approaching nuclear
holocaust in a 1980 pamphlet, *Armageddon and the Coming War with Russia.* "Blood shall flow in the streets up to the bridles of the horses," he assured an interviewer in 1981. Of course, this did not pose a problem to the
faithful, for "if you are saved, you will never go through one hour, not one
moment of the Tribulation." As fundamentalism grew more political in the
1980s, its proponents saw in Reagan's nuclear buildup the working out of
God's alleged plan. Hal Lindsey's 1981 bestseller, *The 1980s: Countdown to
Armageddon,* insisted that the "Bible supports building a powerful military
force," including more nuclear missiles, and that believers must make themselves heard politically. Groups like the Christian Coalition and the Moral
Majority began distributing "moral report cards" on members of Congress,
rating them on their support for military measures. James Robison, the pre-
millennialist television preacher who delivered an invocation at the GOP
national convention of 1984, declared: "Any teaching of peace prior to
[Christ's] return is heresy. . . . It's against the Word of God; it's Anti-
christ."[75]

Falwell's Moral Majority movement worked zealously to foster pro-
nuclear sentiment. In a lengthy fundraising letter of June 17, 1982, Falwell
promised "a major campaign" against "the 'freez-niks.'" They were "hys-
terically singing Russia's favorite song: a unilateral U.S. nuclear freeze—
and the Russians are loving it!" Starting in the spring of 1983, Falwell placed
full-page newspaper ads in the *Washington Post, New York Times,* and more
than 70 other newspapers, denouncing "the 'freeze-niks,' 'ultra libs,' and
'unilateral disarmers,'" and exhorting "patriotic, God-fearing Americans to
speak up" for military defense. He also aired a one-hour, prime-time TV
special attacking the Freeze. Using his weekly Sunday morning sermons,
broadcast over 400 television stations around the country, Falwell lashed
out again and again at the antinuclear movement. On March 20, 1983, he told
listeners: "In the Kremlin, Andropov or somebody decides that we need
300,000 to march in Stockholm or Berlin or New York, and the robots stand
up and start marching for a nuclear freeze. This idea of unilateral disarmament is nothing more than slavery for our children." Reporting on Falwell's
"formidable travels across the nation" with his new crusade, reporter Hay-
nes Johnson remarked that the televangelist had "a single, well-orchestrated,
well-financed political purpose. As he would put it, he's rallying support for
the president's nuclear arms policy of 'peace through strength.' Others, less
charitable, would say he's selling the bomb."[76]

Freeze campaigners could live with these wild attacks from the Right, but they found it more difficult to shrug off the problems they encountered with having their plan adopted by Congress and the President. The Senate had bottled up the Freeze resolution, while the House, which had passed it, had also supported legislation that funded the MX, cruise, and Pershing II missiles. Moreover, even if Congress endorsed the Freeze, it would be in the form of an advisory resolution, which the President could ignore. As a result, in early 1983, Freeze leaders began to toy with a "No Freeze, No Funds" approach.[77] This idea took form at the December 1983 Freeze convention, in St. Louis, where delegates voted to support legislation that would have Congress withhold funds for the testing of nuclear warheads and for the testing and deployment of ballistic missiles for as long as the Soviet Union halted the same programs. Although this "Quick Freeze" represented a temporary retreat from the goal of a comprehensive halt to the nuclear arms race, it would put teeth in congressional action and bypass the obstruction of the President. At the same time, it would continue the campaign's bilateral approach.[78] Accordingly, in April 1984, the Freeze campaign's congressional allies introduced the Arms Race Moratorium Act into both houses of Congress, and by late May it had 120 co-sponsors in the House and seven in the Senate. Furthermore, the candidates for the Democratic presidential nomination endorsed Quick Freeze action and elements of it were incorporated into the House and Senate versions of the Defense Authorization Bill. Even so, given a lack of enthusiasm for the Quick Freeze in the arms control community, plus considerable congressional resistance to acting on the new proposal in an election year, legislative backers decided to postpone a vote on it until 1985.[79]

A ban on nuclear testing provided another possible step toward freezing the arms race for, without nuclear testing, new nuclear weapons could not be developed. Taking the lead in reviving the campaign for a nuclear test ban, Greenpeace protested at Moruroa against French nuclear testing, at Leningrad against Soviet testing, at the Nevada test site against U.S. testing, and in a balloon above the Berlin Wall against four power nuclear testing. In late 1982, the environmental organization put together a CTBT Working Group to develop support for congressional action on a nuclear warhead testing ban, and in June 1983, the twentieth anniversary of the partial test ban treaty, this Working Group held a news conference at which congressional leaders and prominent arms control advocates raised the demand for a treaty. The following spring, the newly formed International Alliance of Atomic Veterans joined with Greenpeace to conduct a national tour that raised the weapons testing issue in fifteen U.S. cities. It culminated in a press conference that unveiled legislation by Senators Kennedy and Charles Mathias (R-Md.) to urge the President to resume negotiations for a CTBT.[80] On August 6, 1984, the Center for Defense Information, in conjunction with numerous other groups, launched an international Campaign to End All Nuclear Explosions with the goal of securing a nuclear test ban by August 6, 1985. Greenpeace, SANE, PSR, WILPF, UCS, the Freeze campaign, and other peace groups joined to foster this venture, as did the American Physical Society, Common Cause, the Union of American Hebrew Congregations, and other citizens' organizations.[81]

Yet another means of breaking through the congressional-presidential logjam was winning at the polls. In January 1983, Forsberg began discussing the election of a new administration and Congress. That spring, a Freeze campaign task force concluded that an independent political action committee should be organized and, in June, campaign activists created Freeze Voter '84. Rather than dole out money to political candidates, Freeze Voter would use its financial resources to hire staff and mobilize volunteers at the local level, thus putting political muscle behind the campaigns of Freeze-endorsed candidates. "Up to now we've tried to change the politicians' minds," Bill Curry, the executive director, told the December 1983 Freeze convention. "Now we're going to change the politicians."[82] Although few activists were enthusiastic about Mondale, he did endorse the Freeze and sharply attack the Reagan administration's escalation of the nuclear arms race. After he secured the Democratic presidential nomination that July, bolstered by a party platform that strongly backed the Freeze, the Quick Freeze, and other arms control measures, Freeze Voter '84 and most other major antinuclear organizations fell into line behind his candidacy and that of congressional proponents of nuclear arms control and disarmament.[83] Ultimately, Freeze Voter '84, the Council for a Livable World, SANE, WAND, and Friends of the Earth raised $5.6 million for hundreds of election campaigns. Freeze Voter alone put some 260 paid staff into the field and mobilized some 25,000 campaign volunteers.[84]

Despite this substantial investment of resources and credibility, the 1984 elections produced only mixed results. Movement leaders were severely disappointed that Reagan won handily and that the makeup of Congress did not shift substantially. Yet the antinuclear issue did not fare as badly in the elections as these factors imply. Mondale, its standard-bearer in the presidential race, was a lackluster candidate and—in the opinion of numerous leading antinuclear campaigners—did a terrible job of presenting the Freeze to the American public.[85] Opinion surveys continued to report that, on nuclear issues, Reagan was out of step with public opinion. A poll that fall revealed that 78 percent of Americans backed a Nuclear Freeze. Indeed, recognizing his vulnerability on arms race issues, Reagan adopted antinuclear rhetoric. He was reelected *despite* his hawkishness, largely thanks to his personal appeal and to an upturn in the economy. Furthermore, although the Reagan landslide could have swept a militaristic Congress into power on his coattails, the movement's political efforts helped prevent this outcome and produced a somewhat more antinuclear legislature than the previous one. Most of the House members who led the opposition to the Reagan administration's nuclear buildup were returned to office, and five out of the seven new Senators elected in 1984 were committed to the Freeze.[86]

Even so, the minimal progress made in "changing the politicians" highlighted the fact that the movement faced some significant obstacles. As the elections had revealed, many supporters of a Freeze voted on the basis of other issues. Also, a portion of the electorate did not know where the candidates stood on nuclear weapons, providing hawkish candidates with the opportunity to secure their support by adopting antinuclear rhetoric. Furthermore, by claiming that his SDI program would free Americans from the dangers of nuclear war, Reagan managed to blunt the appeal of arms control and disarmament among some Americans.[87] In addition, the top 31 conservative groups—most of whom fiercely opposed antinuclear measures—had a combined income of $130 million in 1984–85, giving them a vast financial advantage over disarmament groups. That year, the Freeze campaign's budget was $1.2 million, but the Heritage Foundation's was $10 million. PSR raised $1 million, but the Moral Majority raised $8 million. During the 1984 elections, Republican Party campaign committees outspent their Democratic rivals by nearly four-to-one.[88] Moreover, some Democratic legislators voted for the Freeze merely to embarrass the Reagan administration or to maintain party loyalty. Kehler was stunned to discover that Representative Les Aspin, then steering the Freeze resolution through the House, did not believe in it. These "Freeze phonies," as activists dubbed them, could not be counted upon to oppose individual weapons programs or to make the antinuclear case to the public.[89]

The movement also had some internal problems. Although bilateralism helped ensure the Freeze's popularity, many activists were impatient with it, arguing that—given the massive nuclear overkill already in existence— some unilateral measures, such as halting specific U.S. weapons programs, were perfectly appropriate. Many were also eager to push beyond freezing the arms race to *dis*armament.[90] Furthermore, the Reagan administration's military meddling in Central America weighed heavily upon peace proponents, and this led to pressure to broaden the movement's focus to include anti-interventionism. Ultimately, SANE, the AFSC, and other groups *did* campaign strongly against U.S. intervention in Central America and, though the Freeze campaign preserved its narrower focus, Freeze leaders finessed the issue by linking nuclear war with great power interventionism at Deadly Connections gatherings.[91] In addition, frustrated with electoral politics, increasing numbers of activists were ready to embark upon nonviolent civil disobedience.[92] Finally, there were tensions between the Freeze national leadership and grassroots activists, who distrusted institutionalization of the movement, centralized authority, and an emphasis upon influencing politicians in Washington. In early 1985, when Forsberg suggested appointing George McGovern head of Freeze Voter, local leaders rejected this as an elitist, centralizing move. Convinced that activists were more interested in process than in success—and also exhausted by years of effort—she withdrew from the campaign she had founded.[93]

Despite its problems, however, the movement had become a formidable force. Membership and financial support for American disarmament groups soared, and by early 1985, the UCS had about 110,000 members, SANE over 100,000, PSR more than 30,000, and WAND some 25,000.[94] In 1982 alone, private foundations contributed over $6 million to nuclear disarmament groups and Harold Willens raised over $4 million to campaign for the California Freeze referendum. During the 1984 elections, the Council for a Livable World drew upon 93,000 donors to raise more than $1 million for congressional candidates, the greatest funding it had ever disbursed.[95] Although the largest of the peace organizations, the Freeze campaign, did not maintain a formal membership, by early 1985 it claimed about 1,400 local chapters with hundreds of thousands of activists, and its grassroots mobilization dazzled political observers. In an October 1983 study, Patrick Caddell, one of the nation's leading political pollsters, called the Freeze campaign "the most significant citizens' movement of the last century. . . . In sheer numbers the freeze movement is awesome; there exists no comparable national cause or combination of causes, left or right, that can match . . . the legions that have been activated."[96] Overall, the antinuclear movement of the early 1980s was probably the largest, best-financed, and most popular disarmament campaign in American history.

It also had a great deal of credibility. Given the support of the movement by large numbers of professionals (including physicians, scientists, lawyers, and teachers), Church leaders, and cultural icons, it could not easily be dismissed as a fringe phenomenon. Indeed, even small numbers of businessmen supported it,[97] as did a number of well-known former U.S. national security officials, such as Averell Harriman, Clark Clifford, and Paul

Warnke. In newspaper columns and on the speakers' circuit, former CIA director William Colby championed the Freeze and denounced the MX missile program. On December 14, 1982, the U.N. General Assembly endorsed the Freeze by a vote of 122 to 16.[98] Given the movement's élite, as well as broad-based, support, charges that it was instigated by Moscow tended to fall flat. Furthermore, they were easily refuted. Asked on television about the claim that the Freeze idea had been instigated by Moscow, Forsberg remarked that that was ridiculous, for she had created it, whereupon the interviewer turned pleasantly to another subject. Writing in the *Washington Post*, Stone pointed out that it was U.S. President Lyndon Johnson who, in 1964, had first called for "a verified freeze" on Soviet and American nuclear weapons and added: "People who will believe that the Soviet Union . . . has somehow succeeded in duping large majorities of the U.S. population will believe anything."[99]

As the movement gathered increasing strength and credibility, it gained substantial influence in Congress. During the Reagan years, the original eight organizations in the Monday Lobby Group grew to at least 39, bringing together groups like the Freeze and SANE with others that displayed a newfound commitment to disarmament, such as Common Cause, the League of Women Voters, and major religious bodies. Working together, they brought growing professionalism to arms control and disarmament lobbying.[100] Their activities were supplemented by a March 1983 Citizens Lobby for a Nuclear Weapons Freeze, in which 5,000 volunteer lobbyists from all fifty states pressured members of Congress, and by mass lobbying efforts of pro-Freeze professionals and clergy. The Monday Lobby Group or its constituent organizations also produced eminent, articulate scientific and defense specialists for briefing sessions with members of Congress and their staffs.[101] Thanks to these and other efforts, a substantial anti-militarist bloc emerged in Congress that not only passed the Freeze resolution in the House, but began to challenge the Reagan administration on other issues, as well. In December 1982, the House voted to block funding for the production of MX missiles—the first time since World War II that a President had lost a vote on a major weapons system. In 1984, responding to a Soviet moratorium on antisatellite testing, it legislated a reciprocal ban. Meanwhile, the Senate passed the Kennedy-Mathias bill, calling upon the administration to negotiate a comprehensive test ban treaty.[102]

The fainthearted in Congress could take solace in public opinion. According to a January 1983 poll, only a plurality of Americans (45 percent) believed that, if INF arms control talks failed, Euromissiles should be deployed. That June, a Harris survey showed the public opposed to the MX missile by 53 to 41 percent. Polls on SDI found that it garnered only 35 percent support in 1983 and, although support grew in subsequent years, Americans opposed it by substantial margins when a reference to the price tag was included in the question.[103] More general queries evinced the same reluctance to support a nuclear buildup. Questioned in a March 1982 *Los Angeles Times* poll about U.S. production of "more nuclear bombs," only 34 percent said it would make them feel "more secure," while 43 percent said it would make them feel "more vulnerable." In that same poll, respondents—by 50 to 31 percent—said that the United States did not need more nuclear weapons for its defense. In 1983, a poll found that, by a ratio of more than two-to-one, Americans believed that a U.S. arms buildup would not induce the Soviet Union to negotiate but, rather, would make it more likely to build more weapons.[104] The trend of opinion was particularly startling. Between January 1981 and January 1985, the percentage of Americans favoring U.S. military superiority over the Soviet Union shrank from 52 to 37 percent. In 1981, 51 percent of Americans thought the United States spent too little on the military and 15 percent too much; by January 1985, the figures were virtually reversed: too little, 11 percent; too much, 46 percent—the highest level of opposition to U.S. military spending since the final years of the Vietnam War.[105]

Nor did Americans seem as eager as the President to have a showdown with the Russians. In late November 1982, a Gallup poll found that 68 percent of Americans wanted the U.S. government to go further than it had so far in developing better relations with the Soviet Union. By the following spring, public approval of Reagan's handling of relations with the Soviet Union had sunk to 37 percent. Asked in August 1983 about the President's efforts "to bring about an agreement with the Soviet Union on nuclear weapons," 48 percent said he was not going far enough, 12 percent said he was going too far, and 28 percent said he was doing the right thing. In a November–December 1983 poll about the Reagan administration's defense policies, only 28 percent of respondents said they were bringing the United States closer to peace, while 47 percent said they were bringing the United States closer to war.[106] And this was a war that Americans did not want. In 1984, a poll found that 96 percent of respondents agreed that "picking a fight with the Soviet Union is too dangerous in a nuclear world." Although 66 percent of Americans were prepared to use nuclear weapons if the United States was attacked with them, when it came to using nuclear weapons to defend Western Europe against a Soviet invasion, opinion surveys found consistent and rising opposition: 49 to 37 percent (September 1981); 57 to 28 percent (May 1982); 64 to 26 percent (June 1982); and 65 to 29 percent (Sept.

1984). Indeed, in a May 1984 poll, 74 percent of American respondents agreed that "even relatively small nuclear weapons should never be used in a battlefield situation," and 79 percent said that there was "nothing on earth that could every justify the all-out use of nuclear weapons."[107]

Americans found nuclear arms control and disarmament much more appealing. Throughout the early 1980s, polls revealed that the best-known arms control measure, the bilateral Nuclear Freeze, drew the support of between 70 and 85 percent of the public. Furthermore, although Americans usually frowned on unilateral action, 61 percent of respondents told pollsters in 1984 that they favored a unilateral six-month freeze on U.S. nuclear weapons development to see if the Russians would follow suit.[108] Nuclear disarmament also had overwhelming support. Asked if they favored an international agreement to destroy all nuclear weapons, Americans backed this position by majorities of 61 to 37 percent in March 1982, 72 to 22 percent in May 1982, and 80 to 17 percent in March 1983. In 1949, only 29 percent of American respondents said that the development of nuclear weapons was a bad thing; by 1982, the figure had risen to 65 percent. Commenting on portions of these findings in the summer of 1982, the pollster Louis Harris said that they constituted "an incredible phenomenon," for he could recall nothing quite like the "urgent hunger for peace" that they disclosed. Summing up the latest polls in the fall of 1984, opinion analyst Daniel Yankelovich reported that "the American electorate wants to reverse the present trend toward relying every more heavily on nuclear weapons to achieve the nation's military and political objectives. The public finds the long-term risks of continuing the way we are going to be simply unacceptable."[109]

Canada

Across the border, in Canada, the nuclear disarmament campaign also surged forward, driven by the same factors as elsewhere in the West: the development and deployment of a new generation of nuclear weapons and, above all, a growing fear of nuclear war. Although lagging behind its counterparts in Western Europe and the United States and, also, lacking central coordination or strategy, the Canadian movement was in full flower by 1982, when mass demonstrations and other forms of activism swept the country.[110] The Voice of Women revived and, in the context of the Second U.N. Special Session on Disarmament, dispatched busloads of demonstrators to the June 12, 1982, rally in New York City, along with a Petition for Peace, signed by 125,000 Canadians. By early 1983, the principal focus of VOW's lobbying, vigiling, leafleting, letters, and petitions was support for a minority report in the Canadian parliament, which had urged the government to back a global nuclear freeze, reject cruise missile testing in Canada, back no first use pledges, and champion a U.N. global referendum on nuclear disarmament.[111] This last idea was developed and popularized by a new disarmament organization, Operation Dismantle. Founded by James Stark, a community college teacher, Operation Dismantle grew rapidly and, in November 1982, placed the global referendum proposal on the ballot in cities and towns across Canada. Wherever the proposal appeared that fall, voters approved it, with average support of 76.5 percent. By May 1983, it had been backed by voters in 133 cities and towns, and had been endorsed, as well, by the Federation of Canadian Municipalities, a unanimous vote of the Quebec National Assembly, and 140 members of parliament.[112]

Project Ploughshares backed a proposal that cut closer to home: the establishment of Canada as a nuclear-free zone. Beginning in early 1981, the church-based organization began a campaign that would ban nuclear weapons on Canadian soil, transit of nuclear weapons through Canadian territory, Canadian production of nuclear weapons system components for other nations, and Canadian support systems (including testing) for nuclear weapons. Although this nuclear-free-zone policy, if implemented, would block a number of current nuclear weapons-related projects within Canada, it received widespread support. It served as the focus of the 1981 Disarmament Week, which drew 15,000 people to activities across the country, and was endorsed by groups ranging from the National Farmers Union, to the United Church of Canada, to the New Democratic Party. Furthermore, in response to appeals for local action from Project Ploughshares, Operation Dismantle, and activist mayors, more than 75 cities and towns, including Toronto and Vancouver, proclaimed themselves nuclear-free zones.[113] Meanwhile, Project Ploughshares grew dramatically. Between 1981 and 1985, its income rose from $11,428 to $273,428. By the latter year, it was supported by the Canadian Council of Churches and the major religious denominations, and had acquired nearly fifty local branches.[114]

The emphasis of Project Ploughshares upon a nuclear-free Canada took on specific meaning in the fall of 1982, when a journalist discovered plans to flight-test America's air-launched cruise missiles in northern Alberta. Clashing with Prime Minister Trudeau's earlier rhetoric about suffocating the arms race, Canada's complicity in cruise missile development quickly became *the* central issue for all elements of the Canadian peace movement. That October, 15,000 people participated in a "Refuse the Cruise" rally at the capitol, in Ottawa—one of the largest demonstrations ever held there. Peace groups took out anti-cruise ads in Canadian newspapers and, in December, Project Ploughshares brought a delegation of concerned church leaders to meet with the prime minister. After February 10, 1983, when Trudeau signed a formal agreement with the U.S. government to allow U.S. weapons testing in Canada, protest demonstrations broke out in numerous cities, and a women's peace camp was established near the cruise test range at Cold Lake, Alberta.[115] That September, a coalition of peace groups, unions, and church organizations, led by Operation Dismantle, filed suit against the government, charging that its cruise missile testing violated the Canadian constitution's Charter of Rights and Freedoms. Although protests had begun years before at the Litton Industries plant in Rexdale, Ontario, which manufactured the guidance system for the cruise missile, demonstrations and sit-ins now grew in size and intensity.[116]

Canada's nuclear disarmament campaign drew upon constituencies similar to those in most other Western nations. Not only the small pacifist churches, but the major religious denominations gave it their support. In an antinuclear appeal sent to the prime minister in December 1983, the leaders of the Canadian Council of Churches, the Canadian Conference of Catholic Bishops, the Anglican Church, the Presbyterian Church, the Lutheran Church, and the United Church declared that they opposed the deployment of cruise, Pershing II, and MX missiles, sought reductions in SS-20 missiles, supported a no first-use pledge and a nuclear freeze, rejected Canadian testing of cruise missiles, and did not approve of space weapons.[117] In addition, important antinuclear groups formed among professionals. Physicians for Social Responsibility (renamed Canadian Physicians for the Prevention of Nuclear War) was founded in 1980, and the example was soon followed by antinuclear lawyers, scientists, educators, artists, and other professionals.[118] Labor unions also rallied behind the campaign. Emphasizing its alarm at the nuclear arms race—"this global game of chicken"—the Canadian Labour Congress proclaimed its support for Operation Dismantle, the establishment of Canada as a nuclear-free zone, and the end of cruise missile testing. Women and young people also flocked to the campaign, and a January 1983 poll found disproportionate numbers of both groups opposed to these missile tests.[119]

The antinuclear campaign had less success with Canada's political parties. Only the smallest of the three, the New Democratic Party (NDP), thoroughly aligned itself with the positions of the nuclear disarmament movement. This Social Democratic Party advocated a bilateral nuclear freeze, a pledge of no first use of nuclear weapons, and the establishment of Canada as a nuclear weapons–free zone. Apprised of a poll showing majority public opposition to cruise missile testing, Pauline Jewett, NDP defense spokesperson, called it "a tribute to the terrific efforts, marches, and rallies" of anti-nuclear Canadians. By contrast, the governing Liberals supported Euro-missile deployment, welcomed nuclear armed warships to Canadian ports, and—with occasional hesitations—backed flight-testing U.S. cruise missiles over Canadian territory. The major opposition party, the Conservatives, was, if anything, even more enthusiastic about nuclear missile deployment and testing. "If we won't let NATO test the weaponry, we have very little right to be in NATO," remarked the Conservative defense spokesperson. Thus, although polls showed the Liberals likely to lose parliamentary elections in 1984, antinuclear groups regarded the Conservatives as a very unsatisfactory alternative.[120]

Despite its weakness in electoral politics, however, Canada's antinuclear campaign made considerable progress as a mass movement. In Meadow Lake, Saskatchewan—a small, conservative town about 60 miles south of the proposed cruise testing range—a ballot referendum in the fall of 1982 showed 74 percent of voters in favor of nuclear disarmament and 71 percent against testing of cruise missiles. An April 1983 nuclear disarmament march in Vancouver, sponsored by a coalition of 130 peace, church, and labor groups, drew 65,000 participants, making it the largest single peace demonstration in Canadian history. Overall, more than 100,000 people turned out that weekend for anti-cruise demonstrations in cities and towns throughout Canada, also a record number for a peace venture. In 1983–84, preparing for the coming parliamentary elections, the movement sponsored a Peace Petition Caravan Campaign that gathered half a million signatures on petitions calling for an end to cruise missile testing, the declaration of Canada as a nuclear weapons–free zone, and a redirection of military spending to fund human needs. A study by the Canadian Library of Parliament concluded that "the peace campaign of the 1980s," combined with the proliferation of nuclear weapons, had "made arms reduction a politically irresistible imperative. Media and intellectual debate, books like Jonathan Schell's *The Fate of the Earth*, mass demonstrations, vigils and symbolic displays, letter-writing campaigns, individual protests, have struck a sensitive chord."[121]

Opinion polls provided further evidence of the strong Canadian resistance to the nuclear arms race. A Gallup survey, conducted in January 1983, revealed that Canadians rejected cruise missile testing on their territory by 52 to 37 percent. Another poll, taken that August, found that the margin had shrunk, but that Canadians still opposed such missile tests, 48 to 44 percent.[122] Support for great power nuclear arms control and disarmament measures was substantially greater. According to a spring 1982 study of the views of its own members by the Canadian Institute of International Affairs—which the analysts claimed were roughly similar to those of other Canadians—73 percent rated nuclear arms control and disarmament measures as very important to them, and over 90 percent considered them important to some degree. When asked whether Canada's security would be best enhanced by increasing Western arms levels somewhat, maintaining them, or reducing them somewhat, 73 percent chose the third alternative. Between 1962 and 1982, the percentage believing that "the West should take all steps to defeat Communism, even if it means risking nuclear war," plummeted from 42 to 6 percent. In July 1982, a survey of the entire Canadian population found that, if a worldwide referendum were held, 68 percent of Canadians would vote for total nuclear disarmament.[123] In yet another NATO nation, NATO's nuclear weapons policy was out of line with public sentiment.

Revolt of the Doves

The Movement in the Pacific, Asia, Africa, the Near and Middle East, Latin America, and Eastern Europe, *1981-85*

> We are . . . in solidarity with the peace movements in
> the West which, in their own countries, protest against
> militarism and nuclear armament.
>
> Declaration by East German and Czech
> disarmament activists, 1984

The antinuclear movement became an important political force in many other lands, as well. In Japan, New Zealand, and Australia, it sometimes surpassed in size the mass movements of Western Europe and the United States. To be sure, in most other places, popular movements—confronting an absence of civil liberties and democratic institutions—lacked the political "space" to operate and, consequently, were considerably smaller. Furthermore, many countries in Asia, Africa, the Near and Middle East, and Latin America were far from the front lines of the East-West conflict, and, for this reason, discussions of nuclear weapons and nuclear war often had a rather abstract quality. And yet, some nations, in the Pacific, had undergone their own grim experiences with nuclear weapons and, as a result, their citizens were eager to be rid of them. Other countries, in Eastern Europe, were close enough to the front lines and to the dynamic antinuclear campaigns of Western Europe to spawn small but irrepressible nuclear disarmament movements. Thus, grassroots antinuclear campaigns attained unprecedented strength in some nations and emerged for the first time in others. As a result, during the early 1980s, the movement swept around the globe, stirring an unprecedented popular demand for nuclear disarmament.

Asia and the Pacific

Although the Japanese antinuclear movement entered the 1980s as a multiplicity of groups, without much central direction, it quickly began to coalesce. Once bitter rivals, Gensuikyo and Gensuikin held joint world conferences. Even more important, in 1961, faced with the approach of the 1982 U.N. Special Session on Disarmament, Gensuikyo, Gensuikin, the major *hibakusha* organization, national labor federations, women's and youth associations, a consumers' cooperative union, religious groups, and some eminent individuals established the Japanese National Liaison Committee for Nuclear and General Disarmament. This Liaison Committee was designed to collect millions of signatures on a petition to the United Nations that called for four antinuclear measures: 1) making known to the people of the world the terrible effects of the atomic bombings of Japan and nuclear tests; 2) adopting an international convention outlawing the use of nuclear weapons as a crime against humanity; 3) expanding nuclear free zones where production, possession, introduction, and attack with nuclear weapons would be prohibited; and 4) drafting a treaty for disarmament, with nuclear disarmament given a top priority. Signature gathering began in early 1982, and proceeded rapidly.[1]

At the same time, other groups launched their own antinuclear activities. Working through their professional associations, large numbers of scientists, writers, musicians, artists, actors, lawyers, doctors, journalists, and architects published antinuclear statements. Several large religious groups, working together as the Union of New Religions, began an independent petition campaign, demanding "disarmament and the abolition of nuclear weapons." Similarly, centrist parties and unions circulated yet another antinuclear petition, with a more gradualist approach. Some 38 women's organizations, including most of the major women's associations in Japan, formed a coalition that called for greater involvement of women in the peace movement, and began to assist the Liaison Committee's snowballing petition campaign. Still other Japanese promoted the "ten feet movement," designed to purchase the film footage taken in 1945 by the U.S. Strategic Bombing Survey of the effects of the atomic bombings upon Hiroshima and Nagasaki. For decades, Japan's antinuclear movement had suffered from the widespread impression that it was a politically partisan operation, a product of either the Socialist Party (and the group it dominated, Gensuikin) or the Communist Party (and the group it dominated, Gensuikyo). But the surge of antinuclear activism from a broad range of citizens' organizations helped overcome this assumption, convincing many hitherto uninvolved Japanese that, in resisting the nuclear arms race, they were engaged in a nonpartisan, public-spirited venture.[2]

This broadly based effort produced the greatest burst of antinuclear activism in Japan's history. Some 300,000 people contributed to the purchase of the previously secret film footage of the atomic bombing. This provided the basis for the making of a 20-minute documentary on nuclear destruction that was shown in schools, town halls, and apartment houses throughout Japan. Record numbers of people turned out for antinuclear rallies: 200,000 people in Hiroshima in March 1982, and 400,000 in Tokyo that May. When the Liaison Committee presented its nuclear disarmament petition to the United Nations in June, it had been signed by nearly 29 million people. Moreover, vast numbers of Japanese citizens signed the antinuclear petitions of the other groups, including those of the Union of New Religions (36.7 million), the moderate parties (16 million), and the Catholic bishops (480,000). Although many people apparently signed more than one statement, the petition results nonetheless provided a powerful display of antinuclear sentiment. Impressed by the campaign, more than 1,400 local governments passed resolutions that called upon the Japanese national administration to promote nuclear disarmament at the U.N. Special Session. In May 1982, the House of Representatives adopted a similar resolution.[3]

Despite the importance to this campaign of Japan's history as a nuclear victim, the dramatic efflorescence of antinuclear activism also reflected developments of the early 1980s. The loose talk by American officials about fighting and winning a nuclear war, combined with the Soviet-American confrontation over the Euromissiles, led to a growing sense of nuclear danger. After observing the new documentary about the effects of the 1945 atomic bombing, Japanese viewers wrote: "Hiroshima and Nagasaki are not our past, but our future." According to an April 1982 opinion survey, 63 percent of the Japanese people felt uneasy about the possibility of a nuclear war. Polls in 1983 and 1984 reported that a third of the population ranked nuclear weapons among their greatest concerns. In addition, the development of the mass antinuclear movement in Western Europe helped shatter the government-fed illusion that the Japanese were uniquely sensitive about nuclear weapons and legitimize Japan's nuclear disarmament activism. The 1982 U.N. Special Session on Disarmament had much the same effect and, not surprisingly, provided a central organizing focus for the revived movement.[4]

Japanese fears of nuclear war were exacerbated by a growing concern that its "three non-nuclear principles"—which provided that Japan would not possess, manufacture, or permit the introduction of nuclear weapons on its territory—were being eroded. Increasingly, Japan's military forces engaged in joint military exercises with the armed forces of the United States. Even more alarming, in the early 1980s there were revelations—by former U.S. Ambassador Edwin Reischauer and others—that U.S. warships entering Japanese ports were armed with nuclear weapons.[5] Thus, in the aftermath of the U.N. Special Session, the Japanese movement tended to focus on the issue closest to home: that of the U.S. warships and their armament with Tomahawk cruise missiles. When Reagan visited Tokyo in November 1983, he was greeted with a "Reagan, No! Tomahawk, No!" rally. By 1984, an anti-Tomahawk campaign was well underway, with mass protests outside U.S. military bases. In addition, citizens' groups began petitioning against admitting nuclear vessels and pressuring local governments to proclaim themselves nuclear free. In 1984, about two hundred local governments established the Consortium of Nuclear-Free Local Governments (Nihon Hikaku Sengen Jichitai Kyougikai), although this organization remained more ceremonial than activist.[6]

The Japanese movement also faced some serious difficulties. In the aftermath of the 1982 upsurge around the U.N. Special Session, many ordinary citizens and citizens' groups, satisfied that they had spoken out for nuclear disarmament, returned to their more traditional preoccupations. Furthermore, at the core of the movement, Gensuikin and Gensuikyo remained divided, often for good reasons. Structurally open and democratic, opposed to nuclear power, sympathetic to the Freeze campaign, and close to the Socialist Party and the trade unions, Gensuikin was much like the mass movements in Western Europe. Gensuikyo, on the other hand, though less aligned than most other Communist-led movements, also shared a number of characteristics with them, including authoritarian governance, political purges, and ideological rigidity.[7] In addition, the movement made almost no headway among conservative forces, including the misnamed Liberal Democratic Party, which—largely thanks to the fragmentation of the opposition parties—for decades held onto a parliamentary majority. Thus, despite the unpopularity of nuclear weapons, the Liberal Democrats used their control of the national government to promote nationalist and militarist values in the schools, build up Japan's armed forces, and cooperate with the Reagan administration.[8]

Even so, Japan had an exceptionally popular antinuclear movement. In October 1983, despite the falling off in activism after the U.N. Special Session, some 470,000 people participated in gatherings calling for the abolition of nuclear weapons. Gensuikin alone maintained branches in each of Japan's 46 provinces. Furthermore, unlike their counterparts abroad, key elements of the communications media in Japan—especially two major newspapers, the *Asahi Shimbun* and the *Mainichi Shimbun*—reported zealously on antinuclear issues.[9] Asked about nuclear weapons, remarkably few Japanese saw much value to them. In October 1983, opinion analysts reported that only 21 percent of the public wanted the West to maintain nuclear parity with the Soviet Union, and that only 4 percent favored Western nuclear superiority. Much of the public also looked askance at a military alliance with the United States. Asked earlier that year about Prime Minister Yasuhiro Nakasone's remark that "Japan and the United States share a common destiny," 61 percent expressed objections to it. By contrast, 76 percent of the public supported the "three non-nuclear principles," and 58 percent opposed the use of nuclear weapons under any circumstances. Moreover, in 1982, polls found that 76 percent of the population reacted favorably to citizens' movements to ban the Bomb and that 86 percent wanted their government to advocate either unconditional or gradual abolition of nuclear weapons.[10]

Australia, like its counterparts elsewhere, experienced a phenomenal growth of nuclear disarmament activism during the early 1980s. Hundreds of small, local antinuclear groups sprang up, as did nationwide professional organizations, including the Medical Association for the Prevention of War, Scientists Against Nuclear Arms, and Teachers for Nuclear Disarmament. Church groups like Christians for Peace and Pax Christi threw their weight behind the campaign, producing substantial contingents at antinuclear marches.[11] Women's groups, like Women for Survival, were particularly active, especially in establishing peace camps outside U.S. military bases. In December 1983, hundreds of women—all calling themselves Karen Silkwood, in honor of the martyred American antinuclear activist—staged a nonviolent invasion of the Pine Gap base and, also, tore down its gates.[12] Although the newly formed People for Nuclear Disarmament sought to coordinate activities at the state level and the Australian Coalition for Disarmament and Peace at the national one, the movement usually lacked central direction. Even so, the few united events provided evidence of its unprecedented popularity. On Palm Sunday 1982, an estimated 100,000 Australians took to the streets for antinuclear rallies in the nation's biggest cities, and these rallies grew year by year. In 1985, 350,000 people participated in them.[13]

This remarkable upsurge of Australian protest resulted from numerous factors. A leading one, of course, was the gathering Soviet-American nuclear confrontation, coupled with the resistance to it by citizens' movements in Europe, the United States, and Japan. Beyond this, however, Australians felt a sense of direct nuclear danger—and sometimes complicity—thanks to Australia's uranium mining and exports, French nuclear tests in the Pacific, visits to Australian ports by U.S. nuclear warships, and the location of over a dozen important U.S. military installations in Australia, of which at least three were considered vital to U.S. nuclear war fighting capability. The last item, at least, reflected Australia's membership in the Australia-New Zealand-United States (ANZUS) military alliance.[14] To deal with these and related issues, the bulk of the Australian antinuclear movement rallied around a program of pressing in international fora for the worldwide abolition of nuclear weapons, halting Australia's uranium mining and exports, removing foreign military bases from Australian soil, creating a nuclear-free Pacific, and defending the rights of independent nuclear disarmament activists in foreign lands from government attack.[15]

Despite the substantial size of the movement, it proved difficult to implement this program through electoral politics. Activists found the governing Liberal Party—which had a pro-military, pro-American, and conservative orientation—thoroughly unappealing. Moreover, although peace and disarmament groups traditionally looked to the Labor Party for disarmament initiatives, during 1982 it watered down its anti-uranium mining policy and began taking a less independent position on foreign affairs. Consequently, when Labor emerged victorious in the parliamentary elections of early 1983, the new government, headed by Bob Hawke, adopted policies that did not depart dramatically from the old. The Labor government opposed French nuclear tests, appointed a high profile minister for disarmament, and sent messages of greeting to the Palm Sunday rallies, but its compromising positions on uranium mining, U.S. bases, and a nuclear-free Pacific left most activists disenchanted. Consequently, in June 1984, they formed the Nuclear Disarmament Party, with a platform of no bases, no bombs, and no uranium. Thanks to a spirited campaign, the new party did remarkably well in elections that December. It made nuclear disarmament a major campaign issue, drew 6.5 percent of the vote, elected one senator (and almost elected another), and, together with the antinuclear Australian Democrats, became the balance of power in the upper house of parliament.[16]

Opinion surveys of the time indicate that Australians had rather ambivalent attitudes toward nuclear weapons. When it came to some of the key issues of the Australian antinuclear campaign—such as the entry of U.S. nuclear warships and the presence of U.S. military bases—the movement failed to garner majority support. On the other hand, surveys also found that uranium mining and exporting were opposed by about half the population and that opposition to the visits of U.S. nuclear warships grew during the early 1980s, reaching a plurality of 46 percent in September 1984. According to a 1985 poll, a plurality of Australians (49 percent) also opposed cooperating with the United States in the testing of MX missiles. Moreover, when it came to employing nuclear weapons, Australians were quite clear about their preferences. A 1982 poll found that 72 percent thought the use of nuclear weapons could never be justified. In 1983, 80 percent of Australian respondents told pollsters that they opposed possession of nuclear arms by the nations of the world—presumably indicating that they favored nuclear abolition.[17]

In neighboring New Zealand, the movement enjoyed even greater popularity. As many of its citizens came to the conclusion that the nuclear powers constituted the greatest threat to its security, antinuclear protest swept this small island nation. Older organizations like CND were reinvigorated, while hundreds of new ones were formed, including a crop of professional groups like Physicians for the Prevention of Nuclear War, Psychologists for Human Responsibility, Scientists Against Nuclear Arms, and Poets for Peace. Unions and church groups added their weight to the antinuclear campaign.[18] Although the movement had a very white, middle-class tone, Maori groups eventually joined it. Women's groups, too, became increasingly active, and in May 1983, as part of an International Women's Day of Action for Nuclear Disarmament, staged an antinuclear demonstration of 25,000 in Auckland—the largest public gathering of women in New Zealand's history. Polls found that women and, especially, young people, were disproportionately antinuclear.[19] To give the burgeoning movement some central communication and coordination, activists founded Peace Movement New Zealand in 1981. But, although this central body did provide a national journal (*Peacelink*), outreach to geographically scattered groups, and some degree of networking, for the most part the movement operated on a decentralized, autonomous basis.[20]

The two major projects of the movement centered on making New Zealand a nuclear-free nation. Continuing their program of resistance, Peace Squadrons consistently sought to prevent visiting U.S. nuclear warships from entering their nation's harbors. In June 1982, when the U.S. cruiser *Truxton* attempted to enter Wellington, 30 small peace craft braved stormy seas to protest its arrival. Maritime workers and seamen closed the port for three days through rolling work stoppages, and 15,000 other workers in Wellington halted labor for two hours to hold protest meetings. In March 1984, when a U.S. nuclear submarine, the *Queenfish*, sought to enter Auckland, about a hundred kayaks, rafts, and surfboards—decked out with black streamers and flags—sailed into the path of the vessel. According to an account by CND leader Maire Leadbetter, they created "a symbolic barrier of orange smoke to isolate the death sub from the living citizens of Auckland." Often, land-based protests complemented these ventures. In June 1982, large anti-warship rallies were held in Wellington, and sympathy marches of thousands occurred elsewhere in the country. In August 1983, 50,000 people turned out for an anti-warship protest in Auckland.[21] Meanwhile, in Christchurch, Larry Ross, a "nuclear refugee" from Canada, organized the New Zealand Nuclear Free Zone Committee in 1981. Borrowing an idea from activist women, who symbolically rid themselves of the nuclear menace by proclaiming their homes or offices nuclear-free, the Nuclear Free Zone Committee pressed sympathizers to have their local governments establish nuclear-free municipalities. As a result, by 1984, 65 percent of New Zealanders lived in nuclear-free zones.[22]

The biggest breakthrough for the movement, however, occurred in electoral politics. With the governing National Party (the conservatives) barely able to sustain an effective parliamentary majority against the Labour Party's antinuclear resolutions, Prime Minister Robert Muldoon scheduled a "snap" election for July 1984. Assuming that the warships ban and the consequent reformation of ANZUS were unpopular, the Nationalists made Labour's antinuclear policy the centerpiece of their campaign.[23] For the movement, a crucial moment had arrived. In previous years, it had been skeptical about the willingness of the Labour Party—and particularly Labour's leader, David Lange—to follow through on the party's antinuclear promises. For this reason, and also because it feared co-optation by Labour and the loss of its independence, the movement decided to make antinuclear demands of all parties and to forgo a direct endorsement. On the other hand, when Labour and two minor parties took up the challenge and campaigned vigorously for a nuclear-free New Zealand, the choice was clear. At a conference of movement leaders, it was agreed to ask all disarmament groups to emphasize a simple message: "Don't vote for the Bomb party—get them out of office!" On election day, 63 percent of the voters cast their ballots for the three antinuclear parties, providing Labour with a smashing victory and catapulting it into power.[24]

This proved a turning point. Taking office as prime minister, Lange announced a four-part program: ending French nuclear testing in the Pacific; blocking nuclear waste dumping in that ocean; establishing a South Pacific nuclear-free zone; and keeping nuclear weapons out of New Zealand. The last item was particularly difficult to implement, for it involved challenging U.S. policy. When the U.S. government requested the admission of a nuclear-capable destroyer, the *Buchanan*, refusing to confirm or deny that it carried nuclear weapons, the issue was joined. Fearful that, in the face of U.S. pressure, their government would capitulate, the movement—on 48 hours' notice—turned out 15,000 antinuclear marchers in Auckland on January 30, 1985. On January 31, Lange announced that the warship was banned from New Zealand, and it became, as one activist dubbed it, "Independence Day."[25] Deeply disturbed by the action, American officials called it incompatible with membership in ANZUS, while the Nationalists condemned the Labour government for destroying the alliance. Conservatives formed a Peace Through Security organization, which claimed that the Kremlin directed the antinuclear movement. But Labour's plucky determination to stand up to the enormously powerful U.S. government was popular—not only with antinuclear activists, but with the general public. Between 1978 and early 1984, polls found that opposition to allowing nuclear armed ships into New Zealand's ports rose gradually from 32 to 57 percent. And once Lange had defied the United States, opposition climbed to 76 percent. New Zealand had become a nuclear-free nation—and was proud of it.[26]

In the Philippines, antinuclear protest was also on the upswing. By the early 1980s, the Westinghouse nuclear power plant—under construction at an estimated cost of $2 billion—was inspiring growing opposition amongst Filipinos, who sang derisively of it as "the monster at Morong." In addition, U.S. military bases, particularly the giant ones at Subic Bay and Clark Field, housed nuclear armed planes and warships and, thus, increased the likelihood that the Philippines would become a prime target in a nuclear war. "Why," asked one critic, "should our people be made to suffer in a war that is not of our making?" With the Marcos government's nominal lifting of martial law in January 1981, representatives of church, labor, women's, student, and other groups organized the Nuclear Free Philippines Coalition, dedicated to halting construction of the power plant and closing down U.S. military bases. By early 1983, 82 organizations belonged to the Coalition and, despite the repressive policies of the Marcos regime, protest was growing ever more public.[27] In April 1982, during a visit by U.S. Defense Secretary Weinberger, Filipino students held an antinuclear demonstration outside the U.S. embassy. The following year, activists organized an Anti-Bases Coalition that held an international conference in Manila on military bases and nuclear disarmament. In 1984, opponents of the Marcos regime—including all the major opposition parties—denounced the nuclear reactor project at Morong.[28]

The antinuclear struggle also reached a crescendo in the scattered island nations of the Pacific. Decades of Western use of the region for thermonuclear explosions, nuclear missile tests, and nuclear warship ports, topped off by the latest great power nuclear confrontation, led to a surge of resistance among native peoples. During 1982, in Fiji, the Trade Union Congress organized a one-month boycott of French goods and services to protest French nuclear testing, and the government enacted a ban on the entry of nuclear warships. When, the following year, the government rescinded the ban, church, union, and student groups established the Fiji Anti-Nuclear Group, designed, in the words of its president, R. B. Kumar, "to work towards the achievement of a Nuclear Free Pacific."[29] In Tahiti, thousands of people marched through the streets protesting French nuclear tests and demanding independence from France.[30] On Kwajalein atoll, in 1982, some 1,000 Marshall Islanders—reacting to a U.S. government plan to extend its military rights by fifty years—escaped their crowded squalor on Ebeye Island by staging "Operation Homecoming," an illegal occupation of eleven islands they had left years before to accommodate U.S. nuclear missile tests.[31] In Palau, the U.S. government, stymied by that nation's constitution, sponsored a third and fourth referendum to overturn its antinuclear provision, but without success. A Palau councilwoman remarked: "We have said 'no' four times to the US nuclear intentions in four referenda in four years. When will we be heard? . . . Does democracy apply only in the US?" Her answer came in September 1984, when the U.S. government held a fifth referendum. This time, the Americans waged a $500,000 campaign—quite a lot of money to influence 7,000 voters. Once again, though, the people of Palau voted to keep their islands nuclear free.[32]

Given the common issues affecting Pacific islanders, their scattered movements continued to coalesce. Setting out from Australia in 1982, a large yacht, the *Pacific Peacemaker*, with crew members from diverse lands, sailed from nuclear site to nuclear site, exposing the dangers and publicizing the need for a nuclear-free Pacific. Communications among Pacific peoples and with the international peace movement improved, as did contacts with unions, churches, and professional groups.[33] In July 1983, when the Nuclear Free Pacific movement convened for its fourth conference, in Vanuatu, it was attended by 160 delegates from 33 countries. Deeply resenting the mistreatment of their nations by the great powers, the delegates renamed their organization the Nuclear Free and Independent Pacific (NFIP) movement and adopted a series of pro-independence resolutions, as well as others that protested U.S. involvement in the Philippines, the testing of cruise missiles on native lands, U.S. control over Micronesia, and use of the missile testing range at Kwajalein. The official statement of the conference, the Vanuatu Declaration, concluded: "We go forward from this conference firmly united in our commitment to make our Pacific nuclear free and independent—for ours and future generations." By 1985, the NFIP had 185 constituent organizations.[34]

On the Asian mainland, the antinuclear campaign also gained ground, though not as much. In India, the Gandhi Peace Foundation made occasional forays into the area of antinuclear agitation. In addition, small-scale antinuclear efforts were undertaken by the Indian branch of the FOR and by an Indian CND, which held its first national convention in mid-1983.[35] The best-known antinuclear campaign, however, was launched by the Committee for a Sane Nuclear Policy (COSNUP), an organization founded in June 1981 by Dhirendra Sharma, a science policy specialist at Jawaharlal Nehru University. Increasingly concerned by the Indian government's nuclear power and weapons programs, Sharma pulled together 24 prominent Indians—including Madame Vijayalakshmi Pandit (a former U.N. secretary-general), and eminent jurors, writers, and journalists—for a statement released by COSNUP on June 28. In it, they expressed their "deep concern over the re-emergence of the nuclear bomb lobby in India" and urged the government not to make a rash decision to develop nuclear weapons. Numerous COSNUP antinuclear statements followed, including one directed to the British Commonwealth heads of government, meeting in New Delhi in November 1983, and signed by two hundred prominent Indians. Barnstorming around the country, Sharma and other activists, mostly university students, encountered difficulties explaining nuclear issues to rural Indian villagers and convincing Indian scientists to challenge the government that controlled their research grants. Even so, they managed to break into the mass media and, overall, to spark a public debate about the government's nuclear policies.[36]

In South Korea, as well, nuclear resistance was growing. Given the presence of large numbers of U.S. nuclear weapons in their country, as well as the frightening promises by U.S. officials to employ them in a future war, many South Koreans feared that mass carnage would result from a conflict with North Korea. In June 1981, a survey of South Korean university students found that 89 percent of them rejected nuclear war and that 90 percent were discontented with the world's efforts to secure peace. A report by South Korea's Presbyterian Church on a conference it held in the spring of 1983, attended by 107 ministers, maintained that, thanks to the gathering, "people came to understand . . . that nuclear weapons on our soil are not for Korea's protection. In fact, they could actually cause its destruction!" Given the repressive nature of the South Korean regime, outspoken opposition to government policy was minimal within the country. But, in the United States, Korea support groups, which drew upon substantial South Korean participation, were less reticent. At the massive June 1982 rally in New York City, one of them gathered under the banner: "Nukes Out of Korea." In 1983, they submitted a resolution to the U.S. Congress that called upon the U.S. government to "withdraw its nuclear weapons from South Korea" and "to work diplomatically to create a permanent nuclear-free zone on the Korean peninsula."[37]

Africa, the Near and the Middle East, and Latin America

By contrast, the movement had little presence in Africa. To be sure, in 1983 a small antinuclear group, the Zimbabwe Organization for Nuclear Education, was formed in Harare. And gradually it spread to other parts of the country. There were also occasional public condemnations of the nuclear arms race. In late 1983, *The Weekly Review*, Kenya's foremost news magazine, editorialized: "Nuclear war is not a nightmare only for the northern races. It is a nightmare for everyone, and it is the duty of each one of us to act decisively to avert the holocaust which seems inevitable if the current course of world events is not terminated." Nonetheless, a mass movement failed to develop in Africa. To some degree, this reflected the repressive political climate. In Kenya, one needed a permit to hold a gathering of more than eleven people, even for birthday parties. Furthermore, with no great-power nuclear weapons deployed on the African continent, the nuclear arms race had less relevance and many other issues seemed more urgent. One young African, recently returned from the United States, where he had completed his doctorate, remarked that "many if not most thinking students here" opposed "Reagan's so-called policies," which they viewed as "something out of a spaghetti western." Even so, he added, "attitudes here towards disarmament are similar to those of many blacks in the US. It's not that they don't care. . . . It's just that there are too many other more immediate political and daily struggles to contend with."[38]

These factors also limited antinuclear activism in the Near and Middle East. In this rapidly nuclearizing region, Israel achieved nuclear capability and Iraq, Iran, and Libya worked feverishly to acquire it. Even so, in almost all countries, dictatorial governments circumscribed the possibilities for independent citizen activism. In Turkey, where the antinuclear movement blossomed in the late 1970s, the military coup of 1980 led to its dissolution. Indeed, the new dictatorship utilized a series of military tribunals to prosecute 24 leaders of the Turkish Peace Association.[39] Israel, to be sure, had a democratically elected government, and some organizations—such as Mapam, a leftwing political party—did take antinuclear stands. But the nation's vibrant peace movement was simply too preoccupied with the Israel-Arab confrontation to devote much attention to the nuclear issue.[40]

In Latin America, and especially in countries that had freed themselves from the grip of military dictatorships, the movement made greater progress, but only on a small-scale basis. In August 1982, continued fears that the Brazilian government's nuclear power program was designed to produce nuclear weapons led to the first substantial antinuclear demonstration in Brazil and in Latin America, drawing a thousand participants. Organized by environmental groups and the Social Democratic Workers' Party, it focused on the demand that the Brazilian government accept the nuclear-free terms of the Treaty of Tlatelolco. Nearly two years later, the Brazilian Pacifist Movement—warning that "life on our planet is threatened with extinction by a nuclear holocaust"—brought together representatives of 25 political, religious, labor, and professional organizations to form a coordinating committee in the "struggle for life and against nuclear war."[41] Meanwhile, in January of 1984, a group of prominent Argentine intellectuals organized their own country's Movement for Life and Peace (MOVIP). Well aware that, only recently, their nation's military establishment had operated a bloody dictatorship, MOVIP activists gave their primary attention to opposing homegrown militarism and its attendant incursions upon democracy and civil liberties. Nevertheless, inspired by the overseas antinuclear campaign, MOVIP also raised the nuclear issue. One of its leaders, Alberto Pedace, a biologist, declared: "The possibility of a nuclear tragedy is the greatest problem facing humankind, and we should consider it in every country."[42]

Eastern Europe

To the surprise of most observers, the movement made particularly impressive strides in the nations of Eastern Europe. Certainly, the antinuclear campaign faced major obstacles in this region. The Communist authorities, terrified of grassroots activism—independent of their control and, often, critical of Soviet policy—did their best to stamp it out. Furthermore, much of the population had more immediate concerns than the nuclear arms race, including stagnating economies and the absence of democratic liberties. In addition, many East Europeans felt a deep cynicism about the propaganda-laden "peace" activities of Communist governments and the official Peace Councils, thus arousing suspicion of even legitimate disarmament campaigns.[43] Even so, East European nations were on the front lines of the Soviet-American confrontation and, particularly after 1983, when the Soviet Union began deploying nuclear missiles in East Germany and Czechoslovakia, were becoming prime targets for a nuclear war. Moreover, they housed a restless intellectual-professional class, the cutting edge of antinuclear activism in so many societies.[44] Finally, thanks, in part, to the propaganda of their own governments, East Europeans were well aware of the antinuclear campaign in Western Europe. Some, at least, found it inspirational, a source of outside assistance, and—given Soviet courtship of antinuclear opinion in the West—a potential shield for antinuclear activism in their own countries.[45] Taken together, these items had an explosive potential.

The largest of Eastern Europe's antinuclear movements emerged in East Germany. In March 1981, after meetings with the Dutch IKV, the Study Group on Peace Affairs of the Evangelical Church produced a statement calling for the public renunciation of nuclear deterrence and nuclear war. Although, usually, the church leadership remained cautious, unwilling to challenge the government directly, some church activists were quite daring. Pastor Rainer Eppelmann held immensely popular "Blues Masses" in his East Berlin church, drawing crowds of young East Germans who openly expressed their disdain for militarism and desire for peace. Even during his more conventional religious services, he placed garbage cans before the altar, thus enabling his parishioners to dump their children's war toys "where they belong." In July 1981, Eppelmann sent a letter to Communist Party leader Erich Honecker, suggesting measures to help prevent "the imminent annihilation of Europe."[46] Among intellectuals, too, the issue was simmering. Robert Havemann, a prominent East German scientist and critical Marxist, then under house arrest, wrote an open letter to Brezhnev, signed by over 200 East Germans, calling for the withdrawal of foreign troops from both halves of Germany as a contribution to preventing nuclear war. In December 1981, at an official Berlin writers' gathering, the author Stefan Heym shocked the party faithful by condemning the Euromissiles of both Cold War camps and proposing a joint demonstration against them by East and West Germans.[47]

By 1982, the East German movement was flourishing. In January, Havemann teamed up with Eppelmann to launch the Berlin Appeal—a public plea for a nuclear-free Europe, beginning with the denuclearization and demilitarization of both Germanies. Circulated in schools, factories, and churches, the Berlin Appeal was signed by over 2,000 East Germans, despite the fierce opposition of the government.[48] Meanwhile, although Evangelical church leaders refused to endorse the Berlin Appeal, they did help to secure Eppelmann's release from prison. In addition, to defuse the confrontation that they feared would ensue from youthful plans for a peace march, they agreed to sponsor a "Peace Forum" that February at a Dresden church. This Dresden Forum—drawing some 5,000 people, mostly young and often sporting "Swords into Plowshares" emblems—provided for a remarkably free discussion of disarmament issues. When the Evangelical Church president expressed disagreement with the Berlin Appeal, the audience responded with whistles and boos. At the conclusion of the forum, some 3,000 of the participants poured out to stage an unauthorized (and thus illegal) peace march through the city streets. Although the regime cracked down upon activists and, in March, banned the "Swords into Plowshares" emblem, that June an estimated 3,500 people participated in an unofficial peace action in Potsdam and another 10,000 attended a peace-oriented religious festival in Eisenach.[49]

Indeed, defying arrests, imprisonment, and deportation, the movement became irrepressible. Warning of nuclear destruction, Christa Wolf, one of East Germany's best-known authors, praised the peace movement and called upon writers to "articulate positions of resistance."[50] In Weimar, young people leafleted the public and spray-painted walls with slogans like: "SS-20. No thank you." In Potsdam, activists protested new missile deployments. In Leipzig, peace demonstrations erupted outside the official film festival. In Jena, young activists showed up at an official demonstration bearing signs reading: "No more militarization in our lives." In East Berlin, a disarmament rally on the Alexanderplatz blended East German activists with their counterparts from the West German Green party. Women for Peace initiated a number of antinuclear and anti-military ventures, including yet another demonstration on the Alexanderplatz, in which about thirty women, dressed in black, mailed letters to the government stating their refusal to register for military service.[51] Although the Evangelical Church generally continued its cautious approach, mediating between the movement and the government, its annual "Peace Weeks" and other peace-oriented activities provided activists with vital political "space." Furthermore, in 1982 and 1983, it criticized the deployment of nuclear missiles by both superpowers. The Roman Catholic Church, previously quite reticent on arms race issues, spoke out in January 1983 against militarism and deterrence and, that October, called upon the government to resist plans for deploying nuclear missiles in East Germany.[52]

In Hungary, a more lenient Communist regime provided antinuclear activists with greater opportunities. Alarmed by the nuclear arms race, a group of Budapest University students began to meet for discussions during the summer of 1981. Later that year, they applied to the authorities for the right to hold an independent peace demonstration, but the official Peace Council sidetracked the proposal. Subsequently, studying the arms race and the West European antinuclear campaign, they became convinced of the need for an independent peace movement in the East and for a broad East-West dialogue to counter the nuclear menace. In September 1982, they launched the Peace Group for Dialogue—a group that hoped to avoid repression by keeping the Peace Council apprised of its activities and steering clear of outright opposition to the regime. "If we come to be seen as political dissidents," said one student, "the Hungarian Peace Council will be able to isolate us. We won't oblige them."[53] For a time, this strategy worked. E. P. Thompson met in Budapest with an excited group of young Hungarian activists later that month—in an apartment, rather than in a meeting hall, as the authorities denied a permit for the latter—and was greatly impressed by the vibrancy of this grassroots movement, which he publicized in an END pamphlet that he co-authored with one of Dialogue's founders, Ferenc Köszegi.[54]

As the Hungarian movement gathered momentum, it opened up the nation to a new and far more independent kind of politics. In 1982, Hungarian high school students, acting on their own, organized an Anti-Nuclear Campaign with the slogan: "Let's Melt Down the Weapons." Young antinuclear artists established a group called Indigo, which produced leaflets, buttons, and posters for the movement, including a badge for Dialogue, modeled on the CND nuclear disarmament symbol. In November, at a Dialogue event, this time sanctioned by the Peace Council, END's Mary Kaldor and Mient Jan Faber gave antinuclear speeches before a large public audience in Budapest.[55] Meanwhile, followers of György Bulanyi, the organizer of the Catholic "base communities," formed a Committee for Human Dignity, which publicly expressed its support for the goals of the Western peace movement and its opposition to nuclear weapons in both blocs.[56] Dialogue itself made contacts with independent East German activists, produced its own bulletin, and began organizing affiliates in outlying provinces. In May 1983, some 400 to 500 Dialogue activists joined an official peace march as a separate contingent, under their own banners. Far more colorful than their official counterparts, who trudged along with the usual complacent slogans ("Peace is our future!"), the Dialogue group carried signs reading: "All nuclear weapons out of Europe!" and "Rather active than radioactive!" Through these ventures, the new group attracted the allegiance of thousands of young people.[57]

The Hungarian regime—frightened by this burst of independent activity—soon reversed course, but it could not suppress the movement entirely.

In 1983, the authorities began harassing independent disarmament activists. The government's repressive efforts reached a peak in early July, when it prevented Dialogue from hosting an international peace camp by expelling Western participants, refusing visas to others, and arresting about twenty Dialogue members. In the face of this situation, Dialogue leaders decided later that month to disband the organization.[58] Regarding independent peace action as impossible, a small number of Dialogue activists, led by Köszegi, formed a new group, 4–6–0, to work under the jurisdiction of the Peace Council. In the ensuing years, 4–6–0 promoted peace consciousness, East-West dialogue, and nonviolence training.[59] A substantially larger group, however, taking up the name Peace Group for Dialogue once more, adopted a position of opposition to the regime. Condemning the possible stationing of nuclear weapons in Hungary, they covered a Budapest park with large numbers of antinuclear posters and white flags. They also issued appeals for disarmament and published their own underground newspaper.[60] Though the Anti-Nuclear Campaign fizzled, in the fall of 1983, when an official petition drive, assailing NATO missile deployment, swept through the nation, high school students began circulating a counter-petition, protesting the failure to address Soviet missile deployment. Meanwhile, Hungary's Catholic Church—a loyal servant of the regime—cracked down upon Bulanyi's pacifist movement, denying him the right to celebrate Mass and removing priests allied with him from their parishes. But his movement continued, producing a crop of conscientious objectors.[61]

Czechoslovakia provided a somewhat different model. In 1977, a group of Czech intellectuals and workers, many with roots in the "Prague Spring" of 1968, had established Charter 77 to monitor their government's compliance with the human rights provisions of the 1975 Helsinki Accords. Some 1,000 people signed the group's founding statement and, in the following years, despite constant government harassment, Charter 77 activists managed to sustain a struggling human rights movement.[62] Initially, the Chartists were suspicious of the rising West European antinuclear movement, which—given the distorted picture of it dispensed by Communist propaganda—they feared was indifferent to East bloc militarism and repression. Nevertheless, the Chartists, like many other Europeans, perceived the dangers in the nuclear arms race and, also, admired END's emphasis upon citizen activism in overcoming the military domination of Europe by the great powers. Thus, beginning in 1981, a friendly dialogue ensued between Charter 77 and the Western antinuclear campaign that did much to alleviate the initial Chartist fears.[63]

Gradually, an alliance began to emerge. Languishing in Plzen-Bory prison during 1982, Václav Havel, a leading Chartist, remarked: "If . . . I were a West German, I would probably be . . . collecting signatures for a petition against the installation of Pershings and cruise missiles, and voting 'Green.'" The people who were "doing this, and whom I have the opportunity of watching daily on the television news, are essentially my brothers and sisters." By May 1984, Charter 77 leaders were lauding the Western peace movements as "an expression of profound civic responsibility which, in the face of an undeniable global crisis, does not hesitate to commit itself personally and selflessly in the name of human life and its fundamental values." In an open letter to END's July 1984 convention, in Perugia, which the Czech authorities had barred its delegates from attending, Charter 77 proclaimed that "the emergence of the independent peace movement" was "a major watershed for our strivings to obtain freer and more democratic conditions in our part of Europe." Declaring that "your hopes are our hopes," it called for efforts to "unite all those opposed to the nuclear madness in a mighty democratic coalition."[64]

This unity became a real possibility after October 1983, when the Czech press announced that the Soviet Union would begin deploying nuclear missiles in Czechoslovakia. In response, underground labor movement activists circulated anti-deployment petitions in Czech factories, and called for a public referendum on the issue. Despite police pressure, workers refused to withdraw their signatures from petitions. Students engaged in public protests, while leaders of both the Protestant and the Catholic churches spoke out strongly against missile deployment.[65] By early 1984, well over two thousand Czechs had openly challenged the regime by signing anti-missile petitions. Students at Charles University, not quite as daring, promoted the idea of drawing the sun as an antinuclear symbol. Soon entire walls of building were covered with small, hastily drawn suns.[66] Although Charter 77 continued to emphasize the importance of human rights, its members threw themselves into the antinuclear campaign, and were prominent among the seventeen antinuclear activists arrested for distributing anti-deployment leaflets. In November 1984, leading Chartists from Czechoslovakia and independent activists from East Germany issued a joint statement, expressing their "solidarity with the peace movements in the West" and calling for "no missiles in Europe from the Urals to the Atlantic." In March 1985, Charter 77 sent the END convention the "Prague Appeal," which called for the "removal of all nuclear weapons either sited in or aimed at Europe," the creation of nuclear-free zones, and the development of a democratic European community, living in friendship with all nations.[67]

The antinuclear campaign made less headway in Poland, a country torn politically between the powerful Solidarity labor movement and the Communist regime and, after December 1981, under martial law. In general, Solidarity steered clear of peace and disarmament issues, as did the Roman Catholic bishops.[68] Nevertheless, a variety of underground periodicals and groups in Poland expressed their concern about missile deployment and their support for the European antinuclear movement. In May 1982, preparing for demonstrations against martial law the following month, Cracow's *Solidarity Information Bulletin* proposed the slogans: "We demand the destruction of nuclear arsenals! Begin US-USSR disarmament talks now!" The Workers' Defense Committee (KOR), which drew most of its support from students and intellectuals, also spoke favorably of disarmament. Adam Michnik, a key figure in KOR, proclaimed his respect for the Western peace movement and, when three Solidarity activists went on trial in 1985, urged members of that movement to come to Gdansk to attend the trial, as "your presence might be decisive to our fate." Jacek Kuron, a leading KOR and Solidarity activist, also maintained close connections with the Western antinuclear campaign.[69]

The Polish group most closely aligned with the global antinuclear movement was the Committee for Social Resistance (Komitet Oporu Spolecznego, KOS). Formed almost immediately after the introduction of martial law, KOS was a network of underground cells that operated throughout the nation, from factories to schools. Overlapping with Solidarity and maintaining a working relationship with it, KOS published a newspaper with a print run of 10,000 and was one of the country's key underground organizations. In May 1983, KOS issued an open letter to the West European antinuclear movement, in which it emphasized that "the threat of nuclear annihilation hangs over all the inhabitants of this earth." Declaring that "like you, we say NO to the arms race," KOS looked forward to "future joint activities in defense of peace."[70] In October 1983, KOS followed up with a statement entitled "Peace Is Indivisible," in which it made a series of proposals to the "pan-European peace movement." These included freeing Europe of nuclear weapons and recognizing that the Soviet Union "subjects Europe to military blackmail"—although "the arms race is not the right answer to the existing threat." Future actions, it said, "should be undertaken in solidarity by peace movements in both parts of Europe," for "we are fighting a common battle." Despite the sympathy many average Poles felt for the anti-Soviet Reagan administration, KOS braved their wrath by condemning U.S. military intervention in Grenada. It also participated in END conventions.[71]

An antinuclear campaign was even taking shape in the Soviet Union.

Writers, artists, and other members of the intelligentsia often provided its constituency. At the official Minsk writers conference of 1983 ("War, Literature, and the Nuclear Era"), several prominent authors shocked Communist authorities by denouncing both "capitalist" and "Marxist" nuclear weapons. Young, countercultural types also joined the campaign. A youth group called Independent Initiative, formed after the death of John Lennon and attracted by his phrase "all we need is love," staged an anti-military demonstration on June 1, 1984. Calling for U.S. withdrawal from El Salvador, Soviet withdrawal from Afghanistan, and the withdrawal of both nations' nuclear weapons from Europe, it led to 400 arrests. On December 11, Independent Initiative followed up with another provocative anti-military demonstration in Moscow's Lenin Hills Park, drawing several hundred participants.[72] Although Andrei Sakharov continued to speak out sharply against nuclear war (which he termed "general suicide") and for nuclear disarmament, his new emphasis on maintaining strategic parity placed him at odds with some Western activists.[73] Other Soviet critics, however, eagerly adopted Western ideas. In October 1981, 38 residents of Latvia, Estonia, and Lithuania issued an "Open Letter" calling for the inclusion of the Baltic republics in a Nordic nuclear weapons–free zone. Despite arrests of some of the first group, Estonian activists produced another call for a nuclear-free zone in December 1983.[74]

The largest antinuclear organization to emerge in the Soviet Union was the Trust Group. On June 4, 1982, eleven young people, mostly pacifist intellectuals and artists, launched the Moscow Group to Establish Trust Between the USSR and the USA with a small press conference, attended by Western journalists. Convinced that the nuclear confrontation between the United States and the Soviet Union could not be resolved without the establishment of mutual trust, they called for participation by the public in the trust-building process, including the development of greater interaction between the people of the two societies. Although these activists stated repeatedly that they did not constitute an opposition or dissident movement—and, in fact, did not directly criticize Soviet (or American) policy—the Soviet government reacted angrily to their appearance, packing one Trust Group member (Alexander Shatravka) off to a labor camp, shutting down a Trust Group exhibit of paintings on the Hiroshima bombing, and incarcerating the artist (Sergei Batovrin) in a psychiatric hospital.[75] Despite constant persecution, however, the Trust Group persisted. Soliciting proposals for trust-building from the public, it gathered more than a hundred suggestions along these lines for U.S. and Soviet action (from requiring peace education in the schools to exchanging children during school holidays), which it then disseminated. The Trust Group also held regular peace meetings and seminars in private apartments, organized a photo exhibit on the U.S. nuclear disarmament movement, and received hundreds of visitors from Western antinuclear groups, with whom it eagerly swapped ideas.[76]

Given official harassment and repression, the Trust Group could not build a mass campaign comparable to the Freeze, CND, or IKV, but it did manage to create a viable antinuclear movement—indeed, the only independent movement of any significance that managed to survive in the Soviet Union during these years. Within a fairly short time, the Moscow Trust Group spawned similar groups in Leningrad, Kiev, Odessa, Gorky, Riga, Talinn, Novosibirsk, and other cities, reportedly involving some 2,000 people. Although most of the movement's founders were dispersed through imprisonment or expulsion from the country, new activists arose to take their places.[77] As the campaign continued, it held further exhibits, distributed a hand-printed journal called *Trust*, and began to take political positions. The Odessa Trust Group proposed declaring the Black Sea a "sea of trust," with the removal of all military vessels and coastal military installations, and making Odessa and its twin city of Baltimore nuclear-free cities. The Moscow Trust Group came out in opposition to the MX missile and all new ICBMs, in favor of halting development, testing, and production of all new nuclear weapons delivery systems in East and West, and in support of dissolving NATO and the Warsaw Pact.[78] Previously uneasy about taking to the streets, the Moscow group sent activists out to the Arbat in the summer of 1984 with a petition urging a Soviet-American summit conference. To its delight, it gathered 300 signatures before police rounded up the petitioners. "We are part of an international peace movement," one Trust Group activist told a Western visitor. "We believe this movement can change the world."[79]

The movement was even taking root within officially sanctioned organizations. In the immediate aftermath of Reagan's "Star Wars" speech, the vice president of the Soviet Academy of Sciences, Evgenii Velikhov, a leading physicist, convened a meeting to discuss this latest escalation in the arms race and, in May, he established the Committee of Soviet Scientists for Peace and Against the Nuclear Threat (CSS). The Soviet government planned to respond to a U.S. SDI system by building its own, and apparently viewed the CSS as merely a useful weapon in its propaganda war against the Reagan administration. But the CSS moved in quite a different direction, for it brought together a group of intellectuals familiar with Western antinuclear scientists and genuinely opposed to the nuclear arms race.[80] Velikhov, who chaired the committee, had a great respect for Pugwash participants, and his model for the CSS was the Federation of American Scientists. Roald Sagdeev, a deputy chair who headed the Soviet space program, had been a Pugwash participant and, along with Velikhov, had studied with Lev Artsimovich, a leading Soviet Pugwash activist. The other deputy chair was Andrei Kokoshin, who, like Aleksei Arbatov, another leading CSS member, was a political scientist and reformer employed by a Soviet think tank. In November 1983, when a group of FAS leaders traveled to Moscow to meet with the CSS, they were enormously impressed with its leaders, especially Velikhov, and with its activities. The CSS turned out studies arguing that there was no need for a Soviet SDI program (as the U.S. program could be frustrated through "asymmetric responses"), that nuclear war was suicidal, and that it was vital to drastically reduce nuclear arsenals. Velikhov and Sagdeev also sought to soften the regime's crackdown upon Sakharov.[81]

The activities of the CSS were symptomatic of reformist efforts within official ranks to develop a new approach to world affairs. Although party conservatives dominated Soviet foreign policy, liberal intellectuals, usually housed in academic-advisory posts, promoted an alternative vision for the nation. Georgi Arbatov, deeply influenced by the work of the dovish Palme Commission, in which he participated, sought to promote a program of "common security." Kokoshin, taking up an idea of Western peace researchers, popularized the idea of "nonoffensive defense." Like the others, Georgy Shaknazarov and Fyodor Burlatsky emphasized the necessity of overcoming the nuclear danger. In "The Logic of Political Thinking in the Nuclear Era," an article published in 1984, Shaknazarov argued that the nuclear dilemma necessitated "a new way of thinking"—a phrase and a concept that dated back to Albert Einstein's 1946 plea for nuclear disarmament. One of the most important of the "new thinkers," Aleksandr Yakovlev, exiled a decade before to a diplomatic post in Canada for his liberal ideas, recalled: "We reformers dreamed of ending . . . the division between East and West, of halting the insanity of the arms race, and ending the 'Cold War.'" During the early 1980s, many of them, and particularly Velikhov and Arbatov, became the informal defense and foreign policy advisors to a young party reformer with whom they enjoyed close personal relations, Mikhail Gorbachev.[82]

Gorbachev's conversion to the antinuclear cause, unnoticed at the time, provided another indication of how far the movement had advanced. Addressing the British parliament on December 18, 1984, this rising star within the Soviet party apparatus delivered a message that could as easily have been advanced by a leader of the Western antinuclear movement. Europe, Gorbachev observed, should not be viewed as "a 'theater of operations,'"

but as "our common home" in "a vulnerable, rather fragile, yet interdepend-
ent world." Nuclear weapons, particularly, called for a revolution in consciousness. "When we speak about war and peace, we must bear in mind
that the nature of present-day armaments, and first of all nuclear ones, has
changed the traditional notion of these [political] problems," he said. Those
who still talked lightly of nuclear war "evidently remain prisoners of the
outdated stereotypes characteristic of the time when a war . . . did not
threaten all humankind with annihilation." Thus, "the nuclear age inevitably
dictates new political thinking. Preventing a nuclear war is the most burning
issue for all people on earth."[83]

Although Soviet public opinion polls are not available for these years, it
appears that average citizens shared many of the concerns of their contem-
poraries in other lands. According to numerous experts, there was a growing
belief in the Soviet Union that nuclear war was unthinkable. A study of Soviet teenagers reported that only 3 percent of them believed that they and
their families could survive a nuclear war. The country's most popular
singer, Alla Pugachova, performed a sad antinuclear song in which the
Earth was depicted as a crystal ball on the verge of destruction:

> Tell us, birds, the time has come,
> Our planet is a fragile glass,
> Virgin birch trees, rivers and fields,
> All this, from above, is more delicate than glass.
> Can it be that we shall hear
> From all sides
> The farewell sound of crystal breaking?

The gloomy mood undoubtedly owed much to the heightening Soviet-
American confrontation of the early 1980s, but a number of Soviet citizens,
interviewed about it, also referred to the impact of Soviet television programs, sponsored by International Physicians for the Prevention of Nuclear
War, that had emphasized the vast devastation that would result from a nuclear conflict.[84]

This pessimism about surviving a nuclear war did not necessarily result
in rejection of official Soviet policy, which, given its portrayal in Kremlin
propaganda as opposed to the nuclear arms race, many Soviet citizens found
acceptable. But it did lead to strong popular support for nuclear arms control and disarmament. Walking the streets of Moscow and conversing with
average Soviet citizens in the spring of 1983, a U.S. reporter was struck by
their near-universal disdain for nuclear weapons. "Of course, it's the best
idea, this freeze," a carpenter told him. "More bombs won't help either you

or us." He explained: "In a modern war, everybody will be destroyed." Brushing aside objections, an electrical worker argued that halting the arms race was imperative. A middle-aged typist also turned out to be a nuclear freeze enthusiast. "I think it is a very, very reasonable idea," she said, while walking her dog; "it's only common sense." She added: "And then, in the future, I think they should destroy all the weapons." The sincerity of these views was sometimes exhibited quite directly. In June 1984, as four Moscow Trust Group petitioners were being arrested, passersby shoved aside the police, grabbed the antinuclear petition, and added their names to it. Then they returned it to a Trust Group member through the window of the police car.[85]

In both East and West, the nuclear arms race was creating a crisis of legitimacy.

Revolt of the Doves

International Dimensions, 1981-85

> We must . . . create our own alternative international
> system based on communications between peoples and
> not governments.
>
> Mary Kaldor, 1981

As protest against the nuclear arms race swept around the world during the early 1980s, the antinuclear campaign grew into the largest, most dynamic, international citizens' movement of modern times. Given the need of the rising nonaligned nuclear disarmament organizations to communicate with one another, to coordinate activities across national boundaries, and to develop common strategies, they worked together increasingly through international structures that they organized on a constituency or geographical basis. The success of these nonaligned movements in building a worldwide antinuclear campaign of unprecedented size and influence provides a sharp contrast to the failure of the Communist-led World Peace Council to halt its post–Vietnam War decline. Indeed, suffering not only from its well-deserved reputation for pro-Soviet partisanship but from the comparison with the newer, more dynamic independent movement, the Communist-led peace international continued to decay and to denounce its nonaligned rival. Nor were the more vibrant independent disarmament organizations eager to cooperate with the WPC and its affiliated groups. Thus, as the antinuclear movement shook people, political parties, and governments across the globe, its Communist-led component—despite substantial infusions of Soviet funding—became ever more marginal and irrelevant.

Informal Cooperation

Informal cooperation among antinuclear organizations in non-Communist nations grew rapidly during the early 1980s. Although the Dutch IKV was particularly committed to fostering international communication, nearly all the major nuclear disarmament groups utilized international officers or committees to knit the movement together more closely. Some of the heightening interaction occurred between the antinuclear groups of the Pacific and of the West. Japanese delegations and films played an important part in Western antinuclear activities, and leaders of the Nuclear Free and Independent Pacific movement also worked closely with the Western movement.[1] In the United States, the Friends of the Filipino People and the U.S. Nuclear-Free Pacific Network served as important support groups for antinuclear campaigns in the Pacific.[2] But even closer ties developed between the movements of the United States and Western Europe. In March and April 1982, a delegation of top West European peace movement leaders toured the United States, addressing 88 public meetings and rallies, 56 organizational meetings and receptions, and 32 university gatherings, and giving more than a hundred TV and radio interviews. In turn, the American Friends Service Committee joined the lawsuit brought by Greenham Common women to halt the deployment of U.S. missiles in Britain.[3] Furthermore, movements in Western Europe and the United States frequently exchanged speakers at their respective antinuclear rallies and, on occasion, issued joint communiqués.[4]

These kinds of informal relationships proved important for the movement. At the least, they lifted spirits within the global antinuclear campaign and encouraged further activism. Prodded by their West European counterparts to follow their example by organizing a mass demonstration, the Americans decided to hold their own national antinuclear rally, which led to the unprecedented outpouring of June 1982 in New York City. Furthermore, each movement had opportunities to add credibility to the other. The Europeans were delighted by the development of anti-Euromissile demonstrations among Americans, for such events offset the charge that the European groups were anti-American.[5] For its part, the U.S. movement was able to draw upon top leaders of the British Labour Party, the West German Social Democratic Party, and the Norwegian Labor Party to make the antinuclear case to members of Congress. Above all, widespread international action gave the movement an image of great strength. Between October and December 1981, when millions of people turned out for anti-Euromissile demonstrations in twelve European capitals and several other major cities, it provided impressive evidence that the two major nuclear powers faced an international revolt against their policies.[6]

Organizing by Constituency

The movement's international dimension was also evident among its rapidly growing constituency groups. The most successful of these, International Physicians for Prevention of Nuclear War (IPPNW), began quite modestly. When the three American doctors flew home from their December 1980 meeting with their Soviet counterparts, they established a headquarters in a local drugstore, in Cambridge. "It was a wonderful grass-roots office," one of them recalled. "To prevent nuclear war you walked through the drugstore past the toothpaste section, then up the back stairs past all the mops and brooms toward this huge picture of Einstein at the top." Meanwhile, activists traveled through Europe to encourage national medical groups to join a worldwide federation. In March 1981, IPPNW held its first convention, in Washington, D.C., drawing 70 doctors from twelve countries.[7] Despite fierce internal conflicts, some of them reflecting Cold War divisions, IPPNW grew rapidly. By the time of its fifth international congress, held in Budapest in 1985, IPPNW had affiliates in 41 nations, representing 135,000 physicians.[8] If judged on the basis of attracting large percentages of doctors, the Nordic affiliates were the most successful; 40 percent of Sweden's health care professionals signed up. But most of the funding for IPPNW came from American sources, while the two international presidents—Lown and Chazov—represented the leading Cold War antagonists, the United States and the Soviet Union.[9]

Through most of its activities, IPPNW sought to discredit the very idea of nuclear war. At annual conventions and other meetings, IPPNW repeatedly issued chilling statements on the menace of global annihilation.[10] When the U.S. ambassador to the Soviet Union accused IPPNW of undermining the West by frightening its citizens, while doing little to affect average Russians, Lown and Chazov arranged for a remarkably powerful, hour-long, uncensored IPPNW program on prime time Soviet television in June 1982. Addressing an estimated 100 million Soviet viewers, Lown warned them that the stockpiling of nuclear weapons threatened all people with "unimaginable catastrophe," while Chazov insisted that "nuclear war means death to all human beings."[11] IPPNW also played a key role in the publication of studies of the medical effects of nuclear war by the World Health Organization and by national medical societies and launched a two-year petition drive among physicians calling for an end to the nuclear arms race. The petition netted more than a million signers—about 25 percent of the world's physicians. Like PSR, IPPNW gradually moved toward prescriptions for the world's illness, including a nuclear weapons freeze, an explicit declaration of no first-use by the nuclear powers, and a recognition of the "illusory nature" of civil defense.[12] Frustrated by endless arms control negotiations, Lown turned to the idea of "reciprocating initiatives" by the great powers, the first of which would be the unilateral adoption of a nuclear testing moratorium. Despite Chazov's dismay at the idea, which clashed with the Soviet government's bilateral emphasis, Lown launched it with a speech at IPPNW's Helsinki convention of June 1984.[13]

The rise of IPPNW epitomized the growth of antinuclear campaigns within the professions. Lawyers, teachers, engineers, journalists, psychologists, and scientists created international disarmament organizations, thereby adding their knowledge and prestige to the antinuclear campaign. Among scientists, the Pugwash movement, headed by Joseph Rotblat, remained the pre-eminent international nuclear disarmament organization, drawing together several thousand concerned physicists, chemists, and other researchers from more than 50 nations. Although the Pugwash movement had less of a "cutting edge" role in the antinuclear campaign of the 1980s than it had during the late 1950s and early 1960s, it did reassert its antinuclear emphasis, sponsor working groups on avoiding nuclear war and implementing disarmament, and issue warnings about the dangers of the ongoing nuclear arms race. Its December 1984 Workshop on Nuclear Forces concluded that the steps in the nuclear buildup of the time "increase the chance of nuclear war by mistake, miscalculation, or uncontrollable escalation," "provoke reactions that continue the arms race and further increase the danger," and "perpetuate a pattern of nuclear-weapon-state disregard for their obligations under the Non-Proliferation Treaty that is threatening the entire nonproliferation regime."[14]

Women's antinuclear activism also had a strong international dimension. Polls showed that, in numerous nations, women were more inclined than men to support the antinuclear movement and its positions. This was symbolized by the emergence of women's peace camps—often modeled on the one at Greenham Common—in the United States, West Germany, Canada, Italy, the Netherlands, and elsewhere.[15] Antinuclear activists also staged numerous women's marches and, in 1982, organized an international Women's Peace Day of Action for Nuclear Disarmament. Some of the international women's activity acquired an organizational form, and Women for Peace groups emerged in many West European nations.[16] With its own sections already in place in dozens of countries, WILPF played an important role. On March 8, 1982, WILPF launched its STAR (Stop the Arms Race) campaign, focused on halting the deployment of cruise and Pershing missiles. Through distribution of STAR messages on street corners, radio stations, women's centers, and elsewhere, WILPF hoped to enroll a million women in the antinuclear campaign. A year later, in the campaign's culminating act, WILPF staged a rally outside NATO headquarters in Brussels, drawing some 15,000 women from numerous nations. In 1984, WILPF began an international drive to halt nuclear weapons testing. Gathering signatures on petitions headed "Stop the Arms Race! Start with a Test Ban!" its members called upon the U.N. Secretary General and U.N. member states to conclude a treaty to ban all nuclear tests. In 1985, at the international women's conference in Nairobi, WILPF established a peace tent that became an important meeting center and symbol for the entire gathering.[17]

Religious bodies already had international structures in place, and in general they adopted a critical approach toward nuclear weapons. Pacifist groups like the Quakers and the Buddhists, of course, already participated in antinuclear campaigns. But important new support for nuclear disarmament efforts came from non-pacifist religious groups. Although Pope John Paul II equivocated on nuclear issues—claiming that nuclear deterrence "may still be judged morally acceptable" if it provided "a step on the way toward a progressive disarmament"[18]—the Catholic Pax Christi International, with sections in fourteen countries, took a more sharply antinuclear stand. Focused on the need for nuclear disarmament, Pax Christi frequently sparked the strong condemnations of nuclear weapons by the Catholic bishops in different countries and celebrated well-attended antinuclear masses and prayer meetings before the launching of antinuclear demonstrations. In the spring of 1981, its international council called upon "the governments, trade unions, churches and public opinion of all NATO countries to oppose the deployment of a new generation of nuclear weapons . . . and all further developments of nuclear weaponry."[19] For its part, the General Assembly of the World Council of Churches, meeting in Vancouver in August 1983, declared that "the time has come when the churches must unequivocally declare that the production and deployment as well as the use of nuclear weapons are a crime against humanity, and that such activities must be condemned on ethical and theological grounds." Giving teeth to this resolution, the church body endorsed acts of civil disobedience in resisting preparations for nuclear war.[20]

Social Democratic parties provided another key element of the international campaign for nuclear disarmament. Although their union allies played some role as well,[21] labor's antinuclear activity was less organized and more episodic than the effort of these parties of the moderate Left. During the early 1980s, the antinuclear movement proved remarkably successful in winning the allegiance of the Social Democrats of Northern Europe. These democratic socialists hammered out common policy in the Scandilux group, which, starting in January 1981, brought together representatives of the socialist parties of Denmark, Norway, the Netherlands, Belgium, and Luxembourg, as well as observers from the British, German, and French socialist parties. A key figure in their discussions was Egon Bahr of the West German Social Democratic Party, who provided not only a useful liaison to the Socialist International's president, Willy Brandt, but a highly sophisticated, critical view of the nuclear arms race. Ultimately, their thinking emphasized creating a system of "common security" for Europe, resisting the deployment of the Euromissiles, and denuclearizing Europe. Although some Southern European parties took a more hawkish stance, overall the Socialist International constituted a remarkably antinuclear force in world politics, with figures like Brandt, Bahr, and Olof Palme setting the tone.[22]

The pacifist internationals were also active participants in the antinuclear upsurge. The WRI, which had affiliates in 21 nations, mostly in Europe and North America, had few large ones. But where it did, as in Sweden, they provided a rallying point for anti-missile activities. Usually, however, WRI sections participated in antinuclear campaigns through their work in coalitions, in which they played a fairly modest role. The WRI was particularly eager to inject nonviolent resistance into the antinuclear struggle and, accordingly, its U.S. section, the War Resisters League, was the main organizer of a "Blockade the Bombmakers" action at the 1982 U.N. Special Session on Disarmament, which resulted in over 1,600 arrests.[23] The International FOR, which had some thirty branches and affiliated groups, became especially active in promoting peace camps, for its leaders saw such camps as an important form of grassroots, nonviolent action. It also sought to foster contacts with churches and church activists working for disarmament in Eastern Europe. Seeking to overcome Cold War stereotypes by expanding interpersonal relations between the people of East and West, the International FOR sponsored a "Journey of Reconciliation" to the Soviet Union, photo exchanges, and exchanges of children's artwork.[24] Although many ventures of the pacifist internationals were quite creative, their limited size, the diverse nature of their concerns, and the broad dimensions of the antinuclear upsurge meant that their role in the nuclear disarmament campaign remained relatively small.

Environmental groups provided yet another component of the international campaign. Some organizations engaging in antinuclear activities, such as the Natural Resources Defense Council in the United States, were not components of an international organization. But Friends of the Earth and Greenpeace did pull together a global network of environmental groups that raised nuclear issues. During the early 1980s, Greenpeace was particularly active in challenging nuclear weapons testing, uranium mining, and nuclear waste dumping in the Pacific, honing in on French nuclear testing in Polynesia. Calling attention to the efforts of Pacific islanders to free themselves of great power nuclear colonialism, it publicized and supported efforts to create nuclear-free zones. Greenpeace also assailed the Kremlin's nuclear ventures, staging dramatic, nonviolent invasions of Soviet territory to highlight Soviet nuclear practices. In addition, it launched a campaign to end U.S. and Soviet nuclear testing.[25]

Government officials of a dovish persuasion, mostly out of power, drew together under the auspices of the Palme Commission. Formally known as the Independent Commission on Disarmament and Security Issues, this private body of statesmen from East and West was organized in late 1980 by Olof Palme, the former (and future) prime minister of Sweden. In addition to Palme, who served as its leading light, the commission brought together former U.S. Secretary of State Cyrus Vance, former British Foreign Secretary David Owen, Georgi Arbatov of the Soviet Union's Institute of the U.S.A. and Canada, and thirteen other senior officials. Determined to contribute to peace and disarmament, they met frequently, considered expert papers on a wide range of arms control and security issues, and, in the spring of 1982, issued a widely circulated report, *Common Security: A Blueprint for Survival*. Its numerous recommendations included sharply reducing conventional forces in Europe, establishing a battlefield nuclear weapons–free zone in Central Europe and on each side of the East-West border, and strengthening the security role of the United Nations. In a letter to President Reagan, Palme explained that "we propose to curb the US-USSR nuclear arms race, to achieve a rough parity in conventional forces in Europe, and to reduce the nuclear threat to that continent. . . . Nations must now start to build a structure of common security if the growing risk of nuclear war is to be alleviated." Although the Palme Commission report had far less visibility than the turbulent demonstrations of the era, it had a significant impact. Particularly among Social Democratic parties, then looking for alternative policies to those promoted by the U.S. and Soviet governments, it recommendations received careful scrutiny and, usually, acceptance.[26]

Regional Networks

Although constituency networks played a vital role in the nuclear disarmament movement, regional networks were at least as important. With the antinuclear campaign in full flower by the fall of 1981, leaders of mass movements from fifteen West European countries met in Copenhagen that September and formed the International Peace Communication and Coordination Center (IPCC). Attempting to avoid creating a tightly structured organization with "bureaucratic" procedures, IPCC emphasized its role as a forum for the exchange of ideas and information by "like-minded movements." Furthermore, it never established an executive board, voting procedures, or any formal rules of operation. Instead, the powerful IKV filled the gap by playing a leading role in IPCC affairs, providing it with a free office at the Hague and with an international secretary, Wim Bartels.[27] Above all, IPCC was a West European network, dedicated to creating a nuclear-free Europe. It drew together the leaders of the major nonaligned nuclear disarmament groups, including Britain and Ireland's CND, Norway and Denmark's No to Nuclear Weapons, Belgium's VAKA and CNAPD, Greece's KEADEA, Finland's Committee of 100, France's CODENE, Sweden's Peace and Arbitration Society, and most of the other major nuclear disarmament organizations of Western Europe. At the same time, it also encouraged the participation of representatives from the Nuclear Freeze campaign, SANE, AFSC, and other groups from the United States, Project Ploughshares and Operation Dismantle from Canada, and groups from Australia.[28]

Despite these rather loose and undefined boundaries, both organizational and geographical, IPCC functioned reasonably well. Its meetings, which occurred every three months at different West European sites, were deliberately kept small, to maximize personal interaction and discussion. To provide information to activists on the movement's burgeoning operations in many lands, IPCC took over the production of the magazine *Disarmament Campaigns*, publishing it on a regular basis. With the heightening of the campaign against the deployment of cruise, Pershing, and SS-20 missiles, representatives of IPCC's affiliated groups increasingly used their meetings to swap ideas on tactics, coordinate the timing of demonstrations, arrange for the exchange of speakers, and assess the nuclear policies of the great powers. Attendance at IPCC meetings also impressed the representatives of the Freeze and other U.S. disarmament groups with how crucial their West European counterparts considered blocking Euromissile deployment.[29] The relatively smooth operations of IPCC, in the absence of formal rules, probably reflected not only the political sophistication of IKV, but the overall agreement on essentials among leading activists from the major nonaligned nuclear disarmament groups. At the end of one meeting, a participant asked: "Is it a sign of danger that we don't disagree more?"[30]

It was European Nuclear Disarmament (END), however, which served as the main focus for the European movement. While IPCC drew the top leaders of Western Europe's nonaligned nuclear disarmament groups for small strategy sessions, END provided the conceptual glue, the mass base, and the central rallying point for Europe's popular antinuclear campaign. As nonaligned groups sprang up throughout Europe, often inspired by the END Appeal, an international "consultation" was held in Rome in November 1981. Thereafter, to pull together the organizational signers of the Appeal, END convened annual conventions during these years: in Brussels (1982), West Berlin (1983), Perugia (1984), and Amsterdam (1985).[31] Attracting thousands of antinuclear activists, mostly from Western Europe but also from Eastern Europe, the United States, and Australasia, these END conventions served as sites where the national movements' cadre met, compared notes on events in their home countries, and discussed plans for the future. They were also exciting and turbulent events. Demonstrations broke out not only in the streets—as, for example, in May 1983, when Green Party participants, led by Petra Kelly, demonstrated in East Berlin in support of the Swords into Plowshares group—but inside the convention halls, as well.[32] END's administrative operations also had a chaotic flavor. Although END did manage to publish a journal, establish working groups (mostly dealing with Eastern Europe), and hold meetings in Britain, there was never much central direction or money behind END.[33] Furthermore, a simmering feud between Ken Coates (of the Bertrand Russell Peace Foundation) and E. P. Thompson (END's best-known leader) helped keep the minimal organization that existed, in Britain, divided.[34] Even so, for the millions of West Europeans who participated in the demonstrations and other activities of its constituent groups, END was the very heart and soul of the massive European antinuclear campaign.

A key reason for END's success in rallying much of Western Europe behind its banner was its nonaligned critique of the nuclear arms race and the Cold War that fostered it. In November 1981, for example, Thompson argued that the Cold War was "a habit supported by very powerful material interests in each bloc: the military-industrial and research establishments of both sides, the security services and intelligence operations, and the political servants of these interests. These interests command a large (and growing) allocation of the skills and resources of each society . . . and it is in the interest of these interests to increase that allocation and to influence this direction even more." There existed, then, a *"reciprocal* and inter-active character of the process. . . . Its military and security establishments are *self-reproducing*. Their missiles summon forward our missiles which summon forward their missiles in turn. NATO's hawks feed the hawks of the Warsaw bloc." The military and security services and their political servants needed the Cold War "not only because their own establishments and their own careers depend upon this," but because a need for "the Other" is "intrinsic to human bonding. We cannot define whom 'we' are without also defining 'them.'" Thus, the Cold War was "an ongoing, self-reproducing condition, to which both adversaries are addicted," and was part of the process of "bonding-by-exclusion which must (with our present technologies of death) lead to auto-destruct."[35] Fortified by this kind of analysis, END found it possible to maintain an evenhanded—and popular—approach to the major events of the era.

END's strategy reflected this analysis. If hawkish behavior in one Cold War camp fed hawkish behavior in the other, then dovish behavior would reverse the process, for it would diminish tensions and bring pressure to bear upon "the other side" to reciprocate. Thus, in place of promoting endless negotiations, the movement should press for unilateral initiatives. Thompson told a mass antinuclear rally in October 1981: "We demand the halting of NATO's plans for new missiles, unconditionally. There is no need for negotiations. We demand also the halting and the reduction in numbers of the SS-20s. Unconditionally, without negotiations." That was "the way to get multilateral disarmament—take two unilateral initiatives and put them together."[36] Furthermore, although END and its constituent movements worked zealously to prevent the deployment of the Euromissiles, they were also, in Thompson's words, "contesting the bloc system itself, from whose antagonism the rival militarisms arise."[37] Finally, END leaders recognized that promoting unilateral initiatives and destroying the bloc system could move forward only on a rising tide of transnational resistance. For this reason, among others, it was vital to create a popular campaign that spanned the Cold War divide. As Thompson told a gathering of independent peace activists in Hungary, in 1982: "If the Western peace movement is to break through" the political barriers confronting it, "then we must be able to clasp hands with a non-aligned movement, totally independent of the state, on your side also. What has been epidemic must become pandemic."[38] With independent antinuclear groups sprouting not only in Western Europe, but in the unpromising soil of the East, realizing this hope seemed increasingly possible.

Global Networks

The nonaligned movement also made modest progress in building a global network. Despite the antinuclear upsurge of the early 1980s, neither of the two nonaligned internationals—the International Confederation for Disarmament and Peace (ICDP) and the International Peace Bureau (IPB)—initially benefited from it. With both organizations pathetically weak and underfunded, neither seemed an attractive option. However, after the death of the ICDP's hard-driving secretary, Peggy Duff, in April 1982, a crisis was reached in that organization. Lacking staff and funds, it closed its offices. At END's May 1983 convention in Berlin, members of the executive councils of the two groups held informal talks to discuss a merger, while nonaligned groups, including those affiliates of the existing organizations, attended an open meeting on what kind of international organization they would like to see established. Meeting in September 1983 at Gothenburg, Sweden, the leaders of the ICDP and the IPB voted to merge, retaining the name IPB for the new organization.[39] At that time, the prospects were not entirely promising, for the IPB was nearly moribund and did nothing along activist lines. Even so, it owned its own offices (in Geneva), maintained some credibility with the United Nations, and could point to a highly regarded president, the elderly Sean MacBride, a former IRA revolutionary who had become a leading peace proponent. Looking for an alternative to the Communist-led WPC on the international level, the new antinuclear groups and leaders began gravitating toward it.[40]

Problems of the Movement

Despite these promising developments, the international movement faced some daunting problems. For one thing, its financial resources were quite limited, and constituted only a tiny fraction of those mobilized by the governments it criticized. In addition, these governments often waged massive campaigns to counter (and sometimes to destroy) their critics. Furthermore, except on rare occasions, the movement could not rely on friendly or even impartial coverage by the communications media. Thompson recalled that, on the eve of the 1983 British elections, he became so infuriated by Thatcher's handling of the nuclear disarmament issue that he wrote a pamphlet in a day and a half to set the record straight. "We called a press conference," he noted, "and that pamphlet was on the desk of every television show presenter, all the news programs, and quite a number of press came.

But not one mention of the pamphlet appeared on any television or radio program."[41] Moreover, the movement had great difficulty translating its popular support on nuclear issues into election victories. In the Communist East, there were no elections. In the democratic West, people often voted on the basis of factors unrelated to disarmament, such as personalities, parties, or other issues. At an IPCC meeting in the fall of 1984, Faber challenged the Freeze representative, Karen Fierke, to explain why, if the Freeze was so popular, Reagan led Mondale in the polls. Meg Beresford of CND responded glumly: "Look at the British experience—there is a majority against Trident and a majority for Thatcher. . . . Elections are fought on a whole range of issues." A leading Dutch activist, Laurens Hogebrink, complained: "The gap between 'movement' and 'politics' has become wider."[42]

Another problem plaguing the antinuclear movement lay in the allure of other peace issues. For the most part, nuclear disarmament activists were also strong peace proponents, and there were plenty of global conflicts during these years to spur their concern: in the Middle East, in Afghanistan, and, above all, in Central America, where the Reagan administration drew upon U.S. military might in an attempt to crush leftist governments and rebels. Consequently, many of the nuclear disarmament groups could not resist making an issue of great power military interventionism in the Third World, and it became a major topic of discussion at their international meetings, as well.[43] Even so, in general the global movement remained determined to focus on the nuclear confrontation, leading to some measure of criticism from activists and groups with a Third World focus. "Everyone accused us of being Eurocentric," recalled END's Mary Kaldor. "We were Eurocentric! . . . We had a job to do in Europe at that moment." People, particularly Americans, would say: "Why are you so preoccupied with Poland; what about Nicaragua? And I would say: Look, Nicaragua is your problem. And if we can change things in Europe, that will have an enormous impact on all of the Third World."[44] Thus, despite some uneasiness within its ranks, the antinuclear movement continued to make ridding the world of nuclear weapons its top priority.

Yet another problem revolved around how to patch together the differing approaches of the Freeze and END. These two mass movements, which developed independently, welcomed each other's efforts, sent representatives to one another's conventions, and interacted well with one another on a personal basis.[45] Strategically, though, the movements failed to mesh. "We have had difficulty, in the European peace movements, in coordinating our campaigns" with those of the Americans, Thompson admitted in 1981. "A freeze makes sense for the superpowers; but here in Europe we have to get *rid* of weapons. To campaign in Europe for a freeze would be a step back from the campaign for a nuclear-free Europe, and also from the unilateralist demand for disarmament by direct initiatives by our own nations." Mary Kaldor claimed years later that the Freeze movement was "too technical"—educating people "in the niceties of arms control" rather than exposing the underlying political dynamic of the arms race.[46] For their part, Freeze leaders did not think that calling for unilateral action made sense in the United States and argued that, far from being a conservative proposal, as END leaders seemed to view it, the Freeze was really quite daring. It would go beyond blocking the deployment of a particular weapons system (i.e. the Euromissiles, then the focal point of the END campaign) to halting the nuclear arms race. Forsberg, citing the fact that she was nearly barred from speaking at END's Berlin convention because she allegedly represented one of the superpowers, also thought that the European campaign was animated by some degree of anti-Americanism. Consequently, despite personal friendships, frequent consultation, and cooperation, these two powerful movements had difficulty developing a common strategy.[47]

Détente from Below

One of the most important aspects of the nonaligned movement was its fostering of links between the independent peace activists of East and West—what it called "détente from below." Although the Freeze campaign hesitated to embark upon this project,[48] END led the way. It built close relationships with the Hungarian Dialogue group, Charter 77, the Moscow Trust Group, and other intrepid antinuclear forces in Eastern Europe, published pamphlets about their activities, and organized working groups to maintain contacts with them and publicize their difficulties. At END's 1984 Perugia convention, participants established a European Network for East-West Dialogue.[49] Hostile East European governments blocked most East European activists from attending END conventions, but the Easterners regularly sent messages to these gatherings and produced numerous statements discussed there and elsewhere. At the suggestion of Charter 77, a joint communiqué was drawn up for the Perugia convention and signed by the Swiss Peace Council, the French CODENE, and Petra Kelly of the West German Greens, as well as by members of Charter 77 and the Hungarian Dialogue group. Setting out a common platform for activists on both sides of the Cold War divide, it called for opposition to "every new missile that is deployed in Europe, West and East."[50] Faced with the inability of most Eastern activists to travel to the West, Western activists traveled to the East, meeting their embattled counterparts in tiny apartments and bringing them news of the Western nuclear disarmament campaign, as well as advice, computer disks, Fax machines, cassettes, and antinuclear literature. On January 1, 1983, in response to a call by the Moscow Trust Group, Western activists held silent vigils for peace in West European and American cities, including New York, Boston, Denver, Milwaukee, and Washington.[51]

In the course of consummating this grassroots East-West alliance, the international movement overcame a significant difference in approach, for the Westerners were driven primarily by their desire to curb the nuclear arms race, while the Easterners were driven primarily by their desire to safeguard human rights. And this difference, in turn, reflected the situation they faced in their own countries.[52] Even so, there was no reason that these two activist movements, so similar in their constituencies and ideals, could not support both. "Cold War dogma insisted that one must be for 'human rights' or for 'peace,'" Thompson recalled, but the nonaligned movement "broke that dogma." Amid earnest discussions, Western activists came to agree with their Eastern allies that there could be no peace without a loosening of the political restrictions on freedom. And Eastern activists came to agree with their Western allies that an easing of the Cold War military confrontation would provide them with the political "space" in which freedom could flourish.[53] As Thompson put it in 1983: "Neither the cause of peace nor that of liberty can wait upon the other: it is natural that they go forward together." Not surprisingly, then, Eastern dissident movements warmed toward the Western antinuclear campaign, championing it in their public pronouncements. And the Western antinuclear movement rallied behind Eastern activists, even when their cause had little direct connection to disarmament. In December 1981, responding to the declaration of martial law and the repression of the Solidarity movement in Poland, END issued a press release declaring that "peace and democracy are indivisible." It called on the Polish government "to end the state of emergency and to free the leaders of Solidarity," on the Soviet government and other members of the Warsaw Pact "to respect the integrity of Poland," and on the people of East and West "to join us in our campaign for nuclear disarmament and human rights throughout Europe."[54]

Naturally, the Western movement was particularly vigorous in defending "peace rights"—the rights of independent activists to agitate freely for peace and disarmament. In December 1982, when the Soviet Peace Committee threatened to undermine END's forthcoming convention unless the group broke its links to the East's independent peace activists, the conference organizers resolutely rejected the ultimatum, and publicized it as well.

Addressing an estimated 400,000 antinuclear demonstrators at Hyde Park in the fall of 1983, Thompson called upon "the authorities in the East to take down their security nets and let the dove of peace fly through." This included, he said, "Charter 77, Hungarian young people working for Dialogue, supporters of Polish Solidarity, and the Soviet Groups for Trust."[55] The following January, dozens of the leaders of West European and North American disarmament groups dispatched a protest letter to East Germany's Erich Honecker, demanding that he "release Bärbel Bohley and Ulrike Poppe and others who have been arrested for peace activities in Weimar, Potsdam, Karl Marx Stadt, and Leipzig, in order to facilitate our continued dialogue with *all* who struggle for peace." Four months later, representatives of European and North American peace groups contacted Andreas Papandreou, and urged him, in his forthcoming meeting with Honecker, "to raise the problem of the peace activists who have been arrested recently for their protest against deployment of nuclear missiles in the GDR."[56] At END's July 1984 convention in Perugia, 57 seats were left empty in honor of the antinuclear activists from Eastern Europe and Turkey who were prevented by their governments from attending the event. During the opening plenary session, some 70 activists, wearing gags and carrying banners, took over the stage to underscore this protest.[57] END, particularly, worked at defending East bloc antinuclear campaigners—from prominent figures like Sakharov, to lesser-known activists in the Soviet Union, Czechoslovakia, Hungary, and East Germany.[58]

The Search for New Approaches

The beginning of cruise and Pershing II missile deployment in Western Europe in November 1983 dealt a heavy blow to the nonaligned movement, and convinced leading activists, especially the Europeans, that they had reached a crossroads. Writing in *END Journal*, Kaldor asked: "What specifically do we campaign for, after cruise?" In her opinion, new arms race strategies should be challenged, opposition to the Cold War sustained, nonnuclear, non-provocative defense policies promoted, and "our friends in Eastern Europe" supported.[59] END's Meg Beresford voiced some of the same positions: "opposition to further nuclear escalation"; "opposition to aggressive warfighting strategies"; "presentation of viable alternatives," such as "non-confrontational foreign policies and defensive military strategies" and "conversion"; and defense of "human rights/peace rights." In July 1984, at the END convention, Kaldor teamed up with Faber to present a plan "to raise consciousness about the political future of Europe, about the possibility of an alternative collective security system, in such a way as to undermine the ideology of the Cold War." This proposal—which called for the withdrawal of U.S. and Soviet "occupation" forces from Europe—attracted considerable interest.[60] At a January 1985 meeting of the IPCC, participants suggested a number of new approaches, ranging from a moratorium on new weapons deployment, to support for the Freeze, to promoting a comprehensive test ban treaty. All seemed possible, though none attracted a consensus.[61]

The new approach that made the greatest headway among leading European and North American activists was what became known as Freeze and Withdrawal. In October 1983, still searching for some way to reconcile the strategies of the European and U.S. movements, Laurens Hogebrink of IKV used the occasion of an IPCC meeting to propose a greatly expanded Freeze that would cover a variety of weapons. But the past differences came up again, as did the fear that a Freeze would legitimize the presence in Western Europe of the new cruise and Pershing II missiles.[62] Shortly thereafter, Kaldor produced a modified proposal, calling for a Freeze on the development and production of all nuclear weapons and for the withdrawal of all nuclear weapons on foreign territory. Forsberg of the Freeze thought that it was excellent; Thompson of END liked it, but thought it needed to be supplemented by "a political dimension."[63] At the January 1984 IPCC meeting, a working group of activists—Hogebrink, Kaldor, Erik Alfsen of Norway's No to Nuclear Weapons, and Pam Solo of the Freeze campaign—was appointed to put together a revised version of Freeze and Withdrawal. Appearing that June, it was a lengthy, complex proposal, albeit one that expressed many of the key ideas of the nonaligned movement. Freeze and Withdrawal set as its goal "a world free of nuclear weapons." To attain that goal, it called for a worldwide nuclear weapons freeze, the withdrawal of all INF missiles to the levels that existed prior to the deployment decision of December 1979, the withdrawal of all nuclear weapons from foreign territory (including the creation of nuclear-free zones), further disarmament measures, and, ultimately, nuclear abolition.[64] Although Freeze and Withdrawal never became the centerpiece of the nonaligned movement's strategy, it did provide a good illustration of that movement's determination to press forward, step by step, to a nuclear-free world.

Decay of the Communist-Led Movement

The Communist-led peace movement continued its campaign as well, though its approach remained totally partisan. Calling attention to "the prin-

cipled stands" for peace "taken by the Soviet Union and other socialist
countries," the WPC contrasted this with "the US drive towards a global
apocalypse." Without mentioning the presence of Soviet SS-20 missiles, the
WPC's journal, *Peace Courier*, warned that "deployment of the new US
first-strike missiles in five West European countries will place the world on
the brink of nuclear extinction." Indeed, the WPC never criticized deployment of Soviet nuclear missiles. Instead, praising "the mass movement
which has swept the world," *Peace Courier* predicted it would provide "the
effective weapon to face up to and defeat all U.S. maniacle [*sic*] plans for
nuclear war."[65] Meanwhile, almost alone in the world, the WPC continued
to ignore the Soviet war in Afghanistan and to portray the United States as
the aggressor. In April 1984, to mark what it called "the international Week
of Solidarity with Afghanistan," the WPC called for worldwide condemnation of "the efforts by imperialism to wreck through war the achievements
of Afghanistan." That December, lauding the heroes who had "rescued the
Afghan democratic revolution from the intrigues of those who sought to
jeopardize it," *Peace Courier* argued that the idea "that Afghanistan is for
the Soviet Union what Vietnam was for the US" is "as insidious as it is lu-
dicrous." According to Johannes Pakaslahti, the WPC's former general secretary: "The WPC followed an openly one-sided line in which the Soviet
Union was always right and the United States wrong."[66]

From the WPC's standpoint, Soviet party leaders stood at the zenith of
the peace pantheon. Responding to Brezhnev's death, the WPC proclaimed:
"Mankind will always cherish comrade Brezhnev's unwavering devotion to
the cause of peace, understanding among peoples," and "freedom. . . . His
name will remain a beacon light to peoples all over the world engaged in
. . . the fight against war." Indeed, "Comrade Brezhnev's energetic pursu-
ance of the peace program of the CPSU was yet another proof of his life-
long dedication and commitment to saving mankind from the horrors of
war, particularly nuclear war." When Andropov died soon thereafter, *Peace
Courier*, in a special supplement dedicated to this "outstanding peace
fighter," printed a message from WPC president Romesh Chandra declaring
that "the world-wide peace and anti-war movement has lost an outstanding
man of peace. . . . When, as a consequence of the United States massive
armament buildup, aggression and intervention, the danger of a global nuclear catastrophe has risen to unprecedented heights, President Andropov's
peace initiatives and proposals . . . have again and again given hope and
confidence to, and won the support of, the peace forces of every country."
Thanks to these efforts, "Comrade Andropov's name will live forever in the
annals of history and in the hearts of the peace fighters in every corner of

the planet." The following year, when Chernenko followed his predecessors to the grave, he was also depicted by *Peace Courier* as "an outstanding fighter for peace." Chandra contended that Chernenko's death was "a great loss . . . for the entire progressive humanity, for worldwide peace and anti-war movements." According to the WPC leader, "millions in the world peace movement know well that the peace policy of the Soviet Union, for which President Chernenko's name had become the symbol, will be carried forward with dedication and devotion by the Party, the Government and the people of the Soviet Union—enjoying the full support of the peace move-ment of all countries." Perhaps because three Soviet deaths in two and a half years exhausted his stock of tributes, Chandra drew upon exactly the same words to describe Chernenko's immortality as he had used to describe Andropov's.[67]

Though loyal, however, the WPC grew ever more marginal. Chandra was thrilled by Ronald Reagan's contention that the European antinuclear movement was controlled by the WPC. Meanwhile, recalled Rob Prince, the organization's U.S. secretary, WPC officials were "all looking at each other and saying: 'If only it were true!' But it wasn't. It was absolutely not true." Quite the contrary, the WPC became "totally isolated from the major peace movements—from any of the groups . . . whether it's CND, or IKV, or the END movement. We were not part of it." Meanwhile, the WPC's "practical peace activities and genuine involvement dwindled in size and scope," though "its penchant for large extravaganza events continued unabated."[68] Pakaslahti recalled that "this era was characterized by big conferences with lots of declarations and substantial financial resources to build empty events. There were a lot of tickets paid, and the motto could have been: Join the WPC and see the world." Prince, who attended the 1983 WPC confer-ence in Prague, recalled it as "very large—several thousand people, from all over the world." And "when it was all over, nothing had changed."[69] For Chandra and other WPC officials, however, these conferences were crucial, for Soviet decisions on funding the WPC were based on how "successful" these conferences were. The accompanying demonstrations were just as ar-tificial. Mark Solomon, a member of the WPC's Presidential Commission, recalled that, during the Prague convention, officials organized a big public rally, with independent activists "pushed far away." As the authorities "herded maybe 50–60 thousand people into this square . . . we stood on the platform and looked out, and all we saw was 60,000 somber faces. And the 'hurrahs' almost seemed stage-managed, as if some anti-Communist was making a movie. . . . It looked like a lampoon of the way things are sup-posed to go in Eastern Europe."[70]

Not surprisingly, the WPC's corruption and ineffectuality sparked internal criticism. "We had some problems" with the WPC, recalled Günther Drefahl, president of the GDR Peace Council. "We tried to use our influence to encourage activities—not only to take part in a big meeting, that's not activity, but to speak about activities. And to do something."[71] Some Soviet officials were also growing restive. Tair Tairov, appointed the WPC's Soviet secretary, was told by Soviet authorities to put all his energy into mobilizing the WPC to prevent implementation of NATO's missile deployment decision. But he failed to convince WPC leaders to make it a priority. Nor, of course, did the WPC have the activists to conduct an effective effort. Thus, he recalled, "as it turned out, the campaign to stop deployment of both Soviet and American missiles was completely independent of the WPC." Assessing the situation during the early 1980s, Tairov increasingly was impressed by the growth, dynamism, and sincerity of END and disturbed by the marginality, sectarianism, and corruption of the WPC. Chandra recognized this and, ultimately, a bitter power struggle erupted between the longtime WPC leader and Tairov, with each drawing upon his contacts in Moscow for support. Given the dominance of conservatives in the Soviet party apparatus and the difficulties in reforming a hidebound system, Chandra won. In 1985, Tairov was recalled to Moscow and a more pliant replacement was sent to Helsinki.[72] Under Chandra's leadership, Prince remarked, the WPC "was not so much an ongoing peace movement as the Soviet version of the court of Louis XIV."[73]

WPC affiliates, as offshoots of Communist parties in their countries, generally reflected the power and orientation of these parties. In East bloc nations, the official peace councils organized vast "peace" demonstrations and other activities. According to the secretary of the GDR Peace Council, a 1984 youth manifestation for peace and disarmament was attended "by over 750,000 boys and girls from all over the country." That same year, *Peace Courier* claimed, "over 100,000" peace activities occurred in the Soviet Union, involving "53 million people."[74] In other countries where powerful Communist parties existed, such as France and Finland, Communist-led peace groups also put together well-attended, albeit much smaller, events. By contrast, in the United States, where the Communist Party was miniscule, the membership of the U.S. Peace Council, at its height, stood at only about 1,000.[75] Although all WPC affiliates had a rather starry-eyed view of the Soviet Union, their degree of adoration varied. Not surprisingly, the Soviet Peace Committee was ultra-orthodox. Assailing the claim that the Soviet Union and the United States bore equal responsibility for the arms race, Yuri Zhukov, its hard-line president, argued that such responsibility "fully lies with the United States." Any other interpretation was "not only irrelevant, but extremely perilous for the cause of peace."[76] The Finnish Peace Committee's position was more nuanced, and it even sent delegations to END conventions. Probably the most dissident organization in the WPC was the Italian Communist Party, whose barely concealed scorn for WPC ventures paralleled its skeptical attitude toward the Soviet Union.[77] But the WPC had few dissidents.

Naturally, the burgeoning of the nonaligned movement, with its critique of both Cold War camps and its growing appeal within Communist nations, caused a panic to erupt within the WPC and its constituent organizations. In January 1982, when END activists organized a large demonstration in Geneva during the arms control negotiations, WPC affiliates—noting its criticism of both the Soviet Union and the United States—refused to support it.[78] In a pamphlet published later that year, the East German Peace Council warned that "the advocates of NATO's arms buildup" were promoting "the establishment of an 'independent peace movement,'" in an apparent attempt to disrupt the joint striving for peace by the government and the people." Visiting the Soviet Union in October 1982, Bruce Kent was struck by the fact that, when he mentioned his plan to meet with members of the Moscow Trust Group, the Soviet Peace Committee argued that that would be "a very offensive and hostile act," and seemed to think the independent group was "the result of some Western scheme."[79] In November, at a board meeting of the U.S. Peace Council, the claim was made that "the new campaign to support the 'independent peace movements' of Eastern Europe" represented "another aspect of the attempt to divide and divert the peace movement." Even the relatively liberal Finnish Peace Committee warned END that it "was moving away from stressing factors that unite towards factors that will make cooperation difficult."[80]

The guiding star of the Communist-led movement, the Soviet Peace Committee, made the break official. In a letter sent in December 1982 to 1,500 disarmament groups and individuals in Western Europe and the United States, Zhukov charged that END was trying to "split the anti-war movement" and "infiltrate 'cold war' elements into it." According to Zhukov, END's first convention, at Brussels, in July 1982, had "shown that the true objective of its sponsors was . . . to disunite the anti-war movements." Participants in this convention did not come from "the real mass peace movements of the socialist countries," but from "a group of people who have left their countries and have nothing in common with the struggle for peace and who, while representing nobody, are busy disseminating hostile slanderous fabrications about the foreign and home policies of their former motherland." Indeed, it was "a truly monstrous design to try and use the banner of peace in order to draw the anti-war movement into what is to all intents and purposes a 'cold war' against the public in socialist countries and to lead them along this path to the impasse of anti-Sovietism and anti-communism." END's talk of "equal responsibility" for the arms race was merely an attempt "to conceal and justify an aggressive militarist policy of the USA and NATO."[81]

Thereafter, the Soviet Peace Committee escalated its attack on the nonaligned movement, and particularly upon END and East bloc activists. In the following months, it organized a boycott of END's May 1983 convention by WPC affiliates and arranged, as well, for the denial of visas to members of independent antinuclear groups from the East who wanted to attend it. Interviewed by the *Guardian* in April 1983, Zhukov claimed that the Trust Group was "a joke—it's not serious. There is no so-called independent peace movement." It had only fifteen members, he maintained, and "nobody persecutes them." Olga Medvedkova, a leading activist, was "a Jew by nationality," and her family was simply looking for an excuse to move to Israel, Zhukov insisted.[82] The Peace Committee had a chance to meet her the following month, when three founders of the peace camp at Greenham Common brought her along, unannounced, to a chat they had scheduled with Committee leaders. Ann Pettit, one of the British women, recalled that, once Medvedkova introduced herself as a member of the Soviet Academy of Sciences and a member of the Trust Group, the Committee members began to fidget and then to shout. In the midst of this abuse, Medvedkova "remained totally calm, sipping tea . . . with no outward sign of her inward terror." Within a short time, Oleg Karkhardin, the Committee's vice chair, interrupted her, saying: "I will not allow her to speak. *I'm* the host here, this is my office, I make the rules." Their action was "a provocation," he stormed, and the Trust Group was only "stealing the banner of peace" from the true peace movement, which had 240 million members (the population of the Soviet Union). Eventually, Medvedkova said: "I don't want to prevent a dialogue . . . and if my presence prevents such a dialogue taking place, then I shall leave." And she did. When Karkhardin resumed his attack, one of the Greenham women cut him off, saying: "You keep talking about '*your*' peace movement," but it is "our peace movement, everybody's peace movement." Karkhardin retorted that "a person who opposes this society cannot expect any reaction other than what we showed Mme Medvedkova."[83]

The Western leaders of the nonaligned movement also came in for ferocious criticism. In early 1984, when Glenys Kinnock and Edna Healey, the wives of the two top British Labour Party leaders, visited the headquarters of the Soviet Peace Committee, recalled Denis Healey, "they were treated to a long tirade of abuse against Mary Kaldor and E. P. Thompson." That June, Zhukov charged that "U.S. and NATO psychological warfare units" were "attempting to sabotage some of the anti-nuclear movements from the inside," and that Thompson led one of these "units." Adding the IPCC and Mient Jan Faber to the list of subversives, Grigory Lokshin, secretary of the Soviet Peace Committee, explained: "In NATO's arsenal of methods of subversion . . . an ever-greater place is being given to ideological warfare. This is carried out partly with the help of various front organizations and groups that insinuate themselves into the anti-war movement." Of all those involved, "E. P. Thompson . . . is the noisiest mouthpiece of these anti-Soviet conceptions."[84] When Mark Solomon of the U.S. Peace Council in-dependently wrote an article criticizing Thompson for anti-Sovietism, the Soviet Peace Committee and the WPC seized upon it with alacrity, had it reprinted in numerous languages, and distributed it around the world, in-cluding END's Perugia convention. Prince recalled that Thompson "repre-sented everything that scared the pants off a movement like the WPC. . . . Someone who represents a Left tradition that's not part of this monopoly." Thus, "the need to discredit Thompson was very important."[85]

Although WPC leaders fretted about all elements of the nonaligned movement, they found END's success particularly infuriating. According to Prince, the Soviet Peace Committee was "really upset" that END took off, and "didn't know how to relate to it." Similarly, the WPC did not "know how to deal with this reality." For the most part, as Tairov recalled, Soviet Peace Committee leaders "described the END conventions as an anti-Soviet happening," while Zhukov, Lokshin, and other Peace Committee leaders depicted END "as a pro-NATO, anti-socialist movement." But that only left them on the outside, with no influence upon the millions of antinuclear ac-tivists mobilized by END. Consequently, the WPC, as Prince remarked, "vacillated between really attacking it, on the one hand, and trying to be-come part of it, on the other."[86] Indeed, Werner Rümpel, one of the leaders of the East German Peace Council, recalled that the Soviet Peace Commit-tee pressed the official East bloc peace groups "to take part in it, and one day we would have the majority. It was really an attempt to control this movement." But although the boycott of END conventions stopped, and a few WPC affiliates even joined the organization, this strategy, too, proved ineffective. END remained independent and, as Prince remarked, the WPC remained "nowhere in this movement." In these circumstances, Zhukov returned to the attack. Speaking at a WPC meeting in Helsinki in October 1984, he again denounced END's top leaders, claiming their arguments were "strangely reminiscent of those used by American propaganda."[87]

Response of the Nonaligned Movement

The nonaligned movement was not especially fond of the Communist-led movement, either. "We do not like the World Peace Council, and we are wary of its affiliated organizations," Thompson told a gathering of independent Hungarian activists in 1982. The WPC "has been an organ of Soviet diplomacy for thirty years," he remarked on another occasion, and the "state-sponsored Peace Committees" of Eastern Europe "have never . . . fluttered an eyelash in protest against any action of Soviet militarism."[88] Wim Bartels of the IPCC regarded these official peace councils as nothing more than "the voice of the government," a view echoed by Melinda Fine, who handled international affairs for the Freeze campaign. She added that, "while criticizing US nuclear policy, they do not criticize the nuclear policy of the Soviet Union." Writing in 1984, David McReynolds of the War Resisters League and the WRI, described Zhukov as "truly a fossil who . . . brings back the old furies. The Soviets simply will not accept the concept of an *independent* peace movement!"[89] That same year, a Freeze governing body, uneasy about any dealings with the Soviet Peace Committee, resolved that the Freeze campaign "should receive no money, directly or indirectly, from any government," and that any agreements with official groups would have to be brought to the executive committee for approval. In 1982, the CND executive committee voted against establishing any formal links with the WPC.[90] Dan Plesch, a top CND elected official and staffer, recalled the WPC and its affiliates as "a pain in the ass, flies at every picnic," though some were "more obnoxious than others." In the view of the FAS's Jeremy Stone, the Soviet Peace Committee was "a phony, a front group," and its leaders were "apparatchik, Soviet-style finks."[91]

Within individual nations, too, nonaligned groups usually had a negative attitude toward their Communist-led counterparts. In Denmark, independent groups like No More War and the United Nations Association left the Cooperation Committee for Peace and Security because of its relationship to the WPC. In Austria, independent began to withdraw from the major peace federation thanks to Communist Party influence within it. When the Swiss Easter March Committee, dominated by the Swiss Peace Movement (Schweize Friedensbewegung), a WPC affiliate, rejected calls for "dismantling the bloc system" and "solidarity with the nonaligned movement in Eastern Europe," independent groups distanced themselves from the committee.[92] In the United States, the tiny U.S. Peace Council, doing its best to eschew sectarianism and be cooperative, tried hard to join broader coalitions. But, as Mark Solomon recalled, "some of the major coalitions would never allow us to participate officially, even though they wouldn't turn us away if we showed up at a meeting." Prince, too, recalled that Freeze leaders "were very uncomfortable with us." Reflecting on the relationship years later, the Freeze's Randy Kehler emphasized that its drawbacks outweighed its advantages for the movement. "I felt we needed to be open to everybody, but they didn't have much to offer. . . . So I didn't want to shun them, but I didn't want to spend much time on them either." Thus, given its miniscule size and tepid reception, the U.S. Peace Council constituted what Sanford Gottlieb called "a non-factor" in the overall U.S. movement.[93]

Despite these chilly relations, nonaligned and Communist-led groups did hold occasional meetings with each other. A key reason for the participation of Western nonaligned groups was that most independent groups in the Eastern bloc urged it upon them. As Zdena Tomin, a Czech activist, summarized things, "practically all" of these groups, "with the exception of our Polish friends . . . urge you not to stop contacts with the official peace councils," and "also urge you to use these contacts to legitimize their own existence." Thus, in 1983, the Hungarian Dialogue groups pressed for continued contacts with the official committees, and Charter 77 pressed nonaligned groups to attend the WPC's Prague Assembly and stress "the indivisibility of peace."[94] Writing in *END Journal*, Jiri Hajek, a founder of Charter 77, also championed contacts with the official peace groups. If Western peace movements "do not permit the other side to impose restrictions on them," he argued, those contacts could "provide an opportunity for a dialogue with the power structure in the East." Some Western activists made a similar case. Snubbing the official peace councils "can be counterproductive for the independent [Eastern] groups," a leading activist wrote in the IPCC's *Disarmament Campaigns*. "By dealing with the officials, the Western groups can help create more room for the independents to operate; it is vital that Westerners express their solidarity with these people, both publicly and privately, in their dealings with officials." Indeed, "in the case of Eastern independents, it may be necessary for their continued existence." Furthermore, "direct contacts with officials" would "prevent them from falling into the propaganda trap of believing that the goals of the Western movement are identical to those of the Warsaw Pact."[95]

Thus, uneasily and usually unproductively, Western nonaligned groups met on occasion with the official groups of the East. To be sure, END refused to accede to Charter 77's plea to attend the WPC's Prague conference and, instead, boycotted it. But CND's national council, after rejecting the idea of sending regular delegates, voted to send two "observers," on the condition that, at the conference, they clearly transmit CND's nonaligned views, defend the rights of independent activists in the East bloc, and meet with members of Charter 77.[96] They managed to do all of these, much to the irritation of Czech authorities and many of the official delegates.[97] SANE, the Freeze, and other U.S. groups also met on occasion with representatives of the official peace councils in the United States and Moscow, using these opportunities to encourage citizen-to-citizen dialogue, criticize Soviet abuses of human rights, and to call for Soviet action to halt the arms race. Privately, many nonaligned leaders considered such meetings of little value. Ken Coates of END thought it would be far more useful to talk directly to governments; Judith Winther of Denmark's No to Nuclear Weapons recommended conversing instead with Soviet researchers and scientists, whom she found less "dependent" and less "ignorant" about disarmament issues.[98] Nevertheless, the meetings continued. In February 1984, the Greek KEA-DEA held the first organized gathering of representatives from nonaligned Western groups and the official East bloc peace councils, in Athens. But, predictably, the officials—with the Soviet Peace Committee's Zhukov riding herd—refused to criticize Soviet missile deployments or discuss the persecution of independent activists in their countries. Consequently, the exchanges were sharp, and the delegates left without being able to agree upon a joint closing statement.[99]

The difficulties in dealing with the official peace groups of the East spilled over into the END conventions as well. In July 1984, when END convened in Perugia, representatives of the Soviet, Polish, and Hungarian official peace committees attended an END gathering for the first time. They were observers rather than delegates, however, for they refused to sign the END Appeal, which placed the blame for the nuclear arms race upon both sides in the Cold War. Although few convention participants opposed their presence, controversy arose over how to treat them in the face of the refusal by Warsaw Pact governments to allow independent activists to attend. This sparked the demonstration at the plenary session in support of the excluded activists, which in turn drew an official Soviet Peace Committee protest against this "provocation in cold war style" and its "primitive anti-communism." Another confrontation occurred when the Soviet delegation staged a press conference that was attended by many other delegates. When Soviet Peace Committee officials said there were no disarmament activists in the Soviet Union outside their organization and that Trust Group members had been arrested for "hooliganism," the audience responded with jeers, boos, and heckling. Asked about why the Peace Committee never criticized Soviet nuclear policy, one official remarked that "public opinion and official opinion are the same in our society"—a statement that drew a burst of laughter from the assemblage. At the least, both nonaligned and aligned groups came away from the convention better aware of the gulf that separated them.[100] In July 1985, when END held another convention, in Amsterdam, the official groups once again boycotted it.[101]

The Strength of the International Movements

By 1985, then, the influence and effectiveness of the WPC was dwindling rapidly. Although the WPC claimed affiliates in 141 nations, few of these had any significant base of activists or did anything very useful, even from the standpoint of Communist governments. Without a Soviet subsidy of millions of dollars a year, it is doubtful that the WPC could have stayed afloat. The publication of *Peace Courier* alone cost from $750,000 to $1 million annually, and although some 16,000 copies were printed, the number of its actual subscribers was fewer than 200.[102] WPC leaders produced "a show," recalled the GDR Peace Council's Günther Drefahl, and usually the show occurred among "the already convinced people. They had no great ability to convince other people. . . . They spoke to themselves." According to the WPC's Rob Prince, the Communist-led organization was "a Cold War relic, more of an embarrassment and barrier than an asset to Soviet foreign policy goals." Indeed, "during the great peace activities of the early 1980s, the WPC was on the sidelines, and played a role of no consequence in Europe."[103] Far from reviving this decaying Soviet operation, the burst of independent antinuclear activism that swept the world during these years merely highlighted its one-sidedness, corruption, and decrepitude.

By contrast, the nonaligned antinuclear campaign emerged during the early 1980s as a global movement of unprecedented size and power. Drawing upon the enthusiastic support of professional groups, women's organizations, churches, environmental groups, unions, and mainstream political parties around the world, and backed by public opinion, it represented one of history's great success stories in grassroots political mobilization. In the fall of 1983, it turned out more than five million antinuclear demonstrators on the streets of Europe and North America alone.[104] The world nuclear disarmament movement was not only a substantially larger phenomenon than its antinuclear predecessor of the late 1950s and early 1960s, but—as END

observed—"the biggest mass movement in modern history."[105] Consequently, despite the ever-escalating nuclear arms race, its leaders refused to
accept defeat. Addressing the hundreds of thousands of demonstrators in
Hyde Park that fall, on the eve of Euromissile deployment, Thompson remained fiery and unrepentant. "We have succeeded in these four years in
putting together the only true resource of peace—an international chain of
activists . . . stretching from Athens to San Francisco, from Japan to Iceland, from Montreal to Oslo," he stated. And the current demonstrations
present "one of the greatest concerted international manifestations of the
political will of ordinary people ever known in world history." Could such
an outpouring of popular protest be resisted indefinitely? "At some point,"
he predicted, "the old structures of militarism must buckle under the peaceful non-violent pressure, as the railings of this Hyde Park . . . buckled under
the pressure of peaceful demonstrators for the vote—and, somewhere, peace
must and will break through."[106]

Governments Confront the Movement, 1981-85

> Only the deaf cannot hear the clamor arising all over the world against the arms race.
>
> Pierre Elliott Trudeau, 1982

The unprecedented upsurge of independent citizen activism made the antinuclear campaign an inescapable object of concern for government officials. As they quickly recognized, it had the potential for altering nuclear policies and, thereby, seriously affecting national security issues of the greatest magnitude. In this connection, the movement provided national security managers with either a great danger or a great opportunity, depending upon their political orientation. If they looked forward to a nuclear buildup by their nation or by their Cold War military bloc, they were inclined to regard the antinuclear campaign as a threat to their national security, perhaps even as part of a conspiracy against them by their foreign "enemies." On the other hand, if they had misgivings about the nuclear arms race, they adopted a more tolerant approach toward antinuclear agitation, sometimes even lauding it or establishing close connections with disarmament groups. Whatever their perspective, however, numerous governments perceived that this mass citizens' uprising, bolstered by major social institutions and public opinion, had become a force to be reckoned with. Accordingly, they invested considerable time, energy, and resources in responding to it.

The United States

From the standpoint of U.S. government policy, the movement was clearly a danger. The Reagan administration saw the Freeze campaign "as a serious threat," recalled Thomas Graham, a top ACDA official of the time. Queried about the Freeze movement years later, Robert McFarlane, the President's

National Security Advisor, observed: "We took it as a serious movement that could undermine congressional support for the [nuclear] modernization program, and potentially . . . a serious partisan political threat that could affect the election in '84."[1] In April 1982, Eugene Rostow, the ACDA director, fired off a memo to the White House proposing that the administration "begin an immediate media campaign" to deal with "the growing stridency and hysteria" of the U.S. antinuclear movement. Although this movement "includes such perennial elements as the old-line pacifists, the environmentalists, the disaffected left, and various communist elements," Rostow stated, "there is participation, on an increasing scale in the U.S., of three groups whose potential impact should be cause for concern. They are the churches, the 'loyal opposition' and, perhaps most important, the unpoliticized public." According to White House communications director David Gergen, "there was a widespread view in the administration that the freeze was a dagger pointed at the heart of the administration's defense program."[2]

This sense of danger was reinforced by discouraging reports on American public opinion. In June 1981, Richard Wirthlin, the President's pollster, informed him that, although he received higher approval ratings among Americans than did Jimmy Carter on almost all aspects of foreign policy, Reagan lagged behind him on "promotion of peace"; indeed, 35 percent of the electorate felt that "over the past few months the risk of war has increased." That December, White House staffers pondered the disturbing news that 52 percent of Americans worried that Reagan might "get us into another war." In April 1982, Wirthlin found that, when Americans were confronted with two alternative perceptions of Reagan—one as a proponent of a rapid nuclear buildup and the other as a proponent of Soviet-American nuclear arms reductions—55 percent chose the former and only 35 percent the latter. The dismaying fact, as Wirthlin recognized, was that Americans preferred nuclear arms reductions by overwhelming margins. Although Reagan did not necessarily set his policies by opinion polls or press reports, the administration took both of them very seriously. Wirthlin alone briefed the President two or three times a month, and sometimes more frequently. He would also spend parts of three to five days a week in the White House conferring with key staffers, and on occasion would brief Haig, Weinberger, and Shultz.[3] Furthermore, according to Adelman, top administration officials devoted up to a third of their time to dealing with the mass media. During his tenure as ACDA director, the news clippings "helped fashion the agency's agenda for at least every morning—if not the entire day."[4]

In the administration's opinion, the situation was at least as bad in Western Europe. In July 1981, Reagan's first National Security Advisor,

Richard Allen, called Haig's attention to "the continuing deterioration in West European public opinion with respect to Western defense efforts." That October, Charles Wick, director of the U.S. International Communications Agency, warned the president that "the public protest actions of intense and vocal minorities could have a significant cumulative impact on the world view and the political will of the larger, more passive segments of European publics." Indeed, "to the extent that West European governments are constrained (or encouraged) by their understanding of the moods and tolerances of their constituencies, public opinion in the end may be decisive."[5] There was "tremendous concern" within the administration about the Euromissile demonstrations, recalled Graham; "we realized we were in a real battle . . . over this." Asked how much discussion of the demonstrations took place within the first year or so of the Reagan administration, Allen responded: "A lot! We did a careful study of the reaction of all of Western Europe. . . . The environmentalists, the Greens . . . those people who went to the streets were the objects of our attention." And the conclusions were quite discouraging. "We were swimming upstream," Allen recalled. "The President was swimming upstream, against the current."[6]

Nor did things improve in subsequent years. Haig recalled the growing resistance of European Social Democrats to U.S. nuclear policies, a sign that "the consensus behind NATO on the part of the center left in Europe" was "in danger of disintegration." In his memoirs, Reagan too displayed an intense frustration at the gathering opposition to his nuclear buildup. Conflating the anti-Euromissile demonstrations with the Nuclear Freeze campaign, he recalled bitterly that, during the later summer and fall of 1982, as he sought to save the world from Soviet aggression, "the streets of U.S. and European cities were filled more and more often with nuclear freeze proponents."[7] When Vice President George Bush returned from a trip to Western Europe in 1983, he also came away with a gloomy assessment—bemoaning the unwillingness of its youth to "pay the continuing price . . . that is necessary to maintain freedom's institutions." Writing in March 1984 on the "important problem we face with our European allies," Under Secretary of State Lawrence Eagleburger declared that "the steady decline of European public confidence in US policies is a real concern and one we must all work to correct."[8]

Confronted with these difficulties, the Reagan administration embarked upon a major campaign to roll back the antinuclear movement. In the United States, it began on March 10, 1982, in response to an announcement that day by Senators Kennedy and Hatfield that they would introduce a freeze resolution in Congress. Haig immediately denounced the Freeze idea as "not only bad defense policy," but "bad arms control policy as well." The next day, in a special address to a State Department press briefing, Richard Burt, the department's Director of Political and Military Affairs, followed up by claiming that the Freeze proposal would lock the United States "into a position of military disadvantage and dangerous vulnerability. . . . We think the President's strategic modernization program is indispensable."[9] As administration officials publicly condemned the Freeze as "destabilizing" and potentially "devastating," they met privately to develop what McFarlane, then assistant national security advisor, called "a huge effort" to combat it. They organized an interdepartmental group, the Arms Control Information Working Group, "that I chaired in the White House that included representatives from all the relevant agencies—from the CIA, from Defense, from the Joint Chiefs, from the State Department, from the USIA." Addressing the assembled officials, McFarlane told them that they should "get out from behind" their desks "and go to Atlanta, San Francisco, Denver, the fourteen major media markets of this country, and make a quota of appearances. . . . Everybody in this room and your deputies have to make at least four appearances within the next thirty days. And every place you go, you have to do four categories of appearance. When you go to Chicago, you have to hit four audiences: a college setting; a drive-time radio setting; a civic group . . . ; and another talk show." Thereafter, they should report back to him.[10]

Throughout 1982, what McFarlane called the administration campaign "to counter the nuclear freeze movement" accelerated in intensity, with participation by the highest level officials. In April, the President used a nationwide radio address to assail the Freeze, while Haig warned that "the stakes are too great and the consequences of error too catastrophic" to scrap time-tested policies "for a leap into the unknown."[11] The following month, Weinberger charged that a nuclear freeze might lead the Soviet Union to attempt nuclear blackmail or a first strike against the United States. Addressing an anniversary gathering of the Knights of Columbus in August, Reagan denounced the Freeze as "sterile" and "obsolete." That same month, in a memo to White House Chief of Staff James Baker, McFarlane reported that "attention now shifts to states where freeze resolutions are on the ballot." His Information Working Group had developed "an aggressive strategy keyed to Wisconsin and then the other freeze vote states." It planned "to have top State, ACDA, and Defense speakers visit major media markets, hitting TV, radio, editorial boards, etc., and at the same time conducting an outreach program to inform religious, ethnic, veterans, women and other interest groups." The Defense Department had "an internal information program, to include an interview by Cap Weinberger, aimed at active duty

military personnel, retirees, reservists, civilian employees, and families."
Gergen had already "distributed a two-minute speech insert with back-up
fact sheets to the 350 top administration spokesmen." Beyond using the
president, the secretary of state, and other luminaries, "we are even looking
into the innovative idea of asking the American Security Council or some
other supportive organization to produce an arms control book with an introduction by a well-known American (Charleton Heston, Clint Eastwood),
who could be privately sponsored on a 'celebrity book tour' nationally to hit
the Phil Donahue-type shows that so many people watch." It was "imperative that we . . . try to avoid a series of lop-sided votes, manipulated by the
freeze movement to bring pressure on us and on the Congress."[12]

Although administration officials denied at the time that a government
campaign existed to defeat the Freeze referenda, its operations became increasingly evident. In Arizona, one of the leading Freeze speakers, retired
Admiral Eugene Carroll of the Center for Defense Information, found himself shadowed at nearly every stop he made by General Richard Boverie of
the National Security Council, thanks to last-minute scheduling operations
by the State Department. Although the State Department refused to provide
an accounting to journalists of its sudden blizzard of speech-making efforts
on nuclear issues, it admitted that three-fourths of them occurred in Freeze
referenda states and that nearly half had been initiated by the department.
California, of course, was the great prize—the nation's largest state, where
Reagan had been governor and where he still maintained his home. In July,
the president himself kicked off the administration campaign there, declaring that the Freeze "would make this country desperately vulnerable to nuclear blackmail." Weinberger, Rostow, and other administration wheel-
horses barnstormed across California, raising the alarm about the Freeze. A
few days before the referendum balloting, Clark volunteered to substitute
for McFarlane in San Diego and deliver "a major policy speech." It turned
out to be a bitter attack on the Freeze, in which he claimed that the Russians, at the Geneva arms talks, were "smirking" on "hearing of the success
of the freeze movement." Harold Willens, the sparkplug of the California
Freeze effort, noticed that he, too, was bird-dogged wherever he spoke by
administration officials, and concluded, correctly, that this pattern reflected
"a covert campaign financed by the taxpayers."[13]

That fall, as the Freeze seemed increasingly likely to emerge victorious
at the polls and in Congress, Reagan grew more strident. Speaking before a
gathering of veterans' groups on October 4, he contended that the Freeze—
"a movement that's sweeping across the country"—was "inspired by not
[sic] the sincere, honest people who want peace, but by some who want the

weakening of America and so are manipulating honest people." On November 11, he told a press conference that "foreign agents" had helped "instigate" the Freeze campaign. There was "plenty of evidence" for this, the President stated, but did not produce any. To buttress the President's case, though, the White House press secretary pointed to a number of articles in conservative publications, including *Reader's Digest*, reportedly one of the President's favorite magazines.[14] On December 10, Reagan—admitting that he had leaned heavily for his information on two *Reader's Digest* articles— also cited a report by the House Intelligence Committee. But the committee chair, Edward Boland, declared that the "bottom line" of testimony from FBI and CIA officials as well as from a prominent Soviet defector, was that there was "no evidence that the Soviets direct, manage, or manipulate the nuclear freeze movement"—a contention confirmed when a declassified version of the FBI report was released in March 1983.[15] Reagan, though, insisted that "the originating organization" for the Freeze was the World Peace Council and that the first person to propose a nuclear freeze was Leonid Brezhnev, who supposedly launched it on February 21, 1981.[16] These allegations were so patently false that even the mass media quickly dropped them from consideration.[17]

Although the administration cut loose from its ill-fated allegations that the Freeze was choreographed by the Kremlin, it continued its relentless assault upon the movement, with the President increasingly wielding the cudgels. While the House of Representatives once again considered a Freeze resolution, he devoted a major address to the Los Angeles World Affairs Council on March 31, 1983. Arguing that "the freeze concept is dangerous for many reasons," he insisted that it would "pull the rug out from under our negotiators in Geneva."[18] That May, he used his weekly radio address to claim that freezing U.S. nuclear weapons production "makes about as much sense as saying that the way to prevent fires is to close down the fire department." In August, speaking before the American Legion, he pulled out all the stops. "'Peace' is a beautiful word, but it is also freely used and sometimes even abused," he declared. "Neville Chamberlain thought of peace as a vague policy in the 1930s, and the result brought us closer to World War II. Today's so-called peace movement—for all its modern hype and theatrics—makes the same old mistake." By contrast, "the members of the real peace movement . . . are people who understand that peace must be built on strength."[19]

The administration also did intensive lobbying in an attempt to turn the tide within key institutions. During preparations for the first draft of the Catholic Bishops' Peace Pastoral, Weinberger and other top administration officials presented testimony before the drafting body in defense of the Reagan nuclear program. Disturbed by the ensuing draft, Weinberger and National Security Advisor William Clark criticized it sharply, while White House representatives urged the drafting commission to meet with the President. The administration also attempted to bring pressure to bear upon the bishops by intervening with the Pope.[20] Congress provided another arena of struggle. In August 1982, Reagan made numerous telephone calls to Republican members of the House, pleading with them to oppose the Freeze. He concluded gloomily: "They are all buffaloed by the public pressure of the freeze movement."[21] In February 1983, warning that "the administration faces an uphill struggle this year in countering the efforts of the nuclear freeze movement," Clark proposed to Vice President Bush that he work to persuade House Foreign Affairs Committee chair Clement Zablocki to delay hearings on the Freeze resolution and to see if he was willing to accept resolution language "palatable to the administration." Despite progress along these lines, this arrangement fell through and, according to one NSC staffer, Zablocki returned "to his original version, since he is afraid of losing in the Committee."[22] Meanwhile, the President sought to rally his troops against the Freeze—holding what one official called "a love feast" with representatives of the Coalition for Peace Through Strength, meeting with dozens of members of Congress, and sending a special letter to administration loyalists in Congress.[23] Although this effort failed to hold the line in the House, the administration proved luckier that year in the Senate, where a "Build-down" proposal—scrapping two missiles for every new missile installed—was seized upon by desperate legislators as a "moderate" alternative and championed just long enough to derail the Freeze resolution.[24]

Because of the sharpness of the confrontation, the administration isolated itself from antinuclear organizations. Although Elizabeth Dole, the Assistant to the President for Public Liaison, maintained that the administration provided "an open door" for all groups to "have their views heard at the highest level of government,"[25] requests from Freeze campaign leaders and their overseas counterparts to meet with top administration officials were routinely denied. Consequently, in the aftermath of the successful Freeze referenda in the fall of 1982, when Randy Forsberg and Randy Kehler proposed a meeting with the President as part of what they called a "dialogue . . . essential to the democratic process," the White House quickly turned down the request. These two "radical freeze organizers," an NSC staffer explained to Clark, "have shown no inclination . . . to learn about, or to support, the Administration's far-reaching arms control efforts." Thus, "there is little to be gained from any such meeting. The group would surely exploit any meeting with the President to heighten their self-importance and to gain additional publicity for their message."[26] For similar reasons, the administration rejected requests for presidential meetings with delegations from the Union of Concerned Scientists, Physicians for Social Responsibility, Council for a Livable World, and WILPF.[27] When Europe erupted in anti-Euromissile demonstrations during the fall of 1983, Kehler proposed a meeting of top West European and U.S. nuclear disarmament group leaders with Secretary of State Shultz, but this, too, was rejected, as was a request for a meeting with him that June by leaders of West Germany's Green Party.[28] To be sure, occasionally there was some contact at lower levels of officialdom.[29] But the highest levels of the U.S. government remained quarantined from contamination by the antinuclear movement.

There were two exceptions to this rule. The first occurred when the President's daughter, Patti Davis, a keen supporter of the Freeze campaign, prevailed upon him to meet with one of its most eloquent leaders, Helen Caldicott. Thus, on the afternoon of December 6, 1982, Reagan and Caldicott conversed at the White House for 75 minutes. Although the meeting was quite civil, the two found themselves far apart on approaches, with the President—Caldicott recalled—candidly stating that he considered the Russians "evil, godless Communists" and that he sought to prevent nuclear war by "building more bombs." Reagan noted in his diary that "she seems like a nice, caring person, but she is all steamed up and knows an awful lot of things that aren't true. I tried but couldn't get through her fixation." Caldicott later remarked that Reagan was "one of the least intelligent people" she had ever met, though he seemed pleasant enough and "would have made a nice chicken farmer."[30]

Another fruitless meeting occurred the following month, when Reagan spoke with Harold Willens. After the Freeze emerged victorious in the California referendum, U.S. Senator Alan Cranston, in accordance with the provisions of the ballot proposition, sought to deliver the text to the White House. But officials there only laughed at him, as they later laughed at California Governor Gerry Brown, who also made an attempt. When Willens related this to Patti Davis, with whom he had become acquainted during the referendum campaign, she immediately telephoned her father at the White House and arranged for Willens to meet with him. The night before the White House meeting, Willens did not sleep at all, but compressed what he considered his most influential remarks into a ten-minute talk. But to no avail. Though Reagan was very polite, he was obdurate about dealings with the Russians: "Mr. Willens, you don't understand. You know, over there, they're not even human beings like we are." Willens recalled that these kinds of comments "scared the hell out of me," as did Reagan's remark that, even if nuclear missiles were launched, they could be recalled. Like Caldicott, Willens left his meeting at the White House thoroughly depressed.[31]

By contrast, to counter the antinuclear campaign, the administration worked closely with ultra-conservative organizations,[32] especially those of the Christian Right. In December 1982, Robert Dugan, the director of the National Association of Evangelicals, wrote to Baker at the White House, inviting Reagan to address the Protestant body at its Orlando convention in March. Such an address could "be strategic politically," he pointed out, for, when it came to the Freeze, evangelicals were "potentially, a major bloc of support for the administration." The NAE's Washington office was "working behind the scenes to counteract some of the drift toward the nuclear freeze position," but Reagan's address would put things over the top.[33] Jumping at the opportunity, Reagan and the White House staff turned the speechwriting job over to Tony Dolan, a conservative ideologue. Dolan produced a fire and brimstone version that dismayed more moderate aides, who softened it somewhat, as did Reagan. This address, delivered to the evangelical convention on March 8, 1983, became widely known because of the President's denunciation of the Soviet Union as an "Evil Empire."[34] But Reagan, determined to enlist the evangelicals in the administration campaign against the Freeze, denounced that movement as well, calling it "a very dangerous fraud." "Simple-minded appeasement or wishful thinking about our adversaries is folly," he declared. "It means the betrayal of our past, the squandering of our freedom."[35]

For similar reasons, the administration cemented its relationship with the Rev. Jerry Falwell. A week after Reagan's address to the evangelicals, he met with the televangelist at the White House, where the President thanked him for his strong support, expressed his appreciation for Falwell's anti-Freeze advertising campaign, and asked him what the Moral Majority leader thought of his speech to the evangelical convention. A White House background memo to the President noted appreciatively that the Moral Majority, "a national conservative lobby with $60 million per year budget," mailed its monthly newsletter to 560,000 homes, and that Falwell's Old Time Gospel Hour broadcasts included Sunday programs on more than 400 TV stations and daily programs on more than 500 radio stations. Furthermore, Falwell "has never criticized you or Reagan Administration policy." As Falwell stepped up his ferocious and well-funded attacks on the Freeze campaign, the rightwing evangelist continued to receive special treatment from the administration, including briefings from NSC staff. The White House also provided at least one briefing for Moral Majority state leaders, hosted by White House aide Pat Buchanan. This would be "beneficial . . . to the President," explained a Moral Majority official, "as these men and women return to their states and defend the President's conservative initiatives."[36]

In addition, the administration worked closely on anti-Freeze operations with the conservative American Security Council and the Coalition for Peace Through Strength. Weinberger played a starring role in the American Security Council's film, *Countdown for America*, a $300,000 hawkish documentary that the organization showed on television throughout most of the nation in the fall of 1982, in an attempt to defeat the Freeze referenda. "It's apparent why the Soviets are for a nuclear freeze," Weinberger said in the film. "It would leave them in a position of permanent superiority." In December 1983, the Coalition for Peace Through Strength, which claimed to have the support of 245 members of Congress, launched its In Defense of America project at a White House luncheon hosted by the President. Nearly a year later, Reagan gave a White House reception to recognize the campaign's accomplishments. These included: the development and distribution of 300,000 copies of a book, *A Strategy for Peace Through Strength*; the production of a TV documentary, *Peace Through Strength*, shown on 183 TV stations during Peace Through Strength Week; and the organization of 46 Peace Through Strength rallies across the United States. The costs of these operations were immense and, in 1985, the Coalition for Peace Through Strength estimated that the next phase of In Defense of America alone would require $6.5 million.[37]

Sometimes, the administration drew upon government intelligence agencies to deal with its nuclear critics. Shortly after Reagan's election, the Heritage Foundation presented his transition team with a detailed plan to tighten internal security procedures, arguing that "individual liberties are secondary to the requirement of national security and internal civil order." The plan delineated "anti-nuclear lobbies" as one of the preferred targets.[38] The degree to which the Reagan administration followed this recipe remains uncertain but, at the least, the federal government placed nuclear disarmament groups under surveillance. This included investigations of antinuclear organizations by the FBI, the CIA, Naval intelligence, and the Federal Emergency Management Administration. In the San Francisco Bay area, the FBI admitted infiltrating Physicians for Social Responsibility and other nuclear disarmament organizations.[39] FBI investigations also came to light when their findings became tangled up in the issue of alleged Soviet "manipulation" of the Freeze campaign. Furthermore, according to Robert Gates, then the CIA's deputy director, the CIA "devoted tremendous effort" to investigating Soviet participation in the West European campaign against the Euromissiles, and sent a report on that subject to Bush, Shultz, Weinberger, and Clark in January 1983. Up to this point, administration officials tended to view this campaign as organized by the Kremlin. Referring to the Euromissile demonstrations, Reagan said they were "all sponsored by a thing called the World Peace Council."[40] But Gates claimed that the CIA's efforts "largely persuaded a very conservative Reagan administration that the Soviets did not 'control' the peace movement . . . and that much of the protest was genuine."[41]

In addition, working through Brian Crozier's private intelligence operation, the U.S. government channeled funds to groups in Western Europe that sought to derail the antinuclear campaign. According to Crozier, he met frequently with Reagan and other government officials—including CIA director Casey, National Security Advisors Allen, Clark, and McFarlane, Admiral John Poindexter, Colonel Oliver North, and Professor Richard Pipes—to discuss secret operations initiated and coordinated by The 61 in non-Communist countries. Among these operations were subsidizing the Freedom, Peace and Defense Foundation in the Netherlands, which hired aircraft to display pro-NATO and anti-Soviet slogans during a peace demonstration, and launching the pro-nuclear Rally for Peace in Freedom in Belgium. It also assisted Britain's Coalition for Peace through Security (which—Crozier assured Clark—"challenges the Campaign for Nuclear Disarmament at public meetings, through the press, in Parliament and in various leaflets and pamphlets") and France's pro-nuclear Committee Against Neutralism. According to Crozier, during 1981 and 1982, funding for The 61 came from the CIA, as well as from businesses and the wealthy. In December 1982, when White House memos indicate Crozier corresponded with Clark and met with McFarlane, he discussed an ambitious plan to "create active awareness of [the] necessity to place cruise and Pershing II missiles in Europe" and to expose "the so-called 'Peace Movement.'" Until the Reagan administration records are fully opened, it remains impossible to determine if Crozier received the $335,000 he requested for this purpose, although it is clear that Clark was enthusiastic about Crozier's operations and recommended that the President meet with him.[42]

In an effort to alter public opinion, the Reagan administration embarked upon a major campaign of what it called "public diplomacy" in Western Europe and around the world. The head of the TV and film branch of the U.S. Information Agency (USIA) recalled that "the U.S. government ran a full-service public relations organization, the largest in the world, about the size of the twenty biggest U.S. commercial PR firms combined. Its full-time

professional staff of more than 10,000, spread out among some 150 countries, burnished America's image and trashed the Soviet Union 2,500 hours a
week" in "more than 70 languages, to the tune of over $2 billion per year."
The largest branch of this "propaganda machine" was the USIA (until 1982,
the International Communications Agency), headed by Charles Wick, a
Hollywood movie magnate and personal friend of Reagan's. Determined to
win the worldwide battle for public opinion, the administration brought
Wick into the policymaking process through attendance at NSC meetings
and the Secretary of State's daily policy sessions. It also reversed a long-
term decline in funding for the USIA, increasing its budget by 74 percent
between 1981 and 1985.[43] In this new, enhanced form, the USIA focused
much of its activity on justifying the installation of the Euromissiles and as-
suring the world of America's peaceful intentions. Through a special program of worldwide TV broadcasts, massive distribution of propaganda literature, and speeches by government leaders, Wick hoped "to mitigate the
impact of anti-nuclear movements on publics and governments abroad."[44]

At Wick's urging, top U.S. officials played an important role in this
public relations extravaganza, embarking upon speaking tours across Western Europe and Asia to rally popular support for U.S. nuclear policies. Addressing a Dutch audience, Weinberger told them that, although he had no
intention of interfering with their internal politics, it was "vital" for them to
install their full complement of cruise missiles. Bush recalled that he was
dispatched to West Germany "to help sell the controversial deployment of
intermediate-range Pershing II missiles" and, while there, "witnessed the
ugly demonstrations against them."[45] Reagan, too, at the request of West
European leaders, traveled to Europe to deliver speeches justifying U.S. nuclear policy. Years later, he acknowledged that his trips to Britain and West
Germany in mid-1982 were designed "to demonstrate that I wasn't flirting
with doomsday." Conflating (as he usually did) the European with the
American movement, he explained the background to this mission: "Several
of our European allies . . . had their hands full with the nuclear freeze
movement, which was being fired up by demagogues depicting me as a
shoot-from-the-hip cowboy aching to pull out my nuclear six-shooter." Indeed, by this point, U.S. officials had concluded that, given the inflamed
state of public opinion, their emphasis should not be upon their willingness
to wage nuclear war, or even to foster a nuclear buildup, but to secure nuclear disarmament and peace.[46]

Certainly, the administration dramatically altered its rhetoric. In April
1982, upon the advice of aides who urged him to counter the antinuclear
campaign, Reagan began declaring publicly that "a nuclear war cannot be

won and must never be fought." He added, on that occasion: "To those who protest against nuclear war, I can only say: 'I'm with you.'"[47] That June, responding to Wick's entreaties, he developed similar themes in an address to the West German Bundestag. Catching the drift of things, *Le Monde* reported: "President Reagan wanted to show himself as the leader of the peace movement. He did his best . . . to convince West German opinion that there never was a U.S. President as concerned for . . . peace" and "missed no opportunity to comfort West German public opinion." Enthusiastic about the President's speech, Wick told Shultz that it was generally perceived as showing a "new sensitivity" to Allied "needs and concerns, including the rising influence of public pressure for nuclear disarmament." Indeed, the "most compelling among the discovered attributes of a new Reagan image was his expression of understanding of the nuclear fears of the peace movement."[48] In line with this approach, Bush proclaimed the following January, in West Berlin, that NATO was "the real peace movement," exactly the words used by the Deputy Secretary of State in two speeches to European audiences the following spring.[49] In March 1983, when Reagan appeared on television to announce his Star Wars program, he deliberately billed it as an alternative to nuclear war.[50] Addressing the Japanese Diet that November, Reagan sounded remarkably like a leader of the antinuclear movement, reiterating his declaration that nuclear war should never be fought and concluding: "Our dream is to see the day when nuclear weapons will be banished from the face of the Earth."[51]

Although this dramatic rhetorical shift was a calculated one, its effects remained uncertain. Preparing Reagan for an interview with *Time* magazine, Jack Matlock of the NSC staff told him that one of his objectives should be "calming fears that we are on a 'collision course'" with the Soviet Union, an assumption "which only feeds the pacifist movement." Nancy Reagan also urged the President, with some success, to soften his rhetoric to allay the popular perception that he was "a warmonger." And what, aside from opinion management, can explain the administration's renaming the MX missile the "Peacekeeper"?[52] Even so, conservative activists were dismayed by the administration's sudden talk of nuclear disarmament and not at all certain that it was having the desired effect. The administration "has attempted to co-opt the peace movement," Terry Dolan, chair of the National Conservative Political Action Committee, wrote to White House aide Michael Deaver in July 1982. "But instead of co-opting the 'peace' issue, the Administration has made it more important, thereby moving the discussions away from our agenda to those of the Administration's opponents." The Freeze "is now a real issue, even among Republican conservatives," and "has severely hampered the Administration's ability to carry out much of its foreign policy initiatives. For example, if the Administration supports arms limitation, then why do we need more defense expenditures? . . . That makes no sense to the average American. . . . As the Administration gives credibility to an arms freeze, it lessens support for a strong defense." Taking sharp issue with White House strategy, Dolan concluded: "The Administration hasn't co-opted the 'peace' movement. The 'peace' movement has co-opted the administration."[53]

The administration's determination to control public opinion on nuclear issues also pulled it into the realm of managing the communications media. SANE found that, after conservative criticism, the NEH grants that had partially subsidized its Shadows of the Nuclear Age radio series were not renewed during the Reagan years. Even more direct intervention occurred in January 1983, when the Justice Department ruled that *If You Love This Planet*, an Academy Award–winning documentary of a campus talk by Caldicott, produced by the National Film Board of Canada, would be designated as "political propaganda" under the Foreign Agents Registration Act. This meant that the film's issuer would have to register with the U.S. Attorney General as an "agent of a foreign principal," the film would have to open with the display of a label identifying it as the product of a foreign agent, and that reports would have to be filed with the U.S. government that identified every organization and theater showing the film. Not surprisingly, *If You Love This Planet* was never shown on national television in the United States.[54] The administration also prevented Georgi Arbatov, the articulate director of the Soviet Union's Institute of the U.S.A. and Canada, plus other members of his reformist think tank, from appearing on American television. In 1982, U.S. authorities cut his visa short to prevent his appearance on Bill Moyers's TV program. In 1983, the State Department offered him a visa on the condition that he have no contacts with the mass media. This treatment reminded Arbatov, a critic of the U.S. and Soviet nuclear buildups, of the behavior of his own party ideologues.[55] Naturally, the administration drew heavily upon the USIA to initiate what it considered appropriate nuclear stories in the press, on the radio, and on television programs around the world.[56]

Although, in fact, the administration had very little to worry about in terms of media coverage of nuclear weapons issues, when ABC television—through the planned showing of *The Day After* on November 20, 1983—actually sought to give viewers some idea of what a nuclear war might be like, the administration panicked. Shultz recalled: "Many people in the State Department were highly apprehensive of the potential impact on the

American public and the effect abroad." Pentagon officials, initially cooperative with the film-makers, changed their minds when they saw the script,
demanding that it be altered. When the producers resisted such pressures,
the Pentagon withdrew its offer to conduct filming at a U.S. Air Force base.
In addition, White House communications director David Gergen and other
officials pressed hard for script changes, including dropping a passage in the
script in which a Pershing II missile, headed for Europe, played a role in the
crisis leading to war. Buckling under this pressure, ABC did censor the
film.[57] Indeed, for the most part, the ABC executives were quite cooperative
with the administration, and gave their old friend, Charles Wick, an advance
copy of the film in July. Although Wick and Baker were uneasy about the
film, they decided not to object to its showing, for they were hopeful that it
would not secure commercial sponsorship and, in that event, did not want
allegations to arise "that the White House had suppressed this program."
Reagan previewed it as early as October 10.[58] Thus, the administration had
plenty of time to prepare its public relations response and, as usual,
launched a massive effort to control public reaction. This included distributing carefully calculated "talking points" to a broad range of public officials, placing Op-ed articles in assorted publications, mobilizing "friendly"
groups (e.g. the American Security Council), producing a pamphlet of selected presidential speeches, and helping to stack the post-film discussion
panel with pro-administration speakers.[59]

Controlling public opinion became especially important during the 1984
presidential election campaign. Although, ultimately, Reagan won by a
landslide, insiders did not expect that outcome earlier in the year. As late as
the summer of 1984, heading into the Republican national convention, "Mondale was within striking distance," recalled the President's pollster, Richard
Wirthlin. And popular fear of Reagan's bringing on a nuclear war was his
greatest vulnerability, Wirthlin warned the President. With Mondale and the
Democrats backing the Freeze and riding the wave of popular discontent
with the administration's nuclear policy, GOP campaign strategists regarded
the popular perception of Reagan as a hawk "as a huge vulnerability." The
idea of "Peace through Strength" did not appeal to the public, Wirthlin recalled, for "people believed that you don't build arms to put them in the
closet. You build arms to fight a war. And when those arms are nuclear, that
smacks . . . of a potential Armageddon." Thus, "we recognized that . . . we
could not let the voter go into the voting booth concerned about the possibility of Reagan's leadership . . . taking us close to war." A flood of campaign
ads followed to soften Reagan's image.[60] Furthermore, responding to Democratic jibes that the Reagan administration was the first to fail to hold a

summit conference with the Russians, the administration sought to arrange one with Chernenko, preferably just before the political conventions. When the Russians rejected this idea, Reagan's aides fell back upon a meeting with Gromyko in the White House that September. A few days before it occurred, McFarlane urged the President to announce the appointment of a high level U.S. official to take charge of arms control measures. This would "show leadership" in this area "and meet persistent criticisms from the Congress and the press of the way the process has been handled these past four years." Although nothing came of the McFarlane proposal, the White House heavily publicized Reagan's get-together with Gromyko.[61]

The Soviet Union

The Soviet government felt just as confounded by nuclear disarmament activism, or at least nuclear disarmament activism that voiced criticism of its policies. Four months after the launching of the Moscow Trust Group, the Soviet foreign policy monthly *International Affairs* proclaimed that "there can be no political or moral basis for an antiwar movement that is directed against the policy of the socialist governments." The following year, it assailed the "bogus 'peace groups' created to counter the genuine antiwar forces." Such groups, it charged, sought to "place 'equal responsibility' for the arms race on the U.S.A. and the U.S.S.R. in a bid to weaken and divide the peace movement."[62] Naturally, Soviet authorities were particularly disturbed by signs that pacifist ideas were spreading within the Soviet Union. In 1982, Marshal Nikolai Ogarkov, the Soviet chief of staff, called for heightened ideological efforts to combat pacifism among his nation's youth, and two official pamphlets circulated attacking this allegedly disgraceful tendency. Indeed, that same year, Andropov himself reportedly complained to a visiting Polish delegation about the problem of youthful pacifism.[63] In addition, of course, there was the menace of Sakharov—under house arrest in Gorky, but still considered dangerous enough to be denounced in the Soviet press.[64]

From the standpoint of the Soviet authorities, however, the worst offenders were the Trust Groups. Consequently, as two Moscow Trust Group representatives reported in September 1983, Trust Group activists underwent "detentions, arrests, threats, interrogations, 'talks' with the police, 'talks' with their bosses, searches, job dismissals, 24-hour shadowing . . . beatings, incarceration in psychiatric hospitals, provocations, automobile accidents, imprisonment, official warnings and charges, vilification in the press, house arrest," and "psychological terrorizing."[65] Many, given the choice of exile or imprisonment, chose to leave for the West. Although, initially, the authorities prosecuted Trust Group activists on the basis of their peace activities, this proved embarrassing in light of the professed Soviet support of peace. Thus, subsequent prosecution occurred on the basis of "hooliganism" and other criminal activities. Olga Medvedkova, who had had been beaten and severely bruised by a policeman as she tried to attend the trial of a fellow peace activist, was convicted of assault. Alexander Shatravka, sentenced to three years in a labor camp for circulating the Trust Group's initial appeal, had his term extended for four years on drugs charges. Thanks to vigorous protests by Western peace groups, the Soviet government sometimes relented. Western antinuclear activists raised Shatravka's case with Evgenii Chazov of IPPNW, and he secured the pacifist's release from the labor camp. After substantial publicity, Medvedkova—pregnant and an unlikely assailant—was given a suspended sentence and allowed to depart for the United States.[66]

Nevertheless, even when Soviet authorities backed away from enforcing substantial prison terms, they continued their pressure on the embattled activists. In August 1984, as Moscow Trust Group members met to plan rallies, speeches, seminars, and a march to mark Hiroshima Day, 36 of the organizers were arrested as they arrived at the home of Vladimir and Maria Fleishgacker, who remained under house arrest after most of the members had been released following interrogation. Several days later, nearly fifty participants in the peace group were arrested at a seminar on Hiroshima Day. Although they were told to sign a pledge stating that they would no longer commemorate it, all refused to do so. Once again, most were released after interrogation. But, after August 1984, the Fleishgackers, who had been harassed since the founding of the Trust Group, found their home almost constantly surrounded by the KGB. In these unpromising circumstances, they, too, departed from the Soviet Union. But other activists took up the antinuclear struggle, and the Soviet government continued its struggle against them.[67]

Although IPPNW fared far better in its dealings with Soviet authorities, it, too, faced difficulties. Of course, IPPNW was an officially approved movement, whose Soviet participants remained in close touch with the government. In early 1981, the Central Committee of the Soviet Communist Party approved Soviet participation in the forthcoming IPPNW international conference and authorized the preparation of papers for the Soviet delegation by the Ministry of Health Care, the Ministry of Foreign Affairs, and other government bodies.[68] But, in fact, top Soviet leaders like Brezhnev and Andropov had mixed feelings about IPPNW. Complaining to Chazov,

Andropov grumbled that the Americans "only talk to the strong." Others were more critical. In 1981, when Chazov prepared a speech for delivery at a session of the Supreme Soviet outlining the views of the international physicians' movement, Boris Ponomarev, the hard-liner who directed the International Department of the Central Committee, insisted upon "corrections." Mikhail Suslov, the party ideologist, also objected strongly to it. But the IPPNW leader managed to get authorization to deliver it from a reluctant Chernenko. In general, Chazov faced opposition not from only senior party leaders, but from many officials in the military and in the Foreign Ministry. Military leaders, for example, criticized Chazov for "demoralizing the Soviet people." Marshal Ogarkov himself hinted at the need to begin a counteroffensive against IPPNW, writing: "It is necessary to bring the truth about the existing . . . military danger to the Soviet people." Lown recalled that, when he pushed Chazov too hard, the latter retorted "that there was a military-industrial complex in the Soviet Union, and that didn't take kindly" to his position. It was "only by virtue of the fact that he was the doctor of these people, that they felt he was indispensable," that he could "get away with a lot of things. Otherwise, he would have been thrown to the wolves long ago."[69]

The Soviet government also felt deeply ambivalent about the antinuclear efforts of the Socialist International (SI). For years, the Kremlin had courted this worldwide organization of Social Democratic parties, but the results were far from satisfactory. "Unfortunately," a Soviet analyst concluded in the early 1980s, "the leaders of the Socialist International have been affected to a certain extent by the anti-Soviet and anti-Communist campaign launched by the United States." Evaluating the SI's work to halt the arms race, Vladimir Kryuchkov, the director of the KGB's foreign operations, concluded that it had made "a definite contribution to the cause of the struggle for peace and disarmament and a return to a policy of détente." And yet, he remained sharply critical of it. At the SI's 1983 congress, he noted, it had falsely conceived "the problems of war and peace as the result of rivalry" between the United States and the Soviet Union, when, in fact, the problem resulted from "the sharp increase in the aggressiveness" of American imperialism. According to Kryuchkov, the SI's warped consciousness and behavior reflected the "opportunist nature of the parties which belong to this organization" and the "right-wing" views of many of them. Worse yet, "their attacks on communist parties and the countries representing real socialism are mounted under the flag of 'democratic socialism,' thereby misleading the broad masses of workers throughout the world."[70]

It is quite true that, as Western conservatives charged, the Soviet government welcomed the upsurge of Western antinuclear activism and sought to encourage it. At the end of March 1982, Vadim Zagladin, deputy chair of the International Affairs department of the party's central committee, told an East German official that the Freeze campaign had become a mass movement, one that he expected would expand. He believed that, confronted with the growing resistance in the United States and Western Europe to the U.S. nuclear buildup, Reagan would have to move in the direction of compromise.[71] That same year, the KGB made stirring up foreign opposition to the cruise missiles a top priority. In July 1983, the party's central committee, warning other Communist parties of the U.S. government's "acceleration of the armaments race" and "threatening of peace," argued that "the movement against missiles and nuclear weapons continues to constitute one of the strongest influences with which even the Western governments following the Reagan administration have to deal." Indeed, "the antimissile movement could frustrate the plans of the NATO warmongers if all possibilities on the national and international level are mobilized."[72] That November, Kryuchkov told his overseas agents that "active measures" of the KGB should include "stimulating further development of the anti-war and anti-missile movements in the West, involving in them influential political and public figures and broad strata of the population, and encouraging these movements to take more decisive and coordinated action." Subsequently, the party and the KGB dispatched similar messages abroad.[73]

Nevertheless, the Soviet government never succeeded in controlling the Western nuclear disarmament movement or even influencing it to a significant extent—a point made not only by the CIA,[74] but, subsequently, by Soviet sources. The Western peace movement "was not our doing," recalled Arbatov, and "in point of fact, things were . . . the other way around—the idea of a nuclear freeze came to us from the United States." Oleg Gordievsky, the second in command of the KGB's British operations during the early 1980s—who simultaneously spied for the West and later defected to it—recalled that, despite his London residency's ambitious plan for organizing mass demonstrations and other protests against the cruise missiles, there was not "any evidence that the KGB had more than a marginal influence on the campaign against cruise conducted by the peace movement." Indeed, "it is reasonable to conclude that the vast expenditure of time and effort by the Center [the KGB's headquarters, in Moscow] in this field achieved little of real importance." Of course, some KGB agents liked to inflate their significance by portraying their efforts as a brilliant success; but sophisticated officials saw through their boasts. In July 1982, when Arkadi

Guk, the KGB chief in London, briefed the new embassy counselor, he insisted that a recent antinuclear demonstration by 250,000 Britons—one that Gordievsky knew had been "wholly organized" by CND—had really been arranged by his own KGB residency. The diplomat nodded politely but, as soon as Guk left the room, he turned to Gordievsky and remarked: "Whoever heard such nonsense?" In 1983, when the KGB Center ordered all its residencies in NATO countries and in many other parts of the world to popularize the slogan "Reagan means War!" not a single one managed this feat.[75]

Indeed, the Soviet government not only failed to control the Western antinuclear movement, but, in the early 1980s, began a fierce attack upon it. The launching of the vitriolic propaganda campaign against END by the Soviet Peace Committee and the WPC[76]—both Soviet-controlled bodies—in late 1982 certainly would not have occurred without the endorsement of officials in Moscow. But why should Moscow approve such an attack, particularly in the crucial period just *before* the installation of the cruise missiles? And why did it have the Eastern bloc peace committees boycott END's Berlin convention, declare Mient Jan Faber and other END leaders *persona non grata* in Eastern Europe, and condone the crackdown upon END's East European allies during this same period? After all, it did hope that the West European movement might block cruise and Pershing missile deployment. The answer lies in the fact that, from the start, Soviet officials had incompatible goals. They wanted a movement that would stymie the Western military buildup. But they also wanted to proceed with their own missile deployment without interference by a nonaligned campaign. By 1982, they recognized that they could not have both. END and its East European allies were staunchly independent, and—like most Social Democratic parties—could not be appeased without a rollback of Soviet nuclear weapons. From the Soviet standpoint, this was impossible. Ultimately, then, the goal of maintaining Soviet nuclear strength triumphed over the competing goal of blocking Western missile deployment.[77] In line with their Bolshevik forebears, Soviet leaders opted for a smaller movement, but—in their view—a better one.

Of course, from the Soviet standpoint, there already existed a better antinuclear movement: the World Peace Council and its national affiliates. The vast bulk of what conservatives called Soviet funding for Western peace movements went to Communist parties or operatives, who either employed it for their own "peace" ventures or passed it along to WPC branches in their countries. During these years, the Soviet government still leaned heavily on the WPC and its affiliates for antinuclear operations, which is one reason its lavish funding produced such meager results. At the May 31, 1983, meeting of the Politburo of the Central Committee of the Soviet Communist Party, when Andropov called for opening up "a wider network . . . to mobilize public opinion of the Western countries of Europe and America against the location of the nuclear weapons in Europe," none of the party leaders suggested implementing this proposal through a Western peace group. Instead, one urged using the WPC's forthcoming Prague conference for such purposes, and another expressed his complete agreement, promising to "begin realization of this idea starting tomorrow." In its July 1983 message to Communist parties, the Soviet party central committee called attention to "the mass movement against nuclear weapons and missiles," but then went on to claim that "its potential was convincingly expressed" at the Prague gathering, whose resolutions should be given "central importance" by foreign party stalwarts in furthering "the effectiveness of the peace movement."[78]

Below the surface, however, a more sophisticated approach was developing among party reformers, who regarded the independent antinuclear campaign with considerable sympathy. Velikhov worked cooperatively with Western antinuclear scientists, Chazov with Western antinuclear physicians, and Arbatov with a range of independent Western intellectuals. Moreover, to promote the work of the independent antinuclear movement, they took risks in challenging official orthodoxy. Jeremy Stone of the Federation of American Scientists recalled that the Soviet authorities, angered at his activities, refused to admit him to their country until Arbatov brought the matter to Andropov, who agreed to scrap this policy. It was Chazov who convinced reluctant Soviet leaders to allow uncensored broadcast of IPPNW conferences, outlining the grim consequences of nuclear war, on Soviet television. Brushing aside the efforts of party propagandists, Velikhov used the meetings he arranged with Western scientists to sincerely confront the issues of the nuclear arms race.[79] Similarly, their close associate within the party hierarchy, Mikhail Gorbachev, was unusually attuned to the antinuclear campaign. In a speech he delivered in Moscow on April 22, 1983, Gorbachev lauded "the powerful upsurge in the antiwar movement, which has embraced the entire globe." Contending that this movement "has become an influential factor in international life," he argued that the governments of the United States and other NATO countries "have to take into account public protests against the arms race and against the deployment of U.S. missiles in Western Europe. These protests reflect a new level of social consciousness and activity of the masses." Nor was this kind of talk only for domestic consumption. Speaking in London on December 20, 1984, Gorbachev asserted that "the European public and the entire world community are ... increasingly sensitive to ... the requirements of the nuclear age." Indeed, the efforts "of all peoples are required in the struggle for peace and for prevention of a nuclear war."[80]

And yet, overall, orthodoxy prevailed. In 1982, as Brezhnev neared death, party reactionaries launched a concerted attack on the reformers. Arbatov came under fire for his work on the Palme commission and for sponsoring the publication of the commission's report in the Soviet Union. In 1983, he was summoned to KGB headquarters to explain the criticism of the Soviet leadership that he supposedly had made to a group of Americans. Others who championed non-ideological approaches to the arms race also encountered withering criticism. Purge activity, even arrests, began at the liberal think tanks, especially in 1984, after the accession of Chernenko. Nor, over time, did the regime warm up toward the independent antinuclear movement. Given the Soviet government's commitment to implementing its own nuclear weapons buildup, it sympathized with that movement no more than did its U.S. counterpart. Indeed, as key leaders of the movement soon understood, the Kremlin worked tirelessly to thwart its progress. By 1985, END's E. P. Thompson had concluded: "If the Geneva negotiations had been, not about cruise, Pershing and SS-20s, but about how to rub out the non-aligned peace movements ... then the negotiators would have come out smiling and arm-in-arm."[81]

The Junior Partners in the Western Bloc

Attitudes toward the antinuclear movement varied among officials from the junior partners of the Western bloc, but for the most part they resembled those of the U.S. leaders of the NATO and ANZUS alliances. NATO Secretary General Joseph Luns was quite critical of the nuclear disarmament campaign, claiming that activists were "more afraid of nuclear weapons that NATO does not have yet than the Soviet SS-20 missile." In November 1982, he claimed that "new reports from the secret services" showed that Western antinuclear campaigns were "strongly aided by the Soviet Union, including financial support." As early as October 1981, in the midst of massive anti-Euromissile protests, Luns announced that NATO defense ministers had agreed to "support a very strong public relations effort" to dampen popular resistance to the missiles.[82] Such efforts escalated thereafter, and in December 1983 an internal report by NATO's Special Consultative Group, charged with handling the Western alliance's arms control negotiations, boasted that "active public affairs efforts by individual Allied governments, drawing on consultations in the SCG, have been successful . . . in reinforcing public support for Allied policy on INF." It added, though, that "these efforts must continue and be intensified." Such activities were merely the tip of the iceberg, for, as indicated by an October 1983 news story in the *Wall Street Journal*, there existed "a multifaceted West European strategy aimed at countering peace movements" and preparing for missile deployment. This included "intensified intelligence gathering . . . placement of missile bases in areas where opposition to them is least, quiet preparation of sites so that missiles can arrive without fanfare, and public relations efforts to offset the influence of peace movements."[83]

Specific developments reinforce these contentions. The French government took a hostile stance toward West European antinuclear protests, with President Mitterrand complaining that "the missiles are in the East and the pacifists are in the West." At France's Pacific testing grounds, the antinuclear voyage of the *Pacific Peacemaker* was disrupted when the French Navy rammed the yacht at Moruroa and French officials impounded it at Tahiti.[84] In Italy, police used considerable violence to disperse nonviolent sit-inners at Comiso, seriously injuring many demonstrators, including Luciana Castellina, a leader of the Italian movement and member of parliament.[85] Other governments, more noted for their tolerance, nonetheless adopted extraordinary measures, including the Belgian, which took increasingly repressive action against demonstrators outside the Florennes base, such as banning assembly in groups larger than three.[86] Stung by the attack upon cruise missile testing in Canada, Prime Minister Trudeau responded with an "Open Letter" to all the daily newspapers, hired a team of public relations advisors, and began a campaign to discredit the disarmament movement. In his open letter, he charged the Canadian movement with having been "relatively silent about the installation of the SS-20s" and with "anti-Americanism."[87] In West Germany, the Christian Democratic government ran a $2.6 million "education" campaign around the theme: "Peace requires security." Even before the opening of the June 1983 Protestant church assembly—rapidly shaping up as an antinuclear festival—the West German interior minister charged that it would be subverted by Kremlin-influenced militants. In further efforts to marginalize the antinuclear movement, Chancellor Kohl cut off federal funding to peace research institutes, while Christian Democratic education ministers in state governments threatened to punish teachers and students participating in the October 1983 anti-missile demonstrations.[88]

Some Western bloc nations adopted a very different approach. Upon its election in 1984, the Lange government in New Zealand promptly established warm relations with antinuclear groups, providing them with assistance for their peace education projects and establishing close liaison between those groups and parliament. Reporting on a meeting with a Cabinet member, one peace group leader remarked: "What a wonderful change to be in a Minister's office and to find that person doing the listening and assenting!"[89] Within NATO, Prime Minister Andreas Papandreou of Greece also proved extraordinarily supportive, arguing that his government "embraces the peace movements," for "the cause of peace cannot advance without popular involvement." This was not just rhetoric, for his government played a major role in organizing conferences of antinuclear activists that met in Athens in 1982 and 1984. Accompanied by 22 ministers and deputy ministers, Papandreou attended the 1982 conference and proclaimed that he was "committed to removing nuclear weapons altogether and unilaterally" from Greece. At that same gathering, he stressed the importance of the peace movement in countering state policies. "Governments have to be persuaded," he said, "and this can only be done by a massive popular presence."[90]

By contrast, officials in Turkey seemed determined to not only destroy their nation's antinuclear movement, but its leading activists, as well. Investigated, arrested, detained, and tried by the military rulers of this NATO nation, eighteen leaders of the Turkish Peace Association were sentenced to eight years of hard labor, plus 32 years of probation. Another five of them received five years in prison and 20 months probation. Their martial law trial, conducted in a converted basketball court over a period of eighteen months, included confessions extracted from witnesses under torture and the exhumation of Peter the Great's Last Will and Testament (1682), which supposedly proved that the Turkish Peace Association, by criticizing NATO bases in Turkey, had been furthering an historic Russian plot. While the convicted men and women—who included a former ambassador, the president of the medical association, the president of the bar association, and distinguished academics, writers, and members of parliament—appealed their sentences to Turkey's supreme court, they were kept crammed together in a small, damp prison cell, where they still resided years later as the military and the courts decided their fate.[91]

The British response provides a striking example of how far a Western government was willing to go to counter its nuclear critics, even when operating within a society with a long tradition of respect for political dissent. In May 1981 Defense Secretary John Nott announced government plans for a publicity campaign to wean "innocent, well-meaning people" away from CND. Although denying any intention of starting a "Reds-under-the-bed" scare, he did state that peace groups were dominated by "a tiny number of left-wingers, neither innocent nor well-meaning." These early government efforts, however, were fairly low-key, and apparently consisted of pressing television and radio stations to limit CND's access to air time, refusing debates with it, and, whenever necessary, dismissing its arguments as unrealistic. But as CND continued its meteoric rise and parliamentary elections loomed, government policy began to toughen. By 1982, recalled Thatcher, CND was "dangerously strong," and something had to be done to halt the progress of "the so-called 'peace movement.'"[92] Late that year, a government decision was made to gear up the campaign and to adopt a harder line. In December, the Conservative Party chair announced that it would be a priority during the new year to provide the nation with the "true facts" about CND, adding: "The Soviets make no secret of the fact that they are giving large-scale funds to the peace movement in Europe." Peter Blaker, the Armed Forces Minister, adopted a similar tack, telling a BBC radio audience that the Russians had given 6 million pounds to the European peace movement. Meanwhile, Thatcher decided to replace Nott as defense secretary with Michael Heseltine, one of the government's most effective communicators and, thus, the logical choice to lead the fight against CND and, by association, the Labour Party.[93]

Taking office in January 1983, Heseltine initially planned to draw upon professional advertising agencies for a multimillion dollar anti-CND campaign, but he dropped this idea when it came under attack in parliament as misuse of the public treasury to fund a partisan political venture.[94] Instead, he established a small team within the Ministry of Defense, DS19, to prepare useful campaign material and coordinate strategy.[95] That April, he took the offensive against CND, sending a letter to Conservative candidates for parliament declaring that behind its "carefully tuned phrases about peace lies the calculating political professionalism of full-time Socialists and Communists." CND's "purpose," he charged, was "the advancement of the Socialist and Communist cause. At its most extreme it is to argue the cause of the Soviet Union at the expense of the free societies of the West." Although CND indignantly retorted that Heseltine's inflammatory letter was "just another attempt to try and smear CND," Heseltine renewed this kind of attack the following month, and went on to contend that the policies of CND and the Labour Party were virtually indistinguishable.[96] Bruce Kent recalled: "They'd be ruthless, really. They didn't mind; they'd smash you. They really didn't care. . . . They could be polite over a glass of sherry, but if they got you outside, finish!" Like the Reagan administration, from which it may have borrowed some ideas, the government, then in the midst of a fierce parliamentary election campaign, also did its best to keep the focus on CND and Labour support for Britain's unilateral nuclear disarmament (which was not popular with the voters) rather than on their critique of cruise missile deployment (which enjoyed strong popular support).[97] As Heseltine took the low road, claiming that every mile marched by CNDers strengthened the Kremlin, Thatcher took the high one. Defending Conservative nuclear policies before parliament at the end of April, she declared: "We are the true peace movement"—drawing laughter from Labour MPs and cheers from Conservatives. Thatcher came away from the heated election campaign well-pleased with Heseltine's efforts. "He defended our approach to nuclear arms with great panache," she recalled, "and inflicted a series of defeats on CND and the Labour Left."[98]

Although, in the aftermath of the spring 1983 campaign, Heseltine boasted that he had destroyed CND and, therefore, that DS19 would no longer be needed, in reality the government continued the struggle against the nuclear disarmament movement. In December, Heseltine became engaged in a public controversy with Britain's Independent Broadcasting Authority over its showing of *The Day After*, a film that he claimed provided an unbalanced portrayal of nuclear deterrence. The way to balance it, he insisted, was to give him the opportunity to present a rebuttal immediately after the film, which is what he finally arranged. Even then, party leaders were not satisfied and, according to the London *Times*, the Conservative Party chairman urged his party's MPs "to prepare themselves to counter the propaganda use which the party expects antinuclear campaigners to make of the showing."[99] Meanwhile, the government conducted an attack on peace studies courses. As early as 1981, the British Secretary of State had publicly attacked peace studies as "appeasement" education and, thereafter, public officials issued dire warnings about peace and antinuclear bias in the nation's schools. Thatcher herself, convinced of pro-CND bias at the nation's only university level peace studies department, located at the University of Bradford, sought to have it shut down, and repeatedly asked officials: "Has that department been dealt with yet?" Well aware of governmental pressures and of the academic quality of their program, members of the department agreed to have it investigated. In these circumstances, it survived.[100] The government also apparently sought to have CND chair Joan Ruddock fired from her position at the Ministry of Health and Bruce Kent brought into line by his church superiors, but neither effort panned out.[101]

A more dramatic confrontation occurred at Greenham Common. Embarrassed by the persistent success of women at cutting through the perimeter wire and staging nonviolent protests on the cruise missile base, Heseltine told a stunned parliament on November 1, 1983, that protesters who ventured too near the missile bunkers would be shot. A Labour spokesperson responded that the Defense Minister's threat was "hysterical," remarking: "There are gradations of defense. You don't defend missiles against unarmed women by shooting them." Although Thatcher claimed that Heseltine's plan was thoroughly appropriate, the government never did shoot any of the Greenham women. But it certainly brought extraordinary pressure to bear upon them. One Greenham peace camper, who later won a law case against the government for wrongful arrest and detention, was arrested on several occasions at night and held by police and soldiers with other women activists in a muddy pit, surrounded by barbed wire, with bright lights focused upon them. On other occasions, without explanation, she was arrested and detained for hours at local police stations.[102] Above all, however, the government was determined to shut down the Greenham Common peace camp. On a night in early April 1984, as hundreds of women slept peacefully in their tents, police and bailiffs sealed all roads to the camp and swooped down upon it. Using a bullhorn, a bailiff awakened them with the announcement that they had five minutes to leave. As they staggered out of their tents into the sub-freezing dawn, police tore down their shelters and other property, hauling it away and arresting thirty of them. Retreating to the surrounding woods, the remaining women vowed to restore their protest site. "The women's peace camp is going to be here until they get rid of the cruise missiles," promised one of them.[103] And it was.

Another confrontation with antinuclear protesters occurred at Molesworth, a second location chosen by the Thatcher government for a cruise missile base. Arriving in the middle of the night in February 1985, 3,000 British soldiers and police rousted some 100 nonviolent peace activists from their encampment ("Rainbow Village") and secured the perimeter of the base with heavy barbed wire, thereby turning the still disused airfield, in the words of the *Guardian*, "into a muddy resemblance of the Somme valley in 1917." The intrepid Michael Heseltine, sporting black boots and a camouflage jacket, flew into Molesworth by helicopter and informed the mass media that the extraordinary action—which he promised to supplement by erecting a 6.5-mile fence at a cost of one million pounds—had been taken to avoid months of civil disobedience on the site. As usual, the Labour spokesperson on defense was less enthusiastic, describing the operation as ridiculous and commenting that when the defense secretary "strutted around Molesworth this morning in his flak jacket," he did not seem to realize that he "was not facing some wild Baader-Meinhof terrorist gang but 100 British citizens, most of them Quakers with a long tradition of honorable protest against the weapons of war."[104] In its monthly magazine *Sanity*, CND published a poem to commemorate the event:

TO GENERAL HESELTINE
Victor of Molesworth

Hail to the conquering hero,
Who came at dead of night
As leader of three thousand
And bravely cleared the site.

He came to quell the Quakers,
He came to safeguard Cruise,
He came in combat jacket
And bravely faced the news.

He came to Rainbow Village
He came to rout the foe,
Who threaten decent values
And all we love and know:

The enemies of Britain
Who work for our defeat
By setting up a chapel
And planting winter wheat.

Thank heaven for Saint Michael,
Who struggles to prevent
The wickedness of conscience,
The evil of dissent.[105]

Although the Thatcher government did not formally classify CND as a "subversive" organization—under British law, a group threatening the safety of the state and seeking to undermine parliamentary democracy—revelations in early 1985 indicate that the authorities treated the nuclear disarmament group as if it were. Cathy Massiter, who spent 14 years working for MI5, the British government's domestic intelligence agency, was given the job of investigating the British peace movement in the spring of 1981. Officially, she was supposed to be watching known Communists (formally categorized as subversives) to discover if they were manipulating peace groups, but unofficially she was pressed to gather information on the entire antinuclear campaign. Files were opened on Bruce Kent, Joan Ruddock, and other CND officials, phone taps were installed, and MI5 agents were placed in CND offices. One of the agents, Harry Newton, an elderly fellow who used to chat amiably with Bruce Kent in the washroom at CND's London headquarters, even provided MI5 with a diagram of the office layout, thus facilitating a future burglary. The results of this surveillance were then passed along to the Prime Minister's office and to DS19, the special group established by Heseltine to combat CND. Concerned that these and other activities—including the opening of intelligence files on thousands of CND members—were unnecessary, violated her agency's charter, and reflected partisan political pressures, Massiter complained to her superiors. When her complaints failed to secure a remedy, she resigned from MI5, and, in early 1985, joined by another MI5 officer, went public with the information.[106]

These espionage activities were supplemented by what, when referring to KGB operations, usually were called "active measures." Sometimes they were quite traceable, as when the Foreign Office began pumping substantial funding into the British Atlantic Committee (BAC), thereby becoming the major source of its support. Formerly a rather somnolent operation, the BAC quickly became a prominent crusader against CND. It dispatched anti-CND speakers around the nation, denounced the antinuclear group on television, local radio, and in the press, formed a welcoming committee for President Reagan, and—when members of parliament began to question its tax status as a charitable organization—launched another government front group to continue its campaign: Peace Through NATO.[107] Other operations were more covert. Brian Crozier's group, The 61, which by the mid-1980s was spending about $1 million per year—some of it from the CIA—on its anti-peace movement ventures, was particularly active in Britain, where it poured money and intelligence information into what he called "peace counter groups." One of them, the Campaign Against Council Corruption, was designed to abolish local governing councils, thereby undermining the nuclear-free zone movement and ending council funding for other peace ventures. Working closely with Thatcher, to whom he reported regularly on his operations, Crozier accomplished this goal through the passage of legislation in 1985. The 61 also fought hard to defeat Michael Foot, the Labour Party candidate for prime minister, during the 1983 election campaign. In Crozier's view, Foot "was deeply committed to . . . policies indistinguishable from those advocated by the Communists." The 61 helped to plant disparaging stories about Foot in the press and to produce a poster comparing Foot to Neville Chamberlain, returning in 1938 from Munich. Along the way, Crozier wrote a number of articles of his own, including one that appeared in the London *Times* ("How CND serves the Russians").[108]

One of Crozier's favorite operations was the Coalition for Peace Through Security. Although the Coalition liked to call itself a "grass-roots campaigning peace movement," it lacked a membership, drew its funding from The 61, and spent virtually all its time attacking CND. Crozier recalled that one of its luminaries, Julian Lewis, "became The 61's leading activist in Britain, notably as the scourge of Monsignor Bruce Kent and the Campaign for Nuclear Disarmament." Another Coalition leader, Edward Leigh, a young Conservative politician, told a gathering of the faithful that the time had come "to fight CND in the streets." Although the Coalition never quite managed this, it did harangue CND marchers from the roof of its expensive London headquarters through 600 watt amplifiers and charter a plane that buzzed a CND festival while trailing a banner reading: "Help the Soviets, Support CND!" (Ironically, only hours earlier, E. P. Thompson had brought a speaker from Polish Solidarity onto the festival stage, where his call for support of Solidarity and an end to Soviet nuclear weapons was greeted with a standing ovation.) Some of the Coalition's favorite slogans included: "Peace is a Soviet weapon of conquest" and "Disarmament equals surrender!"[109] Endorsed by Thatcher and other leading Conservatives, the Coalition distributed vast quantities of posters, stickers, and leaflets attacking CND as a pawn of the Soviet Union. One of its multicolored brochures, adorned with a nuclear disarmament symbol blending into a red hammer and sickle, spelled out the acronym CND as "Communists, Neutralists, Defeatists." The Coalition also briefed MPs in preparation for debates on military and foreign policy.[110]

The Junior Partners in the Soviet Bloc

It was ironic that the Thatcher government got on so badly with East European Communist regimes for, when it came to the nonaligned peace movement, they saw eye to eye. In June 1983, when independent Czech peace activists demonstrated outside the WPC's World Assembly for Peace and Life in Prague, they were assaulted by club-wielding policemen. That July, the Czech government sentenced the Charter 77 spokesperson Ladislav Lis—the foremost figure responsible for initiating a dialogue between his organization and Western antinuclear groups—to fourteen months imprisonment and three years under house arrest. The indictment against him cited his distribution of "hostile and anti-socialist documents," the majority of which were open letters to the Western peace movement. In November, on the eve of their issuing a statement calling for new arms control talks, twenty Charter 77 activists were taken into custody, interrogated about their activities, and then released, but not before being warned against protesting the Soviet Union's forthcoming deployment of nuclear missiles.[111] Attitudes toward foreign groups were not any friendlier. In the spring of 1983, a Czech Communist Party brochure, designed for instruction of its activists and functionaries, asserted that "imperialism" was attempting "to weaken the peace movement by infiltrating it with ideas, persons and whole organizations whose clear aim is to break the peace movement" and "prevent its unification." Such groups were "apparently conducted and financed directly from the center of CIA and similar agencies." And "in Europe, the organization with [that] explicit anti-Communist and anti-Soviet function is European Nuclear Disarmament." In June 1983, when CND representatives sought to make contact with members of Charter 77 during the Prague conference, they were attacked by the secret police. In August, an article in the Czech party newspaper *Rude Pravo* assailed END and E. P. Thompson for attempting to "weaken and paralyze anti-war efforts" and "influence the peace movement according to Washington's ideas."[112]

In Hungary, where the regime previously had shown greater leniency, the pattern now became much the same. Addressing an April 1983 central committee plenum, Communist Party leader Janos Kadar claimed that elements financed by imperialism "have of late become more aggressive," and "some would like to be legalized in order to gain a forum. . . . But we will not legalize hostile endeavors . . . and we will not tolerate the establishment of bases of opposition." That spring, members of the independent Dialogue group were given warnings by their university department chairs or party secretaries at their places of employment. When they attempted to attend the Prague conference, they were met with tear gas, arrests, and deportation back to Hungary.[113] A crisis developed in July 1983, when Western peace activists arrived to participate in a summer peace camp organized by Dialogue. The authorities suddenly denied Dialogue a campsite permit, and when the group sought to proceed with the gathering anyway, they arrested twenty Dialogue members and deported most of the fifteen Western visitors—including four Greenham Common women. A party central committee report that year indicated the authorities' fear that Hungarian peace activists were "turning away from state institutions" and that "opposition to the 'superpowers' had become more or less general." Thus, the central committee concluded that movements "standing outside the Peace Council" would not be tolerated. After all, "the chief task of the Hungarian peace movement" was "to popularize and support the efforts for peace of our country and of the socialist peace community."[114]

Like its counterparts in East and West, the East German regime reacted with considerable hostility to the independent antinuclear campaign. Pastor Rainer Eppelmann was first arrested in February 1982. Though released after two days, he was routinely told to visit the security police for interrogation.[115] Others activists, not as well known, received harsher treatment. Beginning in late 1982 and reaching a peak in the summer of 1983 the authorities cracked down upon the thriving antinuclear community in Jena, arresting some activists and expelling others.[116] In October 1983, while millions elsewhere demonstrated against the Euromissiles, the secret police detained hundreds of independent activists to block a planned "die-in" on East Berlin's Alexanderplatz. In November, another roundup occurred to prevent antinuclear demonstrations at the Soviet and American embassies. In December, the authorities arrested four activists from Women for Peace. Two were quickly released, but the other two—Ulrike Poppe and Bärbel Bohley—remained imprisoned for more than a month on treason charges, carrying a twelve-year sentence, apparently because they had discussed their activities with a British member of CND and END. In the Poppe and Bohley cases, as in numerous others, public protests by Western antinuclear campaigners apparently helped to lighten sentences or speed the release of their East German counterparts. But public policy was clear enough. "When one of our friends died in jail," recalled an antinuclear campaigner from Jena, "we got the message."[117]

Nor, despite the claims of missile enthusiasts in the United States and Britain, did the East German government seem any fonder of the leaders of the West European antinuclear campaign. In June 1982, after an East German official warned Mient Jan Faber about Eppelmann, claiming that he belonged in a psychiatric hospital, the IKV leader promptly went off to visit him that afternoon. This led to Faber's being barred from any further visits to the GDR and to the East German churches—under duress—breaking off relations with IKV.[118] From the standpoint of the East German government, the West German Greens were just as bad. In May 1983, when five prominent members of the Green Party, including Petra Kelly, went into East Berlin and unfurled two banners on the Alexanderplatz—reading "Swords into Plowshares" and "Disarmament East and West"—the East German police attacked them, tore up their banners, and deported them quickly to the West. Embarrassed that his police had assaulted members of the West German Bundestag, East German party leader Erich Honecker publicly expressed regret over the incident and invited Kelly to return to meet with him. Provocative as ever, Kelly arrived at their rendezvous wearing a T-shirt adorned with the Swords into Plowshares symbol and slogan, then banned by the regime. Relationships grew no warmer and, after November 1983, the regime barred all known Green Party activists from entering East Germany.[119] In addition, the East German secret police, the Stasi, like Britain's MI5, compiled intelligence files on CND and its leaders. The East

German government even gathered regular reports on CND from a secret agent inside the nuclear disarmament organization—one working, unsuccessfully, to challenge the CND leadership and to overcome the influence of END.[120]

Indeed, when it came to END, the East German government could hardly have been more hostile. Certainly there was nothing in the Stasi reports on END conventions to provide any comfort to the regime. The May 1983 convention in West Berlin, noted one report, had been characterized by the spreading of "antisocialist and anti-Soviet" theories, "hostile aims toward socialist states," and an "antisocialist direction." The linkage of the disarmament problem and the "imperialist human rights campaign" was the "dominant element" of the convention, it maintained, and a variety of subversive activities were planned in the GDR. The following June, recounting the activities of what it considered subversive forces in the preparations for the Perugia convention, the Stasi maintained that they had increased their activities within END, with the intention of dividing the peace movement, directing it toward an anti-Communist position, and supporting opposition forces in Communist nations in order to secure legalization and their establishment as partners in the West European peace movement. END, it warned, wanted to isolate the peace councils of Communist countries and organize a slanderous anti-Communist campaign.[121] Not surprisingly, then, the East German government followed a policy of total resistance to this key antinuclear movement. It barred entry to East Germany of not only some of END's top leaders, like Faber and Kelly, but even of lesser-known members of its coordinating committee.[122] Like the U.S. and British governments, the East German regime regarded END as a subversive movement, manipulated by foreign agents.

At the same time, East German authorities began a public defense of their military priorities—based, as in the West, upon the idea of peace through strength. In March 1982, Heinz Hoffmann, the Defense Minister, condemned the independent antinuclear movement, arguing that "our soldiers bear their arms for peace, and the better command they have over their weapons, the better peace is assured. . . . We know that one day socialism and peace will need both our plowshares *and* our swords." Concerned that the Swords into Plowshares campaign was getting out of hand, the authorities banned the wearing of its emblem that spring, arguing that it had become a "subversive symbol." Those who wore it, declared state radio, were "blind, deaf and hypocritical." Meanwhile the official youth organization, the Free German Youth, took the lead in a pro-military campaign entitled:

"Peace must be defended—Peace must be armed." Using this theme, it held an estimated 90,000 meetings with over two million participants.[123] In the East, as in the West, the authorities drew upon the rhetoric of peace in a determined effort to keep public opinion in line with their military policies.

Nations Outside the U.S. and Soviet Blocs

Not surprisingly, nations located outside the revived Cold War battleground of the U.S. and Soviet blocs often took a more benign view of the antinuclear campaign. In October 1983, as plans moved forward for mass anti-Euromissile demonstrations in neutral Austria, the education and defense ministers of that nation issued edicts that exempted schoolchildren and soldiers from their regular duties, thus enabling them to participate. One member of the Austrian government even took part in the human chain formed by the demonstrators between the embassies of the rival superpowers.[124] In Sweden, too, government officials firmly aligned themselves with the antinuclear campaign. Addressing a packed meeting in London jointly sponsored by END and the Labour Party, Olof Palme—on the verge of winning reelection as Sweden's prime minister—lauded the work of antinuclear organizations and popular campaigns against the Bomb. "You never reach anywhere," he said, "if you can't mobilize the people. It's public pressure which will create the climate for disarmament and nothing else." He added: "It's particularly important that people *not* adapt, that they don't say O.K., you know better." Instead, they must say: "We know better, because it's our lives and our future that is at stake, and we find this all monstrous, this building up of arsenals." He concluded: "The military complexes are tremendously powerful, but in the end we have the chance of showing that the people are stronger."[125]

Even so, some nations had their own nuclear interests to safeguard, and this could lead to a tough stance against nuclear critics. In India, the government's nuclear hierarchy was deeply distressed by the domestic antinuclear campaign, particularly the work of Dhirendra Sharma and his Committee for a Sane Nuclear Policy. In 1981, a review committee headed by the scientific advisor to the minister of defense—who for years had directed nuclear research at the Bhabha Atomic Research Center—recommended that Sharma's Science Policy Research Center be shut down. Although Jawaharlal Nehru University, where it was located, resisted this drastic a move, it did block the center from admitting new students or supervising doctoral candidates. Two years later, following the growth of Sharma's antinuclear efforts and the publication of his muckraking book, *India's Nuclear Estate*, university officials abruptly transferred him to the school of languages and closed the center. It remained closed until Sharma's retirement in 1992, after which it was promptly reopened. Meanwhile, Sharma's political reputation came under fire, with the claim often made that he was a CIA agent. From his standpoint, this was a particularly low blow, for, during his years in the United States, he had been an active leftwing agitator against the Vietnam War—so much so that a U.S. government fellowship awarded to him was withdrawn at the behest of President Nixon. His only consolation was that the government crackdown inspired better media coverage of the antinuclear crusade.[126]

Government attitudes in some nations fell in between. In China, where the critique of the Soviet-American nuclear buildup dovetailed nicely with public policy, officials began issuing positive statements on Western antinuclear movements in the early 1980s. In August 1983, the government sent a delegation to the World Conference Against A & H Bombs for the first time in sixteen years. Intrigued by what they heard there of the Freeze campaign, the Chinese invited a Freeze representative to visit China to brief a variety of groups on its activities. According to the Chinese, this was only the second time since the Chinese revolution of 1949 that a U.S. peace activist received an official invitation to visit China. In Peking and Shanghai, she met with individuals representing social groups and with government officials, who liked the Freeze movement's emphasis upon bilateral action and the notion that U.S. protest might lead to constraints upon U.S. and Soviet nuclear weapons development. Although the Chinese Association for International Understanding, founded in 1981 to replace the long-defunct Chinese Peace Committee, was fairly well acquainted with the U.S. antinuclear movement, she still found herself questioned "for hours about movement goals, priorities, structures, constituencies, and prospects for political impact." She, in turn, questioned the Chinese about their nuclear testing, policies toward the Tibetans, and their attitudes toward the United States and the Soviet Union. As a result of these conversations, which she considered remarkably candid, the Chinese hosted a visit from ten U.S. antinuclear activists early the following year.[127]

Government Response and Its Meaning

Thus, the rise of the antinuclear movement in the early 1980s met with a very substantial government response. Whether or not officials liked the movement—and fairly few of them did—they could not afford to ignore it. Even the most vigorous government efforts to defame, harass, and destroy the antinuclear campaign attested to its political significance, as well as to its future possibilities for shattering the traditional military foundations of international behavior.

Members of the Clamshell Alliance begin a nonviolent occupation of the nuclear power plant construction site at Seabrook, NH, leading to 1,400 arrests, April 1977. © Grace Hedemann.

U.S. officials confer at the White House when prospects for nuclear arms controls seemed bright, August 1977. Left to right: Zbigniew Brzezinski, Jimmy Carter, and Cyrus Vance. Courtesy of the Jimmy Carter Library.

The New Zealand Peace Squadron confronts a U.S. nuclear submarine, the *Pintado*, 1978. Courtesy of the Fellowship of Reconciliation Archives.

A portion of the Japanese antinuclear delegation, in front of pictures of the atomic bombings of Hiroshima and Nagasaki, at the first U.N. Special Session on Disarmament, May 1978. © Grace Hedemann.

Members of the War Resisters League, with writer Grace Paley on the left, unfurl a banner on the White House lawn, 1978. Photo by Karl Bissinger, courtesy of the War Resisters League.

END leader Mary Kaldor, at a demonstration in Japan, 1981. Courtesy of the Fellowship of Reconciliation Archives.

Randall Forsberg, founder of the
Nuclear Freeze campaign, 1982.
Courtesy of Randall Forsberg.

Leaders of the Moscow Trust Group, including Sergei Batovin (upper left), Vladimir
Brodsky (upper right), and Olga Medvedkova (lower right), ca. mid-1982. Courtesy of
the Fellowship of Reconciliation Archives.

END leader
E. P. Thompson
addresses an anti-
nuclear rally in
Hyde Park, Britain,
June 8, 1982. Cour-
tesy of David and
Katie Urry.

Helen Caldicott delivers one of
her many stirring antinuclear
speeches, early 1980s. Courtesy
of the Fellowship of Reconciliation Archives.

Above: Greenham Common women dance defiantly atop a cruise missile silo, January 1, 1983. Photo by Raissa Page, courtesy of Format Photographers.

Left: Joan Ruddock (left), Bruce Kent (second from right), and Petra Kelly (right) march in a CND demonstration, early 1983. Courtesy of Steve Benbow.

The *Rainbow Warrior*, shortly before it was bombed by French agents in Auckland harbor, July 1985. The explosion sank the vessel and killed the crew member who took this picture. Photo by Fernando Pereira, courtesy of Greenpeace.

Ronald Reagan, besieged by the anti-nuclear campaign, loses his jaunty demeanor, September 1985. Courtesy of the Ronald Reagan Library

Bernard Lown (lower right) and Evgenii Chazov (facing him) press Mikhail Gorbachev (left) to extend the unilateral Soviet nuclear testing moratorium, December 1985. The Soviet leader did so. Courtesy of Bernard Lown.

At right: Frank von Hippel (left) and Andrei Sakharov (right) meet at Sakharov's Moscow apartment and discuss cutting the link between an INF accord and SDI, February 1987. A short time later, Gorbachev followed their recommendation, opening the way for the world's first nuclear disarmament treaty. Photo by Jeremy Stone, courtesy of Frank von Hippel.

Left: The Rev. William Sloane Coffin, Jr., the first president of SANE/Freeze (now Peace Action), 1980s. Courtesy of Paul Tick.

Filipino women demonstrate in Manila for the closure of the nuclear-armed U.S.
military bases in their country, November 1987. Photo by Charlie Scheiner, courtesy of
War Resisters League.

I AM HAPPY TO SAY THAT THE ARMS RACE IS NOW OVER...

Australian activists remain vigilant, as indicated by this cartoon from a peace movement publication, 1988. Courtesy of *Social Alternatives*.

Citizens of Kazakhstan, USSR, protest Soviet nuclear testing near the Semipalatinsk
test site, in a demonstration organized by the Nevada-Semipalatinsk movement,
August 1989. Photo by Yuri Kuidin, courtesy of International Physicians for the
Prevention of Nuclear War.

END holds one of its last conventions, in 1990. Photo by David McReynolds, courtesy
of War Resisters League.

Public Policy Wavers,
1981-85

> Deployment was bound to be a sensitive matter,
> especially with an election campaign ahead [in 1983].
> . . . Elsewhere in Europe the situation was still more
> difficult. . . . I now urged . . . that the American
> administration should take a new initiative in the INF
> negotiations.
>
> Margaret Thatcher, 1993

A more significant indication of the movement's growing strength was its impact upon the nuclear policies of governments around the world. At the time, or in retrospect, many government officials claimed that they were not influenced at all by the pressure of the antinuclear campaign. National defense policy, they insisted, could not be made "in the streets" or on the basis of opinion polls. Thus, they refused to deviate from a policy of "peace through strength."[1] Superficially, there is some plausibility to this contention. Soviet policy apparently remained frozen. Furthermore, despite the massive antinuclear protests in Western Europe, deployment of the cruise and Pershing II missiles went forward. Yet, during the early 1980s, there were some changes, albeit minimal, in Soviet policy, and there might have been more if Soviet leaders had not been terrified by the hawkish rhetoric and proposals of the Reagan administration. Meanwhile, Europe's NATO officials pressured the U.S. government to soften its negotiating position at the Geneva INF talks, delayed implementing missile deployment plans, and even came out in forthright opposition to NATO's deployment decision. In addition, responding to the antinuclear upsurge, they and numerous other national leaders began to alter their countries' nuclear weapons policies, including their positions on nuclear arms control and disarmament. As fairly few of them admitted their policy reversals publicly, little of this was recognized at the time. But, in retrospect, the pattern is fairly clear.

NATO Nations

Certainly NATO's West European governments were less resolute about installing the Euromissiles than often portrayed—a fact deeply irritating to U.S. officials. Reagan recalled that "some European leaders, feeling the heat, began expressing doubts about NATO's 1979 decision to deploy the new weapons." Reflecting on the situation, Weinberger, too, emphasized the erosion of the alliance position in the face of public protest. "Every NATO meeting I attended was undergirded by demonstrations," he recalled, with some bitterness. "As more and more of the demonstrations were held," he wrote, "more and more defense ministers at the NATO meetings urged . . . that more be done on the 'second track' of the December 1979 resolution." If the United States were "to retain support of the host governments for deployment," INF negotiations would have to "widely be seen as being open, active and vigorously conducted." Kenneth Adelman recalled that, during the Euromissile controversy, all the West European governments "were nervous about their public, scared to death," especially the Dutch, Belgian, and West German. Arriving at his office, their representatives would ask him what they should do. In response, Adelman would urge them to "keep on track, stay the course." But they, in turn, would propose "all kinds of schemes" to avoid the domestic political crisis they saw shaping up over deployment of the missiles.[2]

As Weinberger implied, a key demand made by America's junior partners was simply that the U.S. government hold serious negotiations for removal of the missiles. As the disarmament track had been inserted into NATO's 1979 decision by the Carter administration, it was far from clear that the more hawkish Reaganites would accept it. From the onset of the Reagan administration, West European leaders pressed the U.S. government for reassurance that it would resume INF negotiations. Unless Washington set a date for resumption of the arms talks, Schmidt insisted, he could not keep his government committed to missile deployment. Of course, Schmidt, in addition to facing a growing revolt against missiles within his own Social Democratic Party, genuinely wanted them removed.[3] Helmut Kohl, who succeeded him as chancellor of West Germany in late 1982, had far less interest in fostering nuclear disarmament, for his Christian Democrats looked forward to acquiring the new missiles. In their view, talk of a "zero option" represented little more than a useful propaganda cover for missile installation and, hopefully, would never be acceptable to the Soviet Union. Margaret Thatcher took much the same position. "I had always disliked the original INF 'zero option,'" she recalled, "because I felt that these weapons made up for Western Europe's unpreparedness to face a sudden, massive attack by the Warsaw Pact; I had gone along with it in the hope that the Soviets would never accept."[4] Thus, it was particularly striking that these and other NATO governments—hard-pressed by the antinuclear revolt—now demanded that Washington conduct genuine negotiations for missile removal. The INF meeting must be "a real negotiation, not just a show," Kohl told Shultz in November 1982. Thatcher said virtually the same thing to him that winter, as did Italian officials. A Bonn government spokesperson told the press: "The more we can prove to people that we are serious about negotiations, the less trouble we are going to have in Europe."[5]

It is also telling that, faced with the antinuclear upsurge, NATO's West European leaders sought to soften the terms for an arms control agreement. Impressed by the widespread opposition within his nation to the Euromissiles, Schmidt began by championing the zero option—the most radical disarmament proposal. But after late 1981, when the U.S. government adopted this position, it became clear that rigid insistence upon it was contributing to an impasse over a Soviet-American arms control agreement, for the Russians were unwilling to trade their missiles already in place for a promise not to install missiles that had not yet been built. Consequently, West European leaders—determined to produce signs of progress for their restive publics—began to call for greater U.S. flexibility at the Geneva negotiations. Even Thatcher, the hardest of the hard-liners, now asked the U.S. government to revise its negotiating position. Concerned about her reelection prospects and about the overall West European situation, she urged Vice President Bush in February 1983 to get the administration to "take a new initiative in the INF negotiations." This entailed seeking "an interim agreement whereby limited reductions on the Soviet side would be balanced by reduced deployments on the part of the United States." When Reagan failed to alter his stance, she recalled, "I continued the private pressure for further movement, while remaining in public totally supportive of the American position."[6]

Other NATO governments, too, saw a Euromissile agreement—or, at the least, the appearance of U.S. negotiating flexibility—as vital in heading off a dangerous domestic crisis. Schmidt pressed hard for such flexibility, although without much success. When, soon after Thatcher's entreaties, the U.S. government did shift its INF negotiating position, only to once again meet a Soviet rebuff, West German officials lobbied privately and spoke out publicly for yet another compromise proposal, the "Walk in the Woods" formula first broached by Paul Nitze.[7] Neither the U.S. nor the Soviet government would accept this position, however, and—with elections looming in the fall of 1983—the West German government grew increasingly desperate. Shultz recalled that West German Foreign Minister Genscher phoned him on September 20, "urging that an announcement be made of new INF moves ... before Sunday's elections." According to Shultz, West German officials "were uneasy and were looking for every scrap of evidence that they could find that we were serious about pursuing a negotiating track with the Soviets." Frequently, then, NATO's West European leaders sought to modify the hard-line position preferred by the U.S. government. Recalling their role in the INF controversy, Richard Perle remarked delicately that "some of them did not want as tough an arms control policy as we had."[8]

To head off a political crisis, the Dutch and Belgian governments followed another tack—delaying missile deployment. Recognizing that cruise missile deployment had become politically impossible, the Dutch government chose to stall on the issue, thus breaking with the NATO policy of installing the missiles in November 1983. "We simply cannot get a yes from the Dutch parliament," the Dutch foreign minister told Shultz in May 1984. "Therefore the strategy is to avoid a no and also to avoid losing both the cabinet and the missiles." From the standpoint of the U.S. government, this represented a dangerous retreat in the face of popular pressure. "Everyone knows that the Dutch have blinked," Shultz complained. In June 1984, Prime Minister Ruud Lubbers announced yet another ingenious compromise—one accepted by the parliament. It entailed postponing a final decision on cruise missile installation until November 1, 1985, and, moreover, moving forward with deployment at that time only if a Soviet-American missile agreement had not been reached and if the Soviets installed *additional* SS-20 missiles. Furthermore, if a deployment decision were taken in November 1985, construction of the missile base would not occur until 1986 and the missiles would not be installed until 1988. This was hardly a ringing endorsement of NATO policy. But, in the circumstances, Lubbers considered it the best he could do. Meanwhile, the Belgian government, facing similar political difficulties, voted on November 30, 1984, to postpone a decision on the missiles.[9]

NATO leaders championed a variant of the delay strategy in the form of a NATO deployment moratorium. In May 1983, the Danish parliament adopted a resolution ordering the government to press for an extension of the INF negotiations, if necessary, and for a ban on missile deployment while the negotiations were in progress.[10] As the missile crisis deepened, the moratorium idea caught on with several deployment countries as well. In May 1984, Prime Minister Craxi of Italy publicly proposed that NATO halt its missile deployment if the Soviet Union resumed missile negotiations. Naturally, Reagan and Shultz strongly opposed what the latter called "this significant break—without any consultation—with our NATO position." But the Dutch and Belgian governments, both blocked from deployment by domestic opposition, liked the moratorium idea, for it would enable them to further delay a deployment decision.[11]

Some NATO nations directly opposed the deployment of cruise and Pershing missiles. In Greece, the Papandreou government steadily criticized NATO missile deployment. Although Papandreou favored the removal of the Soviet SS-20s, he argued that the deployment of the Western missiles would make removal of the Soviet missiles more difficult.[12] The Danish government, initially favorable to the two-track decision, gradually moved toward a de facto repudiation of it. In December 1982, it voted to halt appropriations covering Denmark's share in the funding of NATO's INF missile bases.[13] Both the Canadian and French governments also raised objections to missile deployment on occasion. At the May 1983 economic summit at Williamsburg, Virginia, the attendees agreed on the principles of a statement reaffirming plans for missile deployment that fall. But, the next morning, Reagan recalled, "François Mitterrand and Pierre Trudeau declared that they couldn't support the statement, and in effect called those of us who favored installing the new missiles warmongers." Thatcher remembered Mitterrand as less difficult at the conference, but confirmed that Trudeau "did have a problem with a strong line on deterrence."[14]

Even when a government agreed to install the missiles, changes in the arrangements for their deployment indicated just how shell-shocked the authorities were becoming from their battles with antinuclear forces. Despite Britain's formal agreement with the United States to deploy the cruise missiles at Greenham Common and Molesworth, Heseltine went to the British Cabinet in 1984 to argue that they be confined to Greenham Common. In justifying this sudden change of plans, the defense minister argued that reducing the number of missile sites would limit the antinuclear movement's opportunities for protest. Furthermore, despite the mobile nature of the missiles, the British government apparently decided to avoid conducting missile training exercises outside Greenham Common for a time. According to a January 1984 report in *Jane's Defence Weekly*: "No dates have been fixed for any 'off-base' exercises, and the continuing presence of 'peace' protesters has forced the Pentagon and the UK MoD [Ministry of Defense] to wait to see if current protests cool." Although Weinberger and Heseltine did not want "to admit the influence of the protest movement, they have been unable to plan for any deployment outside the perimeter fence." One Pentagon official predicted that there would "be a less emotional spectacle in the future . . . when the British population gets used to them."[15]

Some West European NATO governments also challenged NATO policy by taking up the antinuclear movement's demand for the creation of nuclear weapon-free zones. Greece's Papandreou was a particularly vocal proponent of the establishment of a nuclear-free zone in the Balkans. Bringing together officials from Bulgaria, Rumania, Greece, Turkey, and Yugoslavia for discussions of the issue, he vowed to free that region from the threat of nuclear war. Even if such a zone took more time than anticipated to materialize, he announced, the Greek government would proceed with the withdrawal of all nuclear weapons on its soil.[16] In the Nordic countries, too, the idea of a nuclear-free zone acquired considerable appeal, not only within the nonaligned nations of Sweden and Finland, but within the NATO nation of Denmark. Although Denmark had traditionally followed a policy of banning nuclear weapons in peacetime but accepting nuclear deployment in the event of war, it moved a step closer toward a total nuclear ban in May 1984. At that time, the Danish parliament passed a resolution, offered by the Social Democrats, that enjoined the government "to work in NATO and in other international organizations to keep Denmark nuclear weapon-free in peacetime as well as during a crisis and in war time by furthering plans to establish a Nordic nuclear weapon-free zone."[17]

The nuclear-free zone movement had a particularly powerful effect in Britain, for it led to the collapse of civil defense measures against nuclear attack. During the autumn of 1982, the British government's planned nuclear civil defense exercise, a nationwide venture termed "Hard Rock," was canceled when twenty county councils, which had proclaimed themselves nuclear-free zones, refused to participate in it. Thereafter, although the Thatcher administration sought to coerce nuclear-free localities into cooperating with national civil defense authorities, it eventually abandoned the struggle. Some civil defense exercises were held, but they were on a much smaller scale and without a nuclear component. When the government launched its "Brave Defender" maneuvers in 1985, nuclear attack did not form part of the scenario. The official in charge explained that the planners did not want "to stir up the Campaign for Nuclear Disarmament." CND also succeeded in blocking the building of civil defense bunkers. In Wales, months of CND picketing and nonviolent occupation of the construction site for a county war headquarters bunker led the government to abandon the project.[18]

In other ways, too, America's NATO partners showed themselves remarkably skittish about anything connected with nuclear weapons. "Some governments were so concerned by the antinuclear demonstrations that regularly took place in their countries," Weinberger recalled, "that they declined to carry out the commitments they had made earlier to serve as hosts" for NATO's Nuclear Planning Group. They seemed considerably more eager for agreements that would reduce the numbers of strategic nuclear weapons.[19] Although Reagan ordered full-scale U.S. production and assembly of the enhanced radiation weapon—the neutron bomb—in 1981, none of America's West European allies would give the administration permission to deploy it on their territory. Fearing a reprise of the tumult of the late 1970s and traumatized by the subsequent anti-Euromissile demonstrations, West European officials considered the weapon untouchable. Deploying the neutron bomb in West Germany, reported one of Schmidt's aides, "was at the moment, out of the question." Nor did acquiring it grow more appealing over time. Unable to find any nation that would accept this weapon, designed to be used against Soviet tanks in Western Europe, the Reagan administration stored it in the United States, where it had no military utility. In these circumstances, the U.S. Congress finally stepped in and, in 1984, prohibited its production.[20]

NATO leaders also expressed wariness of Reagan's SDI proposal. To a great extent, their early dismay with SDI reflected their fears that it would decouple Western Europe from a Fortress America. But other features troubled them as well, including the fact that it would serve as a further provocation to the antinuclear movement that was already causing them so much difficulty. Richard von Weizsäcker, the President of West Germany, recalled: "Most Europeans believed that this plan was technically, strategically, politically, and humanely half-baked."[21] As the U.S. government dangled the prospect of lucrative SDI contracts before its NATO partners, many of them abandoned their critique of the program. McFarlane recalled that, after he explained to Thatcher that "there may be as much as $300 million a year in SDI research and development that ought to be subcontracted to British firms," she became much more enthusiastic about the venture. By 1985, Heseltine was discussing with Weinberger what he called the "steps to secure a substantial proportion of the work for Britain."[22] Even so, grumbling by NATO nations continued, based on a growing concern that SDI research by the United States would leave them behind technologically and, also, on a residual uneasiness about the hostility to SDI of the nuclear disarmament movement. Indeed, the Canadian government apparently rejected official involvement in the SDI project because of determined resistance by the antinuclear campaign.[23]

Caught between pressure from the U.S. government to support a Western nuclear buildup and counter-pressure from the nuclear disarmament movement to abandon it, some NATO leaders sought to reassure their uneasy citizens by engaging in or encouraging high-profile peace diplomacy. In the winter of 1983–84, responding to the public outcry against Canada's testing of cruise missiles, Trudeau embarked upon a well-publicized peace initiative. It entailed flying to West European capitals to meet with NATO officials and delivering speeches calling for "positive political steps in order to reverse the dangerously downward trend-line in East-West relations."[24] In March 1984, with West Germany still torn by fierce debate over nuclear issues, Chancellor Kohl urged Reagan to hold a summit meeting with Soviet party secretary Chernenko. Although the Federal Republic's allies looked with dismay on further *Ostpolitik*—the policy of bettering relations between East and West Germany initiated by the Social Democrats—the Kohl government insisted upon continuing it. An active program of *Ostpolitik*, it argued, was necessary if it were to prevent the peace movement and the political opposition from exploiting popular uneasiness with the escalating arms race.[25] In this fashion, as in others, NATO leaders sought to avoid political disaster by bending gracefully during the storm of popular protest.

ANZUS Nations

America's ANZUS partners responded even more dramatically to the antinuclear campaign. The policy transformation was greatest, of course, in New Zealand, where the new prime minister, David Lange, freely acknowledged the importance of the antinuclear movement and of public opinion in setting his nation on a nuclear-free course. However, despite his Labour Party's 1984 election victory on an antinuclear platform, Lange was reluctant to fully implement it, largely because he recognized that banning nuclear-armed and nuclear-powered warships from New Zealand's ports would place him on a collision course with his ANZUS ally, the United States, the world's most powerful nation. For this reason, Lange responded to U.S. pressure after his election by trying to work out an acceptable compromise with U.S. officials. As late as January 30, 1985, he and the U.S. ambassador expressed confidence that they could resolve the nuclear ships controversy satisfactorily. Yet the Americans did not want a compromise, but a continuation of their ability to bring nuclear weapons into New Zealand's harbors, unannounced, whenever they pleased. And the New Zealand peace movement, plus the Labour Party, wanted a nuclear-free New Zealand. Antinuclear demonstrations filled the streets of the capital and the Labour Cabinet refused to retreat. Ultimately, then, the Lange government remained true to its promises. It barred the visit of the U.S. warship *Buchanan* and stuck to its antinuclear principles. Public support for the warship ban surged, bolstering the government's resolve.[26]

Although his government now came under enormous pressure from the United States and its allies to scrap this policy, Lange and other government leaders not only refused to abandon it, but emerged as eloquent critics of the nuclear arms race. That March, debating the morality of nuclear weapons with the Rev. Jerry Falwell before the Oxford Union, New Zealand's prime minister proclaimed:

Nuclear weapons make us insecure, and to compensate for our insecurity we build and deploy more nuclear weapons. . . . We know that we are seized by irrationality, and yet we persist. We all know that it is wholly without logic or reason to possess the power to destroy ourselves many times over; and yet in spite of that knowledge the nuclear powers continue to refine their capacity to inflict destruction on each other and all the rest of us. . . . There is no humanity in the logic which holds that my country must be obliged to play host to nuclear weapons because others in the West are playing host to nuclear weapons. That is the logic which refuses to admit that there is any alternative to nuclear weapons when plainly there is. It is a self-defeating logic, just as the weapons themselves are self-defeating.

Helen Clark, the chair of the Foreign Affairs Committee in New Zealand's parliament, declared:

To a world overawed by the complexities of arms negotiations between the super-powers—and impatient with the lack of results from them—New Zealand's move . . . cuts right across the impasse and the stagnation of bloc politics. Its real significance is that yet another small, aligned nation is prepared to place conditions on the nature of its strategic alignment and to disengage from and withdraw support for the nuclear weapons strategies of the superpowers.

Further challenging the U.S. government, New Zealand became a leading proponent of a comprehensive test ban treaty and of a South Pacific nuclear weapons–free zone. Speaking before the Labour Party's annual conference, which overwhelmingly endorsed the government's antinuclear policy, Lange stated that it had shown that "a small country could speak up for itself and stand up for what is right."[27]

The change in Australia's policy, though far less sweeping, was nonetheless significant. After the Australian Labor Party won the March 1983 elections, the new prime minister, Bob Hawke, displayed considerably greater caution than did his neighbors in New Zealand. Determined to avoid a break with the U.S. government and with the ANZUS alliance, Hawke told Lange, as he recalled, that "it was nonsense to suggest you could have an alliance relationship but tell your ally that its ships couldn't enter your

ports." In addition, after intense lobbying, he succeeded in getting his party
to drop its opposition to uranium mining and to giving the go-ahead to a
mining project in South Australia—an action that, like his repudiation of
New Zealand's antinuclear stand, deeply dismayed Australia's nuclear disarmament movement.[28] Even so, responding to years of antinuclear agitation, Hawke appointed Australia's first minister for disarmament, tripled the
size of the disarmament section of Australia's Department of Foreign Affairs, established a peace research center at Australian National University,
instructed Australia's representative to vote in favor of a Freeze resolution
at the United Nations, and—rejecting a personal appeal from Reagan—refused to allow Australia to become involved with SDI. In addition, with the
resumption of French nuclear testing in the Pacific and the eruption of new
protests, Australia became a key force in world efforts to secure a comprehensive test ban treaty. It also played the leading role in efforts to establish
a South Pacific nuclear-free zone. At times, the movement pushed Hawke
further than he wanted to go. In February 1983, after a public outcry over the
discovery of his offer to the U.S. government to help test the MX missile,
the prime minister was forced to withdraw it.[29]

Elsewhere in Asia and the Pacific

The changing policies of New Zealand and Australia spilled over into the
other eleven nations of the South Pacific through their work in negotiating
the Treaty of Rarotonga, designed to prohibit the testing, production, acquisition, or stationing of nuclear weapons in the region. Without the support
of these two countries, the treaty probably would not have emerged, for the
other parties to it—all tiny island nations—lacked the requisite influence in
world affairs. Even so, not all of these nations were entirely pleased with
the proposed treaty, for it would not bar the transit of nuclear weapons—as,
for example, on board U.S. warships—and would have no immediate impact on French nuclear testing at Moruroa. Hawke pointed out that individual nations would retain the right to ban port calls by such nuclear-armed
vessels. And, in fact, both New Zealand and Vanuatu already banned their
visits. Stopping French nuclear testing enjoyed far greater support among
South Pacific nations, which viewed it as not only dangerous, but as a continuation of great power colonialism. Walter Lini, the Prime Minister of
Vanuatu, observed acidly that "colonization and nuclearism in the Pacific"
were intimately linked. To eradicate nuclearism, "we have to deal with it
from its root, which is colonization itself. It is morally wrong for an alien
power to occupy someone else's territory, suppress its people, and use that

territory's environment to test deadly weapons." From the standpoint of both Vanuatu and the Nuclear Free and Independent Pacific Movement, it was preferable to develop a stronger treaty, as well as one including the Micronesian islands, located north of the equator. But, ultimately, advocates of a more militant position (generally from Melanesia) compromised with the advocates of a more conservative one (generally from Polynesia).[30]

The movement fared more poorly in Japan, largely thanks to the fact that its keenest political supporters—the Socialist and Communist parties—remained outside the government. The conservative prime minister, Yasuhiro Nakasone, prided himself on his good relations with Washington, including a reputed "Ron-Yasu" friendship, and did his best to mesh Japanese policy with that of the West. In testimony before the Japanese Diet, he went so far as to express support for Reagan's SDI program. Nevertheless, despite Japan's sophisticated level of industrial and technological development, its three non-nuclear principles remained officially enshrined, with no sign of any effort to develop a nuclear weapons capability. Furthermore, unlike the missile plan for Western Europe, there remained no plan for U.S. nuclear deployments in Japan. If the Japanese government, as most Japanese believed, allowed U.S. warships to bring nuclear weapons into its ports, thus violating the third non-nuclear principle—the ban on "introducing" nuclear weapons into Japan—it never dared to admit this fact. At the same time, hundreds of local governments publicly proclaimed themselves nuclear-free zones.[31]

Elsewhere in Asia, where antinuclear movements were nonexistent, public policymakers felt fewer inhibitions at participating in the nuclear arms race. Although Pakistani President Zia ul-Haq denied that his government had any intention of building nuclear weapons, Pakistan was, in fact, developing a nuclear capability, which he implicitly justified by pointing to India's nuclear program. Thanks to China's frosty relationship with the Soviet Union, it tended to endorse nuclear weapons buildups in the West, arguing that they were necessary to preserve the global balance. Thus, in the early 1980s, its leaders contended that Soviet objections to deployment of the neutron bomb were invalid and that NATO missile deployments in Western Europe were an inevitable response to the SS-20s. Even so, justifying its own nuclear weapons program, the Chinese government condemned what it called the "superpower nuclear monopoly," argued for the rights of other nations "to maintain their defense capabilities," and continued to criticize the nuclear nonproliferation treaty.[32] Naturally, neither government placed itself in the vanguard of worldwide antinuclear efforts.

The Soviet Union

Within the Soviet Union, there were some policy modifications, at least partially to appeal to world public opinion. The Kremlin, after all, was engaged in a full-fledged propaganda war with the West and devoted some $3 billion a year to its very extensive overseas propaganda activities—enough to keep an estimated 70,000 employees busy.[33] Not surprisingly, then, at this time of widespread popular dismay with nuclear weapons, government officials used public statements to embarrass the United States and portray the Soviet Union as an avatar of peace. Speaking at the 26th Soviet party congress in February 1981, Brezhnev proclaimed that counting on victory in a nuclear war "is dangerous madness." This position served the Kremlin well over the next year, as the Reagan administration came under increasing public fire for its glib talk of nuclear war. In late October, with Western Europe abuzz at one of Reagan's inflammatory statements along these lines, Brezhnev publicly called on the American president to join the Soviet government in "rejecting the very idea of nuclear attack as criminal" and opposing first use of nuclear weapons.[34] Conversing with American magazine publishers the following day, Leonid Zamyatin, the Kremlin's propaganda chief, reiterated Brezhnev's call for renouncing first use of nuclear weapons. At the June 1982 U.N. Special Session on Disarmament, the Soviet government went still further, pledging unilaterally never to be the first nation to employ nuclear arms. Soviet Defense Minister Ustinov declared that "only extraordinary circumstances—a direct nuclear aggression against the Soviet state or its allies—can compel us to resort to a retaliatory nuclear strike."[35]

The Soviet government's arms control proposals reflected even more clearly a response to pressures from the antinuclear campaign. In May 1982, with Nuclear Freeze resolutions before the U.S. Congress and START talks about to open in Geneva, Brezhnev announced the Soviet government's readiness to support a variant of the Nuclear Freeze proposal. "We would be prepared to reach agreement that the strategic armament of the U.S.S.R. and the U.S.A. be frozen right away," he stated, "as soon as the talks begin, frozen quantitatively—and that modernization be limited to the utmost." Although this was a weaker arms control agreement than promoted by the Freeze campaign, it demonstrated the Kremlin's willingness to tailor its policy proposals to popular antinuclear ideas, as did its introduction of a multilateral Freeze at the United Nations in 1983 and its call for a production Freeze in 1984.[36] In yet another move clearly designed to appeal to public opinion, Brezhnev met in February 1982 with a group of representatives from the Socialist International and publicized the fact that, at Geneva, the Soviet government had proposed a two-thirds cut in U.S. and Soviet arsenals of medium range nuclear missiles in Europe. That December, after becoming the new Soviet party secretary, Andropov delivered his first arms control speech. Shultz recalled that "it contained several proposals, but was mainly propaganda designed to affect European politics and to undermine our ability to proceed with deployments." In fact, the Soviet government made numerous proposals for nuclear weapons reductions—many of them publicly appealing, but none of them acceptable to the U.S. government.[37]

Movement activism produced an important breakthrough in Soviet policy toward space weapons. In March 1983, Velikhov and Sagdeev returned from meetings in Washington, where they had been conferring with American scientists anxious to ban the testing of anti-satellite (ASAT) weapons. Lobbying Soviet government officials, they convinced them of the virtues of this measure, particularly in light of simmering U.S. congressional efforts to initiate a joint U.S.-Soviet moratorium. Consequently, that August, in a meeting with nine U.S. Senators in the Kremlin, Andropov announced a unilateral Soviet moratorium on the testing of ASAT weapons. These efforts to quell the arms race in space might not have gone as far as they did had they not overlapped with the Reagan administration's announcement of SDI. Andropov initially reacted with great anger to the U.S. launching of SDI, proclaiming that if it were built, it would "open the floodgates of a runaway arms race of all types of strategic arms, both offensive and defensive." And there were Soviet scientists and officials eager to counter SDI by developing a Soviet military effort in space. But the Committee of Soviet Scientists, working with its overseas counterparts, sharply rejected the idea of copying SDI and pressed, instead, for arms controls and, if necessary, cheap countermeasures to it. Their recommendations for an "asymmetric response" to SDI were included in a report the committee distributed at home and overseas. As a result, the Soviet government did not move hastily to match the American program but, as the case of ASAT weapons, showed restraint.[38]

Even so, the fundamentals of Soviet policy did not change during these years. Through all its discussions of Euromissile deployment, the Kremlin insisted that it should retain hundreds of its SS-20s while, at the same time, NATO should forgo installation of any cruise and Pershing missiles. Visiting Bonn on November 23, 1981, Brezhnev officially rejected the zero option and proposed instead an agreement that boiled down to Soviet retention of all the SS-20 missiles installed by the end of 1981 (about 250) and Western non-deployment. In addition, while the negotiations proceeded, there would be a moratorium on further missile installation—a provision that opened the possibility of blocking U.S. deployment indefinitely through a strategy of delay. Eliminating all the missiles "cannot be the basis for any U.S.-Soviet agreement," Gromyko told Shultz in September 1982, for the Soviet Union already had the missiles installed and the United States did not; consequently, the zero option amounted to "unilateral disarmament."[39] Nitze's "Walk in the Woods" formula—which proposed to scrap plans for Pershing II missile deployment and balance the numbers of cruise missiles against the numbers of SS-20s—was also thoroughly objectionable to the Soviet government. From its standpoint, the deployment of any cruise missiles was unacceptable, as was the failure to count the existing British and French nuclear forces as part of NATO's INF allotment. Even the Soviet government's INF negotiating offer of October 1983, made on the eve of Western missile deployment, provided that the Soviet Union would scrap only 103 of its 378 SS-20 missiles; in return, NATO would forgo deployment of all 572 cruise and Pershing missiles.[40]

Thereafter, the Soviet government whipsawed missile negotiations between total rejection and its past proposals. When the first NATO missile deployments began in December 1983, the Soviet government withdrew from participation in the INF negotiations and in the START negotiations. This action followed a plan developed a few months before, designed to cast the onus for the collapse of the nuclear arms control talks upon the United States. In fact, however, the Soviet walkout harmed the Soviet image more than it did the American. Consequently, in June 1984—long before Reagan's reelection was assured—Soviet officials began to suggest to their U.S. counterparts that they were ready to resume negotiations. That November, Chernenko made a formal offer along these lines, leading to the resumption of both the INF and START talks in early 1985.[41] But even the installation of the cruise and Pershing missiles and Reagan's reelection triumph did not alter Soviet INF policy. In March 1985, the Soviet position remained exactly where it had been in the past. The Kremlin's chief negotiator simply repeated the old Soviet proposal that, in return for the total renunciation of Western INF missiles, the Soviets would reduce the number of their SS-20s in Europe to the number of French and British nuclear warheads—420, according to him. As the two sides moved into the fifth year of the Reagan administration, the Soviet government had made no significant concessions on missile deployment.[42]

Furthermore, despite its efforts to portray itself as the avatar of peace and disarmament, the Soviet government showed no sign of halting its nuclear and overall military buildup. Taking office in November 1982, Andropov declared that "peace cannot be obtained from the imperialists by begging for it. It can be upheld only by relying on the invincible might of the Soviet armed forces." At the Politburo meeting of May 31, 1983, Defense Minister Ustinov insisted: "All that we do regarding defense we should continue doing. All the missiles that we planned to install should be installed. All the airplanes should be stationed at the spots we agreed upon." Moreover, in the aftermath of its December 1983 withdrawal from the Geneva arms control talks, the Kremlin ordered a provocative escalation of Soviet nuclear efforts. It resumed SS-20 missile deployment, placed SS-23 nuclear missiles in East Germany and Czechoslovakia, and moved Soviet nuclear submarines closer to the coasts of the United States.[43] In late 1984, as Soviet government officials prepared their next five-year plan, covering the 1986–90 period, they incorporated into it a 45 percent rise in military spending.[44]

This inability to depart from traditional military priorities left critics of the nuclear missile buildup thoroughly disgusted. If the Soviet leadership of the 1980s had "shown 10 percent of the initiative of Gorbachev," recalled E. P. Thompson, the Euromissile crisis would have been brought to an early and satisfactory resolution. Inside the Soviet Union, party reformers were equally aghast at the Old Guard's hidebound approach. In June 1984, Anatoly Chernyaev, a reform-minded Central Committee staff member, returning from a briefing given by Marshal Sergei Akhromeyev, deputy chief of the General Staff, was deeply dismayed by the military officer's efforts to "turn the country into a military camp" and his presentation of American documentaries on "amazing" new U.S. missiles and other weaponry. Chernyaev jotted in his diary: "I was watching and thinking that we're spending as much or even more, and for what? We're preparing mankind's suicide. It's insane!" He "wanted to get up and ask the marshal: 'What if we just destroy all those weapons . . . and say to the whole world "Enough already! We've woken up, come to our senses!" What would happen then? Would the Americans attack us the next instant?'" Unfortunately, though, "if I said that they'd surely consider me, the deputy chief of the International Department, a nutcase."[45]

His assessment was surely correct. By the early 1980s, the top Soviet leadership was incapable of creative thinking or initiatives. Recalling the Politburo of the era, Oleg Grinevsky, a key Soviet arms control negotiator, remarked that its members were "sick and old people" who lived "in some kind of an imaginary world. They didn't know what was going on." Consequently, there was no possibility that the Politburo could "go and make reforms." Other Soviet officials, too, pointed to the leadership's physical and mental infirmity, and to the disastrous effects this had upon public policy. "Under Brezhnev, the country was already an embarrassment," wrote Chernyaev; "under Chernenko it became a shameful farce."[46] Furthermore, even if top Soviet leaders possessed the competence to handle public affairs, they died rapidly during these years, providing little opportunity for a significant policy initiative to emerge. Vladimir Slipchenko, who worked at the ministry of defense, recalled the depressing "conveyor belt of funerals" among the party secretaries—Brezhnev, Andropov, and Chernenko—from November 1982 to March 1985. Finally, top Soviet leaders remained prisoners of traditional thinking about international affairs. Even Andropov, the most reformist to appear since Khrushchev, seemed unwilling to undertake any substantial change in Soviet foreign and military policy. Both Arbatov and Gorbachev, two of his reformist protégés, gave him credit for an interest in détente and skepticism about some military programs. But, in retrospect, neither thought that, if he had lived beyond March 1984, he would have endorsed what Gorbachev called "far-reaching transformations." Unfortunately, wrote Gorbachev, Andropov remained "unable to break through the barrier of old ideas and values."[47]

Of course, party reformers did provide an alternative source of ideas but, for the time being, their path to power remained blocked by party conservatives. Arbatov sought to convince Brezhnev of the folly of the SS-20s, but failed thanks to the party secretary's mental incapacity and the rising influence of the military. The influence of the reformers grew somewhat with the accession to power of Andropov who, in 1983, brought the reformist Aleksandr Yakovlev back from his political exile in Canada to head up the Institute of World Economics and International Relations, another of the avant garde think tanks. But, as Gorbachev recalled, "Andropov's death and Chernenko's election as General Secretary instilled fresh hope in the foes of all reform."[48] Yakovlev, Arbatov, and other critics of the missile buildup came under fierce attack from party conservatives, and their modest influence dwindled. Admittedly, Gorbachev, the only reformer on the party's Central Committee, remained relatively unscathed and undaunted. In a public address in Britain, he went so far as to argue that "the nuclear age inevitably dictates a new political thinking."[49] Even so, in February 1984, conservatives deliberately sabotaged his political opportunities. To head off the nomination of Gorbachev as party secretary at the crucial Politburo meeting, Nikolai Tikhonov, a staunch conservative, immediately asked for the floor "on a point of order." Then he proceeded to nominate Chernenko, and the others present—committed to Stalinist style party unity—immediately fell into line. In this fashion, Chernenko—recalled by Dobrynin as "the most feeble and unimaginative Soviet leader of the last two decades"—became the guiding light of Soviet domestic and foreign policy.[50]

Above all, however, the Soviet leadership's commitment to pursuing a nuclear buildup reflected its rising fear of the new U.S. government priorities. Initially, Soviet leaders were disturbed and puzzled by the new administration, for they preferred Republican to Democratic Presidents, and—despite Reagan's hawkish 1980 campaign rhetoric—expected him to resume Nixon's policies of détente. But, with Reagan in the White House, his militantly anti-Soviet statements, the administration's talk of waging and winning a nuclear war, and its massive nuclear arms buildup soon disabused them of this notion. Internal party memoranda and conversations with visiting dignitaries expressed shock at the new administration's plans to build and deploy the B-1 bomber, the neutron bomb, the Trident submarine, and the cruise and MX missiles. "This militaristic program," wrote one Politburo member in October 1981, "shows that Reagan's administration wants to tip the current balance of forces in the U.S.'s favor."[51] Sagdeev recalled that "the Kremlin elite was paranoid about the technical capability" attributed to the Pershing II missiles, for they assumed that these missiles were first strike weapons, designed to kill them in their bunkers. Although, in fact, the Pershing IIs did not have the range to reach Moscow, Soviet leaders assumed that they did, as the manufacturer had made public claims along these lines. In these circumstances, the Kremlin was deeply suspicious of Reagan's newfound peace rhetoric. As Soviet ambassador Dobrynin recalled, Soviet leaders viewed the Reagan administration as "not serious about arms control."[52]

In 1983, particularly, Soviet leaders grew increasingly alarmed that the U.S. government was preparing for a nuclear attack upon their nation. Although Reagan launched his SDI program that March with the claim that it would make nuclear weapons obsolete, Soviet officials regarded it not only as a threat to strategic stability, but as a shield that would facilitate a devastating assault on the Soviet Union. As the KGB later summarized things: "With the aid of this system, the Americans expect to be able to ensure that United States territory is completely invulnerable to Soviet intercontinental ballistic missiles, which would enable the United States to count on mounting a nuclear attack on the Soviet Union with impunity." Consequently, as one official recalled, "the Soviet reaction was highly emotional," and the response emerged "not in a reasoned and careful way but in a tone approaching hysteria."[53] The announcement of SDI, of course, coincided with the approach of the U.S. deployment of cruise and Pershing missiles in Western Europe, which did nothing to ease Soviet fears. "If you look at the events that are taking place in the Western countries," Andropov told the Politburo that May, it is clear that "an anti-Soviet coalition is being formed," creating a "highly dangerous situation." That same month, Ustinov argued that "in the U.S., nuclear war is being shifted into a possible and, under some circumstances, expedient category." In July, the Central Committee secretly warned foreign Communist parties that "we are presently experiencing the destabilization of the entire system of interstate relations, the acceleration of the armaments race, and a serious increase of the danger of war." The installation of cruise and Pershing missiles, it insisted, would ensure "a qualitative advantage for the United States, which would give the USA the possibility of leading a nuclear first strike against our country."[54]

Thereafter, an atmosphere of panic enveloped the nation's leaders. On August 12, Kryuchkov ordered his KGB agents to be watchful for evidence of a surprise NATO nuclear attack. In September, Andropov issued an unusually strident public denunciation of the U.S. government, assailing the "dangerous, inhuman policies" of the Reagan administration and its "militarist course." The Defense Ministry produced a new film for Soviet television, filled with scenes of U.S. missiles and nuclear explosions and warning of war. After the U.S. invasion of Grenada in late October, Soviet Vice President Vasily Kuznetsov, well known in diplomatic circles for his cordiality, charged that U.S. leaders were "making delirious plans for world domination," thus "pushing mankind to the brink of disaster." In the Soviet press, attacks on Reagan reached their zenith, with the U.S. president depicted as a "madman," akin to Hitler. The jitters of the leadership were reinforced on September 26, when the Soviet Union's new launch-detection satellites reported that the U.S. government had fired its Minuteman intercontinental ballistic missiles, and that a nuclear attack upon the Soviet Union was underway. Fortunately, the duty officer in charge of the satellites concluded that they had malfunctioned and, on his own authority, prevented a Soviet nuclear alert. As a result of this incident, he suffered a nervous breakdown, ending his military career, and the nation's leadership went to sleep with the disconcerting knowledge that, on the verge of cruise and Pershing missile deployments, its missile-warning satellites were defective.[55]

That November, Soviet fears of U.S. nuclear aggression nearly propelled the two nations into a nuclear war. From November 2 to 11, 1983, the United States and its NATO allies conducted Able Archer 83, a nuclear training exercise that simulated a full-scale nuclear conflict, with NATO nuclear attacks upon 50,000 Soviet nuclear targets. Although NATO had held such exercises in the past, two things about this one caused the KGB particular alarm: the procedures and message formats for the transition from conventional to nuclear warfare had changed and there appeared to be altered patterns of officer movement and a suspicious radio silence. "In the tense atmosphere generated by the crises and rhetoric of the past few months," Gordievsky recalled, "the KGB concluded that American forces had been placed on alert—and might even have begun the countdown to nuclear war." Terrified that the U.S. government was using Able Archer as a cover behind which it was launching a nuclear attack upon the Soviet Union, the Soviet government alerted its own nuclear forces, readying them for war. Soviet nuclear-capable aircraft in Eastern Europe were placed on higher alert status, command staffs reviewed their strike missions, and nuclear weapons were readied for action. A U.S. government analyst recalled: "On the Soviet side, everyone from the Chief of the General Staff down to pilots and security guards knew that this was not a drill." The situation was particularly dangerous because Soviet military doctrine called for neutralizing an impending nuclear attack by striking enemy forces before it could be launched. However, once again, the crisis eased as it became clear that war was not imminent. "The world did not quite reach the edge of the nuclear abyss," Gordievsky concluded. "But during Able Archer 83 it had . . . come frighteningly close."[56]

Even thereafter, Soviet leaders remained extraordinarily apprehensive. In mid-December 1983, when Grinevsky visited the ailing Andropov at the hospital to report on arms control negotiations, the party secretary snapped: "Are you hoping to talk about trust with the Americans? What kind of trust could you talk to them about?" He continued: "The international situation is very tense. For the first time since the Caribbean Crisis [i.e. the Cuban missile crisis] the United States and the Soviet Union are going at it head on. The United States wants to change the existing strategic situation and they want to have the opportunity of striking the first strategic strike." In these circumstances, "we must have the slogan: 'Russia, concentrate, gather your strength.' If we are strong, we will be respected." Although Reagan delivered an important peace-oriented speech on January 16, 1984, designed to signal his willingness to come to an agreement with Soviet leaders, they reacted to it with bitterness and incredulity. Publicly, Gromyko denounced it as a "hackneyed ploy." Privately, he remarked that "Reagan and his team . . . are trying to destroy us."[57] Later that month, at a high-level KGB conference, Kryuchkov warned that the risk of nuclear war had reached "dangerous proportions," based on the Pentagon's "fantastic idea of world domination." As for Andropov, then on his deathbed, he "spent the last five months of his life," recalled Gordievsky, "as a morbidly suspicious invalid brooding over the possible approach of a nuclear Armageddon."[58]

Given this fear and suspicion of the United States that the Reagan administration's nuclear buildup engendered, Soviet officials decided that they could not possibly let down their guard. As had happened so many times during the Cold War, the hawks on one side bolstered the hawks on the other. "The hostility and militarism of American policy did nothing but create further obstacles on the road to reform," recalled Arbatov. "It posed additional threats to democratic change, justifying both the harsh regime within the country and new Soviet efforts to increase the size of our own military-industrial complex." Indeed, "the reaction to America's military buildup brought out a real Frankenstein monster, which got out of control." Dobrynin recalled that, as Reagan's military buildup manifested itself, "the inclination grew inside the Kremlin not to pacify him but to fight back." Thus, "the impact of Reagan's hard-line policy on the internal debates in the Kremlin and on the evolution of the Soviet leadership was exactly the opposite from the one intended by Washington. It strengthened those in the Politburo, the Central Committee, and the security apparatus who had been pressing for a mirror-image of Reagan's own policy." Reviewing the record of that era, George Kennan, the Soviet policy specialist and former head of the State Department's policy planning staff, drew a similar conclusion. "The general effect of Cold war extremism," he wrote, "was to delay rather than hasten the great change that overtook the Soviet Union at the end of the 1980s."[59] In this fashion, the West's nuclear "strength" did not encourage peace but, ironically, Soviet nuclear "strength."

Eastern Europe

Somewhat greater dissent from the East bloc's nuclear buildup emerged among the Soviet Union's junior partners in Eastern Europe. The East German government, particularly, was dismayed by the plans to install nuclear missiles in both halves of Germany, which provided a near guarantee that the German people would be annihilated in a future nuclear war. Given the independent agitation against nuclear weapons in East Germany, the authorities were also well aware that its citizenry was uneasy about the presence of the missiles. "The GDR leadership was not amused" by the missile installation, recalled Peter Steglich, an East German diplomat who handled European security policy. It was "seriously interested in a big solution between the two superpowers." Thus, among East German officials, there arose the idea: "Let's make a first step. We could withdraw it if the other side is not willing to follow it." This position "created really serious problems for us with the Soviet Union, because they couldn't understand that the GDR was against establishing missiles on the territory of the GDR." Given their subordinate relationship to the Russians, the East Germans never dared to make a formal proposal along these lines. Indeed, the party leadership did not even know what nuclear weapons the Russians maintained in the GDR. Even so, party leader Erich Honecker subtly carved out a position independent from that of the Soviet line on the Euromissiles. As the Soviet negotiators walked out of the Geneva conference, he appealed for "limiting the damage" of the NATO missile deployment and implicitly criticized Soviet intransigence by remarking: "It is better to negotiate ten times than to shoot once."[60]

Other East bloc countries, too, distanced themselves from the Soviet hard line, especially during 1983–84. Although Soviet officials first touched upon possible military countermeasures to NATO missile deployment in May 1983, a Warsaw Pact summit conference the following month unexpectedly failed to produce the announcement. That October, months after the Russians had decided to withdraw from the Geneva conference in the event of Western missile deployment during November—indeed, the same day Moscow broadcast Andropov's statement announcing the decision—the Czech Federal Assembly called for a continuation of the INF talks past the end of the year. After the Soviet government had announced plans for installation of new nuclear missiles in East Germany and Czechoslovakia, a December 1983 meeting of Warsaw Pact defense ministers failed to endorse it. In March 1984, when the Czech *Rude Pravo* criticized unnamed Warsaw Pact nations for deviating from the Soviet line, the Hungarian party organ, *Magyar Hirlap,* responded that Soviet bloc nations "could still play a semi-independent role, especially in helping to maintain a dialogue with the West when the two major protagonists . . . had argued themselves into deadlock." The Hungarian government also reportedly fought hard at Warsaw Pact meetings to ensure that new missiles were not placed on its territory. Not surprisingly, Rumania, long an East bloc gadfly, criticized the missile deployments. But even normally obedient Bulgaria expressed dismay at the new Soviet counter-deployments.[61]

Other Nations

Other nations—usually nonaligned in the Cold War—emerged as even more important actors in the antinuclear struggle, with Sweden often leading the way. Speaking at the U.N. conference on disarmament at Geneva in June

1983, Maj Britt Theorin, who handled disarmament affairs for the recently elected Social Democratic government of Olof Palme, presented a plan for a comprehensive nuclear test ban treaty. That same month, Palme delivered an address to the North Atlantic Assembly meeting that called for a nuclear weapons–free corridor in Europe and a nuclear-free zone in the Nordic region. In 1984, the Swedish government reiterated its demand for a halt to nuclear testing and urged a nuclear weapons freeze. Calling attention to the millions of West Europeans who had demonstrated against the cruise, Pershing and SS-20 missiles in the fall of 1983, Theorin argued that "the Euromissiles and the idea of a limited nuclear war have created strong involvement and resistance in the churches, in trade unions, in many professional groups and in other popular movements. None of the major European political parties (except in France) have been able to avoid the impact of this broad-based public opinion." This was "fortunate," she argued, for "belief in the blessings of the balance of terror is a creed, a dogma—and a dangerous one" and had "brought the world to the verge of destruction." If the superpowers really wanted to disarm, an assumption that Theorin thought "open to serious question," then "the threat of, or plans for, increasing armaments is the wrong way to promote disarmament." Instead, she championed confidence-building and security-building measures, limitations on military research and development, a nuclear weapons freeze, a treaty to counteract plans for weapons in outer space, a nuclear-free corridor in Central Europe and nuclear-free zones, and an agreement on no first use of nuclear weapons.[62]

These efforts found a broader framework within the Five Continent Peace Initiative. Beginning in January 1983, Parliamentarians for World Order, a peace-oriented organization of elected legislators from more than thirty countries, had sought to develop a new approach to nuclear disarmament. Deeply disturbed by the Soviet-American deadlock and working closely with nuclear disarmament organizations, they decided to put together a "small but prestigious group of national leaders" who "could act as an effective third party between the superpowers." With the assistance of Indira Gandhi, then the chair of the Group of Non-Aligned Nations, the organizers traveled from country to country, meeting with national officials and nuclear disarmament group representatives. On May 22, 1984, the heads of state of six nations—Raul Alfonsin of Argentina, Miguel de la Madrid of Mexico, Julius Nyerere of Tanzania, Olof Palme of Sweden, Indira Gandhi of India, and Andreas Papandreou of Greece—formally launched the Five Continent Peace Initiative, calling on the nuclear states "to halt all testing, production, and deployment of nuclear weapons and their delivery systems, to be immediately followed by substantial reductions in nuclear forces." Although Gandhi was assassinated that January, the group's efforts continued, with her son, Rajiv Gandhi, the new Indian prime minister, replacing her. Meeting in Delhi in January 1985, they reiterated their 1984 appeal, but then zeroed in on two additional steps which "today require special attention: the prevention of an arms race in outer space, and a comprehensive test ban treaty." Alfonsin, Nyerere, and Palme immediately flew on to Athens, where Papandreou hosted a meeting of national officials and representatives of IPPNW, the Nuclear Weapons Freeze Campaign, Greenpeace, British CND, IKV, and other nuclear disarmament groups supporting the Five Continent Initiative. "The battle of the streets," insisted the Greek prime minister, "has become the battle of the governments."[63]

Certainly, plenty of governments now publicly adopted the nuclear disarmament campaign's position. Lobbied hard by the antinuclear movement, the United Nations General Assembly passed a variety of Nuclear Freeze resolutions by overwhelming margins. In December 1982, a Mexican-Swedish Freeze proposal, which came closest to the Nuclear Weapons Freeze Campaign's language, called upon the United States and the Soviet Union "to proclaim, either through simultaneous unilateral declarations or through a joint resolution, an immediate nuclear arms freeze" as a first step toward total nuclear disarmament. India sponsored a second Freeze proposal that December, which urged a multilateral Freeze on the production of nuclear weapons and fissionable materials. The General Assembly passed both measures by lopsided votes, with broad support coming from nonaligned nations and the Soviet bloc. Opposition came from the United States and most Western nations, although Greece voted in favor and Denmark and Iceland abstained. China opposed the Mexican-Swedish resolution and abstained on the Indian resolution. This general pattern persisted for years thereafter. Western opposition, however, eroded until, by 1986, a Freeze resolution proposed by Mexico drew the support of Australia, Denmark, Greece, New Zealand, and Norway.[64] In this fashion, the agenda of the antinuclear campaign gradually moved toward the center stage of global politics.

U.S. Policy

The Hard Line Softens, 1981-85

> If things get hotter and hotter and arms control remains
> an issue, maybe I should go see Andropov and propose
> eliminating all nuclear weapons.
>
> Ronald Reagan, 1983

The U.S. government faced a major dilemma in dealing with the nuclear crisis of the early 1980s. Ronald Reagan and his entourage had come into office committed to sponsoring a nuclear buildup and to escaping from the constraints of arms control and disarmament agreements. Furthermore, during the early 1980s, they could see little sign of a change in the Soviet military policy that had frightened them into their drive for a substantially expanded Western nuclear arsenal. On the other hand, administration officials were sensitive to the growing public revolt against the nuclear arms race and, particularly, to two key constituencies through which it brought pressure to bear on them: West European governments and the U.S. Congress. Both constituencies had significant points of leverage. As Strobe Talbott, *Time* magazine's astute analyst of nuclear weapons issues, pointed out: "The Europeans could block the deployment of new missiles in Europe; the Congress could thwart the administration's ambitious plans to build up the nation's strategic defenses." And "in the longer run, of course, the American electorate could even deny Reagan reelection in 1984."[1] In these difficult circumstances, the Reagan administration—and particularly the President and the secretary of state—began to soften U.S. policy in response to the pressures generated by the antinuclear campaign. This transformation of U.S. policy, beginning in late 1981 and accelerating thereafter, was not always evident to the public or to the Kremlin, given the early hawkish pronouncements of the Reaganites and the President's later lapses into confrontational rhetoric. Nevertheless, an important policy reversal occurred. Pressed by antinuclear opinion and in the face of Soviet intransigence, Reagan gradually scrapped his hard line and began to emerge as a nuclear disarmer.

Establishing the Zero Option

The first intimations that the public outcry against nuclear weapons was having an effect emerged in early 1981, during the intra-administration debate over U.S. policy toward the Euromissiles. Under pressure from West European leaders to resume INF negotiations, the Reagan administration divided sharply over the issue. National Security Advisor Richard Allen and his aides argued that the United States should not accept "blackmail" and "pressure tactics" from Western Europe. Weinberger, too, complained that he was fed up with European "moaning and groaning." The State Department, on the other hand, pressed for an early resumption of negotiations. Although Haig was eager to have the cruise and Pershing missiles deployed, as secretary of state he recognized the importance of holding nuclear arms talks to satisfy America's NATO allies. Reagan recalled: "Partly because of concerns in West Germany and European countries, where there was growing political sentiment in favor of unilateral disarmament, Al Haig wanted to go to the arms control bargaining table with the Russians fairly soon." Ultimately, Reagan agreed to accommodate the West Europeans and, that May, after a visit from Schmidt, who once again stressed the political imperative of arms control talks, he issued a communiqué committing himself to "execute both elements of the NATO resolution of December 1979 and to give them equal weight."[2]

But what negotiating position would the administration adopt? The initial winner in the bureaucratic battle was the Pentagon's leading theoretician and hawk, Richard Perle, who convinced the administration to adopt the zero option: the removal of all Soviet intermediate range nuclear weapons from Europe and Asia in exchange for a U.S. promise not to deploy the cruise and Pershing missiles. Haig objected that this was "not negotiable," and, furthermore, would "generate the suspicion that the United States was only interested in a frivolous propaganda exercise or, worse, that it was disingenuously engaging in arms negotiations simply as a cover for a desire to build up its nuclear arsenal." But, as Perle was less than eager to secure arms control agreements on Western INF missiles or other nuclear weapons that might be built and deployed by the United States, he did not see nonnegotiability as a drawback at all. Weinberger, his boss, was initially skeptical about the zero option because—as Perle recalled—"he was afraid that the Soviets would accept it," thus precluding the deployment of the U.S. missiles. However, he soon came around, concluding that the zero option would lead eventually to missile deployment.[3]

Other administration officials, too, have insisted that this initial U.S. position in the INF negotiations was crafted to trigger Soviet rejection and, thus, guarantee deployment of the U.S. missiles. Thomas Graham of ACDA remembered that the zero option "was adopted because it was believed the Soviets would never accept it. It was a formula for stalemate. . . . The real reason that we proposed it" was "to make sure that those negotiations did not succeed, and the deployments would go ahead." Douglas MacEachin, a top CIA official, reported that he knew "from firsthand knowledge that some of the people who designed our zero solution to INF designed it believing that they had come up with a proposal which would not get a yes" from the Russians and "would therefore make it possible to deploy the missiles."[4] Not surprisingly, National Security Decision Directive 15, which laid out the "zero option" formula as U.S. policy, had no fallback position for U.S. arms control negotiators.[5] The Russians would have to take it or, hopefully, leave it.

But there was a second factor behind the Reagan administration's adoption of the zero option: its propaganda value at this time of antinuclear upheaval. "My proposal of the . . . zero option sprang out of the realities of nuclear politics in Western Europe," recalled Reagan. "Now that I was in office and the American-made INF missiles were being scheduled for shipment to Europe, some European leaders were having doubts about the policy. . . . Thousands of Europeans were taking to the streets and protesting." Consequently, "I decided to propose the zero . . . plan." Edwin Meese, counselor to the President, remembered: "There was a tremendous Soviet-inspired and Soviet-funded antinuclear movement in Europe. So the zero option did several things: 1) it carried out one of our primary objectives; 2) it was useful in defusing to some extent the antinuclear sentiment . . . ; and 3) it provided a proper counter-argument or counter-offensive from a propaganda standpoint." According to Reagan, Weinberger, too, argued that the zero option would "put the Soviets on the defensive in the European propaganda war."[6] Analyzing the decision, McFarlane later stated: "You had to have a plausible basis for advocating the [U.S. deployment] program, and the most plausible is that you're willing to do away with it. So the zero option was key to dealing with that popular, street-level criticism." On November 18, 1981, when Reagan unveiled the zero option in a public address, he did it at an hour designed to maximize its impact upon a European audience.[7]

As fate would have it, the State Department's Richard Burt was having a drink that evening with END's Mary Kaldor. He told her, with a chuckle: "We got the idea of the 'zero option' from your banners—the ones that say 'No cruise, no Pershing, no SS-20.'" Burt apparently thought there was a nice irony to this fact.[8] And there was. After all, the Reagan administration—ferociously hostile to nuclear arms control and disarmament—had just adopted a core position of its critics, albeit as a means of undermining their influence and providing the U.S. government with a convenient justification for its nuclear buildup. But, like the administration's shift toward an antinuclear rhetoric, it was altogether too clever. For what if the Soviet government, confounding all expectations, actually agreed to accept the American proposal, thus opening the way for the removal of all intermediate range nuclear missiles from Europe? Would the U.S. government—more comfortable with installing the missiles than with creating a non-nuclear Europe—be able to walk away from its own proposal? At the time, of course, Soviet acceptance seemed highly unlikely. But, in only a few years, the situation would change profoundly.

Compromise in the INF Negotiations

In the meantime, the Reagan administration—under continuous pressure from its NATO allies and from public opinion—began to gravitate toward softening its INF proposal. "We took our allies very seriously," recalled General Rowny, the former chief U.S. arms control negotiator, "and at times . . . they were a handicap. They didn't always agree with us. The first big issue, of course, was whether or not they would take Pershing missiles on their soil. A lot of propaganda had been raised and there were also a lot of opposition movements. . . . At times we said the Soviets are easy and the allies are the problem." Paul Nitze, who handled the INF negotiations for the U.S. government, was particularly unsettled by the extent of West European resistance. Aside from the absence of a military necessity for the Pershing missiles, he wrote in his memoirs, "what also bothered me about the missile decision was its divisive effect on European public opinion, especially West German opinion. Not only did it give the so-called peace movement a ready-made issue; it also threatened to undermine the fragile consensus on defense issues that the West German political parties had struggled so painstakingly to develop and maintain for two decades or more."[9] Indeed, Schmidt warned him that unless there was real progress in the INF negotiations by the fall of 1982, West European support for cruise and Pershing missile deployment would crumble, as would support for U.S. policy more generally. Thus, in July 1982, to break the deadlock at the Geneva negotiations, Nitze took unauthorized action—a walk in the woods with his Soviet counterpart, Yuli Kvitsinsky, to work out "a joint package entailing concessions by both sides." Ignoring the apparently non-negotiable zero option, the two men agreed to present to their respective governments a plan to scrap the deployment of Pershing missiles in exchange for substantial reduction in Soviet SS-20s, thus leaving both nations with roughly equivalent INF forces in Europe.[10]

Ultimately, the Reagan administration rejected Nitze's "walk in the woods" formula, but not without a lengthy internal battle. Leading the charge against the proposal, Perle called Nitze's initiative "an act of intellectual and political cowardice." Following Perle's lead, Weinberger also launched a withering attack upon it. By contrast, the State Department and ACDA liked the "walk in the woods" proposal, and argued in its behalf.[11] Perle recalled: "People who thought it was urgent that we get an agreement naturally wanted to offer terms more to the Soviet liking. But those of us who were indifferent as to whether we got an agreement . . . were happy to wait." The President himself ultimately sided with the Pentagon. Impressed by the fact that the Pershings were "fast-flyers," he did not like the idea of canceling plans for their deployment. Thus, in September 1982, Reagan ruled against Nitze's compromise proposal.[12]

But other compromises had greater viability. Appointed secretary of state in mid-1982, George Shultz found himself at loggerheads with the Pentagon, the CIA, and the NSC in their inflexible approach toward the Soviet Union and arms control negotiations. Shultz thought their attitude not only poor diplomacy, but bad politics, especially in the context of dovish pressures from America's protest-rattled NATO allies. That October, he complained to one of his aides that Weinberger "thinks the allies are like the air traffic controllers," whom Reagan had recently fired. "But we can't fire the allies. We need them." Meanwhile, Nitze, back in Washington at the end of the year, emphasized the importance of antinuclear protest. "We have a political problem in Europe," he told a State Department meeting. "A considerable percentage of European public opinion is not satisfied with our zero-zero position." In Nitze's view, the United States had to begin "exploring an equitable solution above zero."[13] Shultz adopted this idea as well. After meetings with allied leaders, he spoke personally with the President on December 20, telling him that, although zero should remain the "ultimate goal," it was "inevitable" that "we propose intermediate possible outcomes." On December 31, Shultz recalled, he informed Reagan that "our negotiating posture in the coming year would be absolutely crucial. Our allies could not withstand the heat of political pressure against the installation of our INF missiles unless we, at the same time, were advancing reasonable and stabilizing arms control positions at the negotiating table." By early January 1983, the President had begun to retreat, remarking that he was growing worried about "getting too dug in on zero."[14]

The result was what became known as the "interim solution." It provided that, without discarding zero INF weapons as the final goal, the U.S. government would reduce its planned deployments if the Soviet Union would cut back its INF missiles to an equal level.[15] As this outcome seemed far more negotiable with the Russians than did the zero option—and, therefore, would block the deployment of the full complement of U.S. missiles—the more hawkish members of the administration fought ferociously to prevent it from becoming U.S. policy. Perle waged a tough, rearguard campaign, going so far as to argue that the European antinuclear movement had "a stake in U.S. policy as long as we are negotiating toward a zero outcome. Once we give up zero and say we're willing to settle for something other than zero," he added, "the peace movement in Western Europe will be disheartened; their stake in our policy will evaporate" and "the political situation will be worse." However, as there was no indication that the antinuclear movement felt any identification with U.S. policy, this argument carried little weight. In a memo to the President on January 18, 1983, Shultz used the issue of antinuclear sentiment to far greater effect. Predicting that the Soviets would "redouble their appeals to Western publics on issues such as INF," the secretary of state argued that the U.S. government must "win the battle for public opinion by making clear that it is the USSR, not the U.S., that is impeding progress toward agreements." A display of U.S. flexibility had become imperative. Thus, on March 30, 1983, with what Shultz termed "strong support from our NATO allies and Japan," Reagan announced the interim solution.[16]

The Olive Branches of 1983-85

As Soviet-American relations deteriorated, nuclear arms control negotiations stagnated, and antinuclear demonstrations escalated, the Reagan administration—and particularly the President—grew increasingly defensive, as well as increasingly dovish. In July 1983, responding to a letter from Andropov, Reagan personally drafted a response that included a call for the elimination of all nuclear weapons. Horrified by this suggestion, National

Security Advisor Clark and other foreign policy experts at the White House convinced the President to delete this section. Nonetheless, his final message, dated July 11, was an exceptionally friendly one.[17] Reagan and Shultz also refrained from breaking off nuclear arms control negotiations in response to the dramatic Soviet destruction of a Korean airliner in September 1983. In mid-October, Shultz told Reagan that "the absence of dialogue" between the U.S. and Soviet governments was "causing worry both here and among the allies." Consequently, they arranged that Shultz would meet with Soviet officials in the United States and in Europe. Reagan remarked that, "if things get hotter and hotter and arms control remains an issue, maybe I should go see Andropov and propose eliminating all nuclear weapons." Shultz, though, like the President's other advisors, dissuaded him from acting on what he considered an awful idea. By November, the administration was clearly on edge. It found the Soviet response to the Able Archer exercise deeply disconcerting—so much so that McFarlane intervened to reassure the Russians by altering its character. And the deployment of the cruise and Pershing missiles amid widespread protests and a Soviet walkout from the arms control talks produced what Shultz called "gut-wrenching moments."[18]

In this crisis atmosphere, the administration made a further shift toward accommodation with the Soviet Union. Shultz recalled that there was increasing "public alarm, both in Western Europe and America. We were feeling political pressure against our continuing INF deployment and for concessions to the Soviets. . . . We could not leave matters as they stood." The U.S. government had to demonstrate "a readiness to negotiate." Reagan too, remarked that the collapse of the Geneva arms control talks "understandably worried many in the world who were anxious for the superpowers to begin the process of nuclear disarmament" and, as a result, there were "calls from people in Europe and the United States to . . . suspend deployment of the INF missiles." Thus, "from a propaganda point of view, we were on the defensive."[19] Accordingly, the administration gravitated toward a plan for Reagan's delivery of a major "peace" address. Assigned to draft it, Jack Matlock, a Soviet affairs specialist recently added to the NSC staff, recalled that "a significant segment of the Western public worried that the Reagan administration was risking nuclear war by its unwillingness to compromise. It would be useful, therefore, to make clear to our public as well as the Soviet leadership that we wanted to negotiate on a fair basis." Reagan was determined to go even further and speak about building a non-nuclear world. Although Shultz and other administration officials, disconcerted by the prospect of nuclear abolition, discouraged this approach, the President ignored their objections. His only compromise was to postpone delivery of the speech from December 1983 to January 1984, a month when his wife's astrologer expected more auspicious results.[20]

Consequently, on January 16, 1984, Reagan delivered an important policy address that, for a hawkish administration, conveyed a remarkably dovish message. The new year, he predicted, would be a time "of opportunities for peace." The United States was "determined to deal with our differences peacefully through negotiations. We're prepared . . . to work for practical, fair solutions on the basis of mutual compromise. We will never retreat from negotiations." The United States and the Soviet Union had "common interests and the foremost among them is to avoid war and reduce the level of arms," Reagan insisted. Indeed, "I support a zero option for all nuclear arms. . . . My dream is to see the day when nuclear weapons will be banished from the face of the earth."[21] Although it is possible to view this speech as no more than the latest instance in the administration's rhetorical makeover, numerous U.S. officials have contended that it was sincere and meant to be taken seriously—not only by the public, but by Soviet leaders. Advance copies were delivered to Soviet Ambassador Dobrynin, Soviet Foreign Minister Gromyko, and to the Soviet Foreign Ministry. In a subsequent conversation with Gromyko, Shultz made a point of underscoring its importance. According to Matlock, the speech was designed to signal the President's willingness to end the Cold War, and its specific proposals were made "as accommodating as possible." Administration officials did not think that nuclear arms control was "the central issue," Matlock recalled, but that "was where all the public attention in our country was."[22]

The approach of the 1984 presidential election made Reagan's peace offensive all the more imperative. In the fall of 1983, Reagan's pollster, Richard Wirthlin, warned him that, with the economy improving, foreign policy had become his most serious political liability. A poll in early September showed that 51 percent of the public disapproved of how he handled it, and the likely Democratic nominees would undoubtedly attack him on the peace issue. As a result, the President's official campaign plan, drawn up by Wirthlin, argued that "some progress in negotiating an arms settlement" would be helpful in fortifying "the claim that the Reagan administration has maintained the peace." The White House also recognized that a summit meeting with Soviet leaders would bolster's Reagan's peaceful image; but, despite administration efforts, this proved impossible to arrange. Soviet leaders were not eager to enhance Reagan's re-election prospects. Furthermore, they died rapidly.[23] Even worse, from the administration's standpoint, was the fact that, during an August 1984 sound check before a radio speech, a joke that Reagan made about bombing the Soviet Union was picked up by the microphones and, thereafter, made into a public issue.[24] Serious repair efforts followed. Reagan gave a conciliatory speech to the U.N. General Assembly that September and, as Shultz noted, "there was not a word of criticism of the Soviet Union from the cold warrior." On September 28, with Mondale lambasting Reagan for never having held a summit meeting with a Soviet leader, the President's advisors brought Gromyko to the White House, where he was received by the President with great fanfare and a battery of reporters and photographers from around the world. Reagan's actions, however, ran deeper than public relations. At a secret NSC meeting ten days before, Weinberger took a hawkish stance on the content of discussions with the Soviet leader, only to be rebuffed by the President, who insisted: "We must follow the Gromyko meeting with specifics and make concessions."[25]

Even after Reagan's re-election, the administration felt pressured to alter its nuclear policy and, in response, continued the retreat from its early hawkish approach. Meeting with the President on November 14, 1984, Shultz told him bluntly that Congress "will not support key weapons systems without meaningful negotiations. Similarly, allied support will be problematic if arms control efforts unravel." In this context, "extreme positions and inflexibility will not enhance our position, but undermine it." Although he and the President saw eye to eye on the need "to engage with the Soviets and to achieve arms control agreements," Shultz insisted, Weinberger, Casey, and Kirkpatrick were blocking the way. In response to Shultz's threat to resign unless the situation were remedied, Reagan spoke personally to these leading hardliners and, thereafter, told Shultz that they would not cause him difficulties in the future. Shultz did encounter further difficulties, especially with Weinberger, but the President's views, as Shultz recalled, had become "definite: all nuclear weapons should be eliminated." In fact, "he was annoyed at me for expressing reservations." At a meeting of top U.S. national security officials in early 1985, the secretary of state told them that nuclear abolition was now Reagan's position and urged them to "think more about the theme of elimination of nuclear weapons. Everyone thinks it is rhetoric, but rhetoric said often enough by important people tends to wind up with an operational character to it."[26]

That same month, State Department officials managed to get Soviet negotiators back to Geneva to consider the resumption of serious nuclear arms control talks. For the U.S. participants, the political dynamics were clear enough. ACDA's director, Kenneth Adelman, recalled, scornfully: "Secretary Shultz wanted to succeed. He knew his boss, our boss, wanted to succeed; and so did the rest of us. . . . To leave Geneva without resuming the talks would lead to more accusations of Reagan's undying hostility toward the 'evil empire.' Worse yet," as the assistant secretary of state "never stopped emphasizing, were this meeting to break up without even setting the date for another such meeting, the Allies would have conniptions." Given such pressure, as well as a renewed Soviet interest in negotiations, the Soviet and American participants agreed that the two governments would resume nuclear arms control talks in early March 1985. The President was delighted.[27]

Strategic Weapons and Strategic Arms Talks

External pressures also modified the administration's strategic nuclear options. As part of what Reagan called his plan to "regain and sustain a military superiority over the Soviet Union," he had called for a substantial strategic nuclear buildup. This included the construction of large numbers of B-1 (renamed B-1B) bombers, MX (renamed Peacekeeper) intercontinental ballistic missiles, Trident nuclear submarines, and Stealth bombers. But a combination of the antinuclear movement and Congress clipped the wings of this ambitious nuclear program. Only 50 MX missiles, 100 B-1 bombers, and 9 Trident submarines were ever built—a relatively modest addition to the U.S. striking force of thousands of strategic nuclear weapons. Nor were they deployed in time to save the United States from the dreaded Soviet nuclear blackmail or from attack by an allegedly stronger Soviet Union. By 1986, years after the administration's claim of a "window of vulnerability" had been voiced and discarded, there existed no operational MX missiles and only a handful of B-1 bombers.[28] Interviewed on television at the end of 1985, Paul Nitze was asked if he could say which nation then had nuclear superiority. "I'm *sure* I can," he responded gloomily. "The Soviets do in fact have nuclear superiority today." Recalling the situation in 1985, Shultz remarked: "The problem was that the Soviets were able to turn out big and accurate intercontinental ballistic missiles with nuclear warheads, and they were well ahead of us in making them mobile and therefore able to survive an attack from us." He concluded: "Given the political climate in the United States, we could not keep pace in modernization, production, and deployment of these deadly weapons." Or, as McFarlane lamented: "Congress would never let us" build enough missiles, while "the Soviets could build missile after missile . . . without any concern for congressional restraint."[29]

What had happened to the Reagan nuclear buildup? In fact, the administration had requested only 100 B-1 bombers, and it secured the necessary congressional authorization and appropriations for all of them without much of a battle. The problem with deploying these aircraft, each costing $300 million, resulted from their unsatisfactory performance, including crashes by three of them. At the time, it was estimated that their most serious malfunction would not be corrected until at least 1990.[30] In this case, at least, the administration was not foiled by public pressure or by Congress but, rather, by the shoddy nature of the products churned out at the behest of the nation's military-industrial complex.

The real heart of the U.S. strategic buildup was the MX missile. Among the sea, air, and land-based components of America's nuclear strategy, the Reagan administration considered the land-based the most significant and, also, the area in which the United States lagged dangerously behind the Soviet Union. By building the MX missile, a heavyweight ICBM, each of which carried ten nuclear warheads, the administration planned to secure a dramatic upgrading of this land-based system. In the words of National Security Decision Directive 69, the MX missile was "absolutely essential," and its development should be "completed on a priority basis." According to McFarlane: "We were determined to promote it as a centerpiece of the Reagan doctrine's emphasis on restoring our own military strength, a prerequisite to confronting . . . the Soviet Union." But, as he noted, the MX provided "a natural target for liberals and nuclear freeze proponents." Consequently, "as was to be expected, these opponents raised a hue and cry over the missile that reverberated loudly on Capitol Hill."[31]

In fact, the battle in Congress over the MX went remarkably badly for the administration, with antinuclear groups and their legislative allies putting up a strong and effective resistance. Given congressional division over Carter's proposal for 200 MX missiles, as well as opposition from GOP leaders in the proposed basing states, the Reaganites decided at an early date to drop the controversial "race track" basing mode for the MX and to substitute another, dubbed Big Bird—a scheme to place the missiles on airplanes. When this, too, failed to win congressional approval, the Pentagon came up with yet another MX basing mode, called Dense Pack. Endorsed by the President, it would cluster the MX missiles so close together that, according to its proponents, the attacking Soviet ICBMs would destroy each other via "fratricide." Congress, however, was no more impressed by this scheme than by its predecessors. In December 1982, by an overwhelming vote, it denied all funding for production of the MX missile.[32] This was a stunning defeat—the first time in the postwar era that Congress had refused any President a major nuclear weapon. In Adelman's words, the MX had become a "dog, the strategic albatross of the Reagan administration . . . with the President and the Secretaries of State and Defense doling out staggering political capital each time merely to keep this dubious project alive."[33]

Even thereafter, congressional opposition seriously curbed the MX program. To save it from total defeat, the Reagan administration appointed a bipartisan, blue ribbon panel, headed by General Brent Scowcroft. In the spring of 1983, the Scowcroft commission delivered a cautiously crafted proposal, clearly designed to serve as a compromise with nuclear critics. Under its terms, the number of missiles would be cut from 200 to 100, and the basing problem would be solved by placing them in the old Minuteman ICBM silos—an implicit recognition of the fact that the nation's strategic nuclear forces were less vulnerable to Soviet attack than the Reagan administration had contended.[34] Although these compromise positions, now advanced by the administration, peeled away some legislative opposition, the MX proposal still experienced remarkably rough going in Congress. In 1984, in a series of key House votes, no more than six votes separated supporters and opponents of the missile program, and the key vote in the Senate was 48 to 48, with Vice President Bush breaking the tie. Moreover, by 1985, congressional opponents of the MX had managed to cut back the number of missiles authorized to only 50. And here the program remained—at 25 percent of the original request.[35] Leaders of the antinuclear campaign regarded this as a victory, while Reagan administration officials regarded it as a defeat.[36]

Furthermore, to secure even this truncated nuclear buildup, the administration was forced to embark upon strategic nuclear arms control negotiations—negotiations that, given the Reaganites' initial disdain for nuclear arms controls, had been far from assured. As McFarlane put it, in order to build strategic weapons, "you had to have appropriations, and to get them you needed political support, and that meant that you had to have an arms control policy worthy of the name." Although the President mentioned START in the fall of 1981, the administration managed to avoid opening strategic arms negotiations until the spring of 1982, when growing congressional interest in the Freeze and hostility to the MX set the wheels in motion. In a message to the White House, Rostow urged the administration to "combine the decision about starting START with the problem of the 'freeze' resolutions."[37] Early that May, as the Reaganites belatedly hammered out their START position, the *New York Times* reported that, according to Washington officials, "the administration's main concern is to go on record quickly with a simple and comprehensible plan to show that the Reagan team is for peace, thus taking some of the steam out of the nuclear freeze movements in Europe and the United States." Concerned about the growth of the Freeze movement, James Baker, White House chief of staff, pressed for a U.S. START proposal that would be "reasonable-looking." Reagan, too, remarked that he could not afford to subject himself to the charge that "we aren't serious about wanting an agreement." In his instructions to the chair of the U.S. START delegation, the President reminded him that strategic weapons cutbacks would "greatly reduce the nuclear anxiety that has become such a conspicuous feature of public concern throughout the world."[38]

Despite this sudden flurry of efforts to project an image of the Reagan administration as a champion of strategic arms controls, Perle, Weinberger, and other administration hawks won the first round. The U.S. negotiating proposal, announced by Reagan in mid-May 1982, would sharply reduce the number of Soviet ICBMs while setting no limits upon the planned U.S. strategic buildup. Like the administration's initial INF proposal, the first START proposal was, in effect, non-negotiable, and was strongly criticized as such by the State Department. Reagan liked it, however, for it was relatively simple and, if adopted, would certainly reduce the Soviet nuclear threat to the United States. Apparently he did not realize that ICBMs comprised 75 percent of the Soviet strategic nuclear force and only 25 percent of the American, and, therefore, that the demand for deep cuts in these weapons virtually guaranteed Soviet rejection of the American position. General Rowny's appointment as chief START negotiator, as Talbott noted, "provided further assurance that the negotiations would go nowhere." He sat in Geneva "out-frowning, out-waiting, out-stonewalling the Soviets. It was a role for which he was well suited and in which he seemed to take satisfaction."[39]

Nevertheless, to save the MX program from total destruction at the hands of congressional critics, the administration sharply altered its START proposals the next year. Reporting on the congressional attitude toward the MX in April 1983, McFarlane pointed out that two leading Senate moderates, Sam Nunn (D-Ga.) and William Cohen (R-Me.), had stated that "we just don't believe Ronald Reagan wants an arms control agreement." McFarlane added, gloomily: "Their perception is widely shared on the Hill." Somewhat later that year, joined by another group of moderates—Representatives Les Aspin (D-Wis.), Albert Gore, Jr. (D-Tenn.) and Norman Dicks (D-Wash.) and Senator Charles Percy (R-Ill.)—they threatened to oppose the MX unless Reagan shifted his stance on the START talks to a more negotiable position. By October, desperate for support in the MX struggle, Reagan had agreed to their demands and, accordingly, announced that Rowny would return to the Geneva talks with a "major initiative" from the administration.[40]

In this fashion, an arms control–oriented Congress stepped in and co-erced the Reagan administration into a adopting a more accommodating po-sition at the START talks. Kenneth Duberstein, who handled congressional affairs for the White House at the time, told the National Security Council, as he recalled, that "the best method to win MX support had to be our credibility on arms control." Scowcroft, also at that meeting, "spoke in the same vein." And "the President was very much prepared to go in that direc-tion, to go forward on arms control initiatives." According to Duberstein, it was the first time Congress had "had a major role in the formulation of an arms control policy for the United States." Although not happy about the changes in the administration's START position, Perle agreed that congres-sional pressure had been decisive. The administration's START proposals reflected "attitudes in Congress toward modernization, and funding of the modernization program," he recalled. Through START, "we were seen to be doing something. There was a general desire for reduction, and those were reductions." Deputy Secretary of Defense Frank Carlucci also saw a clear link between congressional resistance to the administration's strategic weapons program and the U.S. negotiating position at Geneva. "Our diffi-culty in deploying the MX," he concluded, "tended to drive the arms control process."[41]

The Strategic Defense Initiative

What, then, accounts for the emergence in 1983 of Reagan's Strategic De-fense Initiative? From the outset, SDI was perceived by opponents as a hawkish, isolationist, and risky program—and with some justification. After Senator Kennedy denounced it as "a reckless Star Wars scheme," the name caught on, at least among its many critics. In the Soviet view, by building a shield against incoming missiles, the United States was preparing itself to conduct a first strike. Thus, SDI not only encouraged a Soviet missile buildup to ensure the credibility of the Soviet nuclear deterrent, but en-hanced the possibility of the Soviet government launching a pre-emptive nuclear attack. From the allied standpoint, SDI raised the specter of decou-pling the United States from Western Europe, leaving the latter to face the Soviet Union on its own while the United States hid behind its missile de-fense system.[42] Nor was SDI, as the administration claimed, a non-nuclear program. The version promoted by the scientist Edward Teller, who had helped to mobilize the President behind SDI, relied upon exploding nuclear weapons to power the U.S. destruction of incoming missiles. Furthermore, it was far from certain that the President's proposal to build an invulnerable shield was technologically feasible. A poll of members of the National Academy of Sciences revealed that an overwhelming majority denied the possibility of developing a cost-effective system of defending the populace against missile attack in the foreseeable future. Finally, by providing the United States with the illusion of a defense against nuclear attack, SDI undermined the case for nuclear arms control and disarmament.[43]

Yet, Reagan's decision to champion SDI was based upon more than a drive for U.S. military supremacy. Although the Pentagon had been working on the idea of ballistic missile defense for decades,[44] Reagan's SDI proposal was very much his own and—with its promise of saving the United States from nuclear war—was designed, in part, to counter the flourishing Nuclear Freeze movement. Indeed, his dramatic March 22 television address, announcing the SDI program, devoted a full paragraph to the Freeze, using words that he had substituted for those of his speechwriters. "I know . . . that many of you seriously believe that a nuclear freeze would further the cause of peace," he declared. "But a freeze now would make us less, not more, secure and would raise, not reduce, the risks of war." By contrast, he said, his SDI program would provide "the means of rendering these nuclear weapons impotent and obsolete."[45] Shultz, very uneasy about allied reaction, comforted himself with the thought that the speech "provided a potent argument against the increasingly forceful nuclear freeze movement," as well as "those who argued that the Reagan administration was heedlessly taking the nation down the path to nuclear disaster." George Keyworth, the President's science advisor and a leading figure in the discussions leading up to SDI, remarked to an interviewer on the subject that "the freeze movement in the United States told us something, and . . . what it said was that the public is frightened." Asked if the administration believed that Americans had reached their limits in supporting expenditures on nuclear weapons, Keyworth replied: "Yes. . . . I think the President was sensing and fearing the public's concern. . . . People are . . . telling us to go out and find something new. 'Give us some hope that some day there may be some means by which we don't perceive ourselves to be living under the threat of a nuclear holocaust.' "[46]

Actually, Reagan's circle had recognized for some time that missile defense provided a potentially popular alternative to either a nuclear buildup or the prospect of nuclear war. As early as August 1979, one of Reagan's top advisors, Martin Anderson, had sent him a memo discussing a protective missile system, arguing that it would be difficult for a President to sustain popular support for an offensive military buildup and that an anti-missile system was "fundamentally far more appealing to the American people" than massacring Russians in a nuclear counterattack.[47] This advice seemed especially germane in the winter of 1982–83, when—thanks to the surging antinuclear crusade—Congress had just refused to authorize funds for the MX missile. Although there had been small meetings within the administration on missile defense during its first two years in office, these remained marginal. According to McFarlane, it took the congressional defeat of the MX in December 1982 to put SDI on the front burner. "The defeat of three efforts to make offense solve the problem" of Soviet-American strategic weapons balance, he recalled, "brought us back, in 1983, to exploring a defensive possibility." Recalling the origins of SDI, Keyworth made a similar point. "Strategic modernization was the number one issue of the first two years of the Reagan presidency," he declared, and "was one of the most difficult issues we dealt with." Indeed, the President's March 23 address "came after several months of the most difficult period of introducing MX," when it became clear "that nuclear modernization alone was not going to restore a stable nuclear balance." Boxed in by the nuclear critics, Reagan had adopted what he considered a popular alternative to both a nuclear buildup *and* the Freeze. Two days after his address on SDI, he jotted in his diary that, although "anti-defense propaganda has reduced my rating on foreign affairs," he was "interested to see how that holds for a poll after the speech."[48]

Other factors fed into the SDI proposal, as well. In 1940, Reagan had starred in a Hollywood film, *Murder in the Air*, in which he defended a wonder weapon that would bring down attacking enemy aircraft. Almost four decades later, when he visited the North American air defense command station in Colorado, he was dismayed when he learned that the United States had no effective defense against a nuclear attack.[49] Consequently, at the time of the 1980 presidential campaign he was ready to champion the development of a missile defense system. His political advisors, however, frightened that his suggestion of radical changes in U.S. nuclear weapons policies would terrify voters, convinced him not to mention it.[50] Furthermore, to convince Soviet and American critics of SDI that he was not planning to use SDI to launch a nuclear war but to safeguard against one, he repeatedly offered to share it with the Russians—a proposal that horrified other administration officials at least as much as did his proposal to abolish nuclear weapons. Nevertheless, it is important to recognize that Reagan did not begin to talk seriously about missile defense or about nuclear abolition until 1983,[51] when a number of factors converged: the growth of the antinuclear movement; the frustration of the MX buildup; and the stalemate in nuclear arms control negotiations. In these circumstances, Reagan—for most of his life an actor and politician, attuned to his audiences—made what he considered an important antinuclear proposal.

Other top administration officials viewed SDI differently than did Reagan, for they continued to believe strongly in nuclear deterrence and, furthermore, did not see much possibility of SDI producing either a foolproof defense for the United States or a disarmed world. Nevertheless, Reagan was President of the United States and they served at his pleasure. Therefore, they publicly supported SDI while, at the same time, using it to further their own interests in the intra-administration battle over nuclear arms controls. Contemptuous of SDI when the President first announced it, Perle called the idea of an impregnable shield "the product of millions of American teenagers putting quarters into video machines." But he and Weinberger warmed to it as they recognized its potential for sabotaging arms agreements. By insisting upon Russian acceptance of SDI as the price for a Soviet-American arms accord, they could block progress toward nuclear arms controls. Furthermore, as the ABM treaty stood in the way of any deployment of SDI, they could also exploit the new missile defense priority to undermine it. As Talbott noted: "Perle eventually came to see SDI as an ideal instrument for rendering . . . the ABM treaty itself impotent and obsolete." Conversely, Shultz, Nitze, and McFarlane explored employing SDI as a "bargaining chip" in arms control negotiations. "The arms control potential" of SDI, McFarlane recalled, "was always at the center of my motives."[52]

In the context of a fierce attack upon SDI by the antinuclear campaign, Congress responded with even less enthusiasm for the President's brainchild. "It is difficult to convey the strength and . . . the irrationality and the fury of the opposition to SDI in our Congress," Weinberger recalled. Although the defense secretary's jeremiad is overdrawn, congressional support for the program did remain weak. In fiscal years 1983 and 1984, the administration tried to "reprogram" funds from existing appropriations, but Congress blocked the effort. Thereafter, although Congress did appropriate money for SDI, it voted for substantially smaller amounts than requested by the administration: for fiscal 1985, $1.4 billion out of $1.8 billion requested; for fiscal 1986, $2.67 billion out of $3.75 billion requested. Moreover, given the fact that the U.S. government was already spending money on missile defense, the additional funding for SDI covered by these yearly appropriations probably was less than half the amount Reagan sought.[53]

Finally, like the appropriations for the MX, the congressional appropriations for SDI came at a price for the administration. McFarlane convinced leading congressional moderates like Nunn, Aspin, and Gore to support funding for SDI on the basis that it provided an important bargaining chip—one that would produce a breakthrough in arms control negotiations within two years. Therefore, the administration faced the unpleasant prospect that Congress would cut off SDI appropriations if a nuclear arms control agreement were not secured within a relatively brief time.[54] In this fashion, Congress continued to exercise some degree of leverage over the Reagan administration's arms control policy.

New Troubles Abroad in 1984-85

The 1981–83 crisis over INF deployment did not bring an end to the Reagan administration's troubles abroad, for in 1984–85 it was also beleaguered by antinuclear pressures emanating from numerous non-Communist countries, some of them allies of the United States. There was, for example, the Five Continent Peace Initiative, which the State Department rebuffed in May 1984. A freeze on testing, production, and deployment of nuclear weapons, insisted a department spokesperson, "would not enhance stability or reduce the risk of war." There were also Canadian Prime Minister Pierre Trudeau's global peace activities, which Under Secretary of State Lawrence Eagleburger denounced as the "pot-induced" ravings of an "erratic leftist."[55] In Western Europe, the Dutch and the Belgian governments continued to dismay the Reagan administration by their indecision over INF deployment,[56] while in the Pacific the administration looked with irritation upon an Australian government that refused to allow MX missile testing, criticized the arms race, and promoted the antinuclear Treaty of Rarotonga. In February 1985, after the New Zealand government refused to admit U.S. nuclear warships, the administration's exasperation with other nations reached the boiling point. "Unless we hold our allies' feet to the fire over ship visits and nuclear deployments, one will run away and then the next," a senior Reagan administration official complained. "We will not be put in a position where they want our protection but without the necessary weapons in place to do the job."[57]

But, in the context of the worldwide antinuclear upsurge, it turned out that the U.S. government could do relatively little about this situation. The limits were exemplified by U.S. policy toward New Zealand, a small, allied nation with which the Reagan administration expected to have considerable influence. During New Zealand's 1984 election campaign, in which the question of admitting nuclear armed warships played a major role, the U.S. ambassador released a State Department speech clearly designed to put the nation on notice. It declared that "we view Australia's and New Zealand's willingness to allow us use of their ports as part of their contribution to ANZUS." Visiting U.S. Congressmen implied that, if Lange's Labour Party implemented its plan to bar nuclear-armed warships, the U.S. government would institute trade sanctions. That July, when voters ignored these warnings and gave Labour a landslide victory, Shultz met immediately with Lange and renewed U.S. pressure upon him to back off from his party's warship policy. In December, asked if the U.S. government planned to link trade issues with a nuclear warships ban, William Brock, Reagan's special trade representative, did not answer directly but commented that it was "defying human logic" to "believe that countries don't take into account the actions of other countries as we look at our total relationships." The administration subsequently upped the ante, when a State Department official declared that, "should the visit of the ship we have requested be denied," the U.S. government would "have to consider the implications for overall cooperation with New Zealand under ANZUS."[58] Nevertheless, the New Zealand government stuck to its principles and, at the end of January 1985, declared that it would not admit the U.S. warship *Buchanan*.

New Zealand's action enraged the U.S. government. Weinberger declared that New Zealand was pursuing a course that would do it "great harm," while Perle maintained that, if the Western alliance were to be maintained, New Zealand would have to "pay dearly" for its defiance of the United States. Remarking that "some Western countries have anti-nuclear and other movements which seek to diminish defense cooperation among the allied states," State Department spokesperson Bernard Kalb predicted that the U.S. government's "response to New Zealand would signal that the course these movements advocate would not be cost-free." In Congress, Republican Representative Dick Cheney introduced a bill to bar imports from New Zealand and Australia—the latter guilty of denying support facilities for MX missile tests—based on "their uncooperative attitude towards U.S. international defense policy. . . . If these countries are not willing to share the burden and responsibility of defending freedom, why should we facilitate their enjoyment of freedom's benefits, such as unrestrained access to our markets?"[59]

This was not all talk. Determined to whip the small island nation into line, as well as to halt a domino effect among U.S. allies, particularly Japan, the U.S. government moved quickly and publicly to cut off defense cooperation with New Zealand. Although New Zealand protested that it remained a loyal member of ANZUS, the Reagan administration acted as if it had withdrawn from the alliance. The U.S. government excluded New Zealand from ANZUS defense exercises, banned reciprocal military placements, barred the New Zealand navy from U.S. port facilities, curtailed the exchange of intelligence information between the two nations, and prohibited the sale of U.S.-manufactured spare parts for New Zealand's aging military equipment. In addition, it relegated New Zealand officials to an outer circle of countries at State Department briefings, denied them easy access to the Pentagon and State Department, and instructed New Zealand's close allies (Canada, Britain, and Australia) to remove U.S.-generated intelligence information from the material they passed along to that nation. The Reagan administration was determined to make an example of what one U.S. official called "a piss-ant little country south of nowheresville."[60]

And yet, the U.S. crackdown on New Zealand proved remarkably ineffectual. The Lange government continued to resist U.S. pressure, without suffering any serious repercussions. At home, it won enormous popularity among New Zealanders for its forthright resistance to the United States. Nor did New Zealand's effective exclusion from ANZUS create national security problems. The country remained secure and at peace, with no foreign threat emerging on the horizon. Furthermore, the Australian government—the only other member of ANZUS—argued against the imposition of economic sanctions upon New Zealand, while the U.S. Congress, despite some Republican frothing, seemed unwilling to penalize a nation for dropping out of the nuclear arms race. Apparently as a result of these factors, the Reagan administration never imposed economic sanctions on New Zealand. Indeed, with overseas disarmament groups encouraging people to buy products from a courageous antinuclear nation, New Zealand experienced a trade boom. Thus, despite the ominous rumblings about excluding New Zealand goods from American markets, in the year ending June 1985 New Zealand's exports to the United States jumped by nearly 50 percent.[61]

Retaining SALT II and Other Surprises

The degree to which the Reagan administration found itself hemmed in by antinuclear opinion was also exemplified by its handling of SALT II. The top national security posts in the administration were filled with people who, during the Carter years, had denounced SALT II as the ultimate betrayal of U.S. national security. Reagan himself had campaigned strongly against this arms control agreement. Therefore, as Adelman later noted, "logic would lead one to presume that Reagan would instantly scrap our adherence to this unratified treaty." After all, "that's what Reagan had pledged to the American people." Nevertheless, in 1981, Haig argued that scrapping

SALT II would create problems with U.S. allies and with Congress, who had far greater sympathy for the treaty than did the Reaganites. Thus, the administration adopted a policy, announced by Reagan on Memorial Day 1982, of not undercutting existing nuclear arms accords "so long as the Soviet Union showed equal restraint." As Adelman noted: "This new policy played pleasingly. It showed how sensible Reagan would act as President, despite his wild words as candidate." From the standpoint of the Reaganites, however, this turned into a very bad bargain, for they soon came to believe that the Russians were "cheating" on their SALT II obligations. The "obvious response was to end our interim restraint policy on SALT II," Adelman recalled. But "politics" got in the way, "for by 1984 and 1985 the SALT accords had assumed soaring symbolic salience. They were the sole existing arrangements on strategic arms and the only ones on the horizon." In June 1984, despite GOP control of the Senate, that body voted 82 to 17 for a resolution urging the President to continue observing the terms of the unratified SALT II treaty. Thus, as the next year began, the Reagan administration, despite its loathing of SALT II, continued to observe its limits.[62]

Furthermore, primarily in response to the antinuclear upsurge of the era, the Reagan administration sharply reduced the number of nuclear warheads in Western Europe. In late 1979, at the time of the NATO INF decision, the United States had about 7,200 nuclear weapons in Western Europe. Largely because of the decision at that time to withdraw 1,000 obsolete nuclear warheads, the number of U.S. warheads in Western Europe dropped to 5,840 in 1981. But, thanks to decisions made during the Reagan years, their numbers continued to fall. A key decision came in October 1983, on the eve of NATO's first INF deployments. In a meeting in Montebello, Canada, NATO defense ministers—nervous about the widespread popular opposition to the cruise and Pershing deployments—agreed to withdraw an additional 1,400 nuclear weapons from the continent by the end of the decade, thus reducing the number of U.S. nuclear weapons stationed there to some 4,300. In fact, political considerations led to an even faster decline than anticipated, and as early as 1986 the number of U.S. nuclear weapons in Western Europe had dipped to 4,900—the lowest level since about 1964. Admittedly, the small numbers of new weapons deployed—such as the 572 cruise and Pershing missiles—provided for a qualitative improvement in the U.S. nuclear arsenal. But, in the past, the Reaganites had not been satisfied with quality over quantity; instead, they had called for the deployment of thousands of additional nuclear weapons in Europe. When serving as NATO Supreme Commander, Haig had claimed that the introduction of the 572 cruise and Pershing warheads was totally inadequate—"only political expediency and tokenism." It was one further sign of the antinuclear campaign's strength that—unlike Soviet missile numbers, which climbed appreciably— the number of NATO missiles declined substantially during the Reagan years.[63]

Given the fact that the Reagan administration came into office talking glibly about waging and winning a nuclear war, it is also striking that—as far as can be ascertained—it did not come close to employing nuclear weapons in combat. Although the Reaganites sponsored wars in Central America, the Caribbean, and the Near and Middle East, they do not appear to have factored nuclear weapons into their battle plans. Adelman claimed that he "never heard anyone broach the topic of using nuclear weapons. Ever. In any setting, in any way."[64] Of course, it is possible that the Reagan administration's nuclear restraint reflected the moral inhibitions of U.S. officials or the deterrent power of Soviet nuclear weapons. But it should be remembered that Reagan's phrase, "a nuclear war cannot be won and must never be fought," was first voiced in April 1982 in response to mushrooming antinuclear protest.[65] This oft-repeated mantra, designed for public relations purposes, had the effect of making the waging of nuclear war a less acceptable and, thus, less likely option for his administration. Admittedly, Reagan's public disparaging of nuclear war did not rule out the possibility of waging it. But, by making the case against use of nuclear weapons, it did raise the threshold for the waging of nuclear war.

The Changing of the Line

In this fashion, the Reagan administration gradually modified its nuclear hard line in the years from early 1981 to early 1985. Opposition to nuclear arms control and disarmament gave way to serious negotiations, Cold War confrontation with the Soviet Union was replaced by conciliation, nuclear buildups ground to a halt far short of their objectives, and talk of waging nuclear war came to nothing. These changes in U.S. policy did not occur because of Soviet compromise or capitulation. Certainly, the Reaganites perceived no alteration in Soviet policy during these years—the years of Brezhnev, Andropov, and Chernenko, the years *before the advent of Gorbachev*. Rather, U.S. policy shifted because of pressure generated by the antinuclear campaign and effectively transmitted by U.S. allies and by Congress. Peace was beginning to break out in the American Cold War camp, but it was not based on "strength"—unless, of course, one is referring to the strength of the antinuclear movement.

The Movement Continues, 1985-88

> The paranoid scenario of the superpowers and cold warriors is coming to an end and the possibilities for peace-minded people to have a decisive impact on the future has never been as great.
>
> E. P. Thompson, 1987

A common misconception is that, after the nuclear disarmament movement's spectacular uprising of the early 1980s, it disappeared. According to this view, when the American and Soviet governments refused to retreat from their nuclear buildup of the early 1980s, the frustrated movement withered and died. It is certainly true that, from 1985 to 1988, the immense antinuclear demonstrations gradually abated. In addition, membership in nuclear disarmament organizations waned in many countries. Nevertheless, the movement's decline was a fairly modest one, and throughout the years from 1985 to 1988 it constituted a powerful force—far larger, more active, and more diverse than at any time other than its peak mobilization era of 1981 to early 1985. Indeed, in some nations, the movement grew in strength. On the national and international levels, it began shifting from an unruly upheaval to a more sophisticated form—coalescing into central organizations, developing professional staffs, and conducting coordinated campaigns. The movement also spread to new areas of the world and kept public opinion stirred up about nuclear issues. Overall, then, from 1985 to 1988, the antinuclear campaign remained a mass phenomenon, with substantial resonance in the broader society.

Non-Communist Europe

In the non-Communist nations of Europe, the great wave of antinuclear activism did recede. Although protest demonstrations continued, they were usually smaller than in the preceding years. In October 1985, a disarmament rally at the Hague drew 25,000 people. But, two years earlier, 550,000 people had demonstrated against nuclear weapons in the same city. In Denmark, No to Nuclear Weapons and Women for Peace lost members, particularly among the young.[1] Membership in the same groups also fell in Norway.[2] In Britain, CND's national membership dropped significantly between early 1985 and late 1988. In France, CODENE—which never had a solid base—became weaker. In the Netherlands, the anti-cruise missile coordinating committee officially dissolved in 1987.[3] Unique circumstances undermined the movement in some nations. In West Germany, there were severe internal divisions over strategy. In Austria, the prominent role of the Communist party in the movement caused other groups to abandon it.[4] In Turkey, the government placed the movement's leaders in jail and banned the major organization.[5] More generally, however, the movement suffered from the loss of organizing focus that had been provided by deployment of the cruise, Pershing II, and SS-20 missiles. And it was certainly affected by a growing sense of complacency after Reagan and the new Soviet party leader, Mikhail Gorbachev, began to make progress on nuclear disarmament issues.[6]

Nevertheless, the antinuclear campaign remained very substantial. Some of its demonstrations would have been viewed as startling if they had they not been dwarfed by the enormous antinuclear rallies of the preceding years. In March 1985, a crowd estimated at from 50,000 to 150,000 people surged through Brussels to protest Euromissile deployment. The following month, more than 300,000 antinuclear demonstrators held rallies in West German cities.[7] That October, CND drew 100,000 people to a demonstration in London's Hyde Park, where they rallied under the theme: "Human race, not arms race."[8] As late as 1987, 100,000 protesters turned out in Britain for an antinuclear demonstration sponsored by CND and Friends of the Earth, and another 100,000 demonstrators turned out in Bonn to demand the removal of all Euromissiles.[9] In Spain, huge crowds participated in protests against that nation's membership in NATO, including a February 1986 demonstration in Madrid that may have drawn almost a million people. Even in Turkey, the movement proved surprisingly resilient. Defying government repression, 4,000 people attended a Hiroshima commemoration meeting held in Istanbul.[10] Although CND's national membership waned after the spring of 1985, when it peaked at 110,000, by late 1988 the British antinuclear group still had a very respectable 70,000 national members and perhaps another 130,000 local members. In the Netherlands, IKV continued to sustain more than 300 active local branches.[11]

As they matured, many antinuclear and peace movements grew more efficient. In Italy, they united in February 1987 to form the Association for Peace (Associazione per la pace), the country's first nationwide peace movement. Similarly, an Irish Peace Council was formed in 1986 and, by the following year, had drawn together 26 national peace and solidarity groups as members.[12] Through the mundane but necessary work of hiring staff, collecting dues, keeping records, and distributing antinuclear literature, many organizations compensated for the absence of mass demonstrations with greater political effectiveness. CND employed a staff of more than forty people, many deployed to local branches, thus maintaining the organization's grassroots activity. In May 1988 alone, it was able to distribute some two million antinuclear leaflets, contrasting Britain's Trident nuclear submarine program with nuclear disarmament negotiations between the superpowers. CND also grew quite skillful at lobbying parliament and local governments. Indeed, by 1987, local councils with more than half Britain's population had declared themselves nuclear-free zones.[13] In Norway, No to Nuclear Weapons published two newspapers—one for mass distribution and another for its members—and increased the number of self-proclaimed nuclear-free communities to 97.[14]

The movement's vitality was also exemplified by its persistent activities. In the Netherlands, antinuclear activists launched a massive petition campaign in 1985 against the cruise missiles and, as the government proceeded with the building of the missile base at Woensdrecht, established peace camps outside the base site to block its construction through waves of nonviolent civil disobedience. Preferring a less confrontational approach, IKV emphasized working within the churches for détente, especially "détente from below," and cultivated contacts with East European churches and peace groups.[15] In West Germany, antinuclear groups renewed their pressure against cruise and Pershing missile deployment, opposed SDI, and called for a shift away from military priorities.[16] In Norway, No to Nuclear Weapons opposed the presence of nuclear weapons in Norwegian waters and harbors, assailed plans for SDI, and continued to promote the idea of a Nordic nuclear weapon-free zone.[17] Denmark's No to Nuclear Weapons encouraged its own brand of "détente from below," ranging from exchanges with the people of Eastern Europe, to organizing "sister city" relationships, to establishing contacts with independent peace groups in the East bloc.[18] Throughout non-Communist Europe, but especially in Scandinavia, WILPF's national branches circulated a petition calling for a nuclear test ban, and by September 1986 gathered 600,000 signatures, some 100,000 of them from Sweden.[19]

In Britain, too, the movement engaged in very substantial grassroots activities. Assailing SDI, CND joined with Greenpeace, Scientists Against Nuclear Arms, and other groups to form a Coalition Against Star Wars, which held rallies and other public events. Opposition to the space weapons program was particularly widespread among scientists, and a formal pledge of non-cooperation with SDI was signed by more than half the faculty in the first 29 British science departments in which it was circulated.[20] After the British government's deployment of cruise missiles, much CND energy went into the "Basic Case" campaign—a wide-ranging attempt to convince the public of the necessity for creating a non-nuclear Britain.[21] But the missiles were not forgotten. When an international crisis arose, these nuclear weapons, located at Greenham, were supposed to be driven to assorted secret locations, from which they could be launched. And to practice for such occasions, the armed forces organized cruise missile convoys to periodically rumble up and down the nation's roads. In 1985, responding to Heseltine's boast that these convoys would "melt into the countryside," grassroots antinuclear activists initiated Cruisewatch, a campaign to track, publicize, and disrupt such military maneuvers. Alerted to convoy preparations by women encamped at Greenham or by local residents, thousands of grassroots activists in southern Britain made it a point of pride to harass every convoy—blockading the roads, adorning the trucks with peace symbols, painting the windshields, and cutting the airbrakes. Years later, veterans of Cruisewatch still gathered in pubs to regale one another with stories of the days when they had humiliated the armed forces and frustrated the British government's preparations for nuclear war.[22]

Another sign of the movement's strength was the backing its program received from Western Europe's political parties, especially the Social Democrats. In West Germany, the Greens remained fervently antinuclear, but the Social Democratic Party also championed the removal of the cruise and Pershing II missiles and the negotiation of sharp cuts in strategic nuclear weapons. Both Petra Kelly and Hans Jochen Vogel, the new chair of the Social Democrats, addressed the movement's mass antinuclear rally at Bonn in 1987.[23] Similarly, the Dutch Social Democrats and the two Belgian Socialist Parties campaigned for the removal of the missiles from their countries, while the Danish Social Democratic Party grew more enthusiastic about the creation of a Nordic nuclear weapon-free zone, inviting all the Social Democratic parties in the region for a conference on the subject.[24] In Britain, the Labour Party, under the leadership of Neil Kinnock, gamely carried its support for Britain's unilateral nuclear disarmament into the nationwide elections of 1987.[25] Although the Socialist Workers Party of Spain backed Spanish membership in NATO, it insisted upon banning nuclear weapons from its national territory. Even the French Socialist Party, which stuck by its support for the *force de frappe*, made a modest turn toward championing East-West nuclear weapons reductions.[26] With so much riding on the political fortunes of these parties, leaders of antinuclear groups keenly felt the defeats of the West German, Dutch, and British Social Democrats in the elections of 1986 and 1987.[27]

Despite these election defeats, which often hinged on other issues,[28] West European opposition to nuclear weapons remained widespread. A *Guardian* poll, conducted in late 1986 and early 1987, found that 56 percent of respondents in Britain, 60 percent in France, 66 percent in West Germany, and 78 percent in Italy expressed disapproval of the decision to allow the United States to base nuclear weapons in Europe. The same poll found that only 9 percent of Britons, 17 percent of the French, 8 percent of West Germans, and 5 percent of Italians wanted West European nations to further develop their own nuclear weapons.[29] Indeed, NATO's policy of nuclear deterrence rested on very shaky ground. Although polls in 1986–87 found that small majorities or pluralities of British and French respondents preferred a nuclear to a conventional defense, they also reported that most West German and Dutch respondents rejected nuclear deterrence entirely. In July 1988, a poll in West Germany found that only 30 percent of the population accepted the argument that nuclear deterrence had kept the peace in Western Europe for the previous forty years.[30] And when it came to the actual use of nuclear weapons, there was considerable resistance. A February 1987 poll found that 45 percent of West Germans opposed use of nuclear weapons under any circumstances, 35 percent would use them only if the Soviet Union used them first to attack Western Europe, and only 6 percent would use them to defend their country if a Soviet attack by conventional forces threatened to overwhelm NATO forces (i.e. the NATO policy). Another poll at that time found that 73 percent of Britons rejected first use of nuclear weapons.[31]

Indeed, most West Europeans favored getting rid of nuclear weapons. USIA polls in early 1987 found that large majorities in West Germany, Britain, and France supported the elimination of all intermediate range nuclear missiles from Europe. Polls the following year reported that 74 percent of Britons also supported the elimination of shorter-range nuclear missiles and that 67 percent either agreed or strongly agreed that "the security of Western countries could best be increased by substantial reductions in both American and Soviet nuclear weapons." In June 1988, 79 percent of West German respondents favored the total denuclearization of Europe.[32] Not surprisingly, a Gallup poll in early 1986 found that the signing of a U.S.-Soviet arms control treaty was rated as either important or very important by 73 percent of Belgians, 84 percent of Britons, 82 percent of Danes, 92 percent of Finns, 85 percent of the French, 82 percent of the Irish, 90 percent of the Dutch, 89 percent of Norwegians, 72 percent of Portuguese, 59 percent of Spaniards, and 68 percent of Turks. Although polls in Britain continued to show only a minority of the population backing unilateral nuclear disarmament, unilateral initiatives had considerably greater appeal. Nuclear-free zones also had very substantial backing, with a 1987 USIA poll reporting that 82 percent of Danes favored the creation of a Nordic nuclear-free zone.[33]

Western Europe's changing attitude to Soviet leaders bolstered the popular desire for East-West nuclear arms accords. Although the advent of Gorbachev diminished fears of nuclear war,[34] it also helped create a more favorable image of the Soviet Union and, by contrast, a more negative image of the United States. Between 1983 and December 1987, Dutch poll respondents calling themselves "anti-Soviet" decreased from 56 to 19 percent, while the "pro-Americans" decreased from 28 to 16 percent. Polled in 1986 as to which country was making "the largest contribution to reduction of armaments," 47 percent of the Dutch named the Soviet Union and only 9 percent the United States. By 1987, for the first time since the surveys began, the public in Britain, West Germany, and the Netherlands expressed more confidence in the ability of the Soviet Union to solve world problems than in the ability of the United States.[35] USIA surveys in the fall of 1986 and the spring of 1987 found that most Britons and West Germans no longer viewed the Soviet Union as a threat to the security of Western Europe. Thatcher recalled, irritably: "The British people by and large did not . . . properly appreciate President Reagan," and this was exacerbated by the emergence of Gorbachev, "someone with an unusual understanding of how to play on western public opinion." Thus, there developed "a feeling that the Soviets were the model of sweet reason, the United States of recklessness."[36]

North America

The movement faced some significant problems in the United States. The idea of a Nuclear Freeze—which had provided a focus for the antinuclear campaign in the early 1980s—lost its vibrancy in the following years, as the Freeze resolution remained stalled in Congress and as Gorbachev and Reagan showed signs of moving beyond it to actually eliminate nuclear weapons. Among foundations and other large funders, complained one movement leader, "there's a feeling that 'Peace has broken out, why put money into disarmament?'" The Nuclear Weapons Freeze Campaign was particularly hard-hit by funding cutbacks and, in the summer of 1986, laid off nearly half the staff of its national office.[37] In addition, after years of fierce agitation, leading activists were becoming exhausted or, at the least, impatient. In late 1985, a divisive debate broke out at the annual Freeze convention over adopting a strategy of nonviolent resistance. When, by a narrow margin, the convention rejected it, its angry proponents—convinced that the group had lost its crusading zeal—withdrew from the organization to foster a civil disobedience campaign at the Nevada nuclear test site.[38] Furthermore, the movement was distracted, increasingly, by other peace issues, particularly the U.S. government's war in Central America, thereby diverting its resources and blurring its focus.[39] Finally, the mass media largely ceased to cover the movement's activities. IPPNW's Bernard Lown was astonished that, in late 1985, after he concluded an unprecedented one-on-one meeting with Gorbachev on nuclear issues that lasted more than three hours, highlighted by a press conference on the subject in Moscow, the U.S. communications media ignored the event.[40]

Even so, in a number of respects, the U.S. movement was stronger than ever. Between March 1985 and September 1986, SANE grew from 110,000 to over 150,000 members—about four times its membership of 1983. Although the Freeze campaign did not have a formal membership, its number of state and local affiliates increased from 1,333 in October 1984 to 1,824 by August 1986. As late as 1987, it maintained 109 paid staff members in 56 state and regional offices.[41] Although the membership of both organizations probably peaked in 1986, they increased their potential strength substantially in 1987, when they merged to form SANE/Freeze, the largest peace organization in American history.[42] Other groups with an antinuclear focus were also growing, including Greenpeace (with 650,000 members by late 1987) and PSR (with 37,000 members, another 32,000 contributors, and 154 local chapters by the spring of 1986). Still others, such as the Union of Concerned Scientists (with 100,000 members by late 1987), held their own.[43] Meanwhile, the money raised by the Council for Livable World for U.S. Senate candidates pledged to arms control grew dramatically—from $533,00 in 1982, to $1 million in 1984, to $1.5 million in 1986. Indeed, in the latter year, some candidates received more money through the Council than through any other organization, including the Democratic Senatorial Campaign Committee.[44]

Drawing upon this strength, leading movement groups turned increasingly to promoting a nuclear test ban. This shift of emphasis made sense to many key activists for, by 1985, conservative resistance in the Senate and in the White House blocked implementation of a Nuclear Freeze, while even defeats of individual nuclear weapons programs, such as the MX, did not prevent the emergence of others. By contrast, a test ban seemed politically feasible and, at the same time, an effective way to cut off the development of new types of nuclear weapons. As a result, by early 1985 the campaign launched in 1984 by the Center for Defense Information and Greenpeace to have all nuclear explosions halted by August 6, 1985, had drawn together more than thirty U.S. groups, including SANE, PSR, and the Professionals Coalition. It also claimed to have over 130 groups internationally endorsing the effort.[45] The test ban campaign acquired additional momentum in late July, when Gorbachev announced that the Soviet Union would unilaterally halt its nuclear tests on August 6 and would continue its moratorium indefinitely if the United States would join it. Even groups like Mobilization for Survival, initially critical of a test ban campaign as a retreat from farther-reaching demands, now got behind it. That November, when leading anti-nuclear activists met with Gorbachev at the Geneva summit conference, they brought with them test ban petitions signed by 1.2 million Americans.[46]

These developments also triggered a burst of nonviolent resistance. Convinced of the need for a strong movement response to Gorbachev's initiative, a group of Freeze activists, mostly from Oregon, laid plans for a series of civil disobedience actions—modeled on the Free South Africa protests earlier that year—at the U.S. nuclear test site in Nevada. In the month leading up to the Geneva summit meeting, they staged such actions by anti-nuclear delegations from twenty-eight states. Thereafter, when the convention of the Nuclear Freeze campaign rebuffed their proposal to incorporate this kind of activity into its program, they broke away and created American Peace Test to continue their campaign. As a result, in the following years large numbers of Americans took part in demonstrations at the Nevada test site, and thousands were arrested for civil disobedience. Others engaged in nonviolent resistance to nuclear weapons in other parts of the country. The *Nuclear Resister*, a journal created to report on the burgeoning movement in the United States and Canada, estimated that there were 3,300 arrests of antinuclear activists in 1985, 3,200 in 1986, 5,300 in 1987, and 4,470 in 1988. In March 1988 alone, 2,100 people from more than thirty states were arrested at the Nevada test site, making it one of the largest civil disobedience actions in U.S. history.[47]

The movement had other projects, as well. In addition to the ongoing campaigns for the Freeze and against the MX missile, the largest was probably opposition to SDI or, as it was popularly known, Star Wars. For purposes of assailing the program, Women Strike for Peace produced a critical pamphlet, while Mobilization for Survival put together a devastating packet of materials that it mailed to its 130 affiliates and other supporters.[48] The most effective resistance to Star Wars, however, came from the FAS, the UCS, and grassroots efforts among scientists. In the spring of 1985, when the federal government advertised "the unique opportunity to participate" in this "fascinating and challenging research program" at the University of Illinois, physicists at that university developed an anti-SDI pledge. Promising "not to solicit nor accept SDI funds," they criticized the program as "ill-conceived and dangerous," for it was "not technically feasible" and was likely to encourage "the development of both additional offensive overkill and an all-out competition" in ABM systems. Assisted by United Campuses Against Nuclear War and SANE, the pledge was launched that fall. Ultimately, more than 7,000 American scientists signed this pledge of non-participation, including 57 percent of the faculty in the top twenty physics departments. A poll among members of the National Academy of Sciences found that 79 percent opposed the SDI program and that only 4 percent thought it likely to succeed. In the margins of the poll, they wrote remarks such as: "It is costly, dangerous, and a scientific fraud."[49]

U.S. activists also undertook less visible projects. In many communities, such as Columbia, South Carolina, citizens' groups conducted campaigns to document and protest the dangers of local nuclear weapons production facilities, creating local waves even when their efforts did not draw national attention. Sometimes these groups worked cooperatively with national antinuclear organizations, such as the Natural Resources Defense Council or Greenpeace.[50] Similarly, a nuclear-free zone movement, though never reaching the size of those in Western Europe and Japan, took hold in U.S. towns and cities. Beginning in scattered communities in Hawaii, Montana, and Maryland during the early 1980s, it grew in later years, encouraged by local antinuclear activists, particularly Albert Donnay, an antinuclear campaigner who established an organization called Nuclear Free America. In November 1985, voters in Boulder, Colorado, approved a resolution to make their city nuclear-free. The following March, after a campaign by local activists, the Chicago city council unanimously passed an antinuclear ordinance, making Chicago the nation's largest nuclear-free city. Although Illinois Governor James Thompson denounced the new law as "stupid and un-American," it remained in place, as did more than a hundred other local nuclear-free ordinances that appeared by the late 1980s.[51] Prominent activists also protested the persecution of dissidents in Eastern Europe, with the Campaign for Peace and Democracy/East and West often playing a leading role.[52]

Naturally, the work of the movement's new flagship, SANE/Freeze, was particularly important. It began badly, for ironically the merger of the anti-nuclear campaign's two largest organizations in late 1987 produced some severe problems. These included confusion about the lines of authority, decreased overall funding, and a decision by Freeze Voter to remain independent. In 1988, SANE/Freeze received only $4 million of the $5 million income it had projected, and was forced to lay off a third of its Washington staff.[53] Even so, the new organization had some major strengths, among them a membership estimated at about 200,000, chapters in every part of the United States, an experienced staff, and a new, inspiring president, the Rev. William Sloane Coffin, Jr. The senior minister at New York City's Riverside Church, Coffin was well known as a leading critic of the Vietnam War and of the nuclear buildup.[54] At its merger convention, SANE/Freeze promised to work "to halt and reverse the nuclear arms race" and "to abolish nuclear weapons." In the non-nuclear realm, it hoped to reduce conventional military forces and to secure "new foreign and military policies that exclude military intervention, protect human rights, and promote social and economic development." These ideas were reiterated in its 1988 Peace Platform, which also called upon the victor in that presidential election year "to declare a moratorium on nuclear testing as the first order of business" and "to negotiate a Comprehensive Test Ban Treaty." SANE/Freeze, Coffin declared, was determined to "reconstitute the world."[55]

Given the movement's size and ongoing activity, it retained significant influence in mainstream institutions. In the fall of 1985, the Episcopal Church issued an official critique of U.S. nuclear policy. The following year, the United Methodist Church, the third-largest religious body in the United States, delivered a strong denunciation of nuclear deterrence. The labor movement also continued its support of the antinuclear campaign and, by the summer of 1986, 25 international unions—representing well over half the total membership of the AFL-CIO—backed a Nuclear Freeze and eleven opposed the administration's Star Wars program.[56] Given the support for arms control and disarmament among liberals and Democrats, the movement strengthened its backing in the Democratic-controlled House of Representatives. For a time, it had a smaller constituency in the Republican-controlled Senate, but substantial campaign contributions from the Council for a Livable World and other peace PACs helped produce gains there. In the 1986 elections, thirteen out of seventeen arms controllers supported by the Council emerged victorious, restoring the Senate to Democratic control and rendering it more amenable to the movement's priorities. In the 1988 elections, fourteen of the 22 Senatorial candidates backed by the Council won their elections, giving it a base of 38 Senators (out of 100) it had funded.[57]

As the movement became an important player in electoral politics, its allies began to deliver. In the House, staunchly antinuclear legislators like Pat Schroeder and Ron Dellums were joined by top Democratic leaders like James Wright and Richard Gephardt in promoting key elements of the movement's agenda, such as slashing the MX missile program, blocking development of anti-satellite weapons, restricting Star Wars funding, and legislating a halt to nuclear testing. In the Senate, too, there was a growing responsiveness, though less than in the House. Sympathetic representatives and senators met with movement lobbyists to plan legislative strategy, or contributed to the movement by writing fund-raising letters for it and speaking at its events.[58] As the 1988 presidential election neared, a number of potential candidates had reasonably strong positions on arms control and disarmament issues, including the Rev. Jesse Jackson, Senator Gary Hart, and Governor Michael Dukakis. Jackson, particularly, courted the movement, especially SANE, and spoke glowingly of the prospects of SANE/Freeze at its merger convention. But the movement also had some influence with Dukakis, who edged out Jackson to become the Democratic nominee. In eleventh hour negotiations at the 1988 Democratic national convention, SANE/Freeze leaders secured agreement from the Dukakis forces to add language to the party platform pledging to "promptly initiate a mutual moratorium on missile flight testing and halt all nuclear weapons testing."[59]

The movement could also take heart at the American public's growing dovishness. Although fear of nuclear war continued to dwindle, so did fear of the Soviet Union, and by May 1988 a poll found that only 30 percent of the population viewed it any longer as an "enemy" nation.[60] Gorbachev's approval ratings soared and, in December 1988, 72 percent of Americans had a mostly or very favorable view of him. Indeed, that month, polls found that he was the second most admired man in America, outranking President-elect George Bush.[61] According to Gallup polls, between 1985 and 1987 only 11 to 14 percent of Americans wanted to increase U.S. military spending, but 44 to 46 percent wanted to decrease it—quite a turnabout from 1980, when 70 percent of the public favored an increase in arms spending.[62] Queried in March 1987 as to whether further increases and improvements in nuclear weapons would give either the United States or the Soviet Union a significant advantage over the other, 69 percent said they would not. Admittedly, polls found that the Star Wars program enjoyed majority support. But that was only when it was emphasized as a defensive, research-oriented system;

when its vast cost and dangerous consequences were mentioned, it drew majority opposition.[63] Americans also showed considerable reluctance to use nuclear weapons. In March 1987, 65 percent of poll respondents said that the only time they should be employed was in response to a nuclear attack upon the United States.[64]

This distaste for nuclear weapons was accompanied by a widespread desire for arms control and disarmament. Polls from the fall of 1987 to the spring of 1988 found Americans consistently supporting an INF treaty at levels above 70 percent. In December 1987, a week before such a treaty was signed, Americans backed it by a ratio of six to one.[65] In the summer of 1988, polls found that 71 percent of U.S. respondents favored working with the Soviet Union to eliminate most nuclear weapons by the year 2000. That October, a Gallup survey reported that 63 percent of Americans considered negotiating further arms reductions with the Soviet Union a top priority, 27 percent viewed it as a medium priority, and only 8 percent rated it as a low priority.[66] Similarly, support for the movement's latest goal, a comprehensive test ban treaty, rose between 1984 and 1988 from 69 percent to 85 percent. The Gallup organization noted that, in 1988, there was "broad public displeasure with the way President Ronald Reagan is handling overall foreign policy and the nation's economy." But, in the context of the signing of the INF treaty, he received "the highest marks since taking office for his relations with the Soviet Union." Ironically, Gallup concluded, what popularity Reagan retained was based heavily on scrapping his hard line and fostering nuclear disarmament.[67]

The nuclear disarmament campaign was also a potent force in neighboring Canada. Visiting that country in late 1985, E. P. Thompson found a growing movement—one "full of vitality, with many different accents, many resources," and "a great future." Thousands of small peace groups existed, many of them working together effectively in local coalitions. To provide themselves with some form of national coordination, they held a convention in Toronto in November 1985 and organized the Canadian Peace Alliance. This umbrella group pledged to work to build public and government support for "a freeze and reversal of the arms race on earth and in space," "the declaration of Canada as a Nuclear Weapons Free Zone," "the redirection of funds from wasteful military spending to the funding of human needs," and "the strengthening of world institutions such as the United Nations for the peaceful resolution of international conflict." Thereafter, the Canadian Peace Alliance grew steadily until, by 1988, it had 405 member organizations that, in turn, represented a further 2,500 peace-related groups in the country. Although most of these were small, grassroots groups, others were substantial organizations, including the Canadian Labor Congress, the National Farmers Union, Project Ploughshares, and Greenpeace.[68]

Although Canadian activism and participation declined somewhat, especially in 1987,[69] it retained a substantial presence in the nation's public life. The movement's projects included a well-publicized Stop Star Wars Campaign in 1985 and an ongoing nuclear weapons–free zone campaign that, by June 1987, had led 169 local jurisdictions—with 59.3 percent of Canada's population—to declare themselves nuclear-free. By that time the movement's proposal to have Canada proclaim itself such a zone had the support of two of the three major parties, three provincial and territorial legislatures, major national church bodies, and the major labor federation.[70] Even though Project Ploughshares widened its focus from opposing nuclear weapons to championing alternative security approaches, it remained a staunch backer of antinuclear ventures. Meanwhile, the organization grew, with financial contributions rising steadily during the late 1980s.[71] Other groups, too, retained considerable clout, including Canadian Physicians for Prevention of Nuclear War (4,200 members in 25 chapters), Operation Dismantle (11,000 members and supporters), and Greenpeace (80,000 members).[72] Local actions—including fierce protests against visits of nuclear warships, civil disobedience against weapons testing, and peace festivals—occurred in cities and towns across the nation.[73] Thousands of activists turned out for antinuclear rallies, including a 1987 End the Arms Race walk in Vancouver that drew between 80,000 and 100,000 people.[74]

The movement certainly maintained its very strong base of support in Canadian opinion. Polls conducted from June to September 1987 found that 71 percent of Canadians opposed an increase in Western military strength, and that 86 percent opposed taking "all steps to defeat Communism" if that meant "risking nuclear war." Conversely, 80 percent agreed or strongly agreed that "the security of western countries could best be increased by substantial reductions in both American and Soviet nuclear weapons." Furthermore, 57 percent supported the idea of Canada becoming a nuclear weapons–free zone, 68 percent opposed cruise missile testing on Canadian territory, and 81 percent backed a nuclear test ban.[75]

Asia and the Pacific

In the Pacific, the movement also retained a powerful presence. Australian activists felt discouraged by the positions of the governing Labor Party and, thanks to sectarian Left maneuverings, the collapse of the Nuclear Disarmament Party. Even so, the nuclear disarmament campaign continued to flourish in Australia, with its 1986 Palm Sunday antinuclear rallies drawing 250,000 people, a turnout surpassed only by its rallies in 1985.[76] Concern was growing about the role of U.S. military bases in Australia, particularly the intelligence-gathering stations at Pine Gap, North West Cape, and Nurrungar, which activists believed contributed to the nuclear war-fighting capability of the United States and, also, made Australia a target for a Soviet nuclear attack. Consequently, activists staged numerous demonstrations at these military bases and, in December 1986, established the Australian Anti-Bases Coalition, which gradually grew into the largest peace organization in the country.[77] A great deal of energy also went into resisting the arrival of nuclear warships in Australian ports. In the fall of 1988, Australian protesters—riding surfboards, kayaks, and other small craft—blockaded giant foreign warships, hindering their progress and sometimes "tagging" them with antinuclear slogans. The *Ark Royal*, a British nuclear aircraft carrier, underwent a nonviolent Greenpeace invasion at Sydney and a boycott by the local seamen's union at Melbourne. Even the prostitutes went on strike, announcing that the nuclear behemoths could "take their money, ships, bombs and diseases and go home."[78]

The antinuclear campaign remained especially powerful in New Zealand. Although, to some degree, the movement marginalized itself by its growing radicalism, it remained an impressive force. By 1987, Peace Movement Aotearoa (formerly Peace Movement New Zealand) was serving as the umbrella organization for about 300 peace groups that worked on projects ranging from halting French nuclear tests to persuading their town or city councils to declare their regions nuclear-free.[79] Given such efforts, 72 percent of New Zealand's population lived in municipally proclaimed nuclear-free zones by the fall of 1987. The hottest issue, however, remained the Labour government's ban on nuclear warships. In October 1985, seventeen former senior military officials issued a public statement opposing the ban, arguing that it was inconsistent with New Zealand's membership in the ANZUS alliance. Reinforcing such attacks, the U.S. State Department announced that, if the nation did not rescind the ban, "we will have to revise New Zealand's continued status as a United States ally under ANZUS." Although the nuclear warship ban was popular, so was ANZUS, and the conservative National Party made this an issue in the nationwide August 1987 elections. Labour struck back, using election broadcasts and advertisements focused on the nuclear ships ban—an effort complemented by widespread "vote nuclear-free" campaigns by disarmament groups. On election day, New Zealand's voters handed the Labour Party its first re-election victory since 1938. Labour increased its percentage of the vote and its par-liamentary majority.[80]

Struggles over nuclear weapons were also intense in the small island nations of the Pacific. In Palau, the U.S. government continued its relentless campaign to get this Trust Territory to approve an agreement that would provide for U.S. nuclear weapons facilities, despite antinuclear provisions in its constitution. In August 1987, after upholding their constitution in eight separate national referenda, the people of Palau were subjected to yet an-other referendum campaign—replete with pro-nuclear intimidation, fire-bombings, and murder. According to Palau's pro-American president, the referenda resulted in the amendment of the constitution and the adoption of the agreement. But Palau's women elders launched a court challenge that invalidated these changes, and growing revelations of government corrup-tion led to the president's suicide.[81] In Fiji, a multiracial Labour Party, formed in July 1985, took a strong antinuclear position. That November, it won a majority in municipal elections in the capital, Suva, where the presi-dent of the Fiji Anti-Nuclear Group now became mayor. In April 1987, the Labour Party swept to a nationwide victory, and Dr. Timoci Bavandra, a member of the Fiji branch of IPPNW, became prime minister. Although the new government was ready to implement a nuclear ships ban, the Fijian military staged a coup, precluding this possibility.[82] Meanwhile, the Mar-shallese kept up their occupation of Kwajalein Atoll islands, and the Nu-clear Free and Independent Pacific movement convened its fifth conference that year, in Manila.[83]

The siting of the conference in Manila reflected the progress made by antinuclear forces in the Philippines. In June 1985, defying the Marcos dic-tatorship, tens of thousands of workers, farmers, students, church people, and residents of fishing communities engaged in a "people's strike" against the nuclear power plant at Morong, and for three days the province of Bataan ground to a halt.[84] The following year, when a popular uprising top-pled the dictatorship and elevated the reformer Corazon Aquino to power, it unleashed a new surge of antinuclear activity. Not only could activists now operate in a climate of political freedom, but many Filipinos, resenting the U.S. government's years of support for the cruel and corrupt Marcos re-gime, were determined to terminate the presence of the giant U.S. military bases that housed nuclear weapons. Ten major Filipino organizations launched a campaign to gather a million signatures in support of placing a nuclear-free provision in the nation's new constitution, while the Nuclear Free Philippines Coalition and the Anti-Bases Coalition pressed the constitutional commission for the strongest possible wording. The new constitution that emerged (and was ratified in January 1987) did contain an antinuclear provision, though weaker than disarmament groups would have liked. Meanwhile, antinuclear sentiment spread rapidly. In 19 provinces and 36 municipalities covering some 34 percent of the nation's population, local governments declared themselves nuclear-free zones. At the same time, the growing movement pressed forward with what had become a popular campaign to shut down the U.S. military bases.[85]

The situation was more complex in Japan. Thanks to the widening differences between their patron organizations—the Socialist and Communist parties—the two traditional antinuclear groups, Gensuikin and Gensuikyo, grew increasingly divided and critical of one another. Although both remained powerful groups with loyal constituencies, many Japanese felt alienated by what they considered politically partisan ventures. Younger activists, who regarded Gensuikyo and Gensuikin as overly hierarchical and male-dominated, gravitated toward a multiplicity of new, non-affiliated peace groups, such as the National Movement for Non-Deployment of the Tomahawks, Peace Boat, and Peace Office.[86] Yet, despite some organizational decline and fragmentation, opposition to nuclear weapons remained a powerful current in Japanese life. Fervent antinuclear demonstrations—for example against the port visits of foreign warships—continued. In 1986, the Japanese Scientists Association issued a statement opposing participation in SDI research, declaring that it would damage efforts toward nuclear disarmament and "distort the advance of science." In early 1988, the general assembly of Japan's National Council of Churches called for the abolition of nuclear weapons.[87] Although Japan's conservative rulers did not share the enthusiasm for nuclear disarmament of the Left and Center parties, the strength of antinuclear sentiment was so great that, between late 1984 and February 1987, the number of local governing authorities declaring themselves nuclear-free rose from 300 to 1,104—over 90 percent of them governed by the conservatives.[88]

On the Asian mainland, the movement remained weak, but showed significant signs of growth. In Pakistan, an Islamic Society for International Unity and Peace was established in January 1987. Among its goals was nuclear disarmament, including a total ban on nuclear tests.[89] In India, the government's announcement of a plan to construct a National Testing Range in Orissa in the summer of 1985 sparked a major opposition campaign among the region's people, some 110,000 of whom were to be evicted to make way for this nuclear missile testing facility. A local Resistance Committee was organized among activists from political parties and citizens' groups, and an "outside front" among leftwing parties, unions, student groups, and intellectuals. Using nonviolent resistance, activists organized a "people's curfew" to prevent government officials from entering the area. In February 1988, when 24 magistrates bolstered by 3,000 armed police sought to reach the site, 20,000 villagers formed a human blockade and halted their entry. Furthermore, after the Chernobyl disaster, India's overall antinuclear campaign underwent substantial growth.[90]

Elsewhere in Asia, defying government repression, activists waged an even more dangerous struggle. Angered by China's nuclear tests at Lop Nur in Xinjiang province, which the local Uighur people claimed caused massive increases in cancer, birth defects, and environmental destruction, Uighur students staged street demonstrations in Beijing and other Chinese cities in December 1985. Meanwhile, in West Germany, Uighurs organized protests outside the Chinese embassy in Bonn. Activists drew inspiration from antinuclear demonstrations in the United States and, also, from their sense of mistreatment by China's majority Han population. Sporadic protest activity continued thereafter, blending opposition to nuclear testing with the demand for Xinjiang's independence from China.[91] In South Korea, despite a police state atmosphere, there was rising antinuclear ferment among student, women's, and church groups. The National Council of Churches issued a statement in 1986 that condemned the use of nuclear weapons and called for the removal of "all nuclear weapons deployed on the peninsula or aimed in its direction." In August 1988, a coalition of human rights, opposition, religious, labor, and student groups convened an International Conference on Peace and Reunification of Korea in Seoul. The 700 participants, mostly South Koreans, adopted a Peace Declaration calling for the withdrawal of nuclear weapons from their country and the creation of a nuclear-free zone on the Korean peninsula, the first step toward a Northwest Pacific nuclear-free zone.[92]

Public opinion in the Asia-Pacific region meshed nicely with antinuclear activism. Polls in New Zealand in 1986 found that 92 percent of the population opposed the presence of land-based nuclear weapons in their country and that 69 percent favored maintaining the ban on visits of nuclear warships. Despite internal and external pressure, by 1989 backing for the nuclear warship ban reached 84 percent.[93] In Australia, support for nuclear warship visits and for the presence of U.S. military bases dwindled markedly. Between 1982 and 1988, Australian backing for nuclear warship visits dropped from 47 percent to 24 percent.[94] Among the Japanese, surveys in October 1988 found that 78 percent of the population supported Japan's three non-nuclear principles (i.e. refusing to manufacture, possess, or allow entry to nuclear weapons). Furthermore, by a ratio of two-to-one, the Japanese rejected the idea that nuclear weapons helped to deter war.[95] Asked in early 1986 how important it was that the United States and the Soviet Union sign an arms control treaty, 80 percent of Indians, 84 percent of Japanese, and 88 percent of South Koreans rated it as important or very important. Polled on a similar question that year, 87 percent of New Zealanders favored eliminating nuclear weapons and working strongly for disarmament.[96]

Latin America, Africa, the Middle East, and Eastern Europe

In Latin America and Africa, the movement remained on a much more limited scale. To promote nuclear disarmament, an international gathering of scientists, teachers, politicians, environmentalists, and intellectuals met on August 6, 1986, in Ixtapa, Mexico. The following year, Brazilian scientists took an important antinuclear step, when more than 60,000 of them signed a statement, circulated by the Brazilian Society for the Advancement of Science, that called for banning the "construction, storage, and transport of nuclear weapons" in their country.[97] In Africa, branches of the tiny Zimbabwe Organization for Nuclear Education sponsored small marches, a seminar on "South Africa and the Bomb," and a "die-in" to commemorate the Hiroshima bombing.[98] Although few other movement ventures emerged on these continents, public opinion did have an antinuclear flavor. Polled in early 1986, 72 percent of Argentineans, 76 percent of Brazilians, 66 percent of Uruguayans, 49 percent of Nigerians, and 82 percent of South Africans said they thought it important or very important for the United States and the Soviet Union to sign an arms control treaty.[99]

In the Middle East, as well, the movement remained very weak, and only Israel experienced a surge of antinuclear activism. In October 1986, when Mordechai Vanunu, an Israeli nuclear technician, revealed the story of his country's secret nuclear weapons project to the London *Times*, he was kidnapped by Israeli agents and brought to Israel for trial. Through his act of "whistle-blowing," Vanunu—widely reviled as a traitor—apparently hoped to make Israeli nuclear weapons a political issue. And this, in fact, is what happened. In early 1987, activists organized an Israeli Committee for the Prevention of Nuclear War, and in February it sponsored a large public meeting in Tel Aviv around the theme: "Mushroom Over the Middle East." Together with the activities of the Israeli branch of IPPNW and the support of the leftwing parties for a Middle East nuclear-free zone, the new committee provided the country with a small antinuclear campaign.[100]

Throughout most of Eastern Europe, the movement was beginning to take off. Against all odds, the Soviet Trust Groups continued to grow. In Leningrad and Lvov, they demonstrated against the bloody Soviet war in Afghanistan. In Moscow, Trust Group members held weekly seminars, produced a monthly magazine, and staged an exhibit—quickly shut down by the police—of antimilitarist art in Red Square. After the Chernobyl disaster, the Moscow group held demonstrations calling for an honest report on the accident and for the abolition of nuclear power. In 1987, when the Trust Group adopted a new statement of principles, it condemned the war in Afghanistan.[101] Not at all pleased by this behavior, Soviet authorities responded with harassment, arrests, confinement in psychiatric institutions, and imprisonment. But publicity and protests by Western activists helped shield Trust Group members from the wrath of the regime. When Vladimir Brodsky, a Trust Group member, was sentenced to three years in a labor camp, IPPNW and other peace groups made an issue of his case and secured his freedom. Brodsky later remarked that "I was released only because of the efforts of physicians and the peace movement." Nuclear disarmament groups also succeeded in winning the release of Aleksandr Shatravka, a longtime pacifist and founder of the Moscow Trust Group, from a prison camp.[102]

Indeed, a close alliance developed between Western disarmament organizations and the Moscow Trust Group. Recognizing their ability to provide protection to their embattled East Bloc counterparts, some Western antinuclear campaigners joined with Trust Group members in Moscow demonstrations. In August 1986, American, British, and Soviet activists leafleted together at the entrance to Gorky Park, wearing signs reading: "Peace and environmental safety for all. No more Hiroshimas, no more Chernobyls." Although arrested, they were quickly released. Several days later, two Greenham Common women began a second round of antinuclear leafleting. In this case, the best the police and the KGB managed to do was to warn passersby not to accept the leaflet. But, in fact, they took it anyway.[103] END's Mient Jan Faber and the Trust Group's Yuri Medvedkov conferred at length on strategy and program for the international movement. Medvedkov showed little sympathy for those he called "your own hawks" or for the "Stalinists and hawks" of the Soviet Union. Instead, he told Faber that he hoped to undercut "both sorts of hawks." In 1987, as Gorbachev's *glasnost* eased restrictions on free expression, this seemed increasingly possible. That December, members of the Trust Group even appeared on prime-time Soviet television. In a widely viewed documentary about the antinuclear movement, they complained about Soviet militarism.[104]

Moreover, the Trust Groups were no longer alone. As Soviet authorities loosened the reins in 1987 and 1988, thousands of small, independent citizens' organizations popped up, as a Russian saying went, "like mushrooms after a rain." Composed primarily of young people, they turned eagerly to discussing a broad range of popular issues, from democratization to disarmament. In June 1987, pacifists from cities around the country staged a demonstration in Moscow. That December, one of the new groups, Press Club Glasnost, organized a seminar in Moscow to discuss human rights and world politics, inviting Petra Kelly and other foreign activists.[105] A major concern of the new citizens' groups was nuclear power. Although, initially, the response to the Chernobyl disaster was fairly mild, in late 1987 an antinuclear power movement began developing in communities near Soviet reactor sites. Letters and articles criticizing nuclear power appeared in local newspapers, while independent groups—usually founded by members of the cultural or scientific intelligentsia—took shape. As in the West, the revulsion against nuclear power led to questioning nuclear weapons, for the damage caused by a nuclear reactor raised the issue of the catastrophe produced by a nuclear war. As Gorbachev put it: "Chernobyl was a bell calling mankind to understand what kind of age we live in."[106]

Meanwhile, Velikhov's Committee of Soviet Scientists (CSS), which enjoyed excellent relations with Gorbachev and other party reformers, set off on new ventures. Working closely with the FAS and the Natural Resources Defense Council to develop procedures for verifying nuclear testing, CSS leaders played a key role in emerging efforts to secure a nuclear test ban. They also organized an International Scientists' Forum on Drastic Reductions and Final Elimination of Nuclear Weapons, held in Moscow in February 1987. At the forum, West European advocates of "non-offensive defense" laid out their ideas before Soviet officials and three cooperative East-West ventures were launched: publication of *Science and Global Security*, an international journal focused on arms control and disarmament; a five-year research project on arms reductions under the auspices of the FAS and the CSS; and an International Foundation for the Survival and Development of Humanity. Although the CSS allied itself with the Soviet Union's reform leadership, it did challenge it on occasion, both by taking independent stands and by pushing that leadership to adopt innovative programs, often in line with the disarmament proposals of Western activists. The new foundation, for example, sponsored the formation of a Soviet chapter of Greenpeace and put Andrei Sakharov—only recently the regime's Public Enemy Number One—in charge of a Soviet human rights project.[107]

Although Sakharov denigrated his work for the foundation, his political rehabilitation restored him to leadership in the antinuclear movement. Freed by Gorbachev in late 1986, after nearly seven years of house arrest, the famed Soviet physicist immediately plunged into peace and disarmament politics. He renewed his meetings with Jeremy Stone and Frank von Hippel of the FAS, spoke for the first time with Petra Kelly and Gert Bastian of the West German Greens, and established a working relationship with leaders of the CSS. Addressing the February 1987 forum in Moscow, Sakharov argued that, "without a resolution of political and humanitarian problems, progress in disarmament and international security will be extremely difficult, if not impossible." But, "conversely, democratization and liberalization in the U.S.S.R. . . . will be impeded unless the arms race slows down." For this reason, among others, he insisted that "a significant cut in ICBMs and medium-range and battlefield missiles, and other agreements on disarmament, should be negotiated as soon as possible."[108] Characteristically, during a November 1988 visit to the United States, Sakharov called upon the Soviet Union to cut its armed forces unilaterally and denounced Reagan's SDI program. Overall, he had a positive view of Gorbachev and blamed the failure of the Soviet Union to move faster toward disarmament on "the inertia of a gigantic system, the resistance, both passive and active, of innumerable bureaucratic and ideological windbags."[109]

The movement also showed new signs of vigor in Czechoslovakia. Spontaneous protests against Soviet deployment of nuclear missiles, amplified by the work of Charter 77, continued well into 1985. Moreover, Charter 77 and the Jazz Section of the Prague Musicians Union—an avant garde group with some 7,000 young members and thousands of additional supporters—maintained close contacts with END.[110] But it was the "Lennonists" who proved most rambunctious. Ever since the murder of John Lennon on December 8, 1980, young Czechs had made yearly pilgrimages to the small island of Kampa, in the center of Prague, to honor his memory, adorning its "Lennon Wall" with peace symbols and slogans. When, at the anniversary celebration of 1985, police ordered them to disperse, about 600 of the mourners broke loose and staged an unauthorized peace march through downtown Prague. Along the way, they chanted "No missiles are peaceful!" "Flowers, not weapons!" "Scrap the army!" and—perhaps most provocatively—"Down with the Red bourgeoisie!" Blocked by police from entering the Castle gateway, they drew up a petition against the siting of missiles in Eastern or Western Europe. Some 300 youngsters signed it and, then, sent it off to Czech officials, as well as to the U.S. and Soviet embassies.[111] Despite subsequent interrogations and other harassment by the police, virtually the same thing happened in December 1987, when an estimated 500 young people marched through the streets chanting peace and anti-military slogans. The crowd roared its approval as Ota Veverka, a Charter 77 and Jazz Section activist, called for the replacement of SS-20 missiles with theaters that would stage Václav Havel's plays, with books of banned authors, and with food for the hungry everywhere.[112]

Although relations between Czech and Western activists were sometimes strained, they usually worked together quite amicably. For the most part, Charter 77 took a more pessimistic, human rights-centered view of the possibilities for change—a position exemplified by Havel's eloquent essay, "The Anatomy of a Reticence," that he submitted for discussion to END's 1985 convention. Even so, as Havel later noted, his essay was designed to explain "my uncomfortable opinions to a friend or colleague," and "the dialogue we've had has been beneficial."[113] In April 1988, Czech activists organized the country's first unofficial peace group since the creation of the Communist regime: the Independent Peace Association (Nezavisie Mirove Sdruzeni, NMS). Enthusiastic about disarmament, it nonetheless argued that the simple elimination of armaments would "not ensure either real peace or its permanence." Instead, NMS declared, "the task of every nation is to create internal preconditions for doing without weapons." Charter 77 and NMS invited 35 activists representing independent peace and human rights groups from East and West to an International Peace Seminar, scheduled for June 1988 in Prague. Although Czech police broke up the event—detaining the hosts and deporting the foreign activists—participants were able to make considerable progress on their plans for a European Assembly for Peace and Democracy thanks to substantive discussions they held while incarcerated in Prague's central police station. The same groups, joined by others, held a repeat performance in November. Rising, apparently, from the floorboards, Havel opened the symposium, though he managed to speak only briefly before the police, realizing what was happening, carted him off to prison.[114]

Antinuclear activism was more muted in East Germany. By the mid-1980s, government intimidation, arrests, and expulsions of leading activists to the West had begun to wear down the movement. At least as disheartening was the fact that the Protestant Church, under pressure from the authorities, distanced itself from antinuclear activists. Even so, the struggle continued. Founded in 1986 in East Berlin, the Initiative for Peace and Human Rights—like so many East Bloc groups—blended the cause of political freedom with that of peace and disarmament, as did its underground newspaper, *Grenzfall*. In June 1987, during the official church festival, a coalition of young people organized a "church festival from below." More than a thousand protesters leafleted the opening service and still others unfurled banners at the closing ceremonies attacking church conformity, especially on peace issues. Embarrassed by the protests, the church renewed its ties with the movement. A spirit of revolt was also clear that same month as crowds of young people gathered at the Berlin Wall to listen to rock concerts on the other side. When police sought to disperse them, they defiantly chanted "The Wall must go," "Rosa Luxemburg," and "Gorbachev"—a response publicized by the Initiative for Peace and Human Rights.[115] Visiting East Berlin in 1988, a Canadian disarmament activist was pleased to find a crowd of nearly a thousand people at a peace workshop hosted by the Protestant Church, as well as enthusiastic responses by the young to a related theater performance and poetry reading.[116]

Although, in Hungary, most organized peace and disarmament activism dwindled—leaving in its wake small groups of conscientious objectors, outspoken individuals, and the cautious 4–6–0 organization[117]—it flared up to an impressive degree in Communist Yugoslavia. Inspired by the West European campaign, some official student and Communist youth organizations, as well as citizens' initiatives, especially among urban intellectuals, began independent antinuclear activities in the mid-1980s. On May 9, 1985, to protest the official military parade that day in Belgrade, several hundred young people marched through the center of Ljubljana, Slovenia, denouncing nuclear weapons and the militarization of Yugoslav society. Organized by the Ljubljana Peace Group, the march was followed by unofficial peace marches elsewhere in Slovenia, as well as by numerous arrests. Peace and environmental activism often melded and, in June 1986, when the first congress of the Yugoslav anti-nuclear power movement was held in Belgrade, it was attended by both ecological and peace groups. In Zagreb, activists established a peace and environmental organization called Svarun. Consequently, independent action against nuclear power was widespread in Yugoslavia, with activists holding a protest march of 6,000 people on the first anniversary of the Chernobyl disaster. As in other East European countries, peace groups zealously defended the rights of "civil society" against the power of the state.[118]

The movement was also thriving in Poland. In an April 1985 interview, Jacek Kuron, a leader of the Solidarity movement and of the Committee of Social Resistance (KOS), called for a demilitarized zone across Central Europe, including the withdrawal of nuclear missiles. KOS sent greetings to the July 1985 END convention, as did Solidarity's Lech Walesa, who declared that he was "watching your work toward peace" with "great interest and approval."[119] But a full-fledged peace movement did not emerge in Communist-ruled Poland until the formation of Freedom and Peace (Wolnosc i Pokoj). Inspired by the example of Solidarity and of Western activists, Freedom and Peace was organized in April 1985 after the courts meted out a severe prison sentence to Marek Adamkiewicz, who refused to take the Polish military oath. The new movement, comprised of young people, focused primarily on the rights of conscientious objectors to military service, which they linked to "the struggle for human rights, religious freedom, and national independence." But, as its declaration of principles noted, Freedom and Peace also was concerned about "the seriousness of the threat of nuclear war, of the problem of militarism and of a militaristic education." Despite arrests and other harassment by the authorities, Freedom and Peace activists worked "above ground," staging public meetings, marches, sit-ins, and petitions that spread to more than twenty cities. After the Chernobyl disaster, Freedom and Peace also served as a spearhead for protests against nuclear power.[120]

Not surprisingly, ever-closer relations developed between Polish and Western activists. In its declaration of principles, Freedom and Peace expressed the desire "to work together with the international peace movement," and by May 1987, it had organized an international peace conference in Warsaw. This event was fiercely resisted by the regime, which arrested 22 Freedom and Peace activists, denied visas to Western disarmament campaigners, and pressed the Catholic church leadership hard enough for it to tell churches not to house the gathering. Nonetheless, the meeting occurred. A daring priest opened the doors of the Church of God's Mercy to the conference, more than 60 foreign activists from thirteen countries slipped through the dragnet, and the authorities backed off in embarrassment. Conference attendance grew over its three days, at times reaching 250 people. Freedom and Peace activists, prominent Solidarity leaders, and representatives from West Germany's Green Party, END, CODENE, Charter 77, the Dutch Pax Christi, the War Resisters League, and other groups mingled together happily, strengthening their rapport.[121] In 1988, Solidarity leaders Kuron and Janusz Onyszkiewicz attended the END convention, while Freedom and Peace worked jointly with Solidarity's Intervention and Lawlessness Commission to organize a conference on human rights in Krakow, including a focus on how social movements could promote a demilitarization of life in East and West.[122]

There was also an alliance developing within the East. Repeatedly, activists issued public protests against repression of their counterparts in other East bloc nations.[123] Furthermore, in response to Charter 77's Prague Appeal of March 11, 1985, they began to work together to formulate an all-European peace movement strategy. In June 1985, 21 leading East German activists is-

sued a public response, stating that, although "weapons of mass destruction
... must be abolished and the production of so-called defense systems
which in reality perpetuate the arms race (SDI) must be prevented," activists also must turn "the peace movement" into "an emancipation movement
in the widest sense." By the end of 1986, with the assistance of the European
Network for East-West Dialogue, this joint emphasis had taken shape in a
memorandum, "Giving Real Life to the Helsinki Accords." Signed by hundreds of East European activists—including 33 from Czechoslovakia (most
from Charter 77), 41 from East Germany (most from the Initiative for Peace
and Human Rights), and 61 from Poland (most from Freedom and Peace and
from Solidarity)—the Helsinki memorandum argued against "any tendency
to play off peace against freedom or vice versa." A lasting peace "cannot be
based on the threat of mutual annihilation," it declared, and thus there must
be drastic nuclear arms reductions in Europe, the signing of a test ban
treaty, and the establishment of nuclear-free zones. At the same time, it insisted, "working for civil liberties and social rights is not only a moral obligation for everyone cherishing human dignity and democratic ideas, but
also a political necessity if we want to create the conditions for a really stable, lasting and democratic peace."[124] As East European activists moved
forward with organizing international peace conferences in Warsaw (May
1987), Budapest (November 1987), and Prague (June 1988), the region was
coming alive with cross-border solidarity on peace and disarmament issues.[125]

Although there is no satisfactory way to gauge public opinion in these
dictatorial societies, there were signs of substantial anti-military sentiment.
In Poland, the director of the Institute for Youth Research reported in the
spring of 1987 that, among the young, there was an alarming level of support
for conscientious objection. In Yugoslavia, the official polls during 1986 and
1987 in Slovenia (the only place in the country where surveys were regularly
conducted) showed that some three-quarters of the population sympathized
with peace activism and about half would have liked to participate in it.[126] In
the Soviet Union, there seems to have been widespread distaste for nuclear
weapons and nuclear war. According to a poll conducted among residents of
Moscow in early 1987 by the Institute of Sociological Research of the Soviet
Academy of Sciences, 83 percent of Muscovites said that increases and improvements in nuclear weapons would not give either the United States or
the Soviet Union a significant advantage over the other, and 93 percent
agreed that "a complete liquidation of nuclear weapons" provided "the only
path to escape nuclear war." Moreover, 89 percent thought that, in an all-out

nuclear exchange, "the United States and the Soviet Union would be completely annihilated," and 93 percent believed that no purpose justified use of nuclear weapons.[127]

The International Dimensions of the Nonaligned Movement

One of the remarkable characteristics of the late 1980s was how genuinely international the antinuclear campaign had become. Peace camps established by activists outside missile bases and other military facilities existed around the globe, providing sites for activists from diverse lands to meet, live together, and swap ideas. In March 1985, when U.S.-Soviet arms control talks started up again at Geneva, representatives of major European and North American disarmament groups presented the two superpowers with a long list of their common demands.[128] "Détente from below" flourished. Substantial numbers of American peace activists flocked to the Soviet Union, conducting an unorthodox, peace-oriented "citizen diplomacy" that challenged both U.S. and Soviet foreign policy.[129] Thanks to the efforts of the Center for Defense Information, even former U.S. and Soviet military officers began to meet together to discuss how to prevent war, as they did at conferences organized by the CDI in 1987 and 1988. Using its church connections, IKV encouraged direct discussions between disarmament proponents from Eastern and Western Europe. "We succeeded . . . in establishing real contacts with all kinds of people in Eastern Europe," Faber noted, "and discovered that it was really a common problem we are facing."[130]

A variety of international organizations added their weight to the global antinuclear campaign. Although the pacifist internationals stuck to their broad agenda, opposing nuclear weapons was certainly part of it. Arguing that it was "too late for arms control," the WRI called for "complete and comprehensive disarmament." Somewhat less sweeping in its demands, WILPF pressed for a comprehensive test ban treaty.[131] Similarly, Pax Christi—with more than 100,000 members in sixteen nations by 1988—blended an emphasis on East-West dialogue with a concern for disarmament.[132] Some of the most dramatic antinuclear action was provided by Greenpeace. Long a vigorous foe of nuclear testing, Greenpeace added work against nuclear materials production in 1985 and, in July 1987, launched its most ambitious antinuclear program yet: a Nuclear Free Seas campaign. Designed to rid the oceans of nuclear weapons, the new venture challenged the naval arms race, military exercises on the high seas, and visits of nuclear warships. Greenpeace blockaded nuclear ships off Canada's west coast, fostered civil disobedience in New Zealand and Australia, and "tagged" Soviet warships with radiation symbols off Denmark and Tunisia. Although Greenpeace relied upon small-scale, sensational actions rather than upon mass mobilization, by late 1987 it had three million members in seventeen countries in North and South America, Europe, and the South Pacific—and was growing by 40 percent a year.[133]

A number of internationals provided the movement with traction in the realm of politics and public policy. As in preceding years, the Socialist International (SI)—the world body of social democratic, labor, and socialist parties—served as an important component of the antinuclear campaign. At its October 1985 Bureau meeting, the SI issued an eloquent appeal for disarmament. It followed that up in April 1987, when it demanded "drastic reduction in strategic systems," the elimination of all INF missiles from Europe, and a Central European corridor free from nuclear weapons. The SI also opposed the installation of shorter-range nuclear systems in Europe, as well as the development, testing, and deployment of new anti-missile and space weapons.[134] One of the smallest of the internationals, Parliamentarians Global Action (PGA)—organized in 1977 as Parliamentarians for World Order—began work in 1985 on a campaign to secure a comprehensive test ban treaty through the device of initiating a conference to amend the partial test ban treaty of 1963. Sparked by two veteran peace activists, Aaron Tovish (United States) and Olafur Ragnar Grimmson (Iceland), and bolstered by widespread discontent with the nuclear arms race, the PGA campaign gradually acquired momentum. Meanwhile, PGA expanded to more than 600 legislators from 35 countries.[135]

The international most in the limelight during the late 1980s was International Physicians for the Prevention of Nuclear War. In October 1985, when it was announced that this global physicians' movement had been awarded the Nobel Peace Prize, IPPNW's status soared. Irate at this turn of events, conservative parties and portions of the Western communications media launched a blistering attack upon it, charging that Chazov and other Soviet doctors were agents of the Kremlin and that Western doctors were hopeless naïfs. In an editorial headed "The Nobel Peace Fraud," the *Wall Street Journal* claimed that the Nobel committee had "hit a new low."[136] IPPNW leaders defended the organization's integrity, but the best rebuttal occurred at the Nobel ceremonies that December. Lown and Chazov were doing their best to respond to hostile questions at a crowded press conference when a Soviet journalist tumbled to the floor, felled by a cardiac arrest. Immediately, Lown, Chazov, and other anxious doctors raced to the stricken man's side, taking turns pounding on his chest and giving him mouth-to-mouth resuscitation. Ultimately, they saved his life. When the press conference resumed, Lown, shaken but quick-witted, said: "What you have just seen is a parable of our movement. When a crisis comes, when life is in danger, Soviet and American physicians cooperate. . . . We forget ideology, we forget our differences." And "the big issue confronting humankind today is sudden nuclear death."[137] This dramatic incident rallied support for IPPNW, which pressed forward with its campaign to halt nuclear testing. By late 1988, it had grown to a federation of physicians' groups in 61 countries, with over 200,000 members.[138]

END, the voice of the European campaign, did not fare quite as well. Despite the large number of groups that signed the END Appeal and sent representatives to its annual conventions, it never developed much of an institutional base or coordinating structure. Even a decision in 1985 to create individual END memberships added only minimal strength to the organization.[139] In Western Europe, END—like some of its constituent groups—was beginning to feel the effects of the exhaustion of longtime activists. In Eastern Europe, where the movement had reached a take-off point, governmental obstacles—including harassment, imprisonment, and denials of visas—took their toll. END's Eastern Europe coordinator reported in mid-1986 that relations with East European activists were "difficult" and "fraught with diplomatic and political pitfalls." Conference planners had to be aware of how forlorn the hope was "that any of them will get exit visas to participate."[140] In addition, a growing tension developed within END's ranks between those who emphasized political solutions to the East-West confrontation (usually independent groups, partisans of "détente from below") and those who emphasized nuclear disarmament agreements (usually political parties, partisans of "détente from above").[141]

Even so, END remained a force of considerable significance. Of its annual conventions—Amsterdam (1985), Evry (1986), Coventry (1987), and Lund (1988)—only the one at Evry drew fewer than a thousand participants. West Europeans predominated at these conclaves, but people came to them from a broad range of countries—Japan, China, Afghanistan, India, Argentina, Nicaragua, the United States, Canada, Australia, South Africa, Israel, Palestine, Pacific Island nations, and many more. Forty-two countries were represented in 1987. Despite the legal barriers erected by Communist governments, substantial numbers of East European activists managed to attend and serve as key participants in discussions. Activists attended a broad range of seminars on topics ranging from disarmament, to nuclear-free zones, to Chernobyl, to militarization and underdevelopment, to Third

World intervention. Leaders of the Dutch and West German Social Democratic parties, India's Chipko movement, Pacific island independence groups, and of many other organizations addressed large assemblages, and vigorous debate raged as to priorities and strategies.[142] Covering the 1987 convention in the *Guardian*, a journalist reported that a "mood of optimism and determination was palpable." According to Kaldor, at the 1988 convention, one of the largest in END's history, "there was a real sense of progress both in the level of political discussion and above all, in East-West relations." E. P. Thompson "said that at last, after eight years, we have put peace and freedom together," whereupon Solidarity's Jacek Kuron "hugged him, to huge applause."[143]

Although END was much better known, especially in Europe, the International Peace Bureau increasingly provided the movement with its global structure. In September 1985, the IPB received an infusion of energy and credibility when Bruce Kent, the longtime leader of CND, became its new president. That same month, as befit a genuinely nonaligned movement, the IPB issued statements condemning the Soviet invasion and occupation of Afghanistan, as well as the U.S. economic and military attack upon Nicaragua.[144] Although the IPB, as a peace federation, worked on a broad range of issues, nuclear disarmament was a primary concern. In 1985, it called upon the United Nations "to conclude without delay an international agreement on the total banning of research, development, testing, production, possession, stockpiling, proliferation and use of nuclear weapons." Meanwhile, with the help of its former president, Sean MacBride, IPB launched an appeal and signature campaign for lawyers and parliamentarians that would challenge the legality of nuclear weapons. "Too few have yet understood that the only security possible in the nuclear world is common security," Kent argued, "and the real enemy today is not East or West but a highly dangerous arms race."[145] Casting about for a solid institutional framework, many nuclear disarmament organizations began to affiliate with the IPB, and it underwent a spurt of growth.[146]

As in the past, the international nonaligned movement responded to persecution of activists in East and West with publicity and protests. Committed to supporting beleaguered activists, END involved itself deeply in these efforts, usually through its national working groups. In 1986, END's Soviet working group reported that "support work for the Moscow Trust Group has dominated much of the group's activities this year." There was not only a campaign to free Vladimir Brodsky, but a successful effort for the release of people in psychiatric hospitals and for a speaking tour of Austria, Germany, and the Netherlands by Trust Group members in exile.[147] In 1988, END publicly protested the Czech government's arrests of members of the Independent Peace Association, Charter 77, and the Czech Jazz Section. When the participants in Poland's first Freedom and Peace venture were arrested, protests from Western peace groups helped secure their release. Condemning the arrests of East German activists, WRI president David McReynolds told East German party boss Erich Honecker that "human rights for peace and environmental activists . . . is not something which can be given or taken away at the whim of the state." Furthermore, having participated in the same kinds of ventures in the West, "we feel . . . close to those who were arrested in the DDR, and we cannot remain silent. . . . Our sisters and brothers exist on both sides of the arbitrary political and geographic lines history has imposed."[148]

The Communist-Led Movement

For a brief time, even the Communist-led peace movement displayed a new liveliness. With the advent of the reform-minded Gorbachev, the Soviet Peace Committee decided that the moment had arrived to do something about the very expensive and ineffective World Peace Council. At the WPC's April 1986 conference in Sophia, Bulgaria, Russian officials presented WPC president Romesh Chandra with a speech, in which he was to acknowledge that many of the past criticisms of the WPC were valid and call for "a fresh look" at its structure and at "the norms and framework" of its activity. Recognizing that his decades-long sinecure was in jeopardy, Chandra gave a blistering, unrepentant speech instead. Nevertheless, the Soviet version of Chandra's address was printed and distributed as the speech of record.[149] Moreover, the Russians brought in the chair of the Finnish Peace Committee, Johannes Pakaslahti, to serve as the WPC's general secretary—an alternative source of power to Chandra. Although a Communist, Pakaslahti—like Gorbachev—was a genuine reformer, with no use for the WPC's ineffectiveness, corruption, and isolation from the mass antinuclear campaigns of the time. In stories published in the WPC's *Peace Courier* and in the mainstream European press, Pakaslahti criticized the WPC's marginality and called for the building of an open and unbiased movement.[150]

Despite Chandra's determined resistance, from 1986 to 1988 Pakaslahti did manage to send a current of reform through the WPC. In contrast to *Peace Courier*'s blatantly anti-American articles of the past, it now featured stories like "Save the United Nations," "Easing East-West Tension in Europe," and "Ten Principles for a World Without War."[151] In place of the articles focused on Chandra leading delegations or making speeches, the WPC magazine published contributions by David McReynolds, Bruce Kent, and Ken Coates, plus a friendly interview with E. P. Thompson.[152] Meanwhile, enthusiastic, reform-oriented staffers—usually from North America and Western Europe—embarked upon a program of visiting WPC affiliates to find out how they operated or, for that matter, if they really existed. Pakaslahti supplemented this effort by calling for a dialogue with these groups about what the WPC should be doing and even for meetings with non-WPC organizations to find out what these outsiders had to say about the WPC.[153] Although Chandra and his allies sabotaged portions of the reform program, it picked up additional support in 1988 when Tair Tairov, a former Soviet secretary of the WPC, came to Helsinki and blasted the organization in a published interview. "The future cannot be built around organizing self-contained conferences and offering up free travel tickets for them," he remarked. "The WPC gave medals to Brezhnev and Brezhnev gave medals to the WPC," he added; "but this pattern . . . has absolutely nothing to do with genuine peace work." Lauding END in an interview with *END Journal*, Tairov criticized the WPC as an "authoritarian, hierarchical," and "sectarian" organization that "must change."[154]

WPC affiliates varied in their responses to Pakaslahti's reform course. The most enthusiastic support came from the Swedes, Danes, Norwegians, and Finns, but there was also considerable backing from North Americans and, for the most part, from the West Europeans. In an official report to the WPC, the U.S. Peace Council remarked acidly that "mass peace movements with deep roots have developed . . . without the help or even the attention (and sometimes with the disdain) of the WPC," and the WPC "needs to look at itself to determine what it must do to be . . . a relevant force."[155] Within Communist nations, the official peace committees in Hungary and Poland expressed a desire for change, though others drew back as the full dimensions of the reform program became manifest. The East German committee, long impatient with the ineffectiveness of Chandra, was not any happier with the *glasnost* of Pakaslahti or Gorbachev. Accordingly, it continued its authoritarian, party-line style and gradually tilted against the WPC reformers. Asked by a WPC visitor about its chapters and grassroots activity, Werner Rümpel of the German Peace Council replied scornfully: "We *have* no chapters! This is not the way we function! . . . There are no [independent] initiatives!" In most other regions of the world—and particularly in Latin America, where Chandra retained his popularity—the reform program encountered bitter opposition.[156]

The success of WPC reform, of course, hinged upon the response to it of the Soviet Peace Committee, a particularly hidebound organization then in the throes of its own internal struggles. In April 1987, apparently in response to Gorbachev's calls for *glasnost* and *perestroika*, the SPC underwent a facelift when its aging Stalinist chair, Yuri Zhukov, was replaced with a more personable leader, Genryk Borovik.[157] Meanwhile, within the SPC, a fierce battle erupted between reformers and old-time bureaucrats. The most daring of the reformers was undoubtedly Tairov, then a vice-president of the organization. In June 1988, he published an article in *Komsomolskaya Pravda* in which he condemned the SPC for its "organizationally closed character," "the secrecy practiced by its former leadership," and for "denouncing those who do not share our ideological positions." Interviewed in the CND journal *Sanity*, Tairov remarked tartly that there were "many changes, criticisms, and democratizations" in the Soviet Union—*"except* in the Soviet Peace Committee."[158] These kinds of attacks horrified the SPC's conservative and corrupt officials, terrified that they might lose control of the organization, as well as their comfortable jobs, overseas junkets, and access to Western consumer goods. Thus, while giving lip service to openness, they purged reformers, kept the Moscow Trust Group at arm's length, and began to put the brakes on changes within the WPC. Oleg Kharkhardin, the Soviet WPC secretary, shifted from a position equidistant between Pakaslahti and Chandra to an alliance with Chandra.[159]

In these circumstances, WPC reform was doomed. As Rob Prince, one of its supporters, recalled: "To a movement whose political backbone consisted of communist movements the world round, such 'new thinking' was not popular." Indeed, it was often viewed "as heresy." Furthermore, "reforming or 'renewing' the WPC meant getting rid of a good deal of 'dead wood,' of which there was an extraordinary amount. Like other corrupt and dying organisms, the WPC had attracted a world of parasites, self-seekers and crooks who had 'come along for the ride,' the free food, etc."[160] And these people, now backed by the Soviet Peace Committee, mounted an offensive against reform. It began in late March 1988, when Chandra denounced Pakaslahti's actions and accused the editors of *Peace Courier* of creating a "sort of *END Journal*." Privately, Chandra warned Pakaslahti that "your friends in the Soviet Peace Committee have been defeated, so you better adjust accordingly." But Pakaslahti and most reform-minded staffers refused to retreat, resulting in what Prince described as "full scale war."[161] Although the reformers were able to rally support in sympathetic affiliates,[162] they were no match for their opponents and, especially, for the all-powerful Soviet Peace Committee. At the WPC's November 1988 meeting in Geneva, conservatives—arguing that the WPC faced a dangerous threat "from within"—took firm control of the organization, scrapped the reform course, and decided that there was no longer any need for a general secretary (i.e. Pakaslahti). In late December, Chandra circulated a letter announcing, falsely, that Pakaslahti had resigned.[163] In addition, after holding a secret "trial" of other reformers, the WPC's Old Guard informed them that they had been purged from the WPC secretariat. "In retrospect," Prince recalled, reforming the WPC was "akin to putting make-up on a corpse. We never stood a chance."[164]

The Response of the Nonaligned Movement

The rise of reform elements within the Soviet Union and within the WPC left the nonaligned movement more uncertain than in the past about how to relate to the Communist-led peace movement. As before, nonaligned groups almost invariably rejected invitations to WPC conventions or made their attendance contingent upon significant concessions, such as granting independent East Bloc groups access to the meeting.[165] But encouraging participation by the official East Bloc peace committees in nonaligned conventions—such as those of END—seemed to have greater merit. After all, Gorbachev's initiatives opened new prospects for democratization and disarmament. "We want to embrace the changes at the top," argued END's Ken Coates. "It is a process that could be stopped if it is not supported. We are not a league of oppositions." Moreover, reform currents were beginning to sweep through the WPC and the official peace committees. Another END activist recalled: "There was a feeling that the ice was cracking . . . and here was an opportunity to engage at last with representatives of the official Soviet and Eastern bloc system, who seemed to be wanting to make the move." Furthermore, a modus vivendi with the official peace committees might ease the problems faced in their countries by independent groups. Others, however, argued that the official peace groups were government bodies that had little in common with their independent counterparts. In addition, inviting them to END conventions might offend East Bloc independent groups and, worse yet, undermine the status of independent groups as representatives of disarmament activism in Communist nations.[166]

As a result, relations with the East Bloc's official groups provided the most contentious issue within the nonaligned movement during 1987 and 1988. With its 1988 triennial conference approaching, the WRI decided against inviting the official peace committees to attend.[167] A different approach was adopted by END, which chose to invite both the independent *and* the official groups from East Bloc nations to its conventions. Although most END leaders found this an acceptable compromise, a fierce battle erupted when the END liaison committee—responsible for organizing these conferences—also invited representatives of the East European Communist parties to attend the 1987 convention. Facing a backlash within END's ranks, the committee ultimately cut back the invitations to only three of these parties and limited the issues to be discussed.[168] The hottest of the relationship crises emerged in July 1987, at the END convention in Coventry, when the Hungarian Peace Council announced that it was signing the END Appeal. Supporters of closer ties with the official committees (usually from West European Social Democratic parties) saw the Hungarian move as a welcome sign of East bloc liberalization. Opponents of closer ties (usually from grassroots peace movements), pointing out that the Hungarians could now participate in planning END conventions, viewed it as compromising END's nonaligned status.[169] Ultimately, leaders of the Hungarian Peace Council did participate in END planning and—perhaps because they were surrounded by suspicious Western activists—avoided disruptive behavior.[170]

At no time, however, did the overall relationship become friendly. In secret reports that Stasi agents filed with the East German government, they called attention to a more "realistic" attitude toward the East European peace committees among some elements at the END conventions of 1987 and 1988. Even so, in 1987 the Stasi continued to complain that END's "extreme anticommunist leading forces" were "trying to implement their subversive anti-socialist objectives under the cover of the continuation of the Helsinki process, the realization of 'détente from below' and 'human rights' in order to undermine the political conditions in the socialist states." Furthermore, "there were many attempts to introduce the so-called independent peace forces as equal partners to the socialist states and their peace councils." In 1988, as well, the Stasi reported that the END convention had been used "to attack the socialist states," and that "influential forces" were attempting to turn the Western movement "into an instrument of anti-socialist fight and to split the movement."[171] Sharing these views, the German Peace Council boycotted END's conventions in 1987 and 1988. In addition, the Czechoslovak Peace Committee, badgered by END to safeguard the rights of independent activists, retaliated by refusing to send its own delegation to END's 1988 convention.[172]

Meanwhile, the nonaligned antinuclear campaign swept forward, having surmounted—though not always comfortably—the problems involved in relating to rapidly evolving Communist parties and peace campaigns. In retrospect, this viability of the nonaligned movement proved considerably more important than the fate of the Communist-led peace movement, for the latter stood on the verge of collapse while the former constituted a powerful barrier against the programs of nuclear enthusiasts in East and West. Indeed, from 1985 to 1988, policymakers continued to face a widespread, deeply rooted, and popular nonaligned movement—one that demanded not only nuclear arms controls, but disarmament and human rights. As a result, the stage was set for dramatic public policy changes.

Breakthrough for
Nuclear Disarmament, 1985-88

No task is more important in the world today than to
avert the threat of nuclear annihilation. The more
actively and resolutely members of the public work
towards fulfilling this task, the better are the chances of
success.

Mikhail Gorbachev, 1985

Under enormous pressure from the antinuclear movement, the public policy
dam finally burst in the years from 1985 to 1988. Before that, of course, there
had been important shifts in the nuclear policies of Western nations, most
remarkably those of the United States. But the rise to power of Mikhail Gorbachev in March 1985 provided the final ingredient necessary for a surge of
Soviet-American arms control and disarmament efforts. Ronald Reagan—
hounded by the public, Congress, and U.S. allies—had given ground to the
antinuclear movement in the early 1980s, but his response had been instru-
mental. Despite his newfound antinuclear rhetoric and policies, as well as his
genuine yearnings for a world free of the nuclear menace, he never felt comfortable with the movement. Constrained by his deep-seated anti-Communism, unable to establish a rapport with the fossilized leadership in the
Kremlin, and committed to a buildup of U.S. military "strength," the American President remained ambivalent about working out nuclear arms control
and disarmament agreements with the Soviet Union. By contrast, Gorbachev
was a genuine convert to the antinuclear cause, a true believer in its message
that the nuclear arms race would lead to catastrophe. Forming an alliance
with the nuclear disarmament movement and often adopting its proposals, he
began a dramatic campaign against nuclear weapons and nuclear war that,
eventually, convinced Reagan to make a break with the Old Thinking.
Thereafter, working together, they routed conservative supporters of nuclear
weaponry, opening the way for significant disarmament measures.

The Advent of Gorbachev

With Chernenko's death, Gorbachev was elected Soviet party secretary on March 11, 1985, ushering in a dramatic change in Soviet foreign and military policy. Eleven days later, addressing a visiting group of leaders of the Socialist International, Gorbachev told them that the Soviet Union would "follow unswervingly a course of peace," for "the peace-loving public of the entire world calls for an end to the dangerous arms race and removal of the threat of war." In a speech delivered that May, he argued that "a great deal remains to be done to preserve our planet, the common home of mankind," adding that he had "no doubt that the antiwar movement will continue to grow, more and more effectively obstructing adventurist moves by the forces of aggression." Some of this rhetoric, no doubt, was designed to bring pressure to bear on the Reagan administration. That June, he declared that, if the U.S. government took "a more sensible stand, there would be a prospect for a mutually acceptable agreement on far-reaching, really deep cuts in nuclear arms stockpiles. . . . There would be a way to scrap these weapons altogether and remove the threat of nuclear war, which is what all the peoples of the earth are dreaming about." Nevertheless, there was also a humanitarian, universalistic quality to Gorbachev's speeches that contrasted with the Soviet regime's earlier anti-American diatribes. Addressing the French parliament that October, he declared not only that "there can be no victors in a nuclear war," but that "it is high time to draw a practical conclusion from this: to stop the nuclear arms race. . . . This demand will be supported by . . . all people who cherish their homeland, their lives, the lives of their children and grandchildren." In an age of nuclear weapons, "Europe's security cannot be ensured by military means. . . . This is an absolutely new situation and means a departure . . . from a mentality and manner of action that took centuries—even millennia—to form." Faced with the "self-destruction of the human race," it was time to "burn the black book of nuclear alchemy" and make the twenty-first century one "of life without fear of universal death."[1]

This was what Gorbachev meant by the "new thinking," the phrase he first used publicly in December 1984 and trumpeted increasingly thereafter. In an interview with *Time* magazine in the fall of 1985, he argued that the "primary thing" that defined international relations was "the immutable fact that whether we like one another or not we can survive or perish only together." In 1986, he told Mitterrand, in private discussions, that "the nuclear era requires new thinking from everybody. We all depend upon each other.

. . . In essence, we have no alternative other than to learn to live in the real world."[2] Gorbachev made the same point in *Perestroika*, a book he took great pains writing later that year. "The arms race, just like nuclear war, is unwinnable, " he insisted. "All of us face the need to learn to live at peace in this world, to work out a new mode of thinking." Thus, "the backbone of the new way of thinking is the recognition of the priority of human values, or, to be more precise, of humankind's survival."[3]

To veterans of the antinuclear campaign, Gorbachev's expression of the "new thinking"—as well as his growing calls for a nuclear-free Europe and world—sounded startlingly like the nonaligned nuclear disarmament movement. Rob Prince, then working for its Communist-led rival, the WPC, was flabbergasted: "He took the program of END and he adopted it! . . . What it looked like to me, sitting in Helsinki and watching everything at once, was: 'This guy is starting to talk like E. P. Thompson!' First it's the need for nuclear disarmament. Then it's . . . self-critical stuff: 'We're partly responsible.' You never heard that from a Soviet leader before Gorbachev! And then . . . they're suggesting that there would be cuts in the Warsaw Treaty Organization forces." Thompson agreed that, to a remarkable degree, the new Soviet leader echoed the Western antinuclear campaign. "To our surprise," Thompson recalled, "after 1985 our own words started to come back to us—from Moscow. It was Gorbachev now who took our lines, who spoke of ridding Europe of nuclear weapons 'from the Atlantic to the Urals,' who proposed a practical agenda for the dissolution of both blocs."[4]

Nor was this surprising, for either directly or filtered through his reformist advisors, Gorbachev imbibed the key ideas of the "new thinking" from the nonaligned antinuclear movement. As the first Soviet leader since Lenin to have a university education and as a frequent traveler to Western countries, Gorbachev was a far more sophisticated thinker than his predecessors. While studying at Moscow State University in 1955, he was greatly impressed by the visit of India's antinuclear prime minister, Jawaharlal Nehru, who—as Gorbachev recalled in his memoirs—had "linked the question of peace to the preservation and progress of human civilization."[5] That same year, the Russell-Einstein Appeal, warning humanity of the nuclear peril, had called for "a new way of thinking" if humanity were to survive.[6] Gorbachev's use of the term "new thinking" to reflect this same concept clearly derived from this landmark of the antinuclear campaign. Indeed, his choice for Soviet foreign secretary, his friend and party reformer Eduard Shevardnadze, argued that "the Russell-Einstein Manifesto offered politicians the key to the most troublesome and complex riddles of the age." According to

Arbatov, who became another of Gorbachev's top foreign policy advisors, major ideas for the new thinking "originated . . . outside the Soviet Union with people such as Albert Einstein, Bertrand Russell, and Olof Palme."[7]

Other components of the antinuclear campaign also had an important impact upon Gorbachev. Scientists, he wrote appreciatively, had been "the first to speak out authoritatively" against the "folly" of the nuclear arms race. And he gave particular credit "to the joint efforts of Soviet and American scientists." The Pugwash movement had been especially important in this regard, he told Joseph Rotblat, its longtime leader; indeed, some of his key foreign policy advisors—such as Arbatov, Yakovlev, and Velikhov— had attended Pugwash meetings.[8] Once Gorbachev became party secretary, numerous antinuclear scientists and other intellectuals from abroad met with him and, according to Chernyaev, their "influence on him was huge." Furthermore, Gorbachev may not have known it, but his speechwriters liberally borrowed from END's magazine when preparing his speeches.[9] Tair Tairov, the Soviet secretary of the WPC who reported frequently to Soviet leaders on antinuclear agitation, maintained that, "if it wasn't for the peace movements in the West, there would not have been new thinking at all. . . . Without them Gorbachev would never have proclaimed the idea of a nonviolent, non-nuclear world—he knew that the soil was fertile. They created the historical arena in which he could go ahead."[10] As Gorbachev himself put it: "The new thinking took into account and absorbed the conclusions and demands of the nonaligned movement, of the public and the scientific community, of the movements of physicians, scientists and ecologists, and of various antiwar organizations."[11]

Taking office in March 1985, Gorbachev acted to put the "new thinking" into operation. To reassure party conservatives, many of whom had been wary of him, his statements to party leaders that March and April stressed continuity rather than change in Soviet foreign and military policy.[12] But things soon began to change. Easing Gromyko out of his post as foreign secretary, Gorbachev appointed some of the leading party reformers—Arbatov, Chernyaev, Shevardnadze, Velikhov, and Yakovlov—as his top foreign and military policy advisors. Sharp critics of the nuclear arms race and of the Cold War confrontation with the United States, they helped Gorbachev set Soviet policy on a new course. In April, he announced the cessation of SS-20 deployments in Europe and their reduction to the level prior to the disruption of INF negotiations in late 1983. Responding to the pleas of antinuclear scientists, he refused to order the development of a Soviet SDI program.[13] In July 1985, Gorbachev also proclaimed a unilateral moratorium on Soviet nuclear testing, to begin on August 6, the anniversary of the Hiroshima bombing. He implored the U.S. government to join it while the two powers negotiated a comprehensive test ban treaty. Although these kinds of unilateral moves were not unprecedented and, in addition, were used by Gorbachev to enhance the Soviet Union's image in world affairs,[14] there is little doubt that the new Soviet party secretary was sincere about what he called, in his memoirs, the "vital" need "to bring the costly and dangerous arms race to an end." Chernyaev recalled that the first item on Gorbachev's agenda for his early party meetings was "disarmament."[15]

The "new thinking" and its proponents also brought a dramatically different tone to Soviet-American relations. The NSC's Jack Matlock recalled that the first meeting between Shultz and Shevardnadze "was memorable." The Soviet foreign secretary, a "cheery man with a ready and winning smile, came into the room, shook hands with the Americans, and began the meeting by telling his aides . . . 'I'm new at this. Be sure to correct me if I goof.' With a chuckle, he got down to business." If Shultz did not agree with him, "he would simply say: 'All right, think about it. We think it's a good idea. Maybe you can suggest a better one.'. . . There were no histrionics, no long lectures, no recriminations." At the end of the meeting, Shevardnadze turned to his staff and asked: "OK, fellows, how did I do? How many bloopers did you count?" Then he laughed and said, "'Hold on, tell me when we get out of the room,' shook hands all around, and departed." In shock, one of the American participants turned to another and said: "Don't tell me that's a *Soviet* foreign minister!" At their next meeting, Shevardnadze said to Shultz: "Much in the world depends on the state of Soviet-American relations. And they in turn depend on the relations that you and I have. I intend to do business as your honest and reliable partner, and if you wish, to be your friend." Moved, the U.S. secretary of state stood up abruptly and declared: "Here is my hand. Give me yours!"[16]

By early 1986, the "new thinking" had produced a Soviet blueprint for a nuclear-free world. Announced by Gorbachev on January 15, it consisted of a three-stage program to eliminate all nuclear weapons around the globe by the year 2000. According to the Soviet leader, it was not "another Soviet propaganda trick" but a sincere effort "dictated by a sense of responsibility about preventing nuclear war and preserving peace. Our stance here accorded with world public opinion; among other things, it was a response" to the Five Continent Peace Initiative.[17] But this proposal did have a complex origin. By the spring of 1985, Soviet military officials were worried that Gorbachev and his reformist advisors, in an effort to reach an agreement with the United States, were getting ready to offer serious concessions regarding the Euromissiles. To head this off, they proposed what they thought would be a good combination of useful propaganda and a non-negotiable proposal—rather like the Reagan administration's zero option. As Nikolai Detinov, one of the drafters of the nuclear abolition proposal, put it: "They could show, on the one hand, that the Soviet Union and its General Secretary were eager to eliminate nuclear weapons and, on the other . . . that they understood that such a declaration hardly could lead to any practical results in the foreseeable future, or affect, in any form, the ongoing negotiations." But Gorbachev outmaneuvered them. In late 1985 and early 1986, he used the military's backing of nuclear abolition to legitimize the proposal and, then, to make it official party policy. "In this sense," Detinov recalled, "the real authors of this idea became entrapped by their own gambit."[18]

Gorbachev institutionalized the "new thinking" at the 27th Soviet party congress, held from February 25 to March 6, 1986. "A turning point has arisen," he told the gathering. "The situation created by nuclear confrontation calls for new approaches, methods and forms of relations between the different social systems, states and regions." Indeed, "the present day world has become too small and fragile for wars and policies of force" and, thus, "it is essential above all to considerably reduce the level of military confrontation." Henceforth, he said, Soviet military doctrine would not be based on matching U.S. weaponry, but upon "reasonable sufficiency" and "a path of cooperation to create a comprehensive system of international security." Shevardnadze and other reformers considered this a moment for "rejoicing." The "priority of universal human values," he recalled, was now linked to the idea that "security is gained not by the highest possible level of strategic parity, but the lowest possible level, and nuclear and other weapons of mass destruction must be removed from the equation." From this point on, "our guidelines were precise: to stop the preparations for nuclear war; to move Soviet-American relations onto a track of normal, civilized dialog; to reject the dead, brutally rigid positions in favor of intelligent, mutually acceptable compromises; . . . to seek ways to end nuclear tests and dismantle the American and Soviet intermediate range missiles in Europe"; and to "radically" cut armaments.[19]

Given the central role of the nonaligned antinuclear movement in generating the "new thinking," plus its potential for furthering his program on the world scene, Gorbachev worked to establish an alliance with it. Some of his effort took the unusual form of personal meetings with leaders of antinuclear groups. At the Geneva summit conference of November 1985, SANE's David Cortright, the Freeze campaign's Jane Gruenebaum, and the Rev. Jesse Jackson pressed him hard on controversial issues, including an indefinite extension of the Soviet moratorium on nuclear testing and human rights for Jews and other minorities in the Soviet Union. Although at times the discussion grew heated, Gorbachev insisted that "I appreciate our discussion here and I understand your noble motives and your concern . . . that all nations and political leaders should heed the voice of all the people of the world. We not only heed that voice, we make our policy from that voice." At subsequent summit meetings, as well, Gorbachev carved out time to confer with the leaders of nuclear disarmament groups.[20] On other occasions, he met at length with such leading antinuclear campaigners as Bernard Lown and Admiral Gene LaRocque,[21] fired off thoughtful letters in response to disarmament proposals by Henry Kendall of the UCS, Frank von Hippel of the FAS, and other antinuclear activists, encouraged visits to the Soviet Union by leaders of Pax Christi and other peace groups, and organized the international foundation that pulled together leading activists from the United States and the Soviet Union to work on issues of disarmament, human rights, and the environment.[22] In February 1987, Gorbachev hosted a spectacular Forum for a Nuclear Free World that drew to Moscow several thousand leaders of the global antinuclear campaign.[23]

Gorbachev's courtship of the nonaligned nuclear disarmament movement contrasted sharply with his treatment of its Communist-led rival. To its dismay, the GDR Peace Council was left off the initial invitation list for the Forum for a Nuclear Free World, and one of its leaders recalled bitterly that no one representing the WPC or one of its affiliates was asked to speak at the event. As the leaders of these groups were usually party conservatives, rather than proponents of the "new thinking," Gorbachev marginalized them—leaving them out of his speeches, his writings, and his considerations.[24] By contrast, he lauded other elements of the antinuclear campaign. Referring to the leaders of IPPNW in his book *Perestroika*, he insisted that it was "impossible to ignore what these people are saying," for "what they say and what they do is prompted by accurate knowledge and a passionate desire to warn humanity about the danger looming over it." Thus, "no serious politician has the right to disregard their conclusions or neglect the ideas by which they take world public opinion a stage ahead." Writing to von Hippel and other antinuclear intellectuals, Gorbachev said that he wanted "to underline again that we attach great significance to the active participation of learned people in seeking solutions to what are the most pressing military-political and international problems," for, together, they were confronting "the problem of how to ensure the survival of mankind."[25]

Gorbachev also cultivated prominent political leaders who had taken antinuclear positions. In a speech to a May 1985 luncheon honoring Willy

Brandt, chair of the West German Social Democratic Party and of the Socialist International, Gorbachev claimed that "our views on many current problems are close and even identical in many respects." According to the Soviet leader, "our parties sense the mood of the masses who want a lasting peace and who are strongly opposed to policies escalating the threat of nuclear war." In addition, Gorbachev publicly praised the antinuclear proposals of Olof Palme and established a close rapport with two other leading Social Democratic critics of the nuclear arms race: the British Labour Party's Michael Foot and Denis Healey.[26] The Five Continent Peace Initiative frequently drew his praise. In May 1985, he told an Indian journalist that he had "a high opinion" of the proposals made by the six heads of state, particularly their efforts "to stop the development, production, and deployment of nuclear weapons, to freeze nuclear arsenals and embark on their reduction, to prevent the arms race from spreading to space, and to conclude a treaty banning all nuclear tests." This was also the occasion for Gorbachev's first meeting with one of the Five Continent Initiative's leaders, Rajiv Gandhi, with whom he developed an exceptionally warm relationship. Gandhi heartily endorsed the Soviet leader's nuclear abolition program of January 1986, and when they met again that November, they jointly issued the Delhi Declaration. Arguing that, "in the nuclear age, mankind must develop a new political thinking . . . which provides sound guarantees for the survival of mankind," it emphasized the need to "give priority to universal human values" and to replace the "balance of fear" with "a global system of international security."[27]

In addition, Gorbachev chose to work closely with nuclear disarmament proponents in his own country. One indication of this was the Soviet party secretary's selection of his top foreign and military policy advisors from the ranks of his party's most avant garde reformers—intellectuals long disgruntled by the arms race and the Soviet-American confrontation. Even Andrei Sakharov, the very symbol of nuclear dissent, was now rehabilitated. Long uneasy about keeping Sakharov under house arrest, Gorbachev decided "to rescue Academician Sakharov from exile." On December 1, 1986, the party secretary successfully pushed through the Politburo a proposal to free him. Accordingly, on December 16, Gorbachev phoned the Soviet physicist in Gorky and invited him to return to Moscow. Later that day, when he mentioned this at a meeting with Central Committee officials, sarcastic looks appeared on their faces, and one expressed his concern about the spread of pacifism in Soviet life. Growing irritated, Gorbachev retorted that "the public should participate in the struggle for peace."[28] Once freed, Sakharov frequently presented Gorbachev with demands to release other political prisoners and to undertake disarmament initiatives; remarkably, the Soviet party secretary responded to Sakharov's satisfaction.[29] To be sure, the Moscow Trust Group did not fare as well, and for a time its members continued to be assaulted, imprisoned, deported, or confined in psychiatric hospitals. Nevertheless, with Gorbachev's advent, official tolerance of the Trust Group grew, and most of those confined to psychiatric institutions were released.[30]

Party conservatives were not at all pleased by this turn of events. At the outset, recalled Pavel Palazchenko, who worked as an assistant to Gorbachev, "the conservatives did not immediately catch on to the consequences of the changes they were witnessing and taking part in." Rhetoric calling for peace and nuclear disarmament had long been a staple of Soviet pronouncements on world affairs. What they did not realize, for a time, was that Gorbachev took these items seriously. But as Gorbachev prepared his "new thinking" speech for the 27th party congress, they were beginning to understand—and to object. "What is this 'new thinking'?" expostulated Boris Ponamarev, head of the Central Committee's international department. "Our thinking is correct! Let the Americans change their thinking."[31] Hard-liners in the military-industrial sector and in the KGB opposed making negotiating concessions to the West and denied that military spending was placing an excessive burden on the Soviet economy. In the fall of 1986, when Gorbachev emphasized the theme of universal human values, he noted, "it was if a bomb had gone off" among "the advocates of orthodox thinking." A top party leader objected angrily to this departure from Communist verities. Gorbachev recalled: "I suddenly realized how difficult it would be to make our way through the wall of hardened dogma! It seemed obvious: the nuclear threat, the ecological crisis, the division of the world— it was folly to move further in these directions." But suspicions now "began to arise: 'There is a smell of anti-Marxist heresy here. . . . Gorbachev has shown his hand.'"[32]

Reactions Elsewhere to the Antinuclear Campaign

The response to the antinuclear campaign was more predictable elsewhere. In general, nuclear-armed nations reacted with great hostility to disarmament activism. Under orders from the French government to head off anticipated protest activities against French nuclear testing at Moruroa atoll, French secret service agents attached underwater mines to the hull of the Greenpeace flagship, *Rainbow Warrior*, in July 1985, as it lay at anchor in the harbor of Auckland, New Zealand. The ensuing explosions killed a Greenpeace photographer and set off a major international scandal. Although the French government denied any connection with the murderous blasts, New Zealand's police captured two of the French agents, and the French cover-up gradually unraveled, leading to the resignations of France's defense minister and the head of its secret service. The captured agents entered into a plea bargain with the New Zealand authorities, and received sentences of ten years. But they never served them. The French government signed an agreement with New Zealand for placing them in French custody, contingent upon administering three-year sentences, and then proceeded to violate this agreement by releasing them.[33] In Israel, Mordechai Vanunu, who revealed to the London press the extent of the Israeli nuclear weapons program, was sentenced to an eighteen-year prison term, most of which he has served, thus far, in solitary confinement.[34]

Unlike the new Soviet administration, the governments of other Warsaw Pact nations showed little sign of mellowing toward independent antinuclear agitation. In Poland, the authorities arrested Freedom and Peace activists, charging that the group was an "anti-socialist" and "illegal" force, "hostile to the defense of Poland." In Czechoslovakia, the government prosecuted leading activists in the Independent Peace Association, Charter 77, and the Jazz Section on charges of "incitement" and "illicit trading." In East Germany, the authorities arrested independent peace, human rights, and ecology activists, including leaders of the Peace and Human Rights Initiative, on charges such as "treasonable activity."[35] Nor were these governments any fonder of independent groups in the West. Reporting to the East German authorities, Stasi agents warned that, under the guise of "détente from below," END, IKV, CODENE, and VAKA were working "to inspire and organize internal opposition" in Communist nations, and that END's 1988 convention would "renew the attack" upon them. A Czech government publication argued that, as "Imperialism" was "not able to destroy the movement, it is trying to split it, and bring a part of it under its control," through use of such "disorienting propaganda theses" as the "equal responsibility of the two superpowers."[36]

In Britain, the Thatcher government and its allies used the parliamentary elections of 1987 to launch another campaign of defamation against nuclear critics. "Labour's non-nuclear defense policy is in fact a policy for defeat, surrender, occupation, and finally, prolonged guerilla fighting," Thatcher charged. "Never before has the Labour Party offered the country a defense policy of such recklessness," she contended, "a defense policy of the white flag." Her favorite campaign advertisement, she recalled, depicted " 'Labour's Policy on Arms' with a British soldier, his hands held up in surrender." Even the defense policy of the centrist Liberal-Social Democratic Alliance came in for harsh attack by the prime minister, who claimed that "it amounted to unilateral nuclear disarmament by degrees" and "would just as surely as Labour's produce a 'frightened and fellow-travelling Britain.'"[37] Thatcher's efforts were supplemented by her allies in The 61, who believed, as Crozier noted, that Labour Party leader Neil Kinnock "represented a very real threat," for Kinnock and his wife Glenys were "supporters" of CND. With Thatcher's approval, Crozier met with Keith Joseph, Britain's secretary of education, to work on "psychological actions in the election year." One such action involved briefing TV interviewer David Frost on how best to embarrass Kinnock politically. The 61 also practiced what Crozier called "benign deception," as "unawareness is sometimes essential, to protect those in the public eye and of course the initiator of the action." For example, the group produced and distributed to Conservative candidates a little booklet, *The Vision of St Kinnock*. Covered in red, it was filled with pictures showing the Labour Party leader "playing the fool . . . or in earnest conversation with Fidel Castro, or addressing a CND rally." Other operations included exposing "'loony Left' activities in the councils," producing a study of the mass media showing its supposed "left-wing bias," and distributing useful material to "politically compatible columnists."[38]

Despite the Reagan administration's shift toward a policy of nuclear arms control and disarmament, it continued to regard antinuclear groups with animosity. Repeatedly, White House officials rebuffed requests to meet with Reagan by delegations from antinuclear groups, including SANE, PSR, and SANE/Freeze. Thus, during the same summit meetings at which Gorbachev spoke at length with leading nuclear disarmament activists, Reagan kept his distance from them.[39] During a "Children's Summit," organized by antinuclear groups in December 1987, the children offered armfuls of long-stemmed roses to representatives of each superpower. At the Soviet embassy, officials invited them in for cookies and hot chocolate; at the White House, guards turned the children away and dumped their roses in the trash.[40] Although the President did send messages of greeting to conferences of IPPNW, he repeatedly refused to meet with its leaders.[41] Richard Perle went so far as to publicly denounce the members of PSR as "hopelessly naïve." To be sure, Jeremy Stone of the FAS retained some contact with Paul Nitze. And Andrei Sakharov, as a feted Soviet dissident, managed to speak with both Reagan and Bush, both of whom rebuffed his antinuclear suggestions. But, with these exceptions, antinuclear activists had no entrée to the Reagan administration.[42] Chillingly, the U.S. government—like the British—refused to even comment on the bombing of the *Rainbow Warrior*.[43] Rather than reach out to the concerned public through antinuclear groups, the Reagan administration chose to rely on the "public diplomacy" of the USIA and other propaganda organs.[44]

Some governments were considerably friendlier. Sweden's prime minister, Olof Palme, was a consistent enthusiast. "It is sometimes said that the flamboyant rhetoric of popular movements must be tempered by the realism of statesman," he remarked. But "in these days I rather feel that the rhetoric of statesmen should be tempered by the down-to-earth realism of ordinary people who have come to understand what nuclear war would mean, and demand practical action to prevent it." The Dutch government, though differing from the movement in political perspective, nevertheless retained a civilized relationship with its more respectable elements. Faber of IKV recalled that, in 1986, when preparing for a trip to the Soviet Union to discuss arms control issues, he simply phoned the Dutch defense minister and foreign minister and said: "I want to be briefed by you on what the bottlenecks are in the Geneva negotiations." Soon thereafter, they produced "a paper with all the bottlenecks, saying: 'Well, here it is.'"[45] Even the Chinese government adopted a relatively benign attitude, at least toward overseas activists. When E. P. Thompson visited China in May 1985, he was impressed by the desire of the government to establish good relations with Western antinuclear movements, including the Freeze and CND. He reported that he and his wife, Dorothy Thompson, "were able to lecture quite freely, and no offense was taken when we sharply criticized Marxist orthodoxies. I was able to give public lectures on the Western peace movement at both Nanjing and Nankai universities, saying much the same as I would say in the West. There was a warm welcome." In 1988, the Chinese government's official peace group co-sponsored a symposium on Peace and Security in the Asian-Pacific Region with the Pugwash movement.[46]

Nuclear Policy Elsewhere

Despite the pressure from the antinuclear campaign, some nations clung doggedly to their traditional nuclear priorities. In a heated exchange with Gorbachev in 1987, Britain's Thatcher argued that nuclear weapons were the only guarantee of peace. "We believe in nuclear deterrence," she insisted, "and we do not consider the elimination of nuclear weapons practicable." The British government also reacted angrily to New Zealand's ban on nuclear warship visits, and threatened "loosening of the close and special ties" between the two countries if New Zealand's government passed legislation along these lines.[47] The French government pressed ahead with its nuclear testing program in the Pacific and refused to sign the antinuclear Treaty of

Rarotonga, while the Chinese government—though increasingly amenable to arms control measures—built up its nuclear weapons force, including several new types of ballistic missiles.[48] In 1987, General Mohammad Zia al-Haq, ruler of Pakistan, proudly declared that his country had "reached a stage when it could build nuclear weapons at short notice." Although he subsequently denied this, there were other indications that Pakistan was advancing toward a nuclear weapons capability.[49]

For its part, the U.S. government worked feverishly to hold the line against the growth of antinuclear action by its allies and other friendly nations. Hoping to force the New Zealand government to drop its ban on visits by nuclear warships, the Reagan administration declared in 1986 that it would no longer honor its security guarantees to that nation and in 1987 that it was severing New Zealand's participation in ANZUS. According to the U.S. ambassador, the Reagan administration felt "kicked in the teeth" by New Zealand's ban on nuclear warships and had to "punish" the small nation.[50] Similarly, when the Danish government acted to tighten its ban on visits by nuclear warships, Shultz declared that he was "deeply distressed" by the action, which "would have extremely serious consequences for U.S./Danish defense cooperation." Rejecting the antinuclear Treaty of Rarotonga, a State Department spokesperson told Congress that the administration felt that the treaty "would encourage other areas to adopt similar or stricter nuclear-free zones. It would encourage people to take sections of the Western world and opt out."[51] Although the people of Palau had defeated referenda to amend their antinuclear constitution on numerous occasions, the U.S. government insisted that they vote on the measure once again. While representing the United States in nuclear arms control negotiations at Geneva, Max Kampelman received instructions from the White House to speak with India's Rajiv Gandhi and with Australia's Bob Hawke and change their minds on nuclear issues.[52]

Given the antinuclear tide, however, this was not an easy task. Even within the relatively safe confines of NATO, the "nuclear allergy" was spreading. In September 1985, the Canadian government announced that it would abstain from government-to-government cooperation in connection with SDI. In April 1988, the Danish parliament passed a resolution requiring foreign warships to proclaim that they were nuclear-free before being allowed to enter Danish ports—action that set off a crisis in Danish-American relations, led to new elections, and resulted in an unstable compromise.[53] The Spanish government, which had recently joined NATO but had vowed to keep Spain nuclear-free, insisted successfully upon the withdrawal of 72 nuclear-equipped F-16 fighter planes from a U.S. military base near Madrid.[54] In Greece, the Papandreou government wavered on its commitment to remove all U.S. military bases from the country, but it did reject a U.S. proposal for the installation of new nuclear weapons on its soil and pledge the ultimate withdrawal of all such weapons.[55] Meanwhile, Norway continued to press for the creation of a Nordic nuclear-free zone, while Iceland told the U.S. government that it would enforce its nuclear-free policies and, as a result, would no longer allow the presence of nuclear weapons on board U.S. warships in its harbors. In 1988, NATO's secretary general, Lord Carrington, warned that, although pressure from the "utopian and extremist . . . peace movement" had declined, the new "euphoria" about disarmament was making it difficult for NATO to maintain its military strength.[56]

Antinuclear policies also advanced in the Pacific. Despite intense pressure from the U.S. and British governments, New Zealand refused to retreat from its antinuclear stand. The Lange government drew up legislation to codify its nuclear warships ban, and parliament passed it in June 1987. Together with Australia, New Zealand co-sponsored annual resolutions at the United Nations calling for a comprehensive test ban treaty and laid the groundwork for the Treaty of Rarotonga.[57] The new treaty, formally adopted in August 1985 by the thirteen members of the South Pacific Forum, had provisions that generally resembled those of the Treaty of Tlatelolco, which had established the world's only other nuclear weapons–free zone, in Latin America. But it went somewhat further by banning "peaceful nuclear explosions" and radioactive waste dumping. Probably its most significant nuclear arms control feature was its ban on the stationing of foreign nuclear forces on the territory of South Pacific nations.[58] In the Philippines, as well, antinuclear forces made important gains. The new government of Corazon Aquino—strongly influenced by growing antinuclear sentiment—adopted a constitution stating that "the Philippines shall be nuclear-free, consistent with the national interest." In May 1988, the Philippine Senate passed implementing legislation, thus beginning a confrontation with the government of the United States, which maintained nuclear weapons at its Subic Bay naval base and at its Clark air force base.[59]

Other nations, particularly those involved in the Five Continent Peace Initiative, focused on easing the superpower nuclear confrontation. In 1986, the leaders of the six nations participating in the Five Continent group (Sweden, India, Argentina, Mexico, Greece, and Tanzania) sent a letter to Reagan and Gorbachev, announcing their willingness to help verify a halt to nuclear testing through on-site inspection and monitoring activities. This turned out to be one of the last political acts of Sweden's Olof Palme, who was assassinated soon thereafter.[60] Further action by the six nations—

derisively dubbed the "Gang of 6" by White House operatives—occurred at the June 1988 U.N. Special Session on Disarmament, where they unveiled a proposal for the establishment of "an integrated multilateral verification system within the United Nations" as part of an international security framework to achieve "a nuclear weapons–free world."[61] With Palme's death, Rajiv Gandhi emerged as one of the world's most prominent antinuclear statesmen, pressing the antinuclear case in meetings with both Reagan and Gorbachev. As Gandhi's moral preachments and condemnations of nuclear weapons appealed strongly to the Soviet leader, the two men grew increasingly close, with the Delhi Declaration of November 1986 providing a good summary of their outlook. At the same time, Gandhi scuttled plans for the testing and development of India's own nuclear weapons, evidently preferring his role as an antinuclear leader to his role as a leader of a nuclear power. In June 1988, at the U.N. disarmament conference, he offered India's own "Action Plan for Ushering in a Nuclear-Weapon-Free and Non-Violent World Order."[62]

Reaction to the Advent of Gorbachev

Not all world leaders were this sympathetic to Gorbachev and to his "new thinking." To some of the Reagan administration's leading hawks, the new Soviet leader was just as bad as his predecessors. Weinberger felt that Gorbachev continued to be a dedicated and dangerous Communist, and had merely recognized that "the rhetoric had to be changed." Perle recalled Gorbachev as "thoroughly disingenuous" when it came to peace and disarmament—a man who continued "pumping new money into an aggressive program."[63] Other administration officials were a bit more optimistic, but not much. Writing in the fall of 1985, McFarlane thought it was possible to establish "steady prolonged peaceful competition" with the Soviet Union, although he did not think the USSR would "change ideologically." The State Department's intelligence division reported that June that there was "at least some possibility that Gorbachev may have in mind a 'fast track' on arms control," though it did not view this scenario as "probable." As late as the summer of 1987, the CIA thought Gorbachev's "new thinking" was merely designed to "affect Western opinion" and "to bring Soviet defense and foreign policies in line with . . . the USSR's economic capabilities."[64]

Nor, initially, was Reagan favorably inclined toward the new Soviet leadership. Deeply suspicious of Communists, he did not think, as he wrote in his memoirs, "that Mikhail Gorbachev was going to be a *different* sort of Soviet leader." After conversing with the U.S. ambassador to the Soviet

Union five weeks into Gorbachev's term as party secretary, Reagan jotted in his diary: "He confirms what I believe, that Gorbachev will be as tough as any of their leaders. If he wasn't a confirmed ideologue, he never would have been chosen by the Politburo." Even after Gorbachev sent him courteous messages, emphasizing their "common interest" in not letting things "come to the outbreak of nuclear war" and calling for "an improvement in the relations between the USSR and the U.S.," Reagan believed that the new Soviet leader "was going to be tough to deal with." When Shevardnadze became Soviet foreign minister later that year, he, too, faced a deeply suspicious and hostile American President. Recalling their first meetings, Shevardnadze wrote that Reagan "began just about every one with a reading of a 'bill of indictment' against the Soviet Union, whose charges were crammed with loosely interpreted quotations from the founders of Marxism." America's President "looked at our country through the prism of ideology and saw it as the 'Evil Empire.' To be disabused of such a view, he would have had to begin seeing a country made up of real people." And, "at that time, he still had a long way to go."[65]

In Europe, on both sides of the Cold War barrier, the attitudes toward the new Soviet leadership tended to be less ideological. Hans-Dietrich Genscher, West Germany's foreign minister, told a gathering that "the West has no reason to fear cooperation. We can have only one guiding principle: Take Gorbachev seriously, take him at his word!" Even Margaret Thatcher was impressed by Gorbachev. Although she remained unwilling to let down her nuclear guard, the British prime minister felt from the outset that he was "a man with whom I could do business."[66] In East Germany, Gorbachev's "new thinking" also struck a responsive chord, at least when it came to curbing the nuclear arms race. "There were big differences between the GDR and the Soviets" during the time of Gorbachev, recalled Peter Steglich, an East German diplomat of the era. But when it came to promoting nuclear arms control and disarmament, the party leadership fully "agreed with the Soviets." He added that nuclear disarmament was "impossible" under Brezhnev and "Andropov wasn't ready to go that way." By contrast, Gorbachev and Shevardnadze "were really serious."[67]

The Nuclear Testing Moratorium

Their seriousness was demonstrated by Gorbachev's first dramatic arms control initiative: a unilateral Soviet moratorium on nuclear testing. After meeting overseas with antinuclear scientists in 1982 and 1983, Evgenii Velikhov had returned to the Soviet Union as a proponent of a nuclear test ban. Lobbying for a halt to nuclear testing, he warmly welcomed Bernard Lown's June 1984 proposal for unilateral testing moratoria by the great powers. Greenpeace, too, pressed the U.S. and Soviet governments to halt nuclear testing. In November 1984, retired admirals Gene LaRocque and Eugene Carroll of the Center for Defense Information suggested to Reagan and Chernenko that they initiate a joint testing moratorium on August 6, 1985—exactly 40 years after the Hiroshima bombing. Although Reagan responded negatively and Chernenko died before he could reply, the advent of Gorbachev and the enhanced influence of Velikhov changed the situation significantly. In April 1985, LaRocque and Carroll were invited to the Soviet embassy and handed a letter from the new Soviet party secretary. It said that their proposal was being given "serious consideration" and agreed that a moratorium should begin on August 6.[68] That same month, Lown promoted IPPNW's moratorium proposal in Moscow, where a group of Gorbachev's reformist advisors, including Velikhov and Arbatov, held a small party for him. Velikhov took him aside to say to him: "Congratulations. You have succeeded." When the U.S. physician inquired as to the meaning of this, he was told that, on August 6, "we're stopping nuclear testing."[69] Later that year, Tair Tairov, the renegade Soviet secretary of the WPC, fired off telegrams to Soviet authorities, insisting that the moment had arrived to take a dramatic initiative on the testing issue. "Thousands of people from Australia to Canada are waiting," he said, as were Western peace groups and their leaders. Impressed by the extent of opposition to nuclear testing and uneasy about it himself, Gorbachev acted. On July 29 he announced that, to create favorable conditions for a treaty banning all nuclear tests, the Soviet Union would halt its own nuclear weapons tests on August 6 and continue its moratorium until at least January 1, 1986.[70]

Gorbachev's nuclear test moratorium drew a very mixed reaction. In the view of U.S. officials, it was nothing more than a "propaganda ploy"—a replay of Nikita Khrushchev's action in 1958, when, through a halt to Soviet testing, he succeeded in forcing the U.S. government to stop its own and to begin negotiations for a test ban treaty. Furthermore, they remembered that, three years later, the Soviet government had double-crossed them by resuming nuclear tests. More fundamentally, however, they did not want to end nuclear testing, for they viewed it as vital to the U.S. nuclear weapons program. Consequently, the Reagan administration refused to join the moratorium or to renew test ban negotiations with the Soviet Union.[71] But others found Gorbachev's initiative quite appealing. Around the world, the nuclear disarmament movement was delighted, and focused its efforts increasingly on mobilizing popular support for an end to nuclear testing.[72] In the United States, the House of Representatives passed a resolution by a wide margin that called upon the Reagan administration to reopen test ban negotiations—thus joining the Senate, which had voted overwhelmingly for a similar resolution in June 1984. Responding to a campaign initiated by Parliamentarians Global Action, the Mexican government brought a resolution to the U.N. General Assembly recommending that parties to the partial test ban treaty of 1963 "carry out urgent consultations among themselves as to the advisability and most appropriate method" of converting it to a comprehensive test ban treaty. Opposed only by the governments of the United States, Britain, and France, the resolution sailed through that body in late 1985 by a vote of 121 to 3.[73]

Despite the blunt rejection of his initiative by the U.S. government, Gorbachev repeatedly extended the Soviet nuclear testing moratorium. According to the Soviet party secretary, these extensions were "the result of a serious study of numerous appeals to the Soviet leadership from various intellectuals from other countries." In this connection, he underscored a November 1985 meeting that Velikhov organized, in which Nobel laureates emphasized the importance of banning nuclear tests. But, as the Politburo had decided to resume nuclear testing after the planned expiration of the moratorium in January 1986, the resolution of the issue remained uncertain. Recognizing this, Arbatov and Chernyaev sent Gorbachev a personal appeal to extend the moratorium, referring to Lown's arguments and warning that IPPNW's supporters "might stop believing us." Dobrynin dispatched a message making the same case. Determined to secure an extension of the moratorium, Lown and Chazov held a three-hour private meeting with Gorbachev in December that, as Lown recalled, was "very charged." Gorbachev demanded: "What is the value of our engaging in unilateral activity when the Americans are not going to honor it?"[74] But the pressure brought to bear by the antinuclear campaign tipped the balance, and the moratorium was extended, again and again. Discouraged by the Reagan administration's opposition, Gorbachev would sometimes take a bleak view of the situation. In March 1986, he commented glumly that "we are being forced to end the moratorium." But, on that occasion, he added that "we cannot disregard the huge wave of support that our steps have brought from so many sections of the world community." The Chernobyl nuclear power plant disaster of the following month stiffened his resolve and, ultimately, he continued the Soviet testing moratorium for almost nineteen months—until February 26, 1987.[75]

Movement pressures on the U.S. government meshed nicely with these extensions of the Soviet moratorium. In the United States, nuclear disarmament groups made a nuclear test ban a top priority,[76] helping to generate not only popular support for it (56 to 35 percent, according to an April 1986 poll) but, by mid-1986, passage of pro-test ban resolutions in five states and more than a hundred communities.[77] The most innovative movement response, however, came from Tom Cochran, the senior staff scientist at the Natural Resources Defense Council. Well aware that the U.S. government had long opposed a nuclear test ban with the argument that it would be impossible to monitor in the Soviet Union, Cochran persuaded the FAS's Frank von Hippel to see if he could get Velikhov to agree to having American scientists install seismic monitors at Soviet test sites. Von Hippel broached the idea to Velikhov in May 1986, and by July of that year Cochran and a team of U.S. seismologists were installing the monitors around the Soviet test site at Semipalatinsk. When Velikhov reported this to other Soviet leaders, a heated debate broke out within the Politburo about the program's intrusiveness. After everyone else had left, Gorbachev said to the Soviet scientist: "Well, maybe we shouldn't do this." Velikhov responded: "There's only one problem, boss; they're already there!" U.S. officials were even more disturbed by the scientists' action. Once they learned of it, Perle and others at the Pentagon objected vociferously, particularly to the follow-up plan to place seismic monitors at the U.S. test site in Nevada. Worst of all, from the standpoint of administration hard-liners, Cochran and the antinuclear scientists had seriously undermined the U.S. government's rationale for resisting a nuclear test ban treaty.[78]

The political significance of the scientists' action was demonstrated by developments in Congress. Christopher Paine, a legislative aide to Representative Ed Markey, had been working for some time on what he called a "legislative reciprocal arms control initiative." This entailed cutting a U.S. military program on the condition that the Soviet Union reciprocate in a verifiable way. In 1986, using this approach, he began an effort to end congressional funding for U.S. nuclear test explosions above one kiloton. His campaign in the House was assisted by Representative Les Aspin, then eager for liberal votes that would make him chair of the Armed Services Committee, and especially by news of the scientists' verification activities in the Soviet Union. In the lobby of the House, Paine set up large charts and maps showing where the seismic stations were located. And on the House floor, Markey waved the first seismogram from these stations, demonstrating the possibilities for cooperative verification. As a result, that August the legislation swept through the House by a vote of 234 to 155. This legislation was in sharp contrast to the position of the administration, articulated later that month by White House spokesman Larry Speakes, who insisted that "a nuclear test ban is not in the security interests of the United States, our friends or our allies." Although the Senate bill, sponsored by Senators Hatfield and Kennedy, failed to secure a majority, the House—pressed hard by most nuclear disarmament groups—passed its version again in 1987 and 1988.[79] Meanwhile, the test ban became an important issue among congressional Democrats, substantial numbers of whom now urged the administration to join the Soviet nuclear testing moratorium.[80]

Although the Soviet moratorium fell far short of ending nuclear weapons tests, along with pressures from the movement and from Congress it did restore the issue of curbing nuclear testing to the diplomatic and public agenda. According to ACDA's Kenneth Adelman, "due to pressure from the arms control community, the Congress, and the press," the Reagan administration felt it necessary in 1986 to "do something" about nuclear testing. As a result, an ACDA plan was drawn up to reduce the number and yield of such tests, and in September Reagan brought the plan to the United Nations. The administration subsequently scrapped that approach, but the following month, at the Reykjavik summit conference, the two governments laid plans to begin "step-by-step" test ban negotiations. They jointly experimented with the use of CORRTEX—a complicated and quite possibly unnecessary system of onsite verification insisted upon by the Reagan administration— and resumed discussions of the testing issue.[81] Meanwhile, determined to halt the tests, large numbers of Americans staged protests at the Nevada test site, with thousands arrested there for nonviolent civil disobedience.[82] In March 1988, nuclear disarmament groups from around the world banded together to launch the International Campaign for a Comprehensive Test Ban. Looking back on his moratorium initiative, Gorbachev was disappointed that the U.S. government proved so resistant to it, but nonetheless felt there had been some gains. "We can congratulate ourselves and everyone," he wrote, "for getting the issue moving."[83]

The Geneva Summit Conference

Despite the failure of the Reagan administration to respond more favorably to the nuclear testing moratorium, the President—sensitive to the antinuclear *Zeitgeist*—was anxious to display some progress toward nuclear arms control and disarmament. As soon as Gorbachev became party secretary, Reagan invited him to a summit meeting in the hope that they could "establish a dialogue." Eventually, the meeting was scheduled for November 1985, at Geneva. By this point, Reagan was 74 years old, nearing the end of his career, and with little to show for his years of confrontation with the Soviet

Union. Now, it seemed, as he met for the first time with a top Soviet leader, he finally had a chance to put his mark on history. As McFarlane recalled, Reagan badly wanted the summit: "He couldn't wait. . . . He was eager." According to the national security advisor, the President had come to see himself as a heroic figure, taking the lead in rescuing humanity from the threat of nuclear weapons and nuclear war.[84] His wife, Nancy, encouraged this vision, and badgered administration officials to fall into line with it. Michael Deaver, a top White House aide and friend of hers, later wrote: "It was Nancy who pushed everybody on the Geneva summit. She felt strongly that it was not only in the interest of world peace but the correct move politically." And she was very effective, especially with the President, who doted on her.[85] On the eve of the Geneva conference, Reagan recalled, "I really felt" that "we were at a special moment in history, with a unique opportunity to set the course of peace through the twenty-first century." Addressing the nation, he declared: "Since the dawn of the nuclear age, every American president has sought to limit and end the dangerous competition in nuclear arms. I have no higher priority than to finally realize that dream."[86]

Another sign of Reagan's decision to swim with the antinuclear tide was his handling of the SALT II issue. Although the U.S. administration was keeping its nuclear program within the limits of the 1979 treaty, the agreement had never been ratified. Furthermore, hawkish officials argued that, even if it had been, the Russians were violating its terms and that it would have expired in late 1985. That spring, when top U.S. national security officials met to consider it once again, Weinberger, Casey, and others were determined to scrap it. Adelman recalled: "All of us around the table had opposed SALT II before taking office. It seemed senseless for us to abide by a treaty we opposed when it was unratified and unratifiable, violated, and expired." Even so, the public, Congress, and U.S. allies valued SALT II as a symbol of nuclear arms control. In early June, the U.S. Senate voted overwhelmingly to urge Reagan to continue abiding by the SALT provisions. In the context of the forthcoming summit, these factors tipped the scale. Adelman recalled, with dismay: "Reagan was delighted at the prospect of such a stellar event and would not risk endangering it or its 'atmosphere.'" And this seemed likely enough, for State Department and arms control officials argued that scrapping the treaty "would be a red flag" to the Russians "and those in the world who were hoping for a slowing of the arms race." Consequently, as Adelman noted, "the critical comment came when a White House aide said simply, 'Do we want the Allies and Congress dumping all over the President just as he's about to meet Gorbachev?'" Once again, Reagan decided to continue abiding by the SALT II limits.[87]

Fortunately for the President, Gorbachev, too, recognized the need to address the public's antinuclear concerns. Numerous Soviet officials were dubious about anything useful coming out of the Geneva summit meeting, but Gorbachev was determined to provide it with substance. Conferring with Shultz a few weeks before the event, the Soviet party secretary told him: "The great question is war or peace. That is what preoccupies people everywhere. We should have as our intent the development of a dialogue to reduce confrontation, encourage détente and peaceful coexistence. That is what the world wants." Turning to one of his favorite proposals, Gorbachev told the secretary of state that he was ready to eliminate all nuclear weapons, provided that their two countries agreed to prevent the militarization of space. In his memoirs, he recalled that the last summit meeting had taken place six and a half years before. Since then, the international situation had become "heated to the limit," the rival alliance systems "had fenced themselves behind palisades of nuclear missiles, and people all over the world were full of anxiety." In this context, Soviet leaders had met to prepare numerous initiatives for the Geneva summit, and "the meeting could therefore raise the curtain on the process of resolving the most acute problem of the day—nuclear disarmament."[88]

Despite these good intentions, the Geneva summit proved less than a total success. In line with his soaring hopes, Reagan assured Gorbachev that "we can create history and do some things that the world will remember in a positive way." Even so, the President's fervent anti-Communism immediately led him down an unpromising path. In their first meeting, he recalled: "I took Gorbachev through the long history of Soviet aggression, citing chapter and verse of the Soviet Union's policy of expansionism from 1917 onward." Gorbachev remonstrated that the Soviet Union was a peace-loving state, whereupon "I cited more reasons for our skepticism about the Soviets such as the Soviet betrayal of Stalin's promise at Yalta to hold free elections in the nations of Eastern Europe after World War II."[89] Reagan also launched into a passionate defense of SDI as "a way to end the world's nightmare about nuclear weapons." By contrast, Gorbachev viewed SDI as facilitating a U.S. first strike capability, and thought that Reagan's claim that the United States would share the fruits of SDI research with the Soviet Union was preposterous. "Reagan appeared to me not simply a conservative," Gorbachev wrote in his memoirs, "but a political 'dinosaur.'"[90] On the other hand, the two governments, eager to show some results, agreed on the desirability of a 50 percent cut in strategic nuclear arsenals and of "early progress" toward an "interim INF agreement." At the end of the conference, they adopted a joint communiqué repeating Reagan's now-famous antinuclear statement: "A nuclear war cannot be won and must never be fought." According to Matlock, Reagan—having been accused of warmongering— was "eager to put his commitment to peace on the record."[91]

Even in the absence of concrete agreements, the Geneva summit had a positive effect on the relationship between the two nations, and especially on their top leaders. Reagan recalled that he genuinely "liked Gorbachev, even though he was a dedicated Communist." The American President considered the Soviet party secretary an appealing person, as well as the first Kremlin leader uninterested in expansionism and committed to nuclear arms reductions. Commenting on Gorbachev at a national security meeting that month, Reagan declared: "Maggie Thatcher was right; we can work with this man. . . . He believes in live and let live."[92] Gorbachev was not quite as favorably impressed by Reagan who, he later remarked, "was so loaded with stereotypes that it was difficult for him to accept reason." Nonetheless, he thought that, despite the American President's ignorance and their many differences on specific issues, Reagan was not—as traditional Marxist-Leninist thinking would have it—automatically an enemy. Indeed, starting at this point, Gorbachev increasingly believed that, somehow, he would be able to work with him to reduce Soviet-American confrontation and promote nuclear disarmament.[93] In January 1986, when Kampelman returned to Geneva to head up the U.S. arms control delegation, his Soviet counterpart took him aside and said: "I just want you to know that I've been instructed by my highest authority never to attack Reagan." Laughing a little, he added: "This does not apply to Weinberger."[94]

The Road to Reykjavik, December 1985–September 1986

In the months that followed, the pressures mounted for a nuclear disarmament breakthrough. Reagan and Gorbachev corresponded at length, discussing the need to reduce nuclear arsenals through a variety of means. But Reagan's insistence upon moving forward with SDI and Gorbachev's view of it as a shield for a nuclear first strike hindered progress, as did their disagreement over nuclear testing.[95] Gorbachev's January 15, 1986, announcement of his three-step plan for a nuclear-free world by the year 2000 proved more effective. Reagan, in fact, found it very appealing. When Shultz remarked to him that it should not simply be rejected, the President agreed wholeheartedly, adding: "Why wait until the end of the century for a world without nuclear weapons?" Admittedly, aside from Reagan, U.S. national security officials were almost uniformly hostile. Noting that Gorbachev's plan had been delivered to Reagan only a few hours before it was released to the world, they quickly dismissed it as a propaganda ploy. More fundamentally, as proponents of U.S. military strength, they did not want the United States to dispense with its nuclear arsenal. According to Shultz, Perle told him that "the worst thing in the world would be to eliminate nuclear weapons," and even he considered the idea "utopian." Nevertheless, addressing a group of U.S. officials, Shultz told them that "the President of the United States doesn't agree with you, and he has said so on several very public occasions. . . . He thinks it's a hell of a good idea. And it's a political hot button."[96] At the least, Gorbachev's call for a nuclear-free world added to the U.S. government's anxiety about the public's antinuclear mood. The CIA's Robert Gates recalled: "How to respond to Gorbachev and counter the public image of the Soviet Union leaning far forward to reduce the nuclear threat dominated debate in the Reagan administration in 1986."[97]

The urgency of an American response grew during the second half of the year. On May 27, 1986, Reagan finally acceded to the pleas of his most hawkish advisors and announced that the U.S. government would no longer be bound by the limits of the SALT II treaty. Although Shultz expected an uproar from NATO allies and Congress, he did not think "the President and Weinberger were prepared for the magnitude of what hit them." Fearing "an adverse public reaction in their countries," recalled Adelman, allied leaders, including Thatcher, protested bitterly, and "cables of alarm streamed into the White House." On Capitol Hill, the House reacted angrily by slashing the SDI budget from $5.3 billion to $3.1 billion and by barring funds for the deployment of any strategic weapons that would cause the U.S. government to exceed the SALT II limits. Facing a mutiny, the President backed away from his decision, saying that it was tentative and ordering the military to stay within the treaty limits for the moment.[98] That summer, groping for a dramatic response to Gorbachev's nuclear abolition proposal, Reagan seized upon an idea suggested by Weinberger: abolition of ballistic missiles. Although Reagan may have considered this a sincere offer, it was heavily biased toward the United States. As Nitze pointed out, it was "non-negotiable," for the Russians had "most of their eggs in that one basket," while the Americans enjoyed their advantage in cruise missiles and bombers, which would not be touched by the proposal. Furthermore, Reagan paired it with the development of SDI.[99] Ignoring the idea, Gorbachev nonetheless attempted to open up the stalled negotiating process that September by proposing that they hold a meeting the next month roughly halfway between their capitals, in Reykjavik. Although some of Reagan's advisors opposed holding another summit, Reagan wanted one, at least in part because he assumed it would give his party a political boost in the midterm congressional elections a few weeks later. Furthermore, according to Donald Regan, the White House Chief of Staff: "The President had been speaking out vigorously on disarmament ever since Geneva, and to temporize when he had been offered the chance to negotiate could have incalculable consequences in terms of world opinion."[100]

The Reykjavik Summit, October 1986

In preparing for the summit meeting, the leaders of both governments recognized its political significance. According to Richard Wirthlin, the administration conducted "heavy" polling on U.S. public attitudes before the Reykjavik summit, in the expectation that it would have a major impact. Shortly before the meeting convened, and linked to it, there also occurred what Shultz called "tense negotiations with congressional leaders" over the administration's policy toward nuclear testing and SALT II. At the same time, State Department officials reported to Shultz, as he recalled, that they found "deep desperation" among NATO allies, for they "considered our stance on virtually every issue to be too difficult for Gorbachev to accept." Thus, they hoped and expected that "we would show more flexibility in the direct meetings to come." Confronted by these kinds of pressures—and also because, by this point, he genuinely wanted to reduce nuclear weapons— Reagan was eager to advance a disarmament agenda.[101] In his own pre-Reykjavik analysis, Gorbachev emphasized the influence of the forthcoming U.S. elections and his belief that Reagan was eager "to go down in history as the peace president."[102] There were also the Soviet leadership's own public relations concerns. "Everyone agreed at the Politburo meeting," Gorbachev recalled, "that Reykjavik would improve our image in the world, demonstrating our determination to prevent a new arms race." Yet, like Reagan, he was serious about fostering nuclear disarmament. Instructing the Soviet group preparing for Reykjavik, he outlined their position as cutting all types of nuclear weapons by 50 percent, removing all INF missiles from Europe, and confining SDI to laboratory research—with the ultimate goal of "abolition of nuclear weapons." Of course, "if we fail, then we could say: look what we were willing to do!"[103]

Although the two leaders came closer to meeting their goals at Reykjavik than at Geneva, they once again fell short of a breakthrough. For days, the political climate swept them forward. Appealing to Gorbachev, the President told him: "Our people would cheer if we got rid of the missiles." In turn, Gorbachev insisted that Reagan was "just one step away from going

down in history as the 'peacemaker President.' "[104] They even spoke breez-
ily, if vaguely, about eliminating all nuclear weapons. Although the experts
were aghast, recalled Shultz, the two national leaders "felt what people
wanted in a profound way."[105] Gorbachev's proposals to reduce strategic nuclear weapons systems by 50 percent and to eliminate the INF missiles from
Europe delighted most U.S. officials. To be sure, as Adelman recalled, "one
prominent member" of the U.S. delegation wondered whether the zero option for Europe was really a good idea. "But . . . all of us had supported the
zero option for five long years," and it was impossible to retreat from this
position.[106] The major sticking point was SDI. Viewing SDI as a threat to
Soviet national security, Gorbachev demanded that research on it be confined to the laboratory. By contrast, viewing SDI as a guarantor against nuclear attack, Reagan rejected any curbs on its development. As both men
dug in around this issue, the discussion grew heated and, ultimately, both
left the conference in anger, without coming to any agreement on nuclear
arms control or disarmament.[107]

The events at Reykjavik evoked a generally unfavorable reaction in the
West. Among the hawkish national security élite, there was consternation at
how close Reagan had come to sharply cutting U.S. nuclear weapons programs. Former U.S. Defense Secretary Schlesinger claimed that "Reykjavik
represented a near disaster from which we were fortunate to escape." Nixon
claimed that "no summit since Yalta has threatened Western interests so
much." To Weinberger, NSC officials, and "many" State Department officials, recalled Shultz, "Reykjavik was regarded as a blunder of the greatest
magnitude."[108] Margaret Thatcher was especially critical. "When I heard
how far the Americans had been prepared to go," she recalled, it "was as if
there had been an earthquake beneath my feet. . . . The whole system of nuclear deterrence . . . was close to being abandoned."[109] Ironically, the considerably more dovish general public was irked by the fact that Reagan's
stubborn defense of SDI had destroyed the chances for a major nuclear disarmament accord. Nancy Reagan recalled, ruefully, that her husband
"would have received a great deal of praise for reaching a dramatic agreement with Gorbachev, and as I expected, he took a lot of heat for not signing it." Having surveyed public sentiment for the White House, Wirthlin
concluded that, "initially, many people were upset about the lack of progress." Only "a conscious effort" to convey a positive message "buffered us
against what could have been a very substantial backlash with the public."
Convinced that the public would have greeted a nuclear abolition agreement
"with great joy," Reagan grew ever more critical of nuclear weapons. When
Adelman lectured him on the risks of a nuclear-free world, arguing that nu-

clear weapons had kept the peace in Europe for forty years, the President asked him how he could be so sure of that.[110]

Gorbachev, too, was not ready to abandon his hopes for nuclear disarmament. Although he returned from the summit in an angry mood, irritated by the lack of progress, he soon adopted a more patient attitude. "Let the president consider what happened, let him consult with the Congress," Gorbachev told the Politburo a few days later. "Maybe another attempt will be necessary to breach the distance that separates us. We can wait. And we're not rescinding the proposals we advanced in Reykjavik." After all, "everyone saw that agreement is possible," and "that is why Reykjavik left me an even greater optimist." Not everyone in the Soviet leadership was quite this sanguine. At the Politburo meeting of October 30, 1986, Gromyko charged that the Americans "saw our weakness, and now they are . . . tearing out new concessions from us." To this avatar of party conservatism, nuclear abolition appeared as a major threat. "If we abolish nuclear weapons," he said, "we will be left without something that we have been creating for 25 years, and what are we going to do then? Rely on the honesty of the Americans?" But Gorbachev remained determined to proceed with his disarmament program. As Dobrynin later summarized things: "The old guard in the Politburo and the military-industrial complex covertly opposed his 'new thinking' and his plans for accommodation with the United States, but he overcame them by proclaiming his firm intention to carry out his new foreign policy, fully aware that he could count on the party and on the public support he then enjoyed."[111]

The INF Treaty

For the Reagan administration, the political attractiveness of a nuclear arms control agreement grew substantially in late 1986 and early 1987. According to Wirthlin, "the President was well aware" that such an agreement would give him a political boost, and never was this more important to him than in the months after the Iran-Contra scandal erupted in November 1986. "Politically," wrote Nancy Reagan, this was "the most difficult period he ever went through." The entire federal government "seemed to grind to a halt." On December 1, a *New York Times*-ABC poll revealed that Reagan's overall approval rating had plummeted in a single month from 67 to 46 percent—the sharpest one-month drop in such ratings ever recorded.[112] As the Iran-Contra scandal unfolded, the President's political standing continued to worsen. By early March 1987, Wirthlin informed Reagan, he had reached the lowest point yet of public confidence in his presidency. Furthermore, thanks to victories by Democrats in the November 1986 elections, they had retaken the Senate, giving them control of both houses of Congress. Within the inner circle of the administration, it became clear that the best way to reverse the political slide was through an arms control agreement. The CIA's Robert Gates recalled that a "major effect of Iran-Contra on U.S-Soviet relations was to convince Reagan, his wife, and his closest White House advisers that the terrible stain of the scandal could only be removed, or at least diminished, by the President becoming a peacemaker, by his achievement of a historic breakthrough with the Soviet Union."[113]

Popular sentiment abroad pointed in the same direction. Confronted by Gorbachev's dramatic nuclear disarmament proposals, the U.S. government's overseas image was sinking fast, much to the distress of U.S. officials. According to a panicky USIA report, in the aftermath of the Reykjavik summit most of the public in the largest West European countries saw the Soviet Union as making a greater effort to achieve a nuclear arms control agreement than the United States. By May 1987, Gorbachev outpolled Reagan on arms controls by 72 to 9 percent in West Germany, 63 to 13 percent in Britain, and 45 to 16 percent in France. The USIA noted that, in February 1987, the British public had more confidence in Soviet than in U.S. leadership. Establishing a USIA International Advisory Council that May, USIA director Charles Wick invited the nation's top national security officials to address it on a variety of issues. At the top of the list was: "Why, in many parts of the world, is the U.S. perceived as more of a threat to world peace than the U.S.S.R.? How can we change this?"[114]

It was Gorbachev, however, who cut through the remaining obstacles, thereby enabling both governments to secure a nuclear disarmament agreement. At Reykjavik, the Soviet leader had included a treaty for removal of the Euromissiles as part of the Soviet negotiating package. Therefore, when Reagan insisted upon retaining the right to proceed with SDI, no agreement was possible. But on February 28, 1987, Gorbachev suddenly announced his willingness to separate the INF issue from the issue of SDI. Although Shultz maintained that this announcement came "out of the blue," it actually reflected the influence of antinuclear activism. As early as April 1985, Jeremy Stone of the FAS had begun arguing before Soviet audiences that the best way to block SDI was to "go ahead with disarmament." With nuclear arms reductions underway, "there would be no political support for Star Wars" in the United States.[115] A variant of this "bear-hug strategy" began to be promoted by Andrei Sakharov upon his return from internal exile in December 1986. This "Sakharov finesse," as it came to be known, also involved unlinking INF from SDI, but—unlike Stone's plan—relied for its clout upon the threat of resuming a nuclear weapons buildup if the U.S. government scrapped the ABM treaty and proceeded with SDI. Stone, Sakharov, and von Hippel conferred shortly before the opening of the February 1987 Forum for a Nuclear Free World, and at the Forum—presided over by Gorbachev—all three gave speeches promoting the idea of cutting the INF-SDI linkage. Furthermore, during the final banquet, Stone and von Hippel sat at Gorbachev's table, where they had the opportunity to engage in further advocacy. Two weeks later, Gorbachev made his dramatic announcement.[116]

Was their intervention decisive? Gorbachev's public and private statements indicate that, combined with the widespread public demand for nuclear disarmament, it was. In his book *Perestroika*, Gorbachev wrote that, at the February 1987 Forum, "I had the opportunity to feel the moods and hear the thoughts and ideas of an international intellectual élite. My discussions with them made a great impression on me. I discussed the results of the congress with my colleagues in the Politburo and we decided to make a major new compromise—untie the Reykjavik package and separate the problem of medium-range missiles in Europe from other issues." Records of the Politburo meetings in the days just before the announcement illustrate how intertwined this key Soviet decision was with public pressures for nuclear disarmament. "The biggest measure that would make an impact on the outside world, on public opinion, will be if we untie the package," Gorbachev declared. Yegor Ligachev interjected that, by cutting the missiles, "we will gain a lot in terms of public opinion." Expressing his agreement, Gorbachev promised that "we will pressure the United States through public opinion, arguing that we are in favor of mutual trust." After further discussion, Gorbachev summarized the meeting's consensus that there would be "a statement about untying the package on the medium-range missiles. This will be our response to the state of public opinion in the world." It would also "weaken the negative reaction" to the resumption of Soviet nuclear testing that same month.[117]

With a Euromissile agreement no longer weighted down by SDI, the two nations made rapid progress toward an INF treaty during the following months. Underscoring his willingness to dispense with nuclear weapons, Gorbachev proposed—and the U.S. government agreed—to eliminate shorter-range INF missiles as well, thus making this a "zero-zero agreement." The real opposition now began coming from conservative West European officials—particularly in West Germany and Britain—uneasy about the emergence of a non-nuclear Europe. They had supported the elimination of intermediate range nuclear weapons for propaganda purposes, and now, to their dismay, it was about to become a reality.[118] Yet, as

Rozanne Ridgway, the State Department's top Europeanist, noted, Western Europe's officials were under great political pressure "to do something." Indeed, antinuclear action had become politically irresistible. The general inspector of West Germany's Bundeswehr, admitting that the zero option created strategic difficulties, nonetheless insisted that it could not be opposed, "for the simple reason that no one can deny humanity's desire for denuclearization." Moreover, as Adelman recalled, the "trump card was always that the zero option was *our* proposal, NATO's proposal. All of our elected leaders had been touting it for six years. . . . We had to take yes for an answer." The alternative, he noted, was "a new round of rowdy protests," which NATO leaders dreaded. In this fashion, years of antinuclear agitation, bolstered by public opinion, locked conservative European governments into grudging acceptance of policies they disliked.[119]

Elsewhere, too, conservatives found themselves in a similar bind. In the Soviet Union, as Gorbachev recognized at the time, the main threat to his foreign policy came from party conservatives, who opposed any concessions to the Americans. And, in fact, military-industrial leaders privately despised the emerging INF treaty. But they were constrained from openly opposing it thanks to their earlier support for the idea of a nuclear-free world.[120] In the United States, as Shultz recalled, "the Republican right in congress and some important former officials" began to line up against the prospective treaty. But "if the United States reversed its stand now on our willingness to eliminate INF missiles, after maintaining this position throughout the volatile predeployment period, such a reversal would be political dynamite in Europe!" Furthermore, as Ridgway remarked: "You can't look at an agreement . . . in which you have broad bipartisan support, achieving all the things the United States wanted, including very, very elaborate on-site inspection, and then turn to a world in which you . . . have . . . the committee for this, the committee for that, and the campaign for something else—who have, in fact, put the topic of nuclear arms control and reduction on the agenda and kept it there—. . . and then turn it down."[121]

Ultimately, then, Gorbachev's offer could not be refused. In December 1987, the Soviet leader met with Reagan in Washington for the signing of the INF treaty—the first to eliminate an entire class of nuclear weapons. Both men were quite upbeat about the event, especially Gorbachev, who was clearly in his element. Vice President Bush recalled that, while driving through the city streets in Gorbachev's heavily armored car, surrounded by enthusiastic crowds, he remarked casually to the Soviet leader that "it's too bad you can't stop . . . because I think you'd find warm greetings from the American people." Suddenly Gorbachev ordered the motorcade to screeching halt, and the beaming Soviet leader plunged into the crowds, surrounding by apprehensive security agents and surging mobs of Washingtonians, screaming with delight. Addressing the assemblage, Gorbachev told it—as Palazchenko, his interpreter, recalled—that "the people already understood that our countries should be friends and now the politicians seemed to understand that too. We need your continued support, he said," and the crowd "roared back its approval."[122]

As the Washington summit unfolded, the President received his expected political boost, but Gorbachev was clearly the man of the hour. "'Gorby-mania' . . . seized the capital," Gates recalled. "Senior officers of government, members of congress, top media stars, and celebrities of every stripe fell all over themselves to get close to Gorbachev, to shake his hand—to see this unique man who was . . . changing so much at home and around the world. In my two decades in Washington, I had never seen anything like it."[123] At the treaty signing ceremony—which began at a time insisted upon by Nancy Reagan, based upon the advice of her astrologer[124]— both men gave brief addresses. In line with his hopes, Reagan called the INF agreement "history-making." Gorbachev told the audience that the opportunity had arrived for the two countries to "move together toward a nuclear-free world," a statement that Reagan remembered fondly. A bit later, the Soviet leader added: "Urging us on is the will of hundreds of millions of people, who are beginning to understand that . . . civilization has approached a dividing line . . . between common sense . . . and irresponsibility. . . . We . . . must . . . build a safer and more democratic world, free from the trappings and the psychology of militarism."[125] Returning to the Soviet Union, he told the Politburo: "The world was waiting for that, the world demanded that. Trust in our new foreign policy depended on that. We were striving to put it to the test of life."[126]

For die-hard conservatives in the United States, the INF treaty was the Great Betrayal. Denouncing it as "appeasement," comparable to Neville Chambelain's Munich agreement with Adolf Hitler, the Conservative Caucus called upon Americans to oppose Senate ratification. Leading Republicans like Kissinger, Nixon, Jeane Kirkpatrick, and Brent Scowcroft launched attacks upon it. Among the candidates for the Republican presidential nomination, Vice President Bush was the only one who wholeheartedly endorsed the treaty. Robert Dole, the Republican leader in the Senate, declared that "I don't trust Gorbachev," and accused the President of "stuffing this treaty down the throats of our allies." In March 1988, during treaty hearings before the Senate Foreign Relations Committee, Senator Jesse Helms, the ranking Republican, led off by accusing the administration of "confusion, misstatements and . . . even misrepresentation" in its testimony. Bristling with anger at these remarks, Shultz engaged in a heated exchange with Helms, from which he was rescued by the Democrats. Weinberger and Adelman, both of whom had left the administration, wrote letters to Congress complaining that the treaty did not address the issue of futuristic weapons. The secretary of state also faced unrelenting opposition from Senator Dan Quayle, to whom he finally retorted: "Dan, you have to shut down! We can't have the President's achievement wrecked by Republicans!" Shultz recalled that "the real opposition was all from the GOP side." When he reported that to the President, Reagan "agreed and could only shake his head in dismay."[127] In this context, Reagan's support of the treaty was crucial, for he carried with him enough conservative Senators so that, when their numbers were added to the solid ranks of the Democrats, it had more than enough votes necessary for ratification.[128]

The signing of the INF treaty also dismayed conservatives in other nations. The London *Times*, which frequently reflected the position of the British government, complained that "the objective of the Geneva talks should have been reduction, not elimination. . . . The power blocs are safer with nuclear missiles than without them—and this applies to INF as much as any other weapon category." On the eve of the Washington summit, the *Times* published an article describing the INF treaty as a nuclear Munich. Although Thatcher swallowed her earlier objections and grimly accepted the treaty, she talked increasingly of modernizing NATO's short-range nuclear weapons to compensate for the loss of the INF missiles. For its part, The 6i, which traced the advent of "compromise and appeasement" in the White House to late 1986, deplored the signing of the treaty and "the end of Reaganism."[129] In West Germany, conservatives viewed the INF treaty as decoupling their nation from the United States, as well as subjecting them to increased risk of nuclear attack from the Soviet Union. Ironically, within the Soviet Union, as Gorbachev recalled, "hotheads" began "claiming that the agreement had undermined the Soviet Union's security and upset the balance of weaponry between the superpowers." Indeed, as two leading writers on arms control issues have noted, the criticisms of the INF treaty in the Soviet Union "were very sharp, especially on the part of the retired Soviet military. This group bombarded the Defense and Foreign Affairs Ministries as well as the Central Committee of the CPSU and the KGB with piles of letters and statements trying to prove that the USSR made great concessions without any reasons, that this treaty was presented as an act of unilateral disarmament."[130]

By contrast, nuclear disarmament activists were absolutely delighted with the INF treaty, which they proclaimed a triumph for antinuclear activism. Pointing to END's long and vigorous campaign to rid Europe of cruise, Pershing II, and SS-20 missiles, Mary Kaldor declared that "the real responsibility for the agreement belongs to the peace movement." IPCC stated that the signing of the treaty proved "that politicians could not remain insensitive" to movement and public pressures. In Britain, CND leaders gathered outside the American and Soviet embassies, cracking open bottles of champagne and celebrating. Hailing the treaty at the Molesworth peace camp, CND promised: "INF IS JUST THE BEGINNING!"[131] Meanwhile, in the United States, as SANE/Freeze's newsletter reported, "peace activists publicly toasted the movement's role in bringing about the treaty," and treaty celebrations were held "in almost every major city in the country." In the nation's capital, disarmament groups sponsored a rally and "Bridge to Peace," at which Margaret Papandreou, wife of the Greek prime minister, compared the INF treaty to a baby produced by the "strangest marriage in history," that of Reagan and Gorbachev. "The baby will be baptized by the peace movement because we, after all, arranged the marriage," she told the crowd of thousands, which linked arms to form a human bridge from the Soviet embassy to White House. Nuclear disarmament activists testified in support of treaty ratification before the Senate Foreign Relations Committee and, at the invitation of the Soviet government, before the Supreme Soviet. The following year, when the first Soviet missiles were destroyed under the INF treaty's provisions, an international delegation of antinuclear activists was on hand at the Saryozek military base to witness the event and celebrate their victory.[132]

Escalating Progress, 1987-88

With the agreement on the INF treaty, the character of Soviet-American relations significantly changed. Just as the antinuclear scientists had predicted, Congress responded to the disarmament accord by delivering a hammer blow to SDI, cutting Reagan's budget request for it by a third and mandating that SDI testing remain within the limits of the ABM treaty. For all practical purposes, this blocked further development of Reagan's missile defense dream.[133] "Reagan didn't give up" on SDI, Carlucci recalled. But "we just couldn't get the money" and Congress insisted upon adhering to the ABM treaty. "We had a Democratic Congress" and, consequently, SDI "was not supported."[134] Gorbachev, particularly, was energized by the Soviet-American agreement on eliminating the INF missiles. According to Chernyaev, he viewed it "as the watershed in our entire relationship." Back in Moscow, he dramatically reined in the military, challenging their pet weapons projects. Meeting with Shultz and National Security Advisor Colin Powell in April 1988, Gorbachev told them—as Powell recalled—that "he was going to change the USSR in ways we never imagined. He was saying, in effect, that he was ending the Cold War." Looking directly at Powell, he remarked, with a twinkle in his eye: "What are you going to do now that you've lost your best enemy?"[135] In fact, thanks to growing resistance to a strategic arms agreement by conservatives and military officials, negotiations over START went much more slowly than either Gorbachev or Reagan would have liked. Even so, during 1988, they made some progress on this front, as well.[136]

The atmosphere grew even warmer as the year progressed. In May, Reagan journeyed to Moscow for yet another meeting with Gorbachev. As the two former enemies strolled pleasantly through Red Square, Gorbachev took a small child from a woman's arms and, cradling him in the crook of his own arm, said: "Shake hands with Grandfather Reagan." Addressing a small knot of people that had gathered, Reagan said: "We decided to talk to each other instead of about each other. It's working just fine." When they returned to the Kremlin grounds, a reporter questioned the American President about the "evil empire" he had denounced five years before. "I was talking about another time, another era," he replied.[137] Later that year, Gorbachev acted to implement the ideas of "reasonable sufficiency" and "non-provocative defense" in Soviet military doctrine, laying plans for major, unilateral cutbacks in the Soviet armed forces, particularly in offensive weapons. These were announced on December 7, 1988, in a remarkable address Gorbachev delivered at the United Nations. "The advent of nuclear weapons was just another tragic reminder of the fundamental nature" of changes in the modern world, he declared on that occasion. "A material symbol and expression of absolute military power, nuclear weapons at the same time revealed the absolute limits of that power. The problems of mankind's survival and self-preservation came to the fore." It had become "obvious . . . that the use or threat of force no longer can . . . be an instrument of foreign policy." In their place, the world needed the establishment of strong international security system, under the direction of a revitalized United Nations, as well as a new spirit of Soviet-American cooperation. "I would like to believe that our hopes will be matched by our joint effort to put an end to an era of wars, confrontation and regional conflicts, to aggressions against nature, to the terror of hunger and poverty. . . . This is our common goal and we can only reach it together."[138] Addressing a secret meeting of the Politburo upon his return to the Soviet Union, Gorbachev explained: "We are proposing and willing to build a new world."[139]

The Responsibility for the Breakthrough

In retrospect, it is clear that both Reagan and Gorbachev played important roles in bringing about the INF nuclear disarmament agreement that opened the floodgates for other antinuclear measures and for the end of the Cold War. As Colin Powell observed, Reagan "had the vision and flexibility, lacking in many knee-jerk Cold Warriors, to recognize that Gorbachev was a new man in a new age offering new opportunities for peace." Or, as the British Labour Party's Michael Foot put it: "If he had given a hopelessly dusty answer to Gorbachev, the whole bloody thing wouldn't have happened, and it would have been a terrible disaster for the human race." Instead, of course, Reagan eagerly grasped at the chance for securing nuclear arms control and disarmament agreements, thereby—in Adelman's words—"giving the kiss of life to the very process he had once deplored."[140] But Gorbachev deserves the lion's share of the credit for this turnabout in Soviet-American relations, for he was the more dynamic actor, overcoming Reagan's virulent anti-Communism and effectively playing upon his desire to lead the way toward a nuclear-free world. As Chernyaev later wrote: "If not for Gorbachev's persistence, his dogged determination to prove to all that nuclear weapons were an absolute evil and unacceptable foundation for world politics, the process would not have started and we would not have had the subsequent historical reversal in the arms race." Both national leaders understood that—as Carlucci later remarked—"we were heading in a crazy direction," and acted to apply the brakes.[141] Drawing together, they outwitted conservatives in their own nations and others, leaving them distraught and sputtering.

Yet the bulk of the credit for the new course—or, as Gorbachev liked to call it, the "new thinking"—lay with the nuclear disarmament campaign and the tidal wave of antinuclear sentiment that it generated. So powerful was the antinuclear pressure that it began transforming Reagan's approach to nuclear weapons even *before* the advent of Gorbachev, thus setting the stage for their later agreements. Once Gorbachev appeared on the scene, it became irresistible. Reagan—still uneasy with the nuclear disarmament movement but swept forward by the antinuclear *Zeitgeist*—broke loose from his old moorings. By contrast, Gorbachev was enamored with the movement, and—like his closest advisors—repeatedly adopted its ideas and proposals.

As Jeremy Stone put it: "Gorbachev was the 'dove in place' for which we all devoutly wished. . . . He was ready to be inoculated with every conceptual virus we had." Upon meeting him some time later, Helen Caldicott said simply: "Thank you for saving the world." He thanked her in turn. Indeed, unlike Reagan, Gorbachev recognized the central role of antinuclear activists. Mailing a signed copy of the INF treaty to IPPNW's Bernard Lown, the Soviet leader praised him "for your enormous contribution to preventing nuclear war. Without it and other powerful anti-nuclear initiatives, it is unlikely that this treaty would have come about."[142] As the record of these turbulent years indicates, Gorbachev was correct.

The Movement Tide
Recedes, 1989-93

> We do not want to participate any longer in the great
> powers' senseless nuclear races at the cost of the life
> and health of present and future generations.
>
> Olzhas Suleimenov, 1990

The signing of great power nuclear arms control agreements, the end of the
Cold War, and the disintegration of the Soviet Union had a powerful impact
upon the antinuclear movement in many nations. For the most part, these
developments weakened the movement, especially in the West, for—with
the apparent decline of nuclear danger—campaigns for nuclear disarmament
no longer seemed as crucial to human survival. For much of the public and
even for many movement activists, non-nuclear issues began to assume a
higher priority. And yet, despite its decline, the movement remained a significant political force. Emphasizing the irrationality of preparing for nuclear war in the new, safer, post–Cold War world, antinuclear groups in the
West agitated for further steps toward nuclear disarmament. In turmoil-
wracked Eastern Europe, peace and antinuclear groups thrived, and their
leaders played important roles in promoting democracy, toppling Communist regimes, and in heading up the non-Communist governments that succeeded them. Eastern and Western movements engaged in major joint ventures, including a vigorous, worldwide campaign to end nuclear testing.
Public opinion, though increasingly complacent about nuclear dangers, also
showed substantial impatience with the maintenance of the nuclear arms
race, military spending, and the continued preparations for nuclear war. As
a result, even as the movement waned in most nations, it continued to provide a visible and sometimes powerful source of resistance to nuclear weapons.

The Movement in Decline

The signing of nuclear disarmament treaties, the collapse of East European Communist regimes, and, above all, the end of the Cold War—though welcomed by the nuclear disarmament movement—raised serious problems for it, as well. After the "Reagan-Gorbachev love-in," lamented SANE/Freeze's William Sloane Coffin, Jr., public concern about nuclear weapons dwindled. A May 1990 Gallup poll among Americans found that only 21 percent considered it fairly or very likely that their country would become involved in a nuclear war in the next ten years. This contrasted with 47 percent in 1981 and 1982 and 44 percent in 1983. In early 1991, 56 percent of Americans told pollsters that the Cold War was over, and 62 percent said there was virtually no chance of an all-out nuclear war with the Soviet Union.[1] Although activists were less complacent about the nuclear menace, they, too, felt a pull to put nuclear issues behind them. "When the Berlin Wall came down," recalled Helen Caldicott, "everyone was so exhausted and burned out . . . that they packed their bags and went home and said: 'Thank God *that*'s over!'" A cartoon on the cover of the Italian Peace Association's magazine joked: "I'm taking a nap for peace." Meg Beresford wrote that, "all over Europe, people breathed an enormous sigh of relief. Disarmament was happening. Friendly people began to ask us in CND why we continued. Unfriendly people told us that it was the West's power and resolve that had brought about the change." Thus, "we continued to pump out our message, but it went largely unheard."[2]

Furthermore, even many activists who persisted found the issues somewhat different than those of the past. The end of the Cold War *did* lessen nuclear dangers, just as it opened the door to bloody ethnic and national conflicts, especially in Eastern Europe. To counter these, some of END's top leaders—including Mient Jan Faber and Mary Kaldor—began to withdraw from END to organize the Helsinki Citizens Assembly for Peace and Democracy. Emerging out of the earlier END process of détente from below, and specifically Charter 77's Prague Appeal of 1985, the Helsinki Citizens Assembly (HCA), in Kaldor's words, was an attempt to foster "a pan-European security system that would supplant the military blocs and find ways of solving conflicts in Europe without reliance on military force." It would also seek to sustain and encourage "the creation of a trans-European civil society." An early organizing statement by Faber defined its goal as "a united, democratic, multi-cultural, socially just, ecologically conscious, demilitarized Europe." In October 1990, over 700 people representing 25 European countries, the Soviet Union, Canada, and the United States attended the first HCA convention, in Prague. Addressed by the new Czech president, Václav Havel, a Charter 77 peace and human rights activist only recently released from prison, the convention pulled together a new, international organization that was antiwar, anti-nationalist, and dedicated to the defense of human rights. HCA organized a secretariat in Prague and another at The Hague (headed up by Faber), while branches developed throughout Eastern Europe and in parts of Western Europe. In Kaldor's view, the HCA provided the logical successor to END in the post–Cold War era.[3]

New international conflicts also undermined the antinuclear movement. The Gulf War of 1990–91 was particularly problematic. Given the fact that most antinuclear activists were also peace proponents, they usually condemned both the Iraqi invasion of Kuwait and the U.S. government-led war against Iraq that followed. And this contributed to very substantial antiwar demonstrations, involving an estimated two million people in some 20 countries during the first week of the war against Iraq. But opposition to the Gulf War steered activists and their groups in a non-nuclear direction. In the United States, antinuclear organizations dropped nuclear issues to focus on the Gulf crisis. Even the U.S. movement's *Nuclear Times* published an entire issue on that subject. In June 1991, CND's leaders considered the idea of downplaying nuclear issues and becoming "a more general peace movement."[4] The Gulf War also brought many antinuclear groups into an awkward alliance with sectarian Left organizations, which seized the leadership of anti-war coalitions in a number of countries. Thus, CND found itself working closely with and providing funding for the Trotskyist-dominated Committee to Stop War in the Gulf—a fact that created discomfort and demoralization within CND ranks.[5] In addition, antiwar activists often became cut off from the mainstream of public opinion thanks to popular repugnance at the violent, repressive nature of the Iraqi government and the growing popularity of the war.[6] Other international military action also generated problems for disarmament activists and groups. Although pacifist organizations objected to military intervention in Somalia and Bosnia, many peace-oriented non-pacifists viewed such intervention as a justifiable use of force, especially if it could prevent mass starvation and halt Serbian "ethnic cleansing."[7]

For these reasons, the nonaligned movement underwent a significant organizational decline. In Canada, Project Ploughshares dropped from 47 to 35 local groups between 1988 and 1993. The Canadian Peace Alliance experienced a financial crisis, while Operation Dismantle collapsed and merged with the World Federalists. In Britain, CND lost members and financial resources, especially in the aftermath of the Gulf War.[8] Almost as bad, it lost the support of the Labour Party, which, under Neil Kinnock's leadership, not only abandoned the idea of Britain's unilateral nuclear disarmament, but voted to maintain that nation's nuclear arsenal as long as nuclear weapons existed anywhere in the world.[9] In France, CODENE closed its doors in 1989, in Denmark No to Nuclear Weapons dissolved in 1992, and in Sweden the Swedish Peace and Arbitration Society lost about a third of its members.[10] In the United States, the Professionals Coalition—concluding that it had attained its goals—went out of business in 1991. Mobilization for Survival halted its operations at about the same time. Other organizations, such as SANE/Freeze, PSR, and WAND, experienced losses of membership and volunteers, declines in staffing, and income problems. Often they turned to foundations for financial support, a fact that encouraged them to carve out their own individual niches rather than work in broad coalitions. Moving away from grassroots mobilization and lobbying activities, they became more staff-driven, as well as more research- and education-oriented.[11]

Some of the nonaligned movement's major international organizations also began to wind down or to collapse. "Since the fall of the Berlin Wall," reported Bernard Lown, "people have been asking IPPNW, 'why don't you declare victory and go home? The nuclear threat is over.'" Although IPPNW managed to keep its focus on nuclear abolition, its membership and activism declined.[12] As the West European movement ebbed, IPCC gently faded away in 1991. END held on a bit longer. But, facing financial difficulties, *END Journal* stopped publication at the end of 1989. And, with the collapse of the Cold War blocs, END groped unsuccessfully for a new purpose. In 1992, it convened its last convention, in Brussels. Thereafter, it limped along, uncertain of its future.[13]

The World Peace Council was in even worse shape. Even though conservatives emerged victorious in their power struggle with Pakaslahti and other reformers in late 1988, the dissidents refused to depart quietly. In 1988 and 1989, Tair Tairov publicly criticized the authoritarian traditions, stagnation, and isolated nature of the Soviet Peace Committee and of the WPC. When the Soviet Peace Committee chair arranged to have him forced off the committee and fired from his position at IMEMO, a leading Moscow research institute, Tairov struck back by forming his own independent peace group and stepping up his attack.[14] Meanwhile, Pakaslahti, challenging Chandra's claim that he had agreed to step down as the WPC's general secretary, fought back, proclaiming that he had not resigned and denouncing the WPC's Stalinist tactics. The Communist-led peace groups in the Nordic countries rallied to Pakaslahti's defense, and numerous exposés of the WPC purge appeared in the Communist Party and mainstream press. Protests against the behavior of the Old Guard also arrived from WPC branches in East Germany, Australia, Canada, and the United States.[15] In December 1989, Pakaslahti told a group of WPC affiliates that their organization was in "an ever-deepening crisis." On the world scene, "sweeping political processes of democratization of old structures are taking place," but within the WPC there existed only "stagnation, purges, and other undemocratic practices." Two months later, addressing the WPC's Athens convention, Pakaslahti insisted that the WPC's "line of stagnation and the methods of Stalinist heritage should be openly condemned." The WPC seemed incapable of doing this, he added, so he recommended abolishing the group and building "a new international peace organization."[16]

The impact of this internal criticism, however, did not compare with that of the collapse of the Soviet Union and other East European Communist states. Suddenly, the great source of WPC political direction and funding was gone, leaving the official peace committees in the East and the Communist Party offshoots in the West to fend for themselves. Few of them could. Moreover, the WPC became wrapped up in the scandal surrounding the attempted coup by the Soviet Communist Party's Old Guard against Gorbachev, for it apparently served as a money laundering operation for the coup plotters. The Russian government sent a team of investigators to Finland to explore the Soviet Communist Party-SPC-WPC connection, although the confidentiality policies of Finnish banks prevented its drawing any definite conclusions.[17] With Communism crumbling and discredited, the WPC and its affiliates rapidly disintegrated. After the toppling of the East German regime, the German Peace Council withered away to a very small, chastened operation. The U.S. Peace Council collapsed entirely.[18] By late 1992, hardly any of the WPC's alleged 145 member organizations had paid their dues, and paid subscriptions to its two publications totaled fewer than 50. The WPC probably would have disappeared entirely if—before the disintegration of the Soviet regime—the Soviet Peace Committee had not transferred millions of dollars to the West to keep the Communist-led peace movement afloat. Thereafter, the French Communist Party—and later the Greek Communists—took over the remains of the WPC. But the organization was virtually defunct. The WPC's Old Guard "won," concluded Rob Prince. "But what did they win? Nothing! They won control of nothing."[19]

The Movement Continues in the West

Despite these setbacks, the nonaligned antinuclear movement remained an active force in Western nations. In Britain, CND—though weaker than in the recent past—continued its antinuclear activities, focusing on opposition to the government's Trident nuclear submarines. Utilizing nonviolent resistance, activists disrupted what might have been the first delivery of Trident nuclear warheads. In October 1992, some 2,000 CND demonstrators marched in Glasgow to protest the arrival of these nuclear submarines on the Clyde.[20] In Italy, the Peace Association launched a new campaign, Winds of Peace. Backed by peace, environmental, union, and solidarity groups, as well as by nuclear-free local authorities, it was designed "to develop an alternative peace policy for Italy and Europe, offering analysis, proposals, and actions." In Belgium, CNAPD and VAKA conducted a major campaign against modernization of NATO's short-range nuclear forces, including a demonstration in Brussels on April 16, 1989, that police claimed drew 21,000 people and organizers 75,000. In West Germany, the Physical Society, representing some 15,000 members, issued a resolution on disarmament in March 1989 that called for an end to nuclear testing and "termination of the nuclear arms race."[21] In 1991, joining with six other major peace and environmental organizations, the Norwegian Peace Council formed an alliance for a comprehensive nuclear test ban that lobbied embassies, members of parliament, and governments. Meanwhile, the Australian Coalition for Disarmament and Peace sponsored protests against visits of nuclear-powered and nuclear-armed ships, while Irish CND highlighted the plight of the victims of Chernobyl by sending tons of medical aid and hosting 131 children from the contaminated zones of Belarus on a holiday in Ireland.[22]

In the United States, as well, the movement retained some vigor. In 1989, the city of Oakland, California—as a follow-up to its passage of nuclear-free zone legislation—told the U.S. Department of Energy to move its field office, which oversaw the Lawrence Livermore nuclear weapons lab, out of the city. Although the vast majority of the nation's nuclear-free communities did not take this kind of strong action to implement their antinuclear ordinances, some did ban investments in nuclear weapons–related companies. Moreover, the number of communities proclaiming themselves nuclear-free zones continued to grow. To help the process along, Nuclear Free America branched out to include opposition to nuclear waste dumps, thereby bringing Native American communities—then being pressured to accept nuclear waste by the U.S. government—into the nuclear-free zone movement. Thanks to these efforts, by 1996 there were about 200 self-proclaimed nuclear-free zones in the United States, plus another 20 or so among Native American nations (which, out of respect for their sovereignty, were counted separately).[23]

There were other signs, too, that the U.S. movement retained some strength. In 1990, Mobilization for Survival sent overseas activists on an "After the Cold War" tour of the United States. That same year, the Union of Concerned Scientists began running devastating TV commercials and newspaper ads across the country criticizing the proposed Stealth (B-2) bomber. Decrying the new weapon, the ads contended that "the Cold War is ending," "the plane has no logical mission," and "its costs are out of control." Meanwhile, other B-2 opponents, organized by WAND, PSR, and the Council for a Livable World, sent paper airplanes made of photocopies of $20, $50, and $100 bills winging through the halls of Congress.[24] At the August 1991 national convention of SANE/Freeze, delegates voted to make their organization's 1992 priorities cutting military spending (thus increasing funds available for domestic needs), continuing work on nuclear disarmament, and ending the international weapons trade. Working with coalitions of environmental, labor, public interest, and peace groups it had organized in more than 50 cities, SANE/Freeze sought to develop new, non-military national priorities.[25] Although the membership of SANE/Freeze dropped to about 130,000 by the fall of 1990, this was still more than six times SANE's peak membership in the late 1950s and early 1960s. Furthermore, Greenpeace was growing by 50,000 members a month.[26]

One of the major U.S. antinuclear projects undertaken during these years was a campaign to shut down U.S. and Soviet nuclear weapons production facilities. In 1988, drawing on the momentum developing since the Chernobyl disaster, revelations in the press, and congressional investigations, PSR, the Professionals Coalition, the Sierra Club, the Natural Resources Defense Council, and SANE/Freeze had established the Plutonium Challenge to attack the nuclear weapons complex on health, safety, and environmental grounds. And there was plenty to attack, given the mismanagement and accelerating breakdown of these facilities, which led to frequent contamination of workers and the environment. Joined by the Military Production Network (a coalition of local citizens' groups), as well as by Greenpeace, the campaign utilized informational work, nonviolent civil disobedience, and lawsuits to tangle up the U.S. government's nuclear weapons production in a maze of bad publicity and legal challenges. When the federal government, recognizing the aging and deteriorating nature of its plutonium plants, sought to establish new ones, disarmament and environmental groups worked to block these as well, calling upon Congress to deny funding for them. The best way to avoid unilateral disarmament, the movement argued, was to encourage the Soviet government to shut down its plants as well. And, in fact, beginning in late 1988, SANE/Freeze worked to encourage Gorbachev to halt production of fissile materials as long as U.S. plants remained shut.[27] In April 1989, when the Soviet government announced that it would cease the production of highly enriched uranium and close plutonium reactors, SANE/Freeze leaders William Sloane Coffin and Nick Carter called on the Bush administration to "take immediate steps" to keep the U.S. government's "nuclear reactors shut and to halt the construction of new production facilities."[28]

More conservative groups, of course, promoted quite a different agenda. Despite the disintegration of the Soviet bloc, leading hawks in the United States issued dire warnings of foreign military conquest. A fundraising letter from the American Security Council argued that events in the Communist world were designed "to lull America back to sleep." After all, "how can we justify a full-scale defense when there appears to be no enemy?" In late 1989, Senator Jesse Helms insisted that "the military threat from the Soviet Union and the Warsaw Pact is greater today than it was in 1987, and . . . this capability still continues to grow."[29] In June 1990, more than $600,000 was poured into a campaign to defeat a nuclear-free zone initiative in Alameda County, California, most of it coming from large corporations such as General Electric, AT&T, Hewlett-Packard, Hughes Aircraft, IBM, and Rockwell International. Meeting with federal officials, lobbyists for the Aerospace Industries Association, representing forty of the largest nuclear weapons manufacturers, pressed the U.S. government to take legal action against local nuclear-free zone ordinances—which it did, including the one in Oakland.[30]

Nevertheless, nuclear disarmament activism continued—not only in the United States but around the globe. In Brazil, antinuclear scientists agitated for what they called "a clear, public, official rejection of nuclear weapons in Brazil and elsewhere. Especially in Brazil and Argentina," they noted, "where enrichment and reprocessing technologies could make nuclear weapons possible, enrichment should proceed under conditions of full transparency and complete civil control." In the Philippines, powerful nationalist forces—including the press, the lawyers group, and the peasant group—citing the nuclear-free provision in the new constitution, grew increasingly vocal in their demand for the closure of Subic Naval Base and Clark Air Base, both storage sites for U.S. nuclear weapons. Newspaper columnists decried the degradation of Philippine sovereignty, while students, women, and union members staged demonstrations.[31] Meanwhile, Indian activists continued their three-year effort to block the opening of a nuclear missile testing range in the state of Orissa. In Japan, Gensuikin conducted major campaigns to prevent a plutonium shipment from France, to halt nuclear testing, and to strengthen the nuclear nonproliferation treaty.[32] In Palau, responding once more to pleas by activists, the population voted down the latest attempt by the U.S. government to override that island nation's nuclear-free constitution.[33]

In some nations, antinuclear campaigns made significant progress. As political repression loosened somewhat in South Korea, thirteen peace and environmental organizations, along with 650 individuals, met in March 1991 and formed the Korean Alliance of Anti-Nuclear and Peace Movements. Its goals included the withdrawal of U.S. troops and nuclear weapons, the establishment of a nuclear-free zone, and the end of the arms race between North and South Korea. One of the Alliance's first activities was the issuance of a May 22, 1991, declaration, signed by 1,000 people, calling for the denuclearization of the Korean peninsula. Among the groups collecting endorsements were Chunminryun (the major coalition of political activist associations) and Chondaehyup (the organization representing student governments at nearly all colleges and universities throughout the country). Church and women's groups also joined South Korea's growing antinuclear campaign.[34] Although China remained as repressive as ever, the largest Uighur protest yet against Chinese nuclear testing occurred in May 1992, when some 10,000 people reportedly demonstrated in Kashgar.[35]

The nonaligned movement also continued its operations on the international level. Through its Nuclear Free Seas campaign, Greenpeace produced and publicized a series of reports on naval nuclear weapons deployment and accidents and, also, blocked and "tagged" nuclear vessels of different nations. In July 1989, it nonviolently disrupted a U.S. government test of the Trident II missile program in international waters. It would have done so again that December if U.S. government warships had not repeatedly rammed and nearly sunk the advancing Greenpeace vessel in a violent attack that lasted nearly four hours.[36] Meanwhile, END, celebrating the breakdown of the blocs, turned to dealing with what one leader called "the shape and character of the new Europe." But it did not drop nuclear issues, and it continued to draw large numbers of antinuclear activists to its annual conventions.[37] IPCC groups put together a joint platform for the June 1989 Europe-wide elections to the European parliament, stressing demilitarization, an end to the Cold War, and opposition to modernization of NATO nuclear weapons. Two END leaders, Ken Coates and Peter Crampton, were elected to the parliament, as were activists in the staunchly antinuclear Green parties. In those elections, Green parties made substantial strides, drawing 2.2 million votes— 15 percent of the total.[38]

The Movement Grows in Eastern Europe

Thanks to the spread of political freedom in Communist bloc nations, the movement in the East grew substantially, particularly in the Soviet Union, where large number of small peace groups formed and reformed. Although the Chernobyl disaster and Soviet nuclear testing kept nuclear weapons on the movement's agenda, a broad array of measures was championed by many of the new groups. They included the Society for Demilitarization (focused on reducing the military budget and on abolishing "military-patriotic education" in the schools), Shield (a peace movement within the Soviet military, demanding internal reform), and the Committee of Soldiers' Mothers (which protested against torture and violent deaths within the armed forces).[39] Some of these groups participated in Democratic Russia, a broad coalition of reform groups that included antimilitarism as a priority. An even larger number rallied to Tairov's new movement, the Coalition for Civic Peace. Formed in 1990, Civic Peace was dedicated to "creating a nonviolent, humane community." The world of the future, it argued, should not be based upon force, but on trust, cooperation, civil society, and the cultivation of a planetary, ecological, and peacemaking consciousness.[40] Another group to emerge was the Russian Peace Society. Founded in 1909, it was reestablished in April 1991 by antimilitarist, pacifist, and Tolstoyan organizations, as well as by human rights, cultural, and scientific groups. Among its objectives were alternative military service, a nuclear weapons test ban, a reduction in the military budget, and a non-nuclear world. Usually, antimilitarists supported the Gorbachev-Shevardnadze foreign and military policy, just as party conservatives and neo-fascists fulminated against it.[41]

Elsewhere in Eastern Europe, the movement's gains were less pronounced. During 1989, at least, this reflected the limits still placed upon independent activism by conservative Communist regimes. In May of that year, although members of Czechoslovakia's Independent Peace Association continued their peace and antinuclear activities, numerous activists remained in prison. In Hungary, where the regime was more relaxed about independent activism, peace and disarmament campaigners fared somewhat better.[42] In Poland, where Freedom and Peace continued to promote demilitarization, it worked closely with the Solidarity Movement, and its representatives served on Lech Walesa's Citizens' Committee, a quasi-parliament for the opposition. Freedom and Peace took credit for the fact that, in talks with the regime, Solidarity proposed cutting Poland's military budget by 20 percent. Furthermore, as the struggle heightened against the Communist-led Old Order in East Germany, Czechoslovakia, Hungary, and Poland, independent peace and human rights activists increasingly threw themselves into it, often emerging among its most prominent leaders.[43]

Indeed, just as the guardians of the Old Order had feared, independent peace and human rights activists played key roles in the East European revolutions that toppled their regimes. In East Germany, Bärbel Bohley and Ulrike Poppe, two leading antinuclear campaigners in East Berlin, founded New Forum and Democracy Now, organizations primarily responsible for the peaceful overthrow of the Communist government in the fall of 1989. In Czechoslovakia, Charter 77 provided a crucial ingredient in the "velvet revolution" that overcame the Communist regime.[44] The prominence of peace and human rights activists in the upheavals of 1989 reflected not only their unusual courage but their relatively unique experience in fostering nonviolent opposition movements and nonviolent techniques of resisting militarized, repressive governments: peaceful protest rallies, human chains, mass leafleting, and civil disobedience. Many of these techniques were imparted to them by their West European allies, whose massive, tumultuous agitation in the preceding years also helped to shatter Eastern Europe's climate of fear and cynicism by demonstrating the possibilities for citizen activism. Looking back on the dramatic events of the era, Tairov observed that the "mass demonstrations in the early 1980s were a prelude to the people's revolutions in Eastern Europe in 1989: people learned from each other. And it was the turn of the Eastern Europeans to grasp opportunities created by Gorbachev's new thinking and act non-violently against totalitarian regimes."[45]

Against this backdrop, it was hardly surprising that movement activists emerged as important leaders in the new, democratic governments. In East Germany, after the free elections of 1990, Pastor Rainer Eppelmann, the pacifist priest and antinuclear spokesperson from East Berlin, became the minister for defense and disarmament. His three state secretaries were also veterans of the East German peace movement. In Czechoslovakia, the democratic revolution elevated two top Charter 77 activists—Václav Havel and Jiri Dienstbier—to the posts of president and foreign minister. Another Charter 77 peace and human rights activist, Jaroslav Sabata, became chair of the Czech parliament's foreign affairs committee. Andrei Sakharov was elected to the new Soviet parliament, as was Roy Medvedev, the only Soviet signer of the original END Appeal. In Poland, Jacek Kuron, who had worked closely with END, became the minister of labor. "Civil society is now in power," Dienstbier remarked happily.[46] Drawn into governments, movement leaders were sometimes too preoccupied with other civic responsibilities to continue their earlier agitation. But on occasion they implemented their anti-military beliefs. Eppelmann negotiated the withdrawal of all Soviet military forces from East-Central Europe. In a major speech to the Council of Europe, Havel presented what Sabata termed "basically the original perspective of Charter 77 as it developed through contact with peace groups." Sakharov became a leading critic of Soviet military intervention in Afghanistan—which he denounced as "a war of annihilation, a terrible sin"—and a prominent spokesperson for nuclear disarmament.[47]

Working Together: East and West

Both during and after these dramatic events, nuclear disarmament campaigners from East and West worked closely together. Following up on their successful cooperation in developing on-site monitoring of nuclear testing, antinuclear scientists turned in 1989 to verifying the presence of nuclear weapons on board ships. Senator Helms, ever eager to undermine prospects for arms control, had claimed that this was impossible. In response, von Hippel and Stone of the FAS and Velikhov of the Committee of Soviet Scientists developed a project for studying long distance verification. As a result, in July of that year, Tom Cochran of the Natural Resources Defense Council flew with a scientific team to the Black Sea, near Yalta, where—thanks to Velikhov's efforts—Gorbachev had agreed to anchor the Soviet cruiser *Vega* with a nuclear warhead on board, for their use. Not only did the detection experiments prove successful, but on the return trip Velikhov brought the antinuclear scientists and an accompanying U.S. congressional delegation to visit some of the Soviet Union's top secret plutonium production facilities, then in the process of being shut down by the government. At the suggestion of the U.S. group, he also brought them to what U.S. officials had claimed was a "killer laser" site at Sary Shagan—clear evidence, they insisted, of a Soviet SDI program. It proved to be nothing of the sort. "It looks like a tool that's been left out to dry for 25 years," remarked von Hippel. Drawing upon the Black Sea experiments, Cochran suggested to Soviet officials that both nations take all nuclear warheads off their ships. He later made the same case to U.S. National Security Advisor Colin Powell, in person and by letter.[48]

Much East-West cooperation was also channeled through END. During the stormy year of 1989, END continued to denounce government repression of East European peace and human rights activists, garnering support from movement stalwarts in Western and Communist countries alike.[49] By the time of its July 1990 convention, END had reached a watershed. In the new, post-revolutionary circumstances, independent activists traveled to the END meeting and participated in it without difficulty. Furthermore, some Communist-led peace groups, chastened by the collapse of Communist governments and parties, began to gravitate toward the organization and apply for membership. Thus, formerly illegal movements like the Arche (an environmental movement in East Germany), independent movements like Tairov's Civic Peace, and even some erstwhile official groups in the East now turned to END as an appropriate forum for discussion of European peace and disarmament issues. With the once-powerful Western movement in decline and the Eastern movement growing, this gave END a more balanced East-West representation than in the past.[50]

The rising importance of East European movements within END was reflected by its August 1991 convention. In 1990, Tairov proposed that his Civic Peace Coalition host the gathering in Moscow, pointing out that this would encourage "the process of perestroika," the "emergence of new, independent movements in the USSR, and their contacts with the rest of the world." As plans for a Moscow convention moved forward, the Soviet Peace Committee was thrown into confusion. At first it refused to support the idea, with its leaders arguing that the beneficiaries of such an event remained unclear, that there would be no propaganda gains, and that it should not be led by the Civic Peace Coalition. Meanwhile, independent groups eagerly joined the preparatory committee, including the Association of Student Unions, Shield, the Committee of Soldiers' Mothers, the Moscow Trust Group, and April (an organization of independent writers).[51] Belatedly, the Soviet Peace Committee endorsed the convention, which drew some 600 people from numerous nations in Eastern and Western Europe. Only two days after they departed, Communist Party conservatives launched their coup to oust Gorbachev and restore party reactionaries to power. Soviet peace activists played an important role in the successful popular resistance to the coup, much to the delight of END's leaders. Addressing members of the Soviet preparatory committee, END's coordinating committee congratulated them "on the successful resistance of the Soviet people against an arbitrary, undemocratic and totalitarian coup d'état. At the convention, we assured each other of our common commitment to human rights, democracy and self-determination. Less than two days later, you showed us that that commitment was one for which you were prepared to risk your lives. . . . More than ever, we look forward to working closely with you . . . in all of Europe and beyond."[52]

The most significant East-West antinuclear project was probably the struggle to end nuclear testing. The campaign for a U.S-Soviet ban on nuclear tests, which had been gathering momentum for some years in the

United States, began to take off near the end of the decade. By early 1989, the U.S. Comprehensive Test Ban Coalition, headed by Carolyn Cottom, had drawn together dozens of peace groups, including IPPNW, SANE/ Freeze, and Greenpeace.[53] Moreover, American Peace Test continued its nonviolent protest activities at the Nevada test site, producing thousands of arrests every year.[54] Meanwhile, the campaign of Parliamentarians for Global Action to convene a conference to convert the partial test ban treaty into a CTBT moved forward. To the dismay of the U.S. and British governments, Tovish and Mexican diplomat Miguel Marin Bosch succeeded in lining up the requisite support from governments around the world and, as a result, the conference was slated to begin in January 1991. Prodded by the antinuclear movement, 23 U.S. Senators and 142 Representatives wrote to President Bush, warning against any decision to veto a CTBT amendment and urging him to propose to the Soviet Union a "mutual verified phase-out of nuclear weapons tests leading to conclusion of a comprehensive test ban treaty." By late 1990, the U.S. Coalition had made considerable progress. Although it had almost no money or media coverage, it had mobilized 73 endorsing groups, ranging from Grandmothers for Peace to the national board of the YWCA. In addition, 223 jurisdictions—189 cities, 26 counties, and 8 states—had passed non-binding resolutions in support of a CTBT. That year, the Coalition's lobbying efforts helped push a joint resolution through Congress that called on the Bush administration to negotiate in good faith at the amendment conference.[55]

Parallel activism to halt nuclear testing made a greater splash in the Soviet Union. In February 1989, Olzhas Suleimenov, a renowned Kazakh poet, was about to appear on local television as part of his campaign for a seat in the Congress of People's Deputies when word reached him of radioactive leakage from Soviet nuclear tests at nearby Semipalatinsk. Scrapping his prepared speech, he launched into a description of this latest disaster that nuclear testing had wrought in Kazakhstan, and called on concerned citizens to meet two days later at the writers' union hall in the Kazakh capital of Alma Ata. Five thousand people flocked to the meeting, many standing outside in the winter chill, listening to its proceedings over a makeshift sound system. Inside the hall, participants voted to call for the closing of the Semipalatinsk test site, an end to nuclear weapons production, and a universal ban on nuclear testing. Inspired by reports of U.S. demonstrations at the Nevada test site and seeking to ally themselves with U.S. activists, they called their new group Nevada, although it later came to be known as the Nevada-Semipalatinsk movement. As it developed, it used a logo of a native Kazakh sharing a peace pipe with a Native American. The movement was soon holding demonstrations throughout Kazakhstan. On August 6, 1989, to commemorate the Hiroshima bombing, 50,000 people attended one of its antinuclear rallies—the largest independent event of this type ever held in the Soviet Union. Following the ancient Kazakh custom of flinging stones into the face of evil, thousands of Kazakh citizens hurled rocks toward the test site. In October, the coal miners of Kazakhstan voted to shut down the mines if the government conducted any further nuclear explosions in the region.[56]

Within a short time, this grassroots antinuclear campaign took on national and international dimensions. The Nevada-Semipalatinsk movement staged demonstrations throughout the Soviet Union, and eventually over a million people signed its antinuclear petition. On August 1, 1989, the Supreme Soviet adopted a resolution, written by Suleimenov, calling for a moratorium on all nuclear tests by the United States and by the Soviet Union. By December, when Suleimenov visited the United States to confer with U.S. antinuclear leaders, the Soviet government admitted that, to appease the growing movement, it had cancelled eleven out of eighteen underground nuclear tests.[57] The movement, however, was not placated, and continued to grow. In April 1990, activists in the Soviet far north began a campaign to shut down the Soviet Union's other nuclear test site, located on a pair of islands called Novaya Zemlya. The Nevada-Semipalatinsk movement forged an alliance with the developing Novaya Zemlya-Nevada Committee, with Suleimenov declaring that a "transfer" of nuclear tests to the northern site was unacceptable; only their abolition would do.[58] Meanwhile, Greenpeace joined the fray. That September, as a Greenpeace protest vessel sailed from one Soviet port to another, it was welcomed by local Soviet citizens. But as it entered the Novaya Zemlya testing zone, the ship was fired upon, boarded, and put under tow by far less appreciative Soviet border guards—though not before a group of Greenpeace crew members slipped ashore at the test site and measured its radioactive contamination.[59]

Thanks to these kinds of activities, the alliance among nuclear testing opponents, East and West, grew ever warmer. In late March and April 1990, American Peace Test and the Nevada-Semipalatinsk movement exchanged activists for protests at their respective test sites. Although this venture received virtually no coverage in the American press,[60] IPPNW and the Nevada-Semipalatinsk movement teamed up for an even more dramatic event in May—an International Citizens Congress that convened in Alma Ata. The conference brought together some 300 delegates from dozens of antinuclear, peace, and environmental groups from 25 countries. It also gathered a substantial number of "downwinders" and atomic bomb survivors from the

Soviet Union, the United States, Japan, and the South Pacific, who shared stories on the cancer, genetic deformities, and leukemia that nuclear weapons had brought to their communities. Large crowds of local residents greeted the conference participants, including one of 20,000 cheering people carrying signs, flags, and placards. Delegates agreed that a cohesive international coalition would be necessary to end nuclear testing, which they viewed as the centerpiece of nuclear arms control and disarmament. Consequently, they formed the Nevada-Semipalatinsk-Moruroa International Movement to Halt Nuclear Weapons Testing. Before the conference convened, Lown and Suleimenov met with Soviet Foreign Minister Shevardnadze to urge him to reinstitute the Soviet testing moratorium.[61]

Thereafter, antinuclear movements in Belgium, Britain, France, New Zealand, the Philippines, Polynesia, the Netherlands, Switzerland, the United States, the Soviet Union, and other nations increasingly focused their efforts upon securing an end to nuclear testing, and drew support for this campaign from other citizens' groups as well. In France, the anti-testing movement attracted traditional antinuclear campaigners, a new group called Stop Tests, pacifists, human rights groups, youth groups, unions, women's groups, churches, and Third World support groups. The French movement maintained close contacts with the antinuclear and pro-independence movement in Polynesia, as well as with the victims of nuclear tests in Nevada, Kazakhstan, the Marshall Islands, and Australia. It also publicized the testimony of Tuareg nomads in the South Sahara on the effects of past French nuclear testing in their homelands. Solange Fernex, a member of Stop Tests and of the European parliament, declared that "to continue testing is immoral, a gross violation of human rights, and a danger to the environment. ... We can and we will stop testing in France and the whole world." At the International Peace Bureau's annual conference of 1990, securing a comprehensive test ban treaty provided the main theme.[62]

There were other signs, as well, that the movement had developed a genuinely international presence. Thanks to persistent antinuclear agitation, numerous localities around the world had declared themselves nuclear-free zones—more than 4,000 by the summer of 1990.[63] The IPB grew from a paper organization to a respected network of nonaligned peace and disarmament groups. Despite the decline of many national peace groups, by 1992 the IPB encompassed 128 affiliates in 40 countries on all continents. Its activities included not only close work with the antinuclear testing campaign of the French Stop Tests network, IPPNW, Greenpeace, and other groups, but a World Court Project, designed to obtain an advisory opinion from the International Court of Justice that would outlaw nuclear weapons. Begun by former IPB president Sean MacBride, the project was officially launched in May 1992 at the Palace of Nations, in Geneva, with the submission of an antinuclear petition signed by 11,000 lawyers. The kickoff of the World Court Project was co-sponsored by IPB, IPPNW, and the International Association of Lawyers Against Nuclear Arms, and brought together lawyers, scholars, peace activists, and diplomats from 32 countries for meetings and planning sessions on the campaign. Simultaneous launches were held in New Zealand, Finland, India, and Britain.[64] Although weaker than in the immediate past, the antinuclear movement could still draw upon some powerful resources and conduct imaginative campaigns.

Continued Popular Pressure

The strength of the antinuclear movement was buttressed by a transformation in Western attitudes toward the Soviet Union and its leaders. Although Soviet leaders and policies had been extremely unpopular in recent decades, the situation changed dramatically during these years. Between December 1988 and August 1991, the percentage of the American public approving of Gorbachev ranged from 68 percent to 80 percent—support that any American President or politician might have envied. Indeed, in September 1990, when President Bush's approval rating stood at a remarkable 67 percent, Gorbachev's stood at 70 percent.[65] Polls in December 1989 and December 1990 found that the Soviet leader was the second most popular man among Americans.[66] When Gorbachev visited Stanford University in 1990, students cheered and screamed "Gorby, Gorby!" as if the Soviet President were a rock star. Elsewhere in the West, the attitude toward the Soviet leader was much the same, and the West German President recalled "the warm, spontaneous, enthusiastic welcome the West German people gave him wherever he went." Similarly, although 89 percent of Americans viewed the Soviet Union as an unfriendly or "enemy" nation in May 1984, polls from February 1989 to February 1991 showed that from 51 percent to 62 percent of the American public now had a favorable view of the Soviet Union.[67]

Naturally, as leading hawks had feared, the collapse of Cold War enmities undermined support for military priorities and enhanced sympathy for nuclear arms controls and disarmament. In late 1988, questioned as to whether NATO should modernize its remaining nuclear weapons in Europe or start negotiations for further reductions, 71 percent of Britons favored negotiations. Asked if new nuclear weapons should be brought into Britain and Europe, 78 percent opposed the idea. In January 1989, when Britons were asked what was the best defense for their nation—nuclear or conventional weapons—53 percent still chose nuclear weapons. But, that same month, British respondents, by 48 to 42 percent, told pollsters that they favored the withdrawal of all nuclear weapons from Europe. In April 1990, a Gallup poll in Britain found 58 percent of Britons against Trident, 55 percent against new air and sea-launched cruise missiles, and 75 percent in favor of transferring funds from military spending into social and environmental programs. Two years later, when the French government surprised many observers by unilaterally halting its nuclear testing, polls found that this action had the support of 60 percent of the French public.[68]

Other peoples, too, seemed quite dovish. Back in the late 1940s, between 55 and 69 percent of Americans thought the development of the atomic bomb was a "good thing." But a July 1990 poll found that only 37 percent still viewed its development in a positive light, while 56 percent called it a "bad thing." In July 1991, 84 percent of Americans who knew of the START I treaty, then being negotiated, thought Congress should ratify it. That October, 50 percent of Americans thought that the United States was spending too much money on the military—the highest level since the early 1970s—and 71 percent of Americans polled favored the unilateral nuclear arms reductions announced by President Bush the previous week.[69] In the Soviet Union, top military officers running for public office in the 1989 elections were defeated, and a 1989 poll by a leading sociologist found that 71 percent of the 200,000 respondents named severely curtailing military spending as the first thing the country should do to improve the quality of Soviet life. Even in India, where nationalists had managed to stir up considerable public support for acquiring the Bomb, an October–November 1991 poll found that 50 percent of Indian respondents wanted their country to sign the nuclear nonproliferation treaty.[70]

Nor did the public show much enthusiasm for using nuclear weapons. In July 1990, when a Gallup poll asked Americans whether nuclear weapons should be used by the United States if it became involved in another world war, only 17 percent responded affirmatively, another 18 percent responded affirmatively with qualifications, and 58 percent said "No." During the Gulf War, when Saddam Hussein was widely hated and there seemed no prospect of nuclear retaliation, polls conducted in seven of Europe's largest cities in February 1991 found that fewer than a third of respondents supported use of nuclear weapons against Iraq, even in response to an Iraqi chemical weapons attack. Polls revealed that 56 percent of Britons opposed a resort to nuclear weapons against Iraq in these circumstances. To be sure, a January 1991 poll found that Americans were split evenly—45 to 45 percent—over the use of tactical nuclear weapons against Iraq "if it might save the lives of

U.S. troops." But the following month, when the question was put in a less biased way—simply asking about "U.S. use of tactical nuclear weapons in the Persian Gulf war"—only 28 percent favored it and 66 percent opposed it. At no point in the conflict did a majority of Americans support use of nuclear weapons in response to an Iraqi conventional or chemical weapons attack.[71]

Confronting the Past and the Future

Thus, from 1989 to 1993, even as the antinuclear movement receded from its peak membership and mobilization of the recent past, it produced an impressive array of activism around the globe. From the revolutions that swept Eastern Europe to the far-flung outpourings of opposition to nuclear testing, it helped to stir up broadly based citizens' protest campaigns. Moreover, it succeeded in maintaining the popularity of nuclear arms controls and disarmament with the general public. These factors, joined with its earlier successes in forcing reluctant governments to alter their nuclear policies, left the leaders of the movement not only proud of its past, but hopeful that it would play an important role in the future. Addressing the IPB's 1992 conference, a year before his death, E. P. Thompson continued to argue that "committed peace workers can know no automatic loyalty to their own nation and, indeed, must teach others that such loyalty is against the interests of human survival. Once again, people, across national boundaries, must learn to be loyal to each other, and must build citizens' agencies to enable them to express this loyalty." It was quite possible, he contended, that nuclear weapons had not been used since 1945 because such action "would have outraged the world conscience." Therefore, "it must be our aim in the twenty-first century to enlarge this conscience, and to ensure that war of any kind is restrained in the same way."[72]

Further Victories, 1989-93

The world is crying out for arms control.

George Bush, 1990

From 1989 to 1993, very substantial nuclear disarmament occurred. According to U.S. government officials, this development resulted from a flexing
of their military muscles, after which the Soviet Union simply surrendered
and accepted a disarmed world. Summing up his foreign and defense policy
during the 1992 presidential debates, George Bush declared: "We didn't listen to the nuclear freeze crowd; we said 'peace through strength,' and it
worked." Years later, his secretary of state, James Baker, argued that "what
made sense was to be strong so that we could win the Cold War and achieve
the peace, and that's what we did."[1] Although it's true enough that Bush,
Baker, and most other members of the new administration entered office
committed to a hard-line approach, they did not follow it very long. Like
their predecessors in Washington, they found themselves pushed pell-mell
by a combination of movement pressures and Gorbachev initiatives in an
antinuclear direction. Following much the same trajectory as Reagan, Bush
entered into a partnership with Gorbachev, and the two leaders implemented
the farthest-reaching nuclear arms reductions in world history. They
dropped plans for nuclear modernization, signed strategic arms reduction
treaties, halted nuclear testing, closed nuclear facilities, halted plans for new
weapons systems, and even scrapped substantial portions of their nuclear arsenals unilaterally. Swept along in the antinuclear tide, other nations, too,
accepted significant nuclear constraints. Admittedly, without a Soviet leader
willing to abandon nuclear weapons and the Cold War, it seems unlikely
that much of this would have happened. But it also seems unlikely that Gorbachev, Bush, or most other world leaders would have followed this scenario without the impetus of the nuclear disarmament movement.

The Pause

Despite the antinuclear momentum in U.S. public policy that had built up in 1987 and 1988, the incoming administration of George Bush was reluctant to continue it. During these years, Bush and the men whom he would choose as his top national security officials—Brent Scowcroft (national security advisor), Dick Cheney (secretary of defense), and James Baker (secretary of state)—were deeply skeptical of Reagan's increasingly dovish policies. Privately, Bush was appalled by Reagan's antinuclear talk at Reykjavik and by his "sentimentality" about Gorbachev. In January 1988, he warned that Gorbachev was not a "freedom-loving friend of democracy," but an "orthodox, committed Marxist." When Reagan traveled to Moscow later that year and dismissed the Cold War as part of "another era," Bush warned Americans that "the Cold War isn't over."[2] Scowcroft, a career military officer, expressed his outspoken dismay at Reagan's antinuclear programs, including the INF treaty. "Nuclear weapons were, for me, an indispensable element in the US strategy of keeping the Soviets at bay," he recalled, and the Reagan administration had "rushed to judgment about the direction [*sic*] the Soviet Union was heading." In Scowcroft's opinion, Gorbachev was "potentially more dangerous than his predecessors," for "he was attempting to kill us with kindness, rather than bluster." Cheney, too, was leery of nuclear arms control, and during the years when he served as a Wyoming Congressman and Republican House whip, the Council for a Livable World never gave him a rating higher than zero.[3] As for Baker, he considered his predecessor, George Shultz, much too eager for arms control agreements during his final year as secretary of state. Meeting thereafter with the State Department's Roz Ridgway, Baker asked her: "Don't you think you all went too far?" She recalled that Bush's top officials "were annoyed by the Reagan administration," and "didn't like anything they were handed in the U.S.-Soviet relationship at the time they took over. . . . They simply believed that Reagan had been hornswoggled."[4]

These hawkish views slipped out on occasion during the 1988 presidential election campaign. Although Bush was careful to avoid publicly challenging the foreign and defense policies of his fellow Republican, Ronald Reagan, he had no such scruples in connection with his Democratic opponent, Michael Dukakis, and the antinuclear movement. During the 1988 election campaign, Bush sharply and repeatedly assailed Dukakis as soft on national defense and a partisan of the Kremlin. "Remember the freeze movement?" Bush asked. "My opponent supported it. . . . He wanted to restrain us, not the Soviet Union." Truman and Kennedy, Bush jeered, "never believed in this nuclear freeze," which he depicted, falsely, as a unilateral measure. According to Bush, the INF treaty came about "because we didn't listen to the freeze advocates and strengthened the defenses of this country." Although Bush's portrayal of Dukakis as a pushover for the antinuclear movement might be viewed as no more than a cynical campaign ploy, much like his repeated use of a TV ad linking Dukakis to a black rapist, there were other signs, as well, that Bush and his closest advisors genuinely favored a traditional approach toward nuclear weapons and toward the Soviet Union. As the campaign progressed, Bush argued that "we must maintain the pressure on Moscow," insisting that "this is no time to reduce our leverage" by military cutbacks. In his first televised debate with Dukakis, he warned that, despite the revolutionary changes initiated by Gorbachev, "the jury is still out on the Soviet experiment." Although Bush promised to meet at some point with the Soviet leader, he said he would not try "to achieve any grand breakthrough."[5]

The President was true to his word, and upon taking office in January 1989, he halted the government's nuclear arms control and disarmament program while his administration reconsidered its options. Appearing on television two days after Bush's inauguration, Scowcroft warned that Gorbachev seemed "interested in making trouble within the Western alliance," principally through "a peace offensive." This would throw the West off its guard, giving the Soviet Union time to build up its military power and, then, engage in world conquest. "The Cold War," insisted Scowcroft, "is not over." In mid-February, Bush initiated a "national security review" of U.S. policy toward the Soviet Union. The review was based on a memo, prepared for Bush by Scowcroft, which argued that, as the Soviet Union remained "an adversary with awesome military power," it would be "thoughtless to abandon policies that have brought us this far." The President liked the memo, adding only: "My own sense is that the Soviet challenge may be even greater than before." As the review proceeded, Scowcroft's deputy, Robert Gates, told a private group that the Bush administration needed a "conscious pause" on Soviet policy while it "looks over the landscape and reconsiders its position." Meanwhile, he advised those preparing the review: "Don't be so dazzled by Mikhail Gorbachev, Superstar, that you forget we're in the business of making policy toward a country, not an individual." After all, Gorbachev would probably prove to be an historical aberration, "an exception that proves the rule." Others in the administration did not consider even Gorbachev a worthy negotiating partner. The world was still "defined by superpower rivalry," Scowcroft recalled. "The Cold War strug-

gle had shaped our assumptions about international and domestic politics
. . . our armed forces and military strategy."[6]

Predictably, the Bush administration's national security review and
other early actions did little to put arms control and disarmament back on
track. Completed by March 14, 1989, the review—as Scowcroft admitted—
proved "disappointing," without the "imaginative initiatives need to set US-
Soviet relations on a productive path." Recognizing its shortcomings, the
NSC produced a "think piece" for "coping with Gorbachev." But this, too,
hardly provided an adequate blueprint for dealing with the profound
changes ushered into world politics by the Soviet leader's "new thinking." It
maintained that the United States "would have to prepare carefully for bilateral arms control" and should "underscore the credibility of NATO's nuclear deterrent through modernization" of the West's nuclear weapons. Visiting Washington that March, Jack Matlock, the U.S. ambassador to the Soviet Union, brought along proposals for regular U.S.-Soviet summit meetings, including one to be held that spring or in the early summer, and was
surprised to find top U.S. officials reluctant to hold them. "Wouldn't the
Soviets use a summit meeting to put pressure on us for concessions in arms
control negotiations?" Bush asked him. Scowcroft, too, was cool toward the
idea, arguing that "if the meeting did not produce a major agreement, the
media would term it a failure." Later that spring, while Bush and Baker
talked of their desire to improve Soviet-American relations, Scowcroft,
Gates, and Cheney "stressed the need for the United States to keep up its
guard and at times suggested in public that Gorbachev might not last much
longer."[7]

Soviet leaders were well aware of what they called "the pause" and, as
Shevardnadze noted, "were worried" by it. Gorbachev recalled that Bush
had been pleasant enough in an early telephone conversation, "and it
seemed that we could expect a constructive dialogue and quick progress."
But, then, "weeks and months passed," and it became clear that the new
administration was "in no hurry to develop Soviet-American relations." The
first meeting between Shevardnadze and Baker "left us with the impression
that the new administration was biding its time, waiting for . . . what were
they waiting for? Some of the signals we were receiving were quite alarming."[8] Palazchenko recalled that the pause "created an opening for the conservatives and 'the agencies' in Moscow," who put their own negative interpretation into telegrams and memos to Gorbachev. In this fashion, noted
Palazchenko, the Bush administration "did not always help those in the Soviet Union who counseled patience and a continued emphasis on relations
with the United States." Or, as Matlock put it: Washington's cool behavior

"fed the hard-line opposition to Gorbachev's attempts to scale back the Soviet military." What bolstered the reformers was the growth of grassroots peace sentiment. Gorbachev recalled that Evgenii Primakov, who headed up a Soviet delegation to the United States, "reported a noticeable swing in American public opinion in favor of the Soviet Union, particularly at the grass-roots level. Ingrained mistrust was gradually giving way to sympathy and interest." Thus, "there were reasons to believe that sooner or later the Bush administration would have to follow suit and adapt to the changing mood of the American public."[9]

In fact, that spring, the Bush administration was beginning to feel the pressure—from the public and from allied leaders—for a resumption of arms control and disarmament efforts. To counter Gorbachev's sweeping calls for disarmament, Bush and Baker began putting references into their speeches and press statements that the U.S. government wanted to see "deeds, not words" from the Soviet Union. But, as White House press secretary Marlin Fitzwater recalled, "the rest of America was rushing headlong into its infatuation with Gorbachev, and the press wasn't even printing our admonitions to demand more than promises." "How do we break through?" he asked his deputies, in frustration. "The public thinks Gorbachev is a white knight." Fitzwater urged the President to "put the ball back in Gorbachev's court." At a White House meeting, a reporter asked the President about the "widespread impression" that he had "no foreign policy." Growing angry, Bush replied that "I've never heard such outrageous hypotheses!" A ripple of laughter went through the room. Clearly irked, the President continued: "I don't worry about that. And we *have* a foreign policy." In April, when George Kennan told the Senate Foreign Relations Committee that Bush had been "unresponsive" to recent "encouraging initiatives" from the Soviet Union, legislators, the audience, and even the committee stenographer responded with a standing ovation. Two days later, questioned by the press about his reaction to Gorbachev's shut-down of Soviet plutonium plants, Bush retorted irritably: "We'll be ready to react when we feel like reacting." Pressures for bold U.S. action mounted, as well, among allied leaders, who worried about adverse public reaction, in their nations and others, to the Bush administration's faltering commitment to arms control and disarmament. "Don't let things linger," Thatcher told Baker. Geoffrey Howe, the British foreign secretary, urged the U.S. government to "get back in the game."[10]

The Return to Arms Control and Disarmament:
Blocking New Short-Range Nuclear Forces

When it came to NATO's short-range nuclear forces (SNF), however, the British government joined the American in fiercely resisting nuclear arms controls. The issue went back to the 1987 INF agreement when, to compensate for the withdrawal of intermediate range nuclear forces from West European nations, the Reagan administration agreed to retain NATO's SNF missiles in West Germany and to "modernize" them at a later date. In fact, modernization was a euphemism, for it entailed replacing the Lance missile (which had a range of 70 miles) with one that could travel about 280 miles and, also, substantially increasing the number of launchers for it. In 1988, however, the West German and Belgian governments began criticizing modernization plans. West German Foreign Minister Hans-Dietrich Genscher opposed "straining disarmament negotiations by an ill-timed modernization of short-range nuclear weapons and by closing the door on long-term policies of disarmament and détente."[11] By contrast, Thatcher insisted upon modernization, viewing negotiations over SNF missiles as an invitation to a denuclearized Europe, a prospect that she dreaded. The U.S. government sided with Thatcher. Meeting with his staff in February 1989, Baker told them that "any concession" on Lance "would be a classic slippery slope" toward a nuclear-free Europe. Thus, it risked the "entire strategy that has served NATO well for forty years." That April, speaking at the National Defense University, Cheney declared that "we must not fall into this dangerous trap" of SNF negotiations. "One of the Kremlin's primary goals remains the denuclearization of Europe," and "the Alliance must maintain the will to resist the call for a third zero."[12]

It was clear to all that the SNF controversy had a strong political dimension. Given the unpopularity of the SNF missiles in West Germany, a consensus had formed among all the political parties that no plans should be made for modernization and that negotiations should proceed for the removal of existing SNF missiles from East and West. Thus, although initially at odds with Genscher, the Christian Democrats' Helmut Kohl came around to his position, telling Thatcher bluntly that modernization and a refusal to negotiate on the SNF missiles were "simply not sustainable politically in Germany." Scowcroft recalled bitterly: "The strong and well-organized anti-nuclear movement in the Federal Republic mobilized in vocal opposition to modernization, calling instead for elimination of the remaining weapons." Thus, "facing such a hot political issue and cooling support for the government, Kohl and his coalition partner, Foreign Minister Hans-Dietrich Genscher of the Free Democratic Party, hoped to have a [modernization] decision further delayed, until after the German general elections in 1990." By May of 1989, with nightmares of renewed anti-Euro-missile demonstrations pressing upon them, almost all the governments of NATO's European nations felt similarly. This virtually isolated the governments of Britain and the United States, which still insisted upon opposing SNF weapons reductions and implementing modernization.[13]

The politics of arms control grew considerably hotter after May 11 when, in a meeting with Baker, Gorbachev told the U.S. secretary of state that he had decided to withdraw 500 tactical nuclear weapons from Eastern Europe. And if the United States were willing to take farther-reaching steps, said the Soviet leader, he was willing to withdraw *all* tactical nuclear weapons from Eastern Europe by 1991. Baker was furious, viewing this as an attempt to "score public relations points with European publics." He recalled that, "once again, Gorbachev had taken the political initiative, and we were losing the battle for public opinion. We had to do something." Bush agreed. "We must take the offensive," he said. "We cannot just be seen as reacting to yet another Gorbachev move. We need to do it to keep public opinion behind the alliance." Privately, Bush complained to Scowcroft that he was "sick and tired of getting beat up day after day for having no vision and letting Gorbachev run the show." But what could be done? Thatcher continued to insist that "we have to have SNF modernization," while Kohl said that his government "would collapse if we pushed modernization." When Baker traveled to the Nordic countries, he found massive resistance to the modernization proposal. The Norwegian prime minister and the Danish foreign minister told him that "this debate over a weapons system . . . had everything to do with politics—and their politics were distinctly not Britain's." Also, "the situation in Greece and Turkey was substantially the same—I was really getting an earful." Baker returned to Washington convinced that "NATO could not afford another crisis over deploying nuclear weapons. The Alliance may have been able to endure such a crisis in 1983 . . . but it would not be able to survive with the wily Mikhail Gorbachev in power." Indeed, "the danger was growing that NATO would fragment in the face of Gorbachev's charm offensive."[14]

As a result of this one-two punch from Gorbachev and public opinion, NATO retreated substantially on the issue of SNF missiles. At the May 29–30, 1989, NATO summit conference, a compromise was reached between the hard-liners and the arms controllers. It entailed tabling the proposal for SNF modernization, with the understanding that "partial reductions" in existing

SNF forces would be negotiated with the Soviet Union. Thatcher complained that the new approach "was to subordinate clear statements of intention about the alliance's defense to the political sensibilities of the Germans." She did not "think that this boded well." Although the hard-liners also gained something, it came in the form of yet another arms control arrangement. Specifically, negotiations on SNF reductions would not begin until after reductions in conventional forces had been negotiated.[15] Moreover, within a short time, it became clear that SNF modernization would *never* take place. In November 1989, with elections looming, Genscher informed Bush that his government simply would not accept the new missiles. Furthermore, the U.S. Congress refused to appropriate money for them. Accordingly, in March 1990, Bush told Thatcher that he was ready to announce their cancellation. Two months later, NATO formally cancelled SNF modernization, a move quickly praised by the Soviet government.[16]

On to Malta

NATO's retreat on SNF modernization marked the beginning of the end for the Bush administration's hard-line stance toward the Soviet Union. Pressed to respond to Gorbachev's initiatives, the Bush administration began to warm toward a summit conference. In June 1989, the President had begun considering "what we should do about meeting with Gorbachev." He wanted to hold the summit, he noted in his diary, "but I don't want to get it bogged down on arms control." Fitzwater recalled that "the American people were clamoring for an East-West summit and starting to ask why George Bush was so timid. R.W. 'Johnny' Apple, the *New York Times* political writer, wrote a front-page article stating this proposition and it burned every high-level foreign policy official in government." The President was particularly upset, "and he openly referred to this article in meetings, making everyone aware of the public pressures that were building." Sensitive to "the cries of public opinion," Bush monitored it "carefully," and listened to Fitzwater's press briefings on the intercom. "Every day he heard someone ask, 'When is Bush going to meet with Gorbachev?'" Eventually, Bush called in Fitzwater and told him that, during the summer, he had agreed to hold a summit with Gorbachev at the end of the year. "That's great!" Fitzwater blurted out, for he was "elated that we were going to show the critics wrong." The pressure, however, continued, and in September Senate Democratic leader George Mitchell scored the administration for being "almost nostalgic about the cold war" and urged it to adopt "a more energetic and engaged policy" toward the Soviet bloc. Baker, who had a good sense of public relations, felt these criticisms keenly, and argued for compromises in U.S. positions that would push arms control negotiations forward.[17]

The Soviet government, especially, was ready for action. When it came to disarmament, Dobrynin recalled, Gorbachev—"carried away by the cheering international audience"—was determined "to reach his objectives as soon as possible."[18] And, as things turned out, antinuclear activists showed him the way forward. Since 1987, Soviet and American antinuclear scientists had been arguing that SDI should be delinked from other arms control agreements. In the case of strategic arms reductions, however, the Soviet military and other Old Guard forces had resisted separating the issues, insisting that SDI and START should remain part of the same package. In 1989, however, Shevardnadze organized secret meetings at which leading Soviet scientists—including Velikhov and Sagdeev—called for "unlinking" the two issues. This carried the day with Shevardnadze and Gorbachev, to the intense dismay of the military and other "Old Thinkers." Consequently, when the Soviet foreign minister conferred with Baker in Jackson Hole, Wyoming, in late September, he declared that the Soviet government was prepared to separate the sticky issue of SDI from a START agreement. Baker was delighted, and considered this "a dramatic break-through"—as it was.[19]

This Soviet initiative and others, combined with the popular pressure for the Bush administration to scrap its hard line, put Washington officials on the spot as they prepared for the forthcoming summit conference, at Malta. As late as October 1989, Bush insisted that the summit would provide no more than a get-acquainted meeting. But that fall, as the dramatic events in Eastern Europe unfolded, including the opening of the Berlin Wall, it became impossible to hold to this minimalist position. Robert Blackwill, the NSC official responsible for Europe and the Soviet Union, told his colleagues: "The question now is how to satisfy the wild beast of public opinion." Baker, particularly, was determined not to be "outpropositioned" again by Gorbachev, and therefore made the case for developing nuclear arms control and disarmament proposals that would put the U.S. government on the side of the angels, or at least on the side of public opinion. Scowcroft recalled that, in preparing for the summit, the U.S. secretary of state "came up with the idea of taking the initiative ourselves and trying to put Gorbachev on the defensive." Bush "liked the idea, feeling that, among other things, it would still those critics who continued to accuse us of drift and a lack of direction."[20] Thus, as the summit conference opened at Malta on December 2, 1989, the two governments—competing for public approval—were ready to move forward toward nuclear arms control and disarmament agreements.

At the Malta conference, both Gorbachev and Bush demonstrated that, despite the downturn in Soviet-American relations during the preceding year, they intended to work together toward a more peaceful, disarmed world. Gorbachev remarked that "we need to get rid of the view of one another as enemies," and told the President that the Soviet Union would "not start a war under any circumstances." Instead, we "are open to cooperation with America," and are "devoted to continuation of the process of disarmament in all directions." Somewhat bitterly, Bush noted that "some people in the US accuse me of excessive caution," but added that he was committed to "reducing strategic offensive weapons" and to other disarmament measures. Even privately, he told his staff: "I want substantive and positive proposals that will further the relationship. We are going to have a new relationship." Although Gorbachev avoided the kind of grandstanding for the public that so irritated American officials, within the meeting he did emphasize the public pressure that had brought the two governments together. "Cold War methods, methods of confrontation, have suffered defeat in strategic terms," he told Bush. "We have recognized this. And ordinary people have possibly understood this even better." After all, "people simply meddle in policymaking," a fact that was "completely understandable since we are essentially talking about the issue of survival. And this kind of public sentiment is strongly affecting us, the politicians."[21]

The START I Treaty

Despite the progress made at Malta toward better Soviet-American relations, completing negotiations on a strategic arms reduction treaty proved more difficult than expected. At Malta, recalled Gorbachev, "disarmament was obviously one of the issues of the day," and he assumed that the two nations would have a START treaty ready for the summit meeting that he and Bush planned for the summer of 1990. Indeed, at Malta, Bush told Gorbachev that they should "really get going on this," while Gorbachev told Bush that, when it came to verification, "you can have as many inspectors as you want."[22] Even so, in the aftermath of the meeting, hawkish officials within both governments dug in their heels. In the United States, Scowcroft and Cheney insisted upon taking an uncompromising line on the U.S. START position, leading to frustration within the State Department, which wanted to accelerate progress toward an agreement. In the Soviet Union, the military grew increasingly disdainful of Gorbachev's "new thinking." Marshal Akhromeyev complained that he was "getting sick and tired of the Americans' always having their way," and said that he and his fellow military officers were "very disillusioned" with Gorbachev's policies.[23] By 1991, however, Gorbachev and Bush wanted and expected a START agreement, including the accompanying signing ceremony at a summit meeting that summer. As a result, both sides made concessions and, by mid-July, they had their treaty.[24]

Although long-delayed, START I was an important agreement—the first in history to reduce the numbers of strategic nuclear weapons. Indeed, it required both the United States and the Soviet Union to cut their strategic nuclear forces to 6,000 warheads, a reduction of nearly half of the deployed strategic weapons on each side. It also laid out an ambitious program for the dismantling of the missile launchers under extensive verification.[25] For hardliners in both nations, dedicated to maintaining or expanding their nuclear arsenals, the treaty represented a disaster. In the Soviet Union, some of them sought to embarrass the government on the day of the signing, appearing on television and shouting "Treason!" The following month, convinced that Gorbachev was "making all the concessions" in his relations with the United States, they staged a coup in an attempt to remove him from power. The disgruntled Marshal Akhromeyev was one of the coup leaders. But the presidents of the two nations considered the START treaty a triumph—and not only because they had negotiated it. According to Gorbachev, the signing ceremony was "a moment of glory for the new thinking and the foreign policy stemming from it." Even Bush, not inclined toward sentimentality or toward recognizing the key role played in securing the treaty by legions of antinuclear campaigners, hinted at both in his memoirs. "I really did feel emotionally involved at the ceremony," he wrote. "For me this was more than ritual; it offered hope to young people all over the world that idealism was not dead."[26]

Unilateral Nuclear Disarmament

The START I treaty proved only the prelude to one of the most daring and far-reaching antinuclear actions ever taken by the great powers. On September 27, 1991, Bush announced that all U.S. ground-based tactical nuclear weapons would be destroyed, all sea-borne tactical nuclear weapons would be removed from U.S. warships, and the number of air-delivered tactical nuclear weapons in Europe would be cut by 50 percent. In addition, he said, he was going to take all U.S. strategic bombers, as well as some land-based strategic missiles, off alert and was canceling plans for mobile ICBMs and short-range attack missiles. Although Gorbachev, in response, announced sweeping nuclear reductions of his own on October 5, Bush's action was taken unilaterally, and neither nation bothered with verification. Bush's extraordinary move—which eliminated thousands of U.S. tactical nuclear weapons, including the Lance missiles remaining in Western Europe—reflected in large part his desire to move quickly and dramatically enough to avoid the dispersion of tens of thousands of nuclear warheads located in the rapidly disintegrating Soviet Union.[27] And yet there were movement-driven motives as well. According to Scowcroft, the unilateral weapons withdrawals also resulted from the "undesirable" nature of short-range nuclear weapons in Germany, pressures from South Korea to remove U.S. nuclear weapons from that nation, and the fact that "a number of countries were reluctant to allow our warships carrying nuclear weapons into their ports," particularly Japan and New Zealand.[28]

Another factor behind Bush's unilateral action lay in a growing aversion to nuclear weapons among a handful of top U.S. military leaders. One of them was Colin Powell, chair of the JCS. Months before, he had proposed getting rid of small artillery-fired nuclear weapons, but had been blocked by Cheney and military officers. On September 5, 1991, when the President called for "new ideas on nuclear disarmament," Powell was ready to act, and within days proposed most of the policies the President announced in his September 27 speech. To what extent Tom Cochran's proposals to Powell to remove tactical nuclear weapons from U.S. warships affected Powell's own recommendation along these lines remains unclear.[29] But it is clear that a key figure in the military's chain of decision-making was General George Lee Butler, Powell's former deputy and, after January 1991, head of the U.S. Strategic Air Command (SAC). As the military commander of America's nuclear forces, Butler was an important architect of Bush's 1991 proposals, and the President took SAC's airborne command post and all of its bombers off 24-hour alert on Butler's recommendation. Butler considered nuclear modernization plans "totally divorced from reality," and supported the cancellation of new nuclear weapons systems, cut back SAC's nuclear target list by 75 percent, and secured the administration's permission to shut down SAC entirely in June 1992. Although Butler had harbored doubts about the safety and utility of nuclear weapons for some time, what he called his "intellectual unhinging" began in 1988, when, on his first visit to the Soviet Union, he saw that its miserable condition did not match the image of the mighty nation he had held. "It all came crashing home to me that I really had been dealing with a caricature all those years."[30]

A further factor behind the Bush administration's turn to unilateral nuclear disarmament lay in Congress's growing resistance to funding the administration's weapons programs. "Most Americans know," the President insisted in August 1990, a bit anxiously, "that giving peace a chance does not mean taking a chance on peace. And so they endorse giving the military the tools to do its job—the Peacemaker [the MX missile], the Midgetman, the B-2 and the Strategic Defense Initiative." But with the Cold War clearly at an end and with disarmament groups pressing hard for deep cuts in nuclear weapons programs, Congress delivered heavy blows to the administration's priorities. It slashed funding for the B-2 bomber and for the SRAM-T short-range attack missile, left the fate of the Midgetman missile in doubt, and gave every indication that it would terminate the mobile MX missile. Indeed, only the day before Bush's September 1991 announcement, the Senate defeated the MX mobile basing program by a vote of 67 to 33. As a result, by 1992 the mobile MX, Midgetman, and SRAM-T programs had been discarded, and the B-2 program had been cut back from 132 to 20 bombers.[31] Nor did SDI fare very well. In his first budget request for the program, Bush asked for $4.9 billion, and Congress slashed this to $3.8 billion, at the same time prohibiting SDI tests that would violate the ABM treaty. The next year, Congress cut the funding to $2.9 billion—the lowest level in five years. In early 1991, buoyed by the U.S. triumph in the Gulf war, SDI zealots in Congress sought to push through legislation that would scrap the ABM treaty after two years and initiate SDI testing and development. But GOP sponsors in the Senate, recognizing that the bill faced certain defeat, withdrew the measure from consideration. In the House, where SDI diehards pressed it to a vote, they lost by 281 to 145. "We had a lot of trouble with SDI," Baker recalled. "I think the fact that we got anything for SDI . . . was a moral victory," but "we *were* disappointed that we didn't get more."[32]

The movement also played an important role in shutting down the nuclear weapons production facilities in both the Soviet Union and the United States. Responding to the November 1988 plea of SANE/Freeze's William Sloane Coffin to suspend production of fissile material, Soviet officials summoned him to an official meeting in Washington in late March 1989 to tell him that their government was giving the SANE/Freeze proposal "serious consideration," and that "appropriate steps" would be taken. Two weeks later, Gorbachev announced a Soviet decision to cease the production of highly enriched uranium for military purposes—what he called a "major step toward the complete cessation of the production of fissionable materials for use in nuclear weapons."[33] Meanwhile, in the United States, the campaign to close down the nuclear weapons complex neared success. In June 1989, in response to devastating revelations about the Rocky Flats nuclear weapons facility, a long-term target of antinuclear groups, seventy federal agents raided it, seizing incriminating records and, in one plant alone, 59 pounds of radioactive dust. That same month, after a lengthy local campaign and fierce lobbying by disarmament and environmental groups, a House Armed Services Committee panel voted to delete $75 million from funds for a proposed Special Isotope Separation plant in Idaho, and barred any work on the construction site for a year. Immediately following the congressional vote, the Department of Energy announced that it would abandon this $2 billion nuclear weapons project. This, in turn, was followed by decisions not to fund a new plutonium facility in Rocky Flats or the Special Nuclear Materials Laboratory at Los Alamos and to abandon plans to reopen the plutonium-uranium extraction plant in Washington. Facing popular and legal challenges to the environmental and health hazards at nuclear weapons facilities all over the country, the Bush administration shut them down. By mid-1992, U.S. production and development of nuclear weapons had come to a halt.[34]

Exit Mikhail Gorbachev

The dramatic unilateral actions in the fall of 1991 were the last major nuclear disarmament ventures in which Gorbachev participated. Following the coup attempt of August 1991, Boris Yeltsin, president of the Russian Republic—a bitter opponent of Communist Party conservatives, but also a personal rival of Gorbachev's—elbowed him aside politically, arranged for the break-up of the nation that December, and left Gorbachev with little choice but to resign from his position as president of a Soviet Union that no longer existed. Gorbachev's downfall, however, really resulted from the inability of the Soviet Communist Party leadership to take his path of reform. As Chernyaev remarked years later, the Communist party's conservative leaders followed him "until they understood that he was starting to leave the framework of the system." Then they abandoned him and, even today, still view him as a "traitor." Palazchenko noted: "He wanted to reform the party, to help it transform itself into something similar to a social-democratic party of a Western type. . . . But its leaders preferred suicide." Of course, they did not view their coup attempt in this light, but as a promising route toward the restoration of their power. They arranged for the kidnapping of Gorbachev and for the mobilization of the Soviet armed forces to seize control of the Soviet Union's fragile democratic institutions. Ultimately, thousands of irate citizens took to the streets to prevent the conspirators from seizing power. Speaking at a protest rally, Shevardnadze warned the crowd that, to prevent "the end of democracy and the beginning of civil war," as well as "the resumption of the arms race and a new cold war," the Soviet people "must unite and stand in the way of the dictatorship."[35] And they did, although the process resulted not only in the defeat of the coup but, several months later, in the departure of the remarkable reform leadership that had done so much to end the Cold War and the nuclear arms race.

Certainly, their writings and speeches of the era leave little doubt about where the reformers stood. In his memoirs, published in 1991, Shevardnadze had nothing but criticism for the Soviet nuclear buildup of the past. "Did the paranoid obsession with military security," he asked, "benefit the people?" He thought not. Indeed, "while nuclear weapons exist, national security is a fiction, regardless of the level of armaments." Musing upon his work for Gorbachev, Chernyaev wrote in his diary in September 1990 that he was striving "to help common sense triumph over militarism." As for Gorbachev, his views came through clearly in his June 1991 address upon his receipt of the Nobel Peace Prize. "I have been suspected of utopian thinking more than once, and particularly when five years ago I proposed the elimination of nuclear weapons by the year 2000 and joint efforts to create a system of international security. It may well be that by that date it will not have happened," he said. But "merely five years have passed and have we not actually and noticeably moved in that direction? Have we not been able to cross the threshold of mistrust? . . . Has not the political thinking in the world changed substantially? Does not most of the world community already regard weapons of mass destruction as unacceptable for achieving political objectives?"[36] The answer to these questions was clearly yes, and Gorbachev, as the Nobel authorities recognized, deserved a large share of the credit for it.

Further Unilateral Disarmament

The cascade of antinuclear actions, however, did not depend only upon Gorbachev, particularly when it came to halting nuclear testing. The strength of the Nevada-Semipalatinsk movement was a key factor in this regard, and—in response to it—the number of Soviet nuclear tests dropped from seventeen in 1988, to eleven in 1989, to one in 1990. "If you could exert as much pressure on President Bush as the Kazakh people are putting on me, we would have a test ban," Gorbachev told Bernard Lown. In early 1991, Nikolai Vorontsov, the Soviet cabinet minister responsible for the environment, attributed Soviet test reduction to the growing popular campaign, adding that the Semipalatinsk site "is for all practical purposes not working any more because of a huge grass-roots movement."[37] In December

1990 the Kazakhstan parliament banned nuclear tests on its territory and, in the aftermath of the August 1991 coup attempt, Kazakhstan's president closed down the Semipalatinsk test site. The Soviet government conducted its one nuclear test of 1990 at the Novaya Zemlya site, but this, too, produced widespread protest, particularly among officials of the Russian Republic, where the site was located. On October 5, 1991, responding to these developments, Gorbachev announced a year-long moratorium on Soviet nuclear testing. Later that month, Yeltsin, president of the Russian Republic, banned nuclear tests on Russian territory for the next year, and announced that Novaya Zemlya would no longer be used as a test site. Thus, Soviet nuclear testing, as well as testing in the nations that emerged from the disintegration of the Soviet Union, came to an end, unilaterally.[38]

Stopping U.S. nuclear tests proved considerably more difficult. Although the Bush administration did agree to allow the long-delayed 1974 Threshold Test Ban Treaty and the 1976 Peaceful Nuclear Explosions Treaty to move forward toward Senate ratification, neither had much impact upon nuclear testing. Furthermore, in January 1990, the administration indicated its opposition to additional test limits, stating that it did not believe that "further limitations" on nuclear testing were "in the U.S. national security interest."[39] At the U.N.'s January 1991 partial test ban treaty amendment conference—which the U.S. government had fought against every step of the way—the Bush administration could hardly have been more negative. The U.S. representative told the gathering that the United States did "not support negotiation of a comprehensive test ban at the present time," and that "so long as nuclear weapons continue to play a critical role in our national security, we must have a sensible testing program." Although the United States was committed to a step-by-step approach, she claimed, it had "not identified any further limitations on nuclear weapons tests . . . that would be in our national security interest." Thus, despite the support for a test ban treaty by nearly all the delegates, the conference went nowhere. Later that year, the Bush administration announced plans for a full range of future nuclear explosions, at a cost of $533 million. They included "Diamond Fortune" and "Hunter's Trophy" in 1992, "Mighty Uncle" in 1993, "Mineral Wagon" in 1994, and "Divine Archer" and "Misty Horizon" in 1996.[40]

But this ambitious program of U.S. nuclear testing was never implemented, thanks largely to the antinuclear campaign. The events that led to this dramatic success began in Oregon, in the late 1980s. Ted Koren, one of the leaders of the powerful antinuclear movement in that state, had concluded that the most important thing that he could do for the cause of nuclear disarmament was to oust one of Oregon's leading congressional hawks. In 1988, he approached Mike Kopetski, a dovish Democratic state legislator interested in running for that congressional seat, and offered to help direct his election campaign. Koren had one condition: Kopetski would have to go to Nevada to participate in an anti-testing demonstration there, thus getting a better sense of what the issue was all about. Kopetski agreed and, like many people who went to the Nevada test site and witnessed nuclear explosions, was horrified by these preparations for nuclear war. Running for Congress that year, he lost, though by a very narrow margin. In 1990, he ran again, with Koren as his campaign manager and Oregon Peaceworks, the statewide peace and disarmament movement, working zealously for his election. This time he won. Shortly after Kopetski's victory, the director of Peaceworks phoned the SANE/Freeze lobbyist in Washington, pointed to Kopetski's willingness to follow the movement's lead on nuclear issues, especially nuclear testing, and asked what he wanted Kopetski to do. Propose a bill for a testing moratorium, was the response. Consequently, Kopetski drew up a bill for a twelve-month moratorium on U.S. nuclear testing, convinced House Democratic leader Richard Gephardt to co-sponsor it, and introduced the legislation in October 1991. Disarmament, environmental, and religious groups swung into line behind this Nuclear Testing Moratorium Act. Working methodically, Kopetski lined up majority support for the measure in the House, and then turned to the Senate.[41]

Pushing a nuclear testing moratorium through the U.S. Senate was a much trickier business. In the past, that body had defeated legislation imposing a testing moratorium, and might well do so again—despite the end of the Cold War, the Soviet test moratorium then in place, movement lobbying, and public support for an end to nuclear testing. In late 1991, Oregon's Mark Hatfield and Senate majority leader George Mitchell agreed to lead the fight for the moratorium bill in the Senate, and after patient work for months, had lined up a slender majority. But with the Bush administration threatening to veto the measure, the bill's Senate sponsors decided to put together even broader support through a compromise. Meeting with Senator James Exon, a hawkish Democrat from Nebraska, they fashioned the Hatfield-Exon-Mitchell bill. It provided for a nine-month U.S. testing moratorium, placed strict conditions on further U.S. testing, and required test ban negotiations and an end to U.S. nuclear testing by September 30, 1996. Despite the Bush administration's opposition and continued threats of a veto, the Senate passed the bill by a vote of 68 to 26 in early August. After negotiations, the House accepted the Senate version of the legislation, which, that September, was passed easily by both houses of Congress.[42]

The Bush administration now faced a dilemma. Although the President had nothing but disdain for the anti-testing legislation, he did not want to veto it either. The reason for his reluctance was that the shrewd floor sponsors of the legislation, at the urging of antinuclear lobbyists, had attached it to the energy and water appropriations bill, which provided funding for the construction of the super-conducting super-collider, a $500 million project to be built in Texas. Securing this lucrative project for his home state, with its large bloc of electoral votes, was vital to Bush, who was then engaged in an uphill battle for re-election. Thus, on October 2, 1992, the President reluctantly signed the legislation, remarking that the section on nuclear testing was "highly objectionable," for it might "prevent the United States from conducting underground nuclear tests that are necessary to maintain a safe and reliable nuclear deterrent." Declaring that nuclear deterrence remained "an essential element of our national security," he promised to "work for new legislation to permit the conduct of a modest number of necessary underground nuclear tests."[43] But Bush never had the opportunity to promote new legislation, for that November he went down to defeat in the presidential election. Meanwhile, years of efforts by the antinuclear movement came to fruition, and U.S. nuclear testing came to a halt, unilaterally.

Another type of great power unilateral restraint emerged in the form of rejecting the use of nuclear weapons. In 1990, Adelman complained that "officials have come to consider their use totally out of the question, except when the nation's very survival would be at stake." That April, when NATO leaders were planning a joint communiqué, American officials insisted on inserting the phrase that nuclear arms were "weapons of last resort"—a fact that panicked Thatcher, who felt "we were slipping towards" the "fatal position" of "no first use of nuclear weapons."[44] The Soviet Union did not employ nuclear weapons in its war in Afghanistan, and U.S. government leaders ruled out their use in the 1991 war against Iraq—though neither country faced any danger of nuclear retaliation. Although U.S. officials sometimes issued veiled nuclear threats against Saddam Hussein, they were bluffing. President Bush decided at an early stage that the U.S. government would not employ nuclear weapons, even if the Iraqis launched a chemical weapons attack. When Cheney suggested that Powell draw up some possible plans for use of nuclear weapons in the war, the JCS chair replied: "Let's not even think about nukes. You know we're not going to let that genie loose." Convinced that calling attention to U.S. nuclear weapons during the Gulf War would be politically troublesome, the Bush administration did its best to keep them out of the public eye and to issue reassurances to the public that they would not be used.[45]

New Leaders and Nuclear Disarmament

The progress toward nuclear disarmament during the Bush-Gorbachev years did not show any signs of reversal in 1992, for—in the antinuclear context of the time—their successors were eager to continue and extend these programs. Russian President Boris Yeltsin, unlike his predecessor, had little interest in the "new thinking" or in international relations. But, as Palazchenko noted, Yeltsin "had a gut feeling for what the people wanted, and the people supported Gorbachev's foreign policy." Thus, in the international arena, he sometimes tried to "out-Gorbachev Gorbachev." Sagdeev, too, remarked that, upon taking office, Yeltsin went about "winning the nation and the world's sympathy" through "attractive populist slogans. With a pacifist's simplicity he called for an immediate halt to a wide array of military programs, as if he wanted to become a greater champion of disarmament than Gorbachev."[46] Consequently, eager to improve his image with Russian citizens and with those of the West, Yeltsin proved quite amenable to negotiating a further landmark nuclear arms control agreement, the START II treaty. Signed by Bush and Yeltsin on January 3, 1993, START II made additional deep cuts in the two nations' nuclear arsenals, reducing the number of deployed strategic warheads to between 3,000 and 3,500 each and eliminating all multiple-warhead ICBMs. Yeltsin trumpeted the START II treaty as an historic breakthrough, "a major step toward fulfilling mankind's centuries-old dream of disarmament."[47]

George Bush's successor, Bill Clinton—elected in November 1992 and sworn in as President during January 1993—also seemed ready to foster additional moves toward nuclear disarmament. During the 1992 political campaign, he called for cutbacks in spending on nuclear production and testing, on the SDI program, and on military programs generally. In their place, he urged preservation of the ABM treaty, ratification of the START treaties, and negotiation of a comprehensive test ban treaty. Indeed, on September 18, the day the Senate reaffirmed its support for halting nuclear testing, Clinton told a campaign audience that "the biggest threat in the future" was "the proliferation of nuclear technology. . . . To contain that we ought to get out there and join the parade working toward a comprehensive test ban." The United States, he wrote, should have "smaller nuclear arsenals" and had "no need to develop new nuclear weapons designs." Not surprisingly, SANE/Freeze endorsed Clinton for President. And it seemed a wise choice. Asked about his foreign policy priorities at his first post-election press conference, Clinton named Russian-American negotiations to reduce nuclear weapons as the second item on his agenda.[48]

Public Policy in Other Nations

Although the nuclear arms control and disarmament measures of the super-powers received the most publicity, they were not the only ones undertaken during these years. Three of the new republics formed from the remains of the Soviet Union—the Ukraine, Belarus, and Kazakhstan—agreed within a short time to divest themselves of all nuclear weapons, thus becoming nu-clear-free nations.[49] China agreed to sign the nuclear nonproliferation treaty, as did North Korea, then a potential nuclear power. Brazil and Argentina, two longtime holdouts from the nonproliferation regime, formally re-nounced the manufacture or acquisition of nuclear weapons in late 1990. South Africa, which had produced its first nuclear weapons in 1980, began to dismantle and destroy them in 1990, and signed the nuclear nonprolifera-tion treaty in 1991.[50] To be sure, the Iraqi government worked to develop a nuclear weapons capability, and is believed to have been no more than a year away from having one before the Gulf War and the introduction of U.N. weapons inspectors disrupted the effort. But India and Pakistan, which probably did have the capability, decided—at least for the time being—not to assemble, test, or deploy nuclear weapons.[51] Even the British and French governments, long hostile to any constraints on their own nuclear options, were caught up in the antinuclear tide. Both of them publicly renounced the use of nuclear weapons during the Gulf War, with Mitterrand calling it "a recourse to barbarian methods that I reject." The French government also announced its decision to adhere to the nuclear nonproliferation treaty and to reduce spending on its nuclear forces. In addition, the British and French governments responded to Bush's unilateral withdrawal of non-strategic nu-clear weapons by reducing their own. Consequently, without negotiations or treaties, a large portion of the world's non-strategic nuclear weapons were removed from service.[52]

Many of these and other antinuclear policies reflected popular pressure. The South African apartheid regime, desperate to bolster its international image, had decided in late 1988 to divest itself of its nuclear arsenal. As South African President F. W. de Klerk told his parliament, nuclear weap-ons were "an obstacle to the development of South Africa's international relations." In the Philippines, the presence of nuclear weapons at the Clark Field and Subic Bay U.S military bases could no longer be sustained against public resistance. Although President Aquino wanted to retain the military bases, the popular, nationalist clamor against them was so great that, in 1991, the Philippine legislature voted to close them down, thus ending nearly a century of American military presence in that nation.[53] In New Zealand, popular support for the government's nuclear-free policy was so over-whelming that, in 1990, the opposition National Party reversed its previous stand and campaigned upon an antinuclear platform. Thus, when it won the election, it retained the Labour Party's ban on admitting U.S. nuclear war-ships. As the outgoing prime minister, David Lange, observed: "In the end, it was the ordinary people of New Zealand who made their country nuclear-free."[54] In France, the government announced in April 1992 that it was halt-ing nuclear testing at Moruroa and was urging other nuclear powers to halt testing as well. Although French motives for this policy reversal remain un-clear, two suggested at the time were to stop the embarrassing Greenpeace protests (the latest of which occurred only two weeks before) and to win fa-vor with the 15 percent of French voters who, in nationwide elections, had just startled political observers by voting for antinuclear Green parties.[55]

Elsewhere, too, popular opposition to nuclear weapons played a role. The Indian government's decision not to "go nuclear" reflected, at least in part, many Indians' view of their country as a leader in the campaign for nuclear disarmament. Indeed, nuclear weapons had become a stigma that most nations sought to avoid. During the Gulf War, the U.S. government faced enormous difficulties finding a nation that would provide base facili-ties for twenty B-52 bombers within a 4,000 mile radius of Iraq, for govern-ments did not want to accept aircraft so closely associated in the public's mind with nuclear weapons.[56] Even the reclusive North Korean government could not entirely ignore public pressure. As Secretary Baker noted, with the Bush administration's announcement in the fall of 1991 that all U.S. nu-clear weapons would be removed from South Korea, "Pyongyang's ultimate rationale for developing its own nuclear arsenal—to provide a nuclear deter-rent against an attack from the South—had evaporated. This development in effect forced North Korea to begin discussions with Seoul." That December, the two Koreas signed agreements confirming that the Korean peninsula should be free of nuclear weapons, and North Korea agreed to sign the non-proliferation treaty safeguards agreement and to allow international inspec-tion of its nuclear facilities. "Thus was American diplomacy directly re-sponsible for an end to six years of intransigence by the North," Baker stated.[57] What he downplayed was the fact that the American diplomacy in-cluded unilateral withdrawal of U.S. nuclear weapons and that the context was the worldwide antinuclear sentiment that put the North Korean regime, like the American, on the spot.

Prophets without Honor

Indeed, Baker's remarks were quite typical of most policymakers, who, even when adopting disarmament policies, showed little respect for the antinuclear activists who had generated them. Gorbachev, of course, was an exception. Maintaining close contacts with leaders of the nuclear disarmament campaign, he invited Suleimenov to join him on an official trip to Britain. On one afternoon in June 1990, he spent four hours accepting awards from Western groups, most of them peace and disarmament organizations.[58] By contrast, French officials responded to the crew members of a new *Rainbow Warrior*, who appeared at France's South Pacific test site to study the radiation effects, by arresting and deporting them. In Czechoslovakia, the Communist regime worked right up to its demise to prosecute and imprison members of Charter 77, the Independent Peace Association, and the John Lennon Peace Club.[59] Similarly, while the East German regime lasted, it had nothing but contempt for the nonaligned movement. In June 1989, reporting on preparations for the eighth END convention, an East German spy warned that its organizers were going to use it as a platform "for human rights in the East European countries," and would viciously contrast the "processes of change and democratization" in the Soviet Union, Poland, and Hungary with the politics of East Germany, Czechoslovakia, and Rumania. There would be special forums organized by "anti-socialist persons and organizations" like Faber, IKV, and VAKA. Moreover, independent groups and movements from the East—"the hostile-negative forces" of Communist nations—would be integrated into the Western disarmament movement. Naturally, the government regarded these as subversive activities.[60]

The attitude of the Bush administration was not much different. Although, on one rather surreal occasion, Bush drew upon Forsberg as a consultant on U.S. defense policy,[61] this was a rare departure from the contempt he usually displayed toward leading nuclear critics. Bernard Lown of IPPNW recalled that he had ready entrée to the prime ministers of Scandinavian countries, West Germany, and the Soviet Union, but could not meet with his own nation's President. When, at the request of Semipalatinsk disarmament activists, Lown sought to deliver to Bush a piece of sculpture from Kazakhstan—a mammoth's ivory tusk with "Long live peace without violence" carved on it—Bush refused to receive him.[62] Indeed, to the Bush administration, the antinuclear movement remained useful primarily as a means of undermining its opponents. In 1992, apparently seeking to repeat his 1988 success in discrediting Dukakis, Bush dispatched U.S. government agents to Britain in a fruitless attempt to obtain pictures of the Democratic challenger, Bill Clinton, on a CND march against the Vietnam War. Three times during the televised presidential and vice presidential debates of October 1992, Bush and his running mate, Dan Quayle, denounced the nuclear freeze movement and sought to associate their Democratic opponents with it. Praising his administration for "winning the cold war," the President insisted that "we never would have got there if we'd gone for the nuclear freeze crowd."[63] In January 1992, when Bush delivered his State of the Union address to Congress, even Gorbachev had been airbrushed out of the picture, with Bush proclaiming simply that the U.S. government had "won the Cold War." This self-serving triumphalism drew a standing ovation from the legislators—though, of course, it had little connection with reality.[64]

The reality was that, despite the belittling of the movement by many government leaders, it had secured some remarkable victories. In the late 1980s and early 1990s, the antinuclear campaign mobilized enough public pressure to play a key role in halting the testing, production, and deployment of nuclear weapons by the United States and the Soviet Union. It also helped to secure the removal (and usually the destruction) of short-range, medium-range, and long-range nuclear weapons from nations where they had been deployed by the two superpowers. Moreover, the movement and the antinuclear climate it generated influenced other nations to reduce their nuclear weaponry, to become nuclear-free, or to remain nuclear-free. As a result, the number of nuclear weapons in world arsenals declined very substantially and, perhaps most significant, nuclear powers resisted the temptation to use them. Taking note of these developments, the editors of the *Bulletin of the Atomic Scientists* set back the hands of their famous "doomsday clock" from 6 to 17 minutes to midnight between March 1990 and December 1991—*before* the disappearance of the Soviet Union.[65] Thanks in large part to the efforts of the antinuclear movement, a safer world was emerging, increasingly free of the menace of nuclear annihilation.

Waning Strength,
Reviving Arms Race,
1993-2002

> The fear of nuclear weapons is falling faster than the danger.
>
> Jeremy Stone, 1999

The end of the Cold War, the widespread popular distaste for nuclear weapons, the continued agitation of the antinuclear movement, and the new leadership of the superpowers in the early 1990s enhanced the possibilities for further strides toward a nuclear-free world—indeed, even for the attainment of that long-sought goal. And there was some additional progress through 1996. This included extension of the nuclear nonproliferation treaty, the expansion of nuclear-free zones, and the signing of a comprehensive test ban treaty. But these proved to be the last major victories for the antinuclear campaign. As the nuclear disarmament movement dwindled and hawkish constituencies began to reassert traditional priorities, the antinuclear momentum slowed and, then, disappeared. By the late 1990s, nuclear disarmament groups were once more on the defensive, fighting desperately to stave off attempts to scrap nuclear constraints. Although antinuclear groups and individuals continued their struggle against the Bomb, they no longer had the strength to put up an effective resistance to a reviving nuclear arms race. As a result, the U.S. Senate refused to ratify the comprehensive test ban treaty, India and Pakistan became nuclear powers, SDI was resurrected in the form of national missile defense, and the U.S. government withdrew from the ABM treaty. By the early years of the new century, it was clear enough that the governments of the great powers and their imitators had returned to a policy of enforcing national security through nuclear might.

A Movement in Decline, 1993-96

The popular mood of the early to mid-1990s provided a difficult terrain for the maintenance of antinuclear activism. "In these post–Cold war days," wrote a British CND leader in 1993, "one of the biggest problems for CND is that there is no longer a perception of danger amongst the general public with regard to nuclear weapons." Reporting to CND's national council the following year, the organization's general secretary bemoaned "the complacency associated with the end of the Cold War." Some leaders of the antinuclear campaign were resigned to it, and urged new approaches to generating antinuclear activism. The movement must "stop harping on the way things used to be," argued Irish CND's charismatic national secretary, Adi Roche. "We must accept that there isn't the fear which got the massive numbers of people on the streets in the 70s and 80s." But despite new mobilizing tactics, the situation only grew worse in the following years. "The level of concern in the public mind about nuclear weapons has dropped a long way down the scale," Bruce Kent observed in the spring of 1995. "There is a general impression that all goes well, major cutbacks of warheads are . . . going on and the Cold War is over." Furthermore, new concerns had arisen. "The nuclear weapon issue seems quite irrelevant when one looks at the twenty or so civil wars raging in different parts of the planet. Even many disarmers now see as their priorities concerns about arms sales, landmines and the ineffectiveness of UN peacekeeping."[1]

In these circumstances, the antinuclear movement continued to wane, and the days of mass mobilization receded into the past. By the summer of 1993, the membership of SANE/Freeze—renamed Peace Action—had shrunk to 53,000. "The national office has a smaller staff," reported its executive director, "and we have a smaller network of groups around the country." PSR experienced a membership fall-off of about 10 percent a year after 1987, dropping to 21,000 members by the summer of 1993. By that time, PSR's budget was down by about 50 percent from its heyday, and some 30 percent of its chapters had become inactive. In Britain, CND declined from 51,000 members to 40,000 between January 1993 and the end of 1996.[2] Some groups adopted different priorities. In Russia, peace activists threw themselves into opposition to the war in Chechnya. The Swedish Peace and Arbitration Society focused on cooperating with Russian and Balkan peace groups, campaigning against landmines and the arms trade, and cutting Swedish military expenditures.[3] Other groups disappeared entirely. Among them were American Peace Test, which had sponsored the large anti-testing demonstrations in Nevada, and the Movement for Disarmament, Peace, and

Liberty, which for decades had provided a voice for the nonaligned movement in France. END wobbled along until July 1993, when it held a seminar at Maastricht, designed to "to go more deeply into the prospects and alternatives for Europe." Then that organization—once the great powerhouse of European protest against nuclear weapons—simply expired. With END's demise, recalled the IPB's Colin Archer, "there was a real sense of the end of an era."[4]

Yet despite the decline of the antinuclear movement, it retained a public presence in many nations. In November 1993, British CND stepped up its campaigns against the Trident nuclear submarine and nuclear proliferation, as well as for a comprehensive test ban treaty. CND activists defiantly sailed protest vessels into the path of nuclear submarines and took heart at the Labour Party's vote to scrap the Trident program.[5] A pamphlet from Exeter CND proclaimed that "nuclear weapons are

still dangerous
still useless
still expensive
still immoral and illegal
and still here.

In May 1994, challenging popular and government complacency, CND published a *Blueprint for a Nuclear Weapon-Free World*. Citing recent disarmament treaties and the improved relations among the nuclear powers, CND's vice chair argued that there was "no obvious reason why we cannot build on these historic but limited deals to really move towards the complete elimination of nuclear weapons."[6] That October, CND held its first major demonstration in London for several years, with the theme of "Nuclear-Free World or Nuclear Free-for-All." Featuring music, giant puppets, and speeches by movement leaders, British MPs, and youth activists, the Trafalgar Square event evoked much of the spirit of the past, and attracted over 5,000 participants, mostly young. As a number of nuclear-related events converged in 1995—the fiftieth anniversary of the Hiroshima bombing, the NPT review conference, and the revival of French nuclear testing—Britain experienced a modest renewal of antinuclear activism.[7]

Antinuclear activism also persisted in the United States. Facing a new President and Congress in early 1993, Peace Action promised to continue the struggle for nuclear disarmament. Although it branched out to other issues—among them, slashing the military budget and halting the proliferation of weapons—Peace Action did demand nuclear abolition. Its 1996 Peace Voter campaign, drawing upon some two thousand volunteers to distribute more than a million voter guides on peace and disarmament issues, was its largest grassroots mobilization since the Freeze campaign of the early 1980s. On the fiftieth anniversary of the atomic bombing of Hiroshima, hundreds of Catholic antinuclear activists dramatized its effects by writhing on the ground in front of an entrance to the Pentagon, while still others entered military facilities and damaged nuclear equipment.[8] However, these and other efforts by antinuclear groups received less public attention than did antinuclear appeals by veterans of the policymaking élite. Robert McNamara, Paul Nitze, and other former government officials sharply criticized the maintenance of nuclear arsenals in the post–Cold War era.[9] In an impassioned speech before the National Press Club in December 1996, U.S. General George Lee Butler declared that "nuclear weapons are inherently dangerous, hugely expensive and militarily inefficient." Accepting them as inevitable "codifies mankind's most murderous instincts." The only rational action, he insisted, was to eliminate nuclear weapons entirely. As this speech came from a military officer who, only two years before, had commanded U.S. nuclear forces, it drew nationwide headlines.[10]

Elsewhere, too, the antinuclear struggle continued. In France, some 3,000 people staged a march against a planned nuclear weapons facility near Bordeaux. In India, the Committee for a Sane Nuclear Policy joined with other concerned groups to urge the five declared nuclear weapons powers to halt nuclear testing and move toward complete nuclear disarmament. In Australia, antinuclear activists held Palm Sunday rallies and commemorated Hiroshima Day across the nation. In Finland, the Peace Union organized a large commemoration ceremony on Hiroshima Day, while the Committee of 100 championed a comprehensive test ban treaty. In Canada, the Voice of Women circulated a petition calling for an end to the production and testing of all nuclear weapons. In the Philippines, activists staged a "die-in" outside the French embassy in Manila to protest French nuclear testing. As in previous years, popular support was particularly widespread in Japan. Japanese antinuclear activists circulated a new Appeal from Hiroshima and Nagasaki, drawing nearly 50 million signatures by 1995. Out of 3,300 Japanese municipalities, 1964 had proclaimed themselves nuclear-free zones by that year, and 839 had adopted resolutions calling for the signing of an international treaty to abolish nuclear weapons.[11] Meanwhile, Uighur protests against Chinese nuclear testing at Lop Nor continued to erupt. In March 1993, when Chinese troops opened fire on a crowd of a thousand demonstrators outside the heavily guarded test site, the enraged protesters stormed the complex—damaging equipment, setting fire to military vehicles and airplanes, and tearing down miles of electronic fencing.[12]

On the international level, as well, the movement retained significant organizational assets. Although nuclear disarmament was but one of the many causes that Greenpeace championed, by October 1994 that organization had some 5 million members around the globe. Furthermore, a number of international constituency groups continued their antinuclear activities, including IPPNW, the International Association of Lawyers Against Nuclear Arms (IALANA), and the International Network of Engineers and Scientists for Global Responsibility (INES).[13] Although the WPC maintained no more than a shadow existence, the nonaligned International Peace Bureau grew into a substantial organization. Headed by Maj Britt Theorin—a former Swedish ambassador for disarmament and current member of the European parliament—it had its own publications, projects, and headquarters in Geneva. By late 1994, it claimed more than 150 affiliates in 41 countries, with a combined membership of between 3 and 4 million.[14]

The movement's focus on nuclear abolition was strengthened by events surrounding the official NPT review and extension conference of 1995. As early as 1993, two networks of antinuclear groups began forming in the hope of using the conference to press the nuclear weapons states to honor their commitment in the original treaty to nuclear disarmament. The larger of the networks, the International Coalition for Nuclear Non-Proliferation and Disarmament, was led by four major internationals—IPB, IPPNW, IALANA, and INES—and eventually drew together 64 groups from 20 countries. The smaller, the World Campaign for the Abolition of Nuclear Weapons, was pulled together by the Nuclear Age Peace Foundation in California.[15] In April 1995, when the conference opened at the United Nations in New York City, their constituent groups and others committed to the abolition of nuclear weapons met daily to brainstorm and coordinate their activities, forming what came to be known as the Abolition Caucus. Despite their vigorous lobbying, however, the nuclear powers succeeded in winning an indefinite extension of the NPT without a specific commitment to nuclear abolition. Thanks to this rebuff, disgruntled activists at the conference drafted a statement calling for the conclusion by the year 2000 of an international treaty requiring the phased elimination of all nuclear weapons. Within a month, some 400 organizations around the world signed this statement, which became the basis for Abolition 2000, a global network of sympathetic groups. Although Abolition 2000 remained a very loosely structured umbrella organization, it did provide increasing numbers of groups with a common rhetoric and goal—in the words of the founding statement, the "unconditional abolition of nuclear weapons."[16]

Two high-profile international statements also gave the antinuclear campaign some badly needed publicity. In August 1996, a report by the Canberra Commission—a blue ribbon panel created by the Australian government in late 1995—placed itself firmly behind nuclear abolition. Comprised of figures with great prestige—among them General Butler, Field Marshal Lord Michael Carver (former chief of the British Defense Staff), Michel Rocard (a former prime minister of France), and Joseph Rotblat (winner of the 1995 Nobel Peace Prize)—the commission argued that "the proposition that nuclear weapons can be retained in perpetuity and never be used . . . defies credibility." Thus, "the only complete defense" against this catastrophe "is the elimination of nuclear weapons," accompanied by the "assurance that they will never be produced again."[17] A second call for nuclear abolition occurred only a few months later. On December 5, 1996, in the immediate aftermath of General Butler's antinuclear address, 61 active and retired generals and admirals from seventeen nations issued a strong declaration calling for the abolition of nuclear weapons. Pointing out that the demise of the Cold War had "created conditions favorable to nuclear disarmament," they declared themselves "convinced that the continuing existence of nuclear weapons in the armories of nuclear powers, and the ever present threat of acquisition of these weapons by others, constitute a peril to global peace and security and to the safety and survival of the people we are dedicated to protect."[18]

Public Opinion, 1993-96

Although the public exhibited greater complacency about the nuclear danger, this did not reflect widespread enthusiasm for nuclear weapons. According to polls, in September 1995 only 15 percent of the West European public thought nuclear weapons were still necessary, while 74 percent considered them unnecessary. Even among the citizens of the nuclear powers, nuclear arsenals had limited appeal. Among Britons, only 39 percent considered nuclear weapons necessary for their nation.[19] At roughly the same time, polls in France found that 42 percent of the public opposed French nuclear deterrence, 60 percent were against the resumption of French nuclear tests, and 78 percent opposed the modernization of nuclear weapons.[20] The Indian public, to be sure, showed greater ambivalence. A survey of India's "educated élites" in the fall of 1994 found that 33 percent favored their country's acquisition of nuclear weapons, 57 percent supported the official policy of "keeping the nuclear option open," and only 8 percent favored renunciation of nuclear weapons. But more than half the respondents backed

India's renunciation of nuclear weapons in the event of the international adoption of "a time-bound plan for global nuclear disarmament."[21]

Antinuclear views also predominated in the United States. There was a widespread concern among Americans about nuclear proliferation, and a 1995 study reported that 82 percent of the public thought preventing the spread of nuclear weapons a very important goal. In that same year, according to pollsters, 61 percent of Americans believed that development of the atomic bomb had been a bad idea.[22] Nor was this antinuclear sentiment limited to the weapons of other nations. In late 1993 and early 1994, polls found that 57 percent of Americans opposed having U.S. national laboratories develop new types of nuclear weapons and that 68 percent wanted to decrease U.S. spending for developing and testing new nuclear weapons. Indeed, Americans favored further reductions in the U.S. nuclear arsenal by 57 to 30 percent.[23] In 1994, an opinion survey found that 80 percent of the public backed a nuclear test ban treaty, and the following year a poll reported that 60 percent backed eliminating "all nuclear arms in the world." The persistent GOP alternative to nuclear disarmament—SDI, repackaged as national missile defense—enjoyed far less popularity. A July 1996 poll found that 32 percent of Americans favored it, 31 percent opposed it, and 37 percent were unsure about it or had no opinion.[24]

Indecision and Some Further Progress, 1993-96

In this context of declining organizational pressure for nuclear disarmament, accompanied by lingering antinuclear attitudes, a number of major powers exhibited a new indecisiveness about support for nuclear constraints. In Russia, antinuclear scientists lost some of their influence upon public policy, while the military-industrial complex worked to revive Russia as a military superpower. Although the U.S. nuclear testing moratorium undermined proponents of a new round of Russian nuclear testing, Russian defense and space industries lobbied for the development of a missile defense system, Russian military officers remained obsessed with the danger of a U.S. nuclear attack, and the government scrapped its earlier commitment to no first-use of nuclear weapons. In Russia's December 1995 elections, the Communists and rightwing nationalists did well, securing a majority in the Duma. Hostile to nuclear arms control and disarmament agreements with the United States, they helped block Russian ratification of the START II treaty.[25] In Britain, the government plunged ahead with the Trident nuclear submarine program and refused to join the U.S.-Russian-French moratorium on nuclear testing. British officials announced, with some trepidation, that they were ready to negotiate a comprehensive test ban treaty, but added that a nuclear-free world was not a "practical" policy goal.[26]

Other major nations also took a cautious position. President Mitterrand extended France's nuclear testing moratorium to match that of the superpowers. But opposition to the moratorium grew among France's conservative parties. In 1994, the latest French government military planning study continued to assert the centrality of nuclear weapons in France's national defense strategy. In India, the rising fortunes of the Hindu nationalist Bharatiya Janata Party (BJP) enhanced the possibility that India would make its nuclear capability overt, for party leaders viewed the possession of nuclear weapons as a means of upgrading their nation's status in world affairs. Although the ruling Congress Party resisted pressures from weapons scientists to conduct nuclear tests, it kept India's nuclear options open, rejecting adherence to the non-proliferation treaty or to a comprehensive test ban treaty. For its part, China remained committed to its no first-use policy, but resisted joining the moratorium on nuclear testing.[27]

Many other nations, however, particularly in the Southern Hemisphere, seemed more committed to antinuclear priorities. In 1994, Brazil and Argentina finally ratified the 1967 Treaty of Tlatelolco, thus ending uncertainty about the effectiveness of the South American nuclear-free zone treaty. Two years later, African nations signed the Treaty of Pelindaba, which turned Africa into a nuclear weapon-free zone. That same year, Southeast Asian nations signed the Treaty of Bangkok, which made their region a nuclear-free zone as well. The Bangkok Treaty irked the nuclear powers, for its provisions barred the passage of nuclear-armed ships and their right to call at ports in the region. But nuclear nations did warm to the less restrictive Treaty of Rarotonga, which had established a South Pacific nuclear weapon-free zone; under pressure from non-nuclear nations to show progress toward nuclear disarmament, the U.S., British, and French governments signed it in 1996. These treaties received little public recognition at the time. But, together with the 1959 Antarctic Treaty, they had the effect of banning nuclear weapons from most of the Southern Hemisphere.[28]

Another indication of the antinuclear attitudes of most nations was the resolution of the antinuclear movement's World Court Project. Spearheaded by IPB, IPPNW, and IALANA, the plan to have the World Court rule on the legality of the use of nuclear weapons acquired considerable momentum in the early 1990s. In 1993, activists succeeded in getting the World Health Organization to request an advisory ruling, setting in motion a struggle between the nuclear powers on the one hand and antinuclear nations and citizens' groups on the other. Submitting evidence in the case—the first ever presented by citizens before the World Court—the IPB provided the world body with the critique of nuclear weapons signed by thousands of lawyers, a sample of the 100 million signatures gathered worldwide on the *Appeal from Hiroshima and Nagasaki*, 170,000 Declarations of Public Conscience, and material surveying fifty years of popular opposition to the nuclear arms race. Forty-three governments also submitted materials to the court, a reflection of the momentous nature of the issue. To counter the argument of the nuclear powers that the U.N. General Assembly was the proper agency to request an advisory ruling, sympathetic nations brought an appropriate resolution to that world body as well. Despite a fierce lobbying campaign by the nuclear powers, the General Assembly adopted the resolution by an overwhelming vote, thereby adding its own request for a World Court advisory ruling on nuclear weapons.[29]

In July 1996, when the World Court issued its ruling, it provided the movement with a limited victory. The limits were hardly surprising, for the judges on the World Court owed their positions to their home governments and almost invariably shared the dominant attitudes of their own societies. And, in this case, half the judges came from the nuclear powers or countries that were allied with them. Nonetheless, the World Court ruling bolstered the movement's position. "The threat or use of nuclear weapons," declared the world body, "would generally be contrary to the rules of international law applicable in armed conflict, and particularly the principles and rules of humanitarian law." The court added that it could not "conclude definitively whether the threat or use of nuclear weapons would be lawful or unlawful in an extreme circumstance of self-defense, in which the very survival of a State would be at stake." But although this left a loophole for nuclear use, it was a smaller one than the nuclear powers claimed as their prerogative. Furthermore, the court ruled that "there exists an obligation to pursue in good faith and bring to a conclusion negotiations leading to nuclear disarmament in all its aspects under strict and effective international control." Thereafter, this historic ruling was quoted widely in diplomatic speeches and statements by non-governmental organizations.[30]

U.S. Government Caution, 1993-96

Like the governments of the other nuclear or would-be nuclear powers, the U.S. government adopted a cautious approach to the issue of nuclear disarmament. This challenged expectations, for the new Clinton administration brought to Washington a number of figures with a more antinuclear orientation than their predecessors in the Bush administration. During his 1992 campaign, Bill Clinton had outflanked George Bush in championing nuclear disarmament.[31] His new Secretary of Defense, Les Aspin, ordered a sweeping review of U.S. nuclear weapons policy, blithely proclaimed "the end of the 'Star Wars' era," and even suggested that the United States would fare better in "a world without nuclear weapons."[32] In addition, some movement activists secured posts in ACDA, the Department of Energy, and the White House Office of Science and Technology.[33] Nevertheless, domestic issues had provided the focus of Clinton's presidential campaign; accordingly, progress toward nuclear arms control and disarmament did not have a particularly high priority in the new administration.[34] Furthermore, Clinton was wary of challenging U.S. military officials, both because he had sidestepped military service during the Vietnam War and because they responded angrily to his early attempt to alter the Pentagon's opposition to gays in the armed forces. In addition, Clinton, Gore, and their associates were "New Democrats," eager to distance themselves from Democratic Party liberalism and to capture the center of American politics. Aspin's career, too, had been marked by political expediency, and as chair of the House Armed Services Committee he had veered back and forth between his party's dovish and more hawkish elements. Warren Christopher, who had helped choose him for the defense post, recalled Aspin's "good centrist credentials."[35]

The Clinton administration's proclivities toward compromise were reinforced by its political difficulties. In the 1992 election, Clinton had drawn only 43 percent of the popular vote, securing a majority only in his home state of Arkansas. In that same election, the Democrats lost ten seats in the House; shortly thereafter, in a special election, they lost another seat in the Senate. As White House staffer David Gergen put it: "Clinton had neither a mandate nor coattails. He had won office but not power." Furthermore, his victory appeared to be based more on popular dislike of Bush than on public enthusiasm for him. Indeed, Clinton emerged from the election—in which his character came under withering assault—with the worst popular ratings of any newly elected President in recent history. Although the Democrats controlled Congress in 1993, few of them felt much loyalty to him, for he was an outsider and had distanced himself from Congress during the campaign. His relations with congressional Republicans were even worse. Irate at having lost the White House and recognizing Clinton's political weakness, they refused to give him the usual presidential "honeymoon," but immediately attacked him personally and viciously. Closing ranks, every Republican in Congress voted against his budget plan. When the Republicans swept the 1994 congressional elections, this sharpened the GOP's belligerent approach to the President. Jesse Helms, the new chair of the Senate Foreign Relations Committee, suggested that Clinton would be in personal danger if he dared to visit a U.S. military base.[36] At the same time, the great wave of popular resistance to the nuclear arms race had receded—a fact recognized by administration officials.[37]

Taken together, these factors led to a restrained arms control and disarmament policy. Aspin's 1993–94 Nuclear Posture Review, which could have led to sweeping changes, ended up reaffirming the status quo. Approved by the President, it provided that U.S. strategic forces would drop no lower than START II levels, that nuclear weapons would be maintained in Europe at their current level, and that there would be no significant changes in U.S. operational policies, including the first use of nuclear weapons. The basis for these conclusions was a "lead and hedge" strategy. The U.S. government would lead by retaining its nuclear options, while continuing arms control negotiations and encouraging Russia to ratify START II. It would hedge by retaining the capacity to deploy strategic warheads at a level nearly double the START II limits, as well as a triad of strategic nuclear forces based on "the leading edge of technology." A *Washington Post* headline proclaimed simply: "Clinton Decides to Retain Bush Nuclear Arms Policy." This bolstering of traditional approaches reflected the strong resistance by U.S. military officers to giving up their favorite weapons and programs, as well as abdication of leadership in this area by top administration officials. After Aspin's retirement in early 1994, his successor as defense secretary, William Perry, threw in the towel on changes, while other top officials, including the President, gave the review little attention.[38] Years later, Anthony Lake, Clinton's national security advisor, put the best face on things by stating that the administration had decided that, rather than initiate sudden changes in nuclear policy, it would bring U.S. military officials along on a gradual basis.[39]

The administration's early nuclear policies reflected this timid approach. In the area of nuclear arms controls, it implemented START I reductions, reached an agreement with Russia to retarget long-range missiles that had been aimed at each other's homelands, and pressed the U.S. Senate to ratify the START II treaty. It also proposed an international treaty that would end the production of fissile material for nuclear weapons.[40] But a number of other policies exhibited some hedging on disarmament. Russia proposed beginning START III negotiations while the legislatures of both nations considered the ratification of START II, but the Clinton administration rebuffed this proposal, thus letting strategic arms negotiations lapse for years. Furthermore, the administration considered proposals to absorb ACDA into the

State Department. In addition, after the GOP resurrected SDI in its 1994 "Contract with America," Clinton signed legislation providing a sudden effusion of funds for research on ballistic missile defense.[41] Also, in secret policy meetings and in public statements, administration officials began to widen the circumstances under which the U.S. government would initiate nuclear war against non-nuclear nations.[42]

Within the realm of nuclear arms controls, the administration accorded the highest priority to non-proliferation, a policy that would restrict the nuclear advances of *other* nations. According to Aspin, proliferation was "the most serious security threat to the United States in the future." Secretary of State Warren Christopher claimed that NATO's "most urgent" task was "curbing the spread of weapons of mass destruction and the means of delivering them. This threat constitutes the arms control agenda of the 1990s."[43] With the parties to the nuclear nonproliferation treaty scheduled to meet in the spring of 1995 to decide whether the treaty should be extended, the U.S. government began diplomatic efforts to ensure this extension indefinitely, without conditions. But it met opposition to this approach from non-nuclear countries, which argued that indefinite extension must be accompanied by clear pledges from the nuclear powers that they were committed to a specific agenda for nuclear disarmament. In response, the Clinton administration pledged its leadership for a number of nuclear disarmament measures, including a comprehensive test ban treaty and a ban on producing and stockpiling fissile materials. On March 1, 1995, Clinton gave a major address calling for the nuclear weapons states "to pursue nuclear arms control and disarmament." The original draft of Clinton's speech spoke of the "eventual elimination of nuclear weapons," but the Pentagon balked and the more cautious words were inserted. Thanks to these and other assurances, plus the diplomatic muscle of the nuclear weapons nations, the Clinton administration achieved its goal that year of the indefinite extension of the NPT.[44]

The Clinton administration secured other non-proliferation measures, as well. In 1991, Congress had passed the Nunn-Lugar legislation to provide financial assistance to the states of the former Soviet Union in dismantling their nuclear weapons. But implementing this program did not proceed smoothly. The Ukraine, Kazakhstan, and Belarus began to hesitate about such disarmament, while congressional Republicans—egged on by their friends at the Heritage Foundation—preferred building new U.S. nuclear weapons to eliminating those threatening the United States. Eventually, however, the Clinton administration prevailed, and the three former Soviet republics were denuclearized.[45] An even trickier situation confronted U.S. officials with respect to the nuclear program of North Korea, which was discovered to be separating plutonium in violation of its NPT commitments. Christopher recalled: "Of all the foreign policy challenges the Clinton administration faced upon taking office, none was more immediately dangerous." Although Christopher called upon the North Korean government to abandon its nuclear aspirations, threatening sanctions if it did not, little progress was made until, in June 1994, the administration received the assistance of ex-President Jimmy Carter. Visiting North Korea, Carter reported that the government had agreed to halt its nuclear program as a prelude to negotiations. After months of tough bargaining, an "Agreed Framework" was reached in October. It provided that North Korea would adhere to the NPT, permit comprehensive IAEA inspections, and take specific steps to freeze and later dismantle its plutonium-based nuclear weapons program. In return, the United States assured North Korea that it would not threaten it with nuclear weapons and promised to provide it with heavy fuel oil shipments and light water nuclear reactors, which would supply nuclear power but not the plutonium that could be used for nuclear weapons. In Christopher's view, the agreement with North Korea was "one of the major achievements of our foreign policy."[46]

The Movement's Influence, 1993-96

Given its declining strength, the organized antinuclear campaign had relatively little impact upon these policies. It was completely outmaneuvered by military officials in the preparation of the Nuclear Posture Review, which it derided as "Cold War Lite."[47] The movement also lacked significant influence over nonproliferation policy. Although the Abolition Caucus took a hard line against indefinite extension of the NPT, most of the major arms control and disarmament groups in the United States—including Peace Action, PSR, Council for a Livable World, and the Union of Concerned Scientists—considering the Abolitionists unrealistic, campaigned for it. This not only dissipated the movement's strength, but led to a sense of betrayal on the part of the Abolitionists, who viewed the NPT supporters as overly cozy with the U.S. government.[48] On the other hand, the World Court decision on the use of nuclear weapons and the abolitionist statements by the generals and admirals did receive some attention within the Clinton administration, ultimately generating internal pressure for somewhat stronger antinuclear rhetoric in policy statements.[49] Another small victory for the movement lay in inhibiting official suggestions for wider use of nuclear weapons. When press reports in March 1994 hinted that the Pentagon was changing U.S. policy against targeting non-nuclear states, the administration issued a public denial. "The NGOs went ballistic," an NSC official explained, "and we were forced to kick the can." Eventually, buffeted by conflicting pressures, the administration settled for ambiguity on this score.[50]

Much of the movement's remaining strength went into the fight for a test ban treaty, and on this issue its efforts came none too soon. In early 1993, despite the Hatfield-Exon-Mitchell legislation—which established a nine-month U.S. testing moratorium, circumscribed U.S. testing thereafter, and set as the U.S. goal the negotiation of a comprehensive test ban treaty (CTBT) by September 1996—the Clinton administration was poised to embark on a different course of action. Within the administration, Thomas Graham, the acting director of ACDA, argued for the negotiation of a zero yield CTBT and for the extension of the testing moratorium. But, in taking this stance, he was virtually alone. The Defense Department, the JCS, the weapons laboratories (under the jurisdiction of the Department of Energy), and NSC officials lobbied strongly to resume nuclear testing and to exempt tests below one kiloton from any test ban treaty. As Clinton favored what he called a "phased approach" and Gore supported a threshold test ban, the scales were heavily weighted on the side of continued nuclear testing. At the first Cabinet level meeting on the subject, Graham was supported only by the President's science advisor. Strongly arrayed against them were Aspin, Christopher, and JCS Chair Colin Powell.[51] Apparently viewing the issue as already settled, the NSC staff, the weapons labs, and the Defense Department laid plans for the fifteen additional nuclear tests allowed under the legislation. The governments of other nuclear powers, too, though temporarily abiding by the testing moratorium, indicated their interest in resuming nuclear tests—especially the British and French.[52]

Well aware that it faced a deteriorating situation, the movement embarked on a vigorous effort to extend the moratorium and secure a full-fledged CTBT. In Britain, CND spearheaded the formation of a Nuclear Test Ban Coalition, comprising peace, environmental, and development groups. It picketed, demonstrated, and circulated an anti-testing petition throughout the nation. Similar campaigns emerged in France and other European countries.[53] In the United States, a broad range of antinuclear groups—including AFSC, the Council for a Livable World, FAS, Friends of the Earth, IPPNW, Peace Action, PSR, 20/20 Vision, the Union of Concerned Scientists, WAND, and others—waged a concerted campaign to push the Clinton administration back on track. In late April, having pieced together the details of the emerging administration policy, they alerted knowledgeable reporters and key CTBT advocates in Congress—among them Hatfield, Exon, and Kopetski. On April 30, the *Washington Post* broke the story of the administration's backtracking on nuclear testing. Together with fierce lobbying by antinuclear groups, it led to what the White House congressional liaison called "a firestorm" in the Democratic-controlled Congress. Senator Tom Harkin of Iowa dispatched a protest letter to the White House, signed by 38 Senators. Congressman Kopetski sent another, signed by 159 Representatives. Both expressed congressional opposition to the one-kiloton plan and to further nuclear testing. Activist meetings with newspaper editorial boards helped produce a flood of anti-testing editorials.[54] Meanwhile, a paper on the testing issue written by Frank von Hippel of the FAS and circulated by antinuclear activists brought him to the attention of Hazel O'Leary, the new secretary of the Department of Energy. Unsure whether to go along with the fifteen tests promoted by the weapons labs, she invited von Hippel to two special meetings that she convened in mid-May to discuss the issue.[55]

As a result, the tide turned in an antinuclear direction. By the end of June 1993, the Clinton administration, feeling the heat, had scrapped its one-kiloton threshold test ban treaty plan and had lowered the number of preferred nuclear tests to nine. Even this compromise, however, failed to hold up against nuclear critics, and newspaper stories appeared indicating that the administration was ready to abandon testing altogether. "We got a pretty strong message from the Hill and from editorial pages not to test," a senior administration official told the press. White House political and legislative affairs operatives added their voices against further testing.[56] At a Cabinet meeting, O'Leary—convinced by von Hippel and other movement consultants that further testing to safeguard the U.S. nuclear stockpile was unnecessary—unexpectedly sided with Graham in arguing to extend the moratorium and work for a full-fledged CTBT. Deferring to her authority over the weapons labs, Powell now dropped his opposition to that approach.[57] Thus, on July 3, the President announced that he would extend the U.S. testing moratorium until at least September 1994, provided that no other nation resumed testing, and would strive to secure a comprehensive test ban treaty by September 1996. "The American people demanded common sense," Hatfield exulted, "and that has led us to where we are today—on the road to a safer world."[58] Clinton's decision had the effect of boxing in other nuclear nations, which expressed varying degrees of irritation at the new policy—particularly Britain, which needed to use U.S. facilities if it were to conduct further nuclear tests.[59]

But the victory was far from won, for almost immediately the nuclear powers began to renege on their commitment to ending nuclear tests. On October 5, 1993, the Chinese government—which had never accepted the moratorium but had promised to show "restraint"—resumed nuclear test-ing.[60] Given the Clinton administration's decision to make the extension of its own testing moratorium contingent upon other nations' refraining from tests, this action could have triggered U.S. test resumption. But the U.S. government persisted with its moratorium. Even so, when it came to the terms of a CTBT, the U.S. administration was less principled. In 1994, it proposed to limit the treaty to ten years in duration. It also began to drift toward exempting small-scale nuclear explosions from the treaty provisions. The secretary of defense, the JCS, the weapons labs, and some elements in the State Department favored allowing nuclear explosions with a yield up to 500 tons, although the Department of Energy, ACDA, and the White House Office of Science and Technology resisted this idea. Furthermore, as late as the summer of 1995, the Clinton administration's official position at the test ban negotiations was that a CTBT should allow nuclear "experiments" with yields up to four pounds—a far smaller exemption, but nonetheless one that rendered a CTBT less than comprehensive.[61] In addition, on June 13, 1995, France's new President, the conservative Jacques Chirac, announced that, although France would sign a CTBT in the future, it was resuming nuclear testing in the Pacific that September.[62]

These actions unleashed another wave of popular protest. In a new surge of energy, the movement condemned the Chinese nuclear tests, assailed the limited duration proposed for the CTBT, and demanded a "true zero-yield" treaty.[63] But it was the French plan to resume nuclear testing that, in the words of a *Washington Post* headline, unleashed a "Typhoon of Anger." Antinuclear rallies and protests sprang up across the world. Responding to calls by disarmament groups, consumers boycotted French goods, irate citi-zens poured French wine into the gutters, and Australian unions refused to handle French cargo or French postal and telecommunications services. "You should not underestimate the sense of outrage here," declared New Zealand's prime minister. Sales of French wines and champagne dropped by a third in Australia and New Zealand, and polls in the latter nation found that public opposition to the resumption of French nuclear tests hit an as-tonishing 98 percent. In Papeete, the capital of Tahiti, some 15,000 people turned out to welcome the arrival of Greenpeace's *Rainbow Warrior II*, then en route to another protest at Moruroa, and to call upon the French not to test.[64] Nor was the furor confined to the Pacific. In Sweden, French wine sales dropped by 50 percent. In France, thousands of Parisians demonstrated against the government's policy. When Chirac sought to address the Euro-pean parliament, about two-thirds of that body rose to its feet, chanting "No! No!" and, for at least five minutes, refused to let him speak.[65] In the

United States, a coalition of 40 disarmament, religious, and environmental groups sparked a consumer boycott, while the U.S. Senate unanimously adopted a resolution condemning French and Chinese nuclear testing. "We expected a few angry outbursts, but we never thought it would get this bad," a senior French official remarked. "The world has really changed in recent years."[66]

Confronted by what appeared to be a revival of the antinuclear movement, the nuclear powers retreated. The French government, which had announced plans for nuclear testing through May 1996, abruptly ended its tests in January of that year, cutting their number back from eight to six. Moreover, in the midst of the storm of protest, the French, who had previously demanded loopholes in a test ban treaty, reversed course in early August 1995 and dropped their insistence upon exempting low-yield tests from a CTBT. Indeed, the French foreign ministry now announced that the future treaty should provide for "the banning of any nuclear weapon test."[67] In turn, this put the U.S. government on the spot. Impressed by the upsurge of public protest against French nuclear testing and no longer able to hide its own appetite for low-yield tests behind the obduracy of the French, the Clinton administration announced on August 11, 1995, that, henceforth, it would seek to secure a "zero yield" treaty.[68] To be sure, it cushioned this abandonment of low-yield testing by promising the U.S. weapons labs a $40 billion, ten-year "stockpile stewardship" program, thus enabling them to continue some measure of nuclear research, development, and production.[69] Nonetheless, the U.S. government's decision to back a "zero yield" nuclear test ban represented an important turning point on the road to a full cutoff of nuclear testing. Nuclear disarmament groups hailed it as "a major victory," while the hawkish Heritage Foundation denounced it as a commitment to "unilateral nuclear disarmament."[70]

From the standpoint of test ban supporters, things remained largely on course thereafter. Making the test ban its top priority in 1996, Greenpeace organized demonstrations, confrontations, and even a protest voyage to China, whose government, in response to international pressure, announced in July 1996 that it was joining the worldwide moratorium.[71] In Britain, CND sought to keep the spotlight on halting nuclear tests, while in the United States, the alliance of mainstream disarmament groups backing the NPT reorganized itself as the Coalition to Reduce Nuclear Dangers and plunged into the CTBT campaign.[72] True to its promises, the Clinton administration did use its influence to bring the other declared nuclear powers into line behind a zero yield test ban treaty. Nevertheless, the Indian government emerged as a major barrier. As its own nuclear weapons program would be hindered by a ban on testing, the Indian government maintained that it would not accept the treaty without the inclusion of a timetable for eliminating all nuclear weapons. In turn, Britain, Russia, and China—viewing India's objections as a good way to torpedo the treaty—insisted that the treaty should not enter into force without the support of three non-declared nuclear powers: India, Pakistan, and Israel.[73] With India and Iran refusing to cooperate, the Geneva negotiations collapsed in August. To circumvent this obstacle, the Australian government brought the test ban treaty directly to the United Nations for endorsement. Pro-test ban groups around the world feverishly pressed their nations to back the Australian resolution. And at a U.N. General Assembly session of September 10, the representatives approved it by a vote of 158 to 3, opening the way for the treaty's signature and ratification. Addressing the world body shortly after the vote, Madeleine Albright, U.S. ambassador to the United Nations, declared: "This was a treaty sought by ordinary people everywhere, and today the power of that universal wish could not be denied."[74]

The Downhill Slide, 1997-2000

Securing the test ban treaty proved to be the movement's last major victory for, beginning in 1997, nuclear arms control and disarmament policy began to unravel. The preconditions for this reverse course were set in previous years, and to a great extent reflected the movement's dwindling strength. But it also resulted from the rise of hawkish forces in Russia, France, India, and other nations, the low priority Clinton administration officials accorded to nuclear arms controls, and the conservative Republican dominance of the U.S. Congress that began with the 1994 elections. In addition, after 1996, Clinton himself bore significant responsibility. The sex scandals that engulfed him and his administration distracted Americans from issues of far greater magnitude and, furthermore, destroyed his ability to govern effectively. "Even as he survived," recalled Gergen, "Clinton could take little solace. He was the first president in history to testify before a grand jury as a target of a criminal investigation; the first president forced to make a humiliating confession of infidelity; the first while in office to have his sexual life graphically publicized; and the first elected president to be impeached."[75] The stage was set for policy reversals, and they followed inexorably.

Despite the talk of movement toward a nuclear-free world that had swirled about during the NPT and CTBT conferences, there was little sign of it in subsequent years. In November 1997, Clinton issued a Presidential

Decision Directive reaffirming that the United States would rely on nuclear weapons as a cornerstone of its national security policy for the "indefinite future." The directive called for maintaining the traditional U.S. triad of strategic nuclear forces: ICBMs, sea-launched ballistic missiles, and long-range strategic bombers. Furthermore, the U.S. government continued to develop and deploy "improved" nuclear weapons. Explaining U.S. policy, the new defense secretary, William Cohen, remarked: "The way we maintain deterrence is that we have a very strong deterrent."[76] Instead of eliminating nuclear weapons, the U.S. government scrapped its arms control and disarmament agency. Responding to pressure from Helms, chair of the Senate Foreign Relations Committee, to fold ACDA into the State Department, the administration agreed to the plan in April 1997, provided that Helms free up legislation to pay the U.S. debt to the United Nations. Although this arrangement fell through when the Republicans added anti-abortion provisions to the legislation, the agency was increasingly demoralized. By late 1998, ACDA's future was in such doubt that the administration finally agreed to GOP legislation ending the agency's independent existence, starting in April 1999.[77]

Meanwhile, the nuclear disarmament process ground to a halt. Despite the signing of the START II treaty in January 1993, no further strategic or other nuclear arms reductions followed. The Russian Duma—controlled by a hawkish bloc of Communists and rightwing nationalists and alienated by NATO expansion and Balkan wars—repeatedly refused to ratify START II. This served to preserve strategic nuclear arsenals at the higher levels agreed to in the 1991 START I treaty. Furthermore, as a result of U.S. government policy, the standstill over START II blocked the commencement of any formal negotiations for an agreement on further reductions through a START III treaty.[78] To be sure, in March 1997 Clinton and Yeltsin reached an accord at their Helsinki summit meeting on a START III "framework agreement" that could lead to reductions down to 2,000 to 2,500 strategic weapons. But they also concurred that formal negotiations on START III should await the Duma's ratification of START II. Finally, in April 2000, thanks in part to the efforts of Russia's new president, Vladimir Putin, the Duma did approve the START II pact. Even so, serious hurdles remained, for the Duma had agreed to a different version of the treaty, and its implementation was not scheduled for completion until 2007. Consequently, by the end of Clinton's term of office, each of the two nations still maintained roughly 6,000 strategic nuclear warheads, the number that had been agreed to under the 1991 START I treaty. Moreover, this was just the tip of the nuclear iceberg, for the two nations possessed a total of some 34,000 nuclear weapons, many of them on "hair-trigger alert"—a true doomsday machine, ready to be used.[79]

The crumbling of antinuclear policies was exemplified by the fate of the test ban treaty. Signed by more than 150 nations—the first of them the United States—the treaty was transmitted by Clinton to the U.S. Senate for ratification in September 1997. In October of that year, Sandy Berger, the White House national security advisor, presented a ratification strategy plan to top administration officials. Conceding that Republican attitudes ranged from indifference to opposition—indeed that the 1996 GOP platform had opposed the CTBT—he nonetheless argued that Senate ratification could be achieved within the next six to nine months. "Our greatest asset," he noted, "is the overwhelming support of the American people for the test ban," which the latest polls showed at 70 percent, "with only 12.5 percent opposed."[80] Clinton promised to make the treaty a top priority in 1998, and in his State of the Union address that January called for Senate approval of the treaty by the end of the year. Nevertheless, Helms refused to allow the Senate Foreign Relations Committee to hold hearings on the CTBT. Angered by this policy, Senator Joseph Biden, the ranking Democrat on the committee, attacked the "stealth campaign here to kill this treaty by not allowing it to come up."[81] But, facing a fight, the administration lost interest in promoting the treaty. When listing her legislative priorities, the new secretary of state, Madeleine Albright, failed to mention it. Clinton and White House staffers backed away from the issue, doubtless more concerned with the growing Monica Lewinsky scandal and the President's pending impeachment. Admiral Carroll of the Center for Defense Information recalled that there was "no pressure whatever from Clinton to move that thing forward." There was a total "lack of leadership" from the President. "He just let it vegetate."[82]

Determined to rescue the test ban treaty, U.S. antinuclear organizations vigorously promoted its Senate ratification. Although some antinuclear activists felt that the CTBT had been compromised by the administration's "stockpile stewardship" program,[83] all of the large, mainstream disarmament groups backed it, with the Coalition to Reduce Nuclear Dangers coordinating their campaign. Coalition leaders pressed Clinton to lead the fight for the treaty, conferred on the issue with administration officials, and strategized with sympathetic Senators.[84] They also worked hard to ignite popular support—producing large quantities of pro-test ban literature, generating pro-CTBT editorials in most of the nation's major newspapers, and mobilizing assorted constituencies.[85] By September 1998, they had lined up CTBT endorsements from hundreds of organizations. In addition to many peace groups, these included the African Methodist Episcopal Church, the American Association for the Advancement of Science, the American Baptist Churches, the American Jewish Congress, the American Physical Society, the Episcopal Church, Friends of the Earth, the League of Women Voters, the National Council of Churches, the Presbyterian Church, the Sierra Club, and the United Methodist Church. Although the public appears to have been less interested in the test ban issue than in the President's sex life, polls in May 1998 showed that 73 percent of Americans supported a test ban treaty— a fact that the Coalition trumpeted repeatedly.[86]

In 1999, the test ban issue came to a head. That January, the administration announced that it would make the treaty a priority, and Clinton again used his State of the Union address to champion treaty ratification. Administration officials, including the Joint Chiefs of Staff, expressed their full support for the CTBT, although, even at this late date, the administration had not put together the White House–directed public campaign that invariably accompanied treaty ratification efforts. Meanwhile, Democrats in the Senate, backing the CTBT, concluded that the time had come to force the issue on what they considered a popular measure. By raising it in the context of a forthcoming election, they felt, they could put enough pressure upon Republicans to split their ranks and secure treaty ratification.[87] As bottling up the treaty in the Senate Foreign Relations Committee was causing increasing embarrassment to the Republicans, Helms and GOP Senate Majority Leader Trent Lott decided upon a new strategy to kill it. They would bring the CTBT to the Senate floor and hold a quick vote upon it, thereby giving its supporters insufficient time to mobilize its broad but latent popular support. As a result, they scheduled a sudden Senate vote on the treaty that October. Although test ban supporters, caught off guard, worked desperately to mobilize popular pressure, Helms, Lott, and other opponents had more than enough votes in the Senate, with its Republican majority, to deny the treaty the necessary two-thirds ratification vote. In the end, all of the Democrats save one (who abstained), but only four of the Republicans, voted for the treaty, sending it down to defeat. Thus, the United States failed to join Britain, France, Russia, and other major powers in ratifying the CTBT.[88]

"This vote must not stand," declared the Council for a Livable World, and promised to work for another Senate vote on ratification "when there is more time for the facts and the arguments to be put before the American people." But, in the immediate future, the prospects were not good. The Republicans had apparently calculated that Americans no longer paid attention to such issues and, therefore, they would suffer no political repercussions.[89]

This proved to be correct. Indeed, rather than use the treaty's rejection to embarrass the Republicans in the forthcoming elections, Democratic strategists concluded that, in the interest of winning a future Senate ratification vote, it would be best to avoid making the CTBT a partisan issue. And so a nuclear test ban disappeared from the mainstream political agenda. Assessing the CTBT disaster a few years later, Daryl Kimball, the executive director of the Coalition to Reduce Nuclear Dangers, attributed it to the power of the political Right and its opposition to nuclear arms controls, to the Monica Lewinsky scandal and Clinton's overall inattention to the test ban, and to the drying up of mass, grassroots nuclear disarmament activism.[90] All appear to have played roles in sabotaging this historic nuclear arms control agreement.

The same downhill slide characterized the battle over National Missile Defense (NMD). By the mid-1990s, Republican support for this refurbished SDI program had hardened into a religious faith, which not even its dubious technological feasibility could shake. Most congressional Democrats and all disarmament groups viewed NMD as scientifically unsound, immensely costly, and likely to revive the nuclear arms race. Furthermore, the Republicans were unable to inspire much popular enthusiasm for it, or to get much political mileage out of charges made during the 1996 elections that, by rejecting NMD, the Democrats were betraying the nation's security. Nevertheless, the Clinton administration's compromising approach to the Republican Congress gradually led it to adopt elements of the GOP position. Although Clinton resisted the Republican call to scrap the ABM treaty, in 1996 he agreed to increase NMD funding, to develop a NMD program within three years, and to make a decision on deploying it within another three. Republicans continued to press for a more specific administration commitment and a broader program without success, though they did manage to increase funding for it.[91] Finally, in mid-March 1999, after the Senate completed the Clinton impeachment trial, the President ceased battling GOP plans for NMD, and both houses of congress endorsed its deployment by large margins. This was a remarkable outcome, for after forty years of effort, at a cost of $120 billion, the U.S. government was still far short of developing a workable missile defense. Indeed, U.S. anti-missile systems had failed fourteen of their last eighteen tests. Even so, Clinton—seeking to remove the issue from the 2000 election campaign—signed legislation that would permit the deployment of an NMD system "as soon as is technologically possible."[92]

But the movement managed to eke out a modest victory on missile defense. Thoroughly opposed to it, antinuclear groups made its defeat a key part of their political agenda.[93] Moreover, in the aftermath of the CTBT disaster, the Coalition to Reduce Nuclear Dangers focused the bulk of its energies and resources on a campaign to block NMD by postponing a decision to deploy it into the next administration. The Coalition's principal arguments were that the technological capability of the system could not be proven by the summer of 2000 (when Clinton had said he would make a deployment decision), that the cost was too high, and that the decision to deploy NMD would increase nuclear dangers thanks to its negative impact on arms reductions, non-proliferation objectives, and on U.S. relations with Russia, China, and U.S. allies. Assailing NMD as the dog that "won't hunt," Peace Action attacked it through its Peace Voter 2000 campaign, including anti-NMD ads on television and in newspapers.[94] The Council for a Livable World ran television ads against the system in selected cities, and worked with scientists, foreign policy specialists, and former government officials to publicize NMD's flaws. Leaders of the American Physical Society, the world's largest organization of physicists, joined with scientists from the FAS and the Union of Concerned Scientists in arguing that insufficient evidence existed to make a decision to deploy the NMD system. In addition, the UCS published an influential report showing the ineffectiveness of the proposed system against likely countermeasures, while the FAS put together an open letter to President Clinton from 50 Nobel laureates declaring that a missile defense system "would offer little protection and would do grave harm to this nation's core security interests."[95] Protest demonstrations occurred around the world. Finally, on September 1, 2000, Clinton announced that he would not authorize deployment of NMD, but would leave that decision to his successor.[96]

This victory, albeit a temporary one, could not compensate for the movement's ineffectuality when it came to restricting U.S. policy for the use of nuclear weapons. The Presidential Decision Directive of November 1997 had jettisoned the Reagan administration's 1981 directive that the U.S. government must be able to win a nuclear war. But Leon Sloss, the Pentagon official who had been the principal drafter of the Reagan directive, pointed out that "removing the idea of prevailing" in a nuclear war did "not change the substance very much," because winning "would have been nice, but it was never very realistic." A more significant feature of the Clinton directive was that, despite the demise of the Soviet threat, the United States continued its policy of being the first to employ nuclear arms in a conflict. Moreover, the new directive called for general planning for potential nuclear strikes against other nations that had what Robert Bell, the NSC's senior director for defense policy, called "prospective access" to nuclear weapons and that were then or might become hostile to the United States. It also extended the role of nuclear weapons to permit their use against nations possessing chemical and biological weapons and even against "non-state" actors. As Paul Warnke noted, this widened role for nuclear weapons was inconsistent with past U.S. pledges of restraint, including those made in connection with the 1995 NPT review conference.[97]

Almost universally, antinuclear leaders felt keenly frustrated by developments in the United States. Addressing a conference on nuclear weapons issues in November 2000, Forsberg charged that the U.S. government was failing to live up to the NPT, blocking implementation of the CTBT, building NMD, and scrapping the ABM treaty. Tom Cochran of the Natural Resources Defense Council maintained that "the whole arms control process" was "floundering." Although Jeremy Stone of the FAS was inclined to forgive the Clinton administration on the basis that it had "extremely little political capital,"[98] most antinuclear leaders were more critical. "What we've witnessed since '94 is basically the destruction of arms control under the Clinton administration," complained Chris Paine of the Natural Resources Defense Council. "It's not just Jesse Helms. It's Clinton. . . . Instead of fighting and making a principled case and carrying it to the public," he retreated from the fray and adopted the rhetoric of his opponents. Robert Musil of PSR agreed that "Clinton was not willing to lead." John Isaacs of the Council for a Livable World took an intermediate approach, as well as one that factored in the decline of popular pressure. "The American public moved away from arms control issues after the fall of the Soviet Union," he remarked. "And unfortunately President Clinton's advisors did the same thing. So, instead of taking advantage of an opportunity, they moved on to other issues and left behind a history of failed opportunity."[99]

Developments in Other Nations, 1997-2000

The direction of nuclear arms control and disarmament policy was more positive in some other nations, particularly in Europe. In the spring of 1997, election victories in Britain by the Labour Party and in France by the Socialist Party produced governments with a greater interest in halting the nuclear arms race than those of their conservative predecessors. Although Britain's new prime minister, Tony Blair, emphasized his "New Labour" credentials—which excluded Labour's erstwhile support for unilateral nuclear disarmament—he and a majority of his Cabinet members were either former or current members of CND. The new British foreign secretary, Robin Cook, had also been a leader of END. Consequently, they had a mordant view of nuclear weapons and immediately began studying options for changing British nuclear policy. Not surprisingly, both the British and French governments cut back their nuclear arsenals and quickly ratified the CTBT.[100] Similarly, the victory of the Social Democratic and Green parties in the September 1998 West German elections produced a more antinuclear government in that nation, as well. The new foreign secretary, Joschka Fischer of the Greens, floated the idea of dropping NATO's first-use policy. Leaders from all three governments spoke out against deployment of a missile defense system.[101] Former antinuclear activists also became the foreign secretaries of the Czech Republic, Greece, and Albania, thereby strengthening the ranks of policymakers calling for nuclear restraint.[102]

In a number of other nations, however, nuclear constraints were eroding. Despite some progress in implementing the Agreed Framework with North Korea, that country tested a new long-range ballistic missile in 1998. Meanwhile, with the assistance of outside suppliers, Iran and Iraq continued to pursue efforts to develop nuclear weapons. According to the United Nations, the Iraqi government's nuclear, chemical, and biological weapons programs were mostly dismantled by U.N. and IAEA weapons inspectors. But, at the end of 1998, Iraq's increasing non-cooperation led weapons inspectors to depart. In their absence, Iraq's nuclear weapons program may have resumed, though apparently in the absence of the fissionable materials necessary for a bomb.[103]

Moreover, in the world's second most powerful nuclear nation, Russia, there were a number of very adverse developments. Although the political decline of the Communist and rightwing nationalist parties facilitated the signing of the START II treaty, Russia's economic and military deterioration produced new dangers. With the marked decline of its conventional forces, the government relied increasingly on nuclear weapons for its national defense. Symptomatically, during the war in Chechnya, Russian government officials threatened to use nuclear weapons, as did the Chechens. Russia's slipshod nuclear reactors, leaking into the soil, the rivers, and the seas, provided not only a major source of radioactive contamination, but the possible basis for nuclear explosions and chain reactions. Furthermore, as the country's economy and government controls crumbled, its fissile materials, nuclear expertise, and tactical nuclear weapons constituted an increasingly likely source of nuclear proliferation. And with the gradual collapse of Russia's early warning system, the prospects grew for a mistaken, but automatic, launching of its thousands of strategic missiles, kept on hair-trigger alert.[104]

The most dramatic sign that the nuclear arms race was reviving came in

May 1998, when the Indian and Pakistani governments conducted nuclear weapons tests, thus becoming nuclear powers. The success of the rightwing, Hindu nationalist party, the BJP, in India's March 1998 elections set the stage. Since 1964 the BJP had favored making India a nuclear power but, with the exception of the short-lived coalition it headed up in 1995, it had not had the opportunity to implement its policy. Now the new prime minister, Atal Bihari Vajpayee, gave an immediate order for test preparations. After the first nuclear explosions rocked the test site at Pokhran on May 11, Indian crowds danced and sang in the streets. Vajpayee proclaimed that the tests would "silence India's enemies and show India's strength," for "we have a big bomb now." Most Indian newspapers celebrated India's "great" achievement, and Hindu fundamentalist supporters of the BJP promised to carry the dust from the test site all over the nation. Pakistanis, who viewed themselves as the targets for India's new weapons, were considerably less enthusiastic, and demands immediately arose to stand up to India by testing Pakistan's nuclear weapons. Leading pro-testing demonstrations, former prime minister Benazir Bhutto removed the glass bracelets worn by South Asian women to symbolize effeminacy and flung them into the crowd, urging it to tell Prime Minister Nawaz Sharif "to put these on." A few days later, with Sharif vowing to prevent India's "nuclear domination," Pakistan detonated its own nuclear weapons.[105]

Despite the nationalist appeal of "going nuclear," many Indians and Pakistanis expressed their dismay. Although a May 1998 poll in India showed 91 percent support for the tests, another that October—after the public had a chance to reflect upon the fact that it was now threatened by Pakistani nuclear weapons—revealed that support had dropped to 44 percent. In November, the BJP suffered serious election defeats in four states, where onion prices apparently meant more to voters than national glory. Small antinuclear demonstrations occurred in Indian cities, assailing the nuclear tests as a moral calamity and as a scandalous diversion of resources in an impoverished nation. In Pakistan, too, nuclear weapons opponents protested the escalating arms race. In the aftermath of the Indian tests, demonstrators marched through the streets of Islamabad carrying signs reading: "Schools Not Bombs" and "Pakistan: Respond With Restraint." A coalition of twelve Pakistani peace and human rights groups called upon their government to "renounce the path of nuclearization." In India, scientists publicly condemned the nuclear tests, and the opposition parties began leveling sharp questions and criticisms at the prime minister.[106] New antinuclear coalitions formed in both nations. The Pakistan Action Committee Against the Nuclear Arms Race excoriated the "jingoistic rhetoric of the nuclear lobbies," proclaiming that "it is high time the peoples of South Asia . . . forced their governments to publicly announce the renunciation of nuclear tests and production of nuclear weapons and missiles." The Movement in India for Nuclear Disarmament declared that "the club of nuclear weapons-states has always been a collection of hypocrites," and "India has now put in its application for joining this club." It was "imperative that India return sincerely, seriously and energetically to the nuclear disarmament agenda. Our real security lies in a world free of nuclear weapons."[107]

Appalled by the growth of the nuclear club, as well as by the overall lack of progress toward nuclear disarmament, the foreign ministers of Brazil, Egypt, Ireland, Mexico, New Zealand, Slovenia, South Africa, and Sweden issued a joint declaration, "Towards a Nuclear Weapon-Free World," on June 9, 1998. Known as the New Agenda Coalition (NAC), this group of middle powers called on the nuclear and nuclear-capable states "to commit themselves unequivocally to the elimination of their respective nuclear weapons and nuclear weapons capability and to agree to start work immediately on the practical steps and negotiations required for its achievement." That October, the NAC—reduced to seven nations thanks to NATO pressure upon tiny Slovenia—introduced a resolution at the U.N. General Assembly incorporating its nuclear abolition program. Though strongly opposed by the nuclear powers, the resolution carried that December by a vote of 114 to 18, with 38 abstentions. In a major blow to the United States, numerous nations allied with it abstained, including Australia, Japan, and all of NATO's non-nuclear states except Turkey. Under renewed pressure from the NAC, the General Assembly passed another resolution in December 1999 that called upon the nuclear powers to "make an unequivocal undertaking to accomplish the speedy and total elimination of their nuclear arsenals and to engage without delay in an accelerated process of negotiations, thus achieving nuclear disarmament to which they are committed under . . . the NPT."[108]

This gathering revolt by non-nuclear nations against the nuclear powers fed into an unusually firm antinuclear stand taken by the world's governments at the NPT review conference of April–May 2000. Under strong pressure from the non-nuclear nations, the conferees agreed to take thirteen "practical steps" to implement the provisions of the treaty. Among them were an "unequivocal undertaking by the nuclear weapons states to accomplish the total elimination of their nuclear arsenals"—language demanded by the New Agenda Coalition—the implementation of START II, the conclusion of START III "as soon as possible," and the preservation and strengthening of the ABM treaty. The NPT conference also resolved to support the CTBT, emphasizing "the importance and urgency of signatures and ratifications."[109] Hailing the agreement, Kofi Annan, U.N. secretary general, called it "a significant step forward in humanity's pursuit of a world free of nuclear dangers." Nuclear disarmament groups, by contrast, tended to downplay the significance of commitment to nuclear abolition by the nuclear powers, for they were well aware of the flouting of past commitments under the NPT. "My radio says that the Big 5 have agreed to get rid of their nuclear weapons," remarked Bruce Kent. "I await to read the small print with great interest and some skepticism."[110] And, in fact, nuclear abolition made little headway in subsequent years.

The Movement Continues, 1997-2000

Despite these setbacks, the antinuclear movement persisted. In Norway, No to Nuclear Weapons continued to leaflet, to publish its newspaper, and to promote the idea of nuclear abolition.[111] In Canada, a Canadian Network to Abolish Nuclear Weapons grew to seventeen national member groups and over ninety endorsing organizations. Meanwhile, the leaders of nineteen Canadian religious denominations wrote to the prime minister, calling for immediate action on a nuclear weapons convention, the de-alerting of nuclear weapons, and a commitment to a no first-use policy.[112] In Japan, both Gensuikyo and Gensuikin continued their antinuclear agitation, and protests erupted against Indian nuclear testing.[113] In Sweden, Women for Peace organized a seminar on disarmament and promoted the work of the Abolition 2000 campaign.[114] In Britain, CND persisted with a broad range of nuclear disarmament activities—providing media briefings, producing educational materials, erecting billboards, placing advertisements, lobbying members of parliament, and working with sympathetic groups like the National Union of Students. In addition, women's "peace camps" continued to protest nuclear and other military activities at sites in Aldermaston, Burghfield, Sellafield, and Menwith Hill.[115]

In the United States, as well, movement agitation continued. Protesting the Indian and Pakistani nuclear tests and demanding ratification of the CTBT, Peace Action put together demonstrations and rallies at the home offices of eighteen U.S. senators, and organized two rallies in Washington, highlighted by the appearance of eight giant missiles staging a futile "arms race" down Massachusetts Avenue. The Lawyers Alliance for World Security worked for deep cuts in nuclear weapons programs and to establish a policy of no first-use, while the Center for Defense Information produced new research and educational materials critical of nuclear weapons programs.[116] The FAS called for pressing ahead to START III and continued to churn out ingenious proposals for defusing nuclear confrontation.[117] General Butler and Jonathan Schell delivered numerous speeches designed to stir up abolitionist sentiment, and Helen Caldicott returned to the United States to agitate against the Bomb, determined to destroy the nuclear monster before it consumed the world.[118] In June 1997, the National Academy of Sciences urged the U.S. government to take immediate action to reduce the risks of nuclear war and to move toward the worldwide prohibition of nuclear weapons. Dozens of cities and towns passed resolutions in favor of nuclear abolition. The following year, nearly a hundred Catholic bishops signed a statement, issued by Pax Christi, claiming that "nuclear deterrence as a national policy must be condemned as morally abhorrent," and urging everyone "to join in taking up the challenge to begin the effort to eliminate nuclear weapons now."[119] In 1999, some of the country's major peace groups— including Peace Action, PSR, and WAND—joined in a coalition venture, Project Abolition. By bringing the demand for nuclear disarmament to civil society groups, they hoped to move public policy in this direction.[120]

The movement also drew upon the latest "information age" technology. Via the internet, antinuclear groups communicated rapidly regarding a range of nuclear weapons issues, from nuclear testing to proposals for nuclear disarmament. They also established attractive organizational web sites, providing activists with information on the latest political developments and interested outsiders with a better sense of what antinuclear groups existed, what they did, and how to join them. In addition, international organizations like IPPNW stayed in touch with their scattered chapters and activists through e-mail. The antinuclear campaign's global consciousness and solidarity clearly benefited from the new ease and speed of electronic communications.[121]

But there was no hiding the fact that the movement was also in decline. Although the memberships of a few organizations grew slightly,[122] for the most part they continued to fall during these years. Young people, particularly, failed to join nuclear disarmament groups, and there was a noticeable graying of their membership. CND, which once had mobilized many thousands of the restless young, no longer had a youth section by 1998.[123] Furthermore, even among the members, there was markedly less participation, with minimal attendance at movement events. Mass demonstrations became relics of the past, while meetings grew smaller. In June 1998, when Maine Peace Action kicked off its "Town Meeting" campaign toward nuclear abolition with a public gathering in Portland, featuring a speech by Schell, only ninety people attended the event. "American democracy is rotting from within," concluded Chris Paine. Americans lived in "virtual communities," he remarked gloomily, and spent their time commiserating with one another by e-mail, rather that joining together to influence their government. In addition, many peace and disarmament groups spread themselves quite thin, responding to concerns ranging from the war in Kosovo, to landmines, to the slaughter in East Timor. In these circumstances, there was sometimes little energy to spare for the antinuclear campaign.[124] Nor, in some countries, did the demand for nuclear abolition have much connection with the emerging political reality. In the United States, at least, the antinuclear battle that did rage focused on intermediate issues: nuclear testing, national missile defense, and the START process. By contrast, Project Abolition never got very far.[125]

In spite of these difficulties, the movement did maintain its international presence. By October 1998, the IPB had 186 member groups in over 40 countries.[126] Working with three other international organizations—IPPNW, the International Association of Lawyers Against Nuclear Arms, and the World Federalist Movement—the IPB convened an international gathering in May 1999 to mark the centennial of the Hague peace conference of 1899. This Hague Appeal for Peace meeting was a remarkable event, for it drew ten thousand people from over a hundred countries to discuss the establishment of world peace, including nuclear disarmament. Among the participants were Nobel Prize winners, the secretary general of the United Nations, and even some national government officials.[127] Other international groups, as well, were far from defunct. By the time of the Hague conference, IPPNW had members in 64 countries, including all the nuclear weapons states. In 1997, it drafted a treaty for the abolition of nuclear weapons, which was introduced thereafter into the U.N. General Assembly.[128] Meanwhile, the Abolition 2000 movement continued to grow. By the year 2000, it had spread around the world, with more than 2,000 member groups. That April, it presented the president of the NPT review conference with an abolition petition it had circulated, signed by more than 13.4 million people.[129] Influential individuals added their voices to the international campaign. In January 1998, some 120 former national leaders from 48 countries—including Jimmy Carter, Mikhail Gorbachev, Helmut Schmidt, and Pierre Trudeau—issued an appeal for the abolition of nuclear weapons.[130]

Yet, like the national groups, the international antinuclear campaign had serious weaknesses. With their national organizations losing members, international organizations lost them, too, plus the human and financial resources they provided. Symptomatically, despite the impressive size and universality of the Hague conference, the IPB remained a rather weak organization, sometimes teetering on the brink of bankruptcy. It was also more of a networking than a coordinating body, with little power to implement its wide-ranging priorities.[131] Much the same was true of Abolition 2000, which, despite its impressive breadth, lacked a strong central organization or even much knowledge about what its constituent groups were doing. Furthermore, the international antinuclear campaign faced the same problem as did national campaigns when it stretched its limited resources to cover a broad array of activities. "Disarmament and Human Security" served as only one of four foci for the Hague conference, and measures for nuclear disarmament provided an even smaller proportion of the conference's action proposals. Abolition 2000, of course, focused exclusively on the nuclear disarmament issue. But the same could not be said of its endorsing groups, many of which were national and local peace organizations. "We're becoming large, but it appears that the support may be thin," remarked David Krieger, one of Abolition 2000's top leaders. "A lot of groups have signed on," but "their actions are not really going deep."[132]

Of course, the movement still influenced public policy on occasion. In December 1997, at the instigation of the Canadian Network to Abolish Nuclear Weapons, Douglas Roche, a Canadian senator and former disarmament ambassador to the U.N., began to form a network of leading international citizens' organizations, which came to be known as the Middle Powers Initiative (MPI). Drawing together IPPNW, IALANA, INES, the IPB, and other disarmament groups, the MPI sought to mobilize influential middle-power nations to commit themselves to immediate practical steps to reduce nuclear dangers—including a no first-use policy and the de-alerting of nuclear forces—and to the abolition of nuclear weapons. When the New Agenda Coalition burst on the scene in June 1998, it had had no official contact with the MPI. But its program was virtually identical, and after Roche met with the officials in the Irish and Swedish foreign ministries, the two groups began a close relationship. This proved important, for the MPI, bolstered by groups like Abolition 2000, brought citizen pressure to bear upon governments around the world—particularly in NATO nations—that helped secure passage of the NAC resolutions at the United Nations.[133] Furthermore, a campaign by Canada's Project Ploughshares helped to mobilize the Canadian foreign ministry behind a proposal for NATO to adopt a no first-use policy. Together with the work of the U.S. Lawyers Alliance for World Security, this facilitated the forging of a German-Canadian bloc within NATO that insisted upon a re-examination of the alliance's nuclear strategy.[134]

Recognizing that nuclear disarmament groups retained some influence in their own countries and in world affairs—either current or potential—some governments maintained a close relationship with them. The Norwegian foreign ministry funded about a quarter of the $100,000 annual budget of No to Nuclear Weapons. Even that country's defense ministry worked cooperatively with the antinuclear group, holding joint seminars with it. In 1998, the Swedish ambassador to the U.N. Conference on Disarmament in Geneva invited several dozen representatives of disarmament groups to his residence and fervently appealed to them to keep up the battle for nuclear disarmament.[135] The following year, the Dutch and Swedish governments put substantial funding into the Hague Appeal for Peace conference. Addressing a plenary session at the Hague gathering, Lena Hjelm-Wallem, the deputy prime minister of Sweden, warned of a slowdown in the nuclear disarmament process, the stalemate over START II, and the breakdown of the nuclear nonproliferation regime. Emphasizing the importance of the NAC's U.N. resolution, she called upon citizens' groups to influence their governments and to foster the "mobilization of public opinion." She argued that "political pressure is vital to create a nuclear weapon-free world."[136]

But the movement no longer had much effect upon the overall situation. By the year 2000, the CTBT was stalemated, the ABM treaty was threatened by plans for national missile defense, nuclear proliferation was growing, and there was little sign of nuclear abolition, either then or in the future. "Things are worse now by orders of magnitude," remarked Caldicott, on one of her barnstorming tours of the United States. "My government wants to open up a hundred uranium mines. I just can't believe they keep making more of this waste. And the bombs are still there," still "on a hair-trigger alert."[137] Even in a country like Britain, where most leaders of the Labour government had once belonged to CND, public policy toward nuclear weapons remained stalemated, without any impetus toward divesting the nation of its nuclear submarines, much less toward creating a nuclear-free world. William Peden, CND's director of parliamentary affairs, attributed it to a fear by the Labour government that, if it reverted to its uncompromisingly antinuclear policies of the past, it would suffer political defeat. Hugh Jenkins, a former CND chair, thought Labour's restraint resulted from its unwillingness to challenge the lead of the U.S. government.[138] Whatever the reason, however, CND was too weak to turn this situation around. Indeed, here and in most parts of the world, the political balance had tipped against the movement.

Public Opinion, 1997-2000

Ironically, nuclear disarmament remained popular with the public. A poll released in March 1998 showed that 92 percent of Canadians favored their country playing a leadership role in promoting an international ban on nuclear weapons. Other polls indicated that 87 percent of Americans, 72 percent of Belgians, 87 percent of Britons, 87 percent of Germans, and 92 percent of Norwegians supported a nuclear weapons ban. Asked by pollsters in the fall of 1998 whether countries that possessed nuclear weapons should completely destroy them or keep them to protect themselves, 61 percent of Russians and 78 percent of Japanese favored destroying them.[139] Other polls revealed similar antinuclear sentiments. A survey of Americans in September 1997 found that 66 percent favored de-alerting nuclear forces, 77 percent thought the world would be safer without nuclear weapons, and 80 percent supported the elimination of nuclear weapons through a verifiable and enforceable international agreement. Only 15 percent favored building new or better nuclear weapons.[140] As in the past, polls found that higher percentages of women favored nuclear disarmament than did men.[141]

But these opinions had limited salience. Polls from August through November 1998 found that only 2 to 3 percent of Americans rated "Peace/world peace/nuclear arms" as one of the two most important issues for the nation to address. Far higher percentages were concerned about education, taxes, the Clinton sex scandal, health care, and crime. Given the mass media's failure to adequately cover nuclear arms control and disarmament issues, Americans remained largely ignorant of them. A Gallup poll taken a week after the U.S. Senate voted to defeat the CTBT found that, although most Americans supported the treaty, 34 percent had never heard of it and only 26 percent knew that the Senate had rejected it.[142] This same lack of focus upon nuclear issues, of course, cut the other way as well. In India, where surveys reported popular support for nuclear tests, a poll in May 1998 found that the development of nuclear weapons was ranked as a top priority by only 6 percent of Indian respondents, below nine other items, ranging from population control (19 percent) to water projects (7 percent). From the standpoint of fostering nuclear disarmament, though, the problem of public complacency was more serious. "People aren't worried about these issues," concluded John Isaacs. "There are a lot of reasons why people should be worried, but they aren't."[143] And, inevitably, this undermined the antinuclear campaign.

Reviving the Nuclear Arms Race, 2000-2002

Movement weakness, public indifference, and political regression were all evident in the U.S. elections of 2000. For the most part, nuclear disarmament did not come up as an issue. When references to nuclear weapons occurred, they were usually in the context of discussions of national missile defense. And even this subject failed to arise during the four presidential and vice presidential debates. In their vast advertising campaigns, the congressional and presidential candidates focused on domestic concerns. Only for more specialized audiences did the two major presidential candidates bother to outline their views. George W. Bush, the Republican, called for the building of a national missile defense system "at the earliest possible date," promised to withdraw from the ABM treaty if Russia did not sanction U.S. deployment of NMD, condemned the CTBT as "not verifiable" and "not enforceable," and suggested that U.S. strategic nuclear weapons could be cut below START II levels. Bush advisor Condoleeza Rice said that the GOP candidate was "reserving judgement" as to the development of new nuclear weapons. Al Gore, the Democrat, supported Clinton's stand on building a smaller missile defense system and delaying a decision on NMD deployment, promised to work for the ratification of the CTBT, hedged on the ABM treaty, and backed negotiated reductions in Soviet and U.S. strategic forces to the levels agreed to in 1997. Disarmament activists had a low visibility in the election, although the Council for a Livable World did raise over a million dollars for Senate and House candidates. Despite the fact that Gore outpolled Bush in the nation and in the contested state of Florida, the Supreme Court gave the GOP candidate the presidency and the Republicans retained their control over both houses of Congress.[144]

Within a short time, the victorious Republicans set about scrapping nuclear constraints. Jettisoning the CTBT, they pressed forward instead with plans for national missile defense, the system they believed would guarantee U.S. security and, thus, make arms controls unnecessary—at least for the United States. Their operations received an unexpected setback when a change in party affiliation by one member of the U.S. Senate gave control of that body to the Democrats and put key Senate committees under the direction of arms control-oriented legislators. But the terrorist attacks of September 11, 2001, reversed the situation once again. With the nation swept up in a patriotic frenzy, Bush found it remarkably easy to sharply increase the Pentagon budget and cast aside arms control treaties. On December 13, he gave Russia notice that the United States was withdrawing from the ABM treaty to clear the way for U.S. tests of missile defense plans. Playing upon national fears, the President insisted that this withdrawal was necessary because the ABM treaty "hinders our government's ability to develop ways to protect our people from future terrorist or rogue-state missile attacks." Abandoning the ABM treaty also destroyed START II, as the version of that treaty ratified by the Duma was based on ABM treaty protocols. Schell noted glumly that, out of all the nuclear arms control agreements, only the NPT seemed safe. And that was because "it has never managed to put any constraints on US behavior. Its raison d'être in the eyes of the United States has always been to constrain . . . the 182 nations that have agreed to forgo nuclear weapons."[145]

The Bush administration's heavy reliance upon nuclear weapons was illustrated by its Nuclear Posture Review. Submitted to Congress in January 2002, this Pentagon-prepared document ignored the U.S. commitment, at the NPT conference of 2000, to eliminate nuclear weapons. Instead, based on the assumption that nuclear weapons would be part of U.S. military forces for at least the next half-century, it outlined an extensive range of programs to sustain and modernize America's existing nuclear arsenal. It also outlined plans to develop a new ICBM, a new sea-launched ballistic missile, a new heavy bomber, new nuclear warheads, and smaller nuclear weapons for use in battlefield situations. These weapons would "assure allies and friends," "dissuade competitors," "deter aggressors," and "defeat enemies." Although the Bush administration had the "goal" of decreasing U.S. "operationally deployed weapons," it would warehouse the remainder, thus giving it the ability to deploy as many as 5,000 strategic nuclear warheads within a reasonably short time. Meanwhile, it would reinvigorate the U.S. nuclear weapons production complex. Furthermore, the posture review called for drafting contingency plans for nuclear attacks upon China, Iran, Iraq, Libya, North Korea, Russia, and Syria. As most of these countries did not possess nuclear weapons, the nuclear posture review provided a further indication of the growing willingness of U.S. officials to initiate nuclear war against non-nuclear nations.[146]

Thus, although the U.S. and Russian governments signed a Strategic Offensive Reductions Treaty in May 2002, the nuclear arms control provisions were modest, indeed. It provided for reducing the number of deployed strategic nuclear warheads by almost two-thirds by the year of its complete implementation: 2012. But, under the treaty, the warheads could simply be placed in storage, thus enabling the two nations to reconstitute their previous nuclear arsenals fairly quickly. Furthermore, the warheads that remained deployed could be upgraded and improved, and there were no treaty provisions dealing with the large number of tactical nuclear weapons. According to Jack Mendelsohn, a former member of the U.S. SALT and START negotiating teams, the treaty "only marginally affects the residual nuclear potential of the United States and Russia." In addition, thanks to its absence of inspection procedures, "it creates thousands of 'phantom warheads,' undercutting its own verifiability, and contains no reduction schedule, making it difficult to predict force levels over the next decade." Commenting on the treaty, Strobe Talbott, who served as deputy secretary of state during the Clinton years, welcomed it for keeping the nuclear arms control process alive, but feared its lack of serious disarmament provisions would encourage frustrated non-nuclear nations to go nuclear.[147]

Certainly, the picture did not appear particularly bright. As tensions heightened between India and Pakistan, with both countries preparing for a military showdown on their border, they worked feverishly to develop their nuclear weaponry. By 2002, the Indian government was not only expanding the number of nuclear warheads it possessed, but working to develop new missiles and—like the United States—a complete triad of nuclear delivery systems.[148] Iraq continued to block weapons inspections, while North Korea worked secretly to develop nuclear weapons.[149] Nor, in European nations, did the decline of Social Democratic parties, which above all others had supported nuclear arms controls, and the rising strength of rightwing, nationalist parties augur well for limitations on nuclear weapons in these countries. The nuclear powers, particularly, seemed hostile to nuclear disarmament. During 2001 the U.S. government led the way in opposing nuclear disarmament resolutions at the United Nations, and most of the other nuclear nations were not far behind. The possibility that the Iraqi government was developing nuclear weapons could have reinvigorated efforts to curb nuclear proliferation through strengthening the international arms control and disarmament regime. But the Bush administration's response was to mobilize for war. In 2002, the *Bulletin of the Atomic Scientists* moved the hands of its "doomsday clock" forward to 7 minutes to midnight—the same setting as at the clock's inception, in 1947.[150]

In many nations, the antinuclear movement persisted. As the nuclear situation deteriorated, some groups began to grow once again and to focus more sharply on nuclear issues. PSR added new members, and devoted greater attention and resources to challenging the nuclear arms race. It revived the "bombing run" and encouraged the placement of stories in medical journals on the effects of nuclear war. Although the Coalition to Reduce Nuclear Dangers formally dissolved in December 2001, thanks to a cutoff in foundation funding, representatives of its constituent groups continued to meet in a working group and to discuss how to counter what they saw as an emerging crisis. In June of 2002, three veterans of the antinuclear struggle—Cortright, Forsberg, and Schell—launched a petition campaign around "An Urgent Call to End the Nuclear Danger," with hopes to draw a million signers, secure funding for antinuclear ads, and affect forthcoming elections. "The bomb is back," noted Schell, "but those of us who oppose the bomb are back, too. And we're not going away." Even so, the immediate prospects for the movement in the United States and other nations did not look promising.[151]

Overall, then, the unraveling of nuclear arms control and disarmament policies in the years after 1993—despite the absence of the Cold War or other major conflicts among the great powers—underscored the degree to which progress in controlling nuclear weapons was dependent upon mobilizing public opposition to them. With this mobilization, nations made headway toward a nuclear-free world. Without it, national governments reverted to their traditional policies of seeking national security through military might. And the result of the latter was a nuclear arms race, with the ever-present danger of nuclear war.

Conclusion

Reflections on the
Past and the Future

> We are not doomed to endless bloodletting. . . . The
> challenge for all . . . is to build the structures within
> which our global community can resolve its differences.
> Bruce Kent, 1999

This study—like its predecessors—indicates that the nuclear arms control
and disarmament measures of the modern era have resulted primarily from
the efforts of a worldwide citizens' campaign, the biggest mass movement
in modern history. Admittedly, this citizens' antinuclear crusade was un-
even—stronger in some countries than in others, addressing a variety of national circumstances, and emphasizing priorities that differed from region to
region. It was also rather structurally underdeveloped, drawing upon a shifting multiplicity of organizations. But, in the context of an escalating nuclear
arms race, it had enough strength and cohesion to mobilize key institutions
within civil society: professional associations, unions, religious bodies, and
political parties. Even within Communist-ruled Eastern Europe, where civil
society barely existed, it emerged as a force to be reckoned with—challenging dictatorial regimes and, ultimately, helping to sweep them away. At
the core of the movement lay the educated middle class, and particularly the
liberal intelligentsia. At its periphery, the general public, which, by and
large, agreed with the movement's critique of the nuclear arms race and its
demand for nuclear disarmament. Thus, at an exceptionally dangerous junc-
ture in modern history, when numerous governments scrambled to build nuclear weapons and threatened to employ them for purposes of annihilation,
concerned citizens played a central role in curbing the nuclear arms race
and preventing nuclear war.

Furthermore, this book indicates that most government officials—and particularly those of the major powers—had no intention of adopting nuclear arms control and disarmament policies. Instead, they grudgingly accepted such policies thanks to the emergence of popular pressure. To be sure, a small group of government officials—among them Olof Palme, Andreas Papandreou, Rajiv Gandhi, and Mikhail Gorbachev—did not need pressuring. They welcomed the antinuclear movement, either because they already shared its perspective or found its arguments convincing. But most officials had a more negative view of the nuclear disarmament campaign, for it challenged their reliance upon nuclear weapons to foster national security. And yet they could not ignore the movement, either, particularly when it reached high tide. Confronted by a vast wave of popular resistance, they concluded, reluctantly, that compromise had become the price of political survival. Consequently, they began to adapt their rhetoric and policies to the movement's program. Within a relatively short time, they replaced ambitious plans to build, deploy, and use nuclear weapons with policies of nuclear disarmament and nuclear restraint. Most of this was accomplished, it should be noted, *before* the disappearance of the Soviet Union. Thereafter, when the antinuclear movement waned, the nuclear arms race resumed.

Some readers may find this explanation of events rather startling. After all, within Western nations—and particularly the United States—it is a commonplace that the U.S. nuclear buildup of the early 1980s was responsible for the arms control and disarmament measures that followed. Former U.S. Secretary of State George Shultz has argued: "When our country's military strength was built up to a point where our Soviet rivals recognized that they could not match us, when they perceived that we might actually use our strength to repel aggression . . . then came the turning point." His successor, James Baker III, insisted that Presidents Reagan and Bush "and all of us . . . are firmly convinced . . . that peace through strength . . . is what has kept the peace."[1] Campaigning for the Presidency in 1992, Bush argued that he and Reagan had championed "'peace through strength,' and it worked." In early 1990, to be sure, Reagan emphasized "mutual interest" as the crucial factor behind U.S.-Soviet weapons agreements, including his own belief that "it was a danger to have a world so heavily armed that one misstep could trigger a great war." But, later that year, when his memoirs appeared, they too emphasized "peace through strength."[2]

It is not difficult to see why this line of thought has come to the fore. Chalking up a great overseas victory for U.S. military power plays well among Americans, and especially among ardent nationalists—people who like to wave flags, pledge allegiance, and sing "God Bless America." And what could be more useful, from a political standpoint, than to appear as the grand architect of this national triumph? Against this backdrop, Bush's claims during the 1992 campaign that he had "won the Cold War" are perfectly understandable, even though, as Bill Clinton rejoindered, Bush was behaving like "the rooster who took credit for the dawn."[3] Furthermore, the peace through strength explanation feeds upon the common fallacy of *post hoc, ergo propter hoc*—that because B followed A, it was *caused* by A. This is an appealing but warped logic. If one accepted it, one could as easily believe that the advice from Nancy Reagan's astrologer—put into effect by the President at the signing of the INF Treaty—*caused* this historic disarmament agreement. Amid a fog of nationalist celebration and muddled thinking, pundits have not bothered to ask about the evidence for the triumphalist interpretation; and, in fact, none has been forthcoming.

If the triumphalist explanation were to be bolstered by evidence, it should include admissions by Soviet officials that U.S. "strength" caused them to withdraw from the nuclear arms race. After all, their motives are central to this interpretation of events. But, in fact, Soviet officials have strongly denied that their "new thinking" reflected U.S. military pressure. Asked if the U.S. government's hard line forced the Soviet government into a more conciliatory posture, Aleksandr Yakovlev replied: "It played no role. None. I can tell you with the fullest responsibility. Gorbachev and I were ready for changes in our policy regardless of whether the American President was Reagan, or Kennedy, or someone more liberal." Georgi Arbatov called the idea that the U.S. military buildup helped alter Soviet policy "absolute nonsense." Soviet changes "not only ripened inside the country but originated within it." Writing in his memoirs, Anatoly Dobrynin *did* give the U.S. government some credit, but not for its "strength." If Reagan "had not abandoned his hostile stance toward the Soviet Union," observed the veteran Soviet diplomat, "Gorbachev would not have been able to launch his reforms and his 'new thinking.' Quite the contrary, Gorbachev would have been forced to continue the conservative foreign and domestic policies of his predecessors." Asked about Bush's 1992 claims that the Soviet Union had simply crumpled before U.S. military might, Gorbachev responded: "I suppose these are necessary things in a campaign. But if this idea is serious, then it is a very big delusion."[4]

Overall, citizen activism for nuclear disarmament provides not only a more accurate explanation of events than does military triumph, but a more heartening one, as well. Of course, most government leaders find it embarrassing, for it reveals them not as steely eyed, self-confident shapers of national destiny, but as beleaguered, apprehensive officials, giving way to the demands of a restive public. This is not their preferred image of themselves. And it is certainly not the image they wish to convey to "enemy" nations—nations, they remain convinced, that are eagerly awaiting signs of "weakness" before commencing assaults upon the national ramparts. Nevertheless, persons farther from the centers of national power should take some satisfaction that, even within the closely guarded realm of "national security," citizen activism—which might be considered the highest form of democracy—has some impact. More broadly, there is good news in the fact that, when it comes to nuclear weapons and nuclear war, the human race has shown the good sense, intelligence, and ability to avoid destroying itself.

There is also some bad news: the nuclear arms race continues, with no sign that the Bomb is about to be banned. Despite the herculean efforts of its critics and the popularity of their critique, more than 30,000 nuclear weapons remain in existence. Thousands of them remain on alert, ready to massacre hundreds of millions of men, women, and children and turn what is left of the earth into a radioactive wasteland. In the midst of worldwide recognition that nuclear war means planetary doom, this is a remarkable anomaly—and one that must be confronted. As Eduard Shevardnadze wrote in 1991: "Surely there is not a single intelligent person on the globe who would not understand that nuclear weapons threaten mankind with annihilation." And this leads to an "unavoidable question: Why is it that to this day, people whose intellect cannot be questioned have not come to the only intelligent decision, to destroy this means of universal suicide?"[5]

The answer to this question lies in the pathology of the nation-state system. With no higher authority to set guidelines for national behavior or to resolve international disputes, nations traditionally have resorted to wars to secure their "national interests." Because great powers have fared better than smaller powers in these military conflicts, they usually have embraced wars more enthusiastically. Of course, non-state actors—criminals, terrorists, and revolutionaries—also have resorted to violence, but their capacity for mass killing has always paled beside that of the nation-state. To enhance the prospect of victory or merely to intimidate rival nations, national officials have drawn upon the most lethal weapons available to them. Since the 1940s, these have been nuclear weapons. Although antinuclear groups have argued that nuclear weapons are not weapons at all, but simply instruments of suicide, most national leaders *do* consider them weapons of war. And war is what they are preparing for in a world of rival nation-states. In this context, most national officials—particularly those charged with safeguarding "national security"—view disarmament, and especially nuclear disarmament, as an unnatural act. As U.N. Secretary General Kofi Annan put it, in his characteristically tactful fashion: "In a world where states continue to compete for power, disarmament does not get proper scrutiny."[6]

Furthermore, there is a substantial public constituency that military-oriented officials have been able to tap for support. Probably its most significant component is composed of nationalists or, as they would term themselves, patriots. Nationalism, of course, has been and remains a very powerful force on the world scene. Indeed, even many persons apprehensive about the Bomb also have been wary of limitations on their own nation's power or sovereignty. And yet, arms control and disarmament require such limitations. Thus, nationalists often oppose nuclear restraints for, in their view, the national interest trumps the human interest. This group supplements and sometimes overlaps with another, motivated by a profoundly pessimistic, Augustinian view of human nature. Often drawn from fundamentalist religious groups and conservative parties, its members are zealous believers in curbing individual "sin" through punishment and national misbehavior through war. Indeed, war—including nuclear war—is often considered inevitable, given the wickedness of human nature and the necessity for an expression of God's wrath. Together with defense contractors and the armed forces, the believers in national glory and irremediable human wickedness provide national security officials with useful political leverage.

Given the tension between the widespread desire for nuclear disarmament and the national security priorities of the nation-state and its admirers, nuclear policy usually has proved a rough compromise, unsatisfactory to either the nuclear enthusiast or critic. Often it takes the form of arms control, which regulates or stabilizes the arms race rather than bringing it to an end. The same tension often produces an ambiguous policy, with officials claiming that they favor nuclear disarmament while fostering the development of nuclear weapons or tacitly condoning the nuclear arsenals of their allies. Sometimes, of course, the balance of forces tips decisively and—based upon which side has attained the upper hand—there will be either a surge in the nuclear arms race or a tilt toward nuclear disarmament. But, from the standpoint of abolishing nuclear weapons, the crucial fact remains that the location of the Bomb within the nation-state system—a system that throughout its history has produced arms races and wars—has set limits on progress toward a nuclear-free world.

Another problem for the antinuclear campaign lies in its own internal dynamic. As the three volumes of this study make clear, when the nuclear menace has become particularly grave, the nuclear disarmament movement has grown into a powerful force, inhibiting the nuclear arms race and deterring nuclear war. In the context of reduced danger, however, the movement has declined, providing national security officials with a renewed opportunity to pursue their favorite military schemes without significant opposition. Then the cycle has begun all over again. Specialists on social movements will recognize a familiar pattern here. For example, capitalists exploit workers, workers form militant unions, capitalists make concessions, unions decline, and capitalists resume their exploitation of workers. Facing a systemic evil, there is a need for constant vigilance. And yet a little reform inevitably undermines the reform movement, with the result that the guardians of the system return to their old tricks.

What, then, will it take to abolish nuclear weapons? As this study suggests, it will certainly require a vigilant citizenry, unwilling to settle for anything less than a nuclear-free world. But, in the context of war-making nations, it seems likely that it will take something more, something "deeper" than an attack upon specific weapons. What is that? Humanity's greatest prophets and ethical leaders have implored people to cast aside hatred and embrace love. If they did, they surely would cease murdering one another in wars or threatening one another with nuclear weapons. Unfortunately, however, we seem very far from this state of affairs and faced, instead, with a world in which fanatical nationalism and other forms of tribalism persist. Thus, although replacing hatred with love is desirable and certainly would lead to a nuclear-free world, it does not provide us with a timely solution to the problem of the nuclear arms race and its motor force, the nation-state system.

Fortunately, however, the abolition of nuclear weapons does not require this profound a change in human behavior. If the roots of the nuclear problem lie in a pathological nation-state system, then we need to do no more (and should do no less) than change that system. Some of the necessary changes have been recognized for a century or more. Foremost among them is strengthening international authority so that it can provide an effective system of security for all nations. This process was begun with the creation of the League of Nations and the United Nations. It has been strengthened by the growth of international law, by the development of an International Criminal Court, and by the emergence of international peacekeeping operations. But many nations—and especially the great powers—though grudgingly supportive of this approach during World Wars I and II, when the nation-state system collapsed into anarchy, reneged on their commitment to international security in subsequent years. Rather than transfer some of their sovereignty to a world peacekeeping organization, they clung greedily to their traditional prerogatives. This betrayal of their commitment to an international security approach left the League of Nations and the United Nations too weak to handle many of the international crises that emerged.[7] But if citizens' movements can force nations to follow through on creating an effective international security organization, they can pull the deadly fangs of the nation-state system. Working together, citizens' movements (on the grassroots level) and a strengthened United Nations (on the global level) could rein in war-making states until, like New Jersey and New York, these semi-sovereign jurisdictions would never think of resolving their disputes through war, much less nuclear war.

Adopting a long-term strategy of taming the war-making nation-state through the creation of an international security system does not eliminate the need for pursuing a short-term strategy of fostering nuclear arms control and disarmament. Indeed, the two are complementary. Without a program that goes "deeper" than the weapons—one that addresses their underlying basis in the nation-state system—we seem likely to be left, at best, with the present kinds of unsatisfactory, unstable compromises between arms races and disarmament. Conversely, without an arms control and disarmament strategy, we are likely to be obliterated in a nuclear holocaust long before our arrival in that new world of international peace and security. But by pursuing both strategies simultaneously, we have the possibility of turning back the threat of nuclear annihilation and, along the way, transcending the disgraceful international violence that has accompanied so much of the human experience.

We live at a potential turning point in human history, for the latest advances in the "art" of war—nuclear weapons—have forced upon us a momentous choice. If nations continue to follow the traditional "national security" paradigm, then—sooner or later—their leaders will resort to nuclear war, thus unleashing unspeakable horror upon the world. Conversely, this unprecedented danger could be overcome through arms control, disarmament, and transformation of the nation-state system. Are the people of the world capable of altering their traditional institutions of governance to meet this challenge? Are they ready for the "new thinking" about international relations necessitated by the nuclear age? If one looked solely at their long record of war, plunder, and other human folly, one might conclude that they are not. But an examination of the history of the nuclear disarmament movement inspires a greater respect for human potential. Indeed, defying the national barriers and the murderous traditions of the past, millions of people have joined hands to build a safer, saner world. Perhaps, after all, they will reach it.

Reference Matter

Notes

For complete authors' names, titles, and publication data on works cited in short form in these Notes, consult the Bibliography. The following abbreviations are used:

A	Amsterdam
ACDA	Arms Control and Disarmament Agency
AFSC	American Friends Service Committee
AMM	Adam Matthew microfilm
BAS	*Bulletin of the Atomic Scientists*
C	Cambridge
CDSP	*Current Digest of the Soviet Press*
CLW	Council for a Livable World
CLW	*Council for a Livable World*
CND (B)	Campaign for Nuclear Disarmament (Britain)
CND (NZ)	Campaign for Nuclear Disarmament (New Zealand)
CODENE	Comité pour le Désarmement Nucléaire en Europe
CPSU	Communist Party of the Soviet Union
CWIHP	*Cold War International History Project*
DC	*Disarmament Campaigns*
DDA	*Defense and Disarmament Alternatives*
DDN	*Defense and Disarmament News*
END	European Nuclear Disarmament
END	*END Journal*
FAS	Federation of American Scientists
FOR	Fellowship of Reconciliation
Freeze	Nuclear Weapons Freeze Campaign
GP	*Gallup Poll*
HM	Harvester microfilm
IHT	*International Herald Tribune*
IKV	Interkerkelijk Vredesberaad
IPB	International Peace Bureau
IPCC	International Peace Communication and Coordination Center
L	London
MfS	Mobilization for Survival
NSA	National Security Advisor

NSC	National Security Council
NSDD	National Security Decision Directive
NT	*Nuclear Times*
NVA	*Nonviolent Activist*
NYT	*New York Times*
PA	Peace Action
PA	*Peace Action*
PC	*Peace Courier*
PDN	*Peace and Democracy News*
PM	*Peace Magazine*
PSR	Physicians for Social Responsibility
S	Swarthmore
SANE	Committee for a Sane Nuclear Policy
SL	St. Louis
Stasi	State Security Services of the German Democratic Republic
SW	*Sane World*
TH	The Hague
WHORM	White House Office of Records Management
WILPF	Women's International League for Peace and Freedom
WP	*Washington Post*
WPC	World Peace Council
WRI	War Resisters' International
WRL	War Resisters League
WSP	Women Strike for Peace

Preface epigraph: Gabriel Garcia Marquez, "The Doom of Damocles," *Greenpeace* 12 (June 1987): 19.

Book epigraph: Camus, *La Peste*, p. 292.

Chapter 1

Epigraph: Myrdal, *Game of Disarmament*, p. 317.

1. These upsurges and their impact upon public policy are described in detail in the first two volumes of this trilogy: Wittner, *One World or None* and Wittner, *Resisting the Bomb*.

2. Homer A. Jack, "The Disarmament Scoreboard," *BAS* 33 (Mar. 1977): 54; Powaski, *March*, pp. 127–44; Garthoff, *Détente*, pp. 191, 193.

3. "Text of Basic Principles, May 29," pp. 898–99; Garthoff, *Détente*, pp. 290–91, 334–35; Nixon, *RN*, pp. 880–81.

4. Herbert Scoville, Jr., "Slowing the Arms Race," *BAS* 33 (Sept. 1977): 4; Kosta Tsipis, "Security Blankets of the Superpowers," *BAS* 32 (Nov. 1976): 19–20; Garthoff, *Détente*, pp. 188–89, 194; Barry Schneider, "Big Bangs from Little Bombs," *BAS* 31 (May 1975): 24–25.

5. Cohen, *Israel*; Perkovich, *India's Nuclear Bomb*, pp. 178, 185; Seaborg, *Stemming*, p. 256; Jim McCahon and Murray Robertson, "The Nuclear South Pacific," *BAS* 33 (Apr. 1977): 26; Jack, "Disarmament Scoreboard," pp. 54–55; Giangrande, *Nuclear North*, p. 145.

6. Nolan, *An Elusive Consensus*, p. 23; Talbott, *Deadly Gambits*, p. 21; Holloway, *Soviet Union*, p. 179; MccGwire, *Perestroika*, pp. 38–39.

7. Dobrynin, *In Confidence*, pp. 251–52; Kissinger, *White House Years*, p. 1152; Fitzwater, *Call the Briefing!*, p. 128.

8. *NYT*, Mar. 1, 2002.

9. The Americans were not quite as crazy as the Russians feared. When Kissinger ordered the unprecedented military alert, known as DEFCON III, he did not realize that it entailed the mobilization of nuclear forces. Lebow and Stein, *We All Lost*, pp. 246–88; Dobrynin, *In Confidence*, p. 300.

10. Even Nixon, not the most empathic of individuals, was struck by the morbid discussions of the war by Soviet officials, and concluded: "They have been through some pretty horrible experiences." Comments of Chernyaev and Detinov in Tannenwald, ed., *Understanding*, pp. 23, 32–33; Arbatov, *System*, pp. 179–80; Nixon, *RN*, pp. 1029–30.

11. Arbatov, *System*, pp. 174–75, 180, 246, 248; Dobrynin, *In Confidence*, p. 193; Garthoff, *Détente*, p. 320; Evangelista, *Unarmed Forces*, p. 230.

12. Tsipis, "Security Blankets," p. 19; Carter, *Keeping Faith*, p. 214; Savel'yev and Detinov, *The Big Five*, pp. 9, 32–41; Dobrynin, *In Confidence*, p. 331; Garthoff, *Détente*, pp. 53, 429, 446, 464.

13. At least on paper, the administration did occasionally indicate support for balanced nuclear reductions. But, according to Robert McFarlane, Kissinger's military assistant on the National Security Council, Kissinger "never believed that reductions were conceivable. . . . The idea that . . . we could reduce nuclear weapons was not seriously considered." Henry Kissinger, "National Security Decision Memorandum 271" (Sept. 24, 1974), Box 1, National Security Decision Memoranda and Study Memoranda; interview with Robert McFarlane, July 21, 1999.

14. Nixon, *RN*, pp. 340, 343, 524; Kissinger, *White House Years*, pp. 54–61, 1143; Kissinger, *Nuclear Weapons*; Kissinger, *Necessity for Choice*.

15. Garthoff, *Détente*, pp. 35–36, 56–57, 68, 127–28, 149–50, 191–92; Schulzinger, *Henry Kissinger*, pp. 63–66; Nixon, *RN*, p. 346.

16. Garthoff, *Détente*, pp. 135–37, 141, 145, 184, 320; Nixon, *RN*, p. 1025; Schrag, *Global Action*, p. 23; Small, *Presidency*, pp. 110–11.

17. Nixon, *RN*, p. 1039; Garthoff, *Détente*, pp. 325–30, 418–19, 538–44, 548; Schmidt, *Men and Powers*, p. 170; Adelman, *Great Universal Embrace*, pp. 254–55.

18. York, *Making Weapons*, p. 284; MccGwire, *Perestroika*, p. 67; Garthoff, *Détente*, p. 548.

19. The rise and decline of the nuclear disarmament movement from 1954 to 1970 are covered in detail in Wittner, *Resisting the Bomb*.

20. Minnion and Bolsover, eds., *CND Story*, p. 150; Report of the CND General Secretary, Easter 1974, Reel 17, CND (B) Records, HM; CND, "Information Sheet 5" (1981), CND Records, S.

21. Minutes of the CND Executive Committee meetings of May 19, 1973 and July 13, 1974, minutes of the CND National Council meetings of Dec. 1, 1983 and June 8, 1974, and CND General Secretary's Report to National Council and Executive, No. 5 (1973) and No. 5, 6, 7, and 8 (1974), Reel 17, CND (B) Records, HM.

22. Interview with Sheila Jones, June 19, 1998; Minutes of the CND National Council meeting, June 8, 1974, Reel 17, CND (B) Records, HM; Taylor, "Labour Party," p. 121.

23. "An Interview with Claude Bourdet," *END Bulletin*, No. 6 (Autumn 1981), p. 5; Howorth, *France*, pp. 32–33; Caldwell, "French Socialists' Attitudes," pp. 169–70; "9/23 meeting w/Christian Mellon" (Sept. 23, 1982), Box 133, Series G, SANE Records; Gallup, *Gallup International Public Opinion Polls: France*, pp. 1041–42.

24. Interview with Mient Jan Faber, Aug. 7, 1986; Philip P. Everts, "Where the Peace Movement Goes When It Disappears," *BAS* 45 (Nov. 1989): 28.

25. Jos Béni, "Peace Movement," p. 13; Galand, "Le C.N.A.P.D.—Belgique," p. 1.

26. "The Swedish Peace and Arbitration Society—a brief description" (Nov. 1974), Box 445, WRI Records; interview with Ole Kopreitan, May 14, 1999.

27. Minutes of WILPF National Board meetings, Feb. 13–14, 1971 and Oct. 15–17, 1971, and Ruth Frankel et al., "Report to National Board" (Apr. 1974), Box 24, Series A,2, WILPF Records; interview with Ron Young, July 31, 1999.

28. Interview with Sanford Gottlieb, July 19, 1998; *Philadelphia Inquirer*, Mar. 14, 1978; "Vietnam" Folder, Box 1, Series A,8, WSP Records; address by Robert Schwartz, former SANE national board member, Albany, NY, Oct. 24, 1987; Swerdlow, *Women Strike for Peace*, pp. 125–230; DeBenedetti and Chatfield, *An American Ordeal*, p. 320; interview with David Cortright, June 29, 1987.

29. WRL, *A WRL History*, n.p.; *NYT*, May 20, 1974; Mindy Chadrow Stein to Martha Baker, Oct. 24, 1974, Box 4, Series A,4, WSP Records.

30. Interview with Terry Provance, July 20, 1999; AFSC press release of Jan. 7, 1974, "Roll Out" (Aug. 22, 1974), and "Participation in the B-1 Bomber Campaign," Box 10, Series II, AFSC Records; Kotz, *Wild Blue Yonder*, p. 142.

31. "Fact Sheet on History of Rocky Flats Campaign," Box 1, AFSC-Rocky Flats Project Records; "Pioneering Work Against Nuclear Weapons Plants," *Quaker Service Bulletin* 70 (Winter 1989): 1.

32. Stone, *"Every Man,"* pp. 39–40, 44–46, 65, 73–75, 91–94, 145–49; interview with Frank von Hippel, Aug. 22, 1999.

33. Primack and von Hippel, *Advice and Dissent*, pp. 208–35; Meyer, *Peace Organizations*, pp. 117–18.

34. Interview with Gene LaRocque, Aug. 17, 1999; interview with Harold Willens, May 11, 2000; interview with Eugene J. Carroll, Jr., May 11, 2000.

35. Perkovich, *India's Nuclear Bomb*, pp. 179, 188.

36. "Of the Anti A- and H-Bombs Movement in Japan," Box 448, WRI Records; Kurino and Kodama, "A Study," p. 123; *Meaning of Survival*, p. 237; interview with Koichi Akamatsu, May 15, 1999; Ichiro Moritaki to Raymond Wilson, June 1, 1972, Japan Congress Against A & H Bombs Records; Takako Tatematsu to Ethel Taylor, Oct. 15, 1974, Box 13, Series A,3, WSP Records.

37. Redner and Redner, *Anatomy*, pp. 276–78; Clements, *Back from the Brink*, pp. 66–67, 76; Locke, *Peace People*, pp. 290–98.

38. Helen Caldicott, "Our Own Worst Enemy," *Fellowship* 45 (June 1979): 5; Summy and Saunders, "Disarmament," p. 35; Burgmann, *Power and Protest*, p. 201; Campbell, *Australian Public Opinion*, p. 54.

39. The ATOM Committee to all delegates to the South Pacific Conference, 1970, CND (NZ) Records; Bette Johnson to Ethel Taylor, Aug. 24, 1974, Box 1, Series A,8, WSP Records; Michael Bedford, "Activism in the Pacific," *NT* 8 (Summer 1990): 20.

40. Micronesia Support Committee, "Tinian—An Island for Uncle Sam," *WIN* 18 (Aug. 1, 1982): 22; Clements, *Back from the Brink*, p. 79; Rajendra Prakash to Dear Friends, Mar. 23, 1974, and Conference Planning Committee, Suva, to Organising Groups, Nov. 20, 1974, Greenpeace Pacific Records.

41. Voice of Women, "Eleventh Annual Meeting" (Oct. 1, 1971), Box 1, Series D,3, and "Branch file: Canada, Voice of Women (1970–1973)" Folder, Box 4, Series A,3, WSP Records.

42. Pavlova, "Hundred Years," p. 151; Evangelista, *Unarmed Forces*, pp. 39, 89; Ilukhina and Pavlova, "Totalitarianism," p. 5; Alexeyeva, "Independent Youth Groups," p. 4; Arbatov, *System*, pp. 142–63.

43. Carter, *Peace Movements*, p. 77; David McReynolds to conference of ICDP, May 18, 1981, New Accession, WRL Records; interview with Sheila Oakes, June 6, 1999.

44. Interview with Homer Jack, June 12, 1988; interview with Valerie Flessati, June 7, 1999.

45. Interview with Joseph Rotblat, July 11, 1994; "Despite Detente, A Mounting Danger to World Peace, Health, and Security," *BAS* 30 (Apr. 1974): 24; Rotblat, "Movements," p. 137.

46. "Fifteen Years at the Front Lines," *Greenpeace Examiner* 11 (Oct.–Dec. 1986): 8–9; "Return to Amchitka," *Greenpeace Quarterly* 1 (Fall 1996): 4–5.

47. "Fifteen Years," pp. 9–10; Redner and Redner, *Anatomy*, p. 278; Locke, *Peace People*, pp. 291–92, 301–2.

48. *Greenpeace Pacific Bulletin*, Nos. 1 (Feb. 1974) and 2 (Winter 1974), "Greenpeace Foundation of N.Z. Newsletter," No. 2 (Nov. 1974), and "Fri Peace Odyssey" (Jan. 1976), Greenpeace Pacific Records; Locke, *Peace People*, pp. 299–301.

49. Interview with Rob Prince, July 27, 1999; Rob Prince, "In the Name of Peace" (Mar. 12, 1990), Prince Papers; interview with Günther Drefahl, May 19, 1999; interview with Mark Solomon, July 8, 1999.

50. See, for example, the WPC's endorsement of WSP's "Demand Disarmament Day" in K. Kielan and K. Talbot to Ethel Taylor, Aug. 22, 1974, Box 4, Series A,4, WSP Records.

51. Rob Prince, "A Sketch History of the World Peace Council," Prince Papers; interview with Mark Solomon, July 8, 1999; Peace Council of the German Democratic Republic, "Statement" (Aug. 30, 1974), German Democratic Republic Peace Council Records.

52. Wittner, *Resisting the Bomb*, pp. 94–95.

53. A. Norden to Romesh Chandra, Jan. 4, 1973, 28.140, Deutscher Friedensrat Records; *Bulletin* No. 1 (Feb. 1973), Bulgarian Peace Committee Records; Andrew and Gordievsky, *KGB*, pp. 504–6; interview with Mark Solomon, July 8, 1999; interview with Werner Rümpel, May 20, 1999; interview with Günther Drefahl, May 19, 1999.

54. Homer A. Jack, "The World Congress of Peace Forces: Some Preliminary Thoughts" (Apr. 17, 1973) and Ilona Sebestyén to Sanford Gottlieb, June 29, 1973, Box 59, Series G, SANE Records; "USSR Blocks SANE at Moscow Confab," *SW* (Oct.–Nov. 1973), pp. 2–3.

55. Margaret Gardiner, "Report on the World Congress of Peace Forces Held in Moscow, 25–31 October 1973, by the ICDP Delegate," Box 59, Series G, SANE Records; Maris Cakars, "World Peace Congress, or Maris Goes to Moscow" and "On Soviet Dissidents," enclosures in Mary Clarke to Maris Cakars, Nov. 30, 1973, Box 6, Series B,1, WSP Records. For a more sympathetic account, prepared by a WSP leader, see Mary Clarke, "World Congress of Peace Forces" (1973), Box 6, Series B,1, WSP Records.

56. Nixon, *RN*, p. 1025; DeBenedetti and Chatfield, *An American Ordeal*, pp. 177, 199, 205, 247, 288; "Sanford Gottlieb," Box 1, Gottlieb Papers; "USSR Blocks SANE at Moscow Confab," pp. 2–3.

57. Stone, *"Every Man,"* p. 352; *NYT*, Feb. 11, 1999.

58. "Ob informastii dlya bratskih kommunisticheskih i rabochih partii o provedenii v SSSR kampanii po prekrascheniyu gonki vooruzhenii, za razopuzhenie" (June 8, 1976), f. 89, op. 26, d. 15, Central Committee of the CPSU Records.

59. Evangelista, *Unarmed Forces*, pp. 32–33, 232; interview with Sergei Kapitza, June 28, 1990.

60. "Sanford Gottlieb," Box 1, Gottlieb Papers; Margaret Gardiner, "Report on the World Congress of Peace Forces Held in Moscow, 25–31 October 1973, by the ICDP Delegate," Box 59, Series G, SANE Records; Alexeyeva, "Independent Youth Groups," p. 4; Ilukhina and Pavlova, "Totalitarianism," p. 5; *NYT*, Dec. 16, 1989.

61. Surviving the assault, McTaggart went to Paris to pursue a lawsuit in a French court. Although the court ruled that the French minesweeper had rammed the *Vega* deliberately, it did not address the questions of France's violation of freedom of the seas and its international piracy. Subsequently, McTaggart become chair of Greenpeace. "Fifteen Years," pp. 10–11; King, *Death*, pp. 121–23.

62. Clements, *Back From the Brink*, pp. 67–68, 76–83; Redner and Redner, *Anatomy*, pp. 278–79; Locke, *Peace People*, pp. 298–99, 303–5.

63. Siracusa, "Peace Movements," p. 7; McCahon and Robertson, "Nuclear South Pacific," pp. 26–27; Clements, *Back From the Brink*, pp. 83–85; Locke, *Peace People*, pp. 312–16.

64. Chapman, *Canada*, p. 11; "Fifteen Years," p. 9.

Chapter 2

Epigraph: "Policy Suggestions: David McReynolds, elected member, Council" (Apr. 1977), Box 38, WRI Records.

1. IKV, *Achter de IKV-campagne*, pp. 3, 6–14, 22; IKV, *Help de Kernwapens de Wereld Uit*; interview with Mient Jan Faber, Aug. 7, 1986; Everts, "Reviving Unilateralism," pp. 46–50.

2. In 1977, only 12 percent of the Dutch population thought their nation's security should be based upon nuclear weapons; 81 percent disagreed. That same year, 72 percent maintained that the use of nuclear weapons was not acceptable under any circumstances. L. J. Hogebrink to War Resisters League, May 24, 1978, Box 40, McReynolds Papers; Everts, "Reviving Unilateralism," p. 44; Everts, "Public Opinion," p. 233.

3. Everts, "Reviving Unilateralism," p. 43; *DC*, No. 1 (Feb. 1980), p. 7; Egbert Boeker, "On the way towards consensus?" *END Bulletin*, No. 4 (Feb. 1981), pp. 5–6.

4. Minutes of the CND National Council meetings of May 6, 1978 and Jan. 11, 1975, Reel 17, CND Records (B), HM.

5. Minutes of the CND National Council meetings of May 14, 1977 and Jan. 14, 1978, and Reports of the CND Organizing Secretary, Jan. 14–Mar. 4, 1978 and Aug. 12, 1978, Reel 17, CND (B) Records, HM. The British government pressure that led to the television ban, which lasted until 1985, is discussed in Wittner, *Resisting the Bomb*, pp. 357–58.

6. Interview with Sheila Oakes, June 6, 1999; Stevens, "Importance," p. 78; minutes of the CND National Council meetings of Apr. 3 and Nov. 6, 1976, Sept. 17, 1977, and Jan. 14 and Dec. 16, 1978, and Reports of the CND Organizing Secretary, Mar. 4–May 6 and May 6–July 15, 1978, Reel 17, and Report of the CND Organizing Secretary, Dec. 4–5, 1976, Reel 19, CND (B) Records, HM.

7. Interview with Bruce Kent, June 7, 1999; Reports of the CND Organizing Secretary, May 6–July 15, and Dec. 16, 1978, and minutes of the CND National Council meetings of Jan. 14, Mar. 4, May 6, and Dec. 16, 1978, Reel 17, CND (B) Records; Gallup, ed., *International Gallup Polls: Public Opinion 1978*, p. 143.

8. Minutes of the CND National Council meetings of Mar. 12, 1977, and July 15 and Aug. 12, 1978, Reel 17, CND (B) Records.

9. Reports of the CND Organizing Secretary, Nov. 5, 1976–Jan. 22, Mar. 12–May 14, and May 14–July 9, 1977, and minutes of the CND National Council meetings of Mar. 12 and Sept. 17, 1977, and Sept. 16 and Dec. 16, 1978, Reel 17, CND (B) Records; Minnion and Bolsover, eds., *CND Story*, p. 150.

10. Mushaben, "Cycles," pp. 30–31; Merkl, "Pacifism," p. 88; Weart, *Nuclear Fear*, p. 344; Nelkin and Pollak, *Atom Besieged*, pp. 141–42; Johnstone, *Politics*, p. 53.

11. Kubbig and Risse-Kappen, "Living," pp. 72–73; Beate Roggenbuck to the author, Jan. 25, 1989; Scharrer, "War and Peace," pp. 277–78.

12. Bent Sorensen, "Anywhere but here!" *BAS* 36 (Apr. 1980): 55; Grepstad, "Norway," pp. 6–8.

13. Grepstad, "Norway," p. 8; Ståhle, *Internationella Kvinnoförbundet*, p. 141; Wiberg, *Provstopp nu!*, p. 15.

14. Lindkvist, "Mobilization Peaks," p. 159; Taipale, "Peace Movement," pp. 20–21, 27–28; Kodama, "Red vs. Green," pp. 5–6.

15. Michael Peristerakis, untitled statement of June 18, 1975, Box 21, Series B, WRL Records; Rossi and Ilari, "Peace Movement," p. 142.

16. Lubelski-Bernard, "Euromissile Crisis," p. 59; Pierre Galand, "Le C.N.A.P.D. —Belgique," p. 2.

17. Furtado, *Turkey*, pp. 5, 9, 11; Marjorie Mowlam, "Peace Groups and Politics," *BAS* 39 (Nov. 1983): 30.

18. Touraine, *Anti-Nuclear Protest*, p. 26; Weart, *Nuclear Fear*, pp. 344–45.

19. Howorth, *France*, pp. 37–41; Caldwell, "French Socialists' Attitudes," pp. 173–84; Bourdet, "Désarmement Nucléaire," pp. 9–13; "An Interview with Claude Bourdet," *END Bulletin* 6 (Autumn 1981): 5–6; Christian Mellon, "Histoire du ralliement: 1972–1981," *Alternatives Non Violentes*, No. 46 (Dec. 1982), pp. 14–23.

20. Dorothy Steffens to Board Members, Jan. 2, 1976, and minutes of the WILPF National Board meeting, Apr. 8–10, 1978, Box 25, Series A,2, WILPF Records.

21. Davidon, "A Simple Act," p. 31; David McReynolds to Lee Weingarten, Feb. 23, 1977, Box 38, McReynolds Papers; minutes of WRL National Committee meetings of Aug. 14–16, 1977 and Oct. 6–8, 1978, Box 2a, Series B, WRL Records.

22. Minutes of the FOR National Council meeting, Apr. 16–19, 1978, Box 8, Series A-2, FOR (U.S.) Records; "F.O.R. Program for the Year Ahead," *Fellowship* 44 (Dec. 1978): 15.

23. Interviews with Ron Young and Carol Jensen, July 31, 1999; "Pioneering Work Against Nuclear Weapons Plants," *Quaker Service Bulletin* 70 (Winter 1989): 7–8; Ann Morrissett Davidon, "The U.S. Anti-Nuclear Movement," *BAS* 35 (Dec. 1979): 46; Solo, *From Protest*, pp. 32–33.

24. Dorothy Nelkin, "Anti-nuclear connections: power and weapons," *BAS* 37 (Apr. 1981): 38; "Fact Sheet on History of Rocky Flats Campaign," Box 1, AFSC-Rocky Flats Project Records.

25. Edith Villastrigo to Liaison Office of the People's Republic of China, Nov. 24, 1976, Box 13, Elizabeth S. French to Mary Boyer, Jan. 13, 1978 and Villastrigo to Bob Marcus, Aug. 2, 1977, Box 5, Series A,3, and WSP press release of Nov. 5, 1977, Box 2, Series A,8, WSP Records; Taylor, *We Made a Difference*, pp. 111, 117–20; *Philadelphia Inquirer*, Mar. 14, 1978.

26. Interview with Carol Jensen, July 31, 1999.

27. Musto, *Catholic Peace Tradition*, p. 260; Fahey, "Pax Christi," pp. 61–63.

28. Interview with Eugene J. Carroll, Jr., May 11, 2000.

29. Stone, *"Every Man,"* p. 77; interview with Sanford Gottlieb, July 19, 1998.

30. *SW*, July–Aug. 1975 and Jan. 1977; Statement by Sanford Gottlieb before the Democratic Platform Committee, May 19, 1976, Box 3, Gottlieb Papers.

31. Interview with Sanford Gottlieb, July 19, 1998; interview with Robert Musil, July 20, 1998; Cortright, *Peace Works*, p. 17; interview with David Cortright, June 29, 1987.

32. Stone, *"Every Man,"* pp. 150–61; Jeremy Stone, "Linking SALT to Ethiopia or Unlinking It from Détente," *BAS* 34 (June 1978): 38–39.

33. Davidon, "U.S. Anti-nuclear Movement," p. 45; Meyer, *Peace Organizations*, p. 118; "Declaration on the Nuclear Arms Race," *BAS* 34 (Mar. 1978): 8–10.

34. Bernard Feld, "The Way to Begin Is to Stop," *BAS* 33 (Mar. 1977): 9.

35. "Proposal for a Successor Body to the Coalition to Stop Funding the War" (June 23, 1975), Box 54, and anonymous to Ed, Joyce, Ann and Ira, Oct. 31, 1975, Box 59, Series G, SANE Records; interview with Sanford Gottlieb, July 19, 1998.

36. Joseph Clark to Edward Lawrence, Feb. 3, 1977 and Dick Creecy and E. Raymond Wilson to Members of the Disarmament Working Group, Aug. 2, 1977, PB1, Series G, SANE Records; Atwood, "Mobilizing," p. 144.

37. Interview with Terry Provance, July 20, 1999; interview with John Isaacs, July 20, 1999; Kotz, *Wild Blue Yonder*, pp. 140–60.

38. Interview with Edith Ballantyne, June 1, 1999; "United Nations Special Session on Disarmament Bulletin #1" (Jan. 12, 1978), Box 2, Section IV, Series A,6, WILPF Records; interview with David Atwood, June 1, 1999; David McReynolds to A. Corradini, May 31, 1978, Connie Hogarth and McReynolds to Ron Young et al., Apr. 14, 1978, Box 40, McReynolds Papers; Atwood, "Mobilizing," pp. 144–55.

39. Homer Jack, "An Evaluation of the U.N. Special Session on Disarmament" (June 26, 1978) and Dick Creecy to Persons and Organizations in the Disarmament Movement, Aug. 3, 1978, Box 2, Section IV, Series A,6, WILPF Records; interview with Edith Ballantyne, June 1, 1999; Atwood, "Mobilizing," pp. 147–49, 152–55.

40. Davidon, "U.S. Anti-nuclear Movement," p. 45; William Sweet, "Seabrook, the 'Clams,' and the Commission," *BAS* 34 (Oct. 1978): 53; Walsh, "Antinuclear Protests," p. 746; Nelkin, "Anti-nuclear Connections," p. 36; Wasserman, *Energy War*, pp. 3–150.

41. Interview with Randall Kehler, Aug. 20, 1999; Helen Caldicott, "Our Own Worst Enemy," *Fellowship* 45 (June 1979): 3; interview with Helen Caldicott, Feb. 27, 1999.

42. Interview with Charles Johnson, Aug. 3, 1999; interview with Peter Bergel, Aug. 3, 1999; interview with Frank von Hippel, Aug. 22, 1999; Weart, *Nuclear Fear*, p. 323; Nelkin, "Anti-nuclear Connections," p. 36.

43. Robert Moore, letter to the editor, *BAS* 37 (Oct. 1981): 61; "A Call to Action" (June 1977), Mike Mawby et al. to Dear Friends, Oct. 5, 1977, Minutes of Mobilization Continuations Committee, July 30, 1977, George R. Vickers to Bruce M. Brown, Feb. 23, 1978, Bob Moore, Norma Becker, and Terry Provance to Dear Friend, Nov. 1978, and "Anti-Nuclear Forces Kick Off Mass Movement," *Energy Daily*, Dec. 7, 1977, MfS Records, S.

44. Den Oudsten, "Public Opinion on International Security," n.p.; *Public Attitudes*, p. 20; "The Harris Survey" (July 10, 1978), "Harris Polls" Folder, Box 3, Office of the Assistant to the President for Communications File; Graham, *American Public Opinion*, p. 59; Gallup, *GP: Public Opinion 1978*, pp. 181–82.

45. See, for example, McGovern to Ethel Taylor, June 23 and Dec. 19, 1978, Box 1, Series A,8, WSP Records.

46. Kotz, *Wild Blue Yonder*, pp. 146–50; interview with Terry Provance, July 20, 1999.

47. Jimmy Carter, "Three Steps toward Nuclear Responsibility," *BAS* 32 (Oct. 1976): 8–14; interview with Zbigniew Brzezinski, July 21, 1999; interview with Paul Warnke, July 20, 1999.

48. Oral history interview with Jimmy Carter, Nov. 29, 1982, p. 3; interview with Harold Willens, May 11, 2000; Harold Willens, "Advice to Jimmy Carter," *BAS* 34 (May 1978): 7.

49. Donna Elliott to the Membership, VOW, Nov. 1975, *VOW Newsletter* (Aug. 1978), and "Statement of the Voice of Women . . . to the United Nations Special Session," Voice of Women Records.

50. "Summary of the History of Project Ploughshares," Project Ploughshares Records; Newman, "Surviving," pp. 47–48.

51. Gallup, ed., *International Gallup Polls: Public Opinion 1978*, p. 142.

52. Burgmann, *Power and Protest*, pp. 195–98; Summy and Saunders, "Disarmament," pp. 33–35; Joseph Camilleri, "Nuclear Controversy in Australia: The Uranium Campaign," *BAS* 35 (Apr. 1979): 40–44; interview with Helen Caldicott, Feb. 27, 1999.

53. Summy and Saunders, "Disarmament," pp. 38–39; "Appeal from the Australian People's Disarmament Conference" (Apr. 1978), Australian Peace Liaison Committee Records.

54. Clements, *Back from the Brink*, pp. 108–10; "Peace Squadron," CND (NZ) Records; Landais-Stamp and Rogers, *Rocking*, p. 20; Newnham, *Peace Squadron*, pp. 8, 11–19.

55. Clements, *Back from the Brink*, pp. 111–13; Newnham, *Peace Squadron*, pp. 22–36.

56. Amelia Rokotuivuna to Dear Friend of ATOM, Jan. 1975, Greenpeace Pacific Records; Michael Bedford, "Activism in the Pacific," *NT* 8 (Summer 1990): 20–21; "A Fiji Declaration by the Conference for a Nuclear Free Pacific" (Apr. 7, 1975), Box 500, WRI Records; Charles Scheiner, "The Pacific Ocean—A Source of Peace?" *NVA* 4 (Jan.–Feb. 1987): 9.

57. "Summary of Soka Gakkai" and Daisaku Ikeda, *A Ten-Point Proposal on Nuclear Disarmament* (1979), p. 6, Soka Gakkai International Records; Committee for the Compilation of Materials, *Hiroshima and Nagasaki*, p. 605.

58. Wasserman, *Energy War*, pp. 166–74; *Meaning of Survival*, p. 259; Kamata and Salaff, "Atomic Bomb," p. 49; "Report of the Forum on the Problem of Atomic Power Stations and Atomic Power," in *Documents of 1977 World Conference*, p. 19, World Conference Against A and H Bombs Records.

59. Koschmann, "Postwar Democracy," pp. 16–18; *Japan Times*, May 20, 1977; interview with Koichi Akamatsu, May 15, 1999; interview with Ikuro Anzai, May 15, 1999; *Meaning of Survival*, pp. 253, 255, 259.

60. Noam Chomsky to Sanford Gottlieb, Jan. 16, 1976, Box 59, Series G, SANE Records.

61. Andrei Sakharov, "The Need for an Open World," *BAS* 31 (Nov. 1975): 8–9; Sakharov, *Alarm and Hope*, pp. 25–26.

62. English, *Russia*, pp. 150–57; Arbatov, *System*, pp. 144, 243.

63. Allen, *Germany East*, pp. 96–98; Mleczkowski, "In Search," p. 187; Tismaneanu, "Unofficial Peace Activism," p. 11; interview with Günther Drefahl, May 19, 1999.

64. Minutes of the WRI council meeting of Apr. 4–11, 1977, Box 31, "Policy Sug-

gestions: David McReynolds, elected member, Council" (Apr. 1977), Box 38, and Recommendations made, decisions taken and resolutions passed at WRI council meeting of July 10–14, 1978, Box 39, WRI Records.

65. "Peace Movement for Disarmament and the Abolition of Nuclear Weapons" (1982), Rissho Kosei-kai Records; minutes of WRI emergency council meeting of July 10–15, 1978, Box 39, WRI Records; "Statement of Pax Christi International on Hiroshima Day, 6th August 1977," Pax Christi International Records.

66. "The Arms Race: A Call to Action," *BAS* 33 (Nov. 1977): 6.

67. Minutes of the WRI council meeting of Apr. 4–11, 1977, Box 31, and Devi Prasad, "Message to the WRI Council Meeting" (June 1976), Box 37, WRI Records; Jim Forest to executive staff, July 29, 1975, Box 21, Series B, WRL Records.

68. Interview with Ron Young, July 31, 1999; minutes of the ICDP executive committee meeting, Feb. 4 and 5, 1977, Box 59, Series G, SANE Records; interview with Sheila Oakes, June 6, 1999.

69. "International Statement of Mobilization for Survival" (Aug. 6, 1977), MfS Records, S; "International Mobilisation for Survival" (Mar. 29, 1978), Reel 17, CND (B) Records; "International Mobilization for Survival Strategy for Disarmament Conference" (May 1978), Box 23, Series B, WRL Records.

70. Sylvia Kushner to Dear Friend, n.d. [1975], and WPC, "Declaration on Disarmament" (Jan. 1978), Solomon Papers; N. Voshinin, "Note to Secretariat: Preliminary ideas for the draft programme of the WPC for 1976" (ca. late 1975), 93.456, Deutscher Friedensrat Records.

71. Albert Norden to Romesh Chandra, Apr. 11, 1978, IV B.2/2.028/52, Socialist Unity Party Records; "Unite, Say 'No' to Horror-Bomb!" *PC* 8 (Aug. 1977): 1–2; "WPC Urges Protest Actions," *PC* 8 (Aug. 1977): 1–2.

72. WPC, "Declaration on Disarmament" (Jan. 1978), Solomon Papers.

73. Ilona Sebestyén to Dear Friends, Jan. 1977, Hungarian Peace Council Records.

74. Interview with Rob Prince, July 27, 1999; interview with Mark Solomon, July 8, 1999; Rob Prince, "A sketch history of the World Peace Council," Prince Papers.

75. Taipale, "Peace Movement," p. 34; interview with Rob Prince, July 27, 1999.

76. Turski and Zdanowski, *Peace Movement*, p. 104.

77. See, for example: K. Kielan, "Talks with the World Council of Churches" (Aug. 24, 1976), 93.457, Deutscher Friedensrat Records.

78. "The WRI & Dissent in Eastern Europe" (Apr. 10, 1977), and "Human Rights in the Socialist Countries" (Apr. 1977), Box 38, WRI Records; Bernard Cardinal Alfrink to Gustav Husak, Oct. 19, 1977, and "Statement by Pax Christi International concerning the case of Joeri Orlov" (May 31, 1978), Pax Christi International (Neth.) Records.

79. Interviews with Bruce Kent, July 10, 1990 and June 7, 1999; Ceadel, "Britain's Nuclear Disarmers," p. 226; Taylor, "Marxist Left," pp. 170–73; interview with Sheila Jones, June 19, 1998.

80. Interview with Terry Provance, July 20, 1999; minutes of WRI executive committee meeting of May 20–21, 1978, Box 31, WRI Records.

81. Minutes of the CND National Council meetings, Feb. 9 and July 14, 1973, and Mar. 12, 1977, Reel 17, CND (B) Records.

82. Technically, the U.S. Peace Council did not become an affiliate of the WPC, but an associate—a distinction that its leaders felt would establish and preserve their independence. Nevertheless, the U.S. Peace Council appointed people who served on the Presidential Committee and in the secretariat of the WPC, its members attended WPC world conferences as delegates, and its literature pointed proudly to its WPC connections. Frances Williams et al. to All delegates of the conference to found the U.S. Organizing Committee for the World Peace Council, Oct. 20, 1976, and Sandy Pollack to Dear Friend, Mar. 29, 1978, Solomon Papers; "Biographical Sketch of Rob Prince," Prince Papers; interview with Mark Solomon, July 8, 1999.

Chapter 3

Epigraph: Carter's inaugural address of Jan. 20, 1977, in *Public Papers: Carter 1977*, p. 3.

1. Garthoff, *Détente*, pp. 849–50.

2. Carter, *Keeping Faith*, p. 212; Dobrynin, *In Confidence*, p. 383; Kaufman, *Presidency*, p. 39. Numerous other Carter administration officials have emphasized the sincerity of his support for nuclear disarmament. Interview with Paul Warnke, July 20, 1999; interview with Zbigniew Brzezinski, July 21, 1999; oral history interview with Anne Wexler, Feb. 12–13, 1981, p. 125; oral history interview with Robert Beckel, Nov. 13, 1981, pp. 54–56.

3. Interview with Zbigniew Brzezinski, July 21, 1999; Brzezinski, *Power and Principle*, pp. 3, 7, 49, 54–55.

4. "Minutes of Cabinet Meeting, February 7, 1977," "Cabinet Minutes, 1–5/77" Folder, Box 18, Plains File, Carter Presidential Papers; Vance, *Hard Choices*, pp. 27–28; interview with Paul Warnke, July 20, 1999.

5. Interview with Harold Brown, Aug. 16, 1999; Carter, *Keeping Faith*, pp. 212–17; Vance, *Hard Choices*, p. 33.

6. Väyrynen, "Nordic Region," p. 174; Boel, *Socialdemokratiets atomvåbenpolitik*, p. 58.

7. Giangrande, *Nuclear North*, p. 185; Jewett, "'Suffocation,'" pp. 204–5; Schmitz, *Anti-Nuclear Protest*, pp. 12–13.

8. Byrne, *Campaign*, pp. 191–92; "Memorandum of Conversation" (Oct. 3, 1978), "Memcons: Brzezinski, 9/78–2/79" Folder, Box 33, Subject File, NSA Records; Nitze, *From Hiroshima*, pp. 366–67; interview with Michael Foot, June 19, 1998.

9. Perkovich, *India's Nuclear Bomb*, pp. 188, 200–201, 211; Beker, *Disarmament*, pp. 65–70; "Subject: The UN Special Session on Disarmament" (Mar. 24, 1978), enclosure in Marjorie Craig Benton to Landon Butler, Mar. 27, 1978, "SALT, 2/16/78–3/27/78 [CF, O/A 563]" Folder, Box 128, Chief of Staff's File.

10. "Foreign Reaction to President's Neutron Warhead Decision" (Apr. 11, 1978), p. 3; "Enhanced Radiation Weapons and Radiological Warfare, 2–4/78" Folder, Sub-

ject File, NSA Records; Carter, *Keeping Faith*, p. 189; Brzezinski, *Power and Principle*, p. 215.

11. Gorbachev, *Memoirs*, p. 138.

12. Beker, *Disarmament*, p. 38; Dobrynin, *In Confidence*, p. 393; interview with Peter Steglich, May 21, 1999.

13. Schmidt, *Men and Powers*, p. 63; comments of Anatoly Chernyaev in Tannenwald, ed., *Understanding*, p. 9.

14. Interview with Edith Ballantyne, June 1, 1999; Furtado, *Turkey*, p. 12.

15. "Memorandum of Conversation" (Apr. 11, 1978), "Memcons: Brzezinski, 10/77–8/78" Folder, Box 33, Subject File, NSA Records; interview with Hugh Jenkins, June 20, 1998.

16. Leonid Brezhnev, "To the Participants in the World Forum of Peace Forces" (Jan. 1977), Solomon Papers; "Ob okazanii dopolnitelnoi materialnoi pomoschi dlya realizatsii programmy deystvii Vsemirnogo Soveta Mira" (1978), f. 89, op. 33, d. 20, Central Committee of the CPSU Records; Snyder, *Warriors*, p. 97.

17. David McReynolds to Peggy Duff, Feb. 6, 1978, Box 40, McReynolds Papers; York, *Making Weapons*, p. 278.

18. Interview with Sanford Gottlieb, July 19, 1998; interview with John Isaacs, July 20, 1999; interview with Gene LaRocque, Aug. 17, 1999; Taylor, "On Being 'Consulted,'" pp. 20–21.

19. Interview with Harold Brown, Aug. 16, 1999; interview with Paul Warnke, July 20, 1999; Michael Hornblow to Fran Voorde, Apr. 14, 1977, Brzezinski to James Grant, May 17, 1977, and Henry Owen to the President, Jan. 18, 1978, "New Directions" Folder, Name File, White House Central File.

20. Sanford Gottlieb to Jimmy Carter, Jan. 21, 1977, "Gottlieb, Sanford" Folder, Name File, and Barton Hunter to Carter, Feb. 18, 1977, "ND 18 3/1/77–3/31/77" Folder, Box ND-48, Subject File, White House Central File; Taylor, "On Being 'Consulted,'" p. 20.

21. Taylor, *We Made a Difference*, p. 120; Carter to David Cortright, Jan. 19, 1978, "Cortright, David" Folder, Name File, White House Central File; WILPF press release of May 10, 1978, Box 2, Section IV, Series A,6, WILPF Records; interview with Harold Willens, May 11, 2000; Thomas A. Halsted to the Acting Director, ACDA, "SALT, 2/16/78–3/27/78 [CF, O/A 563]" Folder, Box 128, Chief of Staff's File.

22. Fran Voorde to Ethel Taylor, Jan. 31, 1977, "Women Strike for Peace" Folder, Name File, White House Central File; Taylor, "On Being 'Consulted,'" pp. 20–21.

23. Barton Hunter to Timothy Smith, Mar. 10, 1977, and C. Arthur Borg to Zbigniew Brzezinski, Mar. 22, 1977, "ND 18 3/1/77–3/31/77" Folder, Box ND-48, Subject File, White House Central File; interview with Harold Willens, May 11, 2000.

24. Interview with Zbigniew Brzezinski, July 21, 1999; interview with Harold Brown, Aug. 16, 1999.

25. *WP*, Oct. 23, 1984; Snyder, *Warriors*, p. 99.

26. Brzezinski to Carter, Oct. 21 and Nov. 18, 1977, "Weekly Reports [to the

President], 31–41: [10/77–1/78]" Folder, Box 41, Brzezinski Papers; Patrick Caddell to Carter and Hamilton Jordan, May 10, 1978, "SALT [5]" Folder, Box 6, Office of the Assistant to the President for Communications File.

27. Interview with Terry Provance, July 20, 1999; Kotz, *Wild Blue Yonder*, pp. 160–67; interview with Harold Brown, Aug. 16, 1999; interview with Zbigniew Brzezinski, July 21, 1999; interview with Paul Warnke, July 20, 1999.

28. Interview with Harold Brown, Aug. 16, 1999; Kotz, *Wild Blue Yonder*, pp. 167–71; Stubbing, *Defense Game*, pp. 347–48.

29. Auger, *Dynamics*, pp. 15, 35–48, 53–54, 104; Brzezinski, *Power and Principle*, p. 301; Carter to Melvin Price, July 21, 1977, "ND 17 1/20/77–12/31/79" Folder, Box ND-48, Subject File, White House Central File.

30. Vance, *Hard Choices*, p. 68; Auger, *Dynamics*, pp. 56–59; Brzezinski to Carter, July 22, 1977, "Weekly Reports [to the President], 16–30: [6/77–9/77]" Folder, Box 41, Brzezinski Papers.

31. Brzezinski recalled: "Our own attitude was that both the actual and the political costs did not justify production if the Europeans were not willing to have the weapon." Brzezinski, *Power and Principle*, p. 302; Carter to Schmidt, Sept. 19, 1977, "Germany, Federal Republic of: Chancellor Helmut Schmidt, 5–12/77" Folder, President's Correspondence . . . File, NSA Records.

32. Brzezinski, *Power and Principle*, pp. 302–4; Vance, *Hard Choices*, pp. 69, 92–93; "Chronology of Events Involving Enhanced Radiation Weapons (ERW)," "Defense—Enhanced Radiation Warhead: [3/78–8/78]" Folder, Box 22, Brzezinski Papers; Risse-Kappen, *Zero Option*, pp. 26–29.

33. Carter, *Keeping Faith*, pp. 226–28; Auger, *Dynamics*, pp. 76–77, 108; interview with Ruud Lubbers, May 27, 1999; Zbigniew Brzezinski to Carter, Mar. 18, 1978, and "Presidential Statement on Enhanced Radiation Weapons" (Apr. 7, 1978), "Defense—Enhanced Radiation Warhead: [3/78–8/78]" Folder, Box 22, Brzezinski Papers; Brzezinski, *Power and Principle*, pp. 304–6; oral history interview with Jimmy Carter, Nov. 29, 1982, pp. 33–34.

34. Auger, *Dynamics*, p. 109; Brzezinski, *Power and Principle*, p. 306; interview with Paul Warnke, July 20, 1999; interview with Harold Brown, Aug. 16, 1999.

35. Secretary of State to Deputy Secretary of State, Mar. [?], 1978, "Defense—Enhanced Radiation Warhead: [3/78–8/78]" Folder, Box 22, Brzezinski Papers; Auger, *Dynamics*, pp. 84, 110; Vance, *Hard Choices*, p. 94.

36. Brzezinski, *Power and Principle*, pp. 49–50, 129–32; oral history interview with Zbigniew Brzezinski, Feb. 18, 1982, p. 84; Vance, *Hard Choices*, p. 23; Schmidt, *Men and Powers*, p. 187; Genscher, *Rebuilding*, pp. 145–46.

37. Brzezinski to Carter, July 22, 1977, "Weekly Reports [to the President], 16–30: [6/77–9/77]" Folder, Box 41, Brzezinski Papers; Carter to Schmidt, Sept. 19, 1977, "Germany, Federal Republic of: Chancellor Helmut Schmidt, 5–12/77" Folder, President's Correspondence . . . File, NSA Records.

38. The new policy was to refuse to use or threaten to use nuclear weapons against non-nuclear nations that had signed the Nonproliferation Treaty, unless they were allied with a nuclear nation attacking the United States or its allies. Marjorie

Craig Benton to Landon Butler, Mar. 27, 1978, "SALT, 2/16/78–3/27/78 [CF, O/A 563]" Folder, Box 128, Chief of Staff's File; interview with Paul Warnke, July 20, 1999; "Non-Use of Nuclear Weapons," in *American Foreign Policy*, p. 196.

39. "President Carter Interviewed," p. 124; Herken, *Cardinal Choices*, pp. 188–89; "Record of the Main Content of A. A. Gromyko's Conversation with USA President J. Carter" (Sept. 23, 1977), Archive of Foreign Policy, Russian Federation, in *CWIHP Bulletin*, No. 8–9 (Winter 1996–97), p. 105.

40. Cyrus Vance to William C. Foster, May 19, 1978, Box 3, Alexander Papers; York, *Making Weapons*, pp. 285–88; Herken, *Cardinal Choices*, pp. 189–90; Schrag, *Global Action*, pp. 24–27.

41. Schrag, *Global Action*, p. 24; Warnke to Carter, Sept. 19, 1978, "Serial Xs—[9/78–12/78]" Folder, Box 36, Brzezinski Papers.

42. Carter's written comments on Brzezinski to Carter, Sept. 21, 1978, and Brzezinski to the Vice President, the Secretary of State, and the Secretary of Defense, Sept. 25, 1978, "Serial Xs—[9/78–12/78]" Folder, Box 36, Brzezinski Papers; Herken, *Cardinal Choices*, pp. 189–90; Garthoff, *Détente*, pp. 756–57.

43. [Hamilton Jordan], "Relationship of SALT II to CTB" (ca. early July 1978), Jody Powell to Carter, July 7, 1978, Jerry Rafshoon to Carter, July 7, 1978, and Frank Moore to Carter, July 7, 1978, "Comprehensive Test Ban Treaty/SALT 1978" Folder, Box 34, Chief of Staff's File; interview with Paul Warnke, July 20, 1999.

44. Carter, *Keeping Faith*, pp. 212–16; Brzezinski, *Power and Principle*, pp. 50, 157; Stubbing, *Defense Game*, p. 345.

45. Brzezinski, *Power and Principle*, pp. 48–49, 152; Carter, *Keeping Faith*, pp. 217, 223; Vance, *Hard Choices*, pp. 45, 49; Dobrynin, *In Confidence*, pp. 384–85.

46. Carter, *Keeping Faith*, p. 219; interview with Thomas Graham, Jr., Aug. 23, 1999; Vance, *Hard Choices*, pp. 49–52; Brzezinski, *Power and Principle*, pp. 146, 157–64; interview with Harold Brown, Aug. 16, 1999.

47. Stubbing, *Defense Game*, p. 345; Garthoff, *Détente*, p. 805; Vance, *Hard Choices*, pp. 53–55; Brzezinski, *Power and Principle*, pp. 163–64.

48. Oral history interview with Anne Wexler, Feb. 12–13, 1981, p. 125; oral history interview with Hamilton Jordan, Nov. 6, 1981, p. 55.

49. Brzezinski, *Power and Principle*, p. 165; Vance, *Hard Choices*, p. 66; interview with Paul Warnke, July 20, 1999.

50. Brzezinski, *Power and Principle*, pp. 147–48, 166–67; interview with Brzezinski, July 21, 1999; interview with Paul Warnke, July 20, 1999.

51. Brzezinski to Carter, Apr. 7 and 14, 1978, "Weekly Reports [to the President], 53–60 [4/78–5/78]" Folder, Box 41, Brzezinski Papers; Brzezinski, *Power and Principle*, p. 167; Vance, *Hard Choices*, p. 102.

52. Hamilton Jordan and Frank Moore to Carter, Nov. 17, 1977, "SALT 1977" Folder, Box 37, Chief of Staff's File. See also Dan Tate to Moore, Nov. 18, 1977, "SALT 1977" Folder, and Richard Moe to the Vice President et al., Apr. 10, 1978, "SALT 1978" Folder, Box 37, Chief of Staff's File.

53. Carter, *Keeping Faith*, pp. 224–25; oral history interview with Jimmy Carter, Nov. 29, 1982, p. 60.

54. Landon Butler to Hamilton Jordan, Apr. 14, 1978, "[SALT II Support], 5/17/77–10/26/78 [CF, O/A 563]" Folder, Box 132, and "The Harris Survey" (May 22, 1978), "SALT, 4/19/78–6/20/78 [CF, O/A 563]" Folder, Box 128, Chief of Staff's File.

55. Oral history interview with Anne Wexler, Feb. 12–13, 1981, p. 22; "Americans for SALT," "[SALT II Support], 5/17/77–10/26/78 [CF, O/A 563]" Folder, Box 132, Chief of Staff's File; interview with Zbigniew Brzezinski, July 21, 1999.

56. Carter, *Keeping Faith*, pp. 220–21; interview with Thomas Graham, Jr., Aug. 23, 1999; Vance, *Hard Choices*, pp. 56–58.

57. Brzezinski, *Power and Principle*, pp. 185–89, 317–21, 325–27; Carter, *Keeping Faith*, pp. 223, 229–32; Vance, *Hard Choices*, pp. 58–63.

58. Carter, *Keeping Faith*, pp. 232–34; "Memorandum of Conversation" (Oct. 3, 1978), "Memcons: Brzezinski, 9/78–2/79" Folder, Box 33, Subject File, NSA Records; Brzezinski, *Power and Principle*, pp. 327–31.

59. Vance, *Hard Choices*, p. 96; Adelman, *Great Universal Embrace*, p. 182.

60. Risse-Kappen, *Zero Option*, pp. 10–13, 20; "Memorandum of Conversation" (Sept. 27, 1977), "Memcons: Brzezinski, 1–9/77" Folder, Box 33, Subject File, NSA Records; Garthoff, *Détente*, pp. 417, 879; Bundy, *Danger*, p. 568.

61. Vance, *Hard Choices*, pp. 64–67; Nitze, *From Hiroshima*, pp. 366–67; Schmidt, *Men and Powers*, pp. 184–89.

62. Schmidt, *Men and Powers*, pp. 185, 189; interview with Harold Brown, Aug. 16, 1999; Risse-Kappen, *Zero Option*, pp. 20–25.

63. "Memorandum of Conversation" (Oct. 3, 1978) and "Memorandum of Conversation" (Oct. 5, 1978), "Memcons: Brzezinski, 9/78–2/79" Folder, Box 33, Subject File, NSA Records.

64. Garthoff, *Détente*, pp. 756–57, 768–85, 801–20; "Record of the Main Content of A. A. Gromyko's Conversation" (Sept. 23, 1977), p. 108; Brzezinski to Carter, July 1, 1977, "Weekly Reports [to the President], 16–30: [6/77–9/77]" Folder, Box 41, Brzezinski Papers.

65. Kull, *Burying Lenin*, pp. 18, 164; Dobrynin, *In Confidence*, pp. 379–80; Central Intelligence Agency, "Soviet National Security Policy: Responses to the Changing Military and Economic Environment" (June 1988), in Zubok, Nielsen, and Grant, eds., *Understanding*.

66. Garthoff, *Détente*, pp. 792–95; Dobrynin, *In Confidence*, p. 430; Gorbachev, *Memoirs*, pp. 443–44; Schmidt, *Men and Powers*, pp. 64–67.

67. Dobrynin, *In Confidence*, pp. 402–5; Arbatov, *System*, p. 193.

68. Vance, *Hard Choices*, p. 109; Brzezinski, *Power and Principle*, pp. 517–18; Dobrynin, *In Confidence*, pp. 397–98.

69. Dobrynin, *In Confidence*, pp. 371–73.

70. Ibid., pp. 347, 370–71, 387–91; Andrew and Gordievsky, *KGB*, pp. 538–39; Kaufman, *Presidency*, pp. 39–40; "Record of the Main Content of A. A. Gromyko's Conversation" (Sept. 23, 1977), p. 106.

71. Dobrynin, *In Confidence*, pp. 387–92; interview with Peter Steglich, May 21, 1999; Schmidt, *Men and Powers*, pp. 182–83.

72. Arbatov, "America," p. 318; Vance, *Hard Choices*, p. 55; "Talks Between A. A. Gromyko and C[yrus] Vance, 28–30 March 1977," f. 89, op. 76, d. 1, Storage Center

for Contemporary Documentation, Moscow, in *CWIHP Bulletin*, No. 10 (Mar. 1998), p. 233; Garthoff, *Détente*, p. 809.

73. "Memorandum of Conversation" (June 23, 1977), "Memcons: Brzezinski, 1–9/77" Folder, Box 33, Subject File, NSA Records; Vance, *Hard Choices*, p. 55; Schmidt, *Men and Powers*, pp. 183–84; Garthoff, *Détente*, pp. 806–8; Dobrynin, *In Confidence*, p. 392.

74. Interview with Zbigniew Brzezinski, July 21, 1999; "Memorandum of Conversation" (June 23, 1977), "Memcons: Brzezinski, 1–9/77" Folder, Box 33, Subject File, NSA Records.

75. "Zapis besedy s senatorom Macgovernom" (Aug. 29, 1977), f. 89, op. 76, d. 41, Central Committee of the CPSU Records; "Record of the Main Content of A. A. Gromyko's Conversation" (Sept. 23, 1977), p. 106.

76. Garthoff, *Détente*, pp. 763, 811–19; Dobrynin, *In Confidence*, p. 399; York, *Making Weapons*, pp. 322–23; Savel'yev and Detinov, *Big Five*, pp. 44–49; "Record of the Main Content of A. A. Gromyko's Conversation" (Sept. 23, 1977), p. 108.

77. Arbatov, "US Foreign Policy," p. 79.

78. Meeting of the Politburo of the Central Committee of the CPSU, Apr. 27, 1978, f. 3, op. 120, d. 39, Archive of the President of the Russian Federation, in *CWIHP Bulletin*, No. 8–9 (Winter 1996–97), 112; "Record of Main Content of Conversation Between A. A. Gromyko and U.S. Secretary of State C. Vance" (May 31, 1978), Archive of the President of the Russian Federation, ibid., pp. 113–15; Dobrynin, *In Confidence*, p. 408.

79. "Speech of Com. L. I. Brezhnev at the Politburo Session of the CC CPSU Concerning Several Issues of the International Situation" (June 8, 1978), f. 89, per. 34, dok. 1, Storage Center for Contemporary Documentation, Moscow, in *CWIHP Bulletin*, No. 8–9 (Winter 1996–97), pp. 117–18; Dobrynin, *In Confidence*, p. 412. For another mordant assessment of U.S. policy that year, see "Report on the Meeting Between SED General Secretary E. Honecker and L. I. Brezhnev in the Crimea, 25 July 1978," DY 30, JIV 2/201/1495, Stiftung "Archiv der Parteien und Massenorganisationen der ehemaligen DDR," in *CWIHP Bulletin*, No. 8–9 (Winter 1996–97), pp. 122–23.

80. "Speech of Com. L. I. Brezhnev at the Politburo Session of the CC CPSU Concerning Several Issues of the International Situation" (June 8, 1978), pp. 117–19.

81. Dobrynin recognized that one reason for Carter's criticism of the Soviet Union was to allay the public impression that he was weak and irresolute. Dobrynin to the USSR Ministry of Foreign Affairs, July 11, 1978, f. 89, per. 76, dok. 28, Storage Center for Contemporary Documentation, Moscow, in *CWIHP Bulletin*, No. 8–9 (Winter 1996–97), pp. 119–21; Dobrynin, *In Confidence*, p. 411.

82. Arbatov, "America," p. 318.

Chapter 4

Epigraph: "The END Campaign," *BAS* 36 (Dec. 1980): 54.

1. Jacobsen, "Nuclear Era," pp. 31–32; Inga Thorsson, "Disavowing Violence," *BAS* 36 (Sept. 1980): 1; Bernard T. Feld, "The Hands Move Closer to Midnight," *BAS* 37 (Jan. 1981): 1.

2. Minnion and Bolsover, eds., *CND Story*, p. 150; interview with Bruce Kent, June 7, 1999; "Information Sheet 5," CND (B) Records, S; Bruce Kent, "General Secretary's Report" (ca. late 1980), Reel 19, CND (B) Records, HM; Kent, *Undiscovered Ends*, pp. 169–72.

3. CND estimates for the turnout at the rally were 70,000 to 100,000 demonstrators, although the *New York Times* reported 50,000. In Britain, the event received extensive front-page newspaper coverage. Kent, *Undiscovered Ends*, pp. 172–74; "CND Groups and Activities Report" (ca. late 1980) and "Publications, 'Sanity,' and Presswork Report" (1980), Reel 19, CND (B) Records, HM; *NYT*, Oct. 27, 1980.

4. Byrd, "Development," p. 65; Ceadel, "Britain's Nuclear Disarmers," pp. 228–30; interviews with Bruce Kent, July 10, 1990 and June 7, 1999; National Peace Council, *Annual Report* (1980), pp. 1–2, Reel 17, CND (B) Records, HM; interview with Daniel Plesch, July 21, 1998.

5. Interview with Bruce Kent, June 7, 1999; Thompson and Smith, eds., *Protest and Survive*, pp. 11–12, 25; "Publications, 'Sanity' and Presswork Report" (1980), Reel 19, CND (B) Records, HM.

6. Duncan Rees, "General Secretary's Report" (July 7, 1979), and Minutes of the CND National Council meeting of July 7, 1979, Reel 17, "General Secretary's Report to CND Annual Conference 1979," and "Publications, 'Sanity' and Presswork Report" (1980), Reel 19, CND (B) Records, HM.

7. National Peace Council, *Annual Report* (1980), p. 4, and Minutes of the CND National Council meeting of Dec. 15, 1979, Reel 17, "Draft CND Statement on Soviet Invasion of Poland (If It Happens)," Reel 18, CND (B) Records, HM.

8. Steve Dawe and Tony Webb, "Anti Nuclear Campaign" (Mar. 3, 1980), "Anti Nuclear Campaign—Newsletter No. 4" (June 1980), and "Resolutions Passed at the AGM of the ANC 1980," Reel 18, CND (B) Records, HM.

9. "England," *DC*, No. 1 (Feb. 1980), pp. 17–18; "International Mobilization for Survival News Service" (Apr.–June 1980), Reel 20, CND (B) Records, HM.

10. Interview with Michael Foot, June 19, 1998; "International Mobilization for Survival News Service" (Apr.–June 1980), Reel 20, CND (B) Records, HM; Byrd, "Development," p. 82; Taylor, "Labour Party," p. 122.

11. Ceadel, "Britain's Nuclear Disarmers," p. 229; "CND Groups and Activities Report" (ca. late 1980), Reel 19, CND (B) Records, HM.

12. "National Peace Council Monthly Mailing Service" (Dec. 19, 1980), and Report of the CND General Secretary, Dec. 15, 1979, Reel 17, CND (B) Records, HM; "Medical Campaign Against Nuclear Weapons," Medical Campaign Against Nuclear Weapons Records.

13. Gallup, ed., *International Gallup Polls: Public Opinion 1979*, p. 98.

14. "Netherlands," *DC*, No. 1 (Feb. 1980), pp. 5–8; Tromp, "Alternatives," p. 74.

15. Everts, "Continuity and Change," p. 11; Everts, "Public Opinion," p. 250.

16. "Belgium," *DC*, No. 1 (Feb. 1980), pp. 4–5; Lubelski-Bernard, "Euromissile Crisis," pp. 53, 58–59; Lamot, "Peace Movement," p. 213; Galand, "Le C.N.A.-P.D."—Belgique."

17. Erik Alfsen, *De förste år av Nei til Atomvåpen*, pp. 1–6, Nei til Atomvåpen Records; Grepstad, "Norway," pp. 10–32; interview with Ole Kopreitan, May 14,

1999; Grepstad, "Peace Movement," pp. 11–12; Waldahl, "Norwegian Attitudes," p. 299.

18. Krasner, *Political Influence*, pp. 3–4; *An Introduction to No to Nuclear Weapons Denmark*, pp. 4–5, 9, 11; "Denmark," *DC*, No. 1 (Feb. 1980), p. 11; Gallup, ed., *International Public Opinion Polls: Public Opinion 1979*, p. 98; Haagerup, "Nordic Peace Movements," pp. 157–58.

19. "Kvinder for fred," Kvinder for Fred Records; Grepstad, "Norway," pp. 17–19; Krasner, "Decline," p. 172; Krasner, *Political Influence*, pp. 8–9; interview with Berit Ås, Aug. 12, 2000.

20. "West Germany," *DC*, No. 1 (Feb. 1980), p. 10; "International Mobilization for Survival News Service" (Apr.–June 1980), Reel 20, CND (B) Records, HM; Kubbig and Risse-Kappen, "Living," p. 74; Mushaben, "Cycles," p. 32.

21. Noack and Staude, "Peace Movement," pp. 223–24; Breyman, *Why Movements Matter*, pp. 55–56; Kelly, *Fighting for Hope*, pp. 120–21; "History of Die Grünen" (1983), Box 2, The Greens Records; Noelle-Neumann, *Germans*, p. 437.

22. Rossi and Ilari, "Peace Movement," pp. 142–46; "Italy," *DC*, No. 1 (Feb. 1980), p. 11; "Eurocommunism and the Bomb," pp. 141–49.

23. Bourdet, "Rebirth," pp. 196–97; "International Mobilization for Survival News Service" (June–July 1979 and Apr.–June 1980), Reel 20, CND (B) Records, HM.

24. Furtado, *Turkey*, p. 9.

25. "Moving Ahead," *DC*, No. 18 (Jan. 1983), p. 10; "Ireland," *DC*, No. 1 (Feb. 1980), p. 16; "International Mobilization for Survival News Service" (Apr.–June 1980), Reel 20, CND (B) Records, HM.

26. Gerd Greune, "Action News No. 2" (Jan. 1981), PB1, Series G, SANE Records; "Kvinder for fred," Kvinder for Fred Records; Grepstad, "Peace Movement," p. 10.

27. Andersson and Lindkvist, "Peace Movement," pp. 12–13; "Kvinder for fred," Kvinder for Fred Records; Lindkvist, "Mobilization Peaks," p. 160.

28. "Canada," *DC*, No. 1 (Feb. 1980), pp. 9–10, 14; Kay Macpherson and Sara Good, "Canadian Voice of Women for Peace," *PM* 3 (Oct.–Nov. 1987): 26; Gerd Greune, "Action News No. 2" (Jan. 1981), PB1, Series G, SANE Records.

29. "United States" and "U.S. Catholic Bishops," *DC*, No. 1 (Feb. 1980), pp. 8–9, 18; "Forum: Strategies for Disarmament," *Fellowship* 46 (Jan.–Feb. 1980): 13.

30. Upon appeal, their sentences were reduced to their time served in prison. "An Introduction to the Plowshares Movement" (1985), Box 527, WRI Records; Davidon, "Warheads into Plowshares," pp. 49–51; Myers, "Storming the Gates," p. 898; Polner and O'Grady, *Disarmed*, pp. 344–47.

31. "Resolutions and Statements" (June 27–July 1, 1979), and "Priorities" (July 1, 1979), Box 25, and Tricia Smith, "Legislative Office: Report to National Board for September 1979–April 1980," Box 26, Series A,2, WILPF Records.

32. David Cortright to Eleanor Smeal, May 23, 1980, Box 126, Series G, SANE Records; *NYT*, June 1, 1980; "Demonstration," pp. 43–46.

33. See, for example, Boyer, "Physicians," pp. 633–43.

34. Interview with Helen Caldicott, Feb. 27, 1999; Waitzkin, "Medical Profession," pp. 647–48; Caldicott, *Desperate Passion*, pp. 160–61, 165, 174.

35. Minutes of the Board of Directors meeting, PSR, Feb. 9, 1980, PSR Records; interview with Bernard Lown, July 6, 1999; Holden, "Physicians," pp. 1449–50, 1452; PSR to Carter and Brezhnev, Feb. 1980, *BAS* 36 (Apr. 1980): 16.

36. Interview with Helen Caldicott, Feb. 27, 1999; Caldicott, *Desperate Passion*, pp. 189, 228; interview with Judy Lipton, July 31, 1999.

37. The lack of enthusiasm for SALT II was evident even among the atomic scientists, who had promoted it for years. See, for example: Bernard Feld, "The High Price of SALT," *BAS* 35 (Feb. 1979): 4; Bernard Feld, "No Substitute for SALT," and "On Nuclear Disarmament," *BAS* 35 (Sept. 1979): 7.

38. Interview with David Cortright, June 29, 1987; interview with Christopher Paine, Sept. 14, 1999; interview with Gene LaRocque, Aug. 17, 1999; interview with Harold Willens, May 11, 2000; Glass, *Citizens*, pp. 10–87; Cortright, *Peace Works*, pp. 134–39.

39. MfS, "Progress and Promise: A Decade of Achievement" (Dec. 1987), author's possession; interviews with Charles Johnson and Peter Bergel, Aug. 3, 1999; Weart, *Nuclear Fear*, p. 346.

40. Dorothy Nelkin, "Anti-Nuclear Connections: Power and Weapons," *BAS* 37 (Apr. 1981): 38; *Meaning of Survival*, p. 266; "Mobilization for Survival," Box 2, AFSC-Rocky Flats Project Records.

41. Interviews with Peter Bergel and Charles Johnson, Aug. 3, 1999.

42. Interview with Randall Forsberg, July 7, 1999; "The Nuclear Connection," Box 11, Series II, AFSC Records; Bob Moore to Friend of MFS, Sept. 1979, MfS Records, S; interview with Terry Provance, July 20, 1999; interview with Carol Jensen, July 31, 1999.

43. Interview with Randall Forsberg, July 7, 1999; Forsberg to Mike Jendrzejczyk, Apr. 10, 1980, and "Call to Halt the Nuclear Arms Race," Box 15, Freeze Records, SL.

44. Interview with Randall Forsberg, July 7, 1999; George Sommaripa and Randall Forsberg, "Strategy for a Concerted National Effort to Halt the Nuclear Arms Race" (Aug. 25, 1980), and Forsberg to Marilyn McNabb, Aug. 26, 1980, PB1, Series G, SANE Records.

45. Interview with Randall Kehler, Aug. 20, 1999; Solo, *From Protest*, p. 49.

46. The groups were: American Baptist Churches, Coalition for a New Foreign and Military Policy, Council for a Livable World, Friends Committee on National Legislation, SANE, Unitarian Universalist Association, United Church of Christ, and Friends of the Earth. Minutes of SANE Executive Committee meeting of July 17, 1979, Box 70, Series G, SANE Records; interview with Robert Musil, July 20, 1998; Marianne Szegedy-Maszak, "Rise and Fall of the Washington Peace Industry," *BAS* 45 (Jan.–Feb. 1989): 19.

47. Gallup, ed., *GP: Public Opinion 1979*, pp. 124–26, 195, 198, 272–73; Gallup, ed., *GP: Public Opinion 1980*, pp. 67–69; Schneider, "Peace and Strength," p. 342; Graham, *American Public Opinion*, p. 59.

48. "International Mobilization for Survival News Service" (June–July 1979) and (Apr.–June 1980), Reel 20, CND (B) Records, HM; Gyotsu N. Sato to Dear friends, July 8, 1980, PB1, Series G, SANE Records; *Meaning of Survival*, p. 265.

49. "Japan," *DC*, No. 1 (Feb. 1980), p. 14; Gerd Greune, "Action News No. 2" (Jan. 1981), PB 1, Series G, SANE Records.

50. "Soft-spoken Romy Takes on Nuclear Energy," *FFP Bulletin* (Sept.–Oct. 1979), pp. 3, 7, "Principles of Unity: Campaign for a Nuclear Free Philippines," author's possession; A. Linn Neumann, "Marcos Tightens Grip on Bases," *NT* (Feb. 1983), pp. 21–22.

51. Burgmann, *Power and Protest*, pp. 196–98; "International Mobilization for Survival News Service" (Apr.–June 1980) and (June–July 1980), Reel 20, CND (B) Records, HM; Gerd Greune, "Action News No. 2" (Jan. 1981), PB1, Series G, SANE Records.

52. Newnham, *Peace Squadron*, pp. 39–48; Clements, *Back From the Brink*, pp. 113–14.

53. Giff Johnson, "Kwajalein: Apartheid in the Pacific," *WIN* 18 (Aug. 1, 1982): 22–23; "Micronesia," *DC*, No. 1 (Feb. 1980), p. 14; Roman Bedor, "Protecting the Source of Life," *Mobilizer* 5 (Winter 1986): 8.

54. "Pacific Concerns Resource Centre," *Peace Movement New Zealand Newsletter* (June 1982), p. 6; "International Mobilization for Survival News Service" (Apr.–June 1980), Reel 20, CND (B) Records, HM; Peter Jones, "Towards a Nuclear Free Pacific," *END Bulletin* (Feb. 1981), p. 19; Sharp, "Militarism," pp. 193, 196.

55. "Latin America," *DC*, No. 1 (Feb. 1980), pp. 14–15; "International Mobilization for Survival News Service" (Apr.–June 1980), Reel 20, CND (B) Records, HM.

56. Ilukhina and Pavlova, "Totalitarianism," p. 4; Kapitza to Andropov, Nov. 11, 1980, in Boag, Rubinin, and Shoenberg, eds., *Kapitza*, pp. 416–20; von Hippel, *Citizen Scientist*, pp. 52–54; Stone, *"Every Man,"* pp. 164–66.

57. Tony Simpson, "Protest and Survive: October 1980, London," *END Bulletin* (Feb. 1981), p. 14.

58. Interview with Bernard Lown, July 6, 1999; Evangelista, *Unarmed Forces*, pp. 149–50; Warner and Shuman, *Citizen Diplomats*, pp. 40–41.

59. Interview with Bernard Lown, July 6, 1999; Evangelista, *Unarmed Forces*, pp. 150–51; IPPNW press release of Dec. 6, 1980, PB2, Series G, SANE Records; Irwin Abrams, "The Origins of International Physicians for the Prevention of Nuclear War: The Dr. James E. Muller Diaries," *Medicine, Conflict and Survival* 15 (1999): 22–24.

60. Ehring and Hücking, "Die neue Friedensbewegung," pp. 320–21; Köszegi and Szent-Ivanyi, "A Struggle," p. 164; Köszegi and Thompson, *New Hungarian*, pp. 4–5, 12.

61. Sandford, *Sword*, pp. 40–41, 49–51; Allen, *Germany East*, pp. 98–99; Mushaben, "Swords," p. 129.

62. See, for example: Minutes of the CND National Council meeting of Sept. 22, 1979, Reel 17, CND (B) Records, HM; David Cortright to Dan Smith, Aug. 25, 1980, Box 70, Series G, SANE Records.

63. Michael Harbottle, "World Disarmament Campaign" (Oct. 1980), Reel 17, CND (B) Records, HM; "Something New," *DC*, No. 1 (Feb. 1980), p. 2; "Inter-Church Peace Council" (Jan. 12, 1983), Pax Christi (Belgium) Records, S.

64. Minutes of the WRI Council Meeting, July 14–18, 1980, Box 39, WRI Rec-

ords; "WILPF: 65 and Still Growing," *Fellowship* 46 (Jan.–Feb. 1980): 22; "IFOR: The Successes of a Complete Failure," *Fellowship* 45 (Sept. 1979): 4.

65. "Report of the Second Pugwash Workshop on the Current Crisis on Nuclear Forces in Europe" (Apr. 11–13, 1980), Kaldor Papers; "Pugwash 1980," *BAS* 36 (Nov. 1980): 9.

66. "The Arms Race and the present modernization of Nuclear Weapons in Western Europe" (Nov. 21, 1979), Folder 715, IKV Records, A; *Facts & Comments*, No. 6 (Aug. 15, 1982), pp. 3–32, Pax Christi International (Belgium) Records, S.

67. Grepstad, "Norway," p. 19; Winther, "Danish Peace Movements," p. 4; Petra K. Kelly, "Women and Ecology," *Gandhi Marg* 13 (Apr. 1980): 44–45.

68. Petersen, "Scandilux," pp. 3, 5–6; "Ridding Europe," pp. 151–55.

69. Interview with E. P. Thompson, Nov. 1, 1989; Thompson, *Double Exposure*, p. 10; Coates, *Dynamics*, pp. 277–78; "The END Campaign," *BAS* 36 (Dec. 1980): 1.

70. Thompson, "Notes on Exterminism," pp. 1–34; "END Campaign," pp. 1, 54.

71. Interview with Mary Kaldor, June 7, 1999; Thompson, "Movement," pp. 400–401; Bess, *Realism*, 126–36.

72. Ceadel, "Britain's Nuclear Disarmers," p. 229; Thompson, "Ends and Histories," pp. 7–8; "European Nuclear Disarmament (END) Conference for Western European Peace and Disarmament Movements" (Sept. 12–14, 1980), Folder 200, WRI Records; Thompson, "Resurgence," p. 83; Dorothy and E. P. Thompson, "END—Retrospect and Next Steps" (Aug. 18, 1980), Kaldor Papers; Taylor and Young, "Britain," p. 291.

73. *Special Session of the World Peace Council in Berlin 2–5 February 1979* (1979), and *The World Peace Council Bureau Session* (1980), p. 9, Box 3, WPC Records; "Prevent Implementation of NATO Decision!" *PC* 11 (Jan. 1980): 1–3, 6.

74. "International Conference of Solidarity with Afghanistan," *PC* 10 (Sept. 1979): 4; "The Kabul Declaration," *PC* 10 (Sept. 1979): 5.

75. Santi, *100 Years*, p. 40; Chandra, "Defend Detente!" pp. 7–8; "Stop Imperialist Military Build-Up!" *PC* 11 (May 1980): 6.

76. Interview with Rob Prince, July 27, 1999; Blokhin, "International Cooperation," pp. 25–28; Inozemtsev, "Introduction," pp. 11, 18.

77. Sandford, *Sword*, pp. 20–21; Günther Drefahl, "The Securing of Détente Requires the Struggle of Peoples against the imperialist Arms Race and for Détente," in *No New Missiles in Western Europe* (1980), pp. 7–12, German Democratic Republic Peace Council Records.

78. "International Mobilization for Survival News Service" (Apr.–June 1980), Reel 20, CND (B) Records, HM; "U.S. Peace Council National Founding Conference, November 9–11, 1979," and "Introducing the U.S. Peace Council," U.S. Peace Council Records; Michael Myerson to Dear Friend, 1980, Minutes of the executive board meeting of the U.S. Peace Council, Oct. 11–12, 1980, and "U.S. Peace Groups Conclude Talks with Soviets" (Apr. 7, 1980), Solomon Papers.

79. "US Peace Council Statement on the Current International Crisis around the Events in Iran and Afghanistan" (Jan. 27, 1980), Solomon Papers.

80. Inozemtsev, "Introduction," p. 21; *NYT*, June 24, 1979; Gordon McLennon to

Ken Coates, July 16, 1980, and Dorothy and E. P. Thompson, "END—Retrospect and Next Steps" (Aug. 18, 1980), Kaldor Papers.

81. Kodama, "Red vs. Green," pp. 3–4; Haagerup, "Nordic Peace Movements," pp. 157–58.

82. Minutes of the of the Coalition for a New Foreign and Military Policy board meeting, June 26, 1980, Brewster Rhoads to Michael Myerson, July 10, 1980, and McReynolds to Rhoads, July 7, 1980, Solomon Papers; "The New 'Red Scare': An Open Letter," U.S. Peace Council Records; Dorothy and E. P. Thompson, "END—Retrospect and Next Steps" (Aug. 18, 1980), Kaldor Papers.

83. "Introducing the U.S. Peace Council" (1980), U.S. Peace Council Records; Schlaga, "Peace Movement," p. 139; interview with Rob Prince, July 27, 1999.

Chapter 5

Epigraph: Dobrynin, *In Confidence*, p. 376.

1. "SALT-Leaning Nongovernmental Organizations" (Feb. 14, 1979), "SALT Chron File [Briefing Book]" Folder, Box 129, Chief of Staff's File; Carter to Ethel Taylor, Oct. 25, 1979, Box 1, Series A,8, WSP Records.

2. Caldicott, *Missile Envy*, p. 5; Kay Camp, "Fourteen Females in Fantasyland: A Visit to NATO Headquarters," Box 26, Series A,2, WILPF Records.

3. Furtado, *Turkey*, p. 16; Lashmar and Oliver, *Britain's Secret*, pp. xiv, 67, 123–24; Crozier, *Free Agent*, pp. xii–xiii, 128, 135–36, 144–45, 294–95.

4. A. N. Yakovlev, "Zapis besedy s Kanadskimi uchyenymi—uchastnikami Paguoshskogo dvizheniya" (May 20, 1980), f. 89, op. 76, d. 29, S. Divilkovsky, "O simpoziume 'Meditsinskie posledstviya yadernogo vooruzheniya i yadernoy voyny'" (Oct. 15, 1980), f. 89, op. 76, d. 30, "O propagandistskom obespechenii coglasheniya ob OSV-2" (July 1979), f. 89, op. 76, d. 59, Central Committee of the CPSU Records.

5. Shaposhnikov, "Role of the Public," pp. 118–25; "O dopolnitelnyh meropriyatiyah po activizatsii vystupleniy obschestvennosti protiv resheniya NATO o proizvodstve i razmeschenii novyh americanskih raket v Zapadnoy Evrope" (Apr. 15, 1980), f. 89, op. 39, d. 1, Central Committee of the CPSU Records.

6. "O podgotovke sovetsko-americanskoi Konferentsii uchenyhmedikov za predotvraschenie yadernoi voiny" (Dec. 1980), f. 89, op. 43, d. 48, Central Committee of the CPSU Records; interview with Bernard Lown, July 6, 1999.

7. *NYT*, Dec. 16, 1989; Shatz, *Soviet Dissent*, p. 179; Stone, *"Every Man,"* p. 165.

8. York, *Making Weapons*, p. 301; Vance, *Hard Choices*, p. 121; Garthoff, *Détente*, pp. 720–21; Minutes of the CND National Council meeting of Apr. 7, 1979, Reel 17, CND (B) Records, HM.

9. Dobrynin, *In Confidence*, p. 416; "O materiale dlya sovetckih sredstv informatsii po Norvegii" (Feb. 1980), f. 89, op. 76, d. 10, Central Committee of the CPSU Records.

10. "O propagandistskom obespechenii coglasheniya ob OSV-2" (July 1979), f. 89, op. 76, d. 59, Central Committee of the CPSU Records; "Minutes of the Meet-

ing between SED General Secretary Erich Honecker and Soviet leader Leonid Bre-
zhnev, Crimea, USSR, 27 July 1979," JIV 2/201/1313, DY 30, Bundesarchiv, in *CWI-HP Bulletin*, No. 8–9 (Winter 1996–97), pp. 123–24.

11. MccGwire, *Perestroika*, pp. 39–40; Dobrynin, *In Confidence*, pp. 396, 430; Savel'yev and Detinov, *Big Five*, p. 57; Pry, *War Scare*, pp. 5–8.

12. Dobrynin, *In Confidence*, pp. 420–26; Savel'yev and Detinov, *Big Five*, p. 55; "Minutes of the Meeting between SED General Secretary Erich Honecker and So-viet leader Leonid Brezhnev," p. 124.

13. Savel'yev and Detinov, *Big Five*, pp. 56–59; Schmidt, *Men and Powers*, pp. 72–75, 78, 87; Dobrynin, *In Confidence*, pp. 431–33; U.S. House of Representatives, *Modernization*, p. 50.

14. Dobrynin, *In Confidence*, pp. 423–24, 431; Holloway, *Soviet Union*, pp. 77–78.

15. Dobrynin, *In Confidence*, pp. 434–48; Schmidt, *Men and Powers*, pp. 78–82.

16. Gorbachev, *Memoirs*, pp. 113–14; Dobrynin, *In Confidence*, p. 425. Brzezinski recalled Brezhnev at Vienna as "a genuinely pitiful figure. . . . At times, he ap-peared almost senile." Brzezinski, *Power and Principle*, p. 343.

17. Brzezinski, *Power and Principle*, pp. 31, 34–35, 44–47; Garthoff, *Détente*, pp. 887–1008; Carter, *Keeping Faith*, pp. 471–83.

18. Thatcher, *Downing Street*, pp. 12, 68–69, 463, 472.

19. York, *Making Weapons*, pp. 222, 294–95, 309, 313, 316–22; Herbert F. York, "Sakharov and the Nuclear Test Ban," *BAS* 37 (Nov. 1981): 37.

20. Stubbing, *Defense Game*, p. 15.

21. Herken, *Cardinal Choices*, pp. 192–96; Brzezinski, *Power and Principle*, pp. 332–37; Christopher E. Paine, "MX: The Public Works Project of the 1980s," *BAS* 36 (Feb. 1980): 12; interview with Harold Brown, Aug. 16, 1999; Matt Nimetz to Landon Butler, Aug. 6, 1979, "SALT Memoranda and Correspondence, 8/1/79–1/3/80 [CF, OA 563]" Folder, Box 130, Chief of Staff's Records; Vance, *Hard Choices*, pp. 137–38, 365.

22. Brown, *Thinking*, pp. 81–82; York, *Making Weapons*, pp. 280–81; Garthoff, *Détente*, pp. 789–90; Kaufman, *Presidency*, pp. 192–93.

23. Brzezinski, *Power and Principle*, pp. 307–9; U.S. House of Representatives, *Modernization*, p. 26.

24. Carter, *Keeping Faith*, pp. 234–35; Schmidt, *Men and Powers*, pp. 189–91.

25. Vance and Brown to Carter, May 9, 1979, "Alpha Channel (Miscellaneous)—[5/79–8/79]" Folder, Box 20, Brzezinski Papers; Risse-Kappen, *Zero Option*, pp. 47–48; interview with Harold Brown, Aug. 16, 1999; interview with Ruud Lubbers, May 27, 1999.

26. Vance, *Hard Choices*, p. 392; interview with Zbigniew Brzezinski, July 21, 1999; interview with Harold Brown, Aug. 16, 1999; interview with Paul Warnke, July 20, 1999; Bundy, *Danger*, pp. 568, 570.

27. Thatcher, *Downing Street*, pp. 239–43; U.S. House of Representatives, *Mod-ernization*, pp. 61, 63; Lubelski-Bernard, "Euromissile Crisis," p. 54; interview with Rozanne Ridgway, Sept. 17, 1999.

28. Carter, *Keeping Faith*, p. 535; interview with Ruud Lubbers, May 27, 1999;

U.S. House of Representatives, *Modernization*, pp. 61–63; Thatcher, *Downing Street*, p. 243; Lubelski-Bernard, "Euromissile Crisis," pp. 54–56.

29. Carter, *Keeping Faith*, pp. 535–38; Schmidt, *Men and Powers*, pp. 209–19; Brzezinski, *Power and Principle*, pp. 309–11, 462–63.

30. Talbott, *Deadly Gambits*, pp. 38–39; Risse-Kappen, *Zero Option*, pp. 45–48, 79–80, 168; Schmidt, *Men and Powers*, pp. 109, 277–78; U.S. House of Representatives, *Modernization*, p. 64.

31. Carter, *Keeping Faith*, pp. 239–40; Caddell, "A Memorandum on Current Public Attitudes on SALT," including Carter's hand-scrawled comments, enclosure in Susan to Hamilton Jordan, May 24, 1979, "SALT, 1979" Folder, Box 37, Chief of Staff's Records.

32. Carter, *Keeping Faith*, pp. 243–53; Brzezinski, *Power and Principle*, p. 342; Stone, *"Every Man,"* pp. 213–25.

33. Vance, *Hard Choices*, pp. 137, 350–51; oral history interview with Lloyd Cutler, Oct. 23, 1982, p. 7; Brzezinski to Carter, Sept. 13 and 21, 1979, "Weekly Reports [to the President], 102–120: [7/79–12/79]" Folder, Box 42, Brzezinski Papers.

34. Oral history interview with Robert Beckel, Nov. 13, 1981, pp. 31, 37. Some years later, in his memoirs, Brzezinski recalled with pleasure the fact that the SALT ratification campaign ended up "creating favorable conditions for a shift in our national priorities toward greater efforts in the national security area." Brzezinski, *Power and Principle*, pp. 344–45.

35. Vance, *Hard Choices*, p. 351; Phil Spector to Anne Wexler and Mike Chanin, June 2, 1979, "SALT Memoranda and Correspondence, 5/7/79–7/30/79 [CF O/A 563]" Folder, Box 130, and Hamilton Jordan to the President, Jan. 30, 1979, "SALT Notebook [CF, A/A 648]" Folder, Box 53, Chief of Staff's Records; oral history interview with Robert Beckel, Nov. 13, 1981, pp. 44–45.

36. Vance, *Hard Choices*, pp. 136, 351; Brown, *Thinking*, p. 188; Carter, *Keeping Faith*, pp. 236–37.

37. Carter, *Keeping Faith*, pp. 262–64; Vance, *Hard Choices*, pp. 358, 389; Brown, *Thinking*, p. 188; Brzezinski, *Power and Principle*, pp. 193, 352–53.

38. Carter, *Keeping Faith*, p. 265.

39. Oral history interview with Hamilton Jordan, Nov. 6, 1981, p. 77; interview with Paul Warnke, July 20, 1999.

Chapter 6

Epigraph: Eugene V. Rostow, "The Ruritanian Quotient: A Talk Given at the First Annual Dinner of the Board of Directors of the Committee on the Present Danger" (Nov. 10, 1977), Box 13, Cline Papers.

1. Stubbing, *Defense Game*, p. 386; Garthoff, *Détente*, p. 551.

2. Nitze, *From Hiroshima*, p. 353; "Common Sense and the Common Danger" (Nov. 11, 1976), Box 13, Cline Papers.

3. Tyroler, ed., *Alerting America*, p. xvii; Nitze, *From Hiroshima*, pp. 354, 359.

4. Paul H. Nitze, "Memorandum of Conversation" (Jan. 20, 1977), Box 30, Nitze Papers.

5. Sanders, *Peddlers of Crisis*, pp. 204–10; Talbott, *Master*, p. 152; Nitze, *From Hiroshima*, pp. 354–55; Rostow to Nitze, Mar. 1, 1977, Box 68, Nitze Papers.

6. Rostow to the Executive Committee, CPD, Aug. 10, 1977, Rostow to the Board of Directors, CPD, Aug. 10, 1977 and Aug. 23, 1977, Box 70, Nitze Papers; *WP*, Aug. 13, 1977.

7. Brzezinski to Rostow, Oct. 11, 1977, Box 68, Nitze Papers.

8. Sanders, *Peddlers of Crisis*, p. 191; Rostow to Harriman, Nov. 1, 1977, Box 37, Nitze Papers; Rostow, "The Ruritanian Quotient" (Nov. 10, 1977), Box 13, Cline Papers.

9. Rostow to Vance, June 2, 1978, and Rostow to Stephen Rosen, Nov. 3, 1980, Box 37, and Rostow to Jackson, Nov. 26, 1979, Box 69, Nitze Papers; Rostow to Directors of the CPD, July 7, 1980, Box 13, Cline Papers.

10. Raymond L. Garthoff, "The 'Spending Gap,'" *BAS* 40 (May 1984): 5–6; Stubbing, *Defense Game*, pp. 16–17; Hans A. Bethe and Franklin A. Long, "The Freeze Referendum: What Next?" *BAS* 39 (Feb. 1983): 3; Udall, *Myths of August*, p. 168.

11. Committee on the Present Danger, "Where We Stand on SALT" (July 6, 1977), and Rostow to Friends and Supporters of the Committee, Dec. 5, 1979, Box 13, Cline Papers; Rostow to Kissinger, Oct. 12, 1978, Box 37, Nitze Papers; Adelman, *Great Universal Embrace*, p. 255.

12. Nitze, *From Hiroshima*, pp. 360–63; Scheer, *With Enough Shovels*, p. 37; interview with Richard Allen, June 29, 1999.

13. Rostow to Robert J. Kaiser, Nov. 13, 1980, and Rostow to William J. Casey, Dec. 8, 1980, Box 37, Nitze Papers.

14. Reagan to My Fellow Board Members and Friends of the CPD, Nov. 7, 1980, Box 13, Cline Papers; Anderson, *Revolution*, pp. 74–75.

15. Ronald Reagan, "Peace" (Apr. 1975), "Treaties" (Mar. 13, 1978), "Two Worlds" (Aug. 7, 1978), "SALT II" (Sept. 11, 1979), "SALT Talks II" (July 31, 1978), "SALT II" (Nov. 28, 1978), and "Rostow VI" (Oct. 10, 1978), in Skinner, Anderson, and Anderson, eds., *Reagan*, pp. 8–9, 15, 54–57, 62, 84–86, 99.

16. Reagan opposed the Partial Test Ban Treaty (1963), the Nuclear Nonproliferation Treaty (1968), the SALT I Treaty and the ABM Treaty (1972), the Vladivostok Accord (1974), the Peaceful Nuclear Explosions Treaty (1976), and the SALT II Treaty (1979), among others. George W. Ball, "The President's Nuclear Responsibility," *BAS* 40 (Nov. 1984): 5–6; *NYT*, July 16, Oct. 2, 1980; *Wall Street Journal*, June 3, 1980.

17. Ronald Reagan, "Strategy II" (May 4, 1977), and "Suicide Lobby" (Mar. 13, 1978), in Skinner, Anderson, and Anderson, eds., *Reagan*, pp. 112–13, 139–41.

18. Ronald Reagan, "Communism, the Disease" (May 1975), and "War" (Mar. 13, 1978), in Skinner, Anderson, and Anderson, eds., *Reagan*, pp. 12, 102.

19. Anderson, *Revolution*, p. 71; Talbott, *Deadly Gambits*, p. 7.

20. *NYT*, July 16, 1980; *Wall Street Journal*, June 3, 1980.

21. Bush explained: "You have survivablity of command in control, survivability of industrial potential, protection of a percentage of your citizens, and you have a capability that inflicts more damage on the opposition than it can inflict upon you.

That's the way you can have a winner." *NYT*, Feb. 1 and 14, Mar. 18, July 16, 1980; Adelman, *Great Universal Embrace*, p. 255.

22. Interview with Richard Allen, June 29, 1999.

23. Sanders, *Peddlers of Crisis*, pp. 282–84; Skinner, Anderson, and Anderson, eds., *Reagan*, pp. 92–99; Ray S. Cline to Reagan, Feb. 25, 1981, Box 31, Cline Papers; Nitze, *From Hiroshima*, pp. 364–65.

24. *Register* (New Haven, Conn.), Oct. 3, 1980 and *Washington Star*, Oct. 25, 1980, Box 71, Nitze Papers; Nitze, *From Hiroshima*, p. 365.

25. Carter, *Keeping Faith*, pp. 542–43, 564–65; *NYT*, Oct. 20, 1980; oral history interview with Gerald Rafshoon, Apr. 8, 1983, pp. 55, 57.

26. Anderson, "Foreign Policy and National Security" (Aug. 1979), in Anderson, *Revolution*, pp. 468–72.

27. Interview with Richard Wirthlin, Oct. 6, 1999; *Wall Street Journal*, June 3, 1980; *NYT*, Oct. 20, 1980.

28. Interview with Harold Brown, Aug. 16, 1999; Carter, *Keeping Faith*, p. 543; oral history interview with Gerald Rafshoon, Apr. 8, 1983, p. 56.

29. Sanders, *Peddlers of Crisis*, p. 292; interview with Caspar Weinberger, July 21, 1998; interview with Kenneth Adelman, July 22, 1998; Stubbing, *Defense Game*, p. 19.

30. *WP*, Jan. 2, 1985; Oberdorfer, *Turn*, p. 103; Drew, "A Reporter," p. 144; Reagan, *An American Life*, p. 258.

31. Haig, *Caveat*, pp. 219–20; U.S. House of Representatives, *Modernization*, p. 34.

32. Sanders, *Peddlers of Crisis*, p. 291; Reagan, *My Turn*, p. 242.

33. *NYT*, Mar. 22, 1981; *WP*, Apr. 11, 1983.

34. Deaver, *Behind the Scenes*, p. 129; Shultz, *Turmoil*, p. 275; interview with Robert McFarlane, July 21, 1999.

35. Adelman, *Great Universal Embrace*, p. 24; *NYT*, June 23 and 28, 1981; John D. Isaacs, "Three R's of Arms Control: Reagan, Rostow and Rowny," *BAS* 37 (Aug.–Sept. 1981): 5; *Boston Globe*, Aug. 4, 1981; Drew, "A Reporter," p. 145.

36. Adelman wrote: "I believed that arms control was vastly overvalued in public discussions, even by the Reagan administration." Interview with Kenneth Adelman, July 22, 1998; Adelman, *Great Universal Embrace*, pp. 31, 232.

37. Emphasis in the original. *NYT*, June 28, 1981; Isaacs, "Three R's," p. 6.

38. Scheer, *With Enough Shovels*, p. 90; Drew, "A Reporter," p. 145; Kotz, *Wild Blue Yonder*, pp. 200–201; Gray and Payne, "Victory Is Possible," pp. 14–27.

39. Deaver, *Behind the Scenes*, pp. 111, 131, 170; interview with Richard Wirthlin, Oct. 6, 1999; Reagan, *My Turn*, pp. 63–64.

40. *NYT*, Nov. 23, 1981; Sanders, *Peddlers of Crisis*, pp. 8–9; Tyroler, ed., *Alerting America*, pp. ix–xi.

41. Reagan, *An American Life*, pp. 265, 268, 550.

42. Breyman, *Why Movements Matter*, p. 53; comments of Edward Rowny in Tannenwald, ed., *Understanding*, p. 31; Reagan, *An American Life*, p. 267.

43. *Los Angeles Times*, Jan. 30, 1981; Reagan, *An American Life*, p. 570.

44. Boyer, *When Time*, pp. 141–42; Rogin, *Ronald Reagan*, pp. 36–37.

45. Stubbing, *Defense Game*, pp. 44, 379 383; *NYT*, Aug. 14, 1981; NSDD 12 (Oct. 1, 1981), in Simpson, ed., *National Security Directives*, pp. 46–47; William Arkin,

"The Buildup That Wasn't," *BAS* 45 (Jan.–Feb. 1989): 6–7; Sanders, *Peddlers of Crisis*, p. 309.

46. Drew, "A Reporter," p. 134; *NYT*, Oct. 18, 21, 22, Nov. 5, 1981; Stubbing, *Defense Game*, p. 385.

47. In Wintex '83, NATO's March 1983 command and staff exercise, NATO began a nuclear war within six days of the commencement of a European conventional conflict. *NYT*, May 30, June 10, 1982; *WP*, June 4, Nov. 10, 1982; Simpson, ed., *National Security Directives*, pp. 15–16, 63; Dyer, *War*, p. 196.

48. Gerard C. Smith, "The Arms Control and Disarmament Agency: An Unfinished History," *BAS* 40 (Apr. 1984): 13; York, *Making Weapons*, p. 222; Seaborg, *Stemming*, p. 244; Schrag, *Global Action*, pp. 27–29.

49. *NYT*, June 23, 1981; Scheer, *With Enough Shovels*, p. 90; McFarlane, *Special Trust*, p. 196.

50. McFarlane, *Special Trust*, pp. 219–21; "National Security Decision Directive 75" (Jan. 17, 1983), ibid., pp. 372–80.

51. Risse-Kappen, *Zero Option*, p. 83; Healey, *Time*, p. 513.

52. John Marcum et al. to Brzezinski, Mar. 6, 1980, "[Meetings—Vance/Brown/ Brzezinski: 3/80–9/80]" Folder, Box 34, Brzezinski Papers; Thatcher, *Downing Street*, pp. 157–59, 236–37; McFarlane, *Special Trust*, p. 306.

53. Oral history interview with Robert Beckel, Nov. 13, 1981, p. 50; Risse-Kappen, *Zero Option*, p. 83; Boutwell, *German Nuclear Dilemma*, pp. 138, 144, 161–62; *Boston Globe*, May 27, 1982.

54. Masumi, *Contemporary Politics*, pp. 201, 392, 475; *Times Union* (Albany, NY), Mar. 25, 1993.

55. Howorth, *France*, pp. 4–7, 55; Utley, *French Defense Debate*, pp. 44–47, 74, 113–18.

56. Arbatov, *System*, pp. 189, 201; Schmidt, *Men and Powers*, p. 92. See also Dobrynin, *In Confidence*, pp. 470–76.

57. Andrew and Gordievsky, *KGB*, pp. 582–89; Andrew and Gordievsky, eds., *Comrade Kryuchkov's Instructions*, pp. 69–71, 86–87; Dobrynin, *In Confidence*, p. 523; Pry, *War Scare*, pp. 9–13.

58. Arbatov, *System*, pp. 209–10; comments of Oleg Grinevsky and Vladimir Slipchenko in Tannenwald, ed., *Understanding*, pp. 216, 256–58, 264–65, 293.

59. Shultz, *Turmoil*, pp. 5–6; Arbatov, *System*, pp. 201, 308; Dobrynin, *In Confidence*, pp. 513, 523–24, 551; comments of Anatoly Chernyaev in Tannenwald, ed., *Understanding*, p. 77.

60. Oberdorfer, *Turn*, pp. 31–32.

61. Garthoff, *Great Transition*, pp. 99–100; Powaski, *Return*, pp. 29–31.

62. Interview with Richard Wirthlin, Oct. 6, 1999; Schneider, "Peace and Strength," pp. 322, 334–35; Stubbing, *Defense Game*, p. 18.

63. Heald and Wybrow, *Gallup Survey*, p. 27; Thatcher, *Downing Street*, pp. 264–66.

64. Boutwell, *German Nuclear Dilemma*, p. 139; Drifte, *Japan's Rise*, pp. 23–25; Reiss, *Without the Bomb*, p. 119.

65. Lumsden, "Nuclear Weapons," p. 105.

Chapter 7

Epigraph: Petra Kelly, "No Euroshima!" (June 6, 1982), pp. 3–4, Box 1, The Greens Records.

1. Cortright, "Peace Movement Role," p. 83; Marjorie Mowlam, "Peace Groups and Politics," *BAS* 39 (Nov. 1983): 31; Jane Dibblin, "An Outpouring of Protest— Peaceful and Determined," *END J*, No. 7 (Dec. 1983–Jan. 1984), pp. 10–11.

2. Den Oudsten, "Public Opinion on Peace and War," p. 18; *IHT*, June 7, 1984.

3. De Boer, "The Polls: The European Peace Movement," pp. 120–21, 126; Den Oudsten, "Public Opinion and Nuclear Weapons," pp. 15–17; Den Oudsten, "Public Opinion," pp. 34–36; Shaffer, *Public Image*, pp. 9–13.

4. Lumsden, "Nuclear Weapons," pp. 101–2, 104; Den Oudsten, "Public Opinion on Peace and War," p. 18; Frank Barnaby, "Europe Aroused," *BAS* 38 (Feb. 1982): 8–9; "An Interview with Mary Kaldor," p. 47.

5. Minutes of the CND National Council meeting of Mar. 23–24, 1985, Reel 26, CND (B) Records, HM; "Britain," *END J*, No. 16–17 (Summer 1985), p. 22; Taylor and Young, "Britain," p. 287.

6. Byrd, "Development," pp. 66–67; *Guardian*, Oct. 26, 1981; David Wainwright, "Campaign for Nuclear Disarmament," *DC*, No. 18 (Jan. 1983), pp. 8–9; Kent, *Undiscovered Ends*, pp. 175–76.

7. *Guardian*, Apr. 2, 1983; *Times* (L), Apr. 2, 1983; *Philadelphia Inquirer*, Apr. 2, 1983.

8. "General Secretary's Report to CND Conference, 26–28 November 1982," Reel 26, CND (B) Records, HM; Byrne, *Campaign*, pp. 83, 138–39; Flessati, *Waking*.

9. Untitled leaflet, IPB Records; "General Secretary's Report to CND Conference, 26–28 November 1982," Reel 26, CND (B) Records, HM.

10. George and Marcus, "Unilateralism's Second Wave," pp. 62–63; Byrne, *Campaign*, pp. 55–68, 77, 138; Byrd, "Development," p. 67; Crewe, "Britain," pp. 53–54.

11. Shelley, "Pacifism," p. 47; "Information Sheet 4," CND (B) Records, S; Byrne, *Campaign*, pp. 119–20.

12. "Nuclear Missiles Out of Europe," CND (B) Records, S; James Hinton and Dave Wainwright, "A Framework for '84," *DC*, No. 29 (Jan. 1984), p. 10; minutes of the CND Executive Committee meeting of Mar. 3, 1984, and "Developing the Anti-Trident Campaign" (Apr. 7–8, 1984), Reel 26, CND (B) Records, HM.

13. Byrne, *Campaign*, pp. 164–65; "What Is a Nuclear Free Zone?" and "'Civil Defence' and Peacetime Emergency Planning," author's possession; "General Secretary's Report to CND Conference, 26–28 September 1982," Reel 26, CND (B) Records, HM.

14. Interview with Bruce Kent, June 7, 1999; Byrne, *Campaign*, pp. 104–5; "The Falklands Affair: Points of Concern" (ca. Apr. 1982), "Sanity Report to the Executive Committee" (July 30, 1983), and minutes of CND Executive Committee meeting of July 30, 1983, Reel 26, CND (B) Records, HM; "Campaign for Nuclear Disarmament Expresses Concern over Situation in Poland" (Dec. 14, 1981), Folder 735, IKV Records, A.

15. "CND International Ctee: Terms of Reference" (Sept. 1, 1983), minutes of CND National Council meetings of July 17–18, 1982, July 16–17 and Oct. 15–16, 1983, and Jan. 14–15, 1984, minutes of the CND Executive Committee meetings of July 3 and Sept. 4, 1982, "General Secretary's Report" (Feb. 6, 1982), "Executive Decisions, September 3rd 1983," and Bruce Kent to V. Popov, Sept. 7, 1983, Reel 26, CND (B) Records, HM; "Meeting for the launch of the 'Campaign for the Defense of the Turkish Peace Movement' on February 21 [1984], House of Commons," Folder 742, IKV Records, A.

16. Byrne, *Campaign*, pp. 115–17; minutes of the CND National Council meeting, of Oct. 15–16, 1983, Reel 26, CND (B) Records, HM; Byrd, "Development," pp. 69, 74.

17. Interview with Bruce Kent, July 10, 1990; interview with Valerie Flessati, June 7, 1999.

18. Byrne, *Campaign*, p. 84; Byrd, "Development," p. 70; "A Letter from CND" (1981), CND (B) Records, S.

19. "General Secretary's Report to CND Conference, 26–28 November 1982," and "No Nukes Music" (July 24, 1981), Reel 26, CND (B) Records, HM; Taylor and Young, "Britain," p. 288.

20. "Information Sheet on the Alternative Defence Commission" (Dec. 1980), Folder 711, IKV Records, A; "Alternative Defence Commission" (May 1983), Box 1, Freeze Records, SL.

21. "An Appeal to Expand the World Disarmament Campaign," Box 2, Freeze Records, SL; Ceadel, "Britain's Nuclear Disarmers," p. 234; Taylor and Young, "Britain," p. 289.

22. Raj Thamotheram to Randy Kehler, May 20, 1983, Nicholas Short to Kehler, Feb. 10, 1984, Will Howard to Kehler, Nov. 22, 1984, Box 1, "The Case for an Immediate Nuclear Freeze," Box 2, Freeze Records, SL; Mike Jendrzejczyk to executive committee, July 13, 1983, "The Nuclear Weapons 'Freeze' Advertising Campaign," Freeze Records, C; Taylor and Young, "Britain," p. 289.

23. Harford and Hopkins, eds., *Greenham Common*; Eglin, "Women and Peace," p. 248; Liddington, *Long Road*, pp. 221–86; Nancy Kintner, "Greenham Common Women," *DC*, No. 18 (Jan. 1983), p. 20; "Some of the main actions at Greenham Common, 1984–85," Greenham Common Women's Peace Camp Records.

24. Interview with Bruce Kent, June 7, 1999; interview with Sheila Jones, June 19, 1998; interview with Nigel Young, May 15, 1999; minutes of the CND Executive Committee meeting of Feb. 5, 1983, minutes of the CND National Council meetings of Apr. 16–17, 1983 and Jan. 14–15, 1984, and Annie Tunnicliffe, "Discussion paper for NVDA workshops," Reel 26, CND (B) Records, HM; Byrne, *Campaign*, pp. 134–35, 153–60; Liddington, *Long Road*, pp. 255–59; Kent, *Undiscovered Ends*, pp. 190–92.

25. Byrne, *Campaign*, pp. 193–94, 198; George and Marcus, "Unilateralism's Second Wave," p. 63; Byrd, "Development," pp. 77–78, 82–83; interview with Michael Foot, June 19, 1998.

26. Byrne, *Campaign*, pp. 199–201; *NYT*, Jan. 11, 1983.

27. Byrne, *Campaign*, pp. 65, 208; Flessati, *Waking*, pp. 28–32; George and Marcus, "Unilateralism's Second Wave," p. 65.

28. Edwards, "Great Debate," pp. 13–29; *Guardian*, Feb. 11, 1983; Ormrod, "Churches," pp. 211–13.

29. Byrne, *Campaign*, p. 65; Hanson, *Catholic Church*, pp. 306–7; Kent, *Undiscovered Ends*, pp. 198–200, 202; "General Secretary's Report" (June 27, 1983), Reel 26, CND (B) Records, HM; Ormrod, "Churches," p. 211.

30. "Strategic Tory Attack on the Nuclear Disarmers" (Feb. 14, 1983), unidentified newspaper clipping, Bess Papers; *Guardian*, Oct. 8, 1983; Campbell, "Tories"; *Times* (L), Apr. 2, 1983; Kent, *Undiscovered Ends*, pp. 179–82; "The Men Who Are Dying to Win," *Sanity* (Feb. 1984), pp. 21–24.

31. *IHT*, May 23, 1983; *Times* (L), Apr. 29, 30, 1983; interview with Bruce Kent, June 7, 1999; Campbell, "Tories"; Crozier, *Free Agent*, pp. 243–46.

32. Byrne, *Campaign*, pp. 215–17; Alison Whyte, "Press Report to Executive" (June 18, 1983), minutes of CND National Council meeting of Jan. 14–15, 1984, and "General Secretary's Report to CND Conference, 26–28 November 1982," Reel 26, CND (B) Records, HM; Kent, *Undiscovered Ends*, p. 185; interview with Bruce Kent, June 7, 1999; *Philadelphia Inquirer*, Mar. 10, 1983.

33. Interviews with E. P. Thompson and Dorothy Thompson, Nov. 1, 1989; Thompson, "Ends and Histories," p. 11; Byrne, *Campaign*, pp. 215–16.

34. Kent, *Undiscovered Ends*, p. 180; Byrne, *Campaign*, pp. 61, 64; Ceadel, "Britain's Nuclear Disarmers," pp. 231–32; *Sunday Telegraph*, Sept. 19, 1999; "CND Rejects Claims of Manipulation by Spies" (Sept. 19, 1999), CND (B) Records, L.

35. Interview with Daniel Plesch, July 21, 1998; Byrne, *Campaign*, pp. 83–84; interview with Bruce Kent, June 7, 1999; Kent, *Undiscovered Ends*, pp. 178–79; *Boston Globe*, May 27, 1982.

36. Jane Oberman, "CND and the Next General Election" (June 1983), Reel 26, CND (B) Records, HM; Michael Meadowcroft, "Liberal Disarmers Break New Ground," *END J*, No. 5 (Aug.–Sept. 1983), p. 18; Kent, *Undiscovered Ends*, pp. 192–93.

37. Foot, *Another Heart*, pp. 56–95; Taylor, "Labour Party," pp. 122–23; Thatcher, *Downing Street*, pp. 296–97; *Wall Street Journal*, June 3, 1983.

38. Foot, *Another Heart*, pp. 157–58; George and Marcus, "Unilateralism's Second Wave," pp. 65–67; interview with Daniel Plesch, July 21, 1998; Crewe, "Britain," p. 12; interview with Michael Foot, June 19, 1998.

39. Taylor, "Labour Party," p. 123; "The History of CND," *Sanity* (Aug. 1984), p. 35; "Britain," *END J*, No. 16–17 (Summer 1985), pp. 22–23; Byrne, *Campaign*, pp. 91, 95.

40. Byrd, "Development," p. 67; "History of CND," p. 35; Hinton, *Protests*, p. 183.

41. Byrne, *Campaign*, pp. 195–97, 231; *NYT*, Oct. 23, 1983.

42. Byrd, "Development," p. 72; Byrne, *Campaign*, pp. 165–67.

43. Crewe, "Britain," pp. 33–34; Byrne, *Campaign*, p. 211; *Guardian*, Jan. 24, Oct. 22, 1983; Byrd, "Development," pp. 96–98.

44. Everts, "Mood," pp. 539–40; Hastings and Hastings, eds., *Index . . . 1982–83*, pp. 323–25; DeBoer, "Polls: The European Peace Movement," pp. 119, 122–23; Crewe, "Britain," pp. 30–31.

45. *Guardian*, Jan. 24, Oct. 22, 1983, May 26, 1984; DeBoer, "Polls: The European Peace Movement," pp. 126–27; Crewe, "Britain," pp. 36–38, 51; Byrd, "Britain," pp. 93–95.

46. Blechman and Fisher, *Silent Partner*, p. 213; Crewe, "Britain," p. 23.

47. British confidence in the U.S. government to deal wisely with world problems dropped steadily in the early 1980s. In 1983, 70 percent of Britons told pollsters that they had little, very little, or no confidence in the United States. Den Oudsten, "Public Opinion on International Security," n.p.; *Guardian*, Oct. 22, 1983; Byrd, "Development," p. 96; Crewe, "Britain," p. 42.

48. IKV, *Help De Kernwapens De Wereld Uit*; "Holland," *END J*, No. 16–17 (Summer 1985), pp. 26–27; interview with Mient Jan Faber, Aug. 7, 1986; Everts, "Continuity," p. 2; Everts and Walraven, *Vredesbeweging*, pp. 59–62; Frank Barnaby, "Europe Aroused," *BAS* 38 (Feb. 1982): 8; *Wall Street Journal*, Jan. 28, 1982.

49. Wim Bartels to friends in the international peace movement, June 14, 1984, IPCC Records; interview with Mient Jan Faber, Aug. 7, 1986; *Towards an International*, p. 2.

50. Wilke Ruiter, "Action Week Against Cruise," *DC*, No. 34 (June 1984), p. 15; Nico van Arkel to Ethel Taylor, Mar. 23, 1984, Box 2, Series A,8, WSP Records; Maria Margaronis, "Notes from Abroad," *NT* 2 (Mar. 1984): 10.

51. Mient Jan Faber, "Ontspanningspolitiek en mensenrechten," IKV Records, TH; IKV to Gustav Husak, Sept. 17, 1982, Folder 737, Faber to Geachte Dames en Heren, Mar. 29, 1982, and Erhan Yigitbasioglu to Faber, Apr. 2, 1982, Folder 742, IKV Records, A.

52. Mient Jan Faber to Lech Walesa, Aug. 26, 1982, and Faber and Wim Bartels to the Solidarnosc Office, Oct. 26, 1982, Folder 736, "First concept of a common declaration of Solidarnosc and the interchurch peace council of the Netherlands," Folder 735, "IKV Volgt Tweesporenbeleid Inzake Oost-Europa" (Sept. 23, 1982), Folder 731, IKV Records, A.

53. "The Politics of the Dutch Missile Decision," *PDN* 1 (Winter 1984–85): 21; Serry, "Peace Movement," p. 58.

54. Chris Corry, "Base Blockades," *DC*, No. 35 (July–Aug. 1984), p. 21; Everts, "Continuity," p. 25.

55. Cees Volwater, "Labour Moves on Peace," *DC*, No. 26 (Oct. 1983), p. 7; *Christian Science Monitor*, Jan. 13, 1984; Everts, "Continuity," p. 21.

56. IKV, *Help De Kernwapens De Wereld Uit*; Serry, "Peace Movement," pp. 54–55; Everts, "Churches"; interview with Mient Jan Faber, Aug. 7, 1986.

57. "Netherlands," *END J*, No. 6 (Oct.–Nov. 1983); Everts, "Continuity," pp. 22–24, 29; Serry, "Peace Movement," p. 54; IKV, *Help De Kernwapens De Wereld Uit*.

58. Everts, "Impact," figure 3; De Boer, "Polls: The European Peace Movement," pp. 128–29; Everts, "Public Opinion," pp. 231, 254–56, 260.

59. Blechman and Fisher, *Silent Partner*, p. 213; Everts, "Mood," p. 516; Everts, "Public Opinion," p. 235.

60. Everts, "Public Opinion," p. 263; Everts, "Mood," p. 506; Kenneth P. Adler,

"Dutch Views on Security Issues" (June 25, 1984), "European Defense Issues [5 of 6]" Folder, Cobb Files.

61. Everts, "Public Opinion," pp. 250, 253, 260–61; Everts, "Mood," pp. 513, 516–19, 531–32.

62. Everts, "Mood," p. 539, De Boer, "Polls: The European Peace Movement," pp. 124–25.

63. Everts, "Mood," p. 548; Everts, "Impact," p. 16; Everts, "Public Opinion," pp. 245, 271–72; Everts, "Continuity," pp. 8–11, 18–19.

64. "Belgium," *END J*, No. 16–17 (Summer 1985), p. 22; Melinda Fine to Strategy Committee, May 1984, Box 16, Freeze Records, SL; Galand, "Le C.N.A.P.D.—Belgique."

65. "Human Chain," *DC*, No. 34 (June 1984), p. 17; Lubelski-Bernard, "Euromissile Crisis," pp. 60–62; Pierre Galand to Dear Friend, Oct. 7, 1982, Folder 715, IKV Records, A.

66. Lubelski-Bernard, "Euromissile Crisis," p. 60; "Disarmament for Peace," *DC*, No. 27 (Nov. 1983), pp. 10–11.

67. "Belgium," p. 22; Goedele de Keersmaker, "The Future in the Balance," *END J*, No. 13 (Dec. 1984–Jan. 1985), pp. 20–21; André Bogaert, "The Central Interest," *DC*, No. 29 (Jan. 1984), p. 7.

68. De Boer, "The Polls: The European Peace Movement," p. 126; "Belgium," p. 22; De Smet, "Belgian Peace Movement," pp. 242–48; Blechman and Fisher, *Silent Partner*, p. 213.

69. "Federal Republic of Germany," *END J*, No. 16–17 (Summer 1985), pp. 23–24; Deile et al., eds., *Bonn, 10.10.81*; "Aktion Sühnezeichen/Friedensdienste," Aktion Sühnezeichen/Friedensdienste Records; Mushaben, "Cycles," pp. 32–34.

70. Peter Findlay, "Inside the protean peace movement," *END J*, No. 20 (Feb.–Mar. 1986), pp. 13–14; *Guardian*, Oct. 24, 1983; Hübner-Funk and Schefeld, "Challenge," p. 233.

71. Boutwell, "Politics," pp. 79–80; Clesse, "Peace Movements," pp. 53–54; Merkl, "Pacifism," p. 83; Tromp, "Alternatives," p. 75; Petra Kelly, "Euroschima, Mon Futur" (July–Aug. 1981), Box 1, The Greens Records.

72. Grewe, "West German Peace Movement," p. 130; De Boer, "Polls: The European Peace Movement," p. 120; Hübner-Funk and Schefold, "Challenge," p. 231; Salomon, "Peace Movement," p. 122.

73. Mushaben, "Cycles," p. 33; Cioc, *Pax Atomica*, p. 190; Hanson, *Catholic Church*, pp. 304–5; Kubbig and Risse-Kappen, "Living," pp. 74–75.

74. "The work of Action Reconciliation" (Sept. 12, 1988), Aktion Sühnezeichen/Friedensdienste Records; "Moving Ahead," and Kristin Flory, "Peace Week," *DC*, No. 18 (Jan. 1983), pp. 6–7, 25; "Festivities for German Peace Week," *END J*, No. 1 (Dec. 1982–Jan. 1983).

75. Mushaben, "Cycles," pp. 32–33; *Christian Science Monitor*, June 10, 1983; John Sandford, "West Germany," *END J*, No. 6 (Oct.–Nov. 1983); Sandra Bell, "Evangelical Church," *DC*, No. 27 (Nov. 1983), pp. 6–7.

76. Findlay, "Inside," p. 15; Kelly, *Fighting*, pp. 38–39; Eva Quistorp, "Ger-

many," *END J*, No. 3 (Apr.–May 1983); "West Germany," *END J*, No. 6 (Oct.–Nov. 1983), p. 6.

77. Findlay, "Inside," p. 15; Lutz van Dick, "Teachers for Peace," *DC*, No. 26 (Oct. 1983), p. 8; Grewe, "West German Peace Movement," p. 124.

78. "F.R.G.," *DC*, No. 26 (Oct. 1983), p. 8; Johnstone, "Labour Signs On," p. 8; Grewe, "West German Peace Movement," pp. 117–18.

79. Kelly, *Fighting*, pp. 18, 21, 48; Petra Kelly, "Greening of Germany" (Dec. 9, 1982), Box 1, The Greens Records; Linda Bullard, "Out of NATO: The Green Approach," *PDN* 1 (Winter 1984–85): 3–4; Schlaga, "Peace Movement," p. 140.

80. Petra Kelly, *Offener Brief an Willy Brandt* (Nov. 5, 1982), Box 1, The Greens Records; Kelly, *Fighting*, p. 23.

81. Johnstone, *Politics*, pp. 51, 69–70; *NYT*, Oct. 21, 1983; Risse-Kappen, *Zero Option*, pp. 75–76; "Resolution Adopted by the SPD Conference on Peace and Security" (Nov. 19, 1983), "European Defense Issues [1 of 6]" Folder, Cobb Files.

82. Risse-Kappen, *Zero Option*, pp. 76–77; *NYT*, Oct. 23, 1983; *Wall Street Journal*, Apr. 4, 1983; Breyman, *Why Movements Matter*, p. 107; Cioc, *Pax Atomica*, pp. 193–94.

83. Cioc, *Pax Atomica*, p. 193; Rattinger, "Federal Republic," p. 163.

84. "END Briefing Notes: West Germany" (1986), author's possession; Rattinger, "Federal Republic," pp. 108, 111, 172; Breyman, *Why Movements Matter*, pp. 149–51.

85. Risse-Kappen, *Zero Option*, pp. 72–73; De Boer, "Polls: The European Peace Movement," pp. 126–28; Den Oudsten, "Public Opinion and Nuclear Weapons," pp. 15–16; Den Oudsten, "Public Opionion," p. 35; Rattinger, "Federal Republic," pp. 134–37, 163; Hassner, "Pacifism," p. 123.

86. Den Oudsten, "Public Opinion and Nuclear Weapons," p. 19; Blechman and Fisher, *Silent Partner*, p. 213.

87. Rattinger, "Federal Republic," p. 140; Shaffer, *Public Image*, pp. 6–7.

88. Everts, "Mood," pp. 539–40; De Boer, "Polls: The European Peace Movement," p. 123; Rattinger, "Federal Republic," pp. 129, 159; Grewe, "West German Peace Movement," p. 108.

89. "Federal Republic," p. 24; Margaronis, "Notes," p. 10; Petra Kelly to Dear Friends, Feb. 14, 1984, Freeze Records, C.

90. "END Briefing Notes: West Germany" (1986), author's possession; *Christian Science Monitor*, Jan. 20, 1984.

91. Andersson and Lindkvist, "Peace Movement," p. 24; Grepstad, "Peace Movement," pp. 10–15; Coates, "Conclusion," pp. 303–4; Haagerup, "Nordic Peace Movements," pp. 144–45, 148–56; Lumsden, "Nuclear Weapons," p. 114; interview with Berit Ås, Aug. 12, 2000.

92. Interview with Ole Kopreitan, May 14, 1999; Erik Alfsen, *De första år av Nei til atomvåpen*, pp. 7–8, 11, Nei til Atomvåpen (Norway) Records; Nilson, "Peace Movement," pp. 39–40; Jon Grepstad, "Moving Ahead," *DC*, No. 18 (Jan. 1983), p. 11; Dibblin, "An Outpouring," p. 11.

93. Betsy Taylor, "Report on the European Nuclear Disarmament Movements" (Jan. 1982), Box 71, Series G, SANE Records; Grepstad, "Peace Movement," p. 14; Nils Petter Gleditsch, "The Freeze in Norway," *BAS* 39 (Nov. 1983): 32–34; Jon Grep-

stad, "Lobbying, Rather than Direct Action," *END J*, No. 6 (Oct.–Nov. 1983), pp. 18–19; Nilson, "Peace Movement," pp. 40–44.

94. Lumsden, "Nuclear Weapons," p. 108; Krasner, *Political Influence*, pp. 5–9; "END Denmark," Folder 728, IKV Records, A; "Specialists Week," *DC*, No. 19 (Feb. 1983), p. 11; Dibblin, "An Outpouring," p. 10; Grepstad, "Peace Movement," p. 11.

95. Kaj Bollmann, "Grassroots Leadership," *DC*, No. 27 (Nov. 1983), pp. 8–9; "The Danish position" (ca. Dec. 1985), IPCC Records; Haagerup, "Nordic Peace Movements," p. 155.

96. Toni Liversage and Judith Winther, "Influencing the Decision Makers," *END J*, No. 8 (Feb.–Mar. 1984); "Danish SDP Changes Course," *END J*, No. 13 (Dec. 1984–Jan. 1985), p. 7; Petersen, "Scandilux," pp. 15–17; Judith Winther, "Behind the Infrastructure Vote," *DC*, No. 18 (Jan. 1983), p. 25.

97. Mats Adler, "Points for Thought," *DC*, No. 29 (Jan. 1984), p. 15; Andersson and Lindkvist, "Peace Movement," pp. 16, 21, 24; Katrin Elborgh, "Annual Report 1983/84 from SPAAS," Box 445, and Henrik Westander and Lars Jederlund, untitled report on SPAS (Apr. 1986), Box 446, WRI Records.

98. Mats Adler, "SPAAS," *DC*, No. 18 (Jan. 1983), pp. 13–14; Ståhle, *Internationella Kvinnoförbundet*, p. 43; Dibblin, "An Outpouring," p. 11; Grepstad, "Peace Movement," p. 11.

99. Adler, "Points for Thought," p. 15; Margaretha Ingelstam, "No Compromise," *DC*, No. 27 (Nov. 1983), pp. 7–8; "Sweden," *Freeze Newsletter* 3 (Aug. 1983): 11.

100. Andersson and Lindkvist, "Peace Movement," pp. 24–25; "Swedish Success," *END J*, No. 1 (Dec. 1982–Jan. 1983), p. 6.

101. Taipale, "Peace Movement," pp. 21–23, 40–44; Illka Taipale to Laurens Hogebrink, Oct. 27, 1981, Folder 725, IKV Records, A; Folke Sundman, "Finland Can Start," *DC*, No. 29 (Jan. 1984), p. 9.

102. Finnish Women for Peace to Dear Friends, Aug. 10, 1981, and "Women for Peace in Finland," Women for Peace in Finland Records.

103. Taipale, "Peace Movement," pp. 38–40, 47; Grepstad, "Peace Movement," p. 11; Dibblin, "An Outpouring," p. 10; Vesa, "Peace Movement," p. 278.

104. Den Oudsten, "Public Opinion on Peace and War," p. 18; Vesa, "Finnish Public Opinion," table 3.

105. Krasner and Petersen, "Peace and Politics," p. 171; Waldahl, "Norwegian Attitudes," pp. 304–7; Nilson, "Peace Movement," p. 41.

106. Waldahl, "Norwegian Attitudes," pp. 294–95.

107. Blechman and Fisher, *Silent Partner*, p. 213; De Boer, "The Polls: The European Peace Movement," p. 125.

108. Waldahl, "Norwegian Attitudes," p. 293; Vesa, "Finnish Public Opinion," table 8.15.

109. Vesa, "Peace Movement," pp. 274–77; Vesa, "Finnish Public Opinion," tables 8.28, 9.1, 10.1; Waldahl, "Norwegian Attitudes," p. 300; Krasner and Petersen, "Peace and Politics," p. 171.

110. Waldahl, "Norwegian Attitudes," pp. 300, 307, 310–11; Vesa, "Peace Movement," p. 275; Vesa, "Finnish Public Opinion," tables 3, 8.15, 8.28, 9.1, 10.1, 10.5; Grepstad, "Peace Movement," p. 13; Krasner and Petersen, "Peace and Politics," p. 171.

Chapter 8

Epigraph: Bernard Dreano, "Larzac An II: ou la dynamique du mouvement," *Le bulletin du CO.DE.N.E*, No. 4 (Oct. 1983), p. 4.

1. Howorth, *France*, pp. 86–87; Mellon, "Peace Organizations," pp. 202–4; Thompson, "Postface," p. 248; Jean Chesneaux, "The Peculiarities of the French," *END J*, No. 13 (Dec. 1984–Jan. 1985), p. 22.

2. Mellon, "Peace Organizations," pp. 206–8; Bourdet, "Rebirth," p. 199; Chesneaux, "Peculiarities," p. 22; Howorth, *France*, pp. 58–62; J. C. Billault to Chers amis, July 16, 1982, Folder 748, IKV Records, A.

3. Howorth, *France*, pp. 62–67; Bourdet, "Désarmement Nucléaire," pp. 13–14; Bourdet, "Rebirth," p. 197; "Initiative pour la création de comités pour le désarmement nucléaire en Europe" (Dec. 1981), CODENE Records; Dreano, "Larzac An II," p. 4; Mellon, "Peace Organizations," pp. 207–11.

4. "CODENE," *DC*, No. 18 (Jan. 1983), p. 8; Bourdet, "Rebirth," p. 214.

5. Howorth, *France*, pp. 68–69; Mellon, "Peace Organizations," p. 214; Gnesotto, "All Quiet," p. 253; "Tchecoslovaquie," "Pologne," and "Soutien aux prisonniers pour la Paix d'U.R.S.S." *Le bulletin du CO.DE.N.E.*, No. 4 (Oct. 1983), pp. 10–13; Jan Kozlik, Anna Marvanova, and Jacques Berthelet, "Communiqué" (June 20, 1983), CODENE Records.

6. Howorth, *France*, pp. 74–76; Sylvie Montrant to Chers Amis, June 28, 1983, CODENE Records; "Mobilisation Generale de Paix," *Le bulletin du CO.DE.N.E.*, No. 3 (Summer 1983), n.p.; Harold Schultz, "Larzac: Catalyst for France," *END J*, No. 6 (Oct.–Nov. 1983), p. 7.

7. Mellon, "Peace Organizations," pp. 207–8; Chesneaux, "Peculiarities," p. 23; Claude Bourdet to the author, June 25, 1993; Jane Dibblin, "An Outpouring of Protest—Peaceful and Determined," *END J*, No. 7 (Dec. 1983–Jan. 1984), p. 10; "END Briefing Notes: France" (1985), Bess Papers.

8. Mellon, "Peace Organizations," pp. 205–6; Colard, "Le Pacifisme," pp. 29–30; Sylvie Montrant, "Long March," *DC*, No. 29 (Jan. 1984), p. 3.

9. Johnstone, *Politics*, p. 108; Hanson, *Catholic Church*, pp. 305–6; Colard, "Le Pacifisme," pp. 31–33; "An Interview with a French Freeze Activist," *Freeze Focus* 4 (Apr. 1984): 16.

10. "END Briefing Notes: France" (1985), Bess Papers; Colard, "Le Pacifisme," pp. 27–28; Gnesotto, "All Quiet," pp. 256–57; Howorth, *France*, p. 69; Bourdet, "Désarmement Nucléaire," p. 14.

11. Fisera, "New Left," p. 242; De Boer, "Polls: The European Peace Movement," p. 126; Fritsch-Bournazel, "France," p. 89.

12. Fisera, "New Left," p. 242; Christian Mellon, "Polls and Peace," *DC*, No. 18 (Jan. 1983), p. 26; Gnesotto, "All Quiet," p. 259; Fritsch-Bournazel, "France," pp. 80, 84.

13. Den Oudsten, "Public Opinion and Nuclear Weapons," p. 19; Den Oudsten, "Public Opinion," p. 36.

14. Everts, "Mood," pp. 539–40; Mellon, "Peace Organizations," p. 212; Fritsch-Bournazel, "France," pp. 80–87.

15. Betsy Taylor, "Report on the European Nuclear Disarmament Movements" (Jan. 1982), Box 71, Series G, SANE Records; Pisano, *Dynamics*, p. 107; Brierley, "Italian Politics," p. 21; Thompson, "Pace e guerra," p. 19; "Report from Rome, Italy" (Mar. 24, 1984), Box 4, Freeze Records, SL.

16. *NYT*, Oct. 23, 1983; Dibblin, "An Outpouring," p. 11; *Guardian*, Oct. 24, 1983.

17. Johnstone, *Politics*, p. 144; Thompson, *Comiso*, p. 13; "Summary Report of the September 13–18, 1982 Fact Finding Trip to Comiso, Italy" (Sept. 29, 1982), Folder 718, IKV Records, A.

18. "Italy," *END J*, No. 16–17 (Summer 1985), p. 27; Brierley, "Italian Politics," p. 22; Pisano, *Dynamics*, p. 110.

19. Bruno Gabrielli, "Comiso and Beyond," *END J*, No. 16–17 (Summer 1985), p. 32; Thompson, *Comiso*, pp. 8–10; "Comitato Unitario per il Disarmo e la Pace" (May 1984), Comiso International Peace Camp Records.

20. Gabrielli, "Comiso," p. 32; Thompson, *Comiso*, pp. 12–15; "Sicily, Italy," *END J*, No. 6 (Oct.–Nov. 1983), p. 6; Martine Grice, "International Women's Day," *Al Magliocco*, and untitled WRI statement (Apr. 1983), Comiso International Peace Camp Records; "Sicily," *END J*, No. 3 (Apr.–May 1983), p. 4.

21. Brierley, "Italian Politics," pp. 19–20; Pfaltzgraff, "Antinuclear Protest," pp. 124–26; Peggy and Theresa Hoskins, "Sicilian Women Take Initiative," *END J*, No. 4 (June–July 1983); Umberto DeGiovannangeli and Tom Bennettollo to Dear Friends, Oct. 26, 1981, Folder 718, IKV Records, A; "Italy," *END J*, No. 16–17 (Summer 1985), p. 27.

22. Pisano, *Dynamics*, pp. 105, 109; Pfaltzgraff, "Antinuclear Protest," pp. 128–31; Gianni Novelli, "Church, State and Peace," *DC*, No. 27 (Nov. 1983), pp. 4–5; *Before All Else, Peace* (1983), Italian Christian Workers Associations Records.

23. Mario Pianta, "Italy," *END J*, No. 6 (Oct.–Nov. 1983); "Italy," p. 27; Brierley, "Italian Politics," p. 19.

24. Johnstone, *Politics*, pp. 142–43; Luciana Castellini to Wim Bartels, Aug. 20, 1982, Folder 718, and "International Peace Camp Comiso" (1983), Folder 710, IKV Records, A; Rossi and Ilari, "Peace Movement," pp. 141–43, 147–49; Pfaltzgraff, "Antinuclear Protest," pp. 133–39.

25. Rossi, "Public Opinion," p. 177; Mario Pianta, "New Possibilities to Stop Cruise," *END J*, No. 5 (Aug.–Sept. 1983), p. 19.

26. Rossi, "Public Opinion," pp. 192–93, 195, 205; Pfaltzgraff, "Antinuclear Protest," p. 150; De Boer, "Polls: The European Peace Movement," p. 126; Wertman, *Most Italians*, p. 1.

27. Rossi, "Public Opinion," p. 191; Den Oudsten, "Public Opinion and Nuclear Weapons," p. 19; De Boer, "Polls: The European Peace Movement," p. 125; Pisano, *Dynamics*, p. 98.

28. Rossi, "Public Opinion," pp. 188–90, 216; Den Oudsten, "Public Opinion," p. 36.

29. These polls did not break down responses by gender. Rossi, "Public Opinion," pp. 198, 205–7, 216; Pfaltzgraff, "Antinuclear Protest," p. 151.

30. Marion Sarafis, "Greece—No Room for Manoeuvre?" *END J*, No. 7 (Dec. 1983–Jan. 1984), p. 5; Marion Sarafis to the author, Nov. 14 and 15, 1987.

31. Sarafis, "Greece," p. 5; "KEADEA," *DC*, No. 18 (Jan. 1983), pp. 9–10; C. Marcopoulos to Dear friends, Aug. 27, 1984, IPCC Records; Peter D. Jones, "Conference in Greece," *Peacelink* (Nov. 1984), p. 14.

32. De Boer, "Polls: The European Peace Movement," pp. 125–26, 130.

33. Coates, "Conclusion," p. 304; Randy J. Rydell and Athanassios Platias, "The Balkans: A Weapon-Free Zone?" *BAS* 38 (May 1982): 57; Mary Kaldor, "A Voice of Dissent in NATO," *END J*, No. 2 (Feb.–Mar. 1983), p. 12.

34. Lemkow and Aguirre, "Peace Movement," pp. 226–27; Kettle-Williams, "Birth," pp. 42–43; Andy Dobson, "Gonzales' Subtle Shifts on NATO," *END J*, No. 14 (Feb.–Mar. 1985), pp. 8–9; "The Anti-NATO Movement in Spain" (Mar. 1982), Folder 722, IKV Records, A.

35. Dibblin, "An Outpouring," p. 11; E. P. Thompson, "Barcelona Conference" (May 24, 1984), Kaldor Papers; Ruth Mir, "March to Madrid," *DC*, No. 35 (July–Aug. 1984), p. 18; Lemkow and Aguirre, "Peace Movement," p. 227.

36. In a survey published in *El Pais* on October 20, 1981, 52 percent opposed Spain's entry into NATO and 18 percent supported it. Francisco Pena, "The Referendum Campaign," *DC*, No. 34 (June 1984), p. 16; Marjorie Mowlam, "Peace Groups and Politics," *BAS* 39 (Nov. 1983): 30; "The Anti-NATO Movement in Spain" (Mar. 1982), Folder 722, IKV Records, A.

37. Den Oudsten, "Public Opinion," p. 36; Den Oudsten, "Public Opinion and Nuclear Weapons," p. 19; De Boer, "Polls: The European Peace Movement," pp. 120, 125.

38. Bein and Epple, "Die Friedensbewegung," pp. 91–92, 110–13; Grossi, "From Contempt to Credibility," p. 9.

39. Mathias Erzinger, "Swiss Peace Council," *DC*, No. 18 (Jan. 1983), p. 14; Bein and Epple, "Die Friedensbewegung," pp. 112–15; Ursula Brunner, "Nuclear War Preparations of 'Neutral' Switzerland," *END J*, No. 3 (Apr.–May 1983), pp. 16–17.

40. Jordan, "Peace Activities," pp. 2–3; "Aufruf zum Marsch für Abrüstung und Frieden" (June 27, 1981) and "Menschen Demonstrieren für den Frieden" (Oct. 22, 1983), author's possession; Maislinger, "Peace Movement," pp. 57, 61–62; Maislinger, "Effects," pp. 2–3; *NYT*, Oct. 23, 1983.

41. Maislinger, "Peace Movement," pp. 61–63; Jordan, "Peace Activities," pp. 3–4; "Arbeitsgemeinschaft Unabhängiger Friedens Initiativen" (1984), New Accession, WRL Records; "Working Group of Independent Peace Initiatives in Austria" (1985), author's possession.

42. Coates, "Conclusion," p. 305; Hanson, *Catholic Church*, p. 308; Maislinger, "Peace Movement," pp. 62–64; Jordan, "Peace Activities," pp. 3–4.

43. Jordan, "Peace Activities," p. 3; "Working Group of Independent Peace Initiatives in Austria" (1985), author's possession; "For a Nuclear Free Belt Around Austria," IPCC Records.

44. Eion Dinan, "Campaign for Nuclear Disarmament," *DC*, No. 18 (Jan. 1983), p. 10; "Recent Activities of Irish CND" (1981), Reel 26, CND (B) Records, HM; *Disarmament Quarterly* [Irish CND] (Spring 1981), Box 70, Series G, SANE Records; *NYT*, Oct. 23, 1983; Judy Kowalok, "Reagan's Homecoming," *DC*, No. 35 (July–Aug. 1984), p. 22.

45. Dinan, "Campaign," p. 10; Kowalok, "Reagan's Homecoming," p. 22; Patrick Comerford, "The Storm That Threatens," *DC*, No. 27 (Nov. 1983), p. 5; *Galway Advertiser*, May 27, 1982, Folder 714, IKV Records, A.

46. Kaldor, "Introduction," p. 1; Dibblin, "An Outpouring," p. 10.

47. Wertman, *Most Italians*, p. 2.

Chapter 9

Epigraph: Pam Solo, "Letter from America," *END J*, No. 5 (Aug.–Sept. 1983), p. 6

1. "Three Minutes to Midnight," *BAS* 40 (Jan. 1984): 2; Gallup, *GP: Public Opinion 1998*, p. 79; Den Oudsten, "Public Opinion and Nuclear Weapons," p. 18; Van Voorst, "Critical Masses," p. 86.

2. Interview with William Sloane Coffin, Jr., Oct. 19, 1989; interview with John Isaacs, July 20, 1999.

3. Interview with Gene LaRocque, Aug. 17, 1999; Dunbar, ed., *Nuclear War*; interview with Eugene J. Carroll, Jr., May 11, 2000.

4. Interview with Robert M. Bowman, Oct. 26, 1992; Fred Kaplan, "The Man Who Fell From Space," *NT* 1 (Nov.–Dec. 1983): 25.

5. Interview with Thomas Cochran, Aug. 23, 1999; interview with Frank von Hippel, Aug. 22, 1999.

6. *WP*, Apr. 11, 1982; "Ground Zero/Phase 2," *BAS* (Aug.–Sept. 1982): 64.

7. Interview with Judy Lipton, July 31, 1999; "Workshops: PSR Annual Meeting, January 21–23, 1983," PSR Records; Caldicott, *Desperate Passion*, pp. 197–98.

8. "Excerpts from the New Abolitionist Covenant," *Fellowship* 47 (July–Aug. 1981): 20; "An Introduction to the Plowshares Movement" (1985), Box 527, WRI Records; Myers, "Storming the Gates," p. 898–99.

9. *WRL News* (May–June 1983), p. 3; David McReynolds, "War Resisters League," *DC*, No. 18 (Jan. 1983), p. 15.

10. *Chicago Tribune*, July 12, 1983; AFSC press release of Nov. 19, 1981, Box 11, Series II, AFSC Records; Pam Solo and Mike Jendrzejczyk, "Nuclear Weapons Facilities Project," *DC*, No. 18 (Jan. 1983), pp. 14–15.

11. Tom DeLuca, "The Cutting Edge of Survival," *Mobilizer* 2 (May 1982): 1, 4; Nora Lumley, "Mobilization's Fifth National Conference," *Mobilizer* 2 (Winter 1982): 7; "Mobilization for Survival 1983 Program," *Mobilizer* 3 (Winter 1983): 12–13.

12. MfS, "Progress and Promise: A Decade of Achievement" (Dec. 1987), author's possession; Jerilyn Bowen to Norma, Jan. 27, 1981, MfS Records, S; Minutes of the WRL National Commmittee meeting of Aug. 30–Sept. 1, 1981, Box 2a, Series B, WRL Records; Bruce Cronin, "Mobilization for Survival," *DC*, No. 29 (Jan. 1984), pp. 5–6; Bruce Cronin, "Peace—Not War—in '84," *DC*, No. 35 (July–Aug. 1984), p. 16.

13. Ethel Taylor to Member of Congress, Jan. 1982, Box 1, Series A,8, WSP Records; Taylor, *We Made a Difference*, pp. 133–37; Yvonne Logan to Board Member, May 10, 1982, Box 26, Series A,2, WILPF Records.

14. Interview with Helen Caldicott, Feb. 27, 1999; Jan Meriwether and Mary Jo Kaplan, "Mobilizing the Women's Peace Vote," *Citizen Participation* (Summer

1984), and "Position Paper: The Freeze, the MX, Pershing II, & Cruise Missiles" (June 1983), Box 18, Freeze Records, SL; Caldicott, *Desperate Passion*, pp. 296–99.

15. "Recipe for Disaster" (Feb. 19, 1981), Melman Papers; interview with Robert Musil, July 20, 1998; interview with David Cohen, July 19, 1999; interview with David Cortright, June 29, 1987.

16. Cortright to John Dow, June 26, 1981, and Cortright to Daniel Draper, Feb. 2, 1982, Box 13, Series H, SANE Records; Cortright to Randy Kehler, Oct. 15, 1984, Box 14, Freeze Records, SL.

17. Interview with Jeremy Stone, July 22, 1999; Stone, *"Every Man,"* pp. 227–28; interview with John Pike, July 22, 1999; "Two Roads to Security," *F.A.S. Public Interest Report* 38 (Mar. 1985): 1–2; interview with Frank von Hippel, Aug. 22, 1999.

18. McCrea and Markle, *Minutes to Midnight*, p. 53; Bernard T. Feld, "Perspectives for 1984," *BAS* 40 (Jan. 1984): 3; Chatfield, *American Peace Movement*, p. 161.

19. "Thousands at Colleges Join Drive Against Nuclear Arms," *Fellowship* 47 (Dec. 1981): 17; Butterfield, "Anatomy," p. 17; Meyer, *Peace Organizations*, pp. 118–19; Alice Kimball Smith, "Scientists and Public Issues," *BAS* 38 (Dec. 1982): 43.

20. "1981 Report," "Director's Report" (Dec. 1983), Jane Wales, "Memorandum for the Policy and Legislative Committee" (Dec. 24, 1982), and "Interim Report" (Jan. 1983), PSR Records; Butterfield, "Anatomy," p. 17; interview with Helen Caldicott, Feb. 27, 1999.

21. Interview with Helen Caldicott, Feb. 27, 1999; Caldicott, *Desperate Passion*, pp. 288–89; interview with Judy Lipton, July 31, 1999; Caldicott, "We Women," p. 20; National Staff to the Board of Directors, PSR, Sept. 23, 1983, minutes of the Board of Directors' meetings of June 5, July 22, and Sept. 24, 1983, and Board Conference Call, June 10, 1983, PSR Records.

22. Interview with Judy Lipton, July 31, 1999; "Physicians for Social Responsibility: General Profile," Box 12, Freeze Records, SL; "Director's Report" (Dec. 1983), and "Physicians for Social Responsibility, Inc.: Fall 1983," PSR Records.

23. Renata Rizzo, "Professional Approach to Peace," *NT* 1 (Aug.–Sept. 1983); "Computer Professionals for Social Responsibility" (Jan. 1983), and "Director's Report" (Dec. 1983), PSR Records; interview with David Cohen, July 19, 1999.

24. Robert Leavitt, "Freezing the Arms Race: The Genesis of a Mass Movement" (1983), pp. 22–26, 33–34, Freeze Records, C; "From Popular Mandate to Public Policy" (Feb. 1983), Box 15, Freeze Records, SL; "The Nuclear Freeze Campaign," *Freeze Newsletter* 2 (Oct. 1982): 2.

25. Gordon Faison and Randy Kehler to Active Participants in the Nuclear Weapon Freezes Campaign, July 22, 1981, PB1, Series G, SANE Records; "Freeze: Because Nobody Wants a Nuclear War," "Economic Benefits of the Freeze," and "The Freeze and the Economy," author's possession.

26. Robert Leavitt, "Freezing the Arms Race: The Genesis of a Mass Movement" (1983), pp. 22–33, Freeze Records, C; interview with Peter Bergel, Aug. 3, 1999; *Freeze Newsletter* 1 (July 1981); "Congressional District Activity, by state (as of June 1, 1982)," Box 10, Freeze Records, SL.

27. "From Popular Mandate to Public Policy" (Feb. 1983), Box 15, Freeze Rec-

ords, SL; *NYT*, Mar. 11, Nov. 4, 1982; Van Voorst, "Critical Masses," p. 82; "A Talk with Randall Kehler," *BAS* 39 (Jan. 1983): 53.

28. Gallup, *GP: Public Opinion 1982*, pp. 280, 283; Gallup, *GP: Public Opinion 1983*, p. 72; Yankelovich and Doble, "Public Mood," p. 46; Schneider, "Peace and Strength," pp. 347–48.

29. "Freeze: Because Nobody Wants a Nuclear War" and "Endorsers and Supporters—Nuclear Weapons Freeze" (May 1983), author's possession; Donner, "But Will They Come?" p. 456; Solo, *From Protest*, p. 66; "Congressional Quick Freeze," Box 1, Freeze Records, SL.

30. Interview with Randy Kehler, Aug. 20, 1999; DeLuca, "Cutting Edge," p. 4; minutes of WRL National Committee meetings of Mar. 13–15, 1981, Oct. 1982, and Feb. 18–20, 1983, and David McReynolds, "Staff Report" (Mar. 1, 1982), Box 2a, Series B, WRL Records; David Cortright, "Notes from meeting with Randy Forsberg and staff" (Sept. 7, 1981), PB1, Series G, SANE Records; Thomas A. Halsted to PSR Chapters, Aug. 14, 1981, PSR Records.

31. "Press Statement of Randall Forsberg" (Mar. 10, 1982), Freeze Records, C.

32. Interview with David Cortright, June 29, 1987; "Stop the NATO Missile Buildup" (May 21, 1981), Box 70, and "Statement by Peace Groups on Reagan Administration's Euromissile Proposal," Box 71, Series G, SANE Records.

33. Interview with Dottye Burt, June 29, 1987; Mike Jendrzejczyk, "Freeze: A Mandate to Stop the Nuclear Arms Race," *END J*, No. 3 (Apr.–May 1983), p. 11; "Decisions Made by the Third National Conference" (Feb. 1983), Box 9, Barbara Roche to National Committee Members, June 3, 1983, Box 4, Freeze Records, SL.

34. Randy Kehler to Pam Solo, Mar. 28, 1983, and Solo to Kehler, Mar. 31, 1983, Box 2, Solo to Strategy Task Force, Apr. 22, 1983, Box 15, Debbie Hejl to Freeze Friends, Apr. 28, 1983, Box 4, Freeze Records, SL.

35. Barbara Roche to National Committee Members, June 3, 1983, "The Euromissile Debate: A Call for a Delay," and "Legislative Update" (July 29, 1983), Box 4, Freeze Records, SL.

36. Randall Kehler and Randall Forsberg to Reagan, Sept. 27, 1983, and Kehler and Forsberg to Andropov, Sept. 27, 1983, Box 16, "A Call for Euromissile Actions, October 21–24, 1983," and "Summary of Euromissile Actions by State" (Oct. 1983), Box 4, Freeze Records, SL.

37. "An Appeal on Behalf of Soviet Peace Activists from the American Peace Movement," in Stead and Grünberg, eds., *Moscow Independent*, pp. 27–28; *NYT*, Sept. 5, 1982; "Arms Control Advocates Protest Harassment of Soviet Peace Group," *BAS* 38 (Nov. 1982): 62–63.

38. "Founder of Independent Soviet Peace Group Welcomed to U.S. by American Peace Groups" (June 24, 1983), Box 14, Freeze Records, SL; Stone, *"Every Man,"* pp. 166–79; von Hippel, "Recollections," pp. 327–28.

39. Solo to Joe Volk et al., June 15, 1984, Box 7, Freeze Records, SL; *NYT*, Apr. 10, 1983.

40. Van Voorst, "Churches," pp. 841–42; Kubbig and Risse-Kappen, "Living," p. 69; *NYT*, Mar. 11, 1982; "Freeze: Because Nobody Wants a Nuclear War," author's possession; R. Albert Mohler, Jr., "Southern Baptists," *DC*, No. 27 (Nov. 1983), p. 9.

41. Van Voorst, "Churches," pp. 843–45; "Freeze: Because Nobody Wants a Nuclear War," author's possession; *NYT*, Mar. 11, 1982.

42. Musto, *Catholic Peace Tradition*, pp. 261–62; Castelli, *Bishops*, pp. 57, 60.

43. Van Voorst, "Churches," pp. 831–38; *NYT*, May 3–5, 1981; Castelli, *Bishops*, pp. 177, 229, 233, 242–43, 274.

44. Kubbig and Risse-Kappen, "Living," p. 70; Van Voorst, "Churches," p. 842; David Cortright, "Unfulfilled Promise" (Oct. 9, 1984), and Robert J. Gabriele to Cortright, May 3, 1985, Box 80, Series G, SANE Records.

45. Castelli, *Bishops*, p. 178; interview with David Cohen, July 19, 1999.

46. Gene Carroll, "Is Labor Support for the Freeze Thawing AFL-CIO Cold War Rhetoric?" *Freeze Newsletter* 2 (Oct. 1982): 10, 30; *Los Angeles Times*, Oct. 5, 1983; "Highlights of Labor's Recent Contributions to Peace," *SW* 23 (May 1984): 5; Gene Carroll to Dear Brother or Sister, Feb. 25, 1985, Uncataloged material, Freeze Records, SL.

47. "Endorsers and Supporters-Nuclear Weapons Freeze" (May 1983), author's possession; Day and Waitzkin, "Medical Profession," pp. 648–50; Rizzo, "Professional Approach," p. 10; Lundberg, "Prescriptions," pp. 660–61.

48. Herken, *Cardinal Choices*, pp. 213–14; "Onward and Upward with Space Defense," *BAS* 39 (June–July 1983): 6–8; Weart, *Nuclear Fear*, pp. 382–83.

49. Schneider, "Peace and Strength," pp. 350–51.

50. Myrna Greenfield, "Seneca Falls, USA," *END J*, No. 6 (Oct.–Nov. 1983), pp. 6–7; Women's Encampment to Dear Friends, n.d., Nancy Facher to Dear Friends, Aug. 23, 1983, "Seneca Women Continue Protest on the 'First Front'" (June 7, 1984), and "Seneca Women Are Here to Stay" (Aug. 29, 1984), Women's Encampment for a Future of Peace and Justice Records; Krasniewicz, *Nuclear Summer*.

51. Strandt, "Media"; Gallup, *GP: Public Opinion 1981*, p. 211; Yankelovich and Doble, "Public Mood," p. 44; David Corn, "Will Arms Issues Matter?" *NT* 2 (Mar. 1984): 13. For an example of greater male support for nuclear disarmament, see Smith, "Polls: Gender," p. 390.

52. Jan Meriwether and Mary Jo Kaplan, "Mobilizing the Women's Peace Vote," *Citizen Participation* (Summer 1984), p. 5, Box 18, Freeze Records, SL.

53. Gordon, "Ultimate Single Issue," p. 21; interview with Dottye Burt, June 29, 1987; Paul F. Walker, "Teach-ins on American Campuses," *BAS* 38 (Feb. 1982): 10–11; "The November 11 Convocation," *BAS* 39 (Feb. 1983): 57.

54. Jamie Kalven, "UCS/UCAM," *BAS* 38 (June–July 1982): 73; interview with Sanford Gottlieb, July 19, 1998; Gottlieb to Barbara Roche, July 6, 1985, Box 1, Freeze Records, SL; *Christian Science Monitor*, Jan. 29, 1982; *NYT*, Feb. 2, 1982.

55. Markey to Members of the Denver Conference, Feb. 18, 1982, Box 18, Freeze Records, SL; interview with Jeremy Stone, July 22, 1999; Jeremy Stone, "The Nuclear Build-Down Tops the Freeze," p. 1, author's possession.

56. Schneider, "Peace and Strength," p. 323; *NYT*, Mar. 11, 1982; Kennedy and Hatfield to Randy Kehler, Apr. 30, 1982, Box 2, Kehler to National Committee Members and Others, Mar. 3, 1982, Box 10, Freeze Records, SL; Forsberg to Kennedy et al., Mar. 18, 1982, Freeze Records, C; interview with Randall Forsberg, July 7, 1999.

57. *WP*, Mar. 31, June 27, 1982; *NYT*, June 20, 1982.

58. *Boston Globe*, Mar. 10, 1982; "Gary Hart on the Nuclear Freeze," Box 18, Hart Papers; *WP*, Apr. 27, June 24, 1982; William Sweet, "The 1982 Election," *BAS* 39 (Jan. 1983): 56–57.

59. Waller, *Congress*, pp. 181–291; Karen Fierke, "Overwhelming Victory for the Freeze in the House," *Freeze Newsletter* 3 (June 1983): 5; Cortright, *Peace Works*, pp. 150–55.

60. *WP*, June 14, 1983; *NYT*, Nov. 6, 1983, Jan. 4, 1984; "Freeze Movement Rates Presidential Candidates," Freeze Records, C; "Meeting of Walter F. Mondale with Representatives of Arms Control Groups" (Jan. 23, 1984), Box 63, Series G, SANE Records; "Meeting with Senator Gary Hart and Arms Control Leaders" (May 16, 1984), Box 19, Hart Papers.

61. Interview with Robert Musil, July 20, 1998.

62. Kehler to Jules Yanover, Mar. 30, 1982, Box 2, Freeze Records, SL; Chatfield, *American Peace Movement*, p. 160; interview with Randall Forsberg, July 7, 1999; Butterfield, "Anatomy"; interview with Helen Caldicott, Feb. 27, 1999.

63. *Turnabout*, p. 24; Rojecki, *Silencing*, pp. 143, 148, 152.

64. *NYT*, May 16, Oct. 24, 1982; *Chicago Tribune*, Sept. 23, 1982; Rojecki, *Silencing*, pp. 137–38.

65. Donner, "But Will They Come?" pp. 460–61; interview with Randall Kehler, Aug. 20, 1999.

66. Barron, "KGB's Magical War"; Terry Provance to Editor, *Reader's Digest*, Sept. 30, 1982, "Memorandum on the Opposition" (June 29, 1982), Freeze Records, C; Asia Alderson Bennett to Edward T. Thompson, Oct. 7, 1982, Box 55, Series G, SANE Records.

67. Schell, *Fate of the Earth*; "The Fate of the Book," *BAS* 38 (Oct. 1982): 63.

68. Interview with Robert Musil, July 20, 1998; Cortright, *Peace Works*, pp. 65–68.

69. Waters, "Fallout"; Cortright, *Peace Works*, pp. 70–75; Meyer, *A Winter*, pp. 131–32.

70. *NYT*, Nov. 22, 1983; *WP*, Nov. 23, 1983; Feldman and Sigelman, "Political Impact."

71. Schlafly, "Six Fatal Fallacies"; Schipper, "Some Girls," p. 23; *Herald American*, Apr. 25, 1982.

72. Donner, "But Will They Come?" pp. 463–64; "The Men Who Are Dying to Win," *Sanity* (Feb. 1984).

73. Donner, "But Will They Come?" pp. 457–58, 464–65; *NYT*, Oct. 2, 1982.

74. *Christian Science Monitor*, Mar. 9, 1983; John Fisher to Unni Cheryan, Oct. 9, 1982, Box 13, Freeze Records, SL; *Interchange* (Jan. 20, 1983), Freeze Records, C; "Men Who Are Dying."

75. Boyer, *When Time*, pp. 126–51; Kotz, *Wild Blue Yonder*, p. 212.

76. Falwell to Dear Friend, June 17, 1982, Freeze Records, C; Robert Friedman, "The Bomb and Jerry Show," *NT* 1 (Aug.–Sept 1983): 25; *NYT*, Mar. 7, 1983; *WP*, Apr. 3, 1983.

77. Towell, "Reagan," p. 108; Randy Kehler to Jeremy Stone, Mar. 9, 1983, Box

5, Kehler to Barbara Roche et al., June 1, 1983, Box 16, Kehler to National Committee Members, June 3, 1983, Box 10, Freeze Records, SL.

78. "Decision Made by the Fourth National Conference of the Nuclear Weapons Freeze Campaign" (Dec. 1983), Box 9, "The New Legislative Strategy Adopted at the National Conference in St. Louis" (Dec. 1983), Box 1, Freeze Records, SL; David Corn, "Freeze Sets New Strategy," *NT* 2 (Jan. 1984): 16.

79. *Washington Times*, Apr. 26, 1984; Chap Morrison to Local Organizers, May 31, 1984, and "Where We Stand: A Progress Report on the Quick Freeze," Box 1, Freeze Records, SL; George Sommaripa to Randy Forsberg, July 24, 1984, Freeze Records, C.

80. Interview with Eric Fersht, Sept. 9, 1989; WRL, *A WRL History*; Fersht to Arms Control/Disarmament Organizations, Nov. 26, 1984, Freeze Records, C.

81. Charles F. Brown, "August 6, 1985" (Jan. 1985), and Christie Balka et al. to WILPF Branch Chairs, Jan. 1985, Sweet Files, WILPF Records; "1985 Strategy Paper" (Dec. 1984), Box 17, Freeze Records, SL.

82. Forsberg to Freeze Strategy Committee, Jan. 8, 1982 (actually, 1983), Box 15, Freeze Records, SL; Randall Kehler, "Message from the National Coordinator," *Freeze Newsletter* 3 (Dec. 1983): 16; David Corn, "The New PAC on the Block," *NT* 2 (Mar. 1984): 11–12; Pressman, "Nuclear Freeze," p. 1021.

83. Interview with Randall Kehler, Aug. 20, 1999; *WP*, Feb. 19, 1984; *NYT*, Apr. 25, July 19, 1984; Bill Curry to Freeze Supporters, Box 6, Freeze Records, SL; Chatfield, *American Peace Movement*, p. 161.

84. John Isaacs, "Congress and the Arms Control Paradox," *BAS* 41 (Jan. 1985): 10; "Impact '84" (1984), author's possession; Christopher E. Paine, "Lobbying for Arms Control," *BAS* 41 (Aug. 1985): 126.

85. Interview with Dottye Burt, June 29, 1987; interview with Randall Forsberg, July 7, 1999; interview with Robert Musil, July 20, 1998; interview with Helen Caldicott, Feb. 27, 1999; interview with Charles Johnson, Aug. 3, 1999.

86. Gallup, *GP: Public Opinion 1984*, p. 245; Isaacs, "Congress," p. 10; Bill Curry to Freeze Activists, Nov. 8, 1984, Box 6, Freeze Records, SL; Paine, "Lobbying," p. 126.

87. "Notes for Friday morning, 25 January 1985, Pre-IPCC discussion," IPCC Records; interview with Randall Kehler, Aug. 20, 1999; interview with Robert Musil, July 20, 1998; interview with Dottye Burt, June 29, 1987.

88. *Turnabout*, pp. 41–43; Kleidman, *Organizing*, p. 162; Paine, "Lobbying," p. 126.

89. David Cortright to Randall Forsberg, May 27, 1983, Box 15, Freeze Records, SL; interview with Randall Forsberg, July 7, 1999; interview with Randall Kehler, Aug. 20, 1999.

90. Borosage, "Bilateral Box"; interview with Terry Provance, July 20, 1999; Dan Ebener, "Freeze: For Disarmament Activists," *Mobilizer* 2 (Winter 1982): 8.

91. Pam Solo to Joe Volk et al., June 15, 1984, Box 7, Freeze Records, SL; interview with David Cortright, June 29, 1987; John P. Demeter, "Forsberg, Ellsberg Link Arms Race to Intervention," *NT* 1 (Jan. 1983): 18; David Corn, "Central America Spurs Debate," *NT* 2 (Oct. 1983): 14–15.

92. Kate Conway et al. to Dear Friend, Apr. 9, 1984, Box 3, Steve Ladd, "Direct

Action Strategy" (Aug. 20, 1984), Box 4, and Randall Kehler to Angie O'Gorman, Sept. 28, 1984, Uncatalogued material, Freeze Records, SL.

93. Interview with Peter Bergel, Aug. 3, 1999; interview with Dottye Burt, June 29, 1987; interview with Randall Forsberg, July 7, 1999.

94. *Turnabout*, p. 43; David Cortright to Randall Kehler, Oct. 12, 1984, Box 14, Freeze Records, SL; *Wall Street Journal*, Feb. 5, 1985; Chatfield, *American Peace Movement*, p. 161; Caldicott, *Desperate Passion*, p. 297.

95. "Movement Picks Up Support From Funders," *NT* 1 (Jan. 1983); 18; interview with Harold Willens, May 11, 2000; Jerome Grossman to Council Supporters, Sept. 1985, author's possession; *Turnabout*, p. 40.

96. Kleidman, *Organizing*, pp. 161–62; Patrick H. Caddell, "The State of American Politics" (Oct. 25, 1983), Box 6, Freeze Records, SL.

97. Interview with Harold Willens, May 11, 2000; Willens, *Trimtab Factor*.

98. "For the Nuclear Freeze Referendum" (1982), Box 13, Freeze Records, SL; *WP*, Apr. 19, 1983; *NYT*, June 14, 1983; Randall Kehler, "Message from the National Coordinator," *Freeze Newsletter* 3 (Dec. 1983): 3.

99. Interview with Robert Musil, July 20, 1998; interview with Judy Lipton, July 31, 1999; interview with Randall Forsberg, July 7, 1999; *WP*, Nov. 7, 1982.

100. Mariannee Szegedy-Maszak, "Rise and Fall of the Washington Peace Industry," *BAS* 45 (Jan.–Feb. 1989): 18, 20; interview with Robert Musil, July 20, 1998; Towell, "Reagan," p. 104.

101. Randall Kehler to Whom It May Concern, June 17, 1983, Box 2, Freeze Records, SL; Wendy Silverman to Chapters and Chapters-in-Formation, Sept. 23, 1983, PSR Records; interview with David Cohen, July 19, 1999.

102. Towell, "Reagan," pp. 104–6; Szegedy-Maszak, "Rise and Fall," pp. 20–21; Paine, "Lobbying," pp. 125–26; Eric M. Fersht to Arms Control/Disarmament Organizations, Nov. 26, 1984, Freeze Records, C.

103. Schneider, "Peace and Strength," pp. 343, 356; "A Prospect for Revival," *DDN* 2 (Mar.–Apr. 1987): 1; Den Oudsten, "Public Opinion on Peace and War," p. 24.

104. Schneider, "Peace and Strength," pp. 341, 349; Kramer, Kalick, and Milburn, "Attitudes," p. 22.

105. Den Oudsten, "Public Opinion on Peace and War," p. 23; Gallup, *GP: Public Opinion 1987*, p. 122; *NYT*, Mar. 4, 1985.

106. "U.S.-Soviet Relations," p. 10; Gallup, *GP: Public Opinion 1988*, p. 52; Gallup, *GP: Public Opinion 1983*, p. 265.

107. Yankelovich and Doble, "Public Mood," p. 33; Den Oudsten, "Public Opinion and Nuclear Weapons," p. 19; "Gallup Poll on Nuclear War," p. 35; Schneider, "Peace and Strength," p. 347; Graham, *American Public Opinion*, pp. 47–50.

108. Gallup, *GP: Public Opinion 1982*, p. 94; Gallup, *GP: Public Opinion 1983*, pp. 266–67; Kramer, Kalick, and Milburn, "Attitudes," p. 15; *WP*, Nov. 23, 1983; Schneider, "Peace and Strength," p. 362; "Nuclear Arms," p. 10; Yankelovich and Doble, "Public Mood," p. 46.

109. Schneider, "Peace and Strength," p. 346; Jamie Kalven, "A Talk with Louis Harris," *BAS* 38 (Aug.–Sept. 1982): 3–5; Yankelovich and Doble, "Public Mood," pp. 36, 46.

110. Penner, "A Brief Overview," pp. 45–46; Munton and Slack, "Canadian Attitudes," p. 9; Newman, "Surviving," p. 48; Regehr and Rosenblum, "Canadian Peace Movement," p. 228.

111. Kay Macpherson and Sara Good, "Canadian Voice of Women," *PM* 3 (Oct.–Nov. 1987): 26; Ann Gertler, "Voice of Women," *DC*, No. 18 (Jan. 1983), p. 6.

112. *Winnipeg Free Press*, May 18, 1983, Operation Dismantle Records; Stark and Brown, "Towards a Global Referendum," pp. 235–36; Schmitz, *Anti-Nuclear Protest*, pp. 10, 17.

113. "Summary of the History of Project Ploughshares," and "Nuclear Weapon-free Zones," Project Ploughshares Records; Regehr, "Canada," p. 245; Margot Trevellyan, "On the Cold War's Front Line," *END J*, No. 7 (Dec. 1983–Jan. 1984), p. 24.

114. Newman, "Surviving," p. 52; David Jackman, "Project Ploughshares: R & D for a Peaceful World," *PM* 3 (Oct.–Nov. 1987): 12; "Summary of the History of Project Ploughshares," Project Ploughshares Records.

115. Eric Shragge, "Cruise: The Test of Canada," *END J*, No. 7 (Dec. 1983–Jan. 1984), p. 23; "Summary of the History of Project Ploughshares," Project Ploughshares Records; Dwight Burkhardt, "Project Ploughshares," *DC*, No. 18 (Jan. 1983), pp. 5–6.

116. Schmitz, *Anti-Nuclear Protest*, pp. 10–11; *The Citizen* (Ottawa), Jan. 20, 1983, and "Organizations Jointly Participating (with Dismantle) in Cruise Court Case," Operation Dismantle Records; Shragge, "Cruise," p. 23; Trevellyan, "On the Cold War's Front Line," pp. 24–25.

117. Schmitz, *Anti-Nuclear Protest*, p. 10; *Churches and Nuclear Disarmament*, pp. 1–5.

118. Regehr and Rosenblum, "Canadian Peace Movement," p. 227; "CPPNW: Canadian Physicians for the Prevention of Nuclear War," *PM* 3 (Oct.–Nov. 1987): 29; "Science for Peace," *PM* 3 (Oct.–Nov. 1987): 27–28.

119. Stark and Brown, "Towards a Global Referendum," p. 236; Dennis McDermott to Members of the Canadian Labour Congress Executive Council et al., June 21, 1983, Freeze Records, C; *The Citizen* (Ottawa), Jan. 17, 1983, Operation Dismantle Records.

120. Regehr and Rosenblum, "Canadian Peace Movement," p. 228; *The Citizen* (Ottawa), Jan. 17, 1983, Operation Dismantle Records; Jewett, "'Suffocation,'" pp. 205–6; Trevellyan, "On the Cold War's Front Line," p. 25.

121. Giangrande, *Nuclear North*, pp. 65, 225; Shragge, "Cruise," p. 23; Penner, "Brief Overview," p. 48; Schmitz, *Anti-Nuclear Protest*, p. 11.

122. Schmitz, *Anti-Nuclear Protest*, pp. 11, 17; Jewett, "'Suffocation,'" p. 215.

123. Munton and Slack, "Canadian Attitudes," pp. 9–12; Hastings and Hastings, eds., *Index . . . 1982–83*, pp. 318–19.

Chapter 10

Epigraph: This declaration was signed by 29 independent activists, including Bärbel Bohley, Werner Fischer, and Ulrike Poppe of East Germany and Václav Havel, Ladislav Lis, and Jaroslav Sabata of Czechoslovakia. "Joint Declaration of Independent Peace Defenders in the German Democratic Republic and in Czechoslovakia" (Nov. 22, 1984), Box 512, WRI Records.

1. Kanobu Sekiguchi to friends who are figh4ting for a nuclear-free future, May 31, 1982, Japan Congress Against A & H Bombs Records, S; interview with Ikuro Anzai, May 15, 1999; Ohnishi, "Peace Movement," p. 26; Hook, "Ban the Bomb," pp. 35–36; "Japanese Disarmament Movement," pp. 287–88.

2. Ohnishi, "Peace Movement," pp. 26–29, 33; Sunao Suzuki, "Public Attitudes toward Peace," BAS 40 (Feb. 1984): 29; Hook, "Ban the Bomb," pp. 35–37.

3. Ohnishi, "Peace Movement," pp. 27–28; Hook, "Ban the Bomb," p. 37; Suzuki, "Public Attitudes," p. 29; "Japanese Disarmament Movement," p. 288.

4. Hook, "Ban the Bomb," pp. 35–36; Ohnishi, "Peace Movement," pp. 28–29; Den Oudsten, "Public Opinion," p. 32.

5. "War Exercises Protested," DC, No. 19 (Feb. 1983), p. 13; Berger, Cultures, p. 226; David C. Morrison, "Japanese Principles, U.S. Policies," BAS 41 (June–July 1985): 22–24.

6. Junko Yamaka, "Japan's Anti-Tomahawk Movement," Freeze Focus 4 (Nov. 1984): 15; "Stop Tomahawk," DC, No. 34 (June 1984), p. 19; Kamimura, Japanese Civil Society, p. 9.

7. Ohnishi, "Peace Movement," pp. 29, 31; Kodama, "Red vs. Green," pp. 3, 12; interview with Koichi Akamatsu, May 15, 1999; Betsy Taylor, "Report from a Trip to the Pacific," Freeze Newsletter 3 (Dec. 1983): 9–10; Koichi Akamatsu to friends, July 20, 1984, Japan Council Against A & H Bombs Records.

8. Masumi, Contemporary Politics, p. 418; Suzuki, "Public Attitudes," pp. 28, 31.

9. Mizuno Takashi, "Militarisation Increases," DC, No. 29 (Jan. 1984), p. 11; "What Is Gensuikin?" p. 1, Japan Congress Against A & H Bombs Records, Tokyo; Suzuki, "Public Attitudes," p. 28.

10. Den Oudsten, "Public Opinion and Nuclear Weapons," p. 19; Suzuki, "Public Attitudes," pp. 28, 30–31; Hook, "Ban the Bomb," p. 39; Hastings and Hastings, eds., Index . . . 1982–83, p. 319.

11. Falk, Taking Australia, p. 245; Saunders and Summy, Australian Peace Movement, p. 46; "Medical Association for the Prevention of War Australia" (Sept. 1986), Medical Association for the Prevention of War Records.

12. "International Symposium: Prevention of Nuclear War" (Oct. 1984), p. 9, Japan Council Against A & H Bombs Records; Burgmann, Power and Protest, p. 204; Jenny Skempton, "Peace Camp Inspiration," END J, No. 8 (Feb.–Mar. 1984), p. 6.

13. Saunders and Summy, Australian Peace Movement, pp. 49, 51; Beverly Symons, "Report from Australia," Peace Movement New Zealand Newsletter (Feb. 1983), p. 15; Kate Genge, "Respecting the Autonomy of Affiliates," Peace Paper (Nov.–Dec. 1988), p. 6, Australian Coalition for Disarmament and Peace Records.

14. Camilleri, "Nuclear Disarmament," p. 37; Sharp, "Militarism," p. 188; Richard Tanter, "Three Fingers in the Nuclear Pie," END J, No. 4 (June–July 1983), pp. 16–17.

15. Summy and Saunders, "Disarmament," pp. 36, 41; Annabelle Newbury-Knight, "West Coast," and "People for Peace," DC, No. 18 (Jan. 1983), pp. 3–4; Burgmann, Power and Protest, pp. 202–4; Peter D. Jones, "Report from Australia," Peacelink (June 1984), p. 14.

16. Burgmann, *Power and Protest*, pp. 198–99, 216; Tanter, "Three Fingers," p. 17; Jones, "Report from Australia," p. 14; Marguerite Nealon and Peter Jones, "Senate Seat for Anti-nukes Party," *END J*, No. 14 (Feb.–Mar. 1985), p. 7; Siracusa, "Peace Movements," p. 9; Summy and Saunders, "Disarmament," pp. 41–42, 51.

17. Saunders and Summy, *Australian Peace Movement*, pp. 45, 64; Campbell, *Australian Public Opinion*, pp. 46–47, 51, 55; Redner and Redner, *Anatomy*, p. 281; Mack, "Untangling," p. 14.

18. Kevin P. Clements, "New Zealand's Antinuclear Stand," *BAS* 43 (Mar. 1987): 32; "Auckland," *Peacelink* (Sept. 1983), p. 4; Clements, *Back From the Brink*, p. 116; Dodge and Hinchcliff, "Peace Movement"; *DC*, No. 27 (Nov. 1983), p. 6.

19. Tim Jones, "Peace Movement N.Z. Meeting," *Peacelink* (July 1983), p. 7; "The Beyond ANZUS Conference," *Peacelink* (Aug. 1984), p. 8; Clements, *Back From the Brink*, pp. 118–19; Campaign for Nuclear Disarmament *Newsletter* (June 1983), CND (NZ) Records; Lamare, "Growth," p. 482.

20. Sonja Antonsen, "What Is Peace Movement New Zealand?" *Peacelink* (Apr. 1983), p. 3; Robinson, "Current Peace Research," p. 34; Clements, *Back From the Brink*, p. 114.

21. Newnham, *Peace Squadron*, pp. 49–53; Campaign for Nuclear Disarmament *Newsletter* (July 1982), CND (NZ) Records; Kia Ora, "Truxton Actions," *Peace Movement New Zealand Newsletter* (June 1982), pp. 8–9; "Nuclear Warship Protests," *Peacelink* (May 1984), p. 18; Clements, *Back From the Brink*, p. 117.

22. Clements, *Back From the Brink*, pp. 114–16; Larry Ross, "N.Z. Nuclear Free Zone Committee Report," *Peace Movement New Zealand Newsletter* (Sept. 1982), pp. 14–15; Larry Ross, "Nuclear Weapons Free Zones in New Zealand," *Peacelink* (Oct. 1983), pp. 8–9.

23. Landais-Stamp and Rogers, *Rocking*, pp. 24–26; "New Zealand: Making Waves in the Pacific," *DDN* (Mar.–Apr. 1986), p. 4; Lange, *Nuclear Free*, pp. 49–54.

24. "Catching the Peace Train," *Peacelink* (Sept. 1983), p. 6; Ray Galvin, "Lobbying for Peace," *Peacelink* (Dec. 1984), pp. 8–9; "Nuclear Free New Zealand: The Campaign That Clinched It," Peace Movement Aotearoa Records; "Elections Special," *Peacelink* (July 1984), center section; Landais-Stamp and Rogers, *Rocking*, pp. 26–27.

25. Siracusa, "Peace Movements," p. 10; "Success in Auckland," *Peacelink* (Mar. 1985), p. 18; Lange, *Nuclear Free*, pp. 87–90; Nicky Hager, "A Sea Change," *Peacelink* (Mar. 1985), p. 3.

26. Lange, *Nuclear Free*, p. 92; "New Zealand," p. 4; Landais-Stamp and Rogers, *Rocking*, pp. 103, 105–6; Clements, *Back From the Brink*, pp. 120–21; Lamare, "Growth," pp. 474–76.

27. Emmanuel, *Monster in Morong*, p. 4; John Miller, "Nuclear Free Philippines Coalition," *Pacific Peacemaker*, No. 12 (Dec. 1984–Jan. 1985), p. 2; A. Linn Jeumann, "Marcos Tightens Grip on Bases," *NT* 1 (Feb. 1983): 21–22.

28. Paul Hutchcroft, "U.S. Bases in the Philippines," *CALC Report* (May–June 1982), p. 18; Jose W. Diokno, "Anti-Bases Coalition," *DC*, No. 29 (Jan. 1984), p. 5; *NYT*, Oct. 22, 1984.

29. Michael Bedford, "Activism in the Pacific," *NT* 8 (Summer 1990): 22; Michael Bedford, "Fiji Runs the Nuclear-Free Gauntlet," *DDN* 3 (Aug.–Sept. 1987): 6; Jone Daknunla, "Fijian Anti Nuclear Movement Revives," *Peacelink* (Feb. 1985), p. 9; R. B. Kumar to Dear Friends, May 24, 1984, New Accessions, WRL Records.

30. "Pacific Resistance Grows," *END J*, No. 9 (Apr.–May 1984), p. 4; "For a Nuclear Free and Independent Pacific," Peace Movement Aotearoa Records.

31. "Enough," Peace Movement Aotearoa Records; *Christian Science Monitor*, July 19, 1982; "Marshall Islands," *Peace Movement New Zealand Newsletter* (Nov. 1982), pp. 12–13.

32. The U.S. government secured a majority vote in this referendum, but fell short of the 75 percent required to change the constitution. Roman Bedor, "Protecting the Source of Life," *Mobilizer* 5 (Winter 1986): 8–9; Leonie Caldecott, "Fighting in the Pacific for a Nuclear-free Independence," *END J*, No. 4 (June–July 1983), pp. 20–21; "Enough," Peace Movement Aotearoa Records; Walden Bello, "The Great Pacific Land-Grab," *Freeze Focus* 4 (Nov. 1984): 10; "'Eyes' for Life," *Pacific Peacemaker*, No. 12 (Dec. 1984–Jan. 1985), p. 3.

33. "Pacific Peacemaker," *Peace Movement New Zealand Newsletter* (Aug. 1982), p. 6; "Pacific Peacemaker," CND (NZ) Records; Tim Jones, "Nuclear Free and Independent Pacific Conference 1983," *Peace Movement New Zealand Newsletter* (Mar. 1983), p. 17.

34. Bedford, "Activism," p. 22; "For a Nuclear Free and Independent Pacific," *Peacelink* (Sept. 1983), pp. 16–17; Bedor, "Protecting the Source," p. 8.

35. Narayan Das to Dear Friend, 1982, Folder 743, IKV Records, A; Narayan Desai, "The Nonviolent Movement in India Today" (ca. 1963), Box 445, WRI Records; "Fellowship News Letter" (Sept. 4, 1988), FOR (India) Records; "Indian Campaign for Nuclear Disarmament," Indian CND Records; Peter Jones, "The Movement in Asia Pacific," *WRI Newsletter*, No. 194 (June 1983), p. 9.

36. Interview with Dhirendra Sharma, Oct. 11, 1995; Sharma, "Confronting," pp. 161–63, 166–67; "COSNUP—Campaign," pp. 35–46.

37. *Korea Herald*, July 8, 1981, *PROK News*, No. 18 (Sept. 1983), *The New Korea*, Aug. 12, 1982, and *Voice of Free Korea* 5 (July–Oct. 1983), Committee for a New Korea Policy Records.

38. Andrew Cowell, Letter to the Editor, *END J*, No. 37 (1989), p. 46; Mary Muthoni Nyanjiru, "Kenyan Protest Alive but Living's the Thing," *END J*, No. 11 (Aug.–Sept. 1984), pp. 24–25.

39. *In Defence of Peace*; Mehmet Ali Dikerdem, "Crackdown at Turkish Trial," *END J*, No. 1 (Dec. 1982–Jan. 1983), p. 10.

40. "Profile of MAPAM," pp. 2–3; Melinda Fine, "Transforming Superpower Policies," *New Outlook* 28 (Feb.–Mar. 1985): 30; Hall-Cathala, *Peace Movement*, p. xiii; Schenker, "Israeli Peace Movement," pp. 25–27.

41. Unidentified Dutch newspaper clipping, Aug. 10, 1982, Folder 748, IKV Records, A; "An Appeal from the Brazilian Pacifist Movement" (Apr. 1984), and "Informative Bulletin of the Brazilian Pacifist Movement" (June 1984), Box 506, WRI Records.

42. *Buenos Aires Herald*, Jan. 15, 1984, Box 506, WRI Records; "Declaracion Inicial del Movimiento por la Vida y la Paz—MOVIP," Folder 748, IKV Records, A; "Argentine Group," *END J*, No. 10 (June–July 1984), p. 9.

43. Köszegi and Szent-Ivanyi, "A Struggle," pp. 117, 119–20, 163; Kavan and Tomin, eds., *Voices from Prague*, p. 6; *Towards an International*, p. 9; Janos Laszlo, "I Do Have the Right to Make My Voice Heard," *END J*, No. 3 (Apr.–May 1983), p. 19; Jiri Hajek, "View from the East," *END J*, No. 9 (Apr.–May 1984), p. 25.

44. English, "Eastern Europe's Doves," pp. 46–47; Tismaneanu, "Unofficial Peace Activism," p. 8; Mushaben, "Swords," pp. 132–33; Kavan and Tomin, eds., *Voices from Prague*, pp. 4–6.

45. Fitzpatrick, "Into the Public Eye," p. 21; *From Below*, p. 3; Frank Lipsius, "Soviet Thaw May Cool Protest," *NT* 1 (Jan. 1983): 22; Caesar Voûte to the author, Feb. 2, 1991.

46. Sandford, *Sword*, pp. 42–43, 61–62, 77; Eppelmann to Honecker, June 1981, ibid., pp. 92–94; Gordon, "From the Other Shore," p. 34; Allen, *Germany East*, pp. 102–3.

47. Sandford, *Sword*, pp. 60–61; Havemann to Brezhnev, Sept. 20, 1981, ibid., pp. 89–91; Allen, *Germany East*, pp. 101–4.

48. Sandford, *Sword*, pp. 63–67; "The Berlin Appeal—Make Peace Without Weapons" (Jan. 25, 1982), ibid., pp. 95–96; Woods, *Opposition*, p. 37; Gordon, "From the Other Shore," p. 34.

49. Allen, *Germany East*, pp. 103, 106–8; Wolfgang Müller, "Delicate Compromise between State and Grassroots," *END J*, No. 1 (Dec. 1982–Jan. 1983), p. 13; Sandford, *Sword*, pp. 67–70; Asmus, "Is There a Peace Movement?" pp. 312–13.

50. Woods, *Opposition*, pp. 37–38; Wolf, *Fourth Dimension*, p. 123.

51. END, "German Democratic Republic" (ca. 1985), author's possession; Allen, *Germany East*, pp. 109–11; Jackson, "GDR," p. 60.

52. Mushaben, "Swords," pp. 124, 129–30; Suzanne Gordon, "The View From the East," *NT* 2 (Jan. 1984): 25; Sandford, *Sword*, p. 108; Jim Wurst, "Roman Catholics," *DC*, No. 27 (Nov. 1983), p. 10.

53. Andrew White, "Open dialogue in Hungary," *END J*, No. 1 (Dec. 1982–Jan. 1983), pp. 15–16; Haraszti, "Hungarian," pp. 134–39; Köszegi and Szent-Ivanyi, "A Struggle," p. 164.

54. Köszegi and Thompson, *New Hungarian*; Ehring and Hücking, "Die neue Friedensbewegung," p. 335.

55. Haraszti, "Hungarian," pp. 137–39; "Peace Group for Dialogue," *DC*, No. 20 (Mar. 1983), pp. 5–6; Laszlo, "I Do Have the Right," p. 19; Ehring and Hücking, "Die neue Friedensbewegung," pp. 331–32.

56. Köszegi and Thompson, *New Hungarian*, pp. 12–13; "Hungarian Leadership Reacts to Independent Peace Groups and Initiatives," *PDN* 1 (Winter 1984–85): 6.

57. Laszlo, "I Do Have the Right," p. 20; Haraszti, "Hungarian," pp. 139–41; Jessie Jones, "New Space for Dialogue in Hungary," *END J*, No. 4 (June–July 1983), p. 10; *From Below*, p. 50.

58. Haraszti, "Hungarian," pp. 140–42; Caeser Voûte to the author, Feb. 2, 1991; Lynne Jones, "Keeping the Dialogue Open," *END J*, No. 6 (Oct.–Nov. 1983), p. 11.

59. Interview with Ferenc Köszegi, Aug. 28, 1986; minutes of the IPCC meeting of Nov. 2, 1986, IPCC Records; Ferenc Köszegi, "Hungarian Officials Hold Conference in Budapest," *END J*, No. 14 (Feb.–Mar. 1985), p. 6.

60. Cathy Fitzpatrick, "Update: Independent Peace Groups in the Eastern Bloc," *PDN* 1 (Spring 1984): 12; Jones, "Keeping the Dialogue Open," p. 12; John Bacher, "The Independent Peace Movements in Eastern Europe," *PM* 1 (Dec. 1985): 10; Haraszti, "Hungarian," p. 143.

61. *From Below*, pp. 53, 58–59; Lipsius, "Soviet Thaw," p. 22; Ehring and Hücking, "Die neue Friedensbewegung," pp. 323–26; Fitzpatrick, "Into the Public Eye," p. 23.

62. Hauner, "Anti-militarism," pp. 91, 95–97; *From Below*, pp. 5–6; Gordon, "From the Other Shore," p. 38.

63. See, for example, Vaclav Racek, "Letter from Prague," E. P. Thompson, "Letter to Prague" (Feb. 1983), "Statement on West European Peace Movements" (Nov. 15, 1981), "Open letter to peace movements" (Mar. 29, 1982), "Open letter from Charter 77 to the Dutch Interchurch Peace Council" (Aug. 27, 1982), Ladislav Hejdanek, "What Peace Do We Actually Want?," Jiri Hajek, "Charter 77 and the Present Peace Movement," Václav Havel, "An Interview" (Apr. 3, 1983), Zdena Tomin, "Dialogue," Jaroslav Sabata, "Letter to E. P. Thompson" (Apr. 1983), in Kavan and Tomin, eds., *Voices from Prague*, pp. 13–70; "Joint East-West Statement," *END J*, No. 9 (Apr.–May 1984), p. 7.

64. Pat Hunt, "Cracks in the ice," *END J*, No. 37 (1989), p. 23; "Letter from Charter," *END J*, No. 11 (Aug.–Sept. 1984), p. 28; "Charter Letter to END Convention," *END J*, No. 12 (Oct.–Nov. 1984), pp. 31–32.

65. Fitzpatrick, "Update," p. 3; A. W. Jackson, "Eastern European Peace Activists Face New Repression," *WRL News*, No. 241 (Mar.–Apr. 1984), pp. 6, 8; English, "Eastern Europe's Doves," p. 48; Hanson, *Catholic Church*, p. 314.

66. "Wide Response to Czech Petitions," *END J*, No. 9 (Apr.–May 1984), p. 6; "A Thousand Suns," *END J*, No. 10 (June–July 1984), p. 8.

67. Fitzpatrick, "Update," p. 3; "Czech and East German Independents Call for Nuclear-Free Europe," *PDN* 2 (Summer–Fall 1985): 6–7; "Charter 77 Document No 5/85: The Prague Appeal" (Mar. 11, 1985), END Records, published as "Prague Appeal."

68. Fitzpatrick, "Into the Public Eye," p. 23; Brian Morton and Joanne Landy, "East European Activists Test Glasnost," *BAS* 44 (May 1988): 19; Hanson, *Catholic Church*, p. 314.

69. Fitzpatrick, "Update," p. 12; "A report from Solidarnosc in Cracow," *END J*, No. 1 (Dec. 1982–Jan. 1983), p. 26; Randle, *People Power*, p. 48; "Independent Peace Moves in Poland" and "Open Letter from Kuron," *END J*, No. 11 (Aug.–Sept. 1984), p. 8; *From Below*, pp. 73–74.

70. Wiktor Moszczynski to E. P. Thompson, May 26, 1983, Freeze Records, C; "Committee of Social Resistance Appeals to the Peace and Anti-Nuclear Movement in Western Europe" (May 9, 1983), Box 507, WRI Records.

71. "Poland," *DC*, No. 35 (July–Aug. 1984), p. 7; "Polish Attitudes to Foreign Affairs," *END J*, No. 15 (Apr.–May 1985), p. 6; *Towards an International*, p. 8.

72. Celebrating John Lennon's birthday, they conducted it under the slogan: "Lennon lives, Lennon will live." This was a parody of the well-known Soviet homily: "Lenin lived, Lenin lives, Lenin will live." Ilukhina and Pavlova, "Totalitarianism," p. 4; Bacher, "Independent Peace Movement," p. 13; Alexeyeva, "Independent Youth Groups," p. 4.

73. Sakharov, *Memoirs*, pp. 577–78; *NYT*, June 23, 1983; Sakharov, "A Message."

74. Taagepera, "Inclusion," pp. 33–44; *From Below*, p. 143.

75. END, "Moscow Trust Group," Box 508, and "An Interview with Soviet Emigre Mark Reitman," Box 507, WRI Records; "The Independent Soviet Peace Movement: An Interview with Two Founding Members," *PDN* 2 (Summer–Fall 1985): 14–15; Mark Reitman, "Three Years in the Trust Group's Life," *END J*, No. 16–17 (Summer 1985), p. 9.

76. Sergei Batovrin, "Why We Refuse Our Bowl of Soup," *END J*, No. 4 (June–July 1983), p. 7; Bacher, "Independent Peace Movement," p. 13; "Independent Soviet Peace Movement," pp. 14–15; Fitzpatrick, "Into the Public Eye," p. 24.

77. END, "Moscow Trust Group," Box 508, WRI Records; Sergei Batovrin and Mikhail Ostrovsky to U.S., Canadian, and European Peace Groups, Sept. 1983, Folder 734, IKV Records, A; Fitzpatrick, "Into the Public Eye," p. 24.

78. "Independent Soviet Peace Movement," pp. 14–15; Alice Underwood, in *END J*, No. 4 (June–July 1983), p. 6; Alexeyeva, *Soviet Dissent*, p. 387; Cathy Fitzpatrick, "The Moscow Trust Group," *DC*, No. 20 (Mar. 1983), p. 3; "Interview with Sergei Batovrin" (Jan. 1983), Box 14, Freeze Records, SL.

79. Hosking, *Awakening*, p. 62; "Repression of Independents Continues," *END J*, No. 12 (Oct.–Nov. 1984), p. 7; Jean McCollister, "Affecting the Policymakers," *END J*, No. 3 (Apr.–May 1983), p. 27.

80. Evangelista, *Unarmed Forces*, pp. 156, 236; interview with Frank von Hippel, Aug. 22, 1999; English, *Russia*, p. 179; interview with Sergei Kapitza, June 28, 1990.

81. Evangelista, *Unarmed Forces*, pp. 156–60; Velikhov, "Chernobyl," pp. 158–60; Velikhov, "Science," p. 33; Von Hippel, "Arms Control Physics," pp. 39–40; interview with Jeremy Stone, July 22, 1999; interview with Frank von Hippel, Aug. 22, 1999; interview with Sergei Kapitza, June 28, 1990; Sagdeev, *Making*, pp. 245–55.

82. Evangelista, *Unarmed Forces*, pp. 160–61, 184–92; English, *Russia*, pp. 117, 134, 163, 167–69, 177, 180–85; Arbatov, *System*, pp. 309–11; Velikhov, "Chernobyl," p. 160; Sagdeev, *Making*, p. 266.

83. Gorbachev, *A Time*, pp. 42, 45.

84. Weart, *Nuclear Fear*, pp. 379–80; Stark, "East Meets West," p. 20; Matlock, *Autopsy*, p. 79; *WP*, Jan. 5, 1985; Kull, *Burying Lenin*, p. 18.

85. Holloway, *Soviet Union*, p. 162; Charles J. Hanley, "'The Freeze' Sounds Good in Muddy Moscow," Associated Press dispatch of Apr. 10, 1983, www.lexis-nexis.com/universe; "Repression of independents," p. 7.

Chapter 11

Epigraph: "Bonn, 10th October, 1981," Kaldor Papers.

1. Serry, "Peace Movement," pp. 56–57; L. J. Hogebrink to Hideaki Nagai, Mar.

12, 1982, and J. Roman Bedor, "Appeal to All the People of the World" (Sept. 1, 1981), Folder 744, IKV Records, A; "CND International Committee: Report for National Council" (Jan. 1983), Reel 26, CND (B) Records, HM.

2. "Nuclear Weapons in the Philippines" (ca. 1982), Committee for a New Korea Policy Records; "Introducing the USNFPN" (Mar. 1983), United States Nuclear Free Pacific Network Records.

3. "US-Europeace Tour 1982," and AFSC press release of Dec. 13, 1983, Box 11, Series II, AFSC Records; "U.S.-Europeace Tour Reaches Millions," *CALC Report* (May–June 1982), p. 19.

4. Interview with Bruce Kent, June 7, 1999; Melinda Fine, "Address to Frankfurt Easter March, April 1983," and "Statement to be Issued by Peace Movements from Europe and the USA in Bonn, June 9th" (1982), Freeze Records, C.

5. Interview with Terry Provance, July 20, 1999; "Holland," *Freeze Newsletter* 3 (Aug. 1983): 11; Wim Bartels to the participants in demonstrations and actions against the Euromissiles, Oct. 19, 1983, Box 14, Freeze Records, SL.

6. Melinda Fine, "International Efforts for a Freeze," *Freeze Focus* 4 (Nov. 1984): 3; interview with David Cohen, July 19, 1999; Young, "Peace Movements," p. 151.

7. Warner and Shuman, *Citizen Diplomats*, p. 45; "International Physicians for the Prevention of Nuclear War" (1986), PSR Records.

8. Interview with Bernard Lown, July 6, 1999; Judy Lipton to Irwin Redliner, June 26, 1983, "International Physicians for the Prevention of Nuclear War: Description and Brief History" (Sept. 1985), and Peter Zheutlin, "Medicine, Politics and the Nobel Peace Prize," PSR Records.

9. Interview with Bernard Lown, July 6, 1999; minutes of the Board of Directors meeting, PSR, June 5, 1983, PSR Records.

10. See, for example: "What We Can Do," *BAS* 37 (June–July 1981): 20–21.

11. Ironically, Lown found that, in the United States, the commercial TV networks refused to run the program, and he eventually settled for a late night showing—with some cuts and followed by hostile commentators—on the Public Broadcasting System. Interview with Bernard Lown, July 6, 1999; Warner and Shuman, *Citizen Diplomats*, pp. 48–51.

12. "International Physicians for the Prevention of Nuclear War: Description and Brief History" (Sept. 1985), PSR Records; Warner and Shuman, *Citizen Diplomats*, p. 51.

13. Interview with Bernard Lown, July 6, 1999; Bernard Lown, "The Urgency of a Unique Initiative" (June 4, 1984), Lown Papers.

14. Lumsden, "Nuclear Weapons," p. 111–12; "Pugwash Conferences on Science and World Affairs" (1982), Pugwash Conferences Records; interview with Frank von Hippel, Aug. 22, 1999; interview with Thomas Cochran, Aug. 23, 1999; "Pugwash Workshop on Nuclear Forces," *BAS* 41 (Mar. 1985): 53.

15. DeBoer, "Polls: The European Peace Movement and Deployment," pp. 119–20; Lumsden, "Nuclear Weapons," p. 114; *END J*, No. 6 (Oct.–Nov. 1983), p. 6.

16. Young, "Peace Movements," p. 155; Caldicott, *Desperate Passion*, p. 282; "Kvinder for fred," Kvinder for Fred Records; "Vrouwen voor vrede," Box 2, Series A,8, WSP Records; "1987 IPB General Assembly," Box 522, WRI Records.

17. Foster, *Women*, pp. 86, 92; Margot Miller, "Belgium," *END J*, No. 3 (Apr.–May 1983), p. 10; "WILPF Launches Campaign to Stop Bomb Tests," *Pax et Libertas* 49 (Sept. 1984): cover; interview with Edith Ballantyne, June 1, 1999.

18. Laurens Hogebrink, "Discussion paper for IPCC meeting, 7–9 October 1983," Freeze Records, C; Lumsden, "Nuclear Weapons," p. 115; Hanson, *Catholic Church*, p. 284.

19. Etienne de Jonghe, "Pax Christi," *DC*, No. 18 (Jan. 1983), pp. 16–17; Etienne de Jonghe, "Pax Christi International: Continuing Its Chosen Path," *DC*, No. 29 (Jan. 1984), p. 14; "Deployment of Theatre Nuclear Weapons in Europe" (May 1981), Pax Christi International (Belg.) Records.

20. *DC*, No. 27 (Nov. 1983), p. 3; Schmitz, *Anti-Nuclear Protest*, p. 7.

21. See, for example: Lumsden, "Nuclear Weapons," pp. 112, 115–16; Sandra Ball, "Labour Tour for Peace," *DC*, No. 26 (Oct. 1983), p. 8.

22. Petersen, "Scandilux," pp. 6–20; Mary Kaldor and Mient Jan Faber, "The Peace Movement and Social Democracy" (June 1986), Bess Papers; interview with Michael Foot, June 19, 1998.

23. WRL, *Peace Calendar, 1986*; John Hyatt, "War Resisters International," *DC*, No. 18 (Jan. 1983), pp. 17–18.

24. Joe Peacock, "International Fellowship of Reconciliation," *DC*, No. 18 (Jan. 1983), p. 16; Jim Forest, "International Fellowship of Reconciliation," *DC*, No. 29 (Jan. 1984), p. 13.

25. Interview with Eric Fersht, Sept. 9, 1989; "Enough" (1986), Peace Movement Aotearoa Records; Lumsden, "Nuclear Weapons," p. 113.

26. "Palme Commission Report," *BAS* 38 (Aug.–Sept. 1982): 65; Palme to Reagan, May 28, 1982, Case File 116584, PC, Subject File, WHORM Records; Petersen, "Scandilux," p. 3.

27. "IPCC, An Effort to Stimulate International Communication and Cooperation" and "IPCC Meeting 13–15 January 1984, Stockholm," IPCC Records; Wim Bartels, "Clarification of the IPCC network of peace movements; 2" (Oct. 7–9, 1983), MfS Records, NY; Jim Wurst, "Moving Ahead," *DC*, No. 18 (Jan. 1983), p. 3; Winther, "Danish Peace Movements," p. 4.

28. "IPCC, An Effort to Stimulate International Communication and Cooperation" and "Membership List IPCC, July 1984," IPCC Records; interview with Gerhard Jordan, Aug. 31, 1986.

29. "IPCC, An Effort to Stimulate International Communication and Cooperation," IPCC Records; "History of *Disarmament Campaigns*" (June 28, 1990), IPB Records; Wim Bartels to Dear friends, July 12, 1982, and Mike Jendrzejczyk and Pam Solo to Nuclear Weapons Facilities Task Force, Oct. 20, 1982, Freeze Records, C.

30. Minutes of the IPCC meeting of Sept. 28–30, 1984, IPCC Records.

31. "Second END Convention" (June 1983), Bess Papers; Carla Ferrari, "The European Disarmament Convention in Italy," *DC*, No. 35 (July–Aug. 1984), p. 18.

32. Interview with Nigel Young, May 15, 1999; Gerard Holden, "A Meeting of Minds," *END J*, No. 4 (June–July 1983), p. 5; Jim Wurst, Dorothea Ensel, and Andreas Körner, "Perugia Convention," *DC*, No. 36 (Sept. 1984), p. 7.

33. Interview with E. P. Thompson, Nov. 1, 1989; "END Annual Report, 1984–5," Bruce Kent, "A Few Thoughts About END" (Feb. 9, 1982), and E. P. Thompson, "END in 1984" (Nov. 21, 1983), Kaldor Papers; E. P. Thompson, "END at September 1981" (Aug. 27, 1981), Bess Papers.

34. Thompson to Mary Kaldor, Aug. 24, 1981, Kaldor to Ken Coates, Sept. 3, 1982, Thompson to Dan Smith and Mary Kaldor, Oct. 7, 1982, and Ken Fleet and Tony Simpson to Roger Fieldhouse, Jan. 4, 1983, Kaldor Papers.

35. Thompson, *Beyond the Cold War*, pp. 169–71, 175–76. For other nonaligned analyses, see Mary Kaldor. "END Can Be a Beginning," *BAS* 37 (Dec. 1981): 42–45; Thompson, "Peace Is a Third Way."

36. Köszegi and Thompson, *New Hungarian*, pp. 42–43; Thompson, *Beyond the Cold War*, p. 121

37. Köszegi and Thompson, *New Hungarian*, p. 47; Melinda Fine to Freeze Activists, July 1984, Freeze Records, C.

38. Young, "Sensing," p. 180; Köszegi and Thompson, *New Hungarian*, pp. 41–42.

39. Interview with Sheila Oakes, June 6, 1999; David McReynolds, "Rebuilding the Non-Aligned International Peace Movement," *WRL News* (Jan.–Feb. 1984), p. 2; John Hyatt to McReynolds, Apr. 6, 1982, Box 515, WRI Records; Sheila Cooper to Friend (ca. June 1983), MfS Records, NY.

40. Interview with Rainer Santi, Aug. 18, 1986; David McReynolds to National Committee, WRL, Feb. 9, 1984, Box 2a, Series B, WRL Records; *IPB* (Geneva: IPB, 1985), MfS Records, S.

41. Interview with Bruce Kent, July 10, 1990; "The Future of the European Peace Movement" (Oct.1983), Kaldor Papers.

42. Minutes of the IPCC meeting of Sept. 30, 1984, IPCC Records; Laurens Hogebrink, "Discussion paper for IPCC meeting, 7–9 October 1983, London" (Sept. 28, 1983), Freeze Records, C.

43. Minutes of the IPCC meeting of Sept. 30, 1984, and Melinda Fine to Dear IPCC friends, Oct. 20, 1984, IPCC Records; Melinda Fine to Strategy Committee et al. (May 1984), Box 16, Freeze Records, SL.

44. Interview with Mary Kaldor, June 7, 1999.

45. E. P. Thompson to Jane Sharp, May 18, 1981, END Records; Serry, "Peace Movement," p. 57; interview with Randall Kehler, Aug. 20, 1999.

46. Thompson, *Beyond the Cold War*, pp. 130–31; interview with Mary Kaldor, June 7, 1999.

47. Interview with Randall Kehler, Aug. 20, 1999; Cortright and Pagnucco, "Limits," pp. 166–68; Randall Forsberg to Kaldor, Nov. 11, 1983, Box 9, Freeze Records, SL; interview with Randall Forsberg, July 7, 1999.

48. Randall Kehler's handwritten comments on Pam Solo to Melinda Fine, June 8, 1984, Box 14, Freeze Records, SL; Cortright and Pagnucco, "Limits," p. 172.

49. Kaldor, "Introduction," in Kaldor, ed., *Europe*, p. 1; E. P. Thompson, "Ends and Histories," p. 10; Mient Jan Faber, "Détente from Below," *DC*, No. 35 (July–Aug. 1984), p. 4; E. P. Thompson to Mary Kaldor, July 27, 1983, Kaldor Papers; Kavan, "Helsinki," p. 37.

50. Holden, "A Meeting," pp. 5–6; E. P. Thompson, Letter to the Editor, *Guar-*

dian, Nov. 30, 1984; John Bacher, "The Independent Peace Movements in Eastern Europe," *PM* 1 (Dec. 1985): 11.

51. Interview with Nigel Young, May 15, 1999; Allen, *Germany East*, p. 120; Meg Beresford to Mary Kaldor, Oct. 11, 1982, Kaldor Papers; interview with Mient Jan Faber, Aug. 7, 1986; "A Silent New Year," *DC*, No. 19 (Feb. 1983), p. 13.

52. Van den Dungen, "Critics," p. 276; interview with Nigel Young, May 15, 1999.

53. Thompson, "Ends and Histories," p. 10; Thompson, "Letter to Prague"; Thompson, *Double Exposure*, p. 109; Dan Smith to Dear Sir, Jan. 12, 1983, Kaldor Papers; Dorothy Thompson, Letter to the Editor, *Guardian*, Jan. 13, 1983.

54. Thompson, "END," p. 235; "War Resisters International Statement on Poland—21 December 1981," Box 527, and "E.N.D. Expresses Concern at Grave Situation in Poland" (Dec. 14, 1981), Box 200, WRI Records.

55. *Guardian*, Dec. 2, 1982; E. P. Thompson, "Will 1983 End in Darkness for Europe?" *Sanity* (Dec. 1983), p. 9.

56. Mary Kaldor et al. to Erich Honecker, Jan. 15, 1984, Box 7, Freeze Records, SL; Wim Bartels to Andreas Papandreou, May 11, 1984, IPCC Records.

57. Bacher, "Independent Peace Movements," p. 11; Jones, "Tentative Dialogue," p. 16.

58. Ken Coates to Sakharov, July 21, 1981, and E. P. Thompson, "Work to the East" (Dec. 31, 1983), Kaldor Papers; E. P. Thompson and Dorothy Thompson, Letter to the Editor, *The Times* (L), Feb. 7, 1984.

59. Mary Kaldor, "The crossroads of a campaign," *END J*, No. 6 (Oct.–Nov. 1983), p. 2; Mary Kaldor, "Thoughts on Returning from END Meeting of 17th March 1984," Kaldor Papers.

60. Meg Beresford, "END in 1984" (Mar. 9, 1984), Kaldor Papers; Mient Jan Faber and Mary Kaldor, "Ending the Occupation of Europe: The Only Way to Save Détente" (July 1984), IPCC Records; Falk, "An American view," p. 12.

61. Minutes of the IPCC meeting of Jan. 25, 1985, IPCC Records.

62. Laurens Hogebrink, "Discussion paper for IPCC meeting, 7–9 October 1983, London" (Sept. 28, 1983), and Mike Jendrzejczyk et al., "Report of Meeting of International Peace Communication and Coordination Center" (Oct. 1983), Freeze Records, C; minutes of IPCC meeting of Oct. 7, 1983, IPCC records.

63. Kaldor to Forsberg, Oct. 11, 1983, and Forsberg to Kaldor, Nov. 11, 1983, Freeze Records, C; E. P. Thompson, "Freeze and Withdrawal: Does it need a political dimension?" (Mar. 1984), IPCC Records.

64. Wim Bartels to Dear Friends, Jan. 24, 1984, and "Freeze and Withdrawal" (June 21, 1984), IPCC Records; Erik Alfsen et al., "Freeze and Withdrawal."

65. World Peace Council, *U.S. Space Offensive*, p. 17; "Apocalypse, No!" *PC* 14 (Nov. 1983): 1; "Unite Against Danger of Nuclear War!" *PC* 12 (Nov. 1981): 1–2.

66. "Solidarity with Afghanistan," *PC* 15 (Apr. 1984): 5; "Afghanistan: A Time for Mass Solidarity," *PC* 15 (Dec. 1984): 8; "Remarks of Johannes Pakaslahti, General Secretary of the World Peace Council, to the Meeting of CSCE National Committees of the WPC, Moscow, 3 December, 1989," Prince Papers.

67. "A Great Champion of Peace Mourned," *PC* 13 (Nov. 1982): supplement;

"Tribute to President Andropov," *PC* 15 (Feb. 1984): supplement; "Tribute to President Chernenko," *PC* 16: 3 (1985): 6.

68. Interview with Rob Prince, July 27, 1999; Rob Prince, "In the Name of Peace" (Mar. 12, 1990), Prince Papers.

69. "Remarks of Johannes Pakaslahti, General Secretary of the World Peace Council, to the Meeting of CSCE National Committees of the WPC, Moscow, 3 December, 1989," Prince Papers; interview with Rob Prince, July 27, 1999.

70. Interview with Rob Prince, July 27, 1999; interview with Mark Solomon, July 8, 1999.

71. Interview with Günther Drefahl, May 19, 1999. See also Schlaga, "Peace Movement," pp. 138–39.

72. Tairov, "From New Thinking," pp. 44–45; interview with Rob Prince, July 27, 1999; interview with Mark Solomon, July 8, 1999; Rob Prince, "A sketch history of the World Peace Council," Prince Papers.

73. Rob Prince, "A sketch history of the World Peace Council," Prince Papers.

74. Renate Mielka to Louise Murray, July 11, 1984, 533.2640, Deutscher Friedensrat Records; *NYT*, Oct. 2, 1983; "All-Union Peace Conference Details Record Activity," *PC* 16: 2 (1985): 1.

75. Pierre Sellincourt to Dear Friends, July 10, 1984, U.S. Peace Council Records; *Rauhan Puolesta* (July 1984), Finnish Peace Committee Records; Kodama, "Red vs. Green," pp. 6–7; interview with Rob Prince, July 27, 1999.

76. *Conference of Peace, Disarmament and Anti-War Movements in Europe and North America* (1984), pp. 14–18, Box 4, WPC Records.

77. Taipale, "Peace Movement," pp. 35–36; interview with Rob Prince, July 27, 1999.

78. *Tribune de Genève*, Jan. 25, 1982, and Charling Tao to Dear Friends, Jan. 31, 1982, Folder 723, IKV Records, A.

79. Sandford, *Sword*, p. 20; Bruce Kent, "Report with comments, on Moscow visit 25/27 Oct. 82," Bess Papers; interview with Bruce Kent, June 7, 1999.

80. Minutes of the meeting of the National Executive Board of the U.S. Peace Council of Nov. 20–21, 1982, U.S. Peace Council Records; Sundman, "END Campaign," p. 64.

81. "An exchange of open letters from the Soviet Peace Committee and European Nuclear Disarmament," and Zhukov to Dear Friends, Dec. 2, 1982, Bess Papers.

82. *Guardian*, Apr. 8, 14, 1983; Barna Sarkadi Nagy and Ilona Sebestyén to International Secretariat of the Liaison Committee, END Convention, Apr. 30, 1983, Box 447, WRI Records.

83. Ann Petitt, "Sitting Down with Both the 'Official' and the 'Unofficial,'" *END J*, No. 5 (Aug.–Sept. 1983), pp. 11–12; *Guardian*, May 30, 1983.

84. Healey, *Time*, p. 523; Thompson, *Double Exposure*, pp. 39–40.

85. Interview with Mark Solomon, July 8, 1999; Solomon, *Death Waltz*; interview with Rob Prince, July 27, 1999.

86. Interview with Rob Prince, July 27, 1999; Tairov, "From New Thinking," p. 45.

87. Interview with Werner Rümpel, May 20, 1999; interview with Rob Prince,

July 27, 1999; "Soviet Official Slams Western Independents," *END J*, No. 13 (Dec. 1984–Jan. 1985), p. 6.

88. Köszegi and Thompson, *New Hungarian*, p. 45; Thompson, *Double Exposure*, pp. 51–52, 112.

89. *Towards an International*, p. 6; Melinda Fine to Strategy/Executive Committee members, ca. June 1984, Box 14, Freeze Records, SL; David McReynolds to CNAPD, Apr. 26, 1984, New Accession, WRL Records.

90. Minutes of the joint meeting of the Freeze strategy/executive committee, June 18, 1984, Box 16, Freeze Records, SL; minutes of the CND executive committee meeting of July 3, 1982, Reel 26, CND (B) Records, HM.

91. Interview with Daniel Plesch, July 21, 1998; interview with Jeremy Stone, July 22, 1999.

92. Krasner, "Political Influence," p. 3; Jordan, "Peace Activities," p. 4; Bein and Epple, "Die Friedensbewegung," p. 116.

93. Interview with Mark Solomon, July 8, 1999; interview with Rob Prince, July 27, 1999; "The New 'Red Scare': An Open Letter," U.S. Peace Council Records; interview with Randall Kehler, Aug. 20, 1999; interview with Sanford Gottlieb, July 19, 1998.

94. *Towards an International*, p. 7; Holden, "A Meeting," p. 6.

95. Jiri Hajek, "View from the East," *END J*, No. 9 (Apr.–May 1984), p. 25; Jim Wurst, "On Relations East and West," *DC*, No. 20 (Mar. 1983), p. 4.

96. Ceadel, "Britain's Nuclear Disarmers," p. 236; minutes of the CND executive committee meeting of Mar. 26, 1983 and of the CND national council meeting of Apr. 16–17, 1983, Reel 26, CND (B) Records, HM; Jon Bloomfield, "View from Prague," *END J*, No. 5 (Aug.–Sept. 1983), pp. 10–11.

97. Bloomfield, "View," pp. 10–11; Douglas Peroni to members of the CND executive committee, June 29, 1983, and "Text of Statement from CND National Council" (1983), Reel 26, CND (B) Records, HM; English, "Eastern Europe's Doves," p. 49

98. Cortright and Pagnucco, "Limits," p. 171; Coates to Mient Jan Faber, Mar. 14, 1983, Freeze Records, C; Winther to Faber, Mar. 14, 1983, Box 7, Freeze Records, SL.

99. Serry, "Peace Movement," pp. 58–59; Maria Margaronis, "Notes from Abroad," *NT* 2 (Mar. 1984): 10; E. P. Thompson, "Bumpy but beneficial," *END J*, No 9 (Apr.–May 1984), p. 27.

100. Richard Falk, "Five days of discussion," *END J*, No. 11 (Aug.–Sept. 1984), pp. 9–10; Jim Wurst et al., "Perugia Convention," *DC* (Sept. 1984), p. 7; *NYT*, July 20, 1984.

101. "Looking East," p. 50.

102. *World Peace Council: List of Members*, pp. 170–74; Rob Prince, "In the Name of Peace" (Mar. 12, 1990), Prince Papers.

103. Interview with Günther Drefahl, May 19, 1999; Rob Prince, "A Sketch History of the World Peace Council," and Rob Prince, "In the Name of Peace" (Mar. 12, 1990), Prince Papers.

104. Jane Dibblin, "An Outpouring of Protest—Peaceful and Determined," *END J*, No. 7 (Dec. 1983–Jan. 1984), p. 10.

105. Köszegi and Thompson, *New Hungarian*, inside cover.

106. Thompson, "Will 1983 End in Darkness?" p. 8.

Chapter 12

Epigraph: Dwight Burkhardt, "Project Ploughshares," *DC*, No. 18 (Jan. 1983), p. 5.

1. Interview with Thomas Graham, Jr., Aug. 23, 1999; interview with Robert McFarlane, July 21, 1999.

2. *WP*, May 9, 1982; Knopf, *Domestic Society*, p. 224.

3. Wirthlin to Reagan, June 18, 1981, Case File 030519SS, FO Subject File, WHORM Records; Richard Beal to Senior Staff, Dec. 21, 1981, "Weekly Poll Summaries—Public Opinion Digests 1981 [1]" Folder, Beal Files; interview with Richard Wirthlin, Oct. 6, 1999.

4. Adelman, "Woefully Inadequate," p. 152; interview with Kenneth Adelman, July 22, 1998.

5. Allen to Haig, July 20, 1981, "United States Information Agency (USIA) Vol. I 1/20/81–12/31/83(4)" Folder, Box 91,377, Agency File, Executive Secretariat, NSC Records; Wick to Reagan, Oct. 29, 1981, Case File 045946, FG 298, Subject File, WHORM Records.

6. Interview with Thomas Graham, Jr., Aug. 23, 1999; interview with Richard Allen, June 29, 1999.

7. Haig, *Caveat*, p. 227; Reagan, *An American Life*, pp. 558–59.

8. Bush to Ray Cline, July 29, 1983, Box 31, Cline Papers; Eagleburger to Charles Z. Wick, Mar. 16, 1984, Case File 325900, FG 006–01, Subject File, WHORM Records.

9. *NYT*, Mar. 11, 12,1982; "Department of State Daily Press Briefing" (Mar. 11, 1982), Freeze Records, C

10. *NYT*, Apr. 24, 1982; James A. Baker III to William P. Clark, Apr. 28, 1982, Dole Files; interview with Robert McFarlane, July 21, 1999; McFarlane, *Special Trust*, pp. 197–98.

11. McFarlane, *Special Trust*, p. 197; *Public Papers: Ronald Reagan 1982*, pp. 487–88; *WP*, Apr. 7, 1982.

12. *NYT*, May 20, 1982; Castelli, *Bishops*, pp. 105–6; William Clark to Baker (signed by McFarlane), Aug. 16, 1982, Case File 081456, ND 018, Subject File, WHORM Records.

13. *St. Louis Post-Dispatch*, Oct. 17, 1982; *WP*, Oct. 27, Nov. 2, 1982; interview with Harold Willens, May 11, 2000.

14. *NYT*, Oct. 5, Nov. 12, 13, 1982; *Boston Globe*, Nov. 13, 1982.

15. The FBI concluded that, despite efforts by the Soviet Union, it did not "directly control or manipulate the movement." *NYT*, Dec. 10, 11, 1982, Mar. 26, 1983; *WP*, Dec. 11, 1982; *Congressional Record* 129 (98th Cong., 1st Sess.), Mar. 24, 1983, pp. 7408–12.

16. *WP*, Dec. 11, 1982; *NYT*, Dec. 11, 1982.

17. Nevertheless, Reagan, in his memoirs, continued to maintain that the Freeze was "inspired by a similar movement in Europe with roots in Moscow." Rojecki,

Silencing, p. 168; interview with Randall Forsberg, July 7, 1999; Reagan, *An American Life*, p. 552.

18. *NYT*, Apr. 1, 1983.

19. "Radio Address to the Nation on the Observance of Armed Forces Day" (May 21, 1983), www.reagan.utexas.edu/resource/speeches/1983/52183b.htm; U.S. Department of State, *Building Peace*, p. 2.

20. Van Voorst, "Churches," pp. 845–47; "A Blast," pp. 16–17; *NYT*, Dec. 16, 1982; Ostling, "Bishops," p. 74; George Bush to Mike, Jan. 5, 1983, Case File 137933, PC, and Clark to the Most Reverend Pia Laghi, Jan. 15, 1983, Case File 133251, ND 018, Subject File, WHORM Records.

21. Recommended Telephone Calls regarding Broomfield-Carney-Stratton Nuclear Arms Reduction and Freeze Resolution, Case File 08122SS, "PR 007–02 Presidential Telephone Calls" Folder, PR, Subject File, WHORM Records.

22. Clark to the Vice President, Feb. 15, 1983, Case File 138726, Bush to Clark, Feb. 16, 1983, Case File 126641, and Peter R. Sommer to Robert C. McFarlane, Mar. 8, 1983, Case File 134103, ND 018, Subject File, WHORM Records.

23. Peter R. Sommer to Robert C. McFarlane, Case File 134103, ND 018, Subject File, WHORM Records; Sommer to McFarlane, Apr. 7, 1983, OA 90304, "LA: Nuclear Freeze" Folder, Kimmitt Files.

24. Interview with Jeremy Stone, July 22, 1999.

25. Oral history interview with Elizabeth Dole, Apr. 16, 1983.

26. Forsberg and Kehler to Reagan, Nov. 15, 1982, Box 10, and William K. Sadleir to Forsberg and Kehler, Jan. 6, 1983, Box 13, Freeze Records, SL; Sven Kraemer to William P. Clark, Dec. 9, 1982, Case File 109714, ND 018, Subject File, WHORM Records.

27. Henry W. Kendall to Reagan, Dec. 15, 1984, Robert Kimmitt to Frederick J. Ryan, Jr., Feb. 9, 1985, Case File 258758, PR 007, and Sven Kraemer to William P. Clark, Aug. 26, 1982, Case File 128780, Kraemer to Clark, Feb. 8, 1983, "ND 018 125400–127285" Folder, ND 018, Subject File, WHORM Records.

28. Kehler to Shultz, Aug. 8, 1983, Richard Burt to Kehler, Aug. 19, 1983, Kehler to Burt, Sept. 1, 1983, and Burt to Kehler, Sept. 28, 1983, Freeze Records, C; Shultz to American Embassy, Bonn, June 1983, Case File 151668, PR 007, Subject File, WHORM Records.

29. Interview with Bernard Lown, July 6, 1999; interview with Jeremy Stone, July 22, 1999.

30. Caldicott, *Missile Envy*, pp. 271–77; Caldicott, "We Women," p. 19; Reagan, *An American Life*, p. 566; interview with Helen Caldicott, Feb. 27, 1999.

31. Interview with Harold Willens, May 11, 2000.

32. "Clearance List for Briefing on Nuclear Freeze Movement . . . on July 30, 1982," and Morton C. Blackwell to Elizabeth Dole, Aug. 27, 1982, Blackwell Files; Red Cavaney to Robert C. McFarlane, Apr. 30, 1982, Dole Files.

33. Dugan to Baker, Dec. 3, 1982, "National Assn of Evangelicals; Orlando, FL; 3/8/83 [3 of 3]" Folder, OA 13,666, Research Office File, White House Office of Speechwriting Records.

34. Reagan, *An American Life*, p. 568; Gergen, *Eyewitness*, p. 242; Reagan's

hand-scrawled comments on "Presidential Address" (Mar. 5, 1983), "National Assn of Evangelicals, Orlando, FL; 3/8/83 [1 of 3]" Folder, OA 13,666, Research Office File, White House Office of Speechwriting Records.

35. *NYT*, Mar. 9, 1983.

36. Faith Ryan Whittlesey, "Meeting with Dr. Jerry Falwell" (Mar. 14, 1983), Case File 127515, Office of the President, Presidential Briefing Papers Records; Peter J. Rusthoven to Fred F. Fielding, Oct. 29, 1983, Case File 173619CU, ND 018, Subject File, WHORM Records; Carolyn Sundseth to Patrick Buchanan, Dec. 30, 1985, and Roy C. Jones to Don Eberly, Nov. 25, 1985, Case File 13328, Sundseth Files.

37. *WP*, Oct. 27, 1982; John M. Fisher to Max L. Friedensdorf, July 25, 1985, including enclosure, Case File 335129, PC, Subject File, WHORM Records.

38. *Philadelphia Inquirer*, Nov. 16, 1980.

39. Interview with Sanford Gottlieb, July 19, 1998; *WP*, Jan. 28, 1984; Peck, "Take-Charge Gang," pp. 1, 18–24; Glick, *War at Home*, pp. 1–2.

40. Perle charged that there was "heavy-duty Soviet involvement" in the West European movement. Gates, *From the Shadows*, p. 260; Talbott, *Deadly Gambits*, p. 81; *Boston Globe*, Nov. 26, 1981.

41. Even so, in his memoirs, published in 1990, Weinberger continued to charge that there was "considerable evidence" that the antinuclear demonstrations had been organized "from the outside." Gates, *From the Shadows*, pp. 261–62; Weinberger, *Fighting*, p. 338.

42. Crozier, *Free Agent*, pp. 178–86, 245; Crozier to Bill [Clark], Nov. 11, 1982, and enclosures, Clark to Brian [Crozier], Jan. 31, 1983, Clark to Frederick Ryan, n.d., Case File 126207, PC, Subject File, WHORM Records.

43. Snyder, *Warriors*, pp. xi–xiii; "Charles Wick Completes 4th Year As USIA's Director" (1985), Case File 325900, FG 006–01, Subject File, WHORM Records; interview with Charles Wick, Aug. 16, 1999.

44. Snyder, *Warriors*, pp. 38–39, 76–78, Wick to James A. Baker III, Michael K. Deaver, and Edwin Meese III, Dec. 22, 1981, Case File 054032, and Wick to Baker, Mar. 5, 1983, Case File 128779, FG 298, Wick to Baker, June 17, 1982, Case File 86870, PC, Subject File, WHORM Records; Wick to William P. Clark, Jr., Apr. 28, 1982, "Nuclear Freeze (3 of 3)" Folder, Box 90278, Kraemer Files.

45. *WP*, Mar. 30, 1984; Bush and Scowcroft, *A World*, p. 64.

46. Interview with Robert McFarlane, July 21, 1999; Reagan, *An American Life*, p. 554; "National Security Decision Directive Number 75" (Jan. 17, 1983), in McFarlane, *Special Trust*, p. 374; "The United States International Communication Agency" (1982), Case File 448124, FG 298, Subject File, WHORM Records; Charles Z. Wick to William P. Clark, Jr., Apr. 28, 1982, "Nuclear Freeze (3 of 3)" Folder, Box 90278, Kraemer Files.

47. Although Reagan's first use of this statement appears to have occurred on April 17, 1982, he delivered the same message at his March 31 press conference, shortly after the inception of the administration's anti-Freeze campaign. Asked whether a nuclear war would be winnable, he responded: "I don't believe there could be any winners." If there were a nuclear war, "everybody would be a loser." Knopf, *Domestic Society*, pp. 228–29; Ronald Reagan, Radio address of Apr. 17,

1982, in *Public Papers: Ronald Reagan: January 1 to July 2, 1982*, pp. 487–88; Bundy, *Danger*, p. 583; Reagan, *An American Life*, p. 554; U.S. Department of State, *Renewing*, p. 2; *NYT*, Apr. 1, 1982.

48. "Foreign Media Reaction to Presidential Trip," "Current Wisdom [1982]" Folder, Gergen Files; "President's European Trip" (June 14, 1982), enclosure in Wick to Shultz, July 6, 1982, Case File 448124, FG 298, Subject File, WHORM Records.

49. Bush preceded these remarks by noting that he had come to Europe "in the pursuit of peace" and that "we, too, are against nuclear war." Nine days later, Bush stated in a London address: "We are not preparing to fight a nuclear war." U.S. Department of State, *Peace and Security*, pp. 1–2; U.S. Department of State, *NATO*, p. 4; U.S. Department of State, *Atlantic Alliance*, p. 4; U.S. Department of State, *U.S. Commitment*, p. 2.

50. Interview with Kenneth Adelman, July 22, 1998. See also chapter 14.

51. Five months earlier, Reagan proclaimed: "I pray for the day when nuclear weapons will no longer exist anywhere on earth." Shultz, *Turmoil*, p. 189; *NYT*, June 17, 1983.

52. Matlock to Robert C. McFarlane, Dec. 13, 1983, "Matlock Chron December 1983" Folder, Matlock Files; Reagan, *My Turn*, pp. 63–64; Lumsden, "Nuclear Weapons," p. 125.

53. Dolan to Deaver, July 7, 1982, Case File 095592, ND 016, Subject File, WHORM Records.

54. Interview with Robert Musil, July 20, 1998; Caldicott, *Desperate Passion*, pp. 234–35; Edwin A. Rothschild, "If You Love These Films," *BAS* 39 (June–July 1983): 39.

55. Arbatov, *System*, pp. 318–19.

56. Snyder, *Warriors*, pp. xv, 38–39, 77–78; Charles Z. Wick to James A. Baker III et al., Dec. 22, 1981, Case File 054032, FG 298, Subject File, WHORM Records; Wick to William P. Clark, Feb. 8, 1983, "United States Information Agency Vol I 1/20/81–12/31/83 (1)" Folder, Box 91,377, Agency File, Executive Secretariat, NSC Records.

57. Shultz, *Turmoil*, p. 373; Cortright, *Peace Works*, pp. 73–74.

58. Interview with Charles Wick, Aug. 16, 1999; Wick to Reagan, Oct. 7, 1983, Case File 167806SS, PR 016–01, Subject File, WHORM Records; Reagan, *An American Life*, p. 585.

59. Robert B. Sims to Robert C. McFarlane and David Gergen, Nov. 9, 1983, Case File 190087, and David B. Waller to Fred F. Fielding, Nov. 14, 1983, Case File 183666, PR 016–01, and "White House Talking Points" (Nov. 17, 1983), Case File 188541, PR 011, Subject File, WHORM Records.

60. Reagan, *My Turn*, p. 270; interview with Richard Wirthlin, Oct. 6, 1999; Oberdorfer, *Turn*, p. 52.

61. Beschloss and Talbott, *At the Highest Levels*, pp. 6–7; Shultz, *Turmoil*, pp. 483–84; McFarlane to Reagan, Sept. 17, 1984, in Blanton, ed., *White House*, p. 171.

62. U.S. Department of State, *Soviet Antipacifism*, pp. 1, 4.

63. *IHT*, Apr. 20, 1982; "An Interview with Mary Kaldor," p. 45; Shultz, *Turmoil*, p. 124.

64. See, for example: Anatoly Dorodnitsyn et al., "When Honor and Conscience Are Lost," *Izvestia*, July 3, 1983, in Lozansky, ed., *Andrei Sakharov*, pp. 267–69.

65. Sergei Batovrin and Mikhail Ostrovsky to U.S., Canadian, European Peace Groups, Sept. 1983, Folder 734, IKV Records, A. See also "The Trials of Moscow's Independent Disarmament Activists" (Fall 1984), Group to Establish Mutual Trust Records.

66. "Moscow Trust Group," Box 508, WRI Records; Mark Reitman, "Three Years in the Trust Group's life," *END J*, No. 16–17 (Summer 1985), p. 9; "Aleksandr Shatravka—Briefing Sheet," Group to Establish Mutual Trust Records; Maria Margaronis, "Notes from Abroad," *NT* 2 (Mar. 1984): 10; Catherine Fitzpatrick to the author, May 4, 1990; "Stop Press," *END J*, No. 9 (Apr.–May 1984), p. 6.

67. "Trust Group Activities and Arrests," *END J*, No. 14 (Feb.–Mar. 1985), p. 6; "Moscow Trust Group," Box 508, WRI Records.

68. "O podgotovke sovetsko-americanskoi Konferentsii uchenyh medikov za predotvraschenie yadernoi voiny" (Jan. 13, 1981), f. 89, op. 43, d. 48, Central Committee of the CPSU Records.

69. Evangelista, *Unarmed Forces*, pp. 151–55; Warner and Shuman, *Citizen Diplomats*, p. 60; English, *Russia*, p. 170; interview with Bernard Lown, July 6, 1999.

70. Andrew and Gordievsky, eds., *Comrade Kryuchkov's Instructions*, pp. 176–78; Kryuchkov to KGB Residents, Apr. 9, 1985, ibid., pp. 179–81.

71. Grabowski (Moscow) to Comrades Axen, Sieber, Feist, Krolikowski, and Loeschner, Jan. 31, 1982, IV 2/2.035/70, Socialist Unity Party Records.

72. Andrew and Gordievsky, eds., *Comrade Kryuchkov's Instructions*, p. 137; Central Committee of the CPSU to foreign Communist parties, July 11, 1983, IV 2/2.035/70, Socialist Unity Party Records.

73. Kryuchkov, "Planning and organization of the work of sections of the Service and organizations abroad in 1984," enclosure in G. G. Titov to Residents, Nov. 2, 1983, in Andrew and Gordievsky, eds., *Comrade Kryuchkov's Instructions*, p. 20; To members and candidates of the Political Bureau, Nov. 28, 1983, IV 2/2.035/70, Socialist Unity Party Records; Andrew and Gordievsky, *KGB*, pp. 628–29.

74. Gates, *From the Shadows*, pp. 261–62.

75. Arbatov, *System*, p. 318; Andrew and Gordievsky, eds., *Comrade Kryuchkov's Instructions*, pp. 137–38; Andrew and Gordievsky, *KGB*, pp. 585–90.

76. This is discussed in chapter 11. See also Thompson, "Ends and Histories," pp. 8–10.

77. Dobrynin, *In Confidence*, p. 557; Tairov, "From New Thinking," p. 45.

78. *WP*, Nov. 29, 1981; *IHT*, Aug. 1, 1983; interview with Rob Prince, July 27, 1999; "Session of Politburo of CC CPSU" (May 31, 1983), f. 89, op. 42, d. 53, ll. 1–14, Central Committee of the CPSU Records, in "Excerpts from Politburo Minutes, 1983–86," pp. 78–80; Central Committee of the CPSU to foreign Communist parties, July 11, 1983, IV 2/2.035/70, Socialist Unity Party Records.

79. Evangelista, "Transnational Relations," pp. 158–59; Evangelista, *Unarmed Forces*, pp. 154–55; interview with Victor Malkov, Dec. 4, 1994; interview with Jeremy Stone, July 22, 1999; interview with Frank von Hippel, Aug. 22, 1999.

80. Gorbachev, *A Time*, pp. 26–27, 50–51.

81. English, *Russia*, pp. 160–61, 170–72; Thompson, *Double Exposure*, p. 2.

82. *Boston Globe*, Nov. 19, 1982; *NYT*, Oct. 22, 1981.

83. "INF: Progress Report to Ministers" (Dec. 8, 1983), p. 4, Box 114, Nitze Papers; *Wall Street Journal*, Oct. 6, 1983.

84. Hassner, "Pacifism," p. 131; "Pacific Peacemaker," *Peacelink* (June 1984).

85. Ken Fleet to the Liaison Committee, Aug. 12, 1983, Box 447, WRI Records; Ben Thompson, "Comiso on the Brink," *END J*, No. 7 (Dec. 1983–Jan. 1984), p. 13.

86. Brandon, *Burning Question*, p. 130; Margaronis, "Notes from Abroad," p. 27; interview with Martin Butcher, July 19, 1999.

87. Steve Lee to Melinda Fine, May 26, 1983, Freeze Records, C; Margot Trevellyan, "On the Cold War's Front Line," *END J*, No. 7 (Dec. 1983–Jan. 1984), p. 24; "Text of an Open Letter to All Canadians From Pierre Elliott Trudeau" (May 9, 1983), Case File 148719, CO 028, Subject File, WHORM Records.

88. Watson, "Battle," p. 43; *Christian Science Monitor*, June 10, 1983; Johnstone, "Labor Signs On," p. 8; Lutz van Dick, "Teachers for Peace," *DC*, No. 26 (Oct. 1983), p. 8.

89. Jim Chapple, "New Directions for Peace People," *Peacelink* (Dec. 1984), p. 6.

90. "The Demand for a Denuclearised Europe: The Role of Greece in Denuclearising the Balkans" (Dec. 10, 1982), p. 10, Folder 717, IKV Records, A; Iatrides, "Papandreou's Foreign Policy," p. 139; Mike Jendrzejczyk, "Report on Conference on Nuclear Free Zones in Europe, Athens, Dec. 10–12, 1982," Freeze Records, C; Mary Kaldor, "A Voice of Dissent in NATO," *END J*, No. 2 (Feb.–Mar. 1983), pp. 12–13, 28.

91. Furtado, *Turkey*, pp. 13, 26–27, 44; Demir, "Turkey," p. 6; Maria Margaronis, "Where Peace Is Treason," *NT* 2 (Jan. 1984): 25; "Turkish Trial," *DC*, enclosure in *END J*, No. 26 (Feb.–Mar. 1987).

92. *Observer*, Apr. 25, 1982; Byrne, *Campaign*, p. 182; Thatcher, *Downing Street*, pp. 259, 267.

93. Byrne, *Campaign*, pp. 182–83; *Financial Times* (L), Dec. 13, 1982; *Sunday Telegraph*, Jan. 2, 1983.

94. *The Times* (L), Jan. 31, Feb. 1, 1983; *Guardian*, Feb. 5, 1983; *Philadelphia Inquirer*, Mar. 10, 1983.

95. *The Times* (L), Mar. 2, July 20, 1983; Byrne, *Campaign*, pp. 183–84.

96. *The Times* (L), Apr. 23, 25, May 18, 20, 26, 1983.

97. Interview with Bruce Kent, June 7, 1999; interview with E. P. Thompson, Nov. 1, 1989; interview with Bruce Kent, July 10, 1990.

98. *Guardian*, Apr. 24, 1983; *The Times* (L), Apr. 29, 1983; Thatcher, *Downing Street*, p. 424.

99. *The Times* (L), Dec. 7, 10, 1983.

100. Taylor and Young, "Britain," p. 288; *Boston Globe*, May 27, 1982; *Guardian*, Oct. 16, 1993; *The Times* (L), Oct. 25, 1993.

101. Interview with Bruce Kent, June 7, 1999.

102. *The Times* (L), Nov. 2, 1983; *Philadelphia Inquirer*, Nov. 2, 1983; *Guardian*, July 2, 1994.

103. *Philadelphia Inquirer*, Apr. 5, 1984; *NYT*, Apr. 5, 1984.

104. *The Times* (L), Feb. 7, 1985; *Manchester Guardian Weekly*, Feb. 17, 1985.

105. Roger Woddis, "To General Heseltine," *Sanity* (Mar. 1985), p. 5.

106. *Observer*, Feb. 24, 1985; *Guardian*, Mar. 1, 1985; Reeve and Smith, *Offence*, p. 27; Byrne, *Campaign*, pp. 185–90.

107. "He Who Pays the Piper," *Sanity* (Nov. 1982), p. 24; "The British Atlantic Committee," and "Peace Through NATO," CND Records, L; *Observer*, Apr. 25, 1982; *Sunday Telegraph*, July 11, 1982.

108. Crozier, *Free Agent*, pp. 187, 244–45, 249–51, 255–57; *The Times* (L), Aug. 24, 1982. Crozier's propaganda also appeared in the United States. See, for example: Crozier, "Great Nuclear Freeze Trap."

109. "The Whitehall Web Which Challenges Your Peace," *Sanity* (Oct. 1982), p. 29; Crozier, *Free Agent*, pp. 243–44, 246, 256–57; "Anti-CND Plot Thickens," *Sanity* (Apr.–May 1982), p. 5; *Observer*, Apr. 25, 1982. Lewis and Leigh are now Tory MPs.

110. *Philadelphia Inquirer*, Mar. 10, 1983; "CND: Communists, Neutralists, Defeatists," CND Records, L; Crozier, *Free Agent*, pp. 246, 257.

111. John Bacher, "The Independent Peace Movements in Eastern Europe," *PM* 1 (Dec. 1985): 11–12; Suzanne Gordon, "The View from the East," *NT* 2 (Jan. 1984): 24–25; English, "Eastern Europe's Doves," p. 49; "An Open Letter from Charter 77," p. 15; Jan Kavan, "Lis Appeal," *END J*, No. 6 (Oct.–Nov. 1983), p. 4.

112. "Who's Paying the Piper?" *END J* , No. 9 (Apr.–May 1984), p. 9; Kent, *Undiscovered Ends*, p. 181; "Trust Group Member Defends Thompson," *END J*, No. 12 (Oct.–Nov 1984), p. 7.

113. Hall, "Church," p. 199; Haraszti, "Hungarian," p. 141; Bacher, "Independent," p. 10.

114. Thompson, *Double Exposure*, p. 72; Gerard Holden, "Soviets Face Warsaw Pact Worries on New Missiles," *END J*, No. 5 (Aug.–Sept. 1983), p. 7; Lynne Jones, "Keeping the Dialogue Open," *END J*, No. 6 (Oct.–Nov. 1983), p. 11; "Hungarian Leadership," pp. 6–7, 22.

115. Allen, *Germany East*, p. 103; Gordon, "From the Other Shore," pp. 39–40.

116. Allen, *Germany East*, pp. 112–15; Fitzpatrick, "Update," p. 3; Sergio Andreis, "We Live Out Our Ideals Every Day," *END J*, No. 6 (Oct.–Nov. 1983), pp. 9–10.

117. Jackson, "Eastern European Peace Activists," p. 6; Fitzpatrick, "Update," pp. 3, 12; "Imprisoned Peace Women Released—Charges Dropped," *END J*, No. 8 (Feb.–Mar. 1984), p. 5; Gordon, "View From the East," p. 31; *From Below*, pp. 31–32.

118. Interview with Mient Jan Faber, Aug. 7, 1986; Faber, "Good Morning," p. 142.

119. Allen, *Germany East*, p. 119; John Sandford, "East German Notebook," *END J*, No. 13 (Dec. 1984–Jan. 1985), p. 6.

120. *Sunday Telegraph*, Sept. 19, 1999; CND press release of Sept. 19, 1999, CND Records, L; *Guardian*, Sept. 22, 1999.

121. "Erkenntnisse zu feindlichen Angriffsrichtungen, Mittel und Methoden während der '2. Konferenz für europäische atomare Abrüstung' vom 9. bis 14.5.1983 in Westberlin" (June 1, 1983), Bl. 321–27, and "Erkenntnisse über die Aktivitäten der Spalterkräfte in Vorbereitung des Konvents in Perugia/Italien" (June 1984), Folder 5351, AKG, HA XX, ZA, Stasi Records.

122. Julian Harber to the GDR Ambassador, Oct. 1984, Bess Papers; interview with Günther Drefahl, May 19, 1999.

123. Asmus, "Is There a Peace Movement?" pp. 313–15; Sandford, *Sword*, pp. 70–73; Kelly, *Fighting*, p. 58; Mushaben, "Swords," p. 130.

124. Maislinger, "Peace Movement," p. 58.

125. "Meeting Between Olof Palme, Edward Thompson and Michael Foot . . . at the Caxton Hall on 2 September 1981," Bess Papers.

126. Sharma, "Confronting," pp. 163–72; Martin, "Nuclear suppression," pp. 312–13; interview with Dhirendra Sharma, Oct. 11, 1995.

127. Betsy Taylor to Nuclear Weapons Freeze Campaign Key Contacts, Sept. 1983, Freeze Records, C; Barbara Roche, "A Visit to the People's Republic of China," *Freeze Focus* 4 (Apr. 1984): 14.

Chapter 13

Epigraph: Thatcher, *Downing Street*, p. 269.

1. In 1988, for example, Ronald Reagan told a broadcast audience that the INF treaty "was made possible by the solidarity . . . of NATO. . . . The Alliance did not waver" in "its decision . . . to go forward with the deployment of INF missiles." "Remarks by the President to Worldnet" (May 24, 1988), Case File 561386, SP1266, Subject File, WHORM Records.

2. Reagan, *An American Life*, p. 601; interview with Caspar Weinberger, July 21, 1998; Weinberger, *Fighting*, pp. 338–39; interview with Kenneth Adelman, July 22, 1998.

3. Risse-Kappen, *Zero Option*, pp. 66–67; Talbott, *Deadly Gambits*, pp. 45–48; Schmidt, *Men and Powers*, pp. 243–44; *Wall Street Journal*, June 18, 1981.

4. Blechman and Fisher, *Silent Partner*, pp. 75–76, 84; Thatcher, *Downing Street*, p. 472.

5. Shultz, *Turmoil*, pp. 149–50, 153; *Wall Street Journal*, Oct. 6, 1983.

6. Risse-Kappen, *Zero Option*, pp. 80–81; Talbott, *Deadly Gambits*, pp. 172–73; Thatcher, *Downing Street*, pp. 269–70.

7. Risse-Kappen, *Zero Option*, pp. 98–101; "Visit of Ambassador Paul Nitze, Bonn, Germany, June 2–3, 1983," Box 114, Nitze Papers; Talbott, *Deadly Gambits*, pp. 187, 190.

8. Shultz, *Turmoil*, p. 371; interview with Richard Perle, June 29, 1999.

9. *NYT*, May 13, 1984; interview with Ruud Lubbers, May 27, 1999; Shultz, *Turmoil*, pp. 475–76; Leo van der Linde, "Missile Decision?" *DC*, No. 34 (June 1984), p. 14; Risse-Kappen, *Zero Option*, p. 103.

10. Toni Liversage and Judith Winter, "Influencing the Decision Makers," *END J*, No. 8 (Feb.–Mar. 1984), p. 14; Johnstone, *Politics*, pp. 176–77.

11. Shultz, *Turmoil*, p. 475; Risse-Kappen, *Zero Option*, p. 103.

12. Jamie Dettmer, "PASOK Returned to Power in Greece," *END J*, No. 16–17 (Summer 1985), p. 4; Mary Kaldor, "A Voice of Dissent in NATO," *END J*, No. 2 (Feb.–Mar. 1983), p. 13.

13. Petersen, "Scandilux," pp. 15–16; Judith Winther, "Behind the Infrastructure Vote," *DC*, No. 18 (Jan. 1983), p. 25.

14. Shultz agrees with Thatcher's interpretation. Reagan, *An American Life*, p. 353; Thatcher, *Downing Street*, p. 300; Shultz, *Turmoil*, pp. 355–56.

15. Ron Lehman to John Poindexter, June 5, 1984, Case File 8404538, Office of the Assistant to the President for National Security Affairs Records; Geoffrey Manners and Hugh Lucas, "Cruise Missiles Locked Inside Greenham Base," *Jane's Defence Weekly*, Jan. 14, 1984, Greenham Common Women's Peace Camp Records.

16. Iatrides, "Papandreou's Foreign Policy," pp. 144–47; "The Demand for a Denuclearised Europe: The Role of Greece in Denuclearising the Balkans" (Dec. 10, 1982), pp. 7–10, Folder 717, IKV Records, A; Nikos Andrikos, "A Balkan Nuclear-Weapons-Free Zone," *BAS* 41 (June–July 1985): 29–31.

17. Det sikkerheds- og nedrustningspolitiske Udvalg, *Dansk sikkerhedspolitik*, pp. 176–90; "Resolution passed by the Danish Folketing (parliament) on Maj 3 1984," IPCC Records.

18. Byrne, *Campaign*, pp. 165, 167, 171; interview with Bruce Kent, June 7, 1999; Brandon, *Burning Question*, p. 131; Tony Simpson, "No Bunkers Here," *DC*, No. 19 (Feb. 1983), p. 4.

19. Weinberger, *Fighting*, p. 335; interview with Daniel Plesch, July 21, 1998; Thatcher, *Downing Street*, p. 158.

20. Auger, *Dynamics*, p. 93; *WP*, Oct. 23, 1984.

21. *Boston Globe*, July 30, 1984; interview with Kenneth Adelman, July 22, 1998; Healey, *Time*, p. 518; von Weizsäcker, *From Weimar*, p. 225.

22. Interview with John Pike, July 22, 1999; Weinberger, *Fighting*, p. 315; McFarlane, *Special Trust*, pp. 306–7; Heseltine to Weinberger, ca. late July to Aug. 1, 1985, Case File 8506227, Presidential Advisory File, Executive Secretariat, NSC Records.

23. Bernd W. Kubbig, "Star Wars Fizzles for European Contractors," *BAS* 44 (Nov. 1988): 17; interview with John Pike, July 22, 1999; Erik Poole, "Peace in Power in Ontario!" *PM* 7 (May–June 1991): 5.

24. Epstein, "Canada," pp. 179–80; Schmitz, *Anti-Nuclear Protest*, p. 14; Pierre Elliott Trudeau, "A Peace Initiative from Canada," *BAS* 40 (Jan. 1984): 15–16, 18–19.

25. Reagan, *An American Life*, p. 595; Berger, *Cultures*, pp. 126–29; von Weizsäcker, *From Weimar*, pp. 264–65.

26. Lange's speech in Los Angeles, Feb. 26, 1985, in "Nuclear Policy Sparks Debate," pp. 3–4; Lange, *Nuclear Free*, pp. 9, 55–105; Barbara Einhorn, "NZ Stands by Non-nuclear Position," *END J*, No. 22–23 (Summer 1986), pp. 16–17; Clements, *Back From the Brink*, pp. 123, 128–35, 138–39.

27. Clements, *Back From the Brink*, pp. 136–39, 141; Lange's speech at Oxford, Mar. 1, 1985, in "Nuclear Policy Sparks Debate," pp. 7–11; Clements, "New Zealand's Relations," p. 598; "Labour Unites," p. 69.

28. Hawke, *Hawke Memoirs*, pp. 219, 280–81; "Uranium Minings Go-Ahead," *DC*, No. 29 (Jan. 1984), p. 16; Caldicott, *Desperate Passion*, p. 152.

29. Hawke, *Hawke Memoirs*, pp. 215, 217–21, 286–92; Siracusa, "Peace Movements," pp. 7, 9, 11–13; Saunders and Summy, *Australian Peace Movement*, pp. 49, 70.

30. Greg Fry, "Toward a South Pacific Nuclear-Free Zone," *BAS* 41 (June–July 1985): 16–20; "Pacific States Go for Nuclear-Free Zone," *END J*, No. 12 (Oct.–Nov. 1984), p. 11; "For a Nuclear Free and Independent Pacific," Peace Movement Aotearoa Records.

31. Akaha, "Japan's Three Nonnuclear Principles," pp. 77–86; Toshiyuki Toyoda, "Japan's Policies Since 1945," *BAS* 41 (Aug. 1985): 62.

32. Shultz, *Turmoil*, p. 494; Drifte, "China," pp. 47–53; John Prados, "China's 'New Thinking' on Nuclear Arms," *BAS* 45 (June 1989): 32.

33. Snyder, *Warriors*, pp. 96–97; Hansen, *USIA*, pp. 181–82; *NYT*, Dec. 10, 1982.

34. Holloway, *Soviet Union*, p. 75; *Pravda*, Feb. 24, 1981, cited in Garthoff, *Détente*, p. 65; *NYT*, Oct. 21, 1981.

35. "O besede s rukovoditelyami amerikanskoy kompanii 'Time-Life'" (Oct. 21, 1981), f. 89, op. 76, d. 31, Central Committee of the CPSU Records; Saxton, "Nuclear Diplomacy," p. 502; McNamara, "Military Role," p. 66.

36. Talbott, *Deadly Gambits*, p. 279; Cortright and Pagnucco, "Limits," p. 171; Melinda Fine, "International Efforts for a Freeze," *Freeze Focus* 4 (Nov. 1984): 4.

37. *NYT*, Feb. 4, 1982; Shultz, *Turmoil*, p. 127; Reagan, *An American Life*, pp. 576–77; MccGwire, *Perestroika*, pp. 71–72; Savel'yev and Detinov, *Big Five*, pp. 72–77.

38. Evangelista, *Unarmed Forces*, pp. 234–39: English, *Russia*, pp. 179–80, 313–14.

39. Risse-Kappen, *Zero Option*, pp. 85–86; Talbott, *Deadly Gambits*, pp. 86–91; Shultz, *Turmoil*, p. 123.

40. Savel'yev and Detinov, *Big Five*, pp. 64–65; Talbott, *Deadly Gambits*, p. 146; Risse-Kappen, *Zero Option*, p. 99.

41. Savel'yev and Detinov, *Big Five*, pp. 67–68, 78–79; Oberdorfer, *Turn*, pp. 83–85; Shultz, *Turmoil*, p. 500.

42. Risse-Kappen, *Zero Option*, p. 105; Evangelista, *Unarmed Forces*, p. 245.

43. Dobrynin, *In Confidence*, p. 512; "Session of Politburo of CC CPSU" (May 31, 1983), f. 89, op. 42, d. 53, Central Committee of the CPSU Records, in "Excerpts from Politburo Minutes, 1983–86," p. 79; Savel'yev and Detinov, *Big Five*, p. 78; Oberdorfer, *Turn*, p. 68.

44. English, *Russia*, p. 190; MccGwire, *Perestroika*, pp. 383–85.

45. Interview with E. P. Thompson, Nov. 1, 1989; Chernyaev, *My Six Years*, pp. 8–9.

46. Comments of Oleg Grinevsky and Georgy Shaknazarov in Tannenwald, ed., *Understanding*, pp. 19, 27; Chernyaev, *My Six Years*, p. 5.

47. Comments of Vladimir Slipchenko in Tannenwald, ed., *Understanding*, p. 25; Gorbachev, *Memoirs*, pp. 141, 153; Arbatov, *System*, p. 277.

48. English, *Russia*, p. 163; Yakovlev, "Perestroika," pp. 33, 71; Gorbachev, *Memoirs*, p. 156.

49. English, *Russia*, pp. 187–91; Arbatov, *System*, pp. 292–93; Gorbachev, *Memoirs*, p. 427.

50. Gorbachev, *Memoirs*, p. 155; comments of Anatoly Chernyaev in Tannenwald, ed., *Understanding*, p. 10; Dobrynin, *In Confidence*, p. 551.

51. Oberdorfer, *Turn*, p. 75; comments of Alexander Bessmertnykh in Wohlforth, ed., *Witnesses*, p. 106; L. Zamyatin, "O novoy programme modernizatsii strategicheskikh vooruzheniy SshA" (Oct. 8, 1981), f. 89, op. 76, d. 72, Central Committee of the CPSU Records; Healey, *Time*, pp. 514–17

52. Sagdeev, *Making*, p. 256; interview with Thomas Graham, Jr., Aug. 23, 1999; Talbott, *Deadly Gambits*, pp. 114–15, 325; Dobrynin, *In Confidence*, pp. 481, 512, 533, 545.

53. Savel'yev and Detinov, *Big Five*, pp. 164–70; comments of Nikolai Detinov in Tannenwald, ed., *Understanding*, pp. 37–40; Healey, *Time*, pp. 517–18; Briefing No. 453/PR/52, enclosure in Gribin to [KGB] Residents, Feb. 13, 1985, in Andrew and Gordievsky, eds., *Comrade Kryuchkov's Instructions*, p. 112; Palazchenko, *My Years*, p. 41.

54. "Session of Politburo of CC CPSU" (May 31, 1983), f. 89, op. 42, d. 53, ll. 1–14, Central Committee of the CPSU Records, in "Excerpts from Politburo Minutes, 1983–86," p. 77; Pry, *War Scare*, p. 35; Central Committee of the CPSU to foreign Communist parties, July 11, 1983, IV 2/2.035/70, Socialist Unity Party Records.

55. Dobrynin, *In Confidence*, p. 523; Pry, *War Scare*, pp. 36–38; Oberdorfer, *Turn*, pp. 64–65.

56. Oberdorfer, *Turn*, pp. 65–67; Andrew and Gordievsky, *KGB*, pp. 599–600, 605; Pry, *War Scare*, pp. 33, 38–44.

57. Comments of Oleg Grinevsky in Tannenwald, ed., *Understanding*, pp. 15–16, 103–5; Talbott, *Deadly Gambits*, p. 345; Oberdorfer, *Turn*, pp. 73–76.

58. "Chief Conclusions and Views Adopted at the Meeting of Heads of Service" (Feb. 1, 1984), enclosure in V. V. Kirpichenko to Residents and Representatives, Feb. 1, 1984, in Andrew and Gordievsky, eds., *Comrade Kryuchkov's Instructions*, p. 6; Pry, *War Scare*, p. 45.

59. Arbatov, *System*, pp. 321–22; Dobrynin, *In Confidence*, pp. 482, 495; *NYT*, Oct. 28, 1992.

60. Interview with Peter Steglich, May 21, 1999; English, "Eastern Europe's Doves," p. 51; *NYT*, Dec. 21, 1983.

61. Chernyaev, *My Six Years*, p. 15; English, "Eastern Europe's Doves," pp. 51–53; "Independent Initiatives," *DC*, No. 20 (Mar. 1983), p. 3.

62. Wiberg, *Provstopp nu!* pp. 18–19; "Address by Prime Minister Olof Palme at the North Atlantic Assembly meeting in Copenhagen, June 13, 1983," Freeze Records, C; Maj Britt Theorin, "Deploy Missiles, Delay Peace," *BAS* 40 (Apr. 1984): 2–3.

63. Olafur Grimsson and Nicholas Dunlop, "Indira Gandhi and the Five Continent Initiative," *BAS* 41 (Jan. 1985): 46; "Four Continent Peace Initiative," *DC*, No. 34 (June 1984), p. 15; Christopher Paine, "The 'Other Nations' Speak Up," *BAS* 41 (Apr. 1985): 6–7.

64. Alan Cohen, "Freeze Work at the 37th U.N. General Assembly: A Preliminary Report" (Dec. 2, 1982), Freeze Records, C; Cortright and Pagnucco, "Limits," pp. 163–64; Melinda Fine, "International Efforts for a Freeze," *Freeze Focus* 4 (Nov. 1984): 4; Jack, *Nuclear Politics*, p. 59.

Chapter 14

Epigraph: Shultz, *Turmoil*, p. 372.

1. Talbott, *Deadly Gambits*, p. 7.

2. Ibid., pp. 45–49, 59; Reagan, *An American Life*, pp. 270, 296; Schmidt, *Men and Powers*, p. 243.

3. Haig, *Caveat*, p. 229; interview with Richard Perle, June 29, 1999; Talbott, *Deadly Gambits*, pp. 56–62.

4. According to Talbott, a leading chronicler of U.S. nuclear arms control policy of this era: "The real purpose of the INF negotiation was not to achieve an agreement before deployment of the American missiles. Rather, it was to make sure that the deployment proceeded on schedule." Interview with Thomas Graham, Jr., Aug. 23, 1999; comments of Douglas MacEachin in Tannenwald, ed., *Understanding*, pp. 135–36; Talbott, *Master*, p. 170. See also Bundy, *Danger*, p. 569; Risse-Kappen, *Zero Option*, pp. 81–82, 84.

5. NSDD 15 (Nov. 16, 1981), in Simpson, ed., *National Security Directives*, p. 52.

6. Reagan, *An American Life*, pp. 295–96; interview with Edwin Meese III, Aug. 23, 1999.

7. Interview with Robert McFarlane, July 21, 1999; Adelman, *Great Universal Embrace*, p. 240.

8. Interview with Mary Kaldor, June 7, 1999; Kaldor, "We Got the Idea," p. 14.

9. Comments of Rowny in Tannenwald, ed., *Understanding*, p. 224; Nitze, *From Hiroshima*, pp. 367–68.

10. Talbott, *Deadly Gambits*, pp. 92, 116–30; Nitze, *From Hiroshima*, pp. 374–82.

11. Talbott, *Master*, p. 176; Gates, *From the Shadows*, p. 259; Nitze, *From Hiroshima*, pp. 386–87; Talbott, *Deadly Gambits*, pp. 141–44.

12. Nitze, however, kept trying. In July 1983, with Western Europe torn by antimissile protests, he once again urged the President to authorize him to return to Geneva and tell Kvitsinsky that the U.S. government was prepared to accept the "walk in the woods" formula. Such action, he insisted, would help to "head off disaster" with West European public opinion. But Nitze made no headway, for Reagan remained set against it. Interview with Richard Perle, June 29, 1999; Talbott, *Master*, pp. 176–77; Talbott, *Deadly Gambits*, pp. 187–88, 190.

13. Gates, *From the Shadows*, pp. 259–60, 280, 288–89; Shultz, *Turmoil*, pp. 117, 141, 165; Talbott, *Deadly Gambits*, p. 163.

14. Shultz, *Turmoil*, pp. 155, 160; Talbott, *Deadly Gambits*, p. 171.

15. NSDD 86 (Mar. 28, 1983), in Simpson, ed., *National Security Directives*, p. 288.

16. Talbott, *Deadly Gambits*, pp. 156–57; Shultz to the President, Jan. 19, 1983, in Zubok, Nielsen, and Grant, eds., *Understanding*; Shultz, *Turmoil*, p. 351.

17. Oberdorfer, *Turn*, pp. 37–38; Reagan to Andropov, July 11, 1983, in Anderson, *Revolution*, p. xxxvii.

18. Shultz, *Turmoil*, pp. 365–67, 372–74, 463; comments of Douglas MacEachin and Jack Matlock in Tannenwald, ed., *Understanding*, pp. 243–44, 261–62; interview with Robert McFarlane, July 21, 1999.

19. Shultz, *Turmoil*, p. 464; Reagan, *An American Life*, p. 590.

20. Matlock, *Autopsy*, pp. 84–85; Oberdorfer, *Turn*, p. 71; Shultz, *Turmoil*, pp. 376, 465–66.

21. Reagan, *U.S.-Soviet Relationship*.

22. Comments of Matlock and Robert McFarlane in Tannenwald, ed., *Understanding*, pp. 74, 85–92, 272; interview with Robert McFarlane, July 21, 1999; comments of Matlock in Wohlforth, ed., *Witnesses*, p. 77; Oberdorfer, *Turn*, p. 72.

23. Oberdorfer, *Turn*, pp. 70–71; Talbott, *Deadly Gambits*, p. 321; Reagan, *An American Life*, pp. 602, 611; Matlock, *Autopsy*, p. 69; Shultz, *Turmoil*, p. 275.

24. *WP*, Aug. 13, 1984; interview with Richard Wirthlin, Oct. 6, 1999; Oberdorfer, *Turn*, pp. 85–86.

25. Shultz, *Turmoil*, pp. 482–84; Gates, *From the Shadows*, pp. 324–25.

26. Shultz, *Turmoil*, pp. 496–99, 504–5, 512.

27. Adelman, *Great Universal Embrace*, pp. 89–91, 100, 116.

28. Reagan, *An American Life*, p. 294; Meyer and Marullo, "Grassroots Mobilization," pp. 5–6; Bundy, *Danger*, p. 583.

29. Talbott, *Master*, pp. 15–16; Shultz, *Turmoil*, p. 527; McFarlane, *Special Trust*, pp. 225–26.

30. John Isaacs, "Washington Report," *BAS* 45 (Sept. 1989): 3; Kotz, *Wild Blue Yonder*, pp. 3–4.

31. Interview with Edwin Meese III, Aug. 23, 1999; Bundy, *Danger*, pp. 563–64; Reagan, *An American Life*, pp. 560–62; NSDD 69 (Nov. 22, 1982), in Simpson, ed., *National Security Directives*, pp. 221–22; McFarlane, *Special Trust*, pp. 222–23.

32. Interview with Robert McFarlane, July 21, 1999; Herken, *Cardinal Choices*, pp. 205–7; Reagan, *An American Life*, p. 560; Stubbing, *Defense Game*, p. 384; John D. Isaacs and Katherine Magraw, "The Lobbyist and the MX," *BAS* 39 (Feb. 1983): 56.

33. Towell, "Reagan," p. 103; Adelman, *Great Universal Embrace*, pp. 173, 306.

34. Bundy, *Danger*, pp. 563–64; Talbott, *Master*, pp. 202–3; Herken, *Cardinal Choices*, p. 207.

35. Herbert Scoville, Jr., "Congressional Cliffhanger," *BAS* 40 (Oct. 1984): 5–6; interview with Christopher Paine, Sept. 14, 1999.

36. Interview with David Cortright, June 29, 1987; interview with David Cohen, July 19, 1999; John Isaacs, "Showdown on Military Budget," *BAS* 42 (Apr. 1986): 4; interview with Thomas Graham, Jr., Aug. 23, 1999; interview with Edwin Meese III, Aug. 23, 1999.

37. Interview with Robert McFarlane, July 21, 1999; Talbott, *Deadly Gambits*, pp. 223, 246–47.

38. *NYT*, May 2, 1982; Talbott, *Deadly Gambits*. 267; Reagan to Edward L. Rowny, June 25, 1982, Blackwell Files.

39. Gerard C. Smith, "The Arms Control and Disarmament Agency: An Unfinished History," *BAS* 40 (Apr. 1984): 13; Talbott, *Master*, pp. 165–66; Haig, *Caveat*, pp. 222–23; Talbott, *Deadly Gambits*, p. 263.

40. McFarlane to William P. Clark, Apr. 29, 1983, "Arms Control-Congressional Vol. I, 1/1/83–12/31/83 (5)" Folder, Box 91,391, Subject File, Executive Secretariat,

NSC Records; Towell, "Reagan," p. 103; interview with John Isaacs, July 20, 1999; Talbott, *Deadly Gambits*, pp. 301–14; "Presidential Statement" (Oct. 4, 1983), Box 18, Hart Papers.

41. Oral history interview with Kenneth Duberstein, Dec. 15, 1983; interview with Richard Perle, June 29, 1999; comments of Carlucci in Wohlforth, ed., *Witnesses*, p. 56.

42. Evangelista, *Unarmed Forces*, p. 233; Bundy, *Danger*, pp. 570–75; Talbott, *Master*, pp. 206–7; interview with Robert McFarlane, July 21, 1999.

43. Jay Keyworth to Ronald Reagan, July 29, 1982, Meese Files; interview with John Pike, July 22, 1999; Weart, *Nuclear Fear*, p. 384; York, *Making Weapons*, pp. 244–45.

44. Interview with Robert M. Bowman, Oct. 26, 1992; FitzGerald, *Way Out There*, pp. 114–17.

45. "NSC/Bakshian/RR" (Mar. 22, 1983), "Address to the Nation: Defense (Bakshian) 3/23/83 [2 of 4]" Folder, and "Address by the President to the Nation" (Mar. 23, 1983), "Address to the Nation: Defense (File #2) [1 of 4]" Folder, Box 80, Special Drafts File, White House Office of Speechwriting Records.

46. Shultz, *Turmoil*, pp. 246–60; William Hartung, "Star Wars Pork Barrel," *BAS* 42 (Jan. 1986): 20.

47. Anderson, *Revolution*, pp. 85–86; Talbott, *Master*, p. 189.

48. Comments of McFarlane in Tannenwald, ed., *Understanding*, pp. 45–46, 59; interview with Robert McFarlane, July 21, 1999; oral history interview with George Keyworth, Sept. 28, 1987, pp. 3–4; FitzGerald, *Way Out There*, pp. 187–209; Reagan, *An American Life*, p. 572.

49. Wills, *Reagan's America*, p. 361; Anderson, *Revolution*, pp. 81–83.

50. Anderson, *Revolution*, pp. 86–87.

51. Shultz, *Turmoil*, p. 260; Fitzwater, *Call the Briefing!*, p. 138; Adelman, *Great Universal Embrace*, pp. 65–69, 313–14; interview with Kenneth Adelman, July 22, 1998.

52. Talbott, *Master*, pp. 7, 18–19, 204–5, 212–16, 231–34; interview with Thomas Graham, Jr., Aug. 23, 1999; Adelman, *Great Universal Embrace*, p. 300; Shultz, *Turmoil*, p. 264.

53. Weinberger, *Fighting*, pp. 312–13, 316; Bundy, *Danger*, p. 571.

54. Interview with Robert McFarlane, July 21, 1999; McFarlane, *Special Trust*, p. 234.

55. *Washington Times*, May 23, 1984; Maria Margaronis, "Notes from Abroad," *NT* 2 (Mar. 1984): 10.

56. The Belgian deployment decision was not made until March 1985. *WP*, Mar. 27, 1984; Shultz, *Turmoil*, p. 506; "Address by Belgian Prime Minister Martens" (Mar. 15, 1985), in U.S. Arms Control and Disarmament Agency, *Documents on Disarmament, 1985*, pp. 194–96.

57. Clements, *Back From the Brink*, pp. 171–72; Andre Carothers, "The Story of the South Pacific Nuclear-Free Zone Treaty," *Greenpeace* 14 (Jan.–Feb. 1989): 10; Simpson, ed., *National Security Directives*, p. 644; *NYT*, Feb. 14, 1985.

58. Landais-Stamp and Rogers, *Rocking*, pp. 61–62, 64–65, 70, 77; Lange, *Nu-*

clear Free, pp. 54–58; Lamare, "Growth," p. 473; Hawke, *Hawke Memoirs*, pp. 282–83.

59. Clements, *Back From the Brink*, p. 136; Landais-Stamp and Rogers, *Rocking*, pp. 80–81, 93–94.

60. Interview with Frank Carlucci, July 20, 1999; "Statement by the Assistant Secretary of State for East Asian and Pacific Affairs" (Mar. 18, 1985), in U.S. Arms Control and Disarmament Agency, *Documents on Disarmament*, pp. 196–99; Hawke, *Hawke Memoirs*, pp. 283–84; Clements, *Back From the Brink*, pp. 136–38; *WP*, Feb. 20, 21, 1985; *NYT*, Mar. 5, 1985; Lange, *Nuclear Free*, p. 99; Landais-Stamp and Rogers, *Rocking*, pp. 80–81.

61. Clements, *Back From the Brink*, pp. 138–39; Hawke, *Hawke Memoirs*, pp. 284–86; Landais-Stamp and Rogers, *Rocking*, pp. 108–9.

62. Adelman, *Great Universal Embrace*, pp. 251, 260–61, 266–68; *Wall Street Journal*, June 20, 1984.

63. William M. Arkin, "Fewer Warheads in Europe," *BAS* 42 (Aug.–Sept. 1986): 4–5; *Guardian*, Nov. 16, 1985; Christopher Paine, "Last Roundup for NATO?" *BAS* 38 (Feb. 1982): 6.

64. Adelman, *Great Universal Embrace*, p. 167.

65. This point is discussed in chapter 12.

Chapter 15

Epigraph: Hans Sinn, "Sixth Annual END Conference: Success," *PM* 3 (Oct.–Nov. 1987): 46.

1. Penner, "A Brief Overview," p. 54; Krasner, "Decline," pp. 174–76; Krasner, *Political Influence*, pp. 5, 17.

2. Interview with Berit Ås, Aug. 12, 2000; "Nei til Atomvåpen (No to Nuclear Weapons), Norway, Status Report" (Sept. 1988), Nei til Atomvåpen (Norway) Records.

3. *Guardian*, May 17, 1985; "Membership Figures," CND Records, L; Bourdet, "Désarmement Nucléaire," p. 16; Dion van den Berg, "Conciliar Process," *END J*, No. 34–35 (Summer 1988), p. 18.

4. Peter Findlay, "Pulling Through a Difficult Patch," *END J*, No. 21 (Apr.–May 1986), pp. 11–13; Maislinger, "Effects," pp. 3, 5.

5. John Mepham, "A Turkish Diary," *END J*, No. 28–29 (Summer 1987), pp. 26–28; John Mepham, "Testing 'Democracy,'" *END J*, No. 33 (May–June 1988), p. 14.

6. *Christian Science Monitor*, Nov. 16–22, 1985; James Hinton, "Good News, Bad News," *END J*, No. 34–35 (Summer 1988), p. 15; interview with Berit Ås, Aug. 12, 2000.

7. Meg Beresford, Mark Salter, and Moira Weaver, "Belgians Deploy Cruise on Time," *END J*, No. 15 (Apr.–May 1985), p. 5; *Guardian*, Apr. 9, 1985.

8. Jamie Dettmer, Paul Anderson, and Mark Thompson, "CND to Campaign on 'Basic Case,'" *END J*, No. 19 (Dec. 1985–Jan. 1986), p. 9.

9. Byrne, *Campaign*, p. 153; interview with Martin Butcher, July 19, 1999; Johnstone, "German Peace Movement."

10. Maria Margaronis, "Notes From Abroad," *NT* 4 (Mar.–Apr. 1986): 41; *Friedens Info*, No. 11 (Apr. 1989), p. 9; "END Briefing Notes: Turkish Peace Association" (1986), author's possession.

11. *Guardian*, May 17, 1985 and Apr. 2, 1988; "Membership Figures," CND (B) Records, L; Den Berg, "Conciliar Process," p. 23.

12. Mario Pianta, "A New Road," *END J*, No. 34–35 (Summer 1988), p. 14; "1987 IPB General Assembly," Box 522, WRI Records.

13. Interview with Martin Butcher, July 19, 1999; interview with Janet Bloomfield, May 14, 1999; Hinton, *Protests*, p. 194; Kaldor, "Introduction," *Campaigns*, p. 1.

14. "Nei til Atomvåpen (No to Nuclear Weapons), Norway, Status Report" (Sept. 1988), Nei til Atomvåpen Records.

15. "END Briefing Notes: The Netherlands" (1985), New Accession, WRL Records; van Essen, "Dutch Cruise Resistance"; den Berg, "Conciliar Process," pp. 18, 23.

16. Findlay, "Pulling Through," pp. 12–13; Otfried Nassauer, "Defining 'Peace,'" *END J*, No. 34–35 (Summer 1988), p. 18.

17. Mette Klouman, "Paying for Detente?" *END J*, No. 34–35 (Summer 1988), p. 16; "Hva Skjer I Norske Havet?" (1987), Erik Alfsen, "A New Zero Option" (1988), and "Nei til Atomvåpen (No to Nuclear Weapons), Norway, Status Report" (Sept. 1988), Nei til Atomvåpen Records.

18. Winther, "Danish Peace Movements," pp. 10–11; Krasner, "Decline," p. 15.

19. Rigmor Risbjerg Thomsen to Geneva, et al., Nov. 12, 1984, Sweet Files, WILPF Records; Ståhle, *Internationella Kvinnoförbundet*, pp. 45, 47; "Stoppa Kärnvapenkapprustningen!" Internationella Kvinnoförbundet för Fred och Frihet (Sweden section) Records.

20. Minutes of the CND executive committee meeting of Sept. 17, 1985, Reel 26, CND (B) Records, HM; "British Peace Groups Strike Back," *DC* (Aug. 1986); "The British Star Wars Research Boycott," Box 446, WRI Records.

21. Byrne, *Campaign*, pp. 146–47, 228–29; Hinton, *Protests*, pp. 193–94.

22. Judy Kowalok, "Wearing Away a Stone: An Interview with Gwyn Kirk," *NVA* 4 (Jan.–Feb. 1987): 7; interview with Martin Butcher, July 19, 1999; interview with Daniel Plesch, July 21, 1999; Hinton, *Protests*, pp. 192–93.

23. Patrick Burke, "SPD Confirms Stance—But Will It Win?" *END J*, No. 24 (Oct.–Nov. 1986), p. 5; Johnstone, "German Peace Movement," p. 11.

24. "Peace Movement Leader Slams Dutch Labour Party," *END J*, No. 22–23 (Summer 1986), p. 5; Beresford, Salter, and Weaver, "Belgians," p. 5; Judith Winther, "Moving towards a Nordic NWFZ," *END J*, No. 16–17 (Summer 1985), pp. 18–19.

25. "Labour Shows United Front," *END J*, No. 25 (Dec. 1986–Jan. 1987), p. 6; Shaw, *Labour Party*, pp. 177–78.

26. "Referendum Confirms"; Jolyon Howorth, "End of Consensus," *END J*, No. 34–35 (Summer 1988), p. 24.

27. Dan Smith, "Beyond a Defeat," *Sanity* (July 1987), p. 4; Mary Kaldor, "Lessons of Defeat," *END J*, No. 28–29 (Summer 1987), pp. 2, 36; Kent, *Undiscovered Ends*, pp. 193–95.

28. Everts, "Continuity," p. 31; Smith, "Beyond," p. 4; Shaw, *Labour Party*, pp. 179–80.

29. *Guardian*, Feb. 16, 1987.

30. USIA, "West European Publics Favor Eliminating INF Missiles" (May 20, 1987), Case File 475427SS, FG 298, Subject File, WHORM Records; den Oudsten, "Public Opinion on International Security"; "Thaw in West German Public Opinion on Soviets," *DDA* 2 (Feb.–Mar. 1989): 10–11.

31. Den Oudsten, "Public Opinion on International Security."

32. USIA, "West European Publics Favor Eliminating INF Missiles" (May 20, 1987), Case File 475427SS, FG 298, Subject File, WHORM Records; Hastings and Hastings, eds., *Index . . . 1988–89*, p. 265; Breyman, *Why Movements Matter*, p. 271.

33. Gallup, *GP: Public Opinion 1986*, p. 129; Hastings and Hastings, eds., *Index . . . 1988–89*, p. 265; den Oudsten, "Public Opinion on Peace and War," p. 30; Joergen Dragsdahl, "NATO Bullies Denmark," *NT* 6 (July–Aug. 1988): 7.

34. Hastings and Hastings, eds., *Index . . . 1988–89*, p. 269.

35. Philip P. Everts, "Where the Peace Movement Goes When It Disappears," *BAS* 45 (Nov. 1989): 30; Everts, "Continuity," p. 17; den Oudsten, "Public Opinion on International Security."

36. USIA, "West European Publics Favor Eliminating INF Missiles" (May 20, 1987), Case File 475427SS, FG 298, Subject File, WHORM Records; Thatcher, *Downing Street*, p. 437. See also Gallup, *GP: Public Opinion 1987*, p. 13.

37. *Christian Science Monitor*, Aug. 17–23, 1985; John Trinkl, "Disarmament: Activism Thrives, But Is There a Movement?" *NVA* 6 (July–Aug. 1989): 6; Dottye Burt, "Progress Report and Recommendations for Revisions in Development Plan" (June 20, 1986), and Burt and Bernice Bild to National Committee Members and State Contacts, July 28, 1986, Uncatalogued material, Freeze Records, SL.

38. Randy Kehler to Freeze executive committee, July 14, 1984, Box 4, Freeze Records, SL; interview with Peter Bergel, Aug. 3, 1999; Renata Rizzo, "The Freeze Carries On," *NT* 4 (Jan.–Feb. 1986): 15.

39. Robert Schaeffer, "Going South: Peace Activists Turn Their Attention to Central America," *NT* 6 (Nov.–Dec. 1987): 10–11, 20; "War Resisters League—U.S. Section Report" (July 1986), Box 524, WRI Records; Boxes 78, 160, 167, and 172, Series G, SANE Records.

40. Kleidman, *Organizing*, p. 161; interview with Bernard Lown, July 6, 1999.

41. SANE, "1986 Members' Report," Nuclear Weapons Freeze Campaign, "Status of State Level Freeze Organizations: August 1986," and Nick Carter to Freeze supporters, spring 1987, author's possession; Kleidman, *Organizing*, pp. 161–62.

42. "SANE Votes to Merge with Freeze," *SW* 26 (Spring 1987): 3; Renata Rizzo-Harvi, "Grass Roots Opt for Unity," *NT* 5 (Jan.–Feb. 1987): 29–31.

43. Robert Schaeffer, "Making Waves," *NT* 6 (Nov.–Dec. 1987): 23, 25; "Physicians for Social Responsibility," *NT* 4 (Mar.–Apr. 1986): 34.

44. The Council did almost as well in 1988, when it raised $1.44 million. CLW, "We Raise $1,500,000 for Congressional Candidates" (Dec. 1986), and CLW, "We Raise $1,440,447 for Congressional Candidates" (Dec. 1988), author's possession.

45. Interview with David Cortright, June 29, 1987; interview with Dottye Burt,

June 29, 1987; Patricia Morgan, "The Next Step," *Mobilizer* 5 (Spring 1985): 10; interview with David Cohen, July 19, 1999.

46. David McReynolds to all groups involved in the Nuclear Test Moratorium network, Oct. 1, 1985, Sweet Files, WILPF Records; Judy Freiwirth, "A Step Backward," *Mobilizer* 5 (Spring 1985): 10–11; interview with Dottye Burt, June 29, 1987; interview with Robert Musil, July 20, 1998.

47. Interview with Peter Bergel, Aug. 3, 1999; interview with Charles Johnson, Aug. 3, 1999; WRL, *A WRL History*; Trinkl, "Disarmament," p. 6.

48. Gene R. LaRocque to Ethel Taylor, May 20, 1986, Box 2, Series A,8, WSP Records; Dorie to Howard, Mar. 13, 1986, Box 506, WRI Records.

49. Interview with Jeremy Stone, July 22, 1999; John Kogut and Michael Weissman, "Taking the Pledge Against Star Wars," *BAS* 42 (Jan. 1986): 27–30; "Scientists Oppose Star Wars," *NT* 5 (May–June 1987): 11; Cortright, "Peace Movement Role," p. 86; *NYT*, Oct. 31, 1986.

50. Daniel Charles, "The People vs. the Complex," *BAS* 44 (Jan.–Feb. 1988): 29–30; interview with Eric Fersht, Sept. 9, 1989.

51. Interview with Charles Johnson, Aug. 3, 1999; "Campaign Results," *NT* 4 (Jan.–Feb. 1986): 4–5; Ron Calogeras, "Windy City Goes Nuclear Free," *NT* 4 (May–June 1986): 39.

52. Orlov, *Dangerous Thoughts*, pp. 285–86; David McReynolds to Ivan Fiala, Nov. 11, 1988, New Accession, WRL Records; Stone, *"Every Man,"* pp. 180–84; "Leading U.S. Peace Movement Figures Protest Trial of Three Polish Solidarity Activists" (May 23, 1985), Box 446, WRI Records.

53. Interview with Robert Musil, July 20, 1998; Marianne Szegedy-Maszak, "Rise and Fall of the Washington Peace Industry," *BAS* 45 (Jan.–Feb. 1989): 18; interview with William Sloane Coffin, Jr., Oct. 19, 1989.

54. Shaffer, "SANE-Freeze Merger"; "Rev. William Sloane Coffin, Jr. Named First SANE/Freeze President," *SW/Freeze Focus* 26 (Autumn 1987): 3.

55. "SANE/Freeze Congress Sets Peace Agenda," *SW/Freeze Focus* 27 (Spring 1988): 5–6; "SANE/Freeze 1988 Peace Platform," *SW/Freeze Focus* 27 (Summer 1988): 19; public address by William Sloane Coffin, Jr., Oct. 24, 1987, Albany, NY.

56. "Bishops Say No to Deterrence," *NT* 4 (July–Aug. 1986): 6–7; Carroll, "Laboring for Peace," p. 1; "Star Wars."

57. Interview with David Cohen, July 19, 1999; Jerome Grossman to CLW supporters, Nov. 1986 and Dec. 1988, author's possession.

58. Interview with David Cohen, July 19, 1999; David Lewis, "Open Doors," *NT* 6 (Sept.–Oct. 1987): 11–12; Renata Rizzo, "You've Got a Friend," *NT* 5 (Oct. 1986): 18–19.

59. Martin Hamburger, "Election '88 Underway," *NT* 5 (Jan.–Feb. 1987): 10; interview with Robert Musil, July 20, 1998; "SANE/Freeze Congress," pp. 5–6; "SANE/Freeze Promotes Peace Agenda at the Democratic Convention," *SW/Freeze Focus* 27 (Fall 1988): 5.

60. Yankelovich and Smoke, "America's 'New Thinking,'" p. 10; Oberdorfer, *Turn*, p. 294.

61. Gallup, *GP: Public Opinion 1987*, p. 212; Gallup, *GP: Public Opinion 1988*, p. 3; Gallup, *GP: Public Opinion 1989*, pp. 3, 231.

62. Gallup, *GP: Public Opinion 1987*, pp. 121–22; Robert K. Musil, "America's Changing Attitudes Toward Peace," *SW* 25 (Nov.–Dec. 1986): 4.

63. Gallup, *GP: Public Opinion 1987*, p. 63; Gallup, *GP: Public Opinion 1986*, p. 268; Musil, "America's Changing Attitudes," p. 5; Robert Schaeffer, "The Tell-Tale Heart," *NT* 6 (Jan.–Feb. 1988): 16.

64. Graham, *American Public Opinion*, p. 43.

65. Yankelovich and Smoke, "America's 'New Thinking,'" p. 9; Gallup, *GP: Public Opinion 1987*, p. 319.

66. Yankelovich and Smoke, "America's 'New Thinking,'" p. 3; Gallup, *GP: Public Opinion 1988*, p. 219.

67. *Public Attitudes*, p. 20; Gallup, *GP: Public Opinion 1988*, pp. 51–52.

68. "Jottings by Edward Thompson" (Nov. 15, 1985), Kaldor Papers; Robert Penner, "Canadian Peace Alliance Breaks New Ground," *NT* 4 (Jan.–Feb. 1986): 10; "The Canadian Peace Alliance," Canadian Peace Alliance Records; "Canadian Peace Alliance Information Sheet" (Feb. 1988), author's possession.

69. Robert Penner, "Peace Movement Needs More Ambitious Strategies," *PM* 3 (Oct.–Nov. 1987): 23; David Langille, "Growing Pains," *PM* 3 (Oct.–Nov. 1987): 21.

70. Penner, "A Brief Review," p. 51; "169 Nuclear Weapons Free Zones in Canada!" *Canadian Peace Alliance News* 2 (Summer 1987): 12; Regehr, Robinson, and Rosenblum, *Making Canada*, p. 1.

71. Newman, "Surviving," pp. 49–52; "Summary of the History of Project Ploughshares," and "Common Security," Project Ploughshares Records.

72. "The Canadian Peace Movement Today," *PM* 3 (Oct.–Nov. 1987): 30–31.

73. Chris Gainor, "Activists Confront Nuclear-Capable Ship in Toronto," *PM* 2 (Oct.–Nov. 1986): 42; "Nuclear Warships Not Welcome," *Greenpeace Examiner* 11 (Oct.–Dec. 1986): 21; Laurie MacBride, "The Motherpeace Action: Building the Circle," *PM* 2 (Oct.–Nov. 1986): 44; "Atlantic," *PM* 3 (Oct.–Nov. 1987): 39.

74. "April 25: Rallies Across the Continent," *Canadian Peace Alliance News* 2 (Summer 1987): 13.

75. Munton, *Peace and Security*, pp. 23, 24, 26, 28, 31. See also *IHT*, Jan. 9, 1987.

76. "She Still Loves This Planet," *PM* 4 (June–July 1988): 17; Burgmann, *Power and Protest*, p. 216; Summy and Saunders, "Disarmament," p. 41.

77. "Pine Gap Fact Sheet," Alice Springs Peace Group Bases Campaign Records; "Action at Nurrungar," *DC* (Aug. 1986); "Disarm the Pacific," *NVA* 9 (Sept.–Oct. 1992): 10–11.

78. Andre Carothers, "The Ties That Blind: Australia's Quest for Relevance," *Greenpeace* 14 (Mar.–Apr. 1989): 14; Michael Ross, "'Nuclear Allergy' Spreads," *NT* 7 (Jan.–Feb. 1989): 7.

79. Lange, *Nuclear Free*, pp. 150–51; "1987 IPB General Assembly," Box 522, WRI Records; "What Is the Peace Movement?" and "Quittez le Pacifique!" Peace Movement Aotearoa Records.

80. Landais-Stamp and Rogers, *Rocking*, pp. 21, 113–14, 134–36, 153–55; Lange, *Nuclear Free*, pp. 176–82; "Labour and Lange."

81. Michael Bedford, "Palau Ends Atom-Arms Ban," *NT* 6 (Jan.–Feb. 1988): 8; Charles Scheiner, "Future in Doubt: Nuclear-Free Belau," *NVA* 3 (Apr.–May 1989): 11.

82. Phil Esmonde, "Letter from Fiji," *PM* 2 (Oct.–Nov. 1986): 5; "From the Editor," *MAPW Pulse* 6 (Winter 1987): 3; Landais-Stamp and Rogers, *Rocking*, p. 151.

83. "A Reunion in the Marshalls Continues the Voyage for Life," *Greenpeace Examiner* 11 (June 1986): 26; Michael Bedford, "Activism in the Pacific," *NT* 8 (Summer 1990): 48.

84. Jorge Emmanuel, "Fighting for a Nuclear Free Philippines," *Mobilizer* 5 (Fall 1985): 16; "The Philippines."

85. Roland G. Simbulan, "How 'The Battle for the Bases' Was Won," *NVA* 9 (Sept.–Oct. 1992): 11; "Philippines: Nuclear Free?" *PM* 2 (Oct.–Nov. 1986): 11; Elmo Gideon Manapat, "On the Nuclear Weapons Free and Foreign Military Bases Provisions of the Proposed Philippine Constitution" (ca. Jan. 1987), author's possession.

86. Kodama, "Red vs. Green," p. 11; interview with Ikuro Anzai, May 15, 1999; "The Japanese Peace Movement," *Gensuikin News*, No. 113 (Summer 1986), pp. 1–3; Joanne Landy to Horst Stasius, Dec. 31, 1986, author's possession.

87. "No Nukes in Japan," *Greenpeace* 13 (Nov.–Dec. 1988): 5; "News from Japan," *END J*, No. 22–23 (Summer 1986), p. 3; "Churches Committed."

88. Interview with Koichi Akamatsu, May 15, 1999; Takahara, "Local Government," p. 51.

89. "1987 IPB General Assembly," Box 522, WRI Records.

90. Paul Routledge, "Blocking Militarism in India," *NVA* 3 (Apr.–May 1989): 9–11; Routledge, "Dispensable Space"; interview with Dhirendra Sharma, Oct. 11, 1995.

91. Day, ed., *Peace Movements*, p. 346; "Chinese to End Tests in Atmosphere," *END J*, No. 22–23 (Summer 1986), p. 5; Enver Tohti to the author, Feb. 28, 2001.

92. Suh, "INF Treaty," p. 10; "Peace News" (May 1988), Australian Quaker Peace Committee Records; "Declaration of the Churches," p. 19; "International Conference."

93. Clements, *Back from the Brink*, p. 159; Lamare, "Growth," p. 477.

94. Carothers, "Ties That Blind," p. 17; John Miller, "NAN/IPB Meet," *NVA* 5 (Dec. 1988): 12–13.

95. Hastings and Hastings, eds., *Index . . . 1988–89*, pp. 268–69.

96. Gallup, *GP: Public Opinion 1986*, p. 129; Kevin P. Clements, "New Zealand's Antinuclear Stand," *BAS* 43 (Mar. 1987): 32.

97. Gabriel Garcia Marquez, "The Doom of Damocles," *Greenpeace* 12 (June 1987): 18; Antonio Rubens Britto de Castro et al., "Brazil's Nuclear Shakeup: Military Still in Control," *BAS* 45 (May 1989): 25.

98. Andrew Cowell, Letter to the Editor, *END J*, No. 37 (1989), p. 46.

99. Gallup, *GP: Public Opinion 1986*, p. 129.

100. Hillel Schenker, "Israel's Whistle-Blower," *END J*, No. 27 (May–June 1987), p. 6; Toscano, *Triple Cross*; *Al Hamishmar*, Dec. 26, 1986; "A Nuclear-Free Middle East," *New Outlook* 30 (Mar. 1987): 39; Newdorf, "Israeli anti-nuclear movement."

101. Howard Clark to Catherine Fitzpatrick, Nov. 25, 1987, Box 517, WRI Records; "The Independent Soviet Peace Movement: An Interview with Two Founding Members," *PDN* 2 (Summer–Fall 1985): 18; "Trust Group latest," *END J*, No. 27 (May–June 1987), p. 4; "Update"; Brian Morton and Joanne Landy, "East European Activists Test Glasnost," *BAS* 44 (May 1988): 24.

102. "Trust Group latest," p. 4; "New Attack"; "Official Attacks"; "Notes from the Underground"; "Shatravka Released—but Repression Continues," *END J*, No. 22–23 (Summer 1986), p. 6.

103. Bob McGlynn, "Peace Mission to Moscow," *NVA* 3 (Oct.–Nov. 1986): 11–12; Sergei Batovrin et al. to Friends, Aug. 1986, USSR Miscellaneous Peace Material; *Times* (L), Aug. 4, 1986; *New York Post*, Aug. 4, 1986.

104. Medvedkov to Faber, Aug. 2, 1985, IPCC Records; Jonathan Steele, "Trust Group—As Seen on TV," *END J*, No. 32 (Feb.–Mar. 1988), p. 16.

105. Personal interview with Ruzanna Ilukhina, May 22, 1991; Morton and Landy, "East European Activists," pp. 24, 26; Alexeyeva, "Independent Youth Groups," pp. 4, 32.

106. Dawson, "Anti-Nuclear Activism," pp. 4–7; Gorbachev, *Memoirs*, p. 193.

107. Von Hippel, "Arms Control Physics," pp. 41–46; Velikhov, "Science," p. 36; Frank von Hippel and Jeremy Stone to Participants in the Organizing Meeting of the Joint Disarmament Project, Apr. 29, 1987, Von Hippel Papers; interview with Frank von Hippel, Aug. 22, 1999.

108. Sakharov, *Moscow*, pp. 27, 41–45; interview with Frank von Hippel, Aug. 22, 1999; Sakharov, "Of Arms," pp. 40–42.

109. *NYT*, Dec. 16, 1989; Sakharov, *Moscow*, p. 10.

110. "Political Opposition," p. 8; "Noose Tightens."

111. Kavan, "Spontaneous Peace Demo"; Tomin, "On Freedom," p. 39; "Let the Bands Play!" p. 29.

112. Kavan, "Is the Ice Finally Melting?"; Morton and Landy, "East European Activists," p. 18.

113. David Charap and Mark Brand, "Charter 77: 'Ignore Who Applauds,'" *END J*, No. 33 (May–June 1988), pp. 19–20; Havel, *Anatomy*; "Interview with Vaclav Havel," *END J*, No. 26 (Feb.–Mar. 1987), p. 14.

114. Lynne Jones to David McReynolds, Dec. 18, 1988, and "The Declaration of the Independent Peace Association" (Apr. 1988), New Accession, WRL Records; "A Touch of Frost-*nost?*" *DDA* 1 (July–Aug. 1988): 8; Judith Hempfling and Joanne Landy, "Prague: The Tale of Two Seminars," *PDN* 3 (Winter 1988–89): 11.

115. "Interview with GDR activist," enclosure in *END J*, No. 26 (Feb.–Mar. 1987); Jackson, "New Samizdat," pp. 15–16; Morton and Landy, "East European Activists," p. 22; Klein, "East Germany," pp. 5–6.

116. Bruce Allen, "Letter from East Berlin," *PM* 4 (Oct.–Nov. 1988): 7.

117. Kiszely, "Pacifism Under Fire"; Ferenc Köszegi, "An Eastern View," *PM* 4 (June–July 1988): 30; interview with Ferenc Köszegi, Aug. 28, 1986.

118. Randle, *People Power*, p. 135; Vjuanovic, "Independent Peace Movement"; Mark Thompson, "In the Laboratory," *END J*, No. 32 (Feb.–Mar. 1988), pp. 17–19; *From Below*, pp. 181–204.

119. John Bacher, "The Independent Peace Movements in Eastern Europe," *PM* 1 (Dec. 1985): 12; "Letter from KOS in Poland to the END Convention in Amsterdam" (June 29), Box 507, WRI Records.

120. Franek Michalski, "'Freedom and Peace' Movement Emerges in Poland," *PDN* 2 (Summer–Fall 1986): 3–4; "'Freedom and Peace,'" pp. 44–48; Morton and

Landy, "East European Activists," pp. 19–20; Steven Becker, "Voices from Mied-zyrzesc," *PDN* 3 (Winter–Spring 1988): 7–8.

121. "'Freedom and Peace' Declaration of Principles," *PDN* 2 (Summer–Fall 1986): 6; *NYT*, May 14, 1987; *WP*, May 11, 1987; Hempfling, "Linking up"; Fleisch-man, "Beyond the Blocs?"; Morton and Landy, "East European Activists," pp. 20–21.

122. Lynne Jones, "What Next for WiP?" *END J*, No. 36 (Oct. 1988–Jan. 1989), p. 25.

123. See, for example, the protests of Charter 77 and the Moscow Trust Group against the arrests of Polish activists: "'Freedom and Peace,'" p. 49.

124. "Oppositionists Debate"; Jan Kavan to David McReynolds, Oct. 24, 1986, New Accession, WRL Records; Kavan, "Helsinki."

125. "From the Editors," *PDN* 3 (Winter–Spring 1988): 1, 25, 28; "Hungarian Meeting a Success," *END J*, No. 31 (Dec.–Jan. 1987–88), p. 8; "International Seminar 'Prague '88.'"

126. "Presidium of the Polish Peace Committee Meets," *Polish Peace Commit-tee Newsletter* (ca. July 1987), p. 11; "Civilizing the System," *END J*, No. 32 (Feb.–Mar. 1988), p. 21.

127. Garthoff, *Deterrence*, pp. 110–11; Gallup, *GP: Public Opinion 1987*, p. 63.

128. Van Essen, "Peace Camps in Europe"; Gwyn Kirk, "Hanging in There: Notes on the Women's Peace Movement," *Peace and Freedom* (June 1987), pp. 6–7, 21, in Box 1, Greenham Women Against Cruise Missiles Records; "Demands Pre-sented by the Representatives of the European and US Peace Movements" (Mar. 12, 1985), Reel 26, CND (B) Records, HM.

129. Renata Rizzo-Harvi, "Americans Invade Soviet Union," *NT* 5 (Nov.–Dec. 1986): 30–32; Lisbeth Gronlund and Daniel Galpern, "Independent Thought and Ac-tion in the U.S.S.R.," *Network News* 7 (Jan. 1987): 1–3; "Golubka" and "Russian-American Humanitarian Initiative," author's possession.

130. "A Historic Meeting" (Apr. 1987) and "Changing the Shape of the Future" (1990), CDI Records; Faber to Vaclav Maly, Oct. 14, 1988, Folder 760, IKV Records, A; interview with Mient Jan Faber, Aug. 7, 1986.

131. "Statement by David McReynolds . . . to the United Nations Special Session on Disarmament" (June 1988), author's possession; Anne to Anne, May 7 and 29, 1985, Sweet Files, WILPF Records.

132. J. Michael Henry, "International Secretary in Australia," *Disarming Times* 13 (Oct. 1988): 1; "1987 IPB General Assembly," Box 522, WRI Records.

133. Interview with Eric Fersht, Sept. 9, 1989; Schaeffer, "Making Waves," pp. 23–26; Ross, "'Nuclear Allergy,'" p. 7.

134. "Socialist International Appeal"; "Socialist International Resolutions."

135. Schrag, *Global Action*, pp. 7, 43–48; "1987 IPB General Assembly," Box 522, WRI Records.

136. Interview with Bernard Lown, July 6, 1999; *NYT*, Oct. 12, 1985; Alex Miller, "Peace Prize Boosts PSR," *NT* 4 (Jan.–Feb. 1986): 11; *Wall Street Journal*, Oct. 14, 1985.

137. Conn Nugent to the Editor, *Wall Street Journal*, Oct. 16, 1985, PSR Records;

interview with Bernard Lown, July 6, 1999; *WP*, Dec. 10, 1985; Warner and Shuman, *Citizen Diplomats*, pp. 31–32.

138. *International Physicians*, p. 7; IPPNW, "You Can Prevent This" (1988), author's possession.

139. Mary Kaldor to "everyone," Apr. 3, 1985, and Edward Thompson, "Planning for Survival" (1985), Kaldor Papers.

140. Interview with Nigel Young, May 15, 1999; Patrick Burke, "END and Eastern Europe," and Judith Eversley, "Eastern Europe" (June 1986), Box 508, WRI Records.

141. Interview with Mient Jan Faber, Aug. 7, 1986; interview with Daniel Plesch, July 21, 1998; Ben Webb, "Split END," *NT* 6 (Sept.–Oct. 1988): 7; Mary Kaldor, "A New Europe," *END J*, No. 30 (Oct.–Nov. 1987), p. 2.

142. "Looking East"; Gerard Holden, "Movements Meet in France," *END J*, No. 22–23 (Summer 1986), p. 3; Mient Jan Faber, "A Few Lessons from the END Convention" (1985), Bess Papers; Mary Kaldor, "Movements Meet in Coventry," *END J*, No. 30 (Oct.–Nov. 1987), p. 9; interview with Martin Butcher, July 19, 1999; Stephen Brown and John Millner to END Convention National Coordinators and Contacts, June 2, 1987, END Records.

143. *Guardian*, July 20, 1987; Mary Kaldor, "From Gloom to Surprise," *END J*, No. 36 (Oct. 1988–Jan. 1989), p. 21.

144. IPB press release of Sept. 9, 1985, "Statement on Afghanistan" (Sept. 1985), and "Statement on Nicaragua" (Sept. 1985), Box 500, WRI Records.

145. "Appeal to the General Assembly of the United Nations" (Sept. 1985), and "Programme of Action for IPB, 1987–88," Box 500, "1987 IPB General Assembly," Box 522, WRI Records; Bruce Kent, "Peace Movement Optimism—A Reply," *PC*, 9–10/87, p. 20.

146. Interview with Rainer Santi, Aug. 18, 1986; Santi to MfS, May 27, 1986, MfS Records, NY.

147. "TPA Prisoners Released," *END J*, No. 21 (Apr.–May 1986), p. 5; Peter Crampton to Dear Friends, May 23, 1985, Box 446, and "Working Groups and Local Groups: Reports for 1986 AGM," Box 508, WRI Records.

148. "Statement about Charges Brought Against Czechoslovak Peace and Civil Rights Activists" (Dec. 18, 1988), Folder 760, IKV Records, A; Randle, *People Power*, p. 168; McReynolds to Honecker, Feb. 3, 1988, Box 517, WRI Records.

149. Interview with Rob Prince, July 27, 1999; Chandra, *Present International Situation*.

150. Interview with Rob Prince, July 27, 1999; interview with Mark Solomon, July 8, 1999; Johannes Pakaslahti, "Growing Optimism in the Peace Movement," *PC*, 8/87, p. 12; *Helsingin Sanomat*, Sept. 20, 1987, Prince Papers; "Renewing the World Peace Council," *PC*, 2/88, pp. 1–2; Johannes Pakaslahti, "It Takes Two to Tango," *PC*, 12/88, p. 2.

151. "Save the United Nations," *PC*, 6/86, p. 4; "Easing East-West Tension in Europe," *PC*, 7–8/86, p. 1; "Ten Principles of a World Without War," *PC*, 1–3/87, p. 7.

152. David McReynolds, "Voice of Non-Violence," *PC*, 5/88, p. 7; Kent, "Peace Movement Optimism"; Ken Coates, "Bringing the Global Family of Peace Movements Together," *PC*, 1/88, p. 16; "A Healing Process?" *PC*, 7–8/88, p. 7.

153. Interview with Rob Prince, July 27, 1999; Rob Prince to Gordie Flowers, May 20, 1988, Prince Papers.

154. *Rauhan Puolesta*, Sept. 1988, Prince Papers; "'The WPC Must Change,'" *END J*, No. 36 (Oct. 1988–Jan. 1989), pp. 21–22.

155. Interview with Rob Prince, July 27, 1999; Hannu Nieminen, "Developing the Peace Movement's International Cooperation," *PC*, 7–8/88, p. 11; Jacques Denis and Bernard LaCombe to Romesh Chandra, Jan. 28, 1988, and Michael Myerson to Chandra and Pakaslahti, Aug. 12, 1988, Prince Papers.

156. Interview with Rob Prince, July 27, 1999; interview with Günther Drefahl, May 19, 1999; interview with Mark Solomon, July 8, 1999.

157. Interview with Mark Solomon, July 8, 1999; *Rauhan Puolesta*, Dec. 1988, Prince Papers; "Peacenik," *END J*, No. 27 (May–June 1987), p. 5.

158. Interview with Rob Prince, July 27, 1999; "Peacenik," *END J*, No. 31 (Dec.–Jan. 1987–88), p. 9; *Komsomolskaya Pravda*, June 25, 1988, Prince Papers; "Pulling No Peace Punches," *Sanity* (Aug. 1988), pp. 20–21.

159. Interview with Rob Prince, July 27, 1999; Prince to Gordie Flowers, May 20, 1988, Prince to Mark Solomon, Sept. 8, 1988, and *Komsomolskaya Pravda*, July 1988, Prince Papers; Jane Mayes, "Trust Group Changes Name," *END J*, No. 28–29 (Summer 1987), p. 6.

160. Rob Prince, "A Sketch History of the World Peace Council," pp. 10–11, and Prince to Gus Newport, Apr. 7, 1988, Prince Papers.

161. Prince to Michael Myerson, Mar. 31, Apr. 15, and Apr. 4, 1988, Prince Papers.

162. See, for example: Johnny Baltzersen to Chandra and Pakaslahti, Sept. 13, 1988, Miklos Barabas and Ilona Sebestyen to European Affiliates of the WPC, Sept. 20, 1988, "Statement of the Executive of the Canadian Peace Congress," Sept. 24, 1988, Michael Myerson and Mark Solomon to Chandra and Pakaslahti, Oct. 26, 1988, Cay Sevon to WPC, Oct. 28, 1988, Urban Karlsson to Chandra and Pakaslahti, Nov. 5, 1988, and Sam Goldbloom to Chandra, Nov. 23, 1988, Prince Papers.

163. Rob Prince, "WPC Secretariat" (June 15, 1988), Rob Prince, "Some Thoughts Concerning the Bureau Meeting of the WPC (Geneva 19–22 November, 1988)," Chandra to Dear Friend, Dec. 28, 1988, and Pakaslahti to Dear Friend, Jan. 12, 1989, Prince Papers.

164. Interview with Rob Prince, July 27, 1999; "Footnotes," Solomon Papers; Rob Prince, "Concerning the Diaries" (Dec. 12, 1996), Prince Papers.

165. Judith Winther to Dear Friends, Dec. 3, 1985, IPCC Records; Jon Grepstad to members of the END Liaison Committee, Feb. 15, 1986, and Niels Gregersen to members of the END Liaison Committee, Feb. 6, 1986, IPB Records; David McReynolds to CSSR Ministry of Internal Affairs, June 16, 1986, New Accession, WRL Records; Mient Jan Faber to Charter 77, Nov. 19, 1987, Folder 760, IKV Records, A.

166. Lynne Jones, "Time for a Change," *END J*, No. 28–29 (Summer 1987), p. 19; interview with Colin Archer, June 1, 1999; Howard Clark to Stephen Brown, Apr. 1, 1987, Box 445, WRI Records; interview with Mary Kaldor, June 7, 1999; *Guardian*, July 20, 1987; Wim Bartels, "Glasnost, Perestroika and the Peace Committees of Eastern Europe," *PM* 3 (Oct.–Nov. 1987): 44–45.

167. Howard Clark to David McReynolds, Aug. 3, 1987, Box 517, WRI Records; minutes from WRL International Task Force meeting of Aug. 17, 1987, New Accession, WRL Records.

168. Interview with Martin Butcher, July 19, 1999; Howard Clark to David McReynolds, Mar. 4, 1987, Box 517, and minutes of the WRI executive committee meeting, May 15–18, 1987, Box 446, WRI Records.

169. "Hungarian Peace Delegaton Signs END Appeal" (July 18, 1987), Folder 761, IKV Records, A; interview with Bruce Kent, June 7, 1999; interview with Martin Butcher, July 19, 1999; Joanne Landy, "Official Peace Councils and the Non-aligned Peace Movement," *PDN* 3 (Winter–Spring 1988): 3–4, 9–11; Joanne Landy to members and friends of END, Sept. 1987, Box 510, WRI Records.

170. Minutes of the END Liaison Committee meeting of Oct. 3–4, 1987, IPB Records; Miklos Barabas to members of the END Liaison Committee, Oct. 17, 1988, Folder 761, IKV Records, A; interview with Martin Butcher, July 19, 1999.

171. "Information über einige politisch-operative Aspekte der Vorbereitung des 6. Konvents der 'Bewegung für Europäische Nukleare Abrüstung' vom 15. 7. bis 19. 7. 1987 in Coventry/Grossbritannien" (July 10, 1987), Bl. 132–42, "Information über einige politisch-operative Aspekte des 6. Konvents der Bewegung für 'Europäische Nukleare Abrüstung' vom 15. Juli bis 19. Juli 1987 in Coventry/Grossbritannien" (Sept. 1987), Bl. 28–34, and "Information über den 7. Konvent der Bewegung für 'Europäische Nukleare Abrüstung' (END) vom 29. Juni bis 2. July 1988 in Lund/Schweden," Bl. 13–17, Folder 5351, AKG, HA XX, ZA, Stasi Records.

172. Bartels, "Glasnost," p. 44; "Information über den 7. Konvent der Bewegung für 'Europäische Nukleare Abrüstung' (END) vom 29. Juni bis 2. Juli 1988 in Lund/Schweden," Bl. 13–17, Folder 5351, AKG, HA XX, ZA, Stasi Records; Ivan Fiala to Dear Friends, July 1988, and Czechoslovak Peace Committee to Gunnar Lassinantti, July 20, 1988, Folder 762, IKV Records, A.

Chapter 16

Epigraph: Gorbachev, *A Time*, p. 100.

1. Ibid., pp. 59–60, 103, 109, 160, 270, 276; Chernyaev, *My Six Years*, p. 59.

2. Kull, *Burying Lenin*, p. 15; "Transcript of Conversation Between Mikhail S. Gorbachev and Francois Mitterrand," in Zubok, Nielsen, and Grant, eds., *Understanding*.

3. Gorbachev, *Memoirs*, p. 238; Chernyaev, *My Six Years*, p. 126; Gorbachev, *Perestroika*, pp. 138, 146.

4. Interview with Rob Prince, July 27, 1999; Thompson, "Ends and Histories," pp. 16–17.

5. Oberdorfer, *Turn*, pp. 108–9; Evangelista, *Unarmed Forces*, p. 26.

6. For a fuller discussion of the Russell-Einstein Appeal and its background, see Wittner, *Resisting the Bomb*, pp. 5–7.

7. Shevardnadze, *Future*, p. 46; Arbatov, "America," p. 315.

8. Evangelista, *Unarmed Forces*, p. 374; interview with Joseph Rotblat, July 12, 1990.

9. The information about Gorbachev's speeches came from one of Gorbachev's speechwriters, Alexei Pankin. Comments of Anatoly Chernyaev in Tannenwald, ed., *Understanding*, p. 198; interview with Mary Kaldor, June 7, 1999.

10. "The WPC Must Change," *END J*, No. 36 (Oct. 1988–Jan. 1989), p. 22. See also Tairov, "From New Thinking," pp. 43–46.

11. *WP*, May 22, 1988.

12. Comments of Georgy Shaknazarov in Tannenwald, ed., *Understanding*, p. 193; Gorbachev, *Memoirs*, pp. 167–68; Evangelista, *Unarmed Forces*, pp. 253–54; Chernyaev, *My Six Years*, p. 29.

13. English, *Russia*, pp. 193–222; Arbatov, *System*, pp. xiii, 349; Risse-Kappen, *Zero Option*, p. 106; interview with Frank von Hippel, Aug. 22, 1999.

14. See, for example: Gorbachev, *A Time*, pp. 75, 244; Gorbachev, *Moratorium*.

15. Gorbachev, *Memoirs*, p. 171; comments of Anatoly Chernyaev in Tannenwald, ed., *Understanding*, pp. 77–79.

16. Matlock, *Autopsy*, pp. 73–74; Shevardnadze, *Future*, p. 71.

17. Gorbachev, *Nuclear Disarmament*; Gorbachev, *Memoirs*, p. 429; Gorbachev, *Perestroika*, p. 230.

18. Savel'yev and Detinov, *Big Five*, pp. 92–93. See, also: Comments of Sergei Tarasenko, Nikolai Detinov, Oleg Grinevsky, Vladimir Slipchenko, and Anatoly Chernyaev in Tannenwald, ed., *Understanding*, pp. 113–14, 120–27, 136–40; Chernyaev, *My Six Years*, pp. 45–46; Schell, "Gift of Time," p. 50.

19. Oberdorfer, *Turn*, pp. 158–60; Evangelista, *Unarmed Forces*, p. 291; Gorbachev, *Memoirs*, pp. 184–85; Shevardnadze, *Future*, pp. 48–51.

20. Cortright and Pagnucco, "Limits," pp. 169–70; "Rough Notes of Meeting with Mikhail Gorbachev, Soviet Embassy, Geneva, November 19, 12:45–1:30 PM" (1985), Box 80, Series G, SANE Records; interview with Robert Musil, July 20, 1998.

21. Interview with Bernard Lown, July 6, 1999; interview with Gene LaRocque, Aug. 17, 1999.

22. Gorbachev to Kendall, July 5, 1985, in Gorbachev, *A Time*, pp. 179–81; Gorbachev to von Mueller, von Hippel, Boserup and Neild, Nov. 16, 1987, in *F.A.S. Public Interest Report* 41 (Feb. 1988): 15; "O priglashenii v SSRR delegatsii katolicheskoi organizatsii Pax Christi" (1987), f. 89, op. 11, d. 52, Central Committee of the CPSU Records; interview with Frank von Hippel, Aug. 22, 1999.

23. Interview with Frank von Hippel, Aug. 22, 1999; interview with Judy Lipton, July 31, 1999; interview with Bernard Lown, July 6, 1999.

24. Interview with Werner Rümpel, May 20, 1999; interview with Nigel Young, May 15, 1999; interview with Rob Prince, July 27, 1999.

25. Gorbachev, *Perestroika*, p. 154; Gorbachev to von Hippel et al., Nov. 16, 1987, in *F.A.S. Public Interest Report* 41 (Feb. 1988): 15.

26. Gorbachev, *A Time*, pp. 136–38; interview with Michael Foot, June 19, 1998.

27. Gorbachev, *A Time*, pp. 114–15; Gorbachev, *Memoirs*, pp. 420–23.

28. Gorbachev, *Memoirs*, p. 296; Chernyaev, *My Six Years*, p. 94; Sakharov, *Moscow*, pp. 3, 5; Anatoly Chernyaev's notes of the conference with heads of department of the Central Committee (Dec. 16, 1986), in Zubok, Nielsen, and Grant, eds, *Understanding*.

29. Gorbachev, *Memoirs*, pp. 296–97; von Hippel, "Recollections," pp. 329–31; interview with Jeremy Stone, July 22, 1999; Sakharov, *Moscow*, pp. 45–46.

30. "Crackdown on 'Moscow Trust Group,'" p. 14; "Trust Group Under Pressure," p. 5; U.S. Department of State, *Soviet Antipacifism*, pp. 5–10.

31. Palazchenko, *My Years*, p. 81; Gorbachev, *Memoirs*, p. 186; Chernyaev, *My Six Years*, p. 44.

32. Evangelista, *Unarmed Forces*, p. 256; Dobrynin, *In Confidence*, pp. 624–26; Gorbachev, *Memoirs*, p. 200.

33. Dyson, *Sink the Rainbow!*; King, *Death*; Chris Masters, "L'affaire Greenpeace," *BAS* 46 (Mar. 1990): 29; "International Law? Qu'est-ce que c'est?" *Greenpeace* 13 (July–Aug. 1988): 4.

34. Paolo Farinella and Venance Journe, "Justice for Vanunu," *BAS* 47 (Jan.–Feb. 1991): 14; *NYT*, Nov. 25, 1999.

35. Jan Minkiewicz to Dear Friends, Mar. 3, 1986, Folder 756, and "Jiri Dienstbier's Open Letter," Folder 760, IKV Records, A; Richard Bloom, "Provoking peace in Poland," *END J*, No. 28–29 (Summer 1987), p. 5; Hana Marvanová, "Degrees of Freedom," *END J*, No. 37 (1989), pp. 26–28; "Jazz Section latest," *END J*, No. 27 (May–June 1987), p. 4; "Passport to exile," *END J*, No. 34–35 (Summer 1988), pp. 28–29.

36. "Stellungnahme zur erfolgten Einladung an die DDR zur Teilnahme an 6. END-Konvent in Coventry/Grossbritannien, 15.–19.7.1987" (Mar. 23, 1987), Bl. 22–23, and "Information über den 7. Konvent der Bewegung für 'Europäische Nukleare Abrüstung' (END) vom 29. Juni bis 2. Juli 1988 in Lund/Schweden," Bl. 13–14, Folder 5351, AKG, HA XX, ZA, Stasi Records; Frana, Krejci, and Pagac, *Peace Movement*, p. 21.

37. Thatcher, *Downing Street*, pp. 578, 580–82.

38. Crozier, *Free Agent*, pp. 277–79.

39. David Cortright to Ronald Reagan, Apr. 23, 1987 and Frederick J. Ryan, Jr. to Cortright, June 25, 1987, Box 87, Series G, SANE Records; Nelson C. Ledsky to Paul Schott Stevens, May 17, 1988, and Stevens to Ryan, n.d., "Soviet Union—1987–1988 (USSR) Memos-Letters-Cables-Reports/Articles (2 of 7)" Folder, Ledsky Files; Cortright and Pagnucco, "Limits," p. 169.

40. "Peace Movement Captures Summit Spotlight," *SW/Freeze Focus* 27 (Spring 1988): 3; interview with Robert Musil, July 20, 1998.

41. John O. Pastore to Reagan, June 26, 1986, Case File 408615, Pastore to Howard H. Baker, Jr., Marybel to Sandy Warfield, Aug. 4, 1987, and Chris McCarrick, "For Files" (Aug. 10, 1987), Case File 497232, and William F. Martin to Ryan, Nov. 8, 1985, Case File 342471, PR 007, Subject File, WHORM Records.

42. *Boston Globe*, Oct. 20, 1985; interview with Jeremy Stone, July 22, 1999; Sakharov, *Moscow*, pp. 69–70.

43. Landais-Stamp and Rogers, *Rocking*, p. 112; Christopher Hitchins, "The Rainbow Warrior Bombing," *Greenpeace Quarterly* 12 (Jan.–Mar. 1987): 23; Clements, *Back From the Brink*, p. 139.

44. James A. Abrahamson to Charles Z. Wick, June 17, 1985, "WORLDNET [5]" Folder, Lenczowski Files; Wick to Ed Djerijian, Dec. 11, 1985, and Djerijian to

Wick, Dec. 17, 1985, Case File 370706, FO 005–03, and John M. Poindexter to Wick, Dec. 19, 1985, Case File 380082, FG 298, Subject File, WHORM Records.

45. Victor F. Weisskopf, "In Memoriam—Olof Palme," *BAS* 42 (May 1986): 49; interview with Mient Jan Faber, Aug. 7, 1986.

46. E. P. Thompson, "Notes on China: for END and CND IC" (May 6, 1985), Kaldor Papers; Liu Yumin, "Symposium on Peace and Security in the Asian-Pacific Region Held in Beijing," *Peace*, No. 12 (Dec. 1988), p. 2.

47. Gorbachev, *Memoirs*, pp. 434–35; Landais-Stamp and Rogers, *Rocking*, pp. 129–30.

48. Gray, *Briefing Book*, p. 14; John Prados, "China's 'New Thinking' on Nuclear Arms," *BAS* 45 (June 1989): 33–35.

49. Praful Bidwai, "'Pakistani Bomb' Claim Stokes Regional Tension," *END J*, No. 27 (May–June 1987), p. 3; Geoffrey Aronson, "Join the Club," *NT* 6 (Jan.–Feb. 1988): 12, 14.

50. Kevin P. Clements, "Kiwi No-Nuke Policy at Risk," *BAS* 48 (Jan.–Feb. 1992): 7–8; Siracusa, "Peace Movements," p. 10; Lange, *Nuclear Free*, p. 148; Landais-Stamp and Rogers, *Rocking*, p. 134; Clements, *Back From the Brink*, pp. 145, 221.

51. Hans M. Kristensen, "Neither Confront nor Deny," *BAS* 48 (Mar. 1992): 3; "U.S. Rejects Pacific Nuclear-Free Zone."

52. "Putting the Squeeze on the Pacific," *Greenpeace Quarterly* 12 (Oct.–Dec. 1987): 4; interview with Max Kampelman, July 21, 1999.

53. William Arkin, "Canada—Too Close for Comfort," *BAS* 42 (Mar. 1986): 5; Jorgen Dragsdahl, "No Defense Against Allies," *END J*, No. 34–35 (Summer 1988), pp. 27–28; "Kiwi Disease in Europe," *Greenpeace* 13 (July–Aug. 1988): 5; Kristensen, "Neither Confront nor Deny," pp. 3–4.

54. Steele, "Spain Says 'Yes, but,'" p. 3; Mariano Aguirre, "Spain: no Deal," *END J*, No. 31 (Dec.–Jan. 1987–88), p. 3; Ben Webb, "Stealing a Base," *END J*, No. 32 (Feb.–Mar. 1988), p. 12.

55. Savvas Paritsis, "The Promises PASOK Could Not Keep," *END J*, No. 26 (Feb.–Mar. 1987), pp. 12–13; William M. Arkin, "Greece's Balancing Act," *BAS* 43 (Mar. 1987): 11–12.

56. Solomon, "Scandinavia"; Michael Ross, "Nuclear Allergy Catches On," *Greenpeace* 14 (Mar.–Apr. 1989): 19; Benn Webb, "Split END," *NT* 6 (Sept.–Oct 1988): 7.

57. Clements, "Kiwi No-Nuke Policy," p. 7; Landais-Stamp and Rogers, *Rocking*, p. 152; Clements, *Back From the Brink*, pp. 142–45.

58. Goldblat, "Multilateral Arms Control," pp. 398–401; Fry, "South Pacific."

59. Michael Bedford and Megan van Frank, "US Bases in the Philippines: A Clouded Future," *DDA* 1 (Sept. 1988): 7; Ross, "Nuclear Allergy," p. 19; Michael Ross, "'Nuclear Allergy' Spreads," *NT* 7 (Jan.–Feb. 1989): 7.

60. Nicholas Dunlop to supporters of Parliamentarians Global Action, n.d., author's possession; Weisskopf, "In memorium," p. 49; Wiberg, *Provstopp nu!*, p. 21.

61. Robert Linhard, "Response to Gang of 6 on Nuclear Testing" (Feb. 28, 1986),

in Blanton, ed., *White House*, p. 229; "Sweden Unveils Six Nation Proposal at SSD III," *World Federalist* 13 (Summer–Fall 1988): 2.

62. Perkovich, *India's Nuclear Bomb*, pp. 261–69, 276, 279, 446; interview with Michael Foot, June 19, 1998; Palazchenko, *My Years*, p. 28; "India Offers World Order Action Plan," *World Federalist* 13 (Summer–Fall 1988): 2.

63. Interview with Caspar Weinberger, July 21, 1998; interview with Richard Perle, June 29, 1999.

64. McFarlane to Bob Pearson, Sept. 9, 1985, in Blanton, ed., *White House*, p. 189; Thomas Thorne to the secretary of state, July 26, 1985, and Central Intelligence Agency, "Gorbachev: Steering the USSR Into the 1990s" (July 1987), pp. 19–20, in Zubok, Nielsen, and Grant, eds., *Understanding*.

65. Reagan, *An American Life*, pp. 612–17; Gorbachev to Reagan, June 10, 1985, "U.S.S.R. General Secretary Gorbachev (8590683–8590713)" Folder, Box 40, Head of State File, Executive Secretariat, NSC Records; Shevardnadze, *Future*, p. 81.

66. Genscher, *Rebuilding*, p. 201; Thatcher, *Downing Street*, p. 463.

67. *Neues Deutschland*, July 24, 1987, in *USSR Seeks Worldwide Double Zero*, pp. 1–3; interview with Peter Steglich, May 21, 1999.

68. Evangelista, *Unarmed Forces*, pp. 170–72, 270; interview with Eric Fersht, Sept. 9, 1989; Cortright, *Peace Works*, pp. 209–10.

69. Evangelista, *Unarmed Forces*, p. 271; interview with Bernard Lown, July 6, 1999.

70. Cortright, *Peace Works*, p. 209; comments of Nikolai Detinov in Tannenwald, ed., *Understanding*, p. 151; Gorbachev, *A Time*, pp. 191–92.

71. Matlock, *Autopsy*, p. 90; comments of Edward Rowny and Jack Matlock in Tannenwald, ed., *Understanding*, pp. 152–54; interview with Rozanne Ridgway, Sept. 17, 1999; Oberdorfer, *Turn*, p. 166; George P. Shultz to Charles McC. Mathias Jr., Feb. 24, 1986, Case File 371329, ND 018, Subject File, WHORM Records.

72. "A Comprehensive Nuclear Test Ban NOW!" Box 522, WRI Records; interview with Dottye Burt, June 29, 1987; *International Physicians*, p. 7.

73. Seaborg, *Stemming*, p. 244; Schrag, *Global Action*, pp. 50–52; William Epstein, "New Hope for a Comprehensive Test Ban," *BAS* 42 (Feb. 1986): 29.

74. Gorbachev, *Perestroika*, p. 153; Evangelista, *Unarmed Forces*, pp. 271–72; Chernyaev, *My Six Years*, p. 45; Warner and Shuman, *Citizen Diplomats*, p. 65.

75. Chernyaev, *My Six Years*, p. 56; Velikhov, "Chernobyl," p. 162; Evangelista, *Unarmed Forces*, pp. 273–76; *WP*, Feb. 27, 1987.

76. "Stop Testing: Freeze Program Focus for 1986," *Freeze Focus* (Summer 1986), p. 1; "Fall Campaign to Press for Test Ban Now" (Sept. 19, 1986), Box 3, Series D, PA Records; Cathy Cevoli, "Putting It On the Line in Nevada" and "CTB Resolutions," *NT* 4 (July–Aug. 1986): 36–38; "WILPF Response to Soviet Extension of Testing Moratorium" (Aug. 20, 1986), Sweet Files, WILPF Records.

77. Gallup, *GP: Public Opinion 1986*, p. 108; "Broad National Support for Nuclear Test Ban" (June 11, 1986), PSR Records.

78. Some administration officials, especially career staffers in ACDA and in the intelligence community, were considerably more enthusiastic about the monitoring

project. Schrag, *Listening*; interview with Frank von Hippel, Aug. 22, 1999; interview with Thomas Cochran, Aug. 23, 1999; interview with Christopher Paine, Sept. 14, 1999.

79. Interview with Christopher Paine, Sept. 14, 1999; interview with Thomas Cochran, Aug. 23, 1999; Martin Hamburger, "Arms Control Takes the Hill," *NT* 5 (Sept.–Oct. 1986): 9; *NYT*, Aug. 19, 1986; Coalition for a CTB to U.S. Representatives, Apr. 14, 1988, PSR Records.

80. Reagan, *An American Life*, p. 660; Dante Fascell et al. to Ronald Reagan, Mar. 21, 1986, Case File 396878, ND 018, Subject File, WHORM Records; "Legislators Ask President to Join A-Testing Moratorium, Negotiate Test Ban Treaty" (Dec. 18, 1986), PSR Records.

81. Adelman, *Great Universal Embrace*, pp. 31–32; Schrag, *Global Action*, pp. 55, 58; NSDD 247, in Simpson, ed., *National Security Directives*, pp. 725–26; Palazchenko, *My Years*, pp. 85–86; Shultz, *Turmoil*, p. 895.

82. Peace groups estimated that there were approximately 4,130 nuclear protest arrests in the United States during 1988, with over 2,800 of them occurring at the Nevada test site. Robert Schaeffer, "Mass Arrests in Nevada," *NT* 5 (May–June 1987): 7; "Thousands Reclaim Nevada Test Site," *SW/FREEZE Focus* 27 (Summer 1988): 4; "In King's Footsteps," *NVA* 3 (Apr.–May 1989): 18.

83. Carolyn Cottom to SANE/Freeze executive committee, Mar. 24, 1988, Cottom to Dear Friends, Apr. 4, 1988, and Cottom to Dear Friends, Apr. 29, 1988, Box 3, Series D, PA Records; minutes of the meeting of the executive committee, Peace Education Division, AFSC, Apr. 23, 1988, Box 3, Series I, AFSC Records; Evangelista, *Unarmed Forces*, pp. 287–88.

84. "Meeting with Soviet Leader in Geneva" (ca. Aug. 1985), "Summit [Geneva 1985] (7)" Folder, Lenczowski Files; interview with Robert McFarlane, July 21, 1999; Oberdorfer, *Turn*, p. 141.

85. Deaver, *Behind the Scenes*, p. 120; interview with Richard Wirthlin, Oct. 6, 1999; McFarlane, *Special Trust*, p. 200.

86. Reagan, *An American Life*, p. 633.

87. Adelman, *Great Universal Embrace*, pp. 268–70; John Isaacs, "November— Critical Month for Arms Control," *BAS* 41 (Sept. 1985): 3–4; Oberdorfer, *Turn*, p. 168; Reagan, *An American Life*, pp. 620–21.

88. Palazchenko, *My Years*, pp. 41–42; Dobrynin, *In Confidence*, pp. 569, 585–87; Oberdorfer, *Turn*, pp. 136–37; Gorbachev, *Memoirs*, pp. 403, 405.

89. Oberdorfer, *Turn*, p. 144; Reagan, *An American Life*, pp. 635–36.

90. Oberdorfer, *Turn*, pp. 148–49; Shultz, *Turmoil*, p. 603; Gorbachev, *Memoirs*, pp. 406–8; Reagan, *An American Life*, p. 639.

91. Shultz, *Turmoil*, p. 605; Gorbachev, *Memoirs*, p. 411; Matlock, *Autopsy*, p. 92.

92. Reagan, *An American Life*, p. 707; Adelman, *Great Universal Embrace*, p. 125; comments of George Shultz in Wohlforth, ed., *Witnesses*, pp. 16–17; interview with Frank Carlucci, July 20, 1999; interview with Max Kampelman, July 21, 1999.

93. Chernyaev, *My Six Years*, pp. 52–53; comments of Anatoly Chernyaev and Nikolai Detinov in Tannenwald, ed., *Understanding*, pp. 112–13, 115, 221–22; Gorbachev, *Memoirs*, p. 405; Dobryinin, *In Confidence*, p. 592.

94. Interview with Max Kampelman, July 21, 1999.

95. Gorbachev to Reagan, Dec. 24, 1985, and Reagan to Gorbachev, Feb. 6 and 22, 1986, in Reagan, *An American Life*, pp. 646–49, 655–58.

96. Shultz, *Turmoil*, pp. 699–705; Nitze, *From Hiroshima*, pp. 421–23; Adelman, *Great Universal Embrace*, pp. 64–65; comments of Jack Matlock, Edward Rowny, and Robert McFarlane in Tannenwald, ed., *Understanding*, pp. 128–29, 132–33, 143–44.

97. Gates, *From the Shadows*, p. 404.

98. Shultz, *Turmoil*, pp. 717–18; Adelman, *Great Universal Embrace*, pp. 280–86; Nitze, *From Hiroshima*, pp. 423–24; Talbott, *Master*, pp. 304–5.

99. Reagan, *An American Life*, pp. 665–66; Nitze, *From Hiroshima*, pp. 425–26; comments of Ed Rowny in Tannenwald, ed., *Understanding*, p. 143; Shultz, *Turmoil*, pp. 719–20.

100. Talbott, *Master*, p. 315; Regan, *For the Record*, pp. 338–41.

101. Interview with Richard Wirthlin, Oct. 6, 1999; Shultz, *Turmoil*, pp. 755–56; Adelman, *Great Universal Embrace*, pp. 26–27, 37.

102. "Anatoly Chernyaev's Notes from the Politburo Meetings" (Oct. 8, 1986), in Zubok, Nielsen, and Grant, eds., *Understanding*. See also Gorbachev, *Memoirs*, p. 415.

103. Gorbachev, *Memoirs*, p. 415; "Anatoly Chernyaev's Notes from the Politburo Session" (Oct. 4, 1986), in Zubok, Nielsen, and Grant, eds., *Understanding*; comments of Anatoly Chernyaev in Wohlforth, ed., *Witnesses*, pp. 15, 166.

104. Shultz, *Turmoil*, p. 771; Gorbachev, *Memoirs*, p. 418; Dobrynin, *In Confidence*, p. 621.

105. Shultz, *Turmoil*, p. 772; Oberdorfer, *Turn*, pp. 202–3; Palazchenko, *My Years*, p. 57.

106. Reagan, *An American Life*, pp. 675–77; Nitze, *From Hiroshima*, pp. 429, 432–33; Shultz, *Turmoil*, pp. 758–59; Adelman, *Great Universal Embrace*, pp. 52–64.

107. Shultz, *Turmoil*, pp. 759–61; Talbott, *Master*, p. 325; "National Security Decision Directive Number 250" (Nov. 3, 1986), "JCS Response—NSDD 250, 12/19/86 [1 of 3]" Folder, Box 92186, Linhard Files.

108. Oberdorfer, *Turn*, p. 183; Shultz, *Turmoil*, pp. 776–78; Reagan, *An American Life*, pp. 684–85.

109. Thatcher, *Downing Street*, pp. 471–72; interview with Ruud Lubbers, May 27, 1999; *Guardian*, Nov. 17, 1986.

110. Reagan, *My Turn*, p. 346; interview with Richard Wirthlin, Oct. 9, 1999; Oberdorfer, *Turn*, p. 203; Adelman, *Great Universal Embrace*, pp. 69, 318.

111. Chernyaev, *My Six Years*, p. 87; "Anatoly Chernyaev's Notes from the Politburo Session" (Oct. 30, 1986), in Zubok, Nielsen, and Grant, eds., *Understanding*; Dobrynin, *In Confidence*, p. 622

112. Interview with Richard Wirthlin, Oct. 6, 1999; Reagan, *My Turn*, pp. 109, 319–20; Cortright, "Peace Movement Role," p. 87.

113. Oberdorfer, *Turn*, p. 244; Gates, *From the Shadows*, p. 421.

114. "European Publics Increasingly Credit Moscow, Narrowing U.S. Lead Over Soviets: Perception of Arms Control Effort Crucial" (July 9, 1987), Case File

475427SS, and Wick to Frank Carlucci, May 27, 1987, Case File 512514, FG 298, Subject File, WHORM Records.

115. Shultz, *Turmoil*, p. 876; Stone, *"Every Man,"* pp. 228–30.

116. Evangelista, *Unarmed Forces*, pp. 328–29; Sakharov, *Moscow*, pp. 15–26; interview with Frank von Hippel, Aug. 22, 1999; von Hippel, "Reducing the Confrontation" (Feb. 15, 1987), in von Hippel, *Citizen Scientist*, pp. 134–36; Stone, *"Every Man,"* pp. 233–34.

117. Gorbachev, *Perestroika*, p. 153; "Anatoly Chernyaev's Notes from the Politburo Sessions of February 23 and 26, 1987," in Zubok, Nielsen, and Grant, eds., *Understanding*.

118. Shultz, *Turmoil*, p. 905; Thatcher, *Downing Street*, pp. 477, 771; interview with Frank Carlucci, July 20, 1999; Blechman and Fisher, *Silent Partner*, pp. 109–14; Risse-Kappen, *Zero Option*, pp. 124–38.

119. Interview with Rozanne Ridgway, Sept. 17, 1999; Blechman and Fisher, *Silent Partner*, pp. 113–14; Berger, *Cultures*, p. 134; Adelman, *Great Universal Embrace*, pp. 204–9, 248; Risse-Kappen, *Zero Option*, p. 169.

120. Palazchenko, *My Years*, pp. 68, 74; Savel'yev and Detinov, *Big Five*, pp. 132–33, 136–38.

121. Shultz, *Turmoil*, pp. 984–95; interview with Rozanne Ridgway, Sept. 17, 1999.

122. Oberdorfer, *Turn*, p. 265; Matlock, *Autopsy*, pp. 150–52; Palazchenko, *My Years*, p. 78.

123. Gates, *From the Shadows*, p. 423.

124. Interview with Frank Carlucci, July 20, 1999; Powell, *My American Journey*, p. 361; Shultz, *Turmoil*, p. 1005.

125. Reagan, *An American Life*, p. 699; Shultz, *Turmoil*, p. 1013.

126. "Anatoly Chernyaev's Notes from the Politburo Session" (Dec. 17, 1987), in Zubok, Nielsen, and Grant, eds., *Understanding*.

127. "Appeasement Is as Unwise in 1988 as in 1938," Case File 563762, ND 018, Subject File, WHORM Records; Shultz, *Turmoil*, pp. 899–900, 988, 990–91, 1007–8, 1081–85; Paul C. Warnke, "INF Treaty a Good Start," *BAS* 44 (Mar. 1988): 18; comments of George Shultz in Wohlforth, ed., *Witnesses*, p. 105.

128. Interview with David Cohen, July 19, 1999; Adelman, *Great Universal Embrace*, p. 249.

129. Joseph Rotblat, "British Fret about 'Vulnerability,'" *BAS* 44 (Mar. 1988): 20–22; Thatcher, *Downing Street*, pp. 771–75, 784–85; Crozier, *Free Agent*, pp. 284–86.

130. Thomas Risse-Kappen, "Odd German Consensus Against New Missiles," *BAS* 44 (May 1988): 16; Gorbachev, *Memoirs*, p. 443; Savel'yev and Detinov, *Big Five*, p. 138.

131. Kaldor, "We Got the Idea"; "After INF: What Next?" *END J*, No. 31 (Dec.–Jan., 1987–88), p. 28; Bruce Kent, "Letter to US Peace Activists," *NVA* 5 (June 1988): 9; "Molesworth Celebration" (1987), IPB Records.

132. "Peace Movement Captures Summit," p. 3; "Testimony on the INF Treaty Before Senate Foreign Relations Committee," *SW/Freeze Focus* 27 (Summer 1988): 7; Evangelista, *Unarmed Forces*, p. 314; "Peace Activist Witnesses INF Weapons Destruction in the USSR," *SW/Freeze Focus* 27 (Fall 1988): 4.

133. Shultz, *Turmoil*, p. 989; Cortright, "Peace Movement Role," pp. 86–87; Talbott, *Master*, pp. 366–67, 370; Oberdorfer, *Turn*, p. 266; comments of Frank Carlucci in Wohlforth, ed., *Witnesses*, p. 56.

134. Reagan told a group of SDI supporters in the spring of 1988 that "it is the funding that is delaying it. . . . Congress has to fund." Interview with Frank Carlucci, July 20, 1999; "Meeting between the President and Conservative Leaders, April 12, 1988," "Weyrich Conservative Event 4/12/88" Folder, Range Files.

135. Comments of Anatoly Chernyaev in Wohlforth, ed., *Witnesses*, p. 49; Powell, *My American Journey*, pp. 369, 375.

136. Talbott, *Master*, pp. 382–83; Shultz, *Turmoil*, p. 1086; Gorbachev to Reagan, Sept. 20, 1988, in Reagan, *An American Life*, pp. 716–19.

137. Oberdorfer, *Turn*, pp. 298–99.

138. Comments of Vladimir Slipchenko in Tannenwald, ed., *Understanding*, pp. 171–72; Matlock, *Autopsy*, p. 142; *NYT*, Dec. 8, 1988.

139. "Minutes of the Meeting of the Politburo of the Central Committee of the Communist Party of the Soviet Union" (Dec. 27–28, 1988), in "On the Eve," p. 24.

140. Powell, *My American Journey*, p. 341; interview with Michael Foot, June 19, 1998; Adelman, *Great Universal Embrace*, p. 294.

141. Chernyaev, *My Six Years*, pp. 103–4; comments of Frank Carlucci in Wohlforth, ed., *Witnesses*, pp. 46–47.

142. Stone, *"Every Man,"* pp. 237–38; interview with Helen Caldicott, Feb. 27, 1999; Evangelista, *Unarmed Forces*, p. 375.

Chapter 17

Epigraph: *Izvestia*, Oct. 2, 1990, in *CDSP* 42 (Nov. 7, 1990): 12.

1. Interview with William Sloane Coffin, Jr., Oct. 19, 1989; Gallup, *GP: Public Opinion 1990*, p. 54; Gallup, *GP: Public Opinion 1991*, p. 52.

2. Interview with Helen Caldicott, Feb. 27, 1999; Mary Kaldor, "Past, Present, Future," *END J*, No. 37 (1989), p. 2; Meg Beresford, "The World as We Knew It," *Sanity* (July–Aug. 1990), inside back cover.

3. Interview with Mary Kaldor, June 7, 1999; Kaldor, ed., *Europe*, pp. 1–3, 199–200; Faber to Citizens Assembly, July 25, 1989, Kaldor Papers; Jiří Dienstbier, "The Helsinki Process 'from Below,'" *END J*, No. 37 (1989), insert; "Assembly in Prague Moves to Shape Europe's Future," *NT* 8 (Winter 1990–91): 8.

4. "Grassroots Action," *SANE/FREEZE News* 30 (Spring 1991): 1; "The Loyal Opposition," *Greenpeace* 16 (Mar.–Apr. 1991): 7; *NT* 8 (Winter 1990–91); Marjorie Thompson and Gary Lefley, "The Choice for CND" (June 1991), Reel 2, CND (B) Records, AMM.

5. Minutes of IPCC meeting of Apr. 5, 1991, IPB Records; minutes of special executive and management committee meeting, Oct. 22, 1990, Reel 2, CND (B) Records, AMM; interview with Martin Butcher, July 19, 1999; interview with Bruce Kent, June 7, 1999.

6. *IPB Annual Report, 1990–91*, p. 1; Tracey Cohen, "Covering the Peace Movement," *NT* 9 (Summer 1991): 24–26.

7. *NYT*, Dec. 21, 1992; interview with Colin Archer, June 1, 1999.

8. Newman, "Surviving," pp. 53–54; interview with Martin Butcher, July 19, 1999; interview with William Peden, June 19, 1998; "membership figures," CND Records, L.

9. E. P. Thompson, letter to the editor, *Guardian*, July 12, 1991; Norman Moss, "Unilateral Disarmament—Labor's Lost Love," *BAS* 45 (Oct. 1989): 9–11; Shaw, *Labour Party*, pp. 187–88.

10. Minutes of the CND executive committee meeting of May 4, 1989, Reel 2, CND (B) Records, AMM; *IPB Annual Report, 1991–92*, p. 9; *IPB Annual Report, 1992–93*, p. 27.

11. Interview with David Cohen, July 19, 1999; *IPB Annual Report, 1991–92*, p. 9; interview with Charles Johnson, Aug. 3, 1999; interview with Daryl Kimball, July 21, 1998; "Downsizing SANE/FREEZE," *NT* 8 (Autumn 1990): 7.

12. Bernard Lown to Dear Friend, Apr. 30, 1993, author's possession; interview with Bernard Lown, July 6, 1999.

13. Interview with Colin Archer, June 1, 1999; Mary Kaldor and Andy Roberts to Dear Friend, Dec. 1, 1989, author's possession; minutes of the END Liaison Committee meeting of Apr. 25–26, 1992, and "The Brussels Convention and What Next?" (Sept. 1992), IPB Records.

14. *Kansan Uutiset*, Jan. 12, 1989, Solomon Papers; *Information*, Dec. 24–25, 1988 and *Land og Folk*, Mar. 3, 1989, Prince Papers; interview with Rob Prince, July 27, 1999.

15. *Kansan Uutiset*, Jan. 12, 1989 and *Uusi Suomi*, Jan. 13, 1989, Solomon Papers; Pakaslahti to Dear Friend, Jan. 12, 1989, *Huvudstadsbladet*, Jan. 13, 1989, *Land og Folk*, Jan. 20, 1989, *Canadian Tribune*, Feb. 26, 1990, "Some Brief Comments on the Recent Decisions of the Ad Hoc Commission on Rules and Regulations of the World Peace Council" (Jan. 13, 1989), Werner Rümpel et al. to Romesh Chandra, Mar. 1, 1989, Brian Henderson to Chandra, Feb. 2, 1989, and Michael Myerson et al. to Chandra, Feb. 9, 1989, Prince Papers.

16. "Remarks of Johannes Pakaslahti, General Secretary . . . 3 December 1989," and "Speech by Johannes Pakaslahti, 7.02.90," Prince Papers.

17. Interview with Mark Solomon, July 8, 1999; Rob Prince, "The Ghost Ship of Lonnrotinkatu," *PM* 8 (May–June 1982): 17, 29.

18. Interview with Edith Ballantyne, June 1, 1999; Günther Drefahl to Dear friends, Jan. 12, 1990, and Bärbel Schindler-Saefkow to Dear Friends, Mar. 9, 1990, Prince Papers; "The GDR Peace Council Will Reconstitute Itself!" *Information*, No. 1/90, p. 1; "German Peace Council of the GDR Newly Set Up," *Information*, No. 2/90, p. 1; Libby Frank to members and friends of the U.S. Peace Council, Sept. 2, 1992, U.S. Peace Council Records.

19. Rob Prince, "Following the Money Trail," *PM* 8 (Nov.–Dec. 1992): 20; Prince, "Ghost Ship," p. 17; interview with Rob Prince, July 27, 1999.

20. Keith Richardson, "Make the Local Trident Connection," *Campaign* (Oct. 1993), p. 3; Phil Jones, "Spotted and Stopped!" *Campaign* (Aug. 1992), p. 1; Janet Williamson, "Thousands March as Trident Arrives on the Clyde," *Campaign* (Nov. 1992), p. 1.

21. "Winds of Peace" (Aug. 10, 1991), Reel 2, CND (B) Records, AMM; "Campagne 'Pas de nouveaux missiles,'" *La Feuille de Liaison du CNAPD*, No. 105 (Apr.–May 1989), pp. 4–18; Mario Birkholz, "German Physicists: 1,700 Tests Are Enough," *BAS* 45 (June 1989): 37.

22. *IPB Annual Report, 1992–93*, pp. 23, 25.

23. "Next, a Nuclear-free Weapons Lab," *BAS* 46 (Jan.–Feb. 1990): 3–4; interview with Charles Johnson, Aug. 3, 1999.

24. "After the Cold War," *Mobilizer* 8 (Summer 1990): 9; interview with Robert Musil, July 20, 1998; William Lanouette, "The Boom in B-2 Bashing," *BAS* 46 (Sept. 1990): 8–9.

25. Ira Shorr, "Peace Economy Campaign Heats Up" and Kevin Martin, "1991 National Congress—Chicago Style!" *SANE/FREEZE News* 30 (Winter 1991–92): 1, 7.

26. "Downsizing," p. 7; "Crisis," *NT* 8 (Spring 1990): 16.

27. Interview with Robert Musil, July 20, 1998; interview with Daryl Kimball, July 21, 1998; interview with Christopher Paine, Sept. 14, 1999; "What Next?" *NT* 7 (Mar.–Apr. 1989): 18–21; "Weapons Plants Ups and Downs," *NT* 8 (Summer 1990): 9; "How Nuclear Weapons Production Brings Peace and Environmental Activists Together," *SANE/FREEZE News* 28 (Fall–Winter 1989): 6.

28. William Sloane Coffin, Jr. to Gorbachev, Nov. 30, 1988, and "SANE/ FREEZE Hails Soviet Gesture of Restraint" (Apr. 7, 1989), Box 6, Series D, PA Records.

29. John Isaacs, "Washington Report," *BAS* 45 (June 1989): 3; John Isaacs, "Hawks Keep Selling War," *BAS* 46 (Mar. 1990): 5.

30. Shawna Moos, "NFZs Lose Ground," *NT* 8 (Autumn 1990): 8–9; interview with Charles Johnson, Aug. 3, 1999.

31. Antonio Rubens Britto de Castro et al., "Brazil's Nuclear Shakeup: Military Still in Control," *BAS* 45 (May 1989): 25; interview with Amina Rasul-Bernardo, Apr. 18, 2002; Bruce Birchard, "U.S. Out of the Philippines!" *NT* 8 (Summer 1990): 21.

32. Paul Routledge, "Protest in India," *NT* 7 (Mar.–Apr. 1989): 6; *IPB Annual Report, 1992–93*, p. 24.

33. "Palau Fights the United States," *NT* 8 (Summer 1990): 48.

34. Committee for a New Korea Policy, "South Korean Voices for Peace," author's possession; "National Democratic Alliance."

35. "China's Nuclear Tests" (1995), www.antenna.nl/wise/438/4335.html.

36. Jacquelyn Walsh and William Arkin, "Nuclear Free Seas," *Greenpeace* 15 (Jan.–Feb. 1990): 13; Shawna Moos, "Nuclear Navy Challenged," *NT* 8 (Autumn 1990): 6–7; William Arkin, "The Folly of Trident," *Greenpeace* 15 (Mar.–Apr. 1990): 12–13.

37. "Now for the Hard Part," *Sanity* (July–Aug. 1990), p. 4; minutes of the END Liaison Committee meetings of Mar. 31–Apr. 1 and June 9–10, 1990, IPB Records.

38. "European, U.S. Peace Leaders Coordinate Efforts," *Quaker Service Bulletin* 70 (Spring 1989): 2; Ken Fleet to END Liaison Committee, June 22, 1989, IPB records; Anna Gyorgy, "Europe Needs Green," *NVA* 6 (Oct.–Nov. 1989): 3–6.

39. Interview with Sergei Kapitza, June 28, 1990; Miranda Spencer, "Nonviolent

Activism Takes Root," *NT* 9 (Spring 1991): 31–32; Ilukhina and Pavlova, "Totalitarianism," pp. 5–6; Ilukhina, "Re-birth," pp. 4–5.

40. "Democratic Russia" (1990), author's possession; Ilukhina, "Re-birth," pp. 11–12; Tairov to END Liaison Committee, Jan. 1, 1992, Box 510, WRI Records.

41. Ilukhina, "Russian Peace Society"; interview with Ruzanna Ilukhina, May 22, 1991; Ilukhina and Pavlova, "Totalitarianism," p. 8; Vitalii I. Goldanskii, "Russia's 'Red-Brown' Hawks," *BAS* 49 (June 1993): 24.

42. Ruth Sormová to Mient Jan Faber, May 23, 1989, Folder 762, and Faber to Julianna Màtrai, Mar. 15, 1989, Folder 761, IKV Records, A.

43. Beverly Woodward, "Changing Poland," *NVA* 6 (Oct.–Nov. 1989): 13; Milan Nikolic and Sonja Licht, "Détente from Below," *NT* 8 (Spring 1990): 27–32.

44. Thompson, "Ends and Histories," pp. 23–24; Evangelista, *Unarmed Forces*, pp. 249–50.

45. Reflecting on these events years later, the German Peace Council's Werner Rümpel, long a dedicated Communist party member, remarked bitterly: "Ultimately, the peace movement is responsible for winning the fight against Communism. It was the winner over Communism!" Galtung, "Europe 1989," pp. 101–5; Randle, *People Power*, pp. 3–67; Tairov, "From New Thinking," p. 45; interview with Werner Rümpel, May 20, 1999.

46. Thompson, "Ends and Histories," pp. 23–24; Faber, "Good Morning," pp. 142–45; Stephen Brown, "A Pacifist in Command," *Sanity* (June 1990), p. 21; "Assembly in Prague," p. 8.

47. Evangelista, *Unarmed Forces*, p. 250; "An Interview with Jaroslav Sabata," pp. 207–8; *NYT*, Dec. 16, 1989.

48. Interview with Frank von Hippel, Aug. 22, 1999; interview with Thomas Cochran, Aug. 23, 1999; Fetter et al., "Gamma-Ray Measurements," p. 828; John Isaacs, "Washington Report," *BAS* 45 (Sept. 1989): 4.

49. Pat Hunt, "Cracks in the Ice," *END J*, No. 37 (1989), pp. 24–25.

50. Joergen Dragsdahl, "European Activists Face New Challenges," *NT* 8 (Aug. 1990): 41; Andrei Melville to Ken Coates and Ken Fleet, Aug. 24, 1989, Jacek Paliszewski and Hieronim Kubiak to Ken Coates, Oct. 9, 1989, and Katrin Zielke, "Official application for a membership from Arche" (ca. spring 1990), IPB Records.

51. Tairov to Sylvie Montrant, Feb. 15, 1990, "Preparations of the X END Convention in Moscow," and "END Convention News" (July 7, 1990), IPB Records; Tair Tairov, "Moscow. Convention-91," Box 510, WRI Records.

52. Minutes of the END Liaison Committee meeting of Aug. 13, 1991, and Coordinating Committee to Soviet Preparatory Committee, Aug. 22, 1991, IPB Records; comments by Igor Ovchinnikov and Ivan Timofeev at public forum in Albany, NY, Sept. 21, 1993; interview with Colin Archer, June 1, 1999.

53. "Campaigning for CTB," *NT* 7 (Jan.–Feb. 1989): 10; "U.S. Endorsers of the International Comprehensive Test Ban Campaign" (Apr. 14, 1989), Box 3, Series D, PA Records.

54. "Anti-Nuclear Arrests," *NVA* 7 (June 1990): 18; "Perspectives," *CND Today* (Summer 1993), p. 12.

55. Geoffrey Aronson, "Global Conference Keeps Test Ban Hopes Alive," *NT* 8

(Winter 1990–91): 43–45; Schrag, *Global Action*, pp. 77–81, 89–90, 132–35; minutes of the U.S. CTBT Coalition meeting of Jan. 8, 1990, Box 3, Series D, PA Records.

56. Peter Zheutlin, "Nevada, U.S.S.R.," *BAS* 46 (Mar. 1990): 10–11; James Lerager, "Kazakhs Stop Soviet Testing," *NT* 8 (Autumn 1990): 12–15; "Semipalatinsk-Nevada"; *NYT*, July 22, 1989.

57. Lerager, "Kazakhs," pp. 13–15; Evangelista, *Unarmed Forces*, p. 352; Zheutlin, "Nevada, U.S.S.R.," pp. 11–12.

58. Ilukhina, "Rebirth," p. 6; *Izvestia*, Apr. 24, 1990, in *CDSP* 42 (May 30, 1990): 30; *Izvestia*, Oct. 2, 1990, in *CDSP* 42 (Nov. 7, 1990): 12.

59. "Novaya Zemlya: Journey into the Soviet Nuclear Testing Zone," *Greenpeace Magazine* 16 (Jan.–Feb. 1991): 13–16.

60. "The Soviet Union's Nevada Movement," *Greenpeace* 15 (Mar.–Apr. 1990): 4; *Los Angeles Times*, Apr. 1, 1990; "Physicians Act Globally for Test Ban," *NT* 8 (Summer 1990): 3.

61. "Physicians Act Globally," p. 3; Peter Zheutlin, "Nuclear Victims of the World Unite," *BAS* 46 (Sept. 1990): 3; Evangelista, *Unarmed Forces*, p. 356; Daniel Young, "Thousands in Alma-Ata Demand Test Ban," *PSR Reports* 10 (Summer 1990): 1.

62. "Time to Stop Testing," *Campaign* (Oct. 1991), p. 2; Gary Lefley, "The Paris Conference and Perspectives for Campaigning" (1992), and "Autumn Campaign 1992" (1992), Reel 2, CND (B) Records, AMM; Solange Fernex, "From a Moratorium to a Comprehensive Test Ban Treaty," *CND Today* (Winter 1992), p. 9; *IPB Annual Report, 1990–1991*, p. 3.

63. "Municipal Defense," *Greenpeace* 15 (July–Aug. 1990): 6.

64. *IPB Annual Report, 1991–92*, pp. 2, 4–5, 9; "IPB" (May 1992), author's possession; interview with Bruce Kent, June 7, 1999.

65. Gallup, *GP: Public Opinion 1991*, pp. 143, 183; Gallup, *GP: Public Opinion 1990*, pp. 121, 126.

66. Gallup, *GP: Public Opinion 1989*, p. 237; Gallup, *GP: Public Opinion 1990*, p. 176.

67. Oberdorfer, *Turn*, pp. 411, 432; von Weizsäcker, *From Weimar*, p. 292; Gallup, *GP: Public Opinion 1991*, p. 51.

68. Elworthy, *In the Dark*, p. 46; Hastings and Hastings, eds., *Index . . . 1988–89*, pp. 265–66; Bruce Kent and Michael Szabo, "Peace and Democracy for the New Decade," *Sanity* (July–Aug. 1990), pp. 18–19; Fernex, "From a Moratorium," p. 9; Utley, *French*, p. 152.

69. Gallup, *GP: Public Opinion 1990*, p. 92; Gallup, *GP: Public Opinion 1991*, pp. 145, 203.

70. Adelman, *Great Universal Embrace*, p. 344; Perkovich, *India's Nuclear Bomb*, p. 322.

71. Gallup, *GP: Public Opinion 1990*, p. 92; Tannenwald, *Nuclear Taboo*, pp. 352–54; Mil Rai and Declan McHugh, "Tackling Nuclear Proliferation," *CND Today* (Summer 1992), p. 11; Gallup, *GP: Public Opinion 1991*, pp. 42, 59.

72. *IPB Annual Report, 1992–93*, p. 6.

Chapter 18

Epigraph: Bush and Scowcroft, *A World*, p. 229.

1. *NYT*, Oct. 12, 1992; interview with James Baker III, Sept. 15, 1999.

2. Oberdorfer, *Turn*, p. 329; Beschloss and Talbott, *At the Highest Levels*, pp. 8–11.

3. Oberdorfer, *Turn*, pp. 331–32; Bush and Scowcroft, *A World*, pp. 12–13; "The Administration View of Gorbachev and Arms Control," *CLW Newsletter* (Summer 1989), p. 2.

4. Beschloss and Talbott, *At the Highest Levels*, pp. 27–28; interview with Rozanne Ridgway, Sept. 17, 1999.

5. Blumenthal, *Pledging*, pp. 284–319; Duane Shank, "Message From the Director," *SW/Freeze Focus* 27 (Fall 1988): 2; *NYT*, Sept. 26, 1988; Oberdorfer, *Turn*, pp. 330–31.

6. Beschloss and Talbott, *At the Highest Levels*, pp. 17–18, 24–25; Bush and Scowcroft, *A World*, p. 564.

7. Bush and Scowcroft, *A World*, p. 40; Matlock, *Autopsy*, pp. 195–97.

8. Shevardnadze, *Future*, p. 98; Gorbachev, *Memoirs*, pp. 496–97.

9. Palazchenko, *My Years*, p. 126; Matlock, *Autopsy*, p. 197; Gorbachev, *Memoirs*, p. 197.

10. Fitzwater, *Call the Briefing!*, pp. 230–31; Beschloss and Talbott, *At the Highest Levels*, pp. 29, 31, 50; Blumenthal, *Pledging*, p. 327.

11. Thatcher, *Downing Street*, pp. 771–76; Thomas Risse-Kappen, "Will NATO Settle for Kohl Cuts?" *BAS* 45 (May 1989): 9–10; Elworthy, *In the Dark*, p. 6; Genscher, *Rebuilding*, pp. 232–33, 238–39.

12. Thatcher, *Downing Street*, pp. 784–87; Beschloss and Talbott, *At the Highest Levels*, p. 36; Genscher, *Rebuilding*, p. 245.

13. Thomas Risse-Kappen, "Odd German Consensus Against New Missiles," *BAS* 44 (May 1988): 14–16; Thatcher, *Downing Street*, pp. 786–88; Bush and Scowcroft, *A World*, pp. 58–59; Elworthy, *In the Dark*, pp. 27–41; Genscher, *Rebuilding*, pp. 237, 244–45.

14. Baker later remarked that the Bush administration "wanted to get out ahead of the power curve, as far as Gorbachev was concerned, on European public opinion." Baker, *Politics*, pp. 82–92; Powaski, *Return*, p. 84; interview with James Baker III, Sept. 15, 1999.

15. Genscher, *Rebuilding*, pp. 257–58; Thatcher, *Downing Street*, pp. 788–89.

16. Beschloss and Talbott, *At the Highest Levels*, pp. 138–39, 207; Bush and Scowcroft, *A World*, p. 265.

17. Bush and Scowcroft, *A World*, p. 130; Fitzwater, *Call the Briefing!*, pp. 246–48; Oberdorfer, *Turn*, pp. 335, 371.

18. Dobrynin, *In Confidence*, p. 626.

19. Palazchenko, *My Years*, pp. 69, 146–47; Evangelista, *Unarmed Forces*, p. 379; Evangelista, "Transnational Relations," pp. 166–67; Beschloss and Talbott, *At the Highest Levels*, pp. 117–19; Baker, *Politics*, p. 151.

20. Beschloss and Talbott, *At the Highest Levels*, pp. 143–45; Bush and Scowcroft, *A World*, p. 160.

21. Transcript of Malta conference, in "At Historic Crossroads," pp. 229–36; Palazchenko, *My Years*, pp. 155–56; Fitzwater, *Call the Briefing!*, p. 256.

22. Gorbachev, *Memoirs*, p. 512; Beschloss and Talbott, *At the Highest Levels*, pp. 155, 157.

23. Beschloss and Talbott, *At the Highest Levels*, pp. 203–4, 370–73; Palazchenko, *My Years*, pp. 221, 258, 273; Dobrynin, *In Confidence*, pp. 525–26; Baker, *Politics*, p. 204.

24. Beschloss and Talbott, *At the Highest Levels*, pp. 402–7; Palazchenko, *My Years*, p. 286.

25. Nolan, *An Elusive Consensus*, p. 32; Powaski, *Return*, pp. 118–23.

26. Shevardnadze, *Future*, p. 216; Palazchenko, *My Years*, p. 371; Gorbachev, *Memoirs*, p. 624; Bush and Scowcroft, *A World*, p. 514.

27. Beschloss and Talbott, *At the Highest Levels*, pp. 445–46; Taylor, *Breaking*, p. 3; Baker, *Politics*, p. 526; interview with Thomas Graham, Jr., Aug. 23, 1999.

28. Bush and Scowcroft, *A World*, p. 545.

29. "An Unexpected Calling," p. 19; Powell, *My American Journey*, pp. 540–41; interview with Thomas Cochran, Aug. 23, 1999.

30. William M. Arkin et al., "Nuclear Weapons Headed for the Trash," *BAS* 47 (Dec. 1991): 17–18; R. Jeffrey Smith, "A Believer No More," *WP National Weekly Edition* (Dec. 22–29, 1997), pp. 6–10; *WP*, Jan. 12, 1997; "An Unexpected Calling," p. 19.

31. John Isaacs, "Short Memories," *BAS* 46 (Nov. 1990): 4; John Isaacs, "Conference fallout," *BAS* 46 (Dec. 1990): 4–5; John Isaacs, "Congress Seizes Bush's Weapons Initiative," *BAS* 47 (Nov. 1991): 3–4; John Isaacs, "Give Bush Some Credit," *BAS* 48 (July–Aug. 1992): 14.

32. John Isaacs, "Clinging to the Cold War," *BAS* 46 (Jan.–Feb. 1990): 10; John Isaacs, "What a Difference a Year Makes," *BAS* 47 (Jan.–Feb. 1991): 11; John Isaacs, "First Shots in the Counter-revolution," *BAS* 47 (May 1991): 3–4; interview with James Baker III, Sept. 15, 1999.

33. "SANE/FREEZE Hails Soviet Gesture of Restraint" (Apr. 7, 1989), and "Transcript of Gorbachev Remarks, London, April 7, 1989," Box 6, Series D, PA Records.

34. Interview with Daryl Kimball, July 21, 1998; "SANE/FREEZE Contributes to Initial Victory Against Nuclear Weapons," *SANE/FREEZE News* 28 (Summer 1989): 4; Russell Mokhiber, "Crime in the Suites," *Greenpeace* 14 (Sept.–Oct. 1989): 14–15; Isaacs, "What a Difference," p. 11; interview with Christopher Paine, Sept. 14, 1999; Magraw, "United States," p. 118.

35. Comments of Anatoly Chernyaev in Tannenwald, ed., *Understanding*, pp. 33–34; Palazchenko, *My Years*, p. 197; Shevardnadze, *Future*, p. 208.

36. Shevardnadze, *Future*, pp. 58, 65; Chernyaev, *My Six Years*, p. 245; Gorbachev, "Nobel Lecture," p. 282.

37. "Clips," *NT* 8 (Autumn 1990): 6; Schrag, *Global Action*, p. 187; "Notes and Comment," p. 31.

38. Evangelista, *Unarmed Forces*, pp. 354–57; "Latest Soviet Test Raises Row," *BAS* 47 (Jan.–Feb. 1991): 47; Chernyaev, *My Six Years*, pp. 306–7; "Disarmament Watch," *BAS* 48 (Jan.–Feb. 1992): 48.

39. William Lanouette, "One Step Forward, Two Steps Back," *BAS* 46 (Apr. 1990): 4; John Isaacs, "Testing Treaties Slip Through," *BAS* 46 (Dec. 1990): 5.

40. Schrag, *Global Action*, pp. 2–3, 144–46, 152; Jim Wurst, "On Hold," *NT* 9 (Spring 1991): 8–10; "Just Curious," *BAS* 47 (July–Aug. 1991): 47.

41. Interview with Peter Bergel, Aug. 3, 1999; interview with Charles Johnson, Aug. 3, 1999; interview with Robert Musil, July 20, 1998; Gephardt and Kopetski to members of the House of Representatives, Nov. 12, 1991, and Bob Tiller et al. to Representatives, Oct. 29, 1991, Kimball Papers.

42. Interview with Christopher Paine, Sept. 14, 1999; John Isaacs, "The Senate That Can Say No," *BAS* 48 (Oct. 1992): 6–7; Tom Zamora-Collina, "Nuclear Weapons Take a Dive," *BAS* 48 (Dec. 1992): 6–8; *Los Angeles Times*, Aug. 4, 1992.

43. Zamora-Collina, "Nuclear weapons," p. 6; Magraw, "United States," p. 119; *Los Angeles Times*, Sept. 25, 1992; interviews with Christopher Paine, Sept. 14, 1999 and Feb. 26, 2002; interview with James Baker III, Sept. 15, 1999; "Statement by the President" (Oct. 2, 1992), Reel 2, CND (B) Records, AMM.

44. Adelman, *Great Universal Embrace*, p. 338; Thatcher, *Downing Street*, p. 811.

45. Tannenwald, *Nuclear Taboo*, pp. 458–62; Nolan, *An Elusive Consensus*, pp. 74–75, 111; Bush and Scowcroft, *A World*, p. 463; Baker, *Politics*, p. 359; Powell, *My American Journey*, pp. 485–86; Arkin, "Calculated Ambiguity," pp. 3–13.

46. Palazchenko, *My Years*, pp. 372–74; Sagdeev, *Making*, p. 326.

47. Powaski, *Return*, p. 153; *NYT*, Jan. 4, 1993.

48. Dunbar Lockwood, "On Clinton's Calendar," *BAS* 49 (Jan.–Feb. 1993): 6–8; John Isaacs, "Bush, Clinton Put Future on Hold," *BAS* 48 (Nov. 1992): 4; Clinton and Gore, *Putting People First*, pp. 42–43, 134, 136, 229; Burt Glass, "Reagan/Bush Era Draws to a Close," *SANE/FREEZE News* 31 (Winter 1992–93): 1.

49. Powaski, *Return*, pp. 136–44; Baker, *Politics*, pp. 658–65.

50. Baker, *Politics*, p. 589; "Argentina and Brazil Renounce Nuclear Weapons," *Disarmament Newsletter* 9 (Feb. 1991): 9; David Albright, "South Africa Comes Clean," *BAS* 49 (May 1993): 3–4.

51. Powaski, *Return*, p. 154; Daryl Kimball to the author, Oct. 31, 2002; Perkovich, *India's Nuclear Bomb*, pp. 293–94.

52. Arkin, "Calculated Ambiguity," pp. 7, 16; Utley, *French*, p. 152; Taylor, *Breaking*, p. 3.

53. Albright, "South Africa," pp. 3–4; interview with Amina Rasul-Bernardo, Apr. 18, 2002; *NYT*, Nov. 25, 1992.

54. Lamare, "Growth," p. 484; Clements, "Kiwi No-Nuke Policy at Risk," *BAS* 48 (Jan.–Feb. 1992): 8; Lange, *Nuclear Free*, p. 9.

55. Tom A. Zamora, "Moruroa-torium," *BAS* 48 (June 1992): 11; Bruno Barrillot, "French Finesse Nuclear Future," *BAS* 48 (Sept. 1992): 22–24; "Greenpeace Hails French Nuclear Testing Moratorium," *Greenpeace* 17 (July–Aug.–Sept 1992): 1.

56. Perkovich, *India's Nuclear Bomb*, p. 317; Arkin, "Calculated Ambiguity," p. 10.

57. Baker, *Politics*, pp. 596–97; Powaski, *Return*, pp. 156–57.

58. "The Soviet Union's Nevada Movement," *Greenpeace* 15 (Mar.–Apr. 1990): 4; Beschloss and Talbott, *At the Highest Levels*, p. 222.

59. Bengt Danielsson, "French Slam 'Open Door' on Greenpeace," *BAS* 47 (Mar. 1991): 6–7; Pat Hunt, "Cracks in the Ice," *END J*, No. 37 (1989), p. 23.

60. "Hinweise im Zusammenhang mit der Vorbereitung zum 8. Konvent der Bewegung für 'Europäisch Nukleare Abrüstung' (END)" (June 22, 1989), Bl. 1–3, Folder 5351, AKG, HA XX, ZA, Stasi Records; interview with Werner Rümpel, May 20, 1999.

61. "IDDS Director Briefs Bush Team," *DDA* 2 (Dec. 1989): 1; interview with Randall Forsberg, July 7, 1999.

62. Interview with Bernard Lown, July 6, 1999.

63. Interview with Sheila Jones, June 19, 1998; *NYT*, Oct. 12, 14, and 16, 1992.

64. Gorbachev felt heartsick at Bush's statement, and remarked charitably that "the end of the Cold War is our common victory." Beschloss and Talbott, *At the Highest Levels*, p. 464.

65. "Ten Minutes to Midnight," *BAS* 46 (Apr. 1990): 3; "A New Era," *BAS* 47 (Dec. 1991): 3.

Chapter 19

Epigraph: Interview with Jeremy Stone, July 22, 1999.

1. "Back to Basics," *Campaign* (Apr. 1993), p. 2; "General Secretary's Report: April Council 1994," CND (B) Records, AMM; "Adi Roche," *CND Today* (Winter 1994), p. 8; Bruce Kent, "Nuclear Disarmament: How Far Have We Got?" *CND Today* (Spring 1995), p. 16.

2. *Daily Gazette* (Schenectady, NY), Aug. 6, 1993; "Membership Statistics" and "membership figures," CND Records, L.

3. "Ilukhina and Pavlova, "Totalitarianism," p. 8; Pavlova, "Hundred Years," pp. 153–54; *IPB Annual Report 1994–95*, pp. 21–22.

4. *IPB Annual Report 1993–94*, p. 11; "END Maastricht Seminar" (July 1993), Box 508, WRI Records; interview with Colin Archer, June 1, 1999.

5. Gary Lefley, "CND Annual Conference 1993," *Campaign* (Dec.–Jan. 1993), p. 9; John Ainslee, "Drive Out Trident, 23 October," *Campaign* (Oct. 1993), p. 1; "Labour Vote to Scrap Trident," *CND Today* (Winter 1993), p. 3; "Campaign for Nuclear Disarmament Annual Report 1994" (1995), Reel 4, CND (B) Records, AMM.

6. Gary Lefley, "Nuclear Weapon . . ." *CND Today* (Summer 1994), p. 23; "Blueprint for a Nuclear Weapon-free World," *CND Today* (Summer 1994), pp. 10–11.

7. Janet Bloomfield, "We Will Prevail," *Campaign* (Dec.–Jan. 1994–95), pp. 1–2; "Campaign for Nuclear Disarmament Annual Report 1994" (1995), Reel 4, CND (B) Records, AMM; Janet Bloomfield, "1995—A Year of Choice," *CND Today* (Spring 1995), p. 2.

8. *PA* 32 (Spring 1993): 1; "Nuclear Abolition Now!" (1996) and "Peace Action and Peace Action Education Fund Annual Reports 1996," author's possession; Polner and O'Grady, *Disarmed*, pp. 13–18.

9. McNamara, *In Retrospect*, pp. 337–46; *WP*, Jan. 16, 1994; Gray, *Briefing Book*, p. 11.

10. Butler, *From Nuclear Deterrence*; *WP*, Jan. 12, 1997; R. Jeffrey Smith, "A Believer No More," *WP National Weekly Edition*, Dec. 22–29, 1997.

11. "3,000 in Bordeaux (France) Against Lab Testing," *Peace-Letter* (Apr. 1996), p. 3; *IPB Annual Report 1994–95*, pp. 15, 18–21.

12. *East Turkestan Information Bulletin* 3 (June 1993), www.caccp.org/et/etib3_3. html.

13. Barbara Dudley to Greenpeace supporters, Oct. 1994, author's possession; "Working Together for a Nuclear Weapon-Free World," IPB Records.

14. "Declaration of the World Assembly for Peace" (Oct. 28, 1996) and "ipb" (1994), author's possession.

15. *IPB Annual Report, 1993–94*, p. 3; interviews with Colin Archer, May 31, June 1, 1999; interviews with David Krieger and Alice Slater, May 14, 1999.

16. Interviews with David Krieger and Alice Slater, May 14, 1999; Janet Bloomfield, "Abolition 2000" (Mar. 2, 1996), IPB Records; "Abolition 2000 Statement," author's possession.

17. Schell, "Gift of Time," p. 22; "The Canberra Commission on the Elimination of Nuclear Weapons," Kimball Papers.

18. "Statement on Nuclear Weapons by International Generals and Admirals" (Dec. 5, 1996), Kimball Papers; "Generals Speak Out for Nuclear Disarmament," *Peacework*, No. 270 (Jan. 1997), pp. 3–7.

19. Janet Bloomfield, "Abolition 2000" (Mar. 2, 1996), IPB Records; Hastings and Hastings, eds., *Index . . . 1995–96*, p. 278.

20. *IPB Annual Report 1994–95*, p. 19; *Peace-Letter* (Apr. 1996), p. 3.

21. Perkovich, *India's Nuclear Bomb*, p. 354. See also Hastings and Hastings, eds., *Index . . . 1995–96*, pp. 278–80.

22. *Public Attitudes*, p. 27; Gallup, *GP: Public Opinion 1999*, p. 234.

23. Jenkins-Smith, Barke, and Herron, *Public Perspectives*, pp. 76, 78, 86.

24. *Public Attitudes*, p. 20; Perkovich, *India's Nuclear Bomb*, p. 357; Gallup, *GP: Public Opinion 1996*, pp. 192–93.

25. Sagdeev, *Making*, p. 326; Kortunov, "Russia," p. 88; Evangelista, *Unarmed Forces*, pp. 11, 372–73; Pry, *War Scare*, pp. xii–xiii; Tannenwald, *Nuclear Taboo*, p. 378; Taylor, *Breaking*, pp. 17–18.

26. Lewis, "United Kingdom," pp. 99, 115; Malcolm Reid, "CND Rejects Latest Government Attempt to Justify UK nuclear Weapons Proliferation," *Campaign* (Dec.–Jan. 1993–94), pp. 1, 7.

27. Utley, *French*, pp. 153–56; Perkovich, *India's Nuclear Bomb*, pp. 334, 353–55, 360–61, 370–84; Tannenwald, *Nuclear Taboo*, pp. 378–79.

28. Tannenwald, *Nuclear Taboo*, p. 399; Schell, "Gift of Time," p. 19; Powaski, *Return*, p. 207.

29. Dewes and Green, "World Court Project"; *IPB Annual Report, 1993–94*, p. 5; *IPB Annual Report, 1994–95*, pp. 4–5; interview with Colin Archer, June 1, 1999.

30. Stone, *"Every Man,"* pp. 104–7, 112–14; International Court of Justice, "Legality of the Threat or Use of Nuclear Weapons" (July 8, 1996), Kimball Papers; World Court Project, "World Court Declares Nuclear Weapons Threat and Use Illegal" (July 8, 1996), author's possession.

31. For details, see chapter 18.

32. Nolan, *An Elusive Consensus*, pp. 38–39; *NYT*, Aug. 18, 1993.

33. Interview with Thomas Cochran, Aug. 23, 1999; Frank von Hippel, "Working in the White House on Nuclear Nonproliferation and Arms Control: A Personal Report," *F.A.S. Public Interest Report* 48 (Mar.–Apr. 1995); interview with John Isaacs, July 20, 1999; interview with Katherine Magraw, May 16, 2002.

34. Interview with Anthony Lake, May 14, 2002; Gergen, *Eyewitness*, p. 276; Morris, *Behind*, pp. 244–45; von Hippel, "Working."

35. Baker, "Clinton Defense," pp. 132–33; Burns and Sorenson, *Dead Center*, p. 63; interviews with Christopher Paine, Sept. 14, 1999 and Feb. 26, 2002; Christopher, *Chances*, p. 173.

36. Gergen, *Eyewitness*, pp. 256–57, 264, 324–25; Christopher, *In the Stream*, p. 22.

37. Interview with Anthony Lake, May 14, 2002; interview with John Holum, Apr. 3, 2002; Nolan, *An Elusive Consensus*, pp. 4–5.

38. Nolan, *An Elusive Consensus*, pp. 50–59, 87, 103; Tannenwald, *Nuclear Taboo*, p. 376; Magraw, "United States," pp. 120, 122; *WP*, Sept. 22, 1994.

39. Interview with Anthony Lake, May 14, 2002.

40. *U.S. Nuclear Policy*, p. 4; Christopher, *In the Stream*, p. 338; Powaski, *Return*, pp. 210–14.

41. "Test Ban Signed—Abolition Next," *PSR Monitor* 11 (Dec. 1996): 4; John Isaacs, "Arms Control in 1998: Congress Maintains the Status Quo," *Arms Control Today* 28 (Oct. 1998): 17–18; interview with Anthony Lake, May 14, 2002; FitzGerald, *Way Out There*, p. 492.

42. Nolan, *An Elusive Consensus*, pp. 65–66; Arkin and Mazarr, "Clinton Defense Policy," pp. 59–60, 63; Paine, "Comprehensive Test Ban Treaty," pp. 47–48; Tannenwald, *Nuclear Taboo*, pp. 376–77.

43. Arkin and Mazarr, "Clinton Defense Policy," p. 59; Christopher, *In the Stream*, p. 137.

44. Nolan, *An Elusive Consensus*, pp. 64–65, 75–76; *NYT*, Apr. 17, 1995; interview with John Holum, Apr. 3, 2002.

45. Nolan, *An Elusive Consensus*, pp. 1, 85, 95–96; Christopher, *In the Stream*, pp. 49, 99–100, 245.

46. Christopher, *In the Stream*, pp. 12, 119, 124–25, 157, 162, 213–21; Powaski, *Return*, pp. 223–25.

47. Tannenwald, *Nuclear Taboo*, p. 376; Jacqueline Cabasso, "Deadly Computer Games," *CND Today* (Spring 1995), p. 18; interview with Christopher Paine, Feb. 6, 2002.

48. Interviews with Alice Slater and David Krieger, May 14, 1999; interviews with Robert Musil, July 20, 1998 and Mar. 14, 2002; "Some Differing Views of the NPT," *CND Today* (Summer 1994), p. 14.

49. "From White House Press Briefing, Dec. 4, 1996," *Peacework*, No. 270 (Jan. 1997), p. 5; interview with Katherine Magraw, May 16, 2002.

50. Nolan, *An Elusive Consensus*, pp. 75, 77–81; Magraw, "United States," pp. 120–21.

51. Kimball, *1993 Campaign*, pp. 4–7; interview with Thomas Graham, Jr., Aug. 23, 1999; interview with Christopher Paine, Sept. 14, 1999.

52. *NYT*, July 1, 1993; Von Hippel, "Working in the White House"; *WP*, June 30, 1993.

53. "Coalition Against Nuclear Testing," *CND Today* (Spring 1993), p. 4; Linda Walker, "Test Ban Coalition," *Campaign* (Mar. 1993), p. 5; Janet Williamson, "Don't Carry on Testing!" *Campaign* (Apr. 1993), p. 1.

54. Kimball, *1993 Campaign*, pp. 6–9; *WP*, June 30, 1993; Burt Glass to Anti-Nuclear Testing Activists, Feb. 24, 1993, Box 3, Series D, PA Records; Daryl Kimball, "Summary of Key Events and Citizen Action" (Nov. 26, 1996), Kimball Papers.

55. Von Hippel, "Working"; *WP*, Dec. 14, 1993; interview with Christopher Paine, Feb. 26, 2002; interview with Thomas Cochran, Aug. 23, 1999.

56. Kimball, *1993 Campaign*, p. 10; *Baltimore Sun*, June 29, 1993; *WP*, June 30, July 4, 1993.

57. *NYT*, July 1, 1993; interview with Katherine Magraw, May 16, 2002; *WP*, July 4, 1993; interview with Thomas Graham, Jr., Aug. 23, 1999; interview with John Holum, Apr. 3, 2002.

58. *WP*, July 4, 1993; "Hatfield Hails Decision to Continue Testing Moratorium" (July 3, 1993), Kimball Papers.

59. "Text of Interview with French President Francois Mitterrand" (July 1, 1993), Kimball Papers; *IHT*, July 5, 1993; *Christian Science Monitor*, July 8, 1993; interview with Thomas Graham, Jr., Aug. 23, 1999.

60. *WP*, July 6, 1993; Office of the Press Secretary, the White House, "Comprehensive Test Ban Treaty Chronology During Clinton Administration" (Sept. 23, 1996), Kimball Papers.

61. Interview with Thomas Graham, Jr., Aug. 23, 1999; Daryl Kimball, "Summary of Key Events and Citizen Action" (Nov. 26, 1996), and "Comprehensive Test Ban in Jeopardy," *CTB Clearinghouse Update* (June 1995), Kimball Papers; *IHT*, Aug. 12–13, 1995.

62. Office of the Press Secretary, the White House, "Comprehensive Test Ban Treaty Chronology" (Sept. 23, 1996), Kimball Papers.

63. Martin Jones, "Focus Shifts to France as China Deals Blow to Test Ban Hopes," *Campaign* (Nov. 1993), p. 1; Daryl Kimball, "Summary of Key Events and Citizen Action" (Nov. 26, 1996), and Daryl Kimball, "Summary of PSR's 'Truly' Comprehensive Test Ban Campaign" (Sept. 6, 1995), Kimball Papers.

64. *WP*, July 10, 1995; *IPB Annual Report 1994–95*, p. 2; interview with Alice Slater, May 14, 1999; *NYT*, Sept. 1, 1995; "France to Conduct Eight Nuclear Tests," *CTB Clearinghouse Update* (June 1995), Kimball Papers.

65. Schell, "Gift of Time," p. 44; "France to Conduct Eight Nuclear Tests," *CTB Clearinghouse Update* (June 1995), Kimball Papers.

66. "Nuclear States Agree to Nuclear Free Zone in Pacific" (Oct. 20, 1995), and Daryl Kimball, "Summary of Key Events and Citizen Action" (Nov. 26, 1996), Kimball Papers; *WP*, July 10, 1995.

67. Schaper, "Comprehensive Test Ban Treaty," pp. 12, 16; Office of the Press

Secretary, the White House, "Comprehensive Test Ban Treaty Chronology During Clinton Administration" (Sept. 23, 1996), Kimball Papers; *NYT*, Aug. 11, 1995.

68. Interview with John Holum, Apr. 3, 2002; interview with Daryl Kimball, July 21, 1998; interview with Katherine Magraw, May 16, 2002; *IHT*, Aug. 12–13, 1995; Office of the Press Secretary, the White House, "Statement by the President: Comprehensive Test Ban Treaty" (Aug. 11, 1995), Kimball Papers.

69. Nolan, *An Elusive Consensus*, p. 82; Paine, "Comprehensive Test Ban Treaty," pp. 45, 54–56; interview with Katherine Magraw, May 16, 2002.

70. "Clinton Backs Total Ban on Nuclear Testing!" *CTB Clearinghouse Action Alert* (Aug. 1995), and "Will America Remain a Nuclear Power?" (Aug. 23, 1995), Kimball Papers.

71. "Ground Zero," *Greenpeace Quarterly* 1 (Summer 1996): 16–21; interview with Christopher Paine, Feb. 26, 2002; "A Dove in Hand," *Greenpeace Quarterly* 1 (Fall 1996): 6.

72. Nicola Butler, "Fool If You Think It's Over," and "Half a Million Signatures," *Campaign* (Feb. 1996), pp. 5, 7; "Coalition to Reduce Nuclear Dangers," Kimball Papers.

73. Interview with Anthony Lake, May 14, 2002; "The Comprehensive Test Ban Treaty," *PSR Monitor* (Apr. 1997): 2; *WP*, June 18, 29, 1996; *NYT*, Aug. 16, 1996.

74. *NYT*, Aug. 21, Sept. 11, 1996; Daryl Kimball, "Summary of Key Events and Citizen Action" (Nov. 26, 1996), Kimball Papers.

75. Interview with John Holum, Apr. 3, 2002; Gergen, *Eyewitness*, pp. 316–17.

76. *WP*, Oct. 31, Dec. 7, 1997; *Los Angeles Times*, July 14, 2000; Hall, "Overkill Is Not Dead."

77. *NYT*, Apr. 18, 1997; Isaacs, "Arms Control in 1998," p. 19.

78. Isaacs, "Arms Control in 1998," p. 19; William Epstein, "Where Do We Go From Here?" *Nuclear Disarmament Commentary* 1 (Apr. 1999): 1–2; Daryl Kimball, "Overview of the Status of Major Strategic Nuclear Weapons Debates" (Feb. 22, 1999), Kimball Papers.

79. *WP*, Mar. 22, 1997; Daryl Kimball, "Overview of the Status of Major Strategic Nuclear Weapons Debates" (Feb. 22, 1999), and Daryl Kimball, "Moving Beyond the Stalled START II Process" (Apr. 17, 2000), Kimball Papers.

80. Samuel R. Berger to the Vice President et al., Oct. 10, 1997, Kimball Papers.

81. Isaacs, "Arms Control in 1998," p. 17; Daryl Kimball, "Holding the CTBT Hostage in the Senate: The 'Stealth' Strategy of Helms and Lott," *Arms Control Today* 28 (June–July 1998): 4.

82. Interview with Christopher Paine, Feb. 26, 2002; interview with Katherine Magraw, May 16, 2002; John Isaacs to Jamie Rubin, Mar. 24, 1998, Kimball Papers; *CLW Newsletter* (Mar. 1999); interview with Eugene J. Carroll, Jr., May 11, 2000.

83. Interview with Alice Slater, May 14, 1999; interview with Daryl Kimball, July 21, 1998.

84. Spurgeon Keeny, Jr. et al. to Clinton, Mar. 4, 1998, and Jan. 11, 1999, and Daryl Kimball to Coalition members attending the Richardson meeting, Mar. 18, 1999, Kimball Papers; interview with Christopher Paine, Feb. 26, 2002.

85. Jenny Smith to Interfaith Community, Mar. 4, 1999, Daryl Kimball, "Arms

Control issues in 1999: The CTBT" (Mar. 26, 1998), "Public Advocacy for the CTBT" (Nov. 3, 1998), and "1997–1998 CTBT Campaign: Lessons Learned," Kimball Papers.

86. "Comprehensive Test Ban Treaty Endorsers" (Sept. 15, 1998), Steven G. Raikin to John Podesta, May 1, 1998, and "Eight in Ten Voters Support Senate Approval of Nuclear Test Ban Treaty" (July 29, 1998), Kimball Papers.

87. Los Angeles Times, Jan. 13, 1999; Associated Press wire story of Jan. 19, 1999, "Richardson Says Senate Passage of CTBT 'Critically Important'" (Mar. 2, 1999), and "The Joint Chiefs of Staff Call for Prompt CTBT Ratification" (Mar. 4, 1999), Kimball Papers; interview with Christopher Paine, Feb. 26, 2002.

88. WP, Oct. 14, 1999; Los Angeles Times, Oct. 14, 1999.

89. Jerome Grossman and John Isaacs to CLW supporters, Oct. 22, 1999, author's possession; interview with Christopher Paine, Feb. 26, 2002.

90. Interview with John Holum, Apr. 3, 2002; interview with Daryl Kimball, May 8, 2002.

91. Towell, "Progress"; Isaacs, "Arms Control in 1998," pp. 16–17; FitzGerald, Way Out There, pp. 493–94; Wall Street Journal, Jan. 22, 1999.

92. FitzGerald, Way Out There, pp. 496–98; CLW Newsletter (Mar. 1999); Wade Boese, "Clinton Says No to NMD as Program Lags; Cites Technology Doubts and Foreign Concerns," Arms Control Today 30 (Sept. 2000): 19.

93. See, for example: CLW, "National Missile Defense: Still a Bad Idea Whose Time Has Not Come" (July 15, 1998), Kimball Papers; Sunflower, No. 31 (Dec. 1999).

94. "Draft NGO Plan of Action on National Missile Defense (NMD), February 28, 2000," and "Panel Examines Readiness of National Missile Defense" (May 3, 2000), Kimball Papers; "The Dog Won't Hunt," PA Report 38 (Winter 1999): 7; "Peace Voter Opens Star Wars Debate," PA Report 39 (Sept. 2000): 1.

95. Barbara Boxer to supporters of the Nuclear Test Ban Treaty, June 2001, author's possession; "Scientists Urge Decision to Delay Missile Defense" (July 6, 2000), Kimball Papers; Kimball to the author, Oct. 31, 2002; NYT, July 6, 2000.

96. Carah Ong, "Criticism and Protest Surround Anti-Missile System," Waging Peace Worldwide 10 (Summer 2000): 13; Boese, "Clinton Says No," p. 19.

97. WP, Dec. 7, 1997; Cortright, "Ban the Bomb II," p. 25; interview with Paul Warnke, July 20, 1999.

98. Speech by Randall Forsberg to the Second Nuclear Age Conference, Graduate Center, CUNY, Nov. 18, 2000; interview with Thomas Cochran, Aug. 23, 1999; interview with Jeremy Stone, July 22, 1999.

99. Interview with Christopher Paine, Sept. 14, 1999; interview with Robert Musil, Mar. 14, 2002; interview with John Isaacs, July 20, 1999.

100. Interview with Mary Kaldor, June 7, 1999; interview with William Peden, June 19, 1998; Nicola Butler and Dan Plesch, "Nuclear Policy Under Review in Blair's Britain" (Sept. 5, 1997), Kimball Papers; comments of Rolf Ekeus, Swedish ambassador to the United States, Ultimate Weapons Panel, John Jay College, Apr. 22, 1999.

101. Los Angeles Times, Oct. 28, 1998; Steve Crawshaw, "Goodbye Greens?" www.prospect-magazine.co.uk; Robert Green, "A Fast Track to Zero Nuclear

Weapons: The Middle Powers Initiative and the New Agenda Coalition," *Medicine, Conflict, and Survival* 16 (2000): 28; Camille Grand, "Missile Defense: The View from the Other Side of the Atlantic," *Arms Control Today* 30 (Sept. 2000): 16.

102. Interview with Mary Kaldor, June 7, 1999.

103. Powaski, *Return*, pp. 226–28, 237–38; Daryl Kimball to the author, Oct. 31, 2002.

104. Cohen, *Failed Crusade*, pp. 197–202, 222, 229–32; Powaski, *Return*, pp. 239–42; Alistair Millar, "The Pressing Need for Tactical Nuclear Weapons Control," *Arms Control Today* 32 (May 1992): 10–11.

105. Perkovich, *India's Nuclear Bomb*, pp. 404–21; Kalpana Sharma, "The Hindu Bomb," *BAS* 54 (July–Aug. 1998): 30–31; Jerome Grossman and John Isaacs to CLW supporters, July 1998, author's possession; Gardezi and Sharma, "Introduction," p. 3; Ayesha Khan, "Pakistan Joins the Club," *BAS* 54 (July–Aug. 1998): 34.

106. Perkovich, *India's Nuclear Bomb*, pp. 422–24, 439; *NYT*, May 15, 1998; Jayaraman, "Indian Scientists"; Sharma, "Hindu Bomb," p. 32

107. Bidwai and Vanaik, *New Nukes*, pp. 90–93; Samad, "Nuclear Pakistan"; "Pakistan Action Committee"; "Indian, Pakistani NGOs," pp. 89–91.

108. Green, "A Fast Track"; "Towards a Nuclear Weapon-Free World" (June 9, 1998), Kimball Papers; *Fast Track*, pp. 2–3, 10–13; *Sunflower*, No. 31 (Dec. 1999).

109. David Krieger, "Non-Proliferation Treaty Stays Alive—For Now," *Waging Peace Worldwide* 10 (Summer 2000): 22–23; "NPT Review Conference."

110. *Guardian*, May 22, 2000; Kent to the author, May 21, 2000.

111. Interview with Ole Kopreitan, May 14, 1999; "The Struggle for a Weapons Free World Must Be Strengthened" (1999), author's possession.

112. "Canadians Support Abolition of Nuclear Weapons," *Canadian Peace Research and Education Association Newsletter* (Nov. 1999), p. 3; "News from Abolition 2000," *CND Today* (Summer 1998), p. 17.

113. Interview with Koichi Akamatsu, May 15, 1999; "Gensuikin," www.jca.ax.apc.org/gensuikin/english/main.html.

114. *IPB Activity Report 1997*, p. 30.

115. Interviews with Louise Edge and William Peden, June 19, 1998; "Women Protesting at the Gates of the Military," Aldermaston Women's Peace Camp Records.

116. "Peace Action 1998 Annual Report," author's possession; interview with Thomas Graham, Jr., Aug. 23, 1999; "The Center for Defense Information" (2000), CDI Records.

117. Interview with Jeremy Stone, July 22, 1999; Stone to Boris Yeltsin, July 13, 1999, and Stone to FAS Council Members and FAS Fund Trustees, July 16, 1999, FAS Records.

118. "Listen to the Voices of Sanity," *Inforum*, No. 24 (Spring 1999), pp. 1–3; "Abolition of Nuclear Weapons," *CLW Newsletter* (Mar. 1999); interview with Helen Caldicott, Feb. 27, 1999.

119. "National Academy of Sciences Urges Deep Cuts and New Nuclear Policy" (June 19, 1997), Kimball Papers; Cortright, "Ban the Bomb II," p. 26.

120. David Cortright to Alan Cranston et al., Apr. 7, 1999, Kimball Papers;

comments of Kevin Martin, Director, Project Abolition, to the Second Nuclear Age Conference, Graduate Center, CUNY, Nov. 18, 2000; "Project Abolition," author's possession.

121. Daryl Kimball to the author, Oct. 31, 2002; Iriye, *Global Community*, p. 188.

122. This included Peace Action, which grew to 67,000 members by the year 2000, perhaps because the setbacks to nuclear arms controls in the United States were particularly disturbing. Public address by Gordon Clark, executive director, Peace Action, Albany, NY, July 22, 2000.

123. "Current membership" (Jan. 16, 1998), CND Records, L; interview with Ole Kopreitan, May 14, 1999; interview with Louise Edge, June 19, 1998.

124. "Three Examples of Local Anti-Nuclear Initiatives," *Peacework*, No. 287 (July–Aug. 1998), p. 27; interview with Christopher Paine, Feb. 26, 2002; *IPB Activity Report 1997*, pp. 21–30.

125. Interview with Daryl Kimball, May 29, 2002.

126. *IPB Activity Report 1997*, inside front cover. For its most recent membership and activities, see www.ipb.org.

127. Interview with Colin Archer, June 1, 1999; Bruce Kent, "Castles or Boarding Houses: A New Concept of Security," *Medicine, Conflict and Survival* 16 (2000): 19–20.

128. Comments of Mary Winn Ashford, co-president, IPPNW, Hague Appeal for Peace Conference, the Hague, May 12, 1999; IPPNW, "Nuclear Weapons Convention: A Treaty to Eliminate Nuclear Weapons," author's possession.

129. Interviews with David Krieger and Alice Slater, May 14, 1999; Carah Ong, "Abolition 2000 Update," *Waging Peace Worldwide* 10 (Summer 2000): 12.

130. Tannenwald, *Nuclear Taboo*, pp. 401–2; Cortright, "Ban the Bomb II," p. 26.

131. Interview with Colin Archer, June 1, 1999; Kent, "Castles," p. 22; interview with Bruce Kent, June 7, 1999.

132. Interview with David Krieger, May 14, 1999; *The Hague Agenda for Peace and Justice for the 21st Century*, author's possession.

133. Green, "A Fast Track"; *Fast Track*, pp. 2–3; interview with Alice Slater, May 14, 1999; interview with Colin Archer, June 1, 1999.

134. Newman, "Surviving," pp. 44–45; interview with Thomas Graham, Jr., Aug. 23, 1999; Tannenwald, *Nuclear Taboo*, p. 404.

135. Interview with Ole Kopreitan, May 14, 1999; interview with Edith Ballantyne, June 1, 1999.

136. Interview with Colin Archer, June 1, 1999; speech by Lena Hjelm-Wallem at the Hague Appeal for Peace Conference, the Hague, May 12, 1999.

137. Interview with Helen Caldicott, Feb. 27, 1999.

138. Kent, "Protest and Survive," p. 14; interview with William Peden, June 19, 1998; interview with Hugh Jenkins, June 20, 1998.

139. "Canadians Support," pp. 2–3; "Canadians on Nuclear Weapons," p. 23; "Abolition 2000: A Survey on Nuclear Weapons" (Apr. 1997), Kimball Papers; Hastings and Hastings, eds., *Index . . . 1998–99*, p. 608.

140. Nolan, *An Elusive Consensus*, p. 15; *Public Attitudes*, pp. 17, 24.

141. *Public Attitudes*, p. 19; "Canadians on Nuclear Weapons," p. 21.

142. Hastings and Hastings, eds., *Index . . . 1998–99*, p. 149; Gallup, *GP: Public Opinion 1999*, p. 230.

143. Hastings and Hastings, eds., *Index . . . 1998–99*, pp. 145, 273; interview with John Isaacs, July 20, 1999.

144. *WP*, Jan. 20, 2000; *CLW Newsletter* (Nov. 2000); "Presidential Election Forum: The Candidates on Arms Control," *Arms Control Today* 30 (Sept. 2000): 2–6; Daryl Kimball to Interested Parties, Sept. 29, 2000, Kimball Papers.

145. *WP*, Dec. 14, 2001; interview with Daryl Kimball, May 29, 2002; Schell, "Disarmament Wars," p. 72.

146. Natural Resources Defense Council, "Faking Nuclear Restraint: The Bush Administration's Secret Plan for Strengthening U.S. Nuclear Forces" (Feb. 13, 2002), author's possession; *Los Angeles Times*, Mar. 10, 2002.

147. *NYT*, May 24, 2002; "Arms Control Association—Media Advisory" (May 24, 2002), author's possession; interview with Daryl Kimball, May 29, 2002; comments of Strobe Talbott on National Public Radio, May 25, 2002.

148. "India's Nuclear Forces, 2002," *BAS* 58 (Mar.–Apr. 2002): 70–72; *WP*, May 27, 2002.

149. *WP*, May 1, 2002; *NYT*, Oct. 19, 2002.

150. *NYT*, May 18, 2002; *Sunflower*, No. 57 (Feb. 2002) and No. 58 (Mar. 2002); Schell, "Bomb Is Back," pp. 58–59.

151. Interview with Robert Musil, Mar. 14, 2002; Schell, "Growing Nuclear Peril"; Schell, "Bomb Is Back," p. 59; interview with Daryl Kimball, May 29, 2002.

Conclusion

Epigraph: Program for the London Philharmonic Orchestra concert, "A Symphony of Mankind," Royal Symphony Hall, Sept. 19, 1999, author's possession.

1. Shultz, *Turmoil*, p. 1131; interview with James A. Baker III, Sept. 15, 1999. See also Thatcher, *Downing Street*, p. 471; Meese, *With Reagan*, p. 171; Genscher, *Rebuilding*, p. 214.

2. *NYT*, Oct. 12, 1992; Oberdorfer, *Turn*, p. 438; Reagan, *An American Life*, p. 549.

3. *NYT*, Oct. 28, 1992; "A Very Big Delusion," p. 5.

4. "A Very Big Delusion," pp. 5–6; Arbatov, *System*, p. 321; Dobrynin, *In Confidence*, pp. 610–11. For similar remarks by Soviet officials, see Tannenwald, ed., *Understanding*, p. 163; Palazchenko, *My Years*, p. 371; Dobrynin, *In Confidence*, pp. 544, 607, 609–12.

5. Speech by Kofi Annan to the Second Nuclear Age Conference, Graduate Center, CUNY, Nov. 17, 2000; Shevardnadze, *Future*, p. 92.

6. Speech by Kofi Annan to the Second Nuclear Age Conference, Graduate Center, CUNY, Nov. 17, 2000.

7. For an excellent history and analysis of the strengths and weaknesses of the United Nations, see Roberts and Kingsbury, "Introduction."

Bibliography

Manuscript Sources

Aktion Sühnezeichen/Friedensdienste Records, Office, Berlin, Germany.

Aldermaston Women's Peace Camp Records, Swarthmore College Peace Collection, Swarthmore, Pa. (hereafter SCPC)

Archibald Stevens Alexander Papers, Archibald S. Alexander Library, Rutgers University, New Brunswick, N.J.

Alice Springs Peace Group Bases Campaign Records, SCPC

American Friends Service Committee Records, SCPC

American Friends Service Committee-Rocky Flats Project Records, Norlin Library, University of Colorado, Boulder, Colo. (hereafter Norlin Library)

Australian Coalition for Disarmament and Peace Records, Office, Sydney, Australia

Australian Peace Committee Records, SCPC

Australian Peace Liaison Committee Records, SCPC

Australian Quaker Peace Committee Records, Office, Victoria, Australia

William L. Ball III Files, Ronald Reagan Library, Simi Valley, Calif. (hereafter Reagan Library)

Richard S. Beal Files, Reagan Library

Michael Bess Papers, Bess Home, Nashville, Tenn.

Morton C. Blackwell Files, Reagan Library

Zbigniew Brzezinski Papers, Jimmy Carter Library, Atlanta, Ga. (hereafter Carter Library)

Bulgarian Peace Committee Records, SCPC

Campaign for Nuclear Disarmament (Britain) Records, Campaign for Nuclear Disarmament Office, London; SCPC; Adam Matthew microfilm; Harvester microfilm

Campaign for Nuclear Disarmament (New Zealand) Records, SCPC

Canadian Peace Alliance Records, SCPC

Canadian Peace Congress Records, Office, Toronto, Canada

Jimmy Carter Presidential Papers, Plains File, Carter Library

Center for Defense Information Records, Office, Washington, D.C.

Central Committee of the Communist Party of the Soviet Union Records, Storage Center for Contemporary Documentation (Tsentr Khraneniia Sovremennoi Dokumentatsii), Moscow, Russia

Chief of Staff's File, Carter Library
Ray S. Cline Papers, Library of Congress, Washington, D.C. (hereafter Library of
    Congress)
Tyrus Cobb Files, Reagan Library
Comiso International Peace Camp Records, SCPC
Comité pour le Désarmement Nucléaire en Europe Records, SCPC
Committee for a New Korea Policy Records, Albany, N.Y.
Committee for a Sane Nuclear Policy Records, SCPC
Council for a Livable World Records, SCPC
Deutscher Friedensrat Records, Federal Archives (Bundesarchiv), Berlin, Germany
Elizabeth Dole Files, Reagan Library
European Nuclear Disarmament Records, SCPC
Federation of American Scientists Records, Office, Washington, D.C.
Fellowship of Reconciliation (India) Records, Kottayam, India
Fellowship of Reconciliation (United States) Records, SCPC
Finnish Peace Committee Records, SCPC
David Gergen Files, Reagan Library
German Democratic Republic Peace Council Records, SCPC
Sanford Gottlieb Papers, Library of Congress
Greenham Common Women's Peace Camp Records, SCPC
Greenham Women Against Cruise Missiles Records, SCPC
Greenpeace (Britain) Records, SCPC
Greenpeace Pacific Records, SCPC
The Greens Records, SCPC
Group to Establish Mutual Trust Between the U.S. and the U.S.S.R. Records, SCPC
Gary Hart Papers, Norlin Library
Hungarian Peace Council Records, SCPC
Indian Campaign for Nuclear Disarmament Records, Office, Calcutta, India
Interkerkelijk Vredesberaad Records, International Institute for Social History
    (International Instituut voor Sociale Geschiedenis), Amsterdam (hereafter In-
    ternational Institute for Social History); Office, the Hague, the Netherlands
International Peace Bureau Records, Office, Geneva, Switzerland
International Peace Communication and Coordination Center, SCPC
Internationella Kvinnoförbundet för Fred och Frihet (Sweden) Records, Office,
    Stockholm, Sweden
Italian Christian Workers Associations Records, SCPC
Homer Jack Papers, SCPC
Japan Congress Against Atomic and Hydrogen Bombs Records, SCPC; Office, To-
    kyo, Japan
Japan Council Against Atomic and Hydrogen Bombs Records, SCPC
Mary Kaldor Papers, Office, London School of Economics, London, Britain
George A. Keyworth Files, Reagan Library
Daryl Kimball Papers, Arms Control Association, Washington, D.C.
Robert Kimmitt Files, Reagan Library
Sven F. Kraemer Files, Reagan Library

Kvinder for Fred Records, SCPC
Nelson C. Ledsky Files, Reagan Library
John Lenczowski Files, Reagan Library
Robert E. Linhard Files, Reagan Library
Bernard Lown Papers, Lown Home, Newton, Mass.
Jack F. Matlock Files, Reagan Library
David McReynolds Papers, SCPC
Medical Association for the Prevention of War Records, SCPC
Medical Campaign Against Nuclear Weapons, SCPC
Edwin Meese III Files, Reagan Library
Seymour Melman Papers, SCPC
Mobilization for Survival Records, Office, New York, N.Y.; SCPC
Mouvement de la Paix Records, SCPC
National Committee for a Sane Nuclear Policy Records, SCPC
National Security Adviser File, Carter Library
         President's Correspondence with Foreign Leaders File
         Subject File
National Security Council Records, Reagan Library
         Agency File
         Head of State File
         Presidential Advisory File
         Subject File
National Security Decision Memoranda and Study Memoranda, Gerald R. Ford Li-
    brary, Ann Arbor, Mich.
Nei til Atomvåpen (Norway) Records, Office, Oslo, Norway
Netherlands Affiliate of International Physicians for the Prevention of Nuclear War
    Records, SCPC
New Zealand Nuclear Weapon Free Zone Records, SCPC
Paul Nitze Papers, Library of Congress
Nuclear Weapons Freeze Campaign Records, Institute for Defense and Disarma-
    ment Studies, Cambridge, Mass.; Western Historical Manuscript Collection,
    Thomas Jefferson Library, University of Missouri, St. Louis, Mo.; Office,
    Washington, D.C.
Office of the Assistant to the President for Communications File, Carter Library
Office of the Assistant to the President for National Security Affairs Records, Rea-
    gan Library
Office of the President, Presidential Briefing Papers Records, Reagan Library
Ohne Rüstung Leben Records, Office, Stuttgart, Germany
Operation Dismantle Records, SCPC
Pax Christi International Records, Office, Antwerp; SCPC
Pax Christi International (Belgium) Records, SCPC
Pax Christi International (Netherlands) Records, SCPC
Peace Action Records, SCPC
Peace Movement Aotearoa Records, Office, Wellington, New Zealand
Rudolf Perina Files, Reagan Library

Physicians for Social Responsibility Records, SCPC

Rob Prince Papers, Norlin Library

Project Ploughshares Records, Conrad Grebel College, Waterloo, Ontario, Canada

Pugwash Conferences on Science and World Affairs Records, SCPC

Rebecca G. Range Files, Reagan Library

Rissho Kosei-Kai Promotion Committee for Disarmament and the Abolition of Nuclear Weapons Records, SCPC

Sellafield Women's Peace Encampment Records, SCPC

Socialist Unity Party Records, Foundation for the Archives of Parties and Mass Organizations of the German Democratic Republic, Federal Archives (Stiftung Massenorganisationen der Deutschen Demokratischen Republic, Bundesarchiv), Berlin, Germany

Soka Gakkai International Records, SCPC

Mark Solomon Papers, Solomon Home, West Newton, Mass.

State Security Services of the GDR Records, the Federal Official for the Documents of the State Security Services of the Former German Democratic Republic Archive (Der Bundesbeauftragte für die Unterlagen des Staatssicherheitsdienstes der ehemaligen Deutschen Demokratischen Republic Archiv), Berlin, Germany

Carolyn Sundseth Files, Reagan Library

Union Pacifiste de France Records, SCPC

United States Nuclear Free Pacific Network Records, SCPC

U.S. Peace Council Records, SCPC

USSR Miscellaneous Peace Material, SCPC

Voice of Women Records, SCPC

Frank von Hippel Papers, von Hippel Home, Princeton, N.J.

War Resisters' International Records, International Institute for Social History

War Resisters League Records, SCPC

White House Central File, Carter Library
    Name File
    Subject File

White House Office of Records Management Records, Reagan Library

White House Office of Speechwriting Records, Reagan Library

White House Office of the Press Secretary Records, Reagan Library

Women for Peace in Finland Records, SCPC

Women Strike for Peace Records, SCPC

Women's Encampment for a Future of Peace and Justice Records, SCPC

Women's International League for Peace and Freedom (United States) Records, SCPC

World Conference Against Atomic and Hydrogen Bombs Records, SCPC

World Peace Council Records, SCPC

Interviews

Personal interviews
    Kenneth Adelman, July 22, 1998, McLean, Va.

Koichi Akamatsu, May 15, 1999, the Hague
Richard V. Allen, June 29, 1999, telephone
John B. Anderson, April 22, 1992, Albany, N.Y.
Ikuro Anzai, May 15, 1999, the Hague
Colin Archer, May 31, June 1, 1999, Geneva
Berit Ås, August 12, 2000, Oslo
David Atwood, June 1, 1999, Geneva
James A. Baker III, September 15, 1999, telephone
Edith Ballantyne, June 1, 1999, Geneva
Anatoly A. Belyayev, June 27, 1990, Moscow
Peter Bergel, August 3, 1999, Salem, Ore.
Janet Bloomfield, May 14, 1999, the Hague
Robert M. Bowman, October 26, 1992, Albany, N.Y.
Harold Brown, August 16, 1999, telephone
Zbigniew Brzezinski, July 21, 1999, Washington, D.C.
Dottye Burt, June 29, 1987, Washington, D.C.
Martin Butcher, July 19, 1999, Washington, D.C.
Helen Caldicott, February 27, 1999, Easthampton, N.Y.
Frank Carlucci, July 20, 1999, Washington, D.C.
Eugene J. Carroll, Jr., May 11, 2000, telephone
Thomas Cochran, August 23, 1999, Washington, D.C.
William Sloane Coffin, Jr., October 19, 1989, Albany, N.Y.
David Cohen, July 19, 1999, Washington, D.C.
David Cortright, June 29, 1987, Washington, D.C.
Günther Drefahl, May 19, 1999, Jena, Germany
Louise Edge, June 19, 1998, London
Mient Jan Faber, August 7, 1986, the Hague
Eric Fersht, September 9, 1989, Washington, D.C.
Valerie Flessati, June 7, 1999, London
Michael Foot, June 19, 1998, London
Randall Forsberg, July 7, 1999, Cambridge, Mass., January 8, 2000, Chicago, Ill.
Sanford Gottlieb, July 19, 1998, Kensington, Md.
Thomas Graham, Jr., August 23, 1999, Washington, D.C.
Kurt Hälker, May 21, 1999, Berlin
Scott Hoffman, May 3, 1991, Albany, N.Y.
John Holum, April 3, 2002, Washington, D.C.
Fred Iklé, July 22, 1998, Washington, D.C.
Ruzanna Ilukhina, May 22, 1991, New Brunswick, N.J.
John Isaacs, July 20, 1999, Washington, D.C.
Homer Jack, June 12, 1988, Swarthmore, Pa.
Hugh Jenkins, June 20, 1998, London
Carol Jensen, July 31, 1999, Stanwood, Wash.
Charles Johnson, August 3, 1999, Monmouth, Ore.
Sheila Jones, July 10, 1990, June 19, 1998, London
Gerhard Jordan, August 31, 1986, Vienna

Mary Kaldor, June 7, 1999, London
Max Kampelman, July 21, 1999, Washington, D.C.
Sergei Kapitza, June 28, 1990, Moscow
Randall Kehler, August 20, 1999, Albany, N.Y.
Bruce Kent, July 10, 1990, June 7, 1999, London
Daryl Kimball, July 21, 1998, May 8, May 29, 2002, Washington, D.C.
Ole Kopreitan, May 14, 1999, the Hague
Ferenc Köszegi, August 28, 1986, Schlaining, Austria
David Krieger, May 14, 1999, the Hague
Anthony Lake, May 14, 2002, Washington, D.C.
Gene LaRocque, August 17, 1999, telephone
Judy Lipton, July 31, 1999, Redmond, Wash.
Bernard Lown, July 6, 1999, Newton, Mass.
Ruud Lubbers, May 27, 1999, the Hague
Edwin Meese III, August 23, 1999, Washington, D.C.
Victor Malkov, December 4, 1994, New Brunswick, N.J.
Robert McFarlane, July 21, 1999, Washington, D.C.
Katherine Magraw, May 16, 2002, telephone
Robert Musil, July 20, 1998, March 14, 2002, Washington, D.C.
Sheila Oakes, June 6, 1999, London
Jack O'Dell, October 2, 1995, Albany, N.Y.
Christopher Paine, September 14, 1999, telephone, February 26, 2002, Washing-
    ton, D.C.
William Peden, June 19, 1998, London
Richard Perle, June 29, 1999, telephone
John Pike, July 22, 1999, Washington, D.C.
Daniel Plesch, July 21, 1998, Washington, D.C.
Rob Prince, July 27, 1999, Denver, Colo.
Terry Provance, July 20, 1999, Washington, D.C.
Amina Rasul-Bernardo, April 18, 2002, Washington, D.C.
Rozanne Ridgway, September 17, 1999, telephone
Joseph Rotblat, July 12, 1990, July 11, 1994, London
Werner Rümpel, May 20, 1999, Berlin
Rainer Santi, August 18, 1986, Geneva
Dhirendra Sharma, October 11, 1995, Albany, N.Y.
Alice Slater, May 14, 1999, the Hague
Mark Solomon, July 8, 1999, West Newton, Mass.
Peter Steglich, May 21, 1999, Berlin
Jeremy Stone, July 22, 1999, Washington, D.C.
Dorothy Thompson, November 1, 1989, New Brunswick, N.J.
E. P. Thompson, November 1, 1989, New Brunswick, N.J.
Frank von Hippel, August 22, 1999, Princeton, N.J.
Paul Warnke, July 20, 1999, Washington, D.C.
Caspar Weinberger, July 21, 1998, telephone
Charles Z. Wick, August 16, 1999, telephone

Harold Willens, May 11, 2000, telephone
Richard Wirthlin, October 6, 1999, telephone
Nigel Young, October 12, 1993, telephone, May 15, 1999, the Hague
Ron Young, July 31, 1999, Stanwood, Wash.
Oral History Interviews
   Jimmy Carter Library, Atlanta, Ga.
      Robert Beckel, November 13, 1981
      Zbigniew Brzezinski, February 18, 1982
      Jimmy Carter, November 29, 1982
      Lloyd Cutler, October 23, 1982
      Hamilton Jordan, November 6, 1981
      Jody Powell, December 2, 1980
      Gerald Rafshoon, April 8, 1983
      Anne Wexler, Februry 12–13, 1981
   Ronald Reagan Library, Simi Valley, Calif.
      Joseph Coors, July 31, 1987
      Elizabeth Dole, April 16, 1983
      Kenneth M. Duberstein, December 15, 1983
      Jacquelin H. Hume, October 28, 1987
      George A. Keyworth, September 28, 1987
      Edward Teller, July 6, 1987

Peace Movement Periodicals

Alternatives Non Violentes (Mouvement pour une Alternative Non-Violente, Montrond, France)
Arms Control Today (Arms Control Association, Washington, D.C.)
Bulletin of the Atomic Scientists (Independent, Chicago)
CALC Report (Clergy and Laity Concerned, New York City)
Campaign (Campaign for Nuclear Disarmament, London)
Canadian Peace Alliance News (Canadian Peace Alliance, Toronto)
Canadian Peace Research and Education Association Newsletter (Canadian Peace Research and Education Association, Brandon, Canada)
CND Today (Campaign for Nuclear Disarmament, London)
Council for a Livable World Newsletter (Council for a Livable World, Washington, D.C.)
Defense and Disarmament Alternatives (Institute for Defense and Disarmament Studies, Cambridge, Mass.)
Defense and Disarmament News (Institute for Defense and Disarmament Studies, Cambridge, Mass.)
Disarmament Campaigns (International Peace Communication and Coordination Center, the Hague)
Disarmament Newsletter (United Nations, New York City)
Disarming Times (Pax Christi Australia, Victoria)
END Bulletin (European Nuclear Disarmament, London)

END Journal (European Nuclear Disarmament, London)

F.A.S. Public Interest Report (Federation of American Scientists, Washington, D.C.)

Fellowship (Fellowship of Reconciliation, Nyack, N.Y.)

Freeze Focus (Nuclear Weapons Freeze Campaign, St. Louis)

Freeze Newsletter (Nuclear Weapons Freeze Campaign, Brookline, Mass. and St. Louis)

Friedens Info (Arbeitsgemeinschaft unabhängiger Friedensinitiativen, Vienna)

Gandhi Marg (Gandhi Peace Foundation, New Delhi)

Gensuikin News (Japan Congress Against Atomic and Hydrogen Bombs, Tokyo)

Greenpeace (Greenpeace, Washington, D.C.)

Greenpeace Quarterly (Greenpeace, Washington, D.C.)

Information (Peace Council of the German Democratic Republic, Berlin)

La Feuille de Liaison du CNAPD (Comité National d'Action pour la Paix et le Développement, Brussels)

Le bulletin du CO.DE.NE (Comité pour le Désarmement Nucléaire en Europe, Montlhery, France)

MAPW Pulse (Medical Association for Prevention of War, Victoria)

Medicine, Conflict and Survival (Medical Action for Global Security, London)

Mobilizer (Mobilization for Survival, New York City)

Network News (United Campuses to Prevent Nuclear War, Washington, D.C.)

New Outlook (Independent, Tel Aviv)

Nonviolent Activist (War Resisters League, New York City)

Nuclear Disarmament Commentary (NGO Committee on Disarmament, United Nations, New York City)

Nuclear Times (Independent, Washington, D.C.)

Pacific Peacemaker (Pacific Peacemaker, Seattle)

Pax et Libertas (Women's International League for Peace and Freedom, Geneva)

Peace (Chinese People's Association for Peace and Disarmament, Beijing)

Peace Action (Peace Action, Washington, D.C.)

Peace Action Report (Peace Action, Washington, D.C.)

Peace and Democracy News (Campaign for Peace and Democracy/East and West, New York City)

Peace Courier (World Peace Council, Helsinki)

Peace-Letter (Mouvement de la Paix, Saint-Ouen, France)

Peacelink (Peace Movement New Zealand, Dunedin)

Peace Magazine (Canadian Disarmament Information Service, Toronto)

Peace Movement New Zealand Newsletter (Peace Movement New Zealand, Dunedin)

Peacework (New England Regional Office, American Friends Service Committee, Boston)

Polish Peace Committee Newsletter (Polish Peace Committee, Warsaw)

PSR Monitor (Physicians for Social Responsibility, Washington, D.C.)

PSR Reports (Physicians for Social Responsibility, Washington, D.C.)

Quaker Service Bulletin (American Friends Service Committee, Philadelphia)

SANE/Freeze News (SANE/FREEZE, Washington, D.C.)
Sane World (Committee for a Sane Nuclear Policy, New York City)
SANE World/FREEZE Focus (SANE/FREEZE, Washington, D.C.)
Sanity (Campaign for Nuclear Disarmament, London)
Sunflower (Nuclear Age Peace Foundation, Santa Barbara, Calif.)
Waging Peace Worldwide (Nuclear Age Peace Foundation, Santa Barbara, Calif.)
World Federalist (World Federalist Association, Washington, D.C.)
WRI Newsletter (War Resisters' International, Brussels)
WRL News (War Resisters League, New York City)

Other Sources

Adelman, Kenneth L. *The Great Universal Embrace: Arms Summitry—A Skeptic's Account.* New York: Simon & Schuster, 1989.
———. "Woefully Inadequate: The Press's Handling of Arms Control," pp. 151–59 in Simon Serfaty, ed., *The Media and Foreign Policy.* New York: St. Martin's Press, 1990.
Alexeyeva, Ludmilla. "Independent Youth Groups in the USSR." *Across Frontiers* 4 (Winter 1988): 4–5, 32.
Alfsen, Erik et al. "Freeze and Withdrawal of Nuclear Weapons." *Bulletin of Peace Proposals* 16:1 (1985): 5–8.
Allen, Bruce. *Germany East: Dissent and Opposition.* Montreal: Black Rose Books, 1989.
American Foreign Policy Basic Documents, 1977–1980. Washington, D.C.: U.S. Department of State, 1983.
"An Interview with Jaroslav Sabata," pp. 207–12 in Mary Kaldor, ed., *Europe from Below: An East-West Dialogue.* London: Verso, 1991.
"An Interview with Mary Kaldor." *Working Papers* 9 (Sept.–Oct. 1982): 42–49.
An Introduction to No to Nuclear Weapons Denmark. Copenhagen: No to Nuclear Weapons, 1986.
"An Unexpected Calling." *Sojourners* 28 (Jan.–Feb. 1999): 16–20.
Anderson, Martin. *Revolution: The Reagan Legacy.* Stanford: Hoover Institution Press, 1990.
Andrew, Christopher, and Oleg Gordievsky, eds. *Comrade Kryuchkov's Instructions: Top Secret Files on KGB Foreign Operations, 1975–1985.* Stanford: Stanford University Press, 1993.
———. *KGB: The Inside Story of Its Foreign Operations from Lenin to Gorbachev.* New York: Harper Collins, 1990.
Arbatov, Georgi. "America Also Needs Perestroika," pp. 307–27 in Stephen F. Cohen and Katrina vanden Heuvel, eds., *Voices of Glasnost: Interviews with Gorbachev's Reformers.* New York: W. W. Norton, 1989.
———. *The System: An Insider's Life in Soviet Politics.* New York: Random House, 1992.
———. "US Foreign Policy at the Onset of the 1980s," pp. 64–80 in Nikolai Inozemtsev, ed., *Peace and Disarmament.* Moscow: Progress Publishers, 1980.

Arkin, William M. "Calculated Ambiguity: Nuclear Weapons and the Gulf War." *Washington Quarterly* 19 (Autumn 1996): 3–18.

———, and Michael J. Mazarr. "Clinton Defense Policy and Nuclear Weapons," pp. 49–69 in Stephen J. Cimbala, ed., *Clinton and Post-Cold War Defense.* Westport, Conn.: Praeger, 1996.

Asmus, Ronald D. "Is There a Peace Movement in the GDR?" *Orbis* 27 (Summer 1983): 301–41.

"At Historic Crossroads: Documents on the December 1989 Malta Summit." *Cold War International History Project Bulletin*, No. 12–13 (Fall-Winter 2001), pp. 229–41.

Atwood, David C. "Mobilizing Around the United Nations Special Sessions on Disarmament," pp. 141–58 in Jackie Smith, Charles Chatfield, and Ron Pagnucco, eds., *Transnational Movements and Global Politics: Solidarity Beyond the State.* Syracuse: Syracuse University Press, 1997.

Auger, Vincent A. *The Dynamics of Foreign Policy Analysis: The Carter Administration and the Neutron Bomb.* Lanham, Md.: Rowman & Littlefield, 1996.

Baker, James A., III. *The Politics of Diplomacy: Revolution, War and Peace, 1989–1992.* New York: G. P. Putnam's Sons, 1995.

Baker, John C. "Clinton Defense Policy-Making: Players, Process, and Policies," pp. 123–38 in Stephen J. Cimbala, ed., *Clinton and Post-Cold War Defense.* Westport, Conn.: Praeger, 1996.

Baldwin, Hugh, ed. *Documents on the Peace Movement in Hungary.* London: European Nuclear Disarmament, 1986.

Bamba, Nobuya. "Peace Movement at a Standstill: Roots of the Crisis." *Bulletin of Peace Proposals* 13:1 (1982): 39–42.

Barron, John. "The KGB's Magical War for 'Peace.'" *Reader's Digest* (Oct. 1982), pp. 205–59.

Bein, Thomas, and Rudolf Epple. "Die Friedensbewegung heute: Rahmenbedingungen und Tendenzen," pp. 91–122 in Thomas Bein, Ruedi Brassel, and Martin Leuenberger, eds., *Handbuch Frieden Schweiz.* Basel: Z-Verlag, 1986.

Beker, Avi. *Disarmament Without Order: The Politics of Disarmament at the United Nations.* Westport, Conn.: Greenwood Press, 1985.

Béni, Jos. "The Peace Movement in Belgium." *Journal of Area Studies*, No. 9 (Spring 1984), pp. 13–18.

Berger, Thomas U. *Cultures of Antimilitarism: National Security in Germany and Japan.* Baltimore: Johns Hopkins University Press, 1998.

Beschloss, Michael, and Strobe Talbott. *At the Highest Levels: The Inside Story of the End of the Cold War.* Boston: Little, Brown, 1993.

Bess, Michael. *Realism, Utopia, and the Mushroom Cloud: Four Activist Intellectuals and Their Strategies for Peace, 1945–1989.* Chicago: University of Chicago Press, 1993.

Bidwai, Praful, and Achin Vanaik. *New Nukes: India, Pakistan and Global Nuclear Disarmament.* New York: Olive Branch Press, 2000.

Blanton, Tom, ed.. *White House E-Mail.* New York: New Press, 1995.

Blechman, Barry M., and Cathleen S. Fisher. *The Silent Partner: West Germany and Arms Control.* Cambridge, Mass.: Ballinger, 1988.

Blokhin, Nikolai. "International Cooperation of Medical Scientists in the Interests of Peace," pp. 25–31 in Nikolai Inozemtsev, ed., *Peace and Disarmament*. Moscow: Progress Publishers, 1980.

Blumenthal, Sidney. *Pledging Allegiance: The Last Campaign of the Cold War*. New York: Harper Collins, 1990.

Boag, J.W., P. E. Rubinin, and D. Shoenberg, eds. *Kapitza in Cambridge and Moscow: Life and Letters of a Russian Physicist*. Amsterdam: North-Holland, 1990.

Boel, Erik, *Socialdemokratiets atomvåbenpolitik: Danmarks atomvåbenfri status*. Aarhus: Aarhus Universitet, 1986.

Borosage, Robert. "The Bilateral Box." *Working Papers* 10 (May–June 1983): 37–40.

Bourdet, Claude. "Désarmement nucléaire en France." Manuscript, 1990, author's possession.

———. "The Rebirth of a Peace Movement," pp. 190–201 in Jolyon Howorth and Patricia Chilton, eds., *Defence and Dissent in Contemporary France*. London: Croom Helm, 1984.

Boutwell, Jeffrey. *The German Nuclear Dilemma*. Ithaca: Cornell University Press, 1990.

———. "Politics and the Peace Movement in West Germany." *International Security* 7 (Spring 1983): 72–92.

Boyer, Paul. "Physicians Confront the Apocalypse: The American Medical Profession and the Threat of Nuclear War." *Journal of the American Medical Association* 254 (Aug. 2, 1985): 633–43.

———. *When Time Shall Be No More: Prophecy Belief in Modern American Culture*. Cambridge, Mass.: Belknap Press, 1992.

Brandon, Ruth. *The Burning Question: The Anti-Nuclear Movement Since 1945*. London: Heinemann, 1987.

Breyman, Steve. *Why Movements Matter: The West German Peace Movement and U.S. Arms Control Policy*. Albany, N.Y.: State University of New York Press, 2001.

Brierley, William. "Italian Politics and the Peace Movement," *Journal of Area Studies*, No. 9 (Spring 1984), pp. 18–23.

Brown, Harold. *Thinking About National Security: Defense and Foreign Policy in a Dangerous World*. Boulder: Westview Press, 1983.

Brzezinski, Zbigniew. *Power and Principle: Memoirs of the National Security Advisor, 1977–1981*. New York: Farrar, Straus & Giroux, 1983.

Bundy, McGeorge. *Danger and Survival*. New York: Random House, 1988.

Burgmann, Verity. *Power and Protest: Movements for Change in Australian Society*. Sydney: Allen & Unwin, 1993.

Burns, James MacGregor, and Georgia J. Sorenson. *Dead Center: Clinton-Gore Leadership and the Perils of Moderation*. New York: Scribner, 1999.

Bush, George, and Brent Scowcroft. *A World Transformed*. New York: Alfred A. Knopf, 1998.

Butler, George Lee. *From Nuclear Deterrence to Nuclear Abolition*. Oxford: Abingdon Peace Group, 1997.

Butterfield, Fox. "Anatomy of the Nuclear Protest." *New York Times Magazine* (July 11, 1982), pp. 14–17, 32, 34–39.

Byrd, Peter. "The Development of the Peace Movement in Britain," pp. 63–103 in Werner Kaltefleiter and Robert L. Pfaltzgraff, eds., *The Peace Movements in Europe and the United States*. London: Croom Helm, 1985.

Byrne, Paul. *The Campaign for Nuclear Disarmament*. London: Croom Helm, 1988.

Caldicott, Helen. *A Desperate Passion*. New York: W. W. Norton, 1996.

———. *Missile Envy: The Arms Race and Nuclear War*. Toronto: Bantam Books, 1986.

———. *Nuclear Madness: What You Can Do*. New York: Bantam Books, 1980.

———. "We Women Have Lacked Guts." *Sojourner* (Oct. 1986), pp. 19–20.

Caldwell, Bill S., III. "The French Socialists' Attitudes Toward the Use of Nuclear Weapons, 1945–1978." Ph.D. diss., University of Georgia, 1980.

Camilleri, Joe. "The Nuclear Disarmament Movement in Europe and Australia." *Social Alternatives* 3:1 (1982): 33–37.

Campbell, David. *Australian Public Opinion on National Security Issues*. Canberra: Australian National University, 1986.

Campbell, Duncan. "Tories Wage Secret war on Peace Campaigners." *New Statesman* 105 (Jan. 28, 1983): 4.

Camus, Albert. *La Peste*, pp. 11–292 in Albert Camus, *Oeuvres complètes d'Albert Camus*. Paris: Gallimard, 1983.

"Canadians on Nuclear Weapons: A Poll by the Canadian Peace Alliance." *Peace Research* 30 (May 1998): 21–26.

Carroll, Gene. "Laboring for Peace." *Economic Notes* 54 (July–Aug. 1986): 1–2.

Carter, April. *Peace Movements: International Protest and World Politics Since 1945*. London: Longman, 1992.

Carter, Jimmy. *Keeping Faith: Memoirs of a President*. New York: Bantam Books, 1982.

Castelli, Jim. *The Bishops and the Bomb: Waging Peace in a Nuclear Age*. Garden City, N.Y.: Doubleday, 1984.

Ceadel, Martin. "Britain's Nuclear Disarmers," pp. 218–44 in Walter Laqueur and Robert Hunter, eds., *European Peace Movements and the Future of the Western Alliance*. New Brunswick, N.J.: Transaction Books, 1985.

"The Challenge of Peace: God's Promise and Our Response," pp. 184–283 in Jim Castelli, *The Bishops and the Bomb: Waging Peace in the Nuclear Age*. New York: Doubleday, 1984.

Chandra, Romesh. *The Present International Situation and the Main Tasks of the Peace Movement*. Helsinki: World Peace Council, 1986.

Chapman, Peter. *Canada and the Movement for a Nuclear Free and Independent Pacific*. Waterloo, Ont.: Project Ploughshares, 1984.

Chatfield, Charles. *The American Peace Movement: Ideals and Activism*. New York: Twayne Publishers, 1992.

Chernyaev, Anatoly S. *My Six Years with Gorbachev*. University Park: Pennsylvania State University Press, 2000.

China and Disarmament. Beijing: Foreign Languages Press, 1988.

Christopher, Warren. *Chances of a Lifetime.* New York: Scribner, 2001.

——. *In the Stream of History: Shaping Foreign Policy for a New Era.* Stanford: Stanford University Press, 1998.

The Church and Nuclear Disarmament. Waterloo, Ont.: Project Ploughshares, 1985.

"Churches Committed to Peace." *Christian Conference of Asia News* 23 (June 1988): 11–12.

Cioc, Mark. *Pax Atomica: The Nuclear Defense Debate in West Germany During the Adenauer Era.* New York: Columbia University Press, 1988.

Clements, Kevin. *Back from the Brink: The Creation of a Nuclear-Free New Zealand.* Wellington: Allen & Unwin/Port Nicholson Press, 1988.

——. "New Zealand's Relations with the UK, the US, and the Pacific." *Alternatives* 10 (1985): 591–605.

Clesse, Armand. "The Peace Movements and the Future of West European Security," pp. 53–67 in Peter van den Dungen, ed., *West European Pacifism and the Strategy for Peace.* London: Macmillan Press, 1985.

Clinton, Bill, and Al Gore. *Putting People First: How We Can All Change America.* New York: Times Books, 1992.

Coates, Ken. "Conclusion," pp. 277–306 in Ken Coates, ed., *The Dynamics of European Nuclear Disarmament.* Nottingham: Spokesman, 1981.

——. *European Nuclear Disarmament.* Nottingham: Bertrand Russell Peace Foundation, 1980.

Cohen, Avner. *Israel and the Bomb.* New York: Columbia University Press, 1998.

Cohen, Stephen F. *Failed Crusade: America and the Tragedy of Post-Communist Russia.* New York: W. W. Norton, 2000.

Colard, Daniel. "Le Pacifisme à la Française." *Arès: Defense et Sécurité* (1985), pp. 15–41.

Committee for the Compilation of Materials on Damage Caused by the Atomic Bombs in Hiroshima and Nagasaki. *Hiroshima and Nagasaki: The Physical, Medical, and Social Effects of the Atomic Bombings.* New York: Basic Books, 1981.

Cortright, David. "Assessing Peace Movement Effectiveness." *Peace and Change* 16 (Jan. 1991): 46–63.

——. "Ban the Bomb II." *Sojourners* 28 (Jan.–Feb. 1999): 25–26.

——. "The Peace Movement Role in Ending the Cold War," pp. 81–90 in Ralph Summy and Michael E. Salla, eds., *Why the Cold War Ended: A Range of Interpretations.* Westport, Conn.: Greenwood Press, 1995.

——. *Peace Works: The Citizen's Role in Ending the Cold War.* Boulder: Westview Press, 1993.

——, and Ron Pagnucco. "Limits to Transnationalism: The 1980s Freeze Campaign," pp. 159–74 in Jackie Smith, Charles Chatfield, and Ron Pagnucco, eds., *Transnational Movements and Global Politics: Solidarity Beyond the State.* Syracuse: Syracuse University Press, 1997.

"COSNUP—Campaign." *Philosophy and Social Action* 24 (July–Dec. 1998): 35–46.

Crewe, Ivor. "Britain: Two and a Half Cheers for the Atlantic Alliance," pp. 11–68 in Gregory Flynn and Hans Rattinger, eds., *The Public and Atlantic Defense.* Totowa, N.J.: Rowman & Allanheld, 1985.

Crozier, Brian. *Free Agent: The Unseen War, 1941–1991.* New York: Harper Collins, 1993.

————. "The Great Nuclear Freeze Trap." *American Legion* (Jan. 1984), pp. 14–15, 45–46.

Davidon, Ann M. "A Simple Act of Walking." *Progressive* 40 (Aug. 1976): 31–32.

————. "Warheads into Plowshares." *Progressive* 45 (May 1981): 49–51.

Dawson, Jane I. "Anti-Nuclear Activism in the Former USSR: A Surrogate for Nationalism?" Paper presented at the Kennan Institute for Advanced Russian Studies, Woodrow Wilson Center, Washington, D.C., Feb. 7, 1994.

Day, Alan J., ed. *Peace Movements of the World: An International Directory.* Essex, Eng.: Longman Group, 1987.

Day, Barbara, and Howard Waitzkin. "The Medical Profession and Nuclear War: A Social History." *Journal of the American Medical Association* 254 (Aug. 2, 1985): 644–51.

De Andreis, Marco. "The Nuclear Debate in Italy." *Survival* 28 (May–June 1986): 195–207.

Deaver, Michael K., with Mickey Herskowitz. *Behind the Scenes.* New York: William Morrow, 1987.

DeBenedetti, Charles, and Charles Chatfield. *An American Ordeal: The Antiwar Movement of the Vietnam Era.* Syracuse: Syracuse University Press, 1990.

DeBoer, Connie. "The Polls: Our Commitment to World War III." *Public Opinion Quarterly* 45 (Spring 1981): 126–34.

————. "The Polls: The European Peace Movement and Deployment of Nuclear Missiles." *Public Opinion Quarterly* 49 (Spring 1985): 119–32.

"Declaration of the Churches of Korea on National Reunification and Peace." *Korea Report* 2 (July 1988): 17–19.

Deile, Volkmar et al., eds. *Bonn 10.10.81: Friedensdemonstration für Abrüstung und Entspannung in Europa.* Bornheim: Lamuv, 1981.

"Demonstration." *New Yorker* 56 (Dec. 8, 1980): 43–46.

den Oudsten, Eymert. "Public Opinion," pp. 31–38 in *World Armaments and Disarmament: SIPRI Yearbook 1985.* London: Taylor & Francis, 1985.

————. "Public Opinion and Nuclear Weapons," pp. 15–20 in *World Armaments and Disarmament: SIPRI Yearbook 1984.* London: Taylor & Francis, 1984.

————. "Public Opinion on International Security: A Comparative Study of the Federal Republic of Germany, the Netherlands, the United Kingdom, and the United States, 1979–1987." M.A. thesis, Groningen University, 1988.

————. "Public Opinion on Peace and War," pp. 17–35 in *World Armaments and Disarmament: SIPRI Yearbook 1986.* Oxford: Oxford University Press, 1986.

De Smet, Luc. "The Belgian Peace Movement Polled," pp. 235–53 in Katsuya Kodama and Unto Vesa, eds., *Towards a Comparative Analysis of Peace Movements.* Hants, Eng.: Dartmouth Publishing, 1990.

Dhavan, Rajeev. "Law and Society: Pokhran and Sanctions." *Philosophy and Social Action* 24 (July–Dec. 1998): 78–81.

Dobrynin, Anatoly. *In Confidence.* New York: Times Books, 1995.

Dodge, Mike, and John Hinchcliff. "The Peace Movement in New Zealand." *Social Alternatives* 3 (Mar. 1983): 41–42.

Donner, Frank. "But Will They Come? The Campaign to Smear the Nuclear Freeze Movement." *Nation* 235 (Nov. 6, 1982): 456–65.

Drew, Elizabeth. "A Reporter in Washington, D.C." *New Yorker* 58 (May 3, 1982): 134–53.

Drifte, Reinhard. *Japan's Rise to International Responsibilities: The Case of Arms Control.* London: Athlone Press, 1990.

Dunbar, Leslie. *Nuclear War in Europe: Report: The First Conference on Nuclear War in Europe, Groningen, The Netherlands, April 22–24, 1981.* Washington, D.C.: Center for Defense Information, 1981.

Dyer, Gwynne. *War.* Homewood, Ill.: Dorsey Press, 1985.

Dyson, John. *Sink the Rainbow!: An Enquiry into the "Greenpeace Affair."* London: Victor Gollancz, 1986.

Edwards, David L. "The Great Debate," pp. 13–31 in John Gladwin, ed., *Dropping the Bomb.* London: Hodder and Stoughton, 1985.

Ehring, Klaus, and Hans-H. Hücking. "Die neue Friedensbewegung in Ungarn," pp. 313–50 in Reiner Steinweg, ed., *Faszination der Gewalt: Politische Strategie und Alltagserfahrung.* Frankfurt: Suhrkamp Verlag, 1983.

Elworthy, Scilla. *In the Dark: Parliament, the Public, and NATO's New Nuclear Weapons.* Oxford: Oxford Research Group, 1989.

Emmanuel, Jorge. *The Monster in Morong.* Ann Arbor, Mich.: Alliance for Philippine Concerns, 1984.

English, Rogert. "Eastern Europe's Doves." *Foreign Policy*, No. 56 (Fall 1984), pp. 44–60.

———. *Russia and the Idea of the West: Gorbachev, Intellectuals, and the End of the Cold War.* New York: Columbia University Press, 2000.

———. "Sources, Methods, and Competing Perspectives on the End of the Cold War." *Diplomatic History* 21 (Spring 1997): 283–94.

Epstein, William. "Canada," pp. 171–84 in Jozef Goldblat, ed., *Non-Proliferation: The Why and the Wherefore.* London: Taylor & Francis, 1985.

"Eurocommunism and the Bomb: Documents from the Communist Party of Italy," pp. 141–49 in Ked Coates, ed., *The Dynamics of European Nuclear Disarmament.* Nottingham: Spokesman, 1981.

Evangelista, Matthew. "The Paradox of State Strength: Transnational Relations, Domestic Structures, and Security Policy in Russia and the Soviet Union." *International Organization* 49 (Winter 1995): 1–38.

———. *Unarmed Forces: The Transnational Movement to End the Cold War.* Ithaca: Cornell University Press, 1999.

Everts, Philip P. "The Churches and Attitudes on Nuclear Weapons: The Case of the Netherlands." *Bulletin of Peace Proposals* 15:3 (1984): 227–42.

————. "Continuity and Change in Public Attitudes on Questions of Security." Paper presented at the Joint Meetings of the World Association for Public Opinion Research and the American Association of Public Opinion Research, Toronto, May 20–23, 1988.

————. "The Impact of the Peace Movement on Public Opinion and Policy-Making: The Case of the Netherlands." Paper presented at the International Peace Research Association conference, University of Essex, England, Apr. 13–18, 1986.

————. "The Mood of the Country: New Data on Public Opinion in the Netherlands on Nuclear Weapons and Other Problems of Peace and Security." *Acta Politica* 17 (Oct. 1982): 497–553.

————. "Public Opinion on Nuclear Weapons, Defense, and Security: The Case of the Netherlands," pp. 221–74 in Gregory Flynn and Hans Rattinger, eds., *The Public and Atlantic Defense*. Totowa, N.J.: Rowman & Allanheld, 1985.

————. "Reviving Unilateralism: Report on a Campaign for Nuclear Disarmament in the Netherlands." *Bulletin of Peace Proposals* 11:1 (1980): 40–56.

————, and G. Walraven. *Vredesbeweging*. Utrecht: Spectrum, 1984.

"Excerpts from Politburo Minutes, 1983–86." *Cold War International History Project Bulletin*, No. 4 (Fall 1994), pp. 76–85.

Faber, Mient Jan. "Good Morning Europe!" pp. 139–49 in Mary Kaldor, ed., *Europe from Below: An East-West Dialogue*. London: Verso, 1991.

Fahey, Joseph. "Pax Christi," pp. 59–71 in Thomas A. Shannon, ed., *War or Peace? The Search for New Answers*. Maryknoll, N.Y.: Orbis Books, 1980.

Falk, Jim. *Taking Australia Off the Map*. Melbourne: William Heinemann, 1983.

Fast Track to Zero Nuclear Weapons: The Middle Powers Initiative: A Briefing Kit. Cambridge, Mass.: Middle Powers Initiative, 1999.

Feldman, Stanley, and Lee Sigelman. "The Political Impact of Prime-Time Television: 'The Day After.'" *Journal of Politics* 47 (May 1985): 556–78.

Fetter, Steve et al. "Gamma Ray Measurements of a Soviet Cruise Missile Warhead." *Science* 248 (May 18, 1990): 828–34.

Fisera, Vladimir Claude. "The New Left and Defence: Out of the Ghetto?" pp. 233–46 in Jolyon Howorth and Patricia Chilton, eds., *Defence and Dissent in Contemporary France*. London: Croom Helm, 1984.

FitzGerald, Frances. *Way Out There in the Blue: Reagan, Star Wars and the End of the Cold War*. New York: Simon & Schuster, 2000.

Fitzpatrick, Cathy. "Into the Public Eye." *Sojourners* 16 (Feb. 1987): 20–25.

Fitzwater, Marlin. *Call the Briefing!* New York: Random House, 1995.

Fleischman, Janet. "Beyond the Blocs? Peace and Freedom Hosts International Seminar in Warsaw." *Across Frontiers* 3 (Summer–Fall 1987): 27–29.

Flessati, Valerie. *Waking the Sleeping Giant: The Story of Christian CND*. London: Christian Campaign for Nuclear Disarmament, 1997.

Foot, Michael. *Another Heart and Other Pulses: The Alternative to the Thatcher Society*. London: Collins, 1984.

Forsberg, Randall. "Confining the Military to Defense as a Route to Disarmament." *World Policy Journal* 1 (Winter 1984): 285–318.

Foster, Catherine. *Women for All Seasons: The Story of the Women's International League for Peace and Freedom*. Athens: University of Georgia Press, 1989.

Frana, Ivo, Josef Krejci, and Zdenek Pagac. *The Peace Movement in Struggle Against Nuclear War and for Disarmament*. Prague: Orbis Press Agency, 1986.

"'Freedom and Peace': Poland's Independent Peace Movement." *East European Reporter* 2 (Spring 1986): 44–49.

Fritsch-Bournazel, Renata. "France: Attachment to a Nonbinding Relationship," pp. 69–100 in Gregory Flynn and Hans Rattinger, eds., *The Public and Atlantic Defense*. Totowa, N.J.: Rowman & Allanheld, 1985.

From Below: Independent Peace and Environmental Movements in Eastern Europe and the USSR. New York: Helsinki Watch, 1987.

Fry, Greg E. "The South Pacific Nuclear-Free Zone," pp. 499–508 in *World Armaments and Disarmament: SIPRI Yearbook 1986*. Oxford: Oxford University Press, 1986.

Furtado, Jean, ed. *Turkey: Peace on Trial*. London: European Nuclear Disarmament and Merlin Press, 1983.

Galand, Pierre. "Le C.N.A.P.D.—Belgique." Brussels, 1984 (mimeographed).

"A Gallup Poll on Nuclear War." *Newsweek* 98 (Oct. 5, 1981): 35.

Gallup, George H. *The Gallup Poll: Public Opinion, 1972–1977*. Wilmington, Del.: Scholarly Resources, 1978.

———. *The Gallup Poll: Public Opinion*. 1978–2001. Wilmington, Del.: Scholarly Resources, 1979–2002.

———, ed. *The Gallup International Public Opinion Polls: France 1939, 1944–1975*. New York: Random House, 1976.

———, ed. *The International Gallup Polls: Public Opinion 1978*. Wilmington, Del.: Scholarly Resources, 1980.

———, ed. *The International Gallup Polls: Public Opinion 1979*. Wilmington, Del.: Scholarly Resources, 1981.

Galtung, Johan. "Europe 1989: The Role of Peace Research and the Peace Movement," pp. 91–105 in Ralph Summy and Michael E. Salla, eds., *Why the Cold War Ended: A Range of Interpretations*. Westport, Conn.: Greenwood Press, 1995.

Gardezi, Hassan, and Hari Sharma. "Introduction." *Bulletin of Concerned Asian Scholars* 31 (Apr.–June 1999): 3–9.

Garthoff, Raymond L. *Détente and Confrontation: American-Soviet Relations from Nixon to Reagan*. Washington, D.C.: Brookings Institution, 1985.

———. *Deterrence and the Revolution in Soviet Military Doctrine*. Washington, D.C.: Brookings Institution, 1990.

———. *The Great Transition: American-Soviet Relations and the End of the Cold War*. Washington, D.C.: Brookings Institution, 1994.

Gates, Robert M. *From the Shadows*. New York: Simon & Schuster, 1996.

Genscher, Hans-Dietrich. *Rebuilding a House Divided: A Memoir by the Architect of Germany's Reunification*. New York: Broadway Books, 1995.

George, Bruce, and Jonathan Marcus. "Unilateralism's Second Wave: The 1983 General Election and After." *Political Quarterly* 55 (Jan.–Mar. 1984): 60–71.

Gergen, David R. *Eyewitness to Power: The Essence of Leadership, Nixon to Clinton.* New York: Simon & Schuster, 2000.

Giangrande, Carole. *The Nuclear North: The People, the Regions, and the Arms Race.* Toronto: Anansi, 1983.

Glass, Matthew. *Citizens against the MX: Public Languages in the Nuclear Age.* Urbana: University of Illinois Press, 1993.

Glick, Brian. *War at Home.* Boston: South End Press, 1989.

Gnesotto, Nicole. "All Quiet on the French Front?" pp. 245–59 in Walter Laqueur and Robert Hunter, eds., *European Peace Movements and the Future of the Western Alliance.* New Brunswick, N.J.: Transaction Books, 1985.

Gorbachev, Mikhail. *For a Nuclear-Free World: Speeches and Statements by the General Secretary of the CPSU Central Committee on Nuclear Disarmament Problems, January 1986–January 1987.* Moscow: Novosti Press Agency, 1987.

———. *Memoirs.* New York: Doubleday, 1995.

———. *The Moratorium: Selected Speeches and Statements by the General Secretary of the CPSU Central Committee on the Problem of Ending Nuclear Tests (January–September 1986).* Moscow: Novosti Press Agency, 1986.

———. "Nobel Lecture, June 5, 1991," pp. 272–83 in Tore Frängsmyr, ed., *Les prix Nobel: The Nobel Prizes, 1990.* Stockholm: Almqvist & Wiksell, 1991.

———. *Nuclear Disarmament by the Year 2000: A Soviet Program.* New York: Richardson & Steirman, 1986.

———. *Perestroika.* New York: Harper & Row, 1987.

———. *A Time for Peace.* New York: Richardson & Steirman, 1985.

Gordon, Suzanne. "From the Other Shore: Movements for Nuclear Disrmament in Eastern Europe." *Working Papers* 10 (Mar.–Apr. 1983): 32–40.

———. "The Ultimate Single Issue." *Working Papers* 9 (May–June 1982): 20–25.

Graham, Thomas. "NATO and Nuclear Weapons Doctrine." *Bulletin of Arms Control,* No 34 (June 1999), pp. 1–4.

Graham, Thomas W. *American Public Opinion on NATO, Extended Deterrence, and Use of Nuclear Weapons.* Lanham, Md.: University Press of America, 1989.

Gray, Colin S., and Keith Payne. "Victory Is Possible." *Foreign Policy,* No. 39 (Summer 1980), pp. 14–27.

Gray, Peter. *Briefing Book on the Nonproliferation of Nuclear Weapons.* Washington, D.C.: Council for a Livable World Education Fund, 1993.

———. *Briefing Book on U.S. Leadership and the Future of Nuclear Arsenals.* Washington, D.C.: Council for a Livable World Education Fund, 1996.

Grepstad, Jon. "Norway and the Struggle for Nuclear Disarmament." Paper presented at the 1981 World Conference Against Atomic and Hydrogen Bombs, Tokyo, Hiroshima and Nagasaki, Aug. 3–9, 1981.

———. "The Peace Movement in the Nordic Countries." *International Peace Research Newsletter* 20:4 (1982): 10–15.

Grewe, Hartmut. "The West German Peace Movement: A Profile," pp. 104–31 in Werner Kaltefleiter and Robert L. Pfaltzgraff, eds., *The Peace Movements in Europe and the United States.* London: Croom Helm, 1985.

Grossi, Verdiana. "From Contempt to Credibility: The Peace Movement in Switzerland, 1945–1992." Paper presented at the International Peace Research Association conference, Malta, Nov. 2, 1994.

Haig, Alexander M., Jr. *Caveat: Realism, Reagan, and Foreign Policy*. New York: Macmillan Publishing, 1984.

Hall, B. Welling. "The Church and the Independent Peace Movement in Eastern Europe." *Journal of Peace Research* 23 (June 1986): 193–208.

Hall-Cathala, David. *The Peace Movement in Israel, 1967–87*. New York: St. Martin's Press, 1990.

Hansen, Allen C. *USIA: Public Diplomacy in the Computer Age*. New York: Praeger, 1989.

Hanson, Eric O. *The Catholic Church in World Politics*. Princeton: Princeton University Press, 1987.

Haraszti, Miklos. "The Hungarian Independent Peace Movement." *Telos*, No. 61 (Fall 1984), pp. 134–43.

Harford, Barbara, and Sarah Hopkins, eds. *Greenham Common: Women at the Wire*. London: Women's Press, 1984.

Hassner, Pierre. "Pacifism and East-West Relations," pp. 112–43 in Walter Laqueur and Robert Hunter, eds., *European Peace Movements and the Future of the Western Alliance*. New Brunswick, N.J.: Transaction Books, 1985.

Hastings, Elizabeth Hann, and Philip K. Hastings, eds. *Index to International Public Opinion*. 1982–1999. Westport, Conn.: Greenwood Press, 1984–2000.

Hauner, Milan. "Anti-militarism and the Independent Peace Movement in Czechoslovakia," pp. 88–117 in Vladimir Tismaneanu, ed., *In Search of Civil Society*. New York: Routledge, 1990.

Havel, Vaclav. *The Anatomy of a Reticence: Eastern European Dissidents and the Peace Movement in the West*. Stockholm: Charta 77 Foundation, 1985.

Hawke, Bob. *The Hawke Memoirs*. Port Melbourne: William Heinemann, 1994.

Heald, Gordon, and Robert J. Wybrow. *The Gallup Survey of Britain*. London: Croom Helm, 1986.

Healey, Denis. *The Time of My Life*. London: Michael Joseph, 1989.

———. *When Shrimps Learn to Whistle: Signposts for the Nineties*. London: Michael Joseph, 1990.

Hempfling, Judith. "Linking up with the East Bloc Peace Movement." *In These Times* 11 (June 10–23, 1987): 4.

Herken, Gregg. *Cardinal Choices: Presidential Science Advising from the Atomic Bomb to SDI*. New York: Oxford University Press, 1992.

Hinton, James. *Protests and Visions: Peace Politics in Twentieth-Century Britain*. London: Hutchinson Radius, 1989.

Holden, Constance. "Physicians Take on Nuclear War." *Science* 207 (Mar. 28, 1980): 1449–52.

Holloway, David. *The Soviet Union and the Arms Race*. New Haven: Yale University Press, 1983.

Hook, Glenn D. "The Ban the Bomb Movement in Japan: Whither Alternative Security?" *Social Alternatives* 3 (Mar. 1983): 35–39.

————. "The Erosion of Antimilitaristic Principles in Contemporary Japan." *Journal of Peace Research* 25 (Dec. 1988): 381–94.

Howorth, Jolyon. *France: The Politics of Peace*. London: Merlin Press, 1984.

Iatrides, John O. "Papandreou's Foreign Policy," pp. 127–59 in Theodore C. Kariotis, ed., *The Greek Socialist Experiment: Papandreou's Greece, 1981–1989*. New York: Pella Publishing, 1992.

Ilukhina, Ruzanna. "Re-birth of Russian Pacifism." Lecture at Society of Friends meeting, Swarthmore, Penn., May 24, 1991.

————, and Tatiana Pavlova. "Totalitarianism and Free Thinking: The Role of Independent Peace and Pacifist Ideas in the USSR in the Ending of the Cold War." Paper presented at the International Congress of Historical Sciences, Montreal, Sept. 1, 1995.

In Defence of Peace. London: Campaign for the Defence of the Turkish Peace Association, 1982.

"Indian, Pakistani NGOs Oppose Nuclear Tests." *Philosophy and Social Action* 24 (July–Dec. 1998): 89–91.

Inozemtsev, Nikolai. "Introduction," pp. 7–21 in Nikolai Inozemtsev, ed., *Peace and Disarmament*. Moscow: Progress Publishers, 1980.

Interkerkelijk Vredesberaad. *Achter de IKV-campagne*. The Hague: Interkerkelijk Vredesberaad, 1981.

————. *Help de Kernwapens de Wereld Uit: Om te Beginnen Uit Nederland*. The Hague: Interkerkelijk Vredesberaad, 1983.

"International Conference on Peace and Reunification of Korea." *Korea Report* 2 (Nov.–Dec. 1988): 11.

International Physicians for the Prevention of Nuclear War: Description and Brief History. Boston: IPPNW, 1986.

"International Seminar 'Prague '88.'" *Across Frontiers* 4–5 (Winter–Spring 1989): 45, 59.

Iriye, Akira. *Global Community: The Role of International Organizations in the Making of the Contemporary World*. Berkeley: University of California Press, 2002.

Jack, Homer A. *Nuclear Politics After Hiroshima/Nagasaki: Unitarian Universalist and Other Responses*. Swarthmore, Penn.: 1987 Minns Lectures, 1987.

Jackson, A. Wynton. "GDR: Appeal on the Occasion of UN Peace Year." *East European Reporter* 2 (Spring 1986): 60–62.

————. "The New Samizdat." *Across Frontiers* 4 (Winter 1988): 15–17.

Jacobsen, Carl G. "The Nuclear Era: Its History; Its Implications," pp. 31–56 in Ken Coates, ed., *The Dynamics of European Nuclear Disarmament*. Nottingham: Spokesman, 1981.

"The Japanese Disarmament Movement on the Upsurge." *Japan Quarterly* 29 (July–Sept. 1982): 287–90.

Jayaraman, K. S. "Indian Scientists Speak Out Against Bomb." *Philosphy and Social Action* 24 (July–Dec. 1998): 86–88.

Jenkins-Smith, Hank C., Richard P. Barke, and Kerry C. Herron. *Public Perspec-*

tives of Nuclear Weapons in the Post–Cold War Environment. n.p.: Sandia National Laboratories, 1994.

Jewett, Pauline. "'Suffocation' of the Arms Race: Federal Policy, 1978–82," pp. 204–15 in Ernie Regehr and Simon Rosenblum, eds., *Canada and the Nuclear Arms Race.* Toronto: James Lorimer, 1983.

Johnstone, Diana. "German Peace Movement Says Scrap All Missiles." *In These Times* 11 (June 24–July 7, 1987): 11.

———. "Labor Signs on with Peace Movement." *In These Times* 7 (Oct. 19–25, 1983): 8.

———. *The Politics of Euromissiles: Europe's Role in America's World.* London: Verso, 1984.

Jones, Lynne. "Tentative Dialogue in Perugia." *New Statesman* 107 (Aug. 3, 1984): 16–17.

Jordan, Gerhard. "Peace Activities in Austria Since 1945." Paper presentated at the European-American Consultation on Peace Research in History, Stadtschlaining, Austria, Aug. 25–28, 1986.

Kaldor, Mary. "The Helsinki Citizens' Assembly," pp. 199–200 in Mary Kaldor, ed., *Europe from Below: An East-West Dialogue.* London: Verso, 1991.

———. "Introduction," pp. 1–4 in Richard Taylor and Nigel Young, eds., *Campaigns for Peace: British Peace Movements in the Twentieth Century.* Manchester: Manchester University Press, 1987.

———. "Introduction," pp. 1–3 in Mary Kaldor, ed., *Europe from Below: An East-West Dialogue.* London: Verso, 1991.

———. "We Got the Idea from Your Banners." *New Statesman* 113 (Mar. 13, 1987): 14–15.

Kamata, Sadao, and Stephen Salaff. "The Atomic Bomb and the Citizens of Nagasaki." *Bulletin of Concerned Asian Scholars* 14 (Apr.–June 1982): 38–50.

Kamimura, Naoki. *Japanese Civil Society, Local Government, and U.S.-Japan Security Relations in the 1990s.* Osaka: Japan Center for Area Studies, 2001.

Kaufman, Burton I. *The Presidency of James Earl Carter, Jr.* Lawrence: University Press of Kansas, 1993.

Kavan, Jan. "Helsinki, the Peace Movement, and the East-West Dialogue." *Across Frontiers* 3 (Spring 1987): 37–45.

———. "Spontaneous Peace Demo in Prague." *Across Frontiers* 2 (Spring–Summer 1986): 19–23.

———, and Zdena Tomin. "Introduction," pp. 3–9 in Jan Kavan and Zdena Tomin, eds., *Voices from Prague: Documents on Czechoslovakia and the Peace Movement.* London: END and Palach Press, 1983.

———. *Voices from Prague: Documents on Czechoslovakia and the Peace Movement.* London: END and Palach Press, 1983.

Kelly, Petra. *Fighting for Hope.* Boston: South End Press, 1984.

Kent, Bruce. "Protest and Survive." *History Today* 49 (May 1999): 14–16.

———. *Undiscovered Ends.* London: Fount, 1992.

Kettle-Williams, Jay. "The Birth of the Peace Movement in Spain." *Journal of Area Studies,* No. 9 (Spring 1984), pp. 42–43.

King, Michael. *Death of the Rainbow Warrior*. Auckland: Penguin Books, 1986.

Kissinger, Henry A. *The Necessity for Choice: Prospects for American Foreign Policy*. New York: Harper & Row, 1961.

———. *Nuclear Weapons and Foreign Policy*. New York: Harper & Row, 1957.

———. *White House Years*. Boston: Little, Brown, 1979.

Kiszely, Karoly. "Pacifism Under Fire." *Across Frontiers* 2 (Spring–Summer 1986): 27–28.

Kleidman, Robert. *Organizing for Peace: Neutrality, the Test Ban, and the Freeze*. Syracuse: Syracuse University Press, 1993.

Klein, Fritz, "East Germany and Eastern Europe." Paper presented at the International Congress of Historical Sciences, Montreal, Sept. 1, 1995.

Knopf, Jeffrey W. *Domestic Society and International Cooperation: The Impact of Protest on US Arms Control Policy*. Cambridge: Cambridge University Press, 1998.

Kodama, Katsuya. "Red vs. Green: A Comparative Study on Peace Movements in Japan, Denmark, and Finland." Paper presented at the Lund Conference on Peace Movements, Lund, Sweden, Aug. 17–20, 1987.

Kortunov, Sergey V. "Russia," pp. 87–98 in Eric Arnett, ed., *Nuclear Weapons After the Comprehensive Test Ban*. Oxford: Oxford University Press, 1996.

Koschmann, J. Victor. "Postwar Democracy and Japanese Ban-the-Bomb Movements." Manuscript, author's possession.

Köszegi, Ferenc, and E. P. Thompson. *The New Hungarian Peace Movement*. London: Merlin Press, 1982.

Köszegi, Ferenc, and Istvan Szent-Ivanyi. "A Struggle Around an Idea: The Peace Movement in Hungary." *New Society* 62 (Oct. 21, 1982): 115–20 and (Oct. 28, 1982): 163–64.

Kotz, Nick. *Wild Blue Yonder: Money, Politics, and the B-1 Bomber*. New York: Pantheon Books, 1988.

Kramer, Bernard M., S. Michael Kalick, and Michael Millburn. "Attitudes Toward Nuclear Weapons and Nuclear War: 1945–1982." *Journal of Social Issues* 39 (Spring 1983): 7–24.

Krasner, Michael A. "Decline and Persistence in the Contemporary Danish and British Peace Movements: A Comparative Political Analysis," pp. 169–91 in Katsuya Kodama and Unto Vesa, eds., *Towards a Comparative Analysis of Peace Movements*. Hants, Eng.: Dartmouth Publishing, 1990.

———. *The Political Influence of the New Danish Peace Movement, 1979–1986*. Aarhus, Denmark: Institute of Political Science, University of Aarhus, 1986.

———, and Nikolaj Petersen. "Peace and Politics: The Danish Peace Movement and Its Impact on National Security Policy." *Journal of Peace Research* 23 (June 1986): 155–73.

Krasniewicz, Louise. *Nuclear Summer: The Clash of Communities at the Seneca Women's Peace Encampment*. Ithaca: Cornell University Press, 1992.

Kubbig, Bernd W., and Thomas Risse-Kappen. "Living Up to the Ethical Dimensions of Nuclear Armament: The Churches as Pace-Setters of Current Thinking on Peace and War." *Bulletin of Peace Proposals* 15:1 (1984): 67–77.

Kull, Steven. *Burying Lenin: The Revolution in Soviet Ideology and Foreign Policy.* Boulder: Westview Press, 1992.

"Labour and Lange break the mould." *Socialist Affairs*, No. 3/87 (1987), p. 62.

"Labour Unites on Economic Policy." *Socialist Affairs*, No. 4/85 (1985), p. 69.

Lamare, James W. "The Growth of Antinuclearism in New Zealand." *Australian Journal of Political Science* 26 (Nov. 1991): 472–87.

Landais-Stamp, Paul, and Paul Rogers. *Rocking the Boat: New Zealand, the United States and the Nuclear-Free Zone Controversy in the 1980s.* Oxford: Berg, 1989.

Lange, David. *Nuclear Free: The New Zealand Way.* Auckland: Penguin Books, 1990.

Lashmar, Paul, and James Oliver. *Britain's Secret Propaganda War.* Gloucestershire: Sutton, 1998.

Lebow, Richard Ned, and Janice Gross Stein. *We All Lost the Cold War.* Princeton: Princeton University Press, 1994.

"Let the Bands Play!" *Across Frontiers* 3 (Fall 1986): 29–34.

Lewis, Patricia M. "The United Kingdom," pp. 99–115 in Eric Arnett, ed., *Nuclear Weapons After the Comprehensive Test Ban.* Oxford: Oxford University Press, 1996.

Liddington, Jill. *The Long Road to Greenham: Feminism and Anti-Militarism in Britain since 1820.* London: Virago Press, 1989.

Lindkvist, Kent. "Mobilization Peaks and Declines of the Swedish Peace Movement," pp. 147–67 in Katsuya Kodama and Unto Vesa, eds., *Towards a Comparative Analysis of Peace Movements.* Hants, Eng.: Dartmouth Publishing, 1990.

Locke, Elsie. *Peace People: A History of Peace Activities in New Zealand.* Christchurch: Hazard Press, 1992.

"Looking East." *Economist* (July 13, 1985), pp. 50–51.

Lubelski-Bernard, Nadine. "The Euromissile Crisis and the Belgian Peace Movements." *Peace Research* 28 (Aug. 1996): 47–65.

Lumsden, Malvern. "Nuclear Weapons and the New Peace Movement," pp. 101–26 in *World Armaments and Disarmament: SIPRI Yearbook 1983.* New York: International Publications Service, 1983.

Lundberg, George D. "Prescriptions for Peace in a Nuclear Age." *Journal of the American Medical Association* 254 (Aug. 2, 1985): 660–61.

Mack, Andrew. "Untangling Public Opinion." *Peace Studies* (June 1985), pp. 13–15.

Magraw, Katherine. "The United States," pp. 116–28 in Eric Arnett, ed., *Nuclear Weapons After the Comprehensive Test Ban.* Oxford: Oxford University Press, 1996.

Maislinger, Andreas. "Effects of the Austrian Peace Movement." Paper presented at the European-American Consultation on Peace Research in History, Stadtschlaining, Austria, Aug. 25–28, 1986.

———. "The Peace Movement in a Neutral Country: On the Subject of the New Peace Movement in Austria." *Wiener Blätter zur Friedensforschung*, No. 42–43 (May 1985), pp. 57–68.

Martin, Brian. "Nuclear suppression." *Science and Public Policy* 13 (Dec. 1986): 312–20.

Masumi, Junnosuke. *Contemporary Politics in Japan*. Berkeley: University of California Press, 1995.

Matlock, Jack F., Jr. *Autopsy on an Empire*. New York: Random House, 1995.

MccGwire, Michael. *Perestroika and Soviet National Security*. Washington, D.C.: Brookings Institution, 1991.

McCrea, Frances B., and Gerald E. Markle. *Minutes to Midnight: Nuclear Weapons Protest in America*. Newbury Park: Sage, 1989.

McFarlane, Robert C., with Zofia Smardz. *Special Trust*. New York: Cadell & Davies, 1994.

McNamara, Robert S. *In Retrospect: The Tragedy and Lessons of Vietnam*. New York: Times Books, 1995.

————. "The Military Role of Nuclear Weapons: Perceptions and Misperceptions." *Foreign Affairs* 62 (Fall 1983): 59–80.

The Meaning of Survival: Hiroshima's 36 Year Commitment to Peace. Hiroshima: Chugoku Shimbun and the Hiroshima International Cultural Foundation, 1983.

Meese, Edwin, III. *With Reagan: The Inside Story*. Washington, D.C.: Regnery Gateway, 1992.

Mellon, Christian. "Peace Organisations in France Today," pp. 202–16 in Jolyon Howorth and Patricia Chilton, eds., *Defence and Dissent in Contemporary France*. London: Croom Helm, 1984.

Merkl, Peter H. "Pacifism in West Germany." *School of Advanced International Studies Review*, No. 4 (Summer 1982), pp. 81–91.

Meyer, David S. *A Winter of Discontent: The Nuclear Freeze and American Politics*. New York: Praeger, 1990.

————, and Sam Marullo. "Grassroots Mobilization and International Politics: Peace Protest and the End of the Cold War." Paper presented at the American Sociological Association convention, Cincinnati, Aug. 25, 1991.

Meyer, Robert S. *Peace Organizations Past and Present*. Jefferson, N.C.: McFarland, 1988.

Mleczkowski, Wolfgang. "In Search of the Forbidden Nation: Opposition by the Young Generation in the GDR." *Government and Opposition* 18 (Spring 1983): 175–93.

Morris, Dick. *Behind the Oval Office: Getting Reelected Against All Odds*. Los Angeles: Renaissance Books, 1999.

"Moscow and the Peace Movement: The Soviet Committee for the Defense of Peace." *Foreign Affairs Note* (May 1987), pp. 1–12.

Munton, Don. *Peace and Security in the 1980s: The View of Canadians*. Ottawa: Canadian Institute for Peace and Security, 1988.

————, and Michael Slack. "Canadian Attitudes on Disarmament." *International Perspectives* (July–Aug. 1982), pp. 9–12.

Mushaben, Joyce Marie. "Cycles of Peace Protest in West Germany: Experiences from Three Decades." *West European Politics* 8 (Jan. 1985): 24–40.

————. "Swords to Plowshares: The Church, the State and the East German Peace Movement." *Studies in Comparative Communism* 17 (Summer 1984): 123–35.

Musto, Ronald G. *The Catholic Peace Tradition*. Maryknoll, N.Y.: Orbis Books, 1986.

Myers, Ched. "Storming the Gates of Hell." *Christian Century* 98 (Sept. 16, 1981): 898–902.

Myrdal, Alva. *The Game of Disarmament: How the United States and Russia Run the Arms Race*. New York: Pantheon, 1976.

"National Democratic Alliance Is Born." *Korea Report* 2 (Jan.–Feb. 1989): 15.

Nelkin, Dorothy, and Michael Pollak. *The Atom Besieged: Extraparliamentary Dissent in France and Germany*. Cambridge, Mass.: MIT Press, 1981.

"New Attack on Soviet Independent Peace Movement." *Across Frontiers* 2 (Winter 1985): 27–28.

Newdorf, David. "Israeli Anti-nuclear Movement Stagnates." *In These Times* 11 (Oct. 21–27, 1987): 17.

Newman, Jacquetta. "Surviving the End of the Cold War: Project Ploughshares in the 1990s." *Peace Research* 31 (Nov. 1999): 44–58.

Newnham, Tom. *Peace Squadron: The Sharp End of Nuclear Protest in New Zealand*. Auckland: Graphic, 1986.

Nilson, Sten Sparre. "The Peace Movement in Norway," pp. 33–48 in Werner Kaltefleiter and Robert L. Pfaltzgraff, eds., *The Peace Movements in Europe and the United States*. London: Croom Helm, 1985

Nitze, Paul H. *From Hiroshima to Glasnost: At the Center of Decision, A Memoir*. New York: Grove Weidenfeld, 1989.

Nixon, Richard. *RN: The Memoirs of Richard Nixon*. New York: Grosset & Dunlap, 1978.

Noack, Paul, and Michael Staude. "Peace Movement in the Federal Republic of Germany," pp. 219–26 in Ervin Laszlo and Jong Youl Yoo, eds., *World Encyclopedia of Peace*, vol. II. Oxford: Pergamon Press, 1986.

Noelle-Neumann, Elisabeth, ed. *The Germans: Public Opinion Polls, 1967–1980*. Westport, Conn.: Greenwood Press, 1981.

Nolan, Janne E. *An Elusive Consensus: Nuclear Weapons and American Security after the Cold War*. Washington, D.C.: Brookings Institution, 1999.

"Noose Tightens Around Czech Jazz Section." *Across Frontiers* 3 (Fall 1986): n.p.

"Notes and Comment." *New Yorker* 67 (May 6, 1991): 31–32.

"Notes from the Underground Soviet Peace Movement." *In These Times* 11 (Apr. 8–14, 1987): 7.

"NPT Review Conference: Agreement on Disarmament at Safeguards' Expense." *Trust & Verify*, No. 92 (July 2000), p. 7.

"Nuclear Arms." *Gallup Report*, No. 208 (Jan. 1983), pp. 10–14.

"Nuclear Disarmament." *Gallup Report*, No. 188 (May 1981), pp. 3–10.

"Nuclear Policy Sparks Debate." *New Zealand Foreign Affairs Review* 35 (Jan.–Mar. 1985): 3–17.

Oberdorfer, Don. *The Turn: From the Cold War to a New Era: The United States and the Soviet Union, 1983–1990*. New York: Poseidon Press, 1991.

"Official Attacks on Independent Soviet Peace Movement Escalate." *Across Frontiers* 2 (Spring–Summer 1986): 12.

Ohnishi, Hitoshi. "The Peace Movement in Japan." *International Peace Research Newsletter* 21 (1983): 26–33.

"On the Eve: A Glimpse Inside the Politburo at the End of 1988." *Cold War International History Project Bulletin*, No. 12–13 (Fall–Winter 2001), pp. 24–29.

"Oppositionists Debate a Strategy for Peace." *Across Frontiers* 2 (Winter 1985): 13–14

Ormrod, David. "The Churches and the Nuclear Arms Race," pp. 189–200 in Richard Taylor and Nigel Young, eds., *Campaigns for Peace: British Peace Movements in the Twentieth Century*. Manchester: Manchester University Press, 1987.

Ostling, Richard N. "Bishops and the Bomb." *Time* 120 (Nov. 29, 1982): 68–77.

Paine, Christopher. "The Comprehensive Test Ban Treaty in the Current Nuclear Context," pp. 45–58 in Matthew McKinzie, ed., *The Comprehensive Test Ban Treaty: Issues and Answers*. Ithaca: Cornell University Peace Studies Program, 1997.

"Pakistan Action Committee Against N-Arms Race." *Philosophy and Social Action* 24 (July–Dec. 1998): 92–93.

Palazchenko, Pavel. *My Years with Gorbachev and Shevardnadze: The Memoir of a Soviet Interpreter*. University Park: Pennsylvania State University Press, 1997.

Pavlova, Tatiana. "Hundred Years of Russian Pacifism." *Journal of Human Values* 5:2 (1999): 147–55.

"The Peace Movement and Eastern Europe." *Labour Focus on Eastern Europe* 5 (Winter 1982–83): 7–10.

Peck, Keenen. "The Take-Charge Gang." *Progressive* 49 (May 1985): 1, 18–24.

Penner, Robert. "A Brief Overview and Analysis of the Canadian Peace Movement Since 1982," pp. 45–57 in Janis Alton, Eric Fawcett, and L. Terrell Gardner, eds., *The Name of the Chamber Was Peace*. Toronto: Science for Peace and Samuel Stevens, 1988.

Perkovich, George. *India's Nuclear Bomb: The Impact on Global Proliferation*. Berkeley: University of California Press, 1999.

Petersen, Nikolaj. "The Scandilux Experiment: Towards a Transnational Social Democratic Security Perspective?" *Cooperation and Conflict* 20 (1985): 1–22.

Pfaltzgraff, Diane K. "The Antinuclear Protest in Italy: A Nonstarter?" pp. 120–51 in James Dougherty and Robert L. Pfaltzgraff, Jr., eds, *Shattering Europe's Defense Consensus: The Antinuclear Protest Movement and the Future of NATO*. Washington, D.C.: Pergamon-Brassey's, 1985.

"The Philippines: Workers Close Westinghouse Nuclear Plant." *Asian Rights Advocate* 9 (Sept. 1985): 2.

"Political Opposition in Czechoslovakia Today." *Across Frontiers* 2 (Winter 1985): 8–9.

Polner, Murray, and Jim O'Grady. *Disarmed and Dangerous: The Radical Lives and Times of Daniel and Philip Berrigan*. New York: Basic Books, 1997.

Powaski, Ronald E. *March to Armageddon: The United States and the Nuclear Arms Race, 1939 to the Present*. New York: Oxford University Press, 1989.

———. *Return to Armageddon: The United States and the Nuclear Arms Race*. New York: Oxford University Press, 2000.

Powell, Colin L., with Joseph Persico. *My American Journey*. New York: Random House, 1995.

"The Prague Appeal." *Across Frontiers* 2 (Summer 1985): 13–15.

"President Carter Interviewed by AP and UPI Corespondents." *Department of State Bulletin* 76 (Feb. 14, 1977): 123–25.

Pressman, Steven. "Nuclear Freeze Groups Focus on Candidates." *Congressional Quarterly* 42 (May 5, 1984): 1021–24.

Primack, Joel, and Frank von Hippel. *Advice and Dissent: Scientists in the Political Arena.* New York: Basic Books, 1974.

"Profile of MAPAM: United Workers Party of Israel." n.p.: MAPAM, 1983.

Pry, Peter Vincent. *War Scare: Russia and America on the Nuclear Brink.* Westport, Conn.: Praeger, 1999.

Public Attitudes on Nuclear Weapons: An Opportunity for Leadership. Washington, D.C.: Henry L. Stimson Center, 1998.

Public Papers of the Presidents of the United States: Jimmy Carter, 1977. Washington, D.C.: U.S. Government Printing Office, 1978.

Public Papers of the Presidents of the United States: Jimmy Carter, 1980–81. Washington, D.C.: U.S. Government Printing Office, 1982.

Public Papers of the Presidents of the United States: Ronald Reagan, 1982. Washington, D.C.: U.S. Government Printing Office, 1983.

Randle, Michael. *People Power: The Building of a New European Home.* Stroud, Eng.: Hawthorn Press, 1991.

Rattinger, Hans. "The Federal Republic of Germany: Much Ado About (Almost) Nothing," pp. 101–74 in Gregory Flynn and Hans Rattinger, eds., *The Public and Atlantic Defense.* Totowa, N.J.: Rowman & Allanheld, 1985.

Reagan, Nancy, with William Novak. *My Turn: The Memoirs of Nancy Reagan.* New York: Random House, 1989.

Reagan, Ronald. *An American Life: The Autobiography.* New York: Simon & Schuster, 1990.

——. *The U.S.-Soviet Relationship.* Washington, D.C.: U.S. Department of State, 1984.

Redner, Harry, and Jill Redner. *Anatomy of the World: The Impact of the Atom on Australia and the World.* Melbourne: Fontana/Collins, 1983.

"Referendum Confirms NATO Membership." *Socialist Affairs*, No. 1/86 (1986), p. 71.

Regan, Donald T. *For the Record: From Wall Street to Washington.* San Diego: Harcourt Brace Jovanovich, 1988.

Regehr, Ernie. "Canada as a Nuclear-Weapons-Free Zone," pp. 241–49 in Ernie Regehr and Simon Rosenblum, eds., *Canada and the Nuclear Arms Race.* Toronto: James Lorimer, 1983.

——, Bill Robinson, and Simon Rosenblum. *Making Canada a Nuclear Weapon–Free Zone.* Waterloo, Ont.: Project Ploughshares, 1987.

——, and Simon Rosenblum. "The Canadian Peace Movement," pp. 225–30 in Ernie Regehr and Simon Rosenblum, eds., *Canada and the Nuclear Arms Race.* Toronto: Jmes Lorimer, 1983.

Reiss, Mitchell. *Without the Bomb: The Politics of Nuclear Nonproliferation.* New York: Columbia University Press, 1988.

"Ridding Europe of Nuclear Weapons: A Statement by the Socialist International," pp. 151–55 in Ken Coates, ed., *The Dynamics of European Nuclear Disarmament*. Nottingham: Spokesman, 1981.

Risse-Kappen, Thomas. *The Zero Option: INF, West Germany, and Arms Control*. Boulder: Westview Press, 1988.

Roberts, Adam, and Benedict Kingsbury. "Introduction: The UN's Roles in International Society since 1945," pp. 1–62 in Adam Roberts and Benedict Kingsbury, eds., *United Nations, Divided World*. Oxford: Clarendon Press, 1993.

Robinson, Wayne. "Current Peace Research and Activism in New Zealand." *International Peace Research Newsletter* 21:3 (1983): 34–38.

Rogin, Michael Paul. *Ronald Reagan, the Movie*. Berkeley: University of California Press, 1987.

Rojecki, Andrew. *Silencing the Opposition: Antinuclear Movements and the Media in the Cold War*. Urbana: University of Illinois Press, 1999.

Rossi, Sergio A. "Public Opinion and Atlantic Defense in Italy," pp. 175–219 in Gregory Flynn and Hans Rattinger, eds., *The Public and Atlantic Defense*. Totowa, N.J.: Rowman & Allanheld, 1985.

———, and Virgilio Ilari. "The Peace Movement in Italy," pp. 140–61 in Werner Kaltefleiter and Robert L. Pfaltzgraff, eds., *The Peace Movements in Europe and the United States*. London: Croom Helm, 1985.

Routledge, Paul. "Dispensable Space, Defensible Space: The Conflict over the National Testing Range in Orissa." *South Asia Bulletin* 8 (Spring–Fall 1988): 98–104.

Sagdeev, Roald Z. *The Making of a Soviet Scientist*. New York: John Wiley, 1994.

Sakharov, Andrei. *Alarm and Hope*. New York: Alfred A. Knopf, 1978.

———. *Memoirs*. New York: Alfred A. Knopf, 1990.

———. "A Message from Gorky," pp. 239–43 in Edward D. Lozansky, ed., *Andrei Sakharov and Peace*. New York: Avon Books, 1985.

———. *Moscow and Beyond, 1986 to 1989*. New York: Alfred A. Knopf, 1991.

———. "Of Arms and Reforms." *Time* 129 (Mar. 16, 1987): 40–43.

Salomon, Kim. "The Peace Movement: An Anti-Establishment Movement." *Journal of Peace Research* 23 (June 1986): 115–27.

Samad, Yunas. "Nuclear Pakistan and the Emergence of a Peace Movement." *Bulletin of Concerned Asia Scholars* 31 (Apr.–June 1999): 14–22.

Sanders, Jerry W. *Peddlers of Crisis: The Committee on the Present Danger and the Politics of Containment*. Boston: South End Press, 1983.

Sandford, John. *The Sword and the Ploughshare: Autonomous Peace Initiatives in East Germany*. London: Merlin Press and END, 1983.

Santi, Rainer. *100 Years of Peace Making*. Geneva: International Peace Bureau, 1991.

Saunders, Malcolm, and Ralph Summy. *The Australian Peace Movement: A Short History*. Canberra: Peace Research Center, Australian National University, 1986.

Saxton, Jon. "Nuclear Diplomacy: The Peace Movement and Declaring No First Use," pp. 493–505 in Paul Joseph and Simon Rosenblum, eds., *Search for Sanity*. Boston: South End Press, 1984.

Savel'yev, Aleksandr, and Nikolay N. Detinov. *The Big Five: Arms Control Decision-Making in the Soviet Union*. Westport, Conn.: Praeger, 1995.

Schaper, Annette. "The Comprehensive Test Ban Treaty from a Global Perspective," pp. 11–26 in Matthew McKinzie, ed., *The Comprehensive Test Ban Treaty: Issues and Answers*. Ithaca: Cornell University Peace Studies Program, 1997.

Scharrer, Siegfried. "War and Peace and the German Church," pp. 273–317 in Walter Laqueur and Robert Hunter, eds., *European Peace Movements and the Future of the Western Alliance*. New Brunswick, NJ: Transaction Books, 1985.

Schell, Jonathan. "The Bomb Is Back." *Sojourners* 31 (Nov.–Dec. 2002): 20–25, 58–59.

———. *The Fate of the Earth*. New York: Avon Books, 1982.

———. "The Gift of Time." *Nation* 266 (Feb. 2–9, 1998): 9–60.

———. "The Growing Nuclear Peril." *Nation* 274 (June 24, 2002): 11–14.

———. "Nuclear Madness." *Nation* 270 (May 29, 2000): 5–7.

Schenker, Hillel. "The Israeli Peace Movement—A Symbol of Hope." *Israel Horizons* 32 (Mar.–Apr. 1984): 25–27.

Schipper, Henry. "Some Girls." *Rolling Stone*, No. 357 (Nov. 26, 1981), p. 23.

Schlafly, Phyllis. "Six Fatal Fallacies of the Nuclear Freezers." *Human Events* (June 25, 1983), p. 17.

Schlaga, Rüdiger. "Peace Movement as a Party's Tool? The Peace Council of the German Democratic Republic," pp. 129–46 in Katsuya Kodama and Unto Vesa, eds., *Towards a Comparative Analysis of Peace Movements*. Hants, Eng.: Dartmouth Publishing, 1990.

Schmidt, Helmut. *Men and Powers: A Political Retrospective*. New York: Random House, 1989.

Schneider, William. "Peace and Strength: American Public Opinion on National Security," pp. 321–64 in Gregory Flynn and Hans Rattinger, eds., *The Public and Atlantic Defense*. Totowa, N.J.: Rowman & Allanheld, 1985.

Schrag, Philip G. *Global Action: Nuclear Test Ban Diplomacy at the End of the Cold War*. Boulder: Westview Press, 1992.

———. *Listening for the Bomb: A Study in Nuclear Arms Control Verification Policy*. Boulder: Westview Press, 1989.

Schulzinger, Robert D. *Henry Kissinger: Doctor of Diplomacy*. New York: Columbia University Press, 1989.

"Semipalatinsk-Nevada as Viewed by a People's Deputy of the USSR." *Moscow News*, No. 51 (Dec. 24–31, 1989), p. 15.

Serry, N. H. "The Peace Movement in the Netherlands," pp. 49–62 in Werner Kaltefleiter and Robert L. Pfaltzgraff, eds., *The Peace Movements in Europe and the United States*. London: Croom Helm, 1985.

Shaffer, Don. "The SANE-Freeze Merger." *In These Times* 11 (Aug. 5–18, 1987): 16.

Shaffer, Stephen M. *Public Image of U.S. Policies Worsens in Britain; German Opinion Remains Largely Negative*. Washington, D.C.: U.S. Information Agency, Feb. 6, 1984.

Shaposhnikov, Vitaly. "The Role of the Public in the Struggle for European Security," pp. 114–26 in Nikolai Inozemtsev, ed., *Peace and Disarmament*. Moscow: Progress Publishers, 1980.

Sharma, Dhirendra. "Confronting the Nuclear Power Structure in India," pp. 155–74 in Brian Martin, ed., *Confronting the Experts*. Albany: State University of New York Press, 1996.

Sharp, Rachel. "Militarism and Nuclear Issues in the Pacific," pp. 176–204 in Rachel Sharp, ed., *Apocalypse No: An Australian Guide to the Arms Race and the Peace Movement*. Sydney: Pluto Press, 1984.

Shaw, Eric. *The Labour Party since 1945*. Oxford: Blackwell, 1996.

Shelley, Diana. "Pacifism, War Resistance, and the Struggle Against Nuclear Weapons: Part II," pp. 36–48 in Gail Chester and Andrew Rigby, eds., *Articles of Peace*. Bridport, Dorset: Prism Press, 1986.

Shevardnadze, Eduard. *The Future Belongs to Freedom*. New York: Free Press, 1991.

Shultz, George P. *Turmoil and Triumph: My Years as Secretary of State*. New York: Charles Scribner's Sons, 1993.

Simpson, Christopher, ed. *National Security Directives of the Reagan and Bush Administrations*. Boulder: Westview Press, 1995.

Siracusa, Joseph M. "Peace Movements in Australia and New Zealand and the Cold War." Paper presented at the International Peace Research Association conference, Malta, Oct. 30–Nov. 4, 1994.

Skinner, Kiron K., Annelise Anderson, and Martin Anderson, eds. *Reagan, In His Own Hand*. New York: Simon & Schuster, 2002.

Small, Melvin. *The Presidency of Richard Nixon*. Lawrence: University Press of Kansas, 1999.

Smith, Tom W. "The Polls: Gender and Attitudes Toward Violence." *Public Opinion Quarterly* 48 (Spring 1984): 384–96.

Snyder, Alvin A. *Warriors of Disinformation: American Propaganda, Soviet Lies, and the Winning of the Cold War, an Insider's Account*. New York: Arcade, 1995.

"The Socialist International Appeal on Disarmament." *Socialist Affairs*, No. 4/85 (1985), p. 36.

"Socialist International Resolutions on Disarmament." *Socialist Affairs*, No. 2/87 (1987), p. 12.

Solo, Pam. *From Protest to Policy: Beyond the Freeze to Common Security*. Cambridge, Mass.: Ballinger, 1988.

Solomon, Mark. *Death Waltz to Armageddon: E. P. Thompson and the Peace Movement*. New York: U.S. Peace Council, n.d.

Solomon, Norman. "Scandinavia 'Zones in' on a Nuclear-free Baltic." *In These Times* 11 (Oct. 14–20, 1987): 5.

Ståhle, Elisabeth. *Internationella Kvinnoförbundet för Fred och Frihet*. Stockholm: IKFF, 1988.

Stark, Elizabeth. "East Meets West." *Psychology Today* 18 (Apr. 1984): 20.

Stark, T. James, and Peter Brown. "Towards a Global Referendum on Disarmament," pp. 231–36 in Ernie Regehr and Simon Rosenblum, eds., *Canada and the Nuclear Arms Race*. Toronto: James Lorimer, 1983.

"Star Wars." *Economic Notes* 54 (July–Aug. 1986): 6.

Stead, Jean, and Danielle Grünberg, eds. *Moscow Independent Peace Group*. London: Merlin Press and END, 1982.

Stevens, Val. "The Importance of the Environmental Movement," pp. 77–79 in John

Minnion and Philip Bolsover, eds., *The CND Story*. London: Allison & Busby, 1983.

Stone, Jeremy. *"Every Man Should Try": Adventures of a Public Interest Activist*. New York: Public Affairs, 1999.

Strandt, Patricia. "Media Freezes Out Women's Meeting." *In These Times* (Mar. 21–27, 1984), p. 16.

Stubbing, Richard A., with Richard A. Mendel. *The Defense Game*. New York: Harper & Row, 1986.

Stützle, Walther. "Introduction: 1986—A Year of Peace?" pp. xxv–xl in *SIPRI Yearbook 1987: World Armaments and Disarmament*. Oxford: Oxford University Press, 1987.

Suh, Hyuk-Kyo. "INF Treaty and Nuclear Weapons in Korea." *Korea Report* 1 (Jan.–Feb. 1988): 10–11, 24–25, 28.

Summy, Ralph, and Malcolm Saunders. "Disarmament and the Australian Peace Movement: A Brief History." *World Review* 26 (Dec. 1987): 15–52.

Sundman, Folke. "The END Campaign and Finland," pp. 50–77 in Kimmo Kiljunen, Folke Sundman, and Ilkka Taipale, eds., *Finnish Peace Making*. Helsinki: Peace Union of Finland, 1987.

Swerdlow, Amy. *Women Strike for Peace: Traditional Motherhood and Radical Politics in the 1960s*. Chicago: University of Chicago Press, 1993.

Taagepera, Rein. "Inclusion of the Baltic Republics in the Nordic Nuclear-Free Zone." *Journal of Baltic Studies* 16 (Spring 1985): 33–51.

Taipale, Ilkka. "The Peace Movement in Finland," pp. 17–49 in Kimmo Kiljunen, Folke Sundman, and Ilkka Taipale, eds., *Finnish Peace Making*. Helsinki: Peace Union of Finland, 1987.

Tairov, Tair. "From New Thinking to a Civic Peace," pp. 43–48 in Mary Kaldor, ed., *Europe from Below: An East-West Dialogue*. London: Verso, 1991.

Takahara, Takao. "Local Government Initiatives to Promote Peace." *Peace and Change* 12:3–4 (1987): 51–58.

Talbott, Strobe. *Deadly Gambits: The Reagan Administration and the Stalemate in Nuclear Arms Control*. New York: Alfred A. Knopf, 1984.

———. *The Master of the Game: Paul Nitze and the Nuclear Peace*. New York: Alfred A. Knopf, 1988.

Tannenwald, Nina. *The Nuclear Taboo: The United States and the Nonuse of Nuclear Weapons Since 1945*. Manuscript. Cambridge: Cambridge University Press, forthcoming.

———, ed. *Understanding the End of the Cold War, 1980–87: An Oral History Conference, Brown University, May 7–10, 1998*. Providence: Watson Institute, 1999.

Taylor, Brian D. *Breaking the Disarmament Deadlock: Nuclear Weapons, Arms Control, and Russian-American Relations*. Washington, D.C.: Council for a Livable World Education Fund, 1998.

Taylor, Ethel. "Reflections: On Being 'Consulted.'" *Progressive* 42 (June 1978): 20–21.

———. *We Made a Difference: My Personal Journey with Women Strike for Peace*. Philadelphia: Camino Books, 1998.

Taylor, Richard. "The Labour Party and CND: 1957 to 1984," pp. 100–30 in Richard

Taylor and Nigel Young, eds., *Campaigns for Peace: British Peace Movements in the Twentieth Century*. Manchester: Manchester University Press, 1987.

———. "The Marxist Left and the Peace Movement in Britain Since 1945," pp. 162–88 in Richard Taylor and Nigel Young, eds., *Campaigns for Peace: British Peace Movements in the Twentieth Century*. Manchester: Manchester University Press, 1987.

———, and Nigel Young. "Britain and the International Peace Movement in the 1980s," pp. 287–301 in Richard Taylor and Nigel Young, eds., *Campaigns for Peace: British Peace Movements in the Twentieth Century*. Manchester: Manchester University Press, 1987.

"Text of Basic Principles, May 29, 1972." *Department of State Bulletin* 66 (June 26, 1972): 898–99.

Thatcher, Margaret. *The Downing Street Years*. New York: Harper Collins, 1993.

Thompson, Ben. *Comiso*. London: Merlin Press and END, 1982.

———. "Pace e guerra." *New Statesman* 105 (Jan. 28, 1983): 19.

Thompson, E. P. *Beyond the Cold War*. New York: Pantheon, 1982.

———. *Double Exposure*. London: Merlin Press, 1985.

———. "END and the Soviet 'Peace Offensive.'" *Nation* 236 (Feb. 26, 1983): 232–36.

———. "Ends and Histories," pp. 7–25 in Mary Kaldor, ed., *Europe from Below: An East-West Dialogue*. London: Verso, 1991.

———. "The Movement for European Nuclear Disrmament." *Bulletin of Peace Proposals* 12:4 (1981): 399–402.

———. "Notes on Exterminism, the Last Stage of Civilization," pp. 1–34 in *Exterminism and Cold War*. London: Verso, 1982.

———. "Peace Is a Third-Way Street." *Nation* 236 (Apr. 16, 1983): 472–81.

———. "Postface: France and the European Peace Movement," pp. 247–52 in Jolyon Howorth and Patricia Chilton, eds., *Defence and Dissent in Contemporary France*. London: Croom Helm, 1984.

———. "Resurgence in Europe, and the Role of END," pp. 80–84 in John Minnion and Philip Bolsover, eds., *The CND Story*. London: Allison & Busby, 1983.

Tismaneanu, Vladimir. "Unofficial Peace Activism in the Soviet Union and East-Central Europe," pp. 1–53 in Vladimir Tismaneanu, ed., *In Search of Civil Society*. New York: Routledge, 1990.

Tomin, Zdena. "On Freedom and Power." *Across Frontiers* 2 (Spring 1986): 39–40.

Toscano, Louis. *Triple Cross*. New York: Carol Publishing, 1990.

Touraine, Alain. *Anti-Nuclear Protest: The Opposition to Nuclear Energy in France*. Cambridge: Cambridge University Press, 1983.

Towards an International Peace Movement: Bridging the Atlantic. Menlo Park, Calif.: Humanitas International, 1985.

Towell, Pat. "Progress on Anti-Missile Program Dulls Bark and Bite of GOP Critics." *Congressional Quarterly Weekly* (Oct. 10, 1998), pp. 2755–56.

———. "Reagan Faces Squeeze on Nuclear Arms Policy." *Congressional Quarterly* 42 (Jan. 21, 1984): 101–8.

Turnabout: The Emerging New Realism in the Nuclear Age. Boston: WAND Education Fund, 1986.

Tyroler, Charles, II, ed. *Alerting America: The Papers of the Committee on the Present Danger*. Washington, D.C.: Pergamon-Brassey's, 1984.

Udall, Stewart L. *The Myths of August: A Personal Exploration of Our Tragic Cold War Affair with the Atom*. New Brunswick, N.J.: Rutgers University Press, 1998.

"Update on Moscow Trust Group." *Across Frontiers* 2 (Winter 1985): n.p.

U.S. Arms Control and Disarmament Agency. *Documents on Disarmament, 1985, 1986*. Washington, D.C.: U.S. Government Printing Office, 1989, 1991.

U.S. Department of State. *Building Peace Through Strength*. Washington, D.C.: U.S. Department of State, 1983.

————. *NATO, Western Security, and Arms Reduction*. Washington, D.C.: U.S. Department of State, 1983.

————. *Peace and Security in Europe*. Washington, D.C.: U.S. Department of State, 1983.

————. *Renewing the U.S. Commitment to Peace*. Washington, D.C.: U.S. Department of State, 1983.

————. *Soviet Antipacifism and the Suppression of the "Unofficial" Peace Movement in the U.S.S.R.* Washington, D.C.: U.S. Department of State, 1988.

————. *U.S. Commitment to Peace and Security in Europe*. Washington, D.C.: U.S. Department of State, 1983.

U.S. House of Representatives, Subcommittee on Europe and the Middle East of the Committee on Foreign Affairs. *The Modernization of NATO's Long-Range Theater Nuclear Forces*. (Report prepared by the Congressional Research Service.) 96th Cong., 2d sess. Washington, D.C.: U.S. Government Printing Office, 1980.

U.S. Nuclear Policy for the 21st Century. Washington, D.C.: Council for a Livable World Education Fund, 1984.

"U.S. Rejects Pacific Nuclear-Free Zone." *Not Man Apart* 17 (Mar.–Apr. 1987): 5.

"U.S.-Soviet Relations." *The Gallup Report*, No. 207 (Dec. 1982), pp. 10–14.

USSR Seeks Worldwide Double Zero Option. Dresden: Verlag Zeit im Bild, 1987.

Utley, R.E. *The French Defence Debate: Consensus and Continuity in the Mitterrand Era*. London: Macmillan Press, 2000.

van den Dungen, Peter. "Critics and Criticisms of the British Peace Movement," pp. 260–86 in Richard Taylor and Nigel Young, eds., *Campaigns for Peace: British Peace Movements in the Twentieth Century*. Manchester: Manchester University Press, 1987.

van Essen, Niek. "Dutch Cruise Resistance." Woensdrecht: mimeographed, 1987.

————. "Peace Camps in Europe." Woensdrecht: mimeographed, 1985.

Vance, Cyrus. *Hard Choices: Critical Years in America's Foreign Policy*. New York: Simon & Schuster, 1983.

van Voorst, L. Bruce. "The Churches and Nuclear Deterrence." *Foreign Affairs* 61 (Spring 1983): 827–52.

————. "The Critical Masses." *Foreign Policy*, No. 48 (Fall 1982), pp. 82–93.

Väyrynen, Raimo. "The Nordic Region and the World Military Order," pp. 169–87 in Ken Coates, ed., *The Dynamics of European Nuclear Disarmament*. Nottingham: Spokesman, 1981.

Velikhov, Yevgeny. "Chernobyl Remains on Our Mind," pp. 157–73 in Stephen F. Cohen and Katrina vanden Heuvel, eds., *Voices of Glasnost: Interviews with Gorbachev's Reformers*. New York: W. W. Norton, 1989.

———. "Science and Scientists for a Nuclear-Weapon-Free World." *Physics Today* 42 (Nov. 1989): 32–36.

"A Very Big Delusion." *New Yorker* 68 (Nov. 2, 1992): 4, 6.

Vesa, Unto. "Finnish Public Opinion and Peace Movement." Paper presented at the Lund Conference on Peace Movements, Lund, Sweden, Aug. 17–20, 1987.

———. "Peace Movement and Public Opinion in Finland," pp. 265–78 in Katsuya Kodama and Unto Vesa, eds., *Towards a Comparative Analysis of Peace Movements*. Hants, Eng.: Dartmouth Publishing, 1990.

von Hippel, Frank. "Arms Control Physics: The New Soviet Connection." *Physics Today* 42 (Nov. 1989): 39–46.

———. *Citizen Scientist*. New York: American Institute of Physics, 1991.

———. "Recollections of Sakharov," pp. 325–33 in P. N. Lebedov Physics Institute, *Andrei Sakharov: Facets of a Life*. Gif-sur-Yvette: Editions Frontières, 1991.

von Weizsäcker, Richard. *From Weimar to the Wall: My Life in German Politics*. New York: Broadway Books, 1999.

Waldahl, Ragnar. "Norwegian Attitudes Toward Defense and Foreign Policy Issues," pp. 275–319 in Gregory Flynn and Hans Rattinger, eds., *The Public and Atlantic Defense*. Totowa, N.J.: Rowman and Allanheld, 1985.

Waller, Douglas C. *Congress and the Nuclear Freeze*. Amherst: University of Masschusetts Press, 1987.

Walsh, John. "Antinuclear Protests Are Busting Out All Over." *Science* 200 (May 19, 1978): 746.

Warner, Gale, and Michael Shuman. *Citizen Diplomats*. New York: Continuum Publishing, 1987.

War Resisters League. *History of the War Resisters League*. New York: War Resisters League, 1980.

———. *Peace Calendar, 1986*. New York: War Resisters League, 1985.

———. *A WRL History of Protest Against Nuclear Testing*. New York: War Resisters League, 1986.

Wasserman, Harvey. *Energy War: Reports from the Front*. Westport, Conn.: Lawrence Hill, 1979.

Waters, Harry F. "Fallout Over 'The Day After.'" *Newsweek* 102 (Oct. 24, 1983): 126.

Watson, Russell. "Battle Over Missiles." *Newsweek* 102 (Oct. 24, 1983): 36–43.

Weart, Spencer R. *Nuclear Fear: A History of Images*. Cambridge, Mass.: Harvard University Press, 1988.

Weinberger, Caspar W. *Fighting for Peace: Seven Critical Years in the Pentagon*. New York: Warner Books, 1990.

Wertman, Douglas A. *Most Italians See NATO as Essential, But Oppose INF Deployment and Increased Defense Spending*. Washington, D.C.: USIA, Sept. 11, 1984.

Wiberg, Ingrid Segerstedt. *Provstopp nu!* Stockholm: Fredsårsdelegationen Skriftserie, 1986.

Willens, Harold. *The Trimtab Factor*. New York: William Morrow, 1984.

Wills, Garry. *Reagan's America: Innocents at Home*. Garden City, N.Y.: Double-day, 1987.

Winkler, Allan M. *Life Under a Cloud: American Anxiety About the Atom*. New York: Oxford University Press, 1993.

Winther, Judith. "The Danish Peace Movements and the Political Development, Nationally and Internationally." Paper presented at the Lund Conference on Peace Movements, Lund, Sweden, Aug. 17–20, 1987.

Wittner, Lawrence S. *One World or None: A History of the World Nuclear Disarmament Movement through 1953*. Vol. I of *The Struggle Against the Bomb*. Stanford: Stanford University Press, 1993.

————. *Resisting the Bomb: A History of the World Nuclear Disarmament Movement, 1954–1970*. Vol. II of *The Struggle Against the Bomb*. Stanford: Stanford University Press, 1997.

Wohlforth, William C., ed. *Witnesses to the End of the Cold War*. Baltimore: Johns Hopkins University Press, 1996.

Wolf, Christa. *The Fourth Dimension: Interviews with Christa Wolf*. London: Verso, 1988.

Woods, Roger. *Opposition in the GDR Under Honecker, 1971–85*. London: Macmillan Press, 1986.

World Peace Council. *The U.S. Space Offensive: Road to Nuclear Annihilation*. Helsinki: Information Center of the World Peace Council, 1985.

————. *World Peace Council: List of Members, 1983–1986*. Helsinki: Information Center of the World Peace Council, n.d.

Yakovlev, Aleksandr. "Perestoika or the 'Death of Socialism,'" pp. 33–75 in Stephen F. Cohen and Katrina vanden Heuvel, eds., *Voices of Glasnost: Interviews with Gorbachev's Reformers*. New York: W. W. Norton, 1989.

Yankelovich, Daniel, and John Doble. "The Public Mood: Nuclear Weapons and the U.S.S.R." *Foreign Affairs* 63 (Fall 1984): 33–46.

Yankelovich, Daniel, and Richard Smoke. "America's 'New Thinking.'" *Foreign Affairs* 67 (Fall 1988–Winter 1989): 1–17.

York, Herbert F. *Making Weapons, Talking Peace: A Physicist's Odyssey from Hiroshima to Geneva*. New York: Basic Books, 1987.

Young, Nigel. "Peace Movements in History," pp. 137–69 in Saul H. Mendlovitz and R. B. J. Walker, eds., *Towards a Just World Peace: Perspectives from Social Movements*. London: Butterworths, 1987.

————. "Sensing Their Strength: Towards a Political Strategy for the New Peace Movements in Europe." *Bulletin of Peace Proposals* (Spring 1983), pp. 175–86.

Zubok, Vladislav, Catherine Nielsen, and Greg Grant, eds. *Understanding the End of the Cold War: Reagan/Gorbachev Years: An Oral History Conference, May 7–10, 1998, Brown University*. Providence: Watson Institute, 1998.

Index

In this index "f" after a number indicates a separate reference on the next page, and "ff" indicates separate references on the next two pages. A continuous discussion over two or more pages is indicated by a span of numbers, e.g., "57–59." *Passim* is used for a cluster of references in close but not consecutive sequence.